Art, Artifact & Architecture Law

Jessica L. Darraby

Volume 1

For Customer Assistance Call 1-800-328-4880

Mat #40179781

Library of Congress Cataloging-in-Publication Data

ISBN 0-87632-221-6

To T.H.B.

About the Author

Jessica L. Darraby, a member of the California Bar, is admitted to practice in the California Supreme Court and U.S. Courts of Appeal for the Ninth Circuit and the District of Columbia Circuit. She is an adjunct professor of law at Pepperdine University School of Law where she teaches art law, and has taught courses and authored chapters on professional ethics, appraisal practice, and international law.

Professor Darraby is a court-appointed expert in state and federal courts, and is a judicially referred mediator and arbitrator for art law matters. She founded the Practitioner's Column on art law for the *Los Angeles Daily Journal*.

Ms. Darraby was a former director of a contemporary art gallery for many years. Recipient of a Canada Council Fellowship, she was awarded degrees of B.A., summa cum laude, University of California; Los Angeles, M.A. from the University of California, Berkeley, and J.D. from Boalt Hall School of Law, Berkeley. Among other boards, she was a member of the national board of directors for ArtTable, Inc. and appointed counsel.

Acknowledgements

Creating this work would not have been possible without the support of my husband. From its inception a decade ago, the project has assumed its own presence. So too has the publisher evolved and changed during this time, resulting in several editorial reassignments of the product. My new editor, Alan Wasserstrom, has been a positive addition offering much-appreciated humour and a sanguinary outlook. He has provided invaluable aid and good perspective. Howard Root, Manuscript Editor, has undertaken diligent and detailed production work. He edits, copyreads and assures in every way the final product.

Research could not have been done for this book in this manner without the support of Professor Daniel Martin, Director of the Law Library at Pepperdine University School of Law. I would especially like to thank Professor Martin for his Legal Bibliography and unflagging support. I would like to express my appreciation to the entire library staff particularly the late Ramona Stahl whose presence is sorely missed, and Don Buffaloe, who was most helpful. Past editions of the treatise were greatly enhanced by the contribution of Linda Kay Zoeckler, Head of the Art Reference Library of the Huntington Library, Art Collections and Botanical Gardens: her superb Artist Bibliography provides an invaluable aid to the reader.

Meyers & McConnell, Jeffrey Meyers and Jay McConnell and their partners and staff throughout the years, have provided a wonderful work environment to update manuscripts. Donna Williams has been particularly helpful in numerous ways, as Nancy Chan has in the past. Grateful acknowledgement is extended to all those who continued their support but cannot be named here, and others to whom credit is overdue. The Getty Center for the History of Art and the Humanities provided valuable access and assistance. The Art Appraisal Services of the Internal Revenue Service provided updated materials. Fayda Aerth, from the former Mead Data Central, provided valuable technical support. Dorthy Kozak and Jacinda Dennison, Pepperdine law school graduates, who worked as research assistants, were extremely helpful; Nick Mallet, partner at Martineau Johnson, London, England, and David Houston, firm librarian, were extremely helpful in tracking down international cases. Fred Backlar and David Jurmain at Sotheby's were very helpful.

I express appreciation to my former editor, Danielle Mazur, who devoted extensive time and expertise in refining this treatise, and whose constancy for three years was a great help.

Preface

A treatise on art law seems daunting because there is no uniform definition of art or consensus about the need to define it. No discrete category of "art" exists from which materials can be rationally included or excluded; art eludes definition even among those for whom it is love and livelihood. How can opinions be rendered and rules developed in the absence of agreement upon the underlying subject matter?

For thousands of years art was generally peripheral to "law" with notable but episodic encounters. But the last two decades have changed the course of history. Today, court dockets and courtrooms are filed with art litigants. Diverse materials and products never before considered art are being preserved for posterity and designated for special handling under legal protection schemes.

Art, architecture, and artifact are now accorded a legal status of cultural preciousness formerly associated with the sublime, the extraordinary, or the antique. Legislative machinery from local to federal levels has spewed more words on art regulation than a laser printer run amok. Administrative agencies nationwide have implemented dozens of art programs with far-reaching implications. Developers and governmental groups have mapped the country with public art, triggering laws that implicate, perpetual custodial care. Prosecutors, assisted by law enforcement, have rerouted trading patterns, exposing the permeable borders between licit market practices and black markets. Corporate America has capitalized on its role as arts sponsor, patron, collector, and connoisseur, thereby wielding power in ways that portend constitutional challenge and impose costs upon use of the visual landscape.

The legal system may be an inadequate one to allocate responsibilities or redress grievances, but the proliferation of cases indicates that parties turn to adjudication to resolve arts disputes. Practitioners and jurists, legislators and regulators in response must conform an amorphous field of "art" to the confining grid of law. That this treatise may help them do so in the interests of justice and with a spirit of cultural imagination is the hope of the author.

Jessica L. Darraby
Los, Angeles, California

How to Use This Book

Section 1: Subject Matter

This treatise examines the policies and laws of the visual arts, which encompasses art, photography, artifacts, antiques, antiquities, and architecture. The subject matter is pertinent to artists, appraisers, arts advisers, museum directors, curators and staff, traders and auctioneers, conservators, collectors, foundations, fabricators, governmental agencies, insurance companies, prosecutors, preservationists, and publishers. Year by year, the individual and collective conduct of these participants in the arts is increasingly subject to legal scrutiny.

Section 2: Approach

The arts are recognized here as a cognate field. The treatise synthesizes laws of the arts as a discrete discipline based upon the rules and regulations affecting creation, production, distribution, display, and preservation of visual art in primary, secondary, and peripheral markets. The analysis is filtered through policy considerations, economic context, and cultural environment.

Section 3: Audience

The treatise is prepared in a format familiar to lawyers and lawmakers, judges and prosecutors, public officials and policymakers, and governmental and quasi-public agencies. The subject matter, however, is relevant to virtually all persons who fall within the arts categories identified earlier, and this presentation is intended to be useful to these persons in their daily decision making and long-term planning, as well as to their legal counsel.

Section 4: Multidisciplinary

Art law characteristically involves hybrid legal issues, some unique to art and some general. A professional approaching an arts transaction or dispute should consider disparate sources of law and be alert to hidden issues. A single object may represent many variegated legal interests. A preliminary analysis is suggested by the following questions:

(1) Is there a tangible asset (contractual and tort warranties; goods and services; breach of contract; personal property)?
(2) What are intangible properties ("moral" rights; intellectual property; First Amendment)?
(3) Is a person portrayed or visible (defamation; rights of publicity; privacy; state trade practices laws)?
(4) Is the imagery portrayed religious (federal-free exercise; establishment clauses; state constitutions)?
(5) Is explicit nudity and/or sex depicted (obscenity)?
(6) Whose First Amendment rights are at issue? Has there been a "transfer" of First Amendment rights (constitutional validity; due process; contract; "moral" rights)?
(7) Is there an artist's promise to perform (personal services; creative services; breach of contract; negligence; indemnification)?
(8) Is architecture--design or structure--involved (real property; copyright; negligence; preservation; "moral" rights)?
(9) Is the object an artifact (archaeological laws; Native American laws; antiquities laws; protected species laws; cultural property)?
(10) Is the object a "multiple" e.g., a print or sculpture (state print laws; federal trade laws; fraud; breach of warranties; breach of contact)?
(11) Has the object been imported or crossed an international border? Are laws of source and transshipment countries relevant to dispute (international cultural property conventions and treaties; executive agreements; foreign laws; federal customs and criminal laws; choice of laws; conflicts of law; export licenses; state laws)?
(12) What are the intangible interests (copyright; trademark; trade dress; "moral" rights)?
(13) How was value determined and by whom, for what purpose, and in what context, e.g., sale, tax filing, estate dissolution (appraisal and valuation; contracts; negligence; fraud; estates and trusts)?
(14) Do consumer uses or purposes exist (consumer protection; consumer warranty; federal trade regulation)?

(15) Has the object been auctioned or has an auction entity or auctioneer been involved in its sale, appraisal, transfer (auction laws; breach of contract; fraud; covenants of good faith and fair dealing, state business practices acts)?
(16) Are there contingent interests (contract; rule against perpetuities)?
(17) Are corporate logos, trademarks, trade names, trade dress, artist's signature, name or likeness, cartoon, comic, or fictional characters depicted or portrayed (trademark; unfair business practices; state art protection; preservation laws; copyright)?
(18) Is there damage to property, persons, product, or business (negligence; unfair competition; interference with contract; business relations; disparagement/defamation)?
(19) Are there reputation interests at stake (negligent; intentional misrepresentation; fraud; defamation)?
(20) Are there insured/insurable acts (insurance; indemnification; subrogation)?
(21) Are public or quasi-public entities or officials involved (sovereign immunities; state action; civil rights statutes; conduct under color of law)?
(22) Are there extrinsic attributes, e.g., good will, cultural iconism, status, or image (heritage laws; preservation laws)?

Section 5: Scope

Two chapters of this treatise provide an overview of the business of visual art and the policies implicated by its creation, trade, and transfer. These chapters introduce the reader to particularities of the arts, describe terms of art, and provide uniform definitions. Subsequent chapters discuss specific business and regulatory issues relating to art, artifact, and architecture.

Section 6: Terms

A confusing aspect of art that overflows into art law is the multiplicity of meanings attached to certain words: provenance, attribution, and authenticity. The multivolume art dictionaries and encyclopedias are often not definitive. The author's usage of terms is identified and, as applicable, cross-referenced in topical chapters. Significant terms can be cross-referenced through the index. The author does not purport to establish the standard but to provide uniformity and clarity for such terms used within this work.

Section 7: Time Period

The time period of this presentation emphasizes development of the law in the United States since the 1970s; the focus is on the era beginning in the 1980s through the present, when arts legislation and litigation rapidly increased. Historical context is provided as applicable.

Section 8: American Law

This treatise is about American law, state and federal. International conventions and treaties adhered to by the United States and international perspectives involving art and artifact, including foreign laws, are covered as applicable.

Section 9: The Unique and Sui Generis

Generalizations and trends recited in the introductory materials are obviously subject to exception. Art is often uniquely handled and imaginatively treated by some counsel and some courts.

Section 10: Connoisseurship Is Not Basis for Selection of Cases

No attempt has been made to eliminate cases by imposing the author's aesthetic judgment upon the quality of work or the caliber of its creator(s). If the art was considered in a regulatory, administrative, or adjudicatory framework, it is included herein. The author has identified the debate about fine art versus applied art, art over craft, and demonstrated how the law has codified these hierarchies while participants in the arts are dissolving them. Efforts have been made to include an eclectic range of art, artifact, and architecture.

Section 11: Charts, Graphs, and Ledger Entries

Charts and graphs, bookkeeping ledgers, and accounting sheets have been specifically created for this book by experts to aid the reader's understanding of the business of art, the practical impact upon trade, and the implications for regulation.

Section 12: Legal Bibliography

This treatise is supported by an extensive legal bibliography providing for the reader's further reference citation to periodicals, books, legislative histories, and legal journal writings. The bibliography can be accessed by topics common and generally recognized at law, and by the various chapters in this treatise where the topic appears. Thus, the reader can use the Bibliography [Appendix 23] as both an external source for additional information and as an internal aid for identifying particular chapter sections.

Section 13: Artist Biography and Bibliography

This treatise is supported by an exceptional additional reference section containing artist biographical information, material, and art bibliographic entries. Originally intended primarily for the legal practitioner who may not be familiar with particular artists or certain schools or art, this new section serves as an aid to any reader seeking additional information. Biographical support was sought for as many artists included herein as was reasonably possible. Usage is straightforward; when art or artist is mentioned on any given page, simply cross-reference alphabetically to this Bibliography [Appendix 24].

Table of Contents

Volume 1

Chapter 1
Fundamentals of Art Law

I. IN GENERAL

II. TIME LINE OF ART HISTORY

III. FORMAL REGULATION OF THE ARTS

IV. DEFINITION OF VISUAL ART

V. CRITERIA OF CONTEXT

XIII. ATTORNEYS AND THE ARTS: PROFESSIONAL RESPONSIBILITY

Chapter 2

Trade Practices Overview

I. STRUCTURE OF ART MARKETS

A. MARKET TERRITORY

B. MARKET IDENTIFICATION

C. BASIC MARKETS

D. ART PRODUCT COMPONENTS: THE CROSSAQ FACTOR (CONDITION, RARITY, OWNERSHIP, SIZE, SUBJECT MATTER, AUTHORSHIP, QUALITY)

II. MARKET PERFORMANCE AND PLAYERS

A. HISTORICAL EVOLUTION OF ART TRADING

B. SALES

XI. TORTS

A. DEFAMATION

B. DISPARAGEMENT

XII. PROVENANCE

XIII. CATALOGUE RAISONNE

XIV. DUE DILIGENCE

Chapter 3
Valuation and Appraisal

I. IN GENERAL

II. APPRAISALS

A. INTRODUCTION

B. APPRAISAL COMPONENTS

1. Appraisal Process

2. Appraisal Assignment

3. Identifying Subject Property

4. Visual Inspection of Subject Property

5. Appraisal Values Are Expressed in Numerical Terms

6. Appraisals Can Be Written or Oral

7. Limiting Conditions and Assumptions

C. COMPARISON OF APPRAISAL AND AUTHENTICATION

III. VALUATION

A. FAIR MARKET VALUE (FMV)

B. METHODOLOGIES OF VALUATION

C. SELECTING THE PROPER MARKET

IV. TAX APPRAISALS

A. CHARITABLE CONTRIBUTIONS

B. OWNERSHIP AS PREREQUISITE TO CONTRIBUTIONS

C. PROPER VALUATION METHODOLOGIES

1. Market Methods

2. Reproduction Cost Methods

D. VALUELESS ART OBJECTS

E. TAXPAYER LIABILITY: DEFICIENCIES, PENALTIES, AND INTEREST

1. Additions to Tax for Negligence: Section 6653

2. Valuation Overstatement: Section 6659

C. APPRAISER-CLIENT RELATIONSHIP

D. APPRAISER'S COMPETENCE

E. DISINTERESTED APPRAISALS

F. SPECIAL APPRAISALS

G. APPRAISAL FEES

H. OWNERSHIP OF APPRAISALS

I. CONFIDENTIALITY OF APPRAISALS

VI. APPRAISAL TORT LIABILITY

A. PROFESSIONAL APPRAISAL MALPRACTICE

B. NEGLIGENT MISREPRESENTATION

C. NEGLIGENCE

D. FRAUD

E. EVIDENTIARY ASPECTS OF APPRAISAL

F. APPRAISER AS PUBLIC OFFICIAL

VII. APPRAISER AS EXPERT IN COURT

Chapter 4

Uniform Commercial Code (UCC)

I. INTRODUCTION

II. UCC Article 2: SALES

A. APPLICATION OF ARTICLE 2 TO ART

B. TITLE

C. EXPRESS WARRANTY

D. IMPLIED WARRANTIES

E. STATUTE OF LIMITATIONS

F. ORAL CONTRACTS TO PURCHASE ARTWORKS

G. MUTUAL MISTAKE

III. ARTICLE 9: SECURED TRANSACTIONS

Chapter 5
Auction

I. INTRODUCTION

II. LAWS OF AUCTION

A. PUBLIC AUCTION

B. AUCTION BUSINESS: PAST AND PRESENT

C. UNIFORM COMMERCIAL CODE (UCC)

D. ART PER SE AUCTIONEERING LAWS

III. MECHANICS OF AUCTION

A. TERMS AND CONDITIONS

B. PREMIUMS, COMMISSIONS, CHARGES

IV. AUCTION LIABILITY: RELATIONSHIP WITH SELLERS

A. IN GENERAL

B. AGENCY

C. CONTRACT

D. INDEMNIFICATION

E. FRAUD

F. REMEDIES

V. LIABILITY: RELATIONSHIP WITH BUYERS

A. IN GENERAL

B. AUTHENTICATION

C. GUARANTEES OF LOT CONTENTS

D. CONSUMER FRAUD

E. VALUE

F. TIME LIMITATIONS FOR SUIT

G. Racketeer Influenced and Corrupt Organizations Act (RICO)

H. PERSONAL LIABILITY OF AUCTIONEER

I. DAMAGES

J. TITLE CLAIMS

VI. THIRD-PARTY ACTIONS AND OTHER ACTIONS

VII. AUCTION AS PLAINTIFF

Chapter 6

International Trade

I. IMPORT-EXPORT

A. OVERVIEW

B. U.S. CUSTOMS SERVICE

1. In General

2. Distinguishing Dutiable Art from Duty-Free Art

3. Duty

4. Customs Review and Examination

C. IMPORTATION: ART DUTY RATES

1. Introduction

2. Paintings

3. Drawings

D. DUTY RATES FOR ART OR ANTIQUE EXCLUSIONS

E. FALSE OR IMPROPER CUSTOMS DECLARATIONS

F. ENFORCEMENT

1. Seizure

2. Forfeiture

G. ADDITIONAL IMPORT RESTRICTIONS

II. ART EXPORTS

III. CULTURAL PROPERTY

A. IN GENERAL

B. FEDERAL LAW

C. ART AS UNIVERSAL HERITAGE

D. UNESCO CONVENTION

E. Cultural Property Implementation Act

F. DIFFERENTIAL IMPORT RESTRICTIONS: Section 12.104a of title 19 of the Code of Federal Regulations CATEGORIES

G. STOLEN CULTURAL PROPERTY IMPORT CONTROLS

H. ARCHAEOLOGICAL AND ETHNOLOGICAL MATERIALS IMPORT RESTRICTIONS

I. IMPORT EXEMPTIONS: Section 312

J. MISCELLANEOUS ISSUES

IV. INTERNATIONAL TRANSACTIONS

A. IN GENERAL

B. PATRIMONY LAWS

C. EXPORT REGULATION

D. ACT OF STATE DOCTRINE

E. DISCOVERY MOTIONS ON RETENTION LAWS

F. MISCELLANEOUS ISSUES

Chapter 7

Copyright

I. GENERALLY

II. HISTORY OF VISUAL ART AND COPYRIGHT LAW

A. CONSTITUTIONAL BASIS

B. JUDICIAL EXPANSION

C. STATUTORY EVOLUTION OF ART COPYRIGHT

III. ART ISSUES IN COPYRIGHT

A. IDEA/EXPRESSION DICHOTOMY

B. IMAGERY

IV. STATUTORY BASICS

A. NOTICE

B. REGISTRATION

1. In General

2. Deposit

a. Identifying Material (I.D. Material)

b. Copies

3. Certificate of Registration

C. PUBLICATION

1. 1909 Act

2. 1976 Act

V. COPYRIGHT ELIGIBILITY

A. GENERAL

1. Reproducing Art in Different Media or Size

2. Functional Art

B. OWNERSHIP OF COPYRIGHT

C. WORK MADE FOR HIRE

D. TRANSFERRING OWNERSHIP, ASSIGNMENTS

1. Writing Requirement

VII. FAIR USE

A. Section 107

B. PURPOSE AND CHARACTER OF USE

C. NATURE OF COPYRIGHTED WORK

D. VOLUME OF TAKING: AMOUNT AND SUBSTANTIALITY

E. MARKET EFFECT AND OTHER FACTORS

VIII. SPECIFIC ART FORMS

A. CARTOONS AND COMIC STRIP CHARACTERS

B. PHOTOGRAPHY

B. DAMAGES

C. ATTORNEY'S FEES AND COSTS

XI. INSURANCE

Chapter 8

Trademark and Unfair Competition

I. GENERALLY

II. Lanham Act

A. SECTION 43(A)

B. TRADE MARK AND TRADE DRESS

Volume 2

Chapter 9
Artists' Rights

III. TRADE

A. CHARACTERIZATION OF "ARTIST"

B. CAREER PROFILE

C. BUSINESS RECORDS RULES FOR ARTISTS

D. STUDIO SALES: DISCLOSURES, WARRANTIES, AND REPRESENTATIONS

H. ACTIONS AGAINST TRADERS FOR FAILURE TO PROMOTE, EXHIBIT, AND SELL ART

I. RECOVERY OF ARTWORKS

J. PRODUCERS, SUPPLIERS, AND MANUFACTURERS

IV. GOVERNMENT FUNDING OF THE ARTS

V. ARTISTS AT WORK

Chapter 10

Fundamentals of Exhibition and Display

I. ART DISPLAY

A. EXHIBITORS

B. PUBLIC FORUM, EXHIBITIONS, AND DISPLAYS

C. ART AUDIENCE

1. Viewers

2. Claims Orientation

3. Specific Types of Viewer

4. Extrinsic Evidence to Aid Viewer's Interpretation of Artworks

D. DISPLAY

1. Quality and Location of Venue

2. Duration

3. Expurgation

4. Privacy and Publicity Rights

II. ART AND THE FIRST AMENDMENT

A. ART AS EXPRESSION AND THE SCOPE OF PROTECTION

B. RESTRICTIONS

C. AMERICAN CURRENCY

D. AMERICAN FLAG

E. DEFAMATION AND LIBEL

F. OBSCENITY

Chapter 11
Art Fraud

I. GENERALLY

II. CIVIL

A. INTRODUCTION

B. FEDERAL TRADE COMMISSION (FTC)

1. Unfair Competition Mandate Includes Art

2. Remedies

C. RACKETEER INFLUENCED AND CORRUPT ORGANIZATIONS ACT (RICO)

1. Mail and Wire Fraud, Fraud

II. PROCESSES OF PRODUCTION AND TERMINOLOGY

A. IN GENERAL

B. FABRICATION

C. STATE MULTIPLES STATUTES

D. PRINT TERMINOLOGY AND PROCESSES

E. LIABILITY

Chapter 13
Archaeology and Artifacts

I. GENERALLY

II. FEDERAL LAWS

A. Antiquities Act of 1906

B. Archaeological Resources Protection Act of 1979 (ARPA)

C. Federal Land Policy and Management Act of 1976 (FLPMA)

D. Archaeological and Historic Preservation Act of 1974

Chapter 14

Historic Preservation and Conservation

D. FIRST AMENDMENT CHALLENGES

IV. CONSERVATION

A. CONSERVATION PROFESSION

B. LEGAL STANDARDS

C. TORT

D. OTHER ISSUES

APPENDICES

Chapter 1

Fundamentals of Art Law

I. IN GENERAL

II. TIME LINE OF ART HISTORY

III. FORMAL REGULATION OF THE ARTS

IV. DEFINITION OF VISUAL ART

V. CRITERIA OF CONTEXT

VI. ART AS PRECIOUS/ART AS PERENNIAL

VII. NOMENCLATURE

VIII. UBIQUITY OF ART

IX. WHAT IS ART: QUESTIONS OF FACT OR ISSUES OF LAW?

X. BACK ROOM RESOLUTION

XI. COURT ROOM LITIGATION

XII. DISPARATE SOURCES OF ART LAW

XIII. ATTORNEYS AND THE ARTS: PROFESSIONAL RESPONSIBILITY

§ 1:42 Generally

KeyCite®: Cases and other legal materials listed in KeyCite Scope can be researched through West's KeyCite service on Westlaw®. Use KeyCite to check citations for form, parallel references, prior and later history, and comprehensive citator information, including citations to other decisions and secondary materials.

I. IN GENERAL

§ 1:1 Arts expertise

> I speak only as an artist. But to speak as an artist is no small thing. Most people ignorantly suppose that artists are the decorators of our human existence, the esthetes to whom the cultivated may turn when the real business of the day is done. But actually what an artist is, is a person skilled in expressing human feeling . . . . Far from being merely decorative, the artist's awareness . . . is one . . . of the few guardians of the inherent sanity and equilibrium of the human spirit that we have.[1]

When people meet mathematicians, they do not purport to understand higher mathematics. But when people meet visual artists, they fancy themselves experts on art. So reflected Robert Motherwell, artist and teacher. Motherwell was not targeting the legal world; nor is his view emblematic. But Motherwell's observation that art is not self-evident and that art expertise is something more than self-proclaimed retains its vitality when transferred to lawyers and lawmakers who are professionally involved in the field commonly called art law.

Lawyers are licensed professionals, as are many of the experts upon whom they rely, like architects and certified public accountants. The arts are, and with minor exception have been, devoid of the accreditation, accountability, registration, and recordation that typically accompany

---

[Section 1:1]

[1]Hearings before the Select Subcomm. on Education re: H.R. Rep. No. 14753, the Environmental Quality Education Act, 91st Cong., 2d Sess. (1970) (testimony of Robert Motherwell, paralleling comments of Marcel Proust).

private or governmental regulation. Artistic genius and creative talent are not easily captured by such measures. However, a strata of art distributors, exhibitors, and sellers exist whose conduct and activities is more susceptible to measure.

Yet arts experts and those whose official capacity cloaks them with authority to judge artworthiness do not necessarily sport objective credentials, nor are their skills and training ordinarily subject to independent review. This allows the trained and the untrained, the knowledgeable and the uninformed, to share unbounded space.

§ 1:2 Custom and usage

Expert testimony on the arts has become an increasingly important aspect of litigation, the result of which is a growing public record revealing the web of relationships and network of transactions that comprise the arts. In a business where handshakes were traditionally favored over executed contracts (notwithstanding statutes of frauds), written records are often sparse, making documented data difficult to obtain.

Massive amounts of "insider" information appear regularly in the general media as a result of unprecedented numbers of lawsuits involving the arts and key players.[1] Even when available, industry statistics, and tax and market figures are not necessarily reliable or compiled under rational or consensual categories, which makes it difficult for comparisons or projections to be made. Since the original publication of this work, that, too, has changed and a variety of organizations and entities now publish, however intermittently, data on the arts.[2] If trade associations, private foundations, and governmental agencies ordinarily do not marshall or publish data on the arts as is commonly done for other businesses, episodic efforts bolstered by sweeping disclosures in the press afford an

---

[Section 1:2]

[1]In re Auction Houses Antitrust Litigation, 193 F.R.D. 162 (S.D. N.Y. 2000) (consolidated class actions seeking damages and other relief for price fixing).

[2]For a dated aggregation of auction data, regional sales, and investment comparisons, *see* Watson, From Manet to Manhattan (1992).

ever widening window on formerly secretive practices.[3] And most museums and art institutions, among the nation's prominent public collectors and exhibitors, are not-for-profit corporations, beyond the scope of the corporate reportorial net. But once again, litigation opened the tent flaps, exposing the practices of museum boardrooms and trustees.[4]

The dearth of data about trade practices and market performance reinforces the potential importance of arts experts in an adjudicatory setting; they elucidate custom and usage not commonly known or accessible. Irrespective of whether these persons would qualify as expert witnesses at trial or offer lay opinion under applicable rules of evidence, artists, critics, appraisers, traders, to name a few, contribute to the development of factually informed legal principles in the arts context through their knowledge about unwritten codes and understood conduct. Such testimony can have, and has had, a pivotal role in the outcome of art law litigation.

Even in the absence of regulation, institutions have had to respond to increasing public pressure on matters like accession and collection practices. Demands from Nazi victims and their heirs for return of artworks dispossessed during World War II have made the front pages of the press daily during the last few years. Major museums have taken the unusual step of listing on websites objects in their collections that have gaps in the provenance.[5] This notification period will presumably spur a variety of claims, from replevin to fraud, and no doubt is an attempt to quiet title once and for all for those half century old claims that even five years ago were considered fruitless.

---

[3]In re Auction Houses Antitrust Litigation, 135 F. Supp. 2d 438 (S.D. N.Y. 2001), opinion superseded on other grounds, 138 F. Supp. 2d 548 (S.D. N.Y. 2001) (auction practices on premiums and commissions publicized in press as a result of civil litigation and indictment and guilty pleas of auction personnel); *see also,* Ch 5 §§ 5:26 to 5:30. Some auction houses publish information regarding sales, but ordinarily do not indicate goods "passed" or bought-in, that is, goods which were not sold publicly at auction; nor are these data independently verifiable. Private treaty sales are sometimes released.

[4]*See, e.g.,* Brooklyn Institute of Arts and Sciences v. City of New York, 64 F. Supp. 2d 184 (E.D. N.Y. 1999) (case settled.)

[5]*See* Ch 6 § 6:2 (museum web site listings).

Revelations about Swiss and American banks, newly released documents and materials from World War II and the Cold War eras are the basis for laying collective blame at the feet of many. Recognition of the role of American museums has been incorporated into institutional guidelines prepared in 1998 by an Association of Art Museum Directors task force. A Presidential Advisory Commission on Holocaust Assets in the United States was established, issuing a report on stolen art and planning to launch a central electronic database for war claims. The House Committee on Banking and Financial Services convened hearings in February 2000. Private and public initiatives like the New York-based Commission for Art Recovery, the Art Loss Register, and a Holocaust Art Restitution Project have been established.

Practices in the arts changed in the last twenty years, as they have among other trades, businesses, and professions, and legislative and other proposals are pending to impose more oversight and require more disclosure.[6] But even as the arts are increasingly regulated and corporatized, the particularly hands-on, apprentice-oriented aspects of artmaking and art selling make custom and usage critical to legal outcomes.

State legislatures have attempted to abrogate customary practices in the arts by enacting laws specifically devoted to art; throughout this work, these laws are termed "art per se" statutes.[7] Some art per se statutes on trade explicitly state their standards must prevail "notwithstanding [arts] custom and usage," provisos that are inconsistent with the goals of the Uniform Commercial Code.[8] Such attempts to legalize the arts may be abortive; reported cases nationwide under art per se statutes are remarkably few with a frequency that remains low

---

[6]The Financial Accounting Standards Board (FASB) withdrew guidelines which would have required museums to capitalize their collections by recording artworks as monetary assets. FASB Proposed Exposure Draft, "Accounting for Contributions Received and Contributions Made" (Nov. 17, 1992) (institution's net assets, revenues, expenses, gains and losses would have been classified according to donor-imposed restrictions). *See also* 24 Sec. Reg. & L. Rep. (BNA) 47, at 1822 (Dec. 4, 1992).

[7]See Chs 2 and 11.

[8]See Ch 4; UCC § 1-205 (course of dealing and usage of trade).

notwithstanding the litigious upsurge in other areas of the arts. Not surprisingly, art per se statutes are largely ignored by those active in the arts, who follow customs and practices prevailing for hundreds, even thousands, of years.

§ 1:3 Former insularity of the arts

Art is no longer the exclusive province of an aesthetic elite, as lawyers who transact or litigate in the arts quickly discover. If art is not entirely democratized, it is assimilated in one form or another in virtually all strata of society. Art in public places programs, redevelopment projects that encourage the coalescing of art and architecture, utilization of landmark public and private properties to showcase art have made art part of the contemporary urban scene. The proliferation of Internet access and websites, profitable licensing agreements that bootstrap culture to consumer products for mass market merchandising merge formerly rarified art viewing into the daily routine: workspaces and public places, parks, hospitals, train stations and subways, homes, businesses, and schools. The most basic objects have been coopted, from screensavers and web wallpaper flashing colorful Impressionist masterpieces to Pop Art bookends and blotters purchased from museum shops or their online counterparts. No longer is the museum institutional setting the exclusive, or even the primary, art viewing source. Ubiquity has insinuated art into otherwise disparate milieus and markets, bringing within art's eclectic embrace diverse viewers, regulators, and participants. Arts issues are as relevant to developers, insurers, corporate advertisers, city planners, and law enforcers as they are to artists, museums, traders, cultural commissions, and appraisers.

For all its popular stretch, art retains a mystique. Until very recently, the arts, for a variety of reasons, have been relatively insular, if not as some contend actually clandestine. Secrecy—perceived or actual—poses a challenge to law professionals. The challenge of this secrecy is evident at the most basic level. Transactional lawyers require market and product information to structure deals. Litigators not only need to apprise themselves about the business and sensibility of art making and art trading, but they must also support their client's position in courts of law according to standards of proof under applicable rules of evidence and procedure.

II. TIME LINE OF ART HISTORY

§ 1:4 Generally

Perhaps the most important thing for the law professional to remember is that art has been part of human existence even before mankind decorated the first cave, but the idea of publicly mandating and regulating arts activities through formal legislative control is relatively recent. Indeed, the appearance of art—and homo sapiens' compulsion to create art for ceremonial, celebratory, religious, decorative, or other reasons—precedes establishment of law by several thousand years.

Remarkably, art has been a relatively unfettered activity. During the multiple millenia wherein art and law have co-existed, few formalized attempts and fewer legalistic ones were undertaken to regulate art creation and production. Other control mechanisms, however, were operative.

III. FORMAL REGULATION OF THE ARTS

§ 1:5 Generally

The contemporary zeal for regulating the art trade is an historical nanosecond in a timeline of almost 30,000 years of art making. Only since the 1970s and almost exclusively in the United States has formal legalistic regulation of various aspects of arts creation, display, and distribution been attempted, although now the European Community and its commercial web of euro-linking directives vie for position as global art regulators.

Art cases reveal the tension in American jurisprudence between the private property rights of the individual and culturally legislated imperatives of the commonality. As the following chapters indicate, the governmental reach can be long indeed. The American legal system appears to be foremost among nations in regulatory efforts. But even before the current trend to legalize the arts, official controls upon art creation, distribution, and display were operative.

Since antiquity, the engine of artistic invention has been fueled, and the mass destruction of art driven, by religion and by power. The power referred to is one of official intervention, not linked to any particular notion of statehood or specific form of political structure or governmental organization. The civic industriousness of the early Romans in making art and the religious zeal of the iconoclasts in destroying it are bound by a similar impetus: hierarchically imposed official directives.

Twentieth and twenty-first century imprimaturs for art making and art destroying retain this officiousness of action, but often include linkage to modern political concepts of sovereignty; for example:

(1) the imperative to produce art in service to a Socialist state after the Russian Revolution;
(2) the ridicule, disposal, and destruction of "degenerate" art by the Nationalist Socialist Party during the Third Reich (while officials cached and warehoused it for their own gain);
(3) destruction of classic artworks and creation of new ones dedicated to cult of Mao Tse-Tong during the Chinese Cultural Revolution; and
(4) destruction of ancient Bamiyan Bhuddas by Al Qaeda in Twenty-First Century Afghanistan as part of Taliban's official fundamentalist policy against idolatry.

These egregious examples illustrate officious interventions where the creative process and artistic output were harnessed to the reins of state power.[1] Yet the amount and diversity of art product that has come down to us through the ages indicate that those in the visual arts have achieved relative distance from governmental intrusion over the course of history.

If the creative process of art making enjoyed relative deference (or indifference) from leaders and governments in terms of official action, ownership of art was another matter. Art "acquisition" has been a state interest from

[Section 1:5]

[1]Artists have shown imagination and ingenuity in pursuing their interests, notwithstanding official intervention.

the ancient world to the modern, whether or not "ownership" was accompanied by consideration and transfer of title, e.g., the Roman investiture, the Napoleanic conquests, and the Nazi appropriations.

That an historical departure of potential magnitude has occurred has not been part of the public debate, although art is considered by the courts to be a matter of public import. The arts have survived, indeed flourished, for thousands of years, give or take a millenia or two, without the aid of legal services. The crush of history in this regard might give the prudent reason to pause before extending the regulatory reach.

IV. DEFINITION OF VISUAL ART

§ 1:6 Defining the definition

Art law is beset by the threshold question, "What is art?" The answer to that question is the same as that to "What is the sum of 2 plus 2?" Of the accountant, philosopher, and lawyer queried, only the last-named counters: "What would you like it to be?"

Art in the legal context is susceptible to a similar riposte. But if artists were asked, "What is art?" many would reject the need to classify it or respond by saying it is what they say it is. Art, according to many, is just that, whatever the artist says it is, notwithstanding evidentiary limitations of such definition.

§ 1:7 Lack of litmus tests

Indeed, any and all things that appeal to artists precipitate or appear in creations, from found objects to found imagery, whether use involves imitation of masters or appropriation of popular advertising, piggybacking creativity to scientific and technological innovations from computers, the internet, infocommunication systems and artificial intelligence. Offerings in the contemporary art scene include a vast visual array of products, processes, performances, videography, sound and light, multimedia installations, scans and morphs, even encrypted interactive "net.art."

If art cannot be defined subjectively or objectively by looking at it, it is equally clear that art is not definable by any particular litmus test. Nor do innate qualities, traits, characteristics, or attributes, either singly or in combination, crystallize identification. Medium, component structure, size, composition, rendition by the artist's hand or by others working in the artist's name,[1] conception or execution by traditional, electronic, photomechanical, digital, encrypted, or other means, such considerations crop up in the opinions, but no one factor is ordinarily dispositive.

Things have been categorized as art if: (1) they sell; (2) creators (or others) offer them for sale as art; or (3) paradoxically, they are designated as art. While consensus might be obtained on images that have become veritable archetypes, like the *Mona Lisa* or a pieta, it is difficult to obtain agreement outside the arts (or even within) as to just what particular things ought to be art and what ought not. This is reflected in the comment: "You call *that* art?" Just what and how much of it the law will permit to be included under the rubric of art is daily being decided.

§ 1:8 Judicial definitions

"[T]he case law which pinpoints the definition of 'art' [is] scarce."[1] The eyeball test—"I know it when I see it"[2]—is as inconclusive for identifying art as it is for rooting out obscenity. Some courts have relied upon dictionary definitions that focus on the classical.[3] Other judicial attempts seem arcane in the contemporary era of multimedia, mixed

---

[Section 1:7]

[1]Lakedreams v. Taylor, 932 F.2d 1103, 1107 (5th Cir. 1991), *quoting* Andrien v. Southern Ocean County Chamber of Commerce, 927 F.2d 132, 135 (3d Cir. 1991) (in copyright "[a]uthors are entitled to copyright protection even if they do not perform with their own hands the mechanical tasks of putting the material into the form distributed to the public"); Rogers v. Koons, 960 F.2d 301 (2d Cir. 1992) (Italian fabricators anonymously fabricate statues for American artist).

[Section 1:8]

[1]In re Leonardo, 102 B.R. 202 (E.D. Cal. 1989).

[2]Jacobellis v. State of Ohio, 378 U.S. 184, 197, 84 S. Ct. 1676, 12 L. Ed. 2d 793 (1964) (Stewart, J. concurring) ("But I know it when I see it.").

[3]Simon v. C.I.R., 103 T.C. 247, 1994 WL 450480 (1994), aff'd, 68 F.3d 41 (2d Cir. 1995) ("Webster's New 20th Century Dictionary . . .

media, and complex processes: An object is art "if it appears to be within the historical and ordinary conception of the term art."[4]

Purely subjective classifications, however, are disfavored by the courts.[5] "[P]ersonal artistic tastes are unpredictable and inexplicable."[6] "One man's mural is another's grafitti."[7] Thus, attempts in law to create aesthetic hierarchies in terms of comparing good art or bad art, or elevating fine art over applied art, art over craft, applied art over industrial art, or fine art over commercial art have been rejected by, among other courts, the U.S. Supreme Court.[8]

§ 1:9 No dispositive definitions

In such circumstances and under such conditions, does a uniform response exist to the question, "What is art?" The question in law is both general and specific; inherent

---

[defines 'work of art' as] anything beautifully made . . . , " a definition adopted by the judge, which would, if applied to art, omit many substantial schools of art and bodies of work, and not only the modern and contemporary).

[4]Rosenthal v. Stein, 205 F.2d 633, 635 (9th Cir. 1953) (defined in context of copyright litigation), *cited approvingly in* Bailie v. Fisher, 258 F.2d 425 (D.C. Cir. 1958).

[5]Skyywalker Records, Inc. v. Navarro, 739 F. Supp. 578 (S.D. Fla. 1990), rev'd, 960 F.2d 134 (11th Cir. 1992) (reversal of bench decision that musical lyrics lacked serious artistic value in obscenity case because judiciary cannot use its personal criteria to determine serious value).

[6]Benchcraft, Inc. v. Broyhill Furniture Industries, Inc., 681 F. Supp. 1190, 1216 (N.D. Miss. 1988), judgment vacated and remanded (unpublished opinion), 871 F.2d 1096 (Fed. Cir. 1989), *citing* Plantronics, Inc. v. Roanwell Corp., 403 F. Supp. 138, 159–60 (S.D. N.Y. 1975), judgment aff'd, 535 F.2d 1397 (2d Cir. 1976).

[7]*See, e.g.,* Cohen v. California, 403 U.S. 15, 25, 91 S. Ct. 1780, 29 L. Ed. 2d 284 (1971) ("one man's vulgarity is another's lyric").

[8]Bleistein v. Donaldson Lithographing Co., 188 U.S. 239, 23 S. Ct. 298, 47 L. Ed. 460 (1903) (pictorial illustrations for advertising purposes are protected as art under copyright law as fine art: "works are not the less connected with the fine arts because their pictorial quality attracts the crowd, and therefore gives them a real use . . . it would be a dangerous undertaking for persons trained only to the law to constitute themselves final judges of the worth of pictorial illustrations . . . . It may be more than doubted, for instance, whether the etchings of Goya or the paintings of Manet would have been sure of protection when seen for the first time.").

in a definitional reply are express and implied values about ourselves, our society, and our culture. Will the act of creation be encouraged and rewarded? By whom, for whom, and to what degree? What about the persons who bring the creation to public purview: What are their entitlements and benefits, obligations and duties? Should the creation itself supersede the interests of its creators?

Art theory, history, and criticism is replete with philosophical, spiritual, and metaphysical responses beyond the scope of this analysis.[1] Is there a seminal "legal" definition, or does there need to be one? To state the question differently, can a field of law arise and survive around a subject matter that it cannot define or circumscribe?

A generic legislative definition, aside from questionable constitutionality, would seem repugnant to the notion of unfettered creativity in a free society. Legislators presumably do not foreclose the artistic options of constituents in a democracy, at least in definitional terms. "It is vital to a democracy [to] support new ideas,"[2] and for America to "recognize . . . the diversity . . . that comprises . . . artistic . . . expression."[3]

§ 1:10 Answer is perceptual

If the definition of art is so elusive that art product seems unbounded, the commonality of art is that each creation is sui generis.[1] The unique aspect of art, which pertains even if the work lacks originality and imagination, is based upon the individualized perception of the viewer in mediating that portrayed by the creator. Perception is key. What contributes to the one-of-a-kind experience of art viewing, irrespective of whether or not the art

---

[Section 1:9]

[1]*See, e.g.*, Tolstoy, *What Is Art? And Essays on Art* (trans. A. Maude, Oxford Univ. Press).

[2]The National Foundation for the Arts and Humanities Act of 1965, as amended by Pub. L. No. 101-512, § 2(10) (Nov. 5, 1990).

[3]The National Foundation for the Arts and Humanities Act of 1965, as amended by Pub. L. No. 101-512, § 2(9) (Nov. 5, 1990).

[Section 1:10]

[1]This is a different issue from whether or not art is unique in the sense of new and original.

is a multiple, is the vision of its maker in conjunction with the interpretation of its viewer; that interaction renders to art its distinguishing attribute of uniqueness.

When viewing the same object, viewers do not "see"—or, in terms of art theory, "read"—the same images and ideas. In other words, the optical facts actually seen by the human eye are not equally perceived by all viewers. Each viewer reads the object differently based upon a distillation of experiences, attitudes, and beliefs, and responds accordingly. Art succeeds over time when it continues to precipitate these individualized interpretative perceptions of viewers beyond the time period of the creator's context.[2]

This personalized subjective viewing militates against definition by scheduled factors or objective criteria, as trial testimony makes clear. A square of canvas whose surface is covered with pigments may be a painting according to the dictionary definition, but it is not ipso facto a work of art in a court of law.

§ 1:11 Who the viewer is

The perceptual call that an object is art is made by the viewer; the legal call that an object is art is made by a subset of viewers, the jury or the judge.[1] Who makes that call is a crucial cultural imperative in a free society. Practitioners must not only determine how art experts can convince viewers, but also consider which viewers make the call: the fact-finder, the law-concluder, or both.

V. CRITERIA OF CONTEXT

§ 1:12 Display

Virtually anything can be transformed into art under presentation by curator, pen of critic, penchant of collector, or passage of time.[1] The "art of exhibiting art" in this century is associated with the role of the "curator-

---

[2]The interaction may be mediated by the exhibitor, *see* Ch 10.

[Section 1:11]

[1]For legal classifications of "viewers" of art, *see* Chs 7 and 10.

[Section 1:12]

[1]California v. LaRue, 409 U.S. 109, 127, 93 S. Ct. 390, 34 L. Ed. 2d 342 (1972) ("Context is the essence of aesthetic judgment.")

impresario."[2] Almost anything can be considered art if it is processed through a curatorial eye and/or presented in a cultural context, at museums, exhibition spaces, recognized commercial settings, international art fairs, expositions, mercantile markets, or on the World Wide Web.

Presentation and context, therefore, are prevailing determinants of and for art. Once presentation and context control, art can and does have infinitely varied manifestations. Even the quotidian can be sacred. Thus, a urinal of industrial manufacture became art when attached by the artist Marcel Duchamp to a base and pseudonymously signed "R. Mutt."[3] This plumbing fixture exhibited publicly introduced at least one art movement and served as a harbinger of others, the aftermath still palpable almost one century later.

§ 1:13 Museums

The evolutionary role of museums in the twentieth century in terms of number, mission reassessment, operational extension resulting in new constituencies—has expanded the lexicon of traditional nomenclature to include a compendium of art products. A museum, which can have encyclopedic or specialty collections, or both, has an historical objective of preservation and a tax-exempt purpose of education.[1] Museums can and do have: (1) critical input into general definitions of what constitutes art; and (2) crucial impact upon specific identifications of particular objects.

The Smithsonian Institution, in Washington, D.C., is a federally owned and operated institution.[2] The Smithso-

---

[2]Kluser & Hegewitsch, Die Uunst der Ausstellung (1991), reviewed by Fanelli, "The Art of Exhibiting Art," 16 Art Newspaper 15 (Mar. 1992).

[3]Marcel Duchamp, "The Fountain" (1917).

[Section 1:13]

[1]IRC § 501(c)(3).

[2]Act of Aug. 10, 1846, ch. 178, 9 Stat. 105. The powers of the Smithsonian Institution and the national museums and art galleries within its jurisdiction are rooted in broad legislation; *See, e.g.,* 20 U.S.C.A. § 50.

nian is chartered by Act of Congress.[3] The confluence of independence and federal regulation are comprehensive and complex. The Board of Directors is composed of federal officials or those selected by them.[4] Federal officials appoint or serve as authorized persons directing business of the member museums of the Smithsonian Institution.[5] Budgets are submitted to Congress[6] and monies recovered by or accruing to it are kept by the Treasury Department.[7] Independent decision making power is authorized for various activities and by various laws.[8] Individual boards of directors for the respective museums are authorized to purchase and sell art and objects.[9]

Classification of a museum impacts upon the propriety of certain legal actions and application of particular rules and regulations.[10] American museums, unlike many, if not most, foreign countries, are private, state, or regional entities that may be operated as quasi-public or private organizations. Museums—private, state and federal—have revised collection policies, expanded exhibition schedules, and added exhibition venues. This has institutionalized wide-ranging and eclectic offerings. To the extent such objects are sold at market, commercial trade supports cultural presentation, and vice versa.

§ 1:14 Contemporary art

Contemporary art movements further the "incessant cross-fertilization between twentieth and twenty-first

---

[3]20 U.S.C.A. § 41.

[4]20 U.S.C.A. § 43.

[5]*See* 20 U.S.C.A. § 76.

[6]20 U.S.C.A. § 49.

[7]20 U.S.C.A. § 53.

[8]*See, e.g.,* 40 U.S.C.A. §§ 193n, r; 20 U.S.C.A. §§ 51–57, 67.

[9]*See, e.g.,* 20 U.S.C.A. § 76cc.

[10]*See, e.g.,* Dong v. Smithsonian Inst., 878 F. Supp. 244 (D.D.C. 1995), judgment rev'd, 125 F.3d 877 (D.C. Cir. 1997) (Smithsonian Institution held to be a federal agency subject to the Privacy Act, 5 U.S.C.A. § 552a).

century art and less exalted forms of visual cultures."[1] Through the university gallery and museum, the nonprofit foundation, the Internet and the mercantile gallery system, a wide variety of products, processes, and materials are offered to the public as contemporary art.

§ 1:15 Multiculturalism

"The arts . . . reflect the high place accorded by the American people to the nation's rich cultural heritage."[1] Since World War II, additional items have been considered art as a result of reassessment of eurocentric orientated classifications and multiculturalism. For example, "primitive" is no longer the description of choice for arts from Africa and Oceana. A goal of democracy according to the legislative purpose of the National Foundation for the Arts and Humanities Act is to "preserve [America's] multicultural artistic heritage."[2]

Thus, Congress passed the Indian Arts and Crafts Act[3] and the American Indian Religious Freedom Act[4] involving "sacred objects" and "cultural rights." Congress established a museum "devoted exclusively to Native American history and art"[5] by the National Museum of the American Indian Act,[6] and the National Museum of African Art and a center for Eastern art.[7] States and localities have opened and supported museums named for and dedicated to ethnic arts and artists.

Congress recognizes diverse cultural interests and

[Section 1:14]

[1]Smith, "High and Low Culture Meet on a One Way Street," N.Y. Times, Oct. 5, 1990, at B1.

[Section 1:15]

[1]The National Foundation for the Arts and Humanities Act of 1965, as amended by Pub. L. No. 101-512, § 2(6), 104 Stat. 1915 (1990).

[2]The National Foundation for the Arts and Humanities Act of 1965, as amended by Pub. L. No. 101-512, § 2(9), 104 Stat. 1915 (1990).

[3]25 U.S.C.A. 3005, amended in 1990 by Pub. L. No. 101-644, 104 Stat. 4662 (1990).

[4]42 U.S.C.A. § 1996, amended by Pub. L. No. 102-485 (Oct. 23, 1992).

[5]20 U.S.C.A. § 80q(2).

[6]Pub. L. No. 101-185, 103 Stat. 1336 (1989).

[7]Pub. L. No. 97-203, §§ 1–3, 96 Stat. 129 (1982).

objects: Acadian immigrants by the Maine Acadian Cultural Preservation Act;[8] native Americans in the Native American Graves Protection and Reparation Act of 1990;[9] and native Hawaiians, Aleuts, and Eskimos by amendment in 1992 of the American Indian Religious Freedom Act. Persons actually or perceptibly disenfranchised, e.g., women, and racial and ethnic minorities, are recognized also by regional governments and private interests, bringing into the mainstream yet more objects and ideas, thereby adding classifications and disposing of others.

§ 1:16 Technological art and the internet

Artists explore for their own uses technologies developed for other purposes. In 1966, Experiments in Art and Technology was established to coalesce arts and inventors. "Montage 93: International Festival of the Image" is considered the first international show of electronically derived images. Digital transmission, laser, holography, light-emitting diodes (LED), computer generated graphics, and the now common videotape are not the first forays of artists into the technological frontier. Artists made newly developed nineteenth century photography a medium of magic, which persists to this day. Nam June Paik aesthetized the television; and Dan Flavin and Jenny Holzer, among others, reinterpreted fluorescence, neon, and LED. Such adaptations and usages are now considered commonplace compared to computer-driven, assisted, or generated works.

New media uses digital technology as tool and as subject. Exhibitions like "BitStreams" and "Data Dynamics" at the Whitney Museum of American Art and acquisitions of interactive virtual art by the Guggenheim Museum in 2002 highlight the quirkiness of collecting and maintaining tech art rapidly made obsolete by new generations of hardware and software. Digital artists today can write their own software to create Net art, send creations into cyberspace with a keystroke, transmute sound, imag-

---

[8]Maine Acadian Culture Preservation Act, Pub. L. No. 101-543, 104 Stat. 2389 (1990).

[9]Native American Graves Protection and Repatriation Act of 1990, 25 U.S.C.A. § 3001.

ery and light into binary codes. Others adapt existing software to morph, transmute and permute combinations of invention and appropriation.

Such process-reprocessed results raise interesting questions of ownership, stewardship, and proprietary rights. How the law will categorize such quasi-product-process creations has yet to be tested. Is the manifestation of the encrypted codes, however temporal or short-lived, "art" within the mission of museums? Tangible or intangible property?

The curatorial challenges are as noteworthy as the legal ones. In 2002 an internet-based artwork titled "Minds of Concern: Breaking News," was removed from the New Museum of Contemporary Art's online site, newmuseum.org, and rendered inactive because it was conducting "surveillance" of outside computers. Titled "Open Source Art Hack," it was designed by Swiss digital artists as a site installation at the museum as well as an internet presence. Its central feature was port-scanning software. Viewers were "prompted to scan ports of organizations that protested . . . the World Economic Forum . . . " Vulnerable ports were identified and methods to penetrate them-or "crack" in the lingo of reconnaissance port-scanning--to obtain private information appeared on screen. The practice has had limited judicial acceptance in certain contexts, providing no damage to or intrusion upon other computers.[1] At the request of its internet service provider, the museum disabled the work. Providers reportedly are hostile to such port-scanning because of possible online jamming.

As artists continue to exploit technological discoveries, more and more material is subsumed within a category of art, or at least curated, housed, and shepherded as such, stretching and subverting stock legislative definitions. Techno- and cyber-art challenge basic premises in both arts and law. Legal system attempts to draw boundaries in virtual space.

[Section 1:16]

[1]See Appendix 1.

§ 1:17 Environmental art

As environmental regulation and federal hazard substance controls[1] mandate public disclosures, and proposed amendments seek to eliminate some traditional materials like lead-based pigments and other toxins, technology continuously introduces new ones. As global ecological concerns mount, artists experiment with recycled and alternative materials, as well as outright toxic and dangerous ones, bringing ever more "stuff" into the province of art.

§ 1:18 Cross-pollination of artistic forms

Integration of art, craft, design, performance, and architecture in all phases of art making and art showing, from conception through production, installation, display, and promotion, blurs the boundaries between theatrical arts, industrial arts, visual arts, and applied arts.

§ 1:19 Functional art

In addition, artists, traders, critics, and scholars have relocated quotidian objects, like forks, clocks, and teakettles, from their original uses, where they were handled for function, to exhibition spaces where both handling and use are prohibited. Objects of contemporary daily life are on display as artifacts, worthy of cultural insignia above and beyond daily uses. That notion of functionalism presents yet again the conflicts between art and craft, and Western and non-Western art. Where objects are functional they fall into a broad category of artifacts that challenge the Western notion of art as a "privileged realm untainted by utility."

§ 1:20 Performance art

Performance art, a hybrid of visual art and stage presentation, is a live presentation that unfolds over time before an audience and is considered a cross between the-

---

[Section 1:17]

[1] *See, e.g.*, "Labeling of Hazardous Art Materials," Pub. L. No. 100-695, 102 Stat. 4568 (1988), to be codified at 15 U.S.C.A. § 1277, amending Federal Hazardous Substances Act.

atre and object oriented art. Interestingly, key challenges to public funding for the arts has come from performance artists.[1] Performance art is included here as relevant to the case law affecting the visual arts.

§ 1:21 Alternative (exhibition) spaces

Expanded participation and demand for exhibition venues was joined by diversification of art participant roles and conduct. As the economy in the 1990s precipitated closing of galleries resulting in loss of spaces to exhibit, artists opened their own venues as alternatives to the dealer system, hence, the term "alternative spaces." Some alternative spaces are located in residences; others are itinerant, moving monthly or periodically from location to location.

VI. ART AS PRECIOUS/ART AS PERENNIAL

§ 1:22 Preserving art for art's sake

The requisite age for historical significance and the attenuated relationship to artistry or craftsmanship has been disposed of in the dialogue on contemporary art, indicating that cultural preciousness associated with preserving for posterity the sublime, the special or the antique, has undergone change.

§ 1:23 Art as perennial recyclable

The law terminates expectations about products by timing warranties to anticipated usage and restricting actionability at law for product misperformance by statutes of limitation. Neither warranties in contract or tort, nor comparable statutes of limitation have been expanded to handle perennial and recyclable products, like art. Art travels complex and circuitous routes; once it is created, it does not enter the trade stream at point *A* for a predictable time period and exit at point *B*. Art is timeless,

---

[Section 1:20]

[1]Finley v. National Endowment for the Arts, 795 F. Supp. 1457 (C.D. Cal. 1992), aff'd, 100 F.3d 671 (9th Cir. 1996), cert. granted, 522 U.S. 991, 118 S. Ct. 554, 139 L. Ed. 2d 396 (1997) and rev'd on other grounds, 524 U.S. 569, 118 S. Ct. 2168, 141 L. Ed. 2d 500 (1998).

transferred and retransferred upon gift, divorce, death, or sale. Nor is market value reduced over time; art often appreciates upon market reentry, the economic basis of the secondary market.[1] Unlike warranties for other products, warranties of authenticity, value, and title are as crucial, or more crucial, for resold art as they are in the immediate years following creation.

Art laws reinforce expectation that art is "permanent" and immutable by making it unlawful to alter, modify, destroy, or mutilate certain artworks, regulation that is complementary to governmental and private preservation of art and architecture. More legislation, and no doubt more litigation, may follow as a result of codification of art and architecture provisions by amendments to federal copyright law and enactment of state and federal legislation to preserve and control, inter alia, monuments, art, artifacts, and historic districts and sites.

VII. NOMENCLATURE

§ 1:24 Generally

> As an artist, I am used to being regarded as a somewhat eccentric maker of refined, but rather unintelligible, objects of perception. . . . I am as well, at other times, an expresser of adoration for the miracle of a world.[1]

§ 1:25 What is an artist?

"Everyone is an artist," to paraphrase the late German conceptual artist Joseph Beuys. That philosophy has not been embraced by the legal system. If courts are uncertain about how and when to classify objects as art, the opinions also reflect disagreement about how to categorize the act

---

[Section 1:23]

[1] See Ch 2.

[Section 1:24]

[1] Hearings before the Select Subcomm. on Education re: H.R. Rep. No. 14753, 91st Cong., 2d Sess. (1970) (testimony of Robert Motherwell).

of art making and the makers.[1] Widespreading applications and adaptations of new technologies available to artists confound neat artistic categorizations to such a degree that museums are naming "new media" curators and creating collections of virtual art. While Michelangelo Buanarotti considered himself first and foremost a sculptor notwithstanding his painterly achievement of the Sistine Chapel, sixteenth century compartmentalization seems quaint to twenty-first art makers. The traditional, the recyclable, the appropriated, the incorporeal virtual product, all are utilized or merged in today's media spectra. Museum exhibitions display voice recognition technology creations, interactive software encrypted net art, and sound and light performances alongside paintings and multimedia video installations. While artists refer to themselves in a multiplicity of ways,[2] their conduct in the cases is referred to as a business,[3] hobby,[4] service,[5] skilled

---

[Section 1:25]

[1]Wills v. C.I.R., 411 F.2d 537, 542 (9th Cir. 1969) ("As the term 'artistic' is ordinarily used, it connotes activities of an aesthetic nature, including for example, painting, drawing, architecture, sculpture"); *see also* Miller v. Civil City of South Bend, 904 F.2d 1081, 1094 (7th Cir. 1990), cert. granted, 498 U.S. 807, 111 S. Ct. 38, 112 L. Ed. 2d 15 (1990) and judgment rev'd, 501 U.S. 560, 111 S. Ct. 2456, 115 L. Ed. 2d 504 (1991) ("The reason we think that art is an intellectual medium . . . is that most of us obtain no enjoyment from art. It requires an educated taste.").

[2]"The Painter's Profession" Artists on Art 129 (ed. R. Goldwater 1972) ("there is no profession . . . in which you may expect less happiness and contentment than painting").

[3]Wildenstein & Co. v. Wallis, 756 F. Supp. 158 (S.D. N.Y. 1991), rev'd without opinion, 983 F.2d 1047 (2d Cir. 1992) (art dealing as commercial business).

[4]Hewitt v. Joyner, 940 F.2d 1561 (9th Cir. 1991) (art making as hobby); Waitzkin v. C.I.R., T.C. Memo. 1992-216, T.C.M. (RIA) ¶ 92216 (1992) (deriving "pleasure" from "creating artwork and seeing it displayed": issue of when the activity is to be classified as for profit or avocational).

[5]Crimi v. Rutgers Presbyterian Church in City of New York, 194 Misc. 570, 89 N.Y.S.2d 813 (Sup 1949) (commission of mural as performance of a service).

occupation,[6] a profession, a calling.[7]

As with art, the term "artist" is subject to multiple interpretations that differ from state to state, and from statute to statute within a given state. Care should be taken to investigate the appropriate, and multiple, definitions. For example, "artist" is defined to include the estate of the artist, and his heirs or representatives under some state laws,[8] the result of which is artist's statutory rights. Graphic artists are excluded from certain definitions of artists but are identified as artists for purposes of some causes of action in the cases.

§ 1:26 Generic media: Painting, sculpture, drawing

Even if a particular painting were deemed a work of art, generic nomenclature like "painting" or "sculpture" no longer adequately categorizes the range of products that constitute art in the twenty-first century. As art materials change, so do art media. Contemporary art movements push the boundaries of traditional media well beyond oil, acrylic, marble, and bronze to include mixed media, multimedia, videotape, televisions, computers, software, and even performance as well as virtual art, sound, and light. Tapestries of scavenged glassine bags containing residues of illegal drugs hang on gallery walls next to mounted bronzes. Given the assortment of material and materiel that comprise the bounteous mix of art, legisla-

---

[6]Mayeske v. International Ass'n of Fire Fighters, 905 F.2d 1548, 1554 (D.C. Cir. 1990).

[7]Haberman v. Gotbaum, 182 Misc. 2d 267, 698 N.Y.S.2d 406 (City Civ. Ct. 1999) (between a "calling" and a "hobby," an artist's work can be "difficult to quantify and to confine"); Rogers v. Koons, 751 F. Supp. 474 (S.D. N.Y. 1990), amended on reargument, 777 F. Supp. 1 (S.D. N.Y. 1991) and judgment aff'd, 960 F.2d 301 (2d Cir. 1992) (plaintiff is "a professional photographer"); Tutton v. Viti, 108 U.S. 312, 2 S. Ct. 687, 27 L. Ed. 737 (1883) ("statues were made by men not really professional sculptors, though calling themselves such"); Young China Daily v. Chappell, 742 F. Supp. 552 (N.D. Cal. 1989) (district court reverses finding of Immigration and Naturalization Service that a graphic designer is not a "profession" under § 101(a)(15)(H)(i) of Immigration and Nationality Act, 8 U.S.C.A. § 1101(a)(15)(H)(i)); Reichman v. Warehouse One, Inc., 173 A.D.2d 250, 569 N.Y.S.2d 452 (1st Dep't 1991), appeal dismissed in part, 78 N.Y.2d 1058, 576 N.Y.S.2d 213, 582 N.E.2d 596 (1991) ("a professional artist").

[8]*See* Appendix 2.

tive attempts to distinguish fine art from the rest may seem risible.

Notwithstanding dated legislative categorizations, fine art for one statutory definition is not necessarily fine art for another. Definitions of art not only vary among states but within each state among the various statutes.[1] Care should be taken to investigate the definition(s) under the applicable laws.

Generic arts nomenclature appears throughout the state and federal regulatory framework and includes, inter alia: painting; sculpture, including construction, assemblage; photography, subclassified by purposes (e.g., photojournalism, photomontage, commercial art); works on paper like prints, subclassified by processes (e.g., etchings, serigraphs, woodblocks, lithographs, monotypes); drawings, subclassified by purpose (e.g., fine art, architectural, mechanical); stained glass; murals (e.g., frescos, stencils, or mosaics); fiber arts (e.g., textiles, weaving). These categories are sometimes limited by the restrictor "fine."

VIII. UBIQUITY OF ART

§ 1:27 Subject matter

Art is no longer esoterica exclusively reserved for an elite. When the world's great museums and Las Vegas casinos coalesce as art exhibitors, attention must be paid. A sea change in the relationship between art and society is occurring. The media presents art in the public dialogue as part of daily coverage of domestic and world affairs: the savings and loan debacle, the banking crisis, insurance industry failures, leveraged buy-outs, shareholder suits and internecine battles for corporate power,[1] international intrigue, politics and finance and last but not least, the

---

[Section 1:26]

[1]*See* Appendix 1.

[Section 1:27]

[1]Hanrahan v. Kruidenier, 473 N.W.2d 184 (Iowa 1991) (shareholder derivative action based upon business judgment rules regarding charitable contributions of art prior to winding up corporation, where court found gift of art within ambit of business judgment rule); Kahn v. Sullivan, 594 A.2d 48 (Del. 1991) (appeal from approval of settlement

internet.[2]

§ 1:28 Commerce

Commerce borrows from the arts, co-opting classic art images and inventing new ones. Advertising reproduces famous art works and agencies commission contemporary artists. Promoters of products from cosmetics to feminine hygiene and purveyors of services from hoteliers to health clubs use art as a marketing strategy to conjure up association with certain lifestyles and reinforce product identification.

Artists in turn co-opt commerce, depicting imagery of icons like Mickey Mouse, the Pink Panther, and original Campbell soup can labels. Dadaism and ready-mades like Marcel Duchamp's repackaged urinal[1] augured new twists on appropriation advanced by contemporary artists. But artworks like the Mona Lisa have functioned as archetypes of cultural iconography from the moment of creation. Artists are professional pilferers and have been from the time the first curves emerged on the Venus Willendorf and the first daubs of carbon grafittied the caves of Lascaux. If copying, borrowing, redacting, recasting and transmuting are artists' stock in trade, their newest find to plunder has no outer limits: cyberspace. The internet, digital technology, encryption are but some of new sources that produce recombatent culture in ways that Marcel Duchamp could never have foreseen but surely would have approved. These borrowings have precipitated a spate of litigation challenging the borders between the First Amendment and intellectual property, unfair business practices, and artist's rights.

---

actions by certain shareholders regarding art collection of Armand Hammer and role of corporation in establishing art museum).

[2]American Intern. Group, Inc. v. Islamic Republic of Iran, 657 F.2d 430 (D.C. Cir. 1981); Golden Budha Corp. v. Canadian Land Co. of America, N.V., 931 F.2d 196, 20 Fed. R. Serv. 3d 388 (2d Cir. 1991) (removal to United States of treasure buried during World War II by Japanese in Philippines).

[Section 1:28]

[1]Phillips de Pury & Luxembourg, Contemporary Art Auction (May 2002), Fountain, glazed cast ceramic urinal with back paint, executed 1917-1964, est. $1,500,000-$2,500,000).

§ 1:29 Corporate support

If business has bandwagoned on the popularity of art as a promotional tool, it has also made financial commitments as sponsors and patrons. In the United States and abroad, businesses are significant sponsors of art exhibitions, cultural projects, antiquities preservation, and architectural restoration, as well as being collectors. By the late 1980s, 1,000 corporate art collections housing countless numbers of objects were in existence, although that number has declined as a result of forced sales by the Resolution Trust Corporation and through bankruptcy, mergers and corporate attrition.

The line between sponsorship and patronage has grown uncomfortably closer, requiring museum associations to revisit ethical considerations relating to corporate subsidized exhibitions that have the look and feel of retail showrooms. Vanity exhibitions of corporate collectors at private and public spaces have raised similar queries about museum missions, curatorial independence and institutional quests for gift-giving and collection building.

§ 1:30 Entertainment

If commerce brought art into the hearts and minds of Americans, no one industry has done more to bring art into the American home than infocommunications and popular entertainment, which appropriate artistic imagery for mass audiences. Art as leisure entertainment means museums, in the same way as amusement parks, are sites for family outings fostered by: mass promotion of "blockbuster" exhibitions, reservations-only admission policies, advance ticket sales through sports and entertainment agencies, on-site and Web site museum gift shops, mail order sales, satellite museum gift shops in commercial malls; and satellite museums in Las Vegas hotel-casinos, remote and foreign locations.

Merchandising art expands public awareness and perhaps encourages public acceptance. In any event, art has been democratized by this popular push, snatched from obscurity to ubiquity, infused with, if not eclipsed by, entertainment and popular culture.

IX. WHAT IS ART: QUESTIONS OF FACT OR ISSUES OF LAW?

§ 1:31 Generally

Justice Oliver Wendell Holmes said: "[I]t would be a dangerous undertaking for persons trained only to the law to constitute themselves final judges of [art]."[1]

Is determination of art made as a finding of fact or an issue of law? Does the decision maker vary depending upon the stage of the litigation, the form of relief requested, or the legal basis on which the claim is predicated?[2] Outside of obscenity cases, no court to date has opined conclusively on these issues, although opinions from other areas, like computer technology, rely upon hybrid blends of fact-finding and legal conclusion.[3] A review of the arts cases indicates disparate views.

That there may attach to a single work of art multiple legal interests in any given transaction or dispute means that the potential exists for ambiguities, inconsistencies or contradictions when definitions from different laws are used.[4]

If the object qualifies as art according to definitions for some claims but not others, it is unclear whether motions based on the pleadings to dispose of the presumed disqualifying claims could or should be sustained. Such

---

[Section 1:31]

[1]Bleistein v. Donaldson Lithographing Co., 188 U.S. 239, 23 S. Ct. 298, 47 L. Ed. 460 (1903). Oliver Wendell Holmes attended the salons of Isabella Stewart Gardner and "extension courses" of Charles Eliot Norton, first professor of art history at Harvard University. Watson, From Manet to Manhattan 127–28.

[2]Harper House, Inc. v. Thomas Nelson, Inc., 889 F.2d 197 (9th Cir. 1989) ("where, as here, 'the question requires us to consider legal conceptions in the mix of fact and law and to exercise judgment about the values that animate legal principles, . . . the question should be classified as one of law and reviewed de novo.' ").

[3]First Comics, Inc. v. World Color Press, Inc., 884 F.2d 1033 (7th Cir. 1989) (sale of art process as sale of goods or sale of process, but "[a]lthough factual findings may clarify the matter, we are unconvinced that the entire issue . . . properly belongs before a trier of fact. Rather it is for the court to decide if a given transaction is within the meaning of a statutory term.").

[4]*See* the litigation checklist in "How to Use This Book."

motions require application of rules of law in the absence of material factual content. Courts have in fact determined whether or not objects were "art" as a matter of law under the guise of statutory construction.[5] If decisions about what art is become purely legal, summary adjudication becomes a proper means to categorize art and dispose of claims, the cultural import of which extends beyond the potential impact of stare decisis and res judicata.

X. BACK ROOM RESOLUTION

§ 1:32 Generally

Whatever one's view of the need to regulate, art law disputes have become art law adjudications at rapidly increasing rates. Whether this litigation is a result of too much or too little regulation remains to be determined. Before litigation fever struck the arts, trade disputes ordinarily were resolved quietly and confidentially in the back rooms of galleries. A back room is a physical area in many galleries that is off limits to the public; it is where dealers broker business, confer with clients, and counsel artists.

Back room resolution is used here to refer to any extra-legal, extra-administrative resolution by the disputants themselves, without the intervention of lawyers, agency officials, or judicial officers. Such resolutions have been made for years, proverbially if not actually, in the back rooms of the nation's galleries. But back room resolution has been joined—if not replaced—by expensive litigation ordinarily associated with big business, which does not characterize most of the small businesses and solo operations prevalent in the arts.

XI. COURT ROOM LITIGATION

§ 1:33 The boom

Why have arts disputants become arts litigants? Dramatic multimillion dollar hammer prices for objects at public auction and soaring prices in private trade during the late 1980s, which the media featured as front-page,

---

[5]Botello v. Shell Oil Co., 229 Cal. App. 3d 1130, 280 Cal. Rptr. 535 (2d Dist. 1991).

prime time stories, may in part explain public (and legal) attention to the art markets and the appearance of participants who are here called new market entrants. That this period of high hammer prices, particularly in the late 1980s, is the only boom in the arts, or even the only modern boom, is an inaccurate perception. This time, however, the boom occurred in an era when information is broadly dispersed over communication networks, so that global participation and reaction, i.e., facsimile and telephone bidding, is immediate.

"Boom" is defined as a period when "the best works set record levels and second-rate works sell for far more than they are worth."[1] By identifying market segments of five-year terms, one analyst places booms throughout the nineteenth century and even before, and in the twentieth century between 1909–1914, 1924–1929, and 1985–1990.

Nor does the 1980s boom mark the only period of astronomical prices. According to data adjusted for present value by certain market analysts, prices realized for Vincent Van Gogh's "Sunflowers" (1987 Christie's auction), "Irises" (1987 Sotheby's auction), or "Portrait of Dr. Gachet" (1990 Christie's auction) are not historically unique.

§ 1:34 Tax laws

Art law formerly derived largely from tax law, the early cases in the 1970s clustering around tax shelters and overvalued or improper charitable contributions of art. But, as mentioned above, a new caste of valuation/investment litigation outside the securities laws has followed market fluctuations, presenting legal issues in an arts context beyond the tax field: contracts and torts, warranties, unfair business practices, false advertising, professional liability, and fraud.

Tax issues in the arts still persist. The resurgence in popularity of auction during the 1980s in turn has been linked to changes in the Tax Reform Act of 1986. Those revisions which calculate certain charitable contributions of tangible personal property, including art, on individual

---

[Section 1:33]

[1]Watson, From Manet to Manhattan 482.

income tax returns deterred, or at least provided a disincentive for, gift-giving to museums. The American Association of Museums (AAM) reports that donations of art to museums in 1986 before the tax law revision were $103.8 million, but by 1990 had dropped to $60 million. Those figures, like other valuations in the arts, are difficult to interpret decisively. Value is established by the donor, not the donee. Whatever the adjusted value of charitable contributions, the AAM study does indicate that the tax laws affected cultural policy.

§ 1:35 Public exposure

Worldwide pre-auction viewings, international catalogue distributions, the internet, web sites of galleries, dealers, museums, artists, art vendors and distributors contribute to increased public access and invite public scrutiny and media attention. Persons whose artworks had disappeared or had been stolen years ago came forward as claimants for newly "discovered" art. Scholars and historians challenged authenticity or sought reattributions. Authenticity and/or ownership disputes ensued, raising a panoply of legal issues, not least of which is the procedural one manifest in the statute of limitations, and its equitable counterpart laches: When is it simply too late to reclaim art even if one's ownership interest is meritorious? Until recently, there were no centralized reporting services to record art thefts and losses. Various private and public arts information services are becoming available.

§ 1:36 Broader participants

Buy-sell, loan-transfer transactions occurred not only at higher prices, but also among a broader base of participants. Ownership transfers of art meant more exhibitions of art. The influx of new market entrants was coupled with additional exhibitors, for example, private arts foundations, corporations, and satellite museums, as well as new distributors, like consultants and agents.

Indeed, art became an integral product within multitiered segments of society. This introduced a swath of additional participants that sprang from administrative and associational fora not ordinarily associated with the arts. These participants' actions nonetheless have affected the process of art regulation, distribution, and display: federal programs, foundations, departments, and agencies, labor unions, common carriers, trade associations, private and public institutions, local and state commissions, state legislatures, and Congress. These persons and entities—individuals, associations, museums, agencies, sovereigns, intermediaries, advisors, and others—entered the arts web; through a domino effect producing rules like joinder and indispensable parties, these also joined the legal fray.

XII. DISPARATE SOURCES OF ART LAW

§ 1:37 Generally

Art law is an amalgamation of laws and rules drawn from diverse legal sources:

(1) specific laws identified here as art per se statutes expressly and facially devoted to art;
(2) stated purpose laws devoted to various goals, e.g., racketeering, consumer protection, and bankruptcy, applied to arts disputes;
(3) general laws, judicial doctrines, and common law; and
(4) federal and state constitutional principles.

If codifying art laws was done to encourage uniformity, establish industry standards, or produce a body of law, those goals have not yet been realized, nor on the face of the statutes could they be. Art per se statutes reinforce a patchwork approach to art law issues and foster quixotic resolution of art law matters.

In the absence of applicable legislation, practitioners, and in turn the courts, have handled each situation as presented, conforming the arts issues to recognized legal claims aimed at existing remedies. Solutions premised on unrelated laws may provide a quick fix for the problems at hand, but do not yield a "body" of art law: Policies pertaining to art are omitted, misstated, or not fully enunciated; few or no discernible rules or principles about the rights and responsibilities of arts participants develop in the jurisprudence; and some legitimate arts disputes never enter the legal system or are dismissed at incipient stages because they have not been, or cannot be, plead in legally cognizable terms.

Reiterating legal principles from other laws, without informing these principles in the arts context, is not useful and is ultimately regressive. The ad hoc approach may have been adequate, if not particularly successful, for a handful of cases filed from the early to mid-1980s. Today, hundreds of arts cases are reported; the number grows monthly. Instead of a clearer picture of jurisprudence on the arts emerging, the ad hoc approach has obfuscated issues and produced anomalous and confusing results. Cobbling claims for arts disputes by applying laws and policies of familiar disciplines, therefore, should be done with caution.

§ 1:38 Art per se laws—Generally

Although no single law or statutory scheme has provided a comprehensive portrait of art's infinite profiles, expressly titled "art" laws do exist, and have been on the books since the late 1970s. They are referred to here as art per se statutes. State art per se statutes were codified at a rapid rate during the 1980s throughout the United States.[1] Congress has federalized comparable and additional legislative interests, and art per se statutes now exist at both state and federal levels.

§ 1:39 Art per se laws—State laws

Art per se statutes, at least at the state level, are unusual in that their impetus, according to the legislative histories, does not spring from the grass roots base they appear to be intended to protect, i.e., artists. Art per se statutes tend to address isolated issues for specified types of artworks. The matters they purport to regulate vary; examples include dealer disclosure laws for sales of particular prints, registration of auctioneers, determination of ownership of artifacts discovered upon public lands, preservation of art, and artist's rights.

[Section 1:38]

[1]Approximately 20 states have codified laws regulating certain aspects of art trading, a trend that began in the 1970s and accelerated and proliferated during the 1980s. These laws, however, have not served as the predicate for claims as often as one might expect; indeed, their usage is relatively rare. *See* Appendix 4.

§ 1:40 Art per se laws—Federal laws—Generally

Federal art per se statutes are largely a product of the 1980s and early 1990s, and they are identified throughout the following chapters. But one federal law bears mention here, legislation begun as early as the 1960s under President John F. Kennedy, whose presidency focused federal attention on the arts. As a result, in the mid-1960s, Congress passed the seminal arts legislation of the century, authorizing a national arts agenda by establishing the National Foundation on the Arts and Humanities (NFAH) in 1965.[1] Among its Declaration of Findings and Purposes,[2] Congress lauded "cultural activity," "creative talent" and celebrated the nation's "realm of ideas and . . . spirit." NFAH was dedicated to "encouraging freedom of thought, imagination and inquiry" in the United States:[3]

DECLARATION OF FINDINGS AND PURPOSES

Sec. 2. The Congress finds and declares the following:

(1) The arts and the humanities belong to all the people of the United States.

(2) The encouragement and support of national progress and scholarship in the humanities and the arts, while primarily a matter for private and local initiative, are also appropriate matters of concern to the Federal Government.

(3) An advanced civilization must not limit its efforts to science and technology alone, but must give full value and support to the other great branches of scholarly and cultural activity in order to achieve a better understanding of the past, a better analysis of the present, and a bet-

---

[Section 1:40]

[1]The National Foundation for the Arts and Humanities Act, Pub. L. No. 89-209 (1965), as amended, Pub. L. No. 101-512, § 2(2), 104 Stat. 1961 (1990). 20 U.S.C.A. §§ 951 et seq.

[2]The National Foundation for the Arts and Humanities Act, Pub. L. No. 89-209 (1965), as amended, Pub. L. No. 101-512, § 2(2), 104 Stat. 1961 (1990).

[3]*See also* S. 856, 104th Cong., 1st Sess. (June 1, 1995), a bill to amend NFAH and other arts legislation.

ter view of the future.

(4) Democracy demands wisdom and vision in its citizens. It must therefore foster and support a form of education, and access to the arts and the humanities, designed to make people of all backgrounds and wherever located masters of their technology and not its unthinking servants.

(5) It is necessary and appropriate for the Federal Government to complement, assist, and add to programs for the advancement of the humanities and the arts by local, State, regional, and private agencies and their organizations. In doing so, the Government must be sensitive to the nature of public sponsorship. Public funding of the arts and humanities is subject to the conditions that traditionally govern the use of public money. Such funding should contribute to public support and confidence in the use of taxpayer funds. Public funds provided by the Federal Government must ultimately serve public purposes the Congress defines.

(6) The arts and the humanities reflect the high place accorded by the American people to the nation's rich cultural heritage and to the fostering of mutual respect for the diverse beliefs and values of all persons and groups.

(7) The practice of art and the study of the humanities require constant dedication and devotion. While no government can call a great artist or scholar into existence, it is necessary and appropriate for the Federal Government to help create and sustain not only a climate encouraging freedom of thought, imagination, and inquiry but also the material conditions facilitating the release of this creative talent.

(8) The world leadership which has come to the United States cannot rest solely upon superior power, wealth, and technology, but must be solidly founded upon worldwide respect and admiration for the Nation's high qualities as a leader in the realm of ideas and of the spirit.

(9) Americans should receive in school, background

and preparation in the arts and humanities to enable them to recognize and appreciate the aesthetic dimensions of our lives, the diversity of excellence that comprises our cultural heritage, and artistic and scholarly expression.

(10) It is vital to a democracy to honor and preserve its multicultural artistic heritage as well as support new ideas, and therefore it is essential to provide financial assistance to its artists and the organizations that support their work.

(11) To fulfill its educational mission, achieve an orderly continuation of free society, and provide models of excellence to the American people, the Federal Government must transmit the achievement and values of civilization from the past via the present to the future, and make widely available the greatest achievements of art.

(12) In order to implement these findings and purposes, it is desirable to establish a National Foundation on the Arts and the Humanities.

§ 1:41 Art per se laws—Federal laws—National endowment for the arts

Within NFAH, the National Endowment for the Arts (NEA) was created.[1] The NEA is charged with, among other tasks, encouraging cultural creation and redistributing cultural products throughout the nation, linking regional America with the cultural coasts. A specific legislative list of the NEA mandate follows:

(c) The [NEA], with the advice of the National Council on the Arts, is authorized to establish and carry out a program of contracts with, or grants-in-aid or loans to, groups or, in appropriate cases, individuals of exceptional talent engaged in or concerned with the arts, for the purpose of enabling them to provide or support—

(1) projects and productions which have sub-

[Section 1:41]

[1] 20 U.S.C.A. §§ 954 et seq.

stantial national or international artistic and cultural significance, giving emphasis to American creativity and cultural diversity and to the maintenance and encouragement of professional excellence;

(2) projects productions, meeting professional standards or standards of authenticity or tradition, irrespective of origin, which are of significant merit and which, without such assistance, would otherwise be unavailable to our citizens for geographic or economic reasons;

(3) projects and productions that will encourage and assist artists and enable them to achieve wider distribution of their works, to work in residence at an educational or cultural institution, or standards of professional excellence;

(4) projects and productions which have substantial artistic and cultural significance and that reach, or reflect the culture of, a minority, inner city, rural, or tribal community;

(5) projects and productions that will encourage public knowledge, education, understanding, and appreciation of the arts;

(6) workshops that will encourage and develop the appreciation and enjoyment of the arts by our citizens;

(7) programs for the arts at the local level;

(8) projects that enhance managerial and organizational skills and capabilities;

(9) projects, productions, and workshops of the kinds described in paragraphs (1) through (8) through film, radio, video, and similar media, for the purpose of broadening public access to the arts; and

(10) other relevant projects.

Congress pledged federal funds to "help create and sustain . . . a climate encouraging freedom of thought, imagination, and inquiry . . . [and] the material conditions facilitating the release of creative talent."[2] The NEA has substantial discretion to award grants under broad funding priorities. NEA awards grants-in-aid through direct and indirect subsidy to groups and individuals whose artistic endeavors have "substantial artistic and cultural significance,"[3] or are otherwise worthy of public support,[4] and through state agencies established to serve same purposes.[5] In response, states have established state art commissions and arts councils that apply for and receive NEA monies for distribution among state approved projects.

The NEA acts through its Chair and a 26 member National Council on the Arts (Council), appointed by the President, with the advice of the Senate.[6] Although the ultimate decisionmaker, the Chair is prohibited from approving or disapproving grant applications until recommendations of the Council have been received.[7] The Chair is authorized to utilize panels of experts to review funding applications;[8] after 1990, "peer review" is mandatory for visual arts applications.[9] Advisory review panels after the 1990 Amendments are to be comprised of experts reflecting "diverse artistic and cultural points of view . . . geographic, ethnic and minority representation . . . [and] lay individuals knowledgeable about the arts."[10]

Controversy arising from NEA visual arts grants in the 1980s prompted Congress to restrict funding[11] and amend

[2]20 U.S.C.A. § 951(7).

[3]20 U.S.C.A. § 954(c)(1).

[4]20 U.S.C.A. § 954(c)(2)–(5).

[5]20 U.S.C.A. § 954(g).

[6]20 U.S.C.A. §§ 954(b)(1) and 955(b).

[7]20 U.S.C.A. § 955(f); some exceptions apply for applications for grants of $30,000 or less.

[8]20 U.S.C.A. § 959(a)(4).

[9]20 U.S.C.A. § 959(c).

[10]20 U.S.C.A. § 959(c)(1)–(2).

[11]Pub. L. No. 101-121, § 304(a) 103 Stat. 701 (1989) ("None of the funds authorized to be appropriated for the [NEA] may be used to promote, disseminate, or produce materials which in the judgment of the [NEA] may be considered obscene, including but not limited to, depictions of sadomasochism, homoeroticism, the sexual exploitation of

NEA grant making criteria.[12] These changes arose from two awards made in the 1980s that still affect the contemporary climate. The Institute of Contemporary Art used $30,000 of an NEA visual arts grant to fund a retrospective of Robert Mapplethorpe and the Southeastern Center for Contemporary Art awarded Andres Serrano a $15,000 grant from NEA support.

To implement the new congressional mandate, the NEA instituted a requirement, which grantees had to certify in writing, that federal funds would not be used in a manner inconsistent with the 1990 criteria. The certification requirement was invalidated as unconstitutionally vague.[13]

After considering various proposed amendments, Congress adopted a bipartisan compromise. Section 954(d)(1) directed the NEA Chair under the new amendments as follows: "[A]rtistic excellence and artistic merit are the criteria by which [NEA] applications are judged, taking into consideration general standards of decency and respect for the diverse beliefs and values of the American public."[14] That statutory language as a criterion for NEA funding eligibility had been declared unconstitutional by a

---

children, or individual engaged in sex acts and which, when taken as a whole, do not have serious . . . artistic . . . value."). This provision was declared unconstitutional in Bella Lewitzky Dance Foundation v. Frohnmayer, 754 F. Supp. 774 (C.D. Cal. 1991).

[12] Pub. L. No. 101-512, § 103(b), 104 Stat. 1915 (1990). 20 U.S.C.A. 954(d)(2), in conjunction with 20 U.S.C.A. 952(j), contains an obscenity exclusion for NEA grants based upon an adjudicative standard rather than mere agency determination, a provision that has been upheld, at least implicitly. *See* Finley v. National Endowment for the Arts, 100 F.3d 671 (9th Cir. 1996), cert. granted, 522 U.S. 991, 118 S. Ct. 554, 139 L. Ed. 2d 396 (1997) and rev'd, 524 U.S. 569, 118 S. Ct. 2168, 141 L. Ed. 2d 500 (1998).

[13] Bella Lewitzky Dance Foundation v. Frohnmayer, 754 F. Supp. 774 (C.D. Cal. 1991).

[14] 20 U.S.C.A. § 954(d)(1). *But see* Finley v. National Endowment for the Arts, 100 F.3d 671 (9th Cir. 1996), cert. granted, 522 U.S. 991, 118 S. Ct. 554, 139 L. Ed. 2d 396 (1997) and rev'd on other grounds, 524 U.S. 569, 118 S. Ct. 2168, 141 L. Ed. 2d 500 (1998) (section 954(d)(1) decency clause declared unconstitutional because of due process infirmities under first and fifth amendments and impermissible first amendment viewpoint discrimination).

federal district court,[15] affirmed on appeal by the Ninth Circuit on the ground that Section 954 on its face impermissibly discriminated on the basis of viewpoint, and was void for vagueness under the First and Fifth Amendments.[16] The United States Supreme Court reversed and remanded, finding Section 954(d)(1) facially valid.[17]

In Finley, four performance artists applied for NEA grants before Section 954(d)(1) was enacted. Their applications were denied. They sued, claiming violation of First Amendment rights. When Section 954 was enacted, the artists amended their complaint to challenge the provision as void for vagueness, arguing that the criteria were sufficiently subjective that the NEA could engage in viewpoint discrimination.

The Court concluded that given the varied interpretations of the criteria and the vague exhortation to "take them into consideration," it was unlikely that the provision would introduce any greater element of selectivity than "artistic excellence."[18]

In 1998, Congress restricted the availability of federal funds for individual artists; NEA grants are now primarily made to certain organizations and state arts agencies that in turn are constrained from sub-granting.[19]

Government localities also subsidize the arts. Federal

---

[15]Finley v. National Endowment for the Arts, 795 F. Supp. 1457 (C.D. Cal. 1992), aff'd, 100 F.3d 671 (9th Cir. 1996), cert. granted, 522 U.S. 991, 118 S. Ct. 554, 139 L. Ed. 2d 396 (1997) and rev'd on other grounds, 524 U.S. 569, 118 S. Ct. 2168, 141 L. Ed. 2d 500 (1998).

[16]Finley v. National Endowment for the Arts, 100 F.3d 671 (9th Cir. 1996), cert. granted, 522 U.S. 991, 118 S. Ct. 554, 139 L. Ed. 2d 396 (1997) and rev'd, 524 U.S. 569, 118 S. Ct. 2168, 141 L. Ed. 2d 500 (1998).

[17]National Endowment for the Arts v. Finley, 524 U.S. 569, 118 S. Ct. 2168, 141 L. Ed. 2d 500 (1998).

[18]National Endowment for the Arts v. Finley, 524 U.S. 569, 118 S. Ct. 2168, 141 L. Ed. 2d 500 (1998) ("a facial constitutional challenge is a heavy burden; the artist must demonstrate a substantial risk that application of the provision will lead to the suppression of speech . . ."); *see also* Broadrick v. Oklahoma, 413 U.S. 601, 613, 93 S. Ct. 2908, 37 L. Ed. 2d 830 (1973) ("facial invalidation is strong medicine . . . employed [only] sparingly . . . as a last resort.").

[19]Pub. L. 106-113, 113 Stat. 1501 (1999).

constitutional standards still apply, including first amendment proscriptions on viewpoint discrimination. Although government is not required to fund the arts, when it does so decision making must be viewpoint-neutral.[20]

XIII. ATTORNEYS AND THE ARTS: PROFESSIONAL RESPONSIBILITY

§ 1:42 Generally

Practitioners provided with the range of arts issues offered here will presumably be in a better position to determine if and when their matters require the arts expertise discussed, an expertise that may have direct bearing on the outcome of their case and perhaps others. Aside from the substantive matters at hand, the role of attorneys in the context of handling arts matters bears particular consideration. The mystery and novelty pervasive in arts transactions and arts disputes have, on occasion, veiled the professional vision of lawyers, bound in art law as in any other area of practice by ethical guidelines and rules of professional responsibility.

Lawyer conduct relating to arts litigation has come before the court, inter alia, as follows: the propriety of time billed and reasonableness of attorneys' fees;[1] prospective awards of attorneys' fees for enforcement of judg-

---

[20]Brooklyn Institute of Arts and Sciences v. City of New York, 64 F. Supp. 2d 184 (E.D. N.Y. 1999)> (withholding appropriated municipal funds to museum because officials called exhibition "sick" and "disgusting" constituted viewpoint discrimination); Cuban Museum of Arts and Culture, Inc. v. City of Miami, 766 F. Supp. 1121 (S.D. Fla. 1991)> (withholding municipal support to museum because exhibition included artists who did not denounce Cuban President Fidel Castro constituted viewpoint discrimination); Esperanza Peace and Justice Center v. City of San Antonio, 2001 WL 685795 (W.D. Tex. 2001)) (municipality's discontinuation of arts funding to nonprofit group based upon opposition to plaintiffs' support of gay and lesbian issues constituted viewpoint discrimination).

[Section 1:42]

[1]Martin v. City of Indianapolis, 28 F. Supp. 2d 1098 (S.D. Ind. 1998) (upholding award of attorneys fees and costs as reasonable in VARA case); Farris v. Todd, 2000 WL 528408 (Tenn. Ct. App. 2000) (assignment and sale of painting by client to attorneys in partial payment for services); Estate of Rothko, 84 Misc. 2d 830, 379 N.Y.S.2d 923, 18 U.C.C. Rep. Serv. 1191 (Sur. Ct. 1975), decree modified, 56 A.D.2d 499,

ments;[2] effectiveness of counsel;[3] roles of attorney participation in art business;[4] representation of adverse interests;[5] conflicts of interest;[6] unconscionable conduct;[7]

---

392 N.Y.S.2d 870 (1st Dep't 1977), order aff'd, 43 N.Y.2d 305, 401 N.Y.S.2d 449, 372 N.E.2d 291 (1977) (for costs); in re determination of legal fees payable to In re Estate of Warhol, 224 A.D.2d 235, 637 N.Y.S.2d 708 (1st Dep't 1996) (award of attorney's fees modified from $7.2 million to $3.5 million, and determination of reasonable legal compensation in artist's estate properly based upon, *inter alia,* time spent, difficulties involved, nature of services, professional standing of counsel, and results obtained).

[2]McCloud v. Lawrence Gallery, Ltd., 1992 WL 6199 (S.D. N.Y. 1992), aff'd, 970 F.2d 896 (2d Cir. 1992) (award of attorney's fees and prospective attorney's fees in underlying action upheld in enforcement of judgment in RICO action).

[3]Grooms v. Solem, 923 F.2d 88 (8th Cir. 1991) (defendant convicted on two counts for selling Native American artifacts stolen from museum appeals on denial of sixth amendment right to effective counsel).

[4]Martin S. Ackerman Foundation v. C.I.R., T.C. Memo. 1986-365, 1986 WL 21569 (1986) (attorney's role in directing private clients to donate artworks purchased from his art business to museums key issue in determining tax-exempt status of foundation he established); Smith's (David) Estate v. Commissioner of Internal Revenue, 57 T.C. 650, 1972 WL 2557 (1972), acq. 1974-2 C.B. and recommendation regarding acquiescence, 1974 WL 36002 (I.R.S. AOD 1974) and aff'd, 510 F.2d 479 (2d Cir. 1975) (role of attorneys in management and administration of artist's estate); *see also* Estate of Rothko, 84 Misc. 2d 830, 379 N.Y.S.2d 923, 18 U.C.C. Rep. Serv. 1191 (Sur. Ct. 1975), decree modified, 56 A.D.2d 499, 392 N.Y.S.2d 870 (1st Dep't 1977), order aff'd, 43 N.Y.2d 305, 401 N.Y.S.2d 449, 372 N.E.2d 291 (1977) (role of gallery directors as executors of artist's will).

[5]Williamsburg Wax Museum, Inc. v. Historic Figures, Inc., 810 F.2d 243, 6 Fed. R. Serv. 3d 1258 (D.C. Cir. 1987) (attorney representing interest adverse to former client); *see also* 56 A.L.R. Fed. 189 §§ 3, 4, 6 (disqualification of law firm for representation of party in federal suit involving former client of firm); *see also* In re: Williamsburg Wax, 52 A.L.R. 2d 1243 supp. §§ 4, 8, 16.

[6]Matter of Friedman, 64 A.D.2d 70, 407 N.Y.S.2d 999 (2d Dep't 1978) (counsel to art gallery purporting to act as counsel for widow of gallery artist drafts contract giving gallery rights in all the artist's artworks).

[7]Matter of Friedman, 64 A.D.2d 70, 407 N.Y.S.2d 999 (2d Dep't 1978), *and see also* 18 A.L.R. 3d 1305 supp. § 4 (unconscionability of lawyer's conduct as grounds for refusing to enforce contracts for sale of goods).

attorney as witness;[8] concealment of evidence;[9] and estate dissolution;[10] and preservation of client confidences from prior representation when defending adverse interest to former client-plaintiff.[11]

---

[8]Keoseian v. von Kaulbach, 707 F. Supp. 150 (S.D. N.Y. 1989) (motion to disqualify counsel brought by Max Beckmann's sister-in-law, claiming counsel previously represented plaintiff on matters substantially related to the litigation and that law firm partners were witnesses who would or could be called to testify at trial).

[9]Matter of John Doe Partnership, 145 Misc. 2d 783, 548 N.Y.S.2d 389 (Sup 1989) (cartoon drawings stolen from museum seized under search warrant at offices of law firm arranging for resale of art to firm client).

[10]Smith's (David) Estate v. Commissioner of Internal Revenue, 57 T.C. 650, 1972 WL 2557 (1972), acq. 1974-2 C.B. and recommendation regarding acquiescence, 1974 WL 36002 (I.R.S. AOD 1974) and aff'd, 510 F.2d 479 (2d Cir. 1975) (conflict of interest of attorney in administration of estate and disposal of assets); *cf.* Estate of Rothko, 84 Misc. 2d 830, 379 N.Y.S.2d 923, 18 U.C.C. Rep. Serv. 1191 (Sur. Ct. 1975), decree modified, 56 A.D.2d 499, 392 N.Y.S.2d 870 (1st Dep't 1977), order aff'd, 43 N.Y.2d 305, 401 N.Y.S.2d 449, 372 N.E.2d 291 (1977) (for costs).

[11]Junior Gallery, Ltd. v. Foreign Resources Corp., 1994 WL 669556 (S.D.N.Y. Nov. 29, 1994) (motion to disqualify law firm because its successive representation of adverse interests created possibility that lawyer would use confidences gained in prior representation of plaintiff in copyright to its detriment in current litigation where it represented defendant).

Chapter 2

Trade Practices Overview

I. STRUCTURE OF ART MARKETS

A. MARKET TERRITORY

B. MARKET IDENTIFICATION

C. BASIC MARKETS

D. ART PRODUCT COMPONENTS: THE CROSSAQ FACTOR (CONDITION, RARITY, OWNERSHIP, SIZE, SUBJECT MATTER, AUTHORSHIP, QUALITY)

II. MARKET PERFORMANCE AND PLAYERS

A. HISTORICAL EVOLUTION OF ART TRADING

B. SALES

C. SERVICES

D. FORMS OF BUSINESS ASSOCIATION

E. TRADER-CLIENT ACTIONS

F. TRADER-LANDLORD ACTIONS

III. TRADER DUTIES AND OBLIGATIONS

A. STATUTORY DEFINITIONS

B. DUTY TO MAINTAIN RECORDS AND ACCOUNT

C. INSURANCE

XI. TORTS

A. DEFAMATION

B. DISPARAGEMENT

XII. PROVENANCE

XIII. CATALOGUE RAISONNE

XIV. DUE DILIGENCE

§ 2:72 Post-War Considerations

KeyCite®: Cases and other legal materials listed in KeyCite Scope can be researched through West's KeyCite service on Westlaw®. Use KeyCite to check citations for form, parallel references, prior and later history, and comprehensive citator information, including citations to other decisions and secondary materials.

I. STRUCTURE OF ART MARKETS

A. MARKET TERRITORY

§ 2:1 Generally

This chapter introduces basic markets, describes market terms typical in the trade and identifies common participants. Art trading is the source of substantial art law litigation; a trade is a mercantile purchase, sale, or transfer ordinarily made by professional traders that include, inter alia, dealers, gallery owners, auctioneers, and, on occasion, major collectors.[1] This cadre of dealers, galleries, and auctioneers is supplemented by numerous persons and entities engaged in art dealing, sometimes on a parttime or intermittent basis.[2] The Internet offers virtually anyone an opportunity to trade on line. Perhaps the most popular site is eBay. Major auction houses have also established Internet sales presences. Online traders have already experienced authenticity and fraud issues that occur in nonvirtual markets. Cases are pending, and no doubt more will be filed.[3] Eclectic traders exist because of absence of licensing or certification requirements for buying or selling artworks; low economic barriers to market entry; and the difficulty of regulating art product.

The term "art market" suggests a unitary trade arena. Such usage is misleading because art is created and collected, bought and sold, devised and disposed of, displayed and resold in various core and peripheral submarkets,

---

[Section 2:1]

[1]Boule v. Hutton, 70 F. Supp. 2d 378 (S.D. N.Y. 1999), judgement entered, 138 F. Supp. 2d 491 (S.D.N.Y. 2001).

[2]Traders, as a category, exclude artists who sell their own art works and charities who sell for fundraising purposes.

[3]*See* § 2:10.

some more stratified than others.[4] On occasion, markets are differentiated by artist, product diversity, market segmentation, and distribution channels.[5] Courts refer to "the fantasy land of marketing in the fine arts,"[6] but art markets do have structure, albeit fluidity of certain products and markets.

B. MARKET IDENTIFICATION

§ 2:2 Significance

What is the significance of the different markets and the separate chains? Specifics are discussed throughout this book, but of general import are two key factors: (1) the courts apply different laws and different principles, obtaining different results, to what otherwise might appear to be a similar transaction; and (2) the Internal Revenue Service evaluates tax claims involving art on the basis of value, i.e., "fair market value," and value is determined by locating the object in the proper market.

---

[4]Estate of O'Keeffe v. C.I.R., T.C. Memo. 1992-210, T.C.M. (RIA) ¶ 92210 (1992) ("a dealer must look within the general art market to the specific markets"); Jennings v. C.I.R., T.C. Memo. 1988-521, 1988 WL 117368 (1988) (expert witness testifies about multiple art markets).

[5]Temporal segmentation: Estate of O'Keeffe v. C.I.R., T.C. Memo. 1992-210, T.C.M. (RIA) ¶ 92210 (1992) ("[art] markets [must be distinguished] for pre-World War II and post-World War II American art"). Geographical segmentation: Estate of O'Keeffe v. C.I.R., T.C. Memo. 1992-210, T.C.M. (RIA) ¶ 92210 (1992) (America and Europe); Boule v. Hutton, 70 F. Supp. 2d 378 (S.D. N.Y. 1999) (testimony regarding a "single, integrated worldwide art market"); *see also* Solomon R. Guggenheim Foundation v. Lubell, 153 A.D.2d 143, 550 N.Y.S.2d 618 (1st Dep't 1990), order aff'd, 77 N.Y.2d 311, 567 N.Y.S.2d 623, 569 N.E.2d 426 (1991) ("The backdrop for this replevin action . . . is the New York City art market"). Product segmentation: Boule v. Hutton, 70 F. Supp. 2d 378 (S.D. N.Y. 1999) (specialized global market of Russian avant garde art); Autocephalous Greek-Orthodox Church of Cyprus v. Goldberg & Feldman Fine Arts Inc., 717 F. Supp. 1374 (S.D. Ind. 1989), judgment aff'd, 917 F.2d 278 (7th Cir. 1990) (antiquities market and modern market). Artist segmentation: Estate of O'Keeffe v. C.I.R., T.C. Memo. 1992-210, T.C.M. (RIA) ¶ 92210 (1992) ("When considering the works of a specific artist, a dealer must look within the general art market to the specific markets that support the value of the artist's work" including other artists.); Vitale v. Marlborough Gallery, 32 U.S.P.Q.2d (BNA) 1283, 1994 WL 654494 (S.D. N.Y. 1994) (submarket of artist Jackson Pollock); *see also* Ch 4.

[6]Porter v. Wertz, 56 A.D.2d 570, 392 N.Y.S.2d 10 (1st Dep't 1977).

Depending upon the market where the transaction occurs, different requirements exist for the level and degree of disclosures by the seller, the actual and presumed reliance of the buyer, the extent to which caveat emptor controls, the type, scope, effect, and duration of warranties, and the interaction of laws like trade regulation, unfair business practices, unfair competition, consumer protection, and others. In tax opinions, courts consider the proper markets offered by the government and those offered by the petitioner, but the court makes its own determination of the proper market and value in that market. Thus, prudent practice suggests locating the transaction in as many markets as appropriate, since courts tend to consider alternative market theories before they arrive at judicially determined values.[1]

§ 2:3 Determination of market identification

Appraisers play a critical role in identifying the proper market, and guidelines for doing so are discussed in Ch 3. In tax cases, the court is the ultimate determiner of the proper market; in nontax cases, the evidentiary base for market identification is usually expert testimony or lay opinion testimony, the admissibility of which is determined by applicable state or federal rules of evidence.

C. BASIC MARKETS

§ 2:4 Primary and secondary markets

A trade is often described in terms of its location in a primary market or a secondary market. A primary market trader takes product directly from its source, i.e., the artist, producer, or publisher, and sells it to various types of buyers, often the ultimate acquirer, i.e., the collector, and often sells or consigns to consultants or other traders. Trader's methods to account for secondary market sales are illustrated in Examples 1 to 4, Journal and Ledger entries, in Appendix 3. Primary describes the relationship of the sellers to its source. A primary market is one where

---

[Section 2:2]

[1]*See generally* Estate of O'Keeffe v. C.I.R., T.C. Memo. 1992-210, T.C.M. (RIA) ¶ 92210 (1992).

art product is obtained by the trader directly from the artist (and sometimes other traders), and is sold directly to collectors and others. The primary connection reduces or eliminates the opportunity for forgery or copying, and reduces the need to investigate prior ownership. The result of this primary relationship between artist and seller is that two major risks of art trading—ownership and title impairment—are greatly reduced.

A secondary market trader obtains product from diverse sources, including estates, auctions, other dealers, foreclosures, bankruptcies, museums, and other collections, and regularly consigns works to other traders, as well as selling to collectors and others. Trader's methods to account for secondary market sales are Illustrated in Example 6, Journal and Ledger entries, in Appendix 3. Works sold in the secondary market typically have a prior chain of sale, i.e., prior owners, lienholders, and title claimants. This is a major difference between trading in the primary market, where authorship can be directly sourced and no prior owners ordinarily exist, and trading in the secondary market, where authorship cannot be directly sourced, and many prior owners and unsecured and secured interests, known and unknown, may exist.[1]

§ 2:5 Adjacent markets

Some creators, producers, distributors, and exhibitors are active in both primary and secondary market trades. These persons and entities work in what is here termed "adjacent markets." These include publishers, foundries, ateliers, agents, consultants, and, at certain times and for certain purposes, art fairs and art expositions, and charitable and estate sales. Adjacent markets can be further distinguished by product line, distribution chains, and, occasionally, customer lists.

§ 2:6 Submarkets and specialty markets

A submarket is a market within a market. Submarkets

[Section 2:4]

[1]Buyers in the secondary market rely upon CROSSAQ, representations and investigations of others, and their own expertise and inquiries to authenticate works and assure good title. *See* § 2:11 regarding CROSSAQ.

are defined by: (1) public recognition of the submarket as one with a separate economic identity; (2) the product of the submarket having peculiar characteristics and uses; (3) existence of distinct customers for the submarket product; and (4) the product's having distinct prices and being sensitive to price changes and specialized factors.[1]

Submarkets for the visual arts have been identified by experts, although not all are accepted by the trade, while others are useless.[2]

§ 2:7 Gray markets

Art has been traded in a gray market,[1] in which "legitimately priced goods are [traded] without the authorization of the trademark or copyright holder."[2] A gray market often involves imported products "sold in the United States outside the manufacturer's distribution system, often contrary to the wishes of the manufacturer."[3] Gray market trading often includes "obscuring the chain of title."[4]

§ 2:8 Black market

In addition to licit trades in the various markets, a black

[Section 2:6]

[1]Vitale v. Marlborough Gallery, 1994 WL 654494, ¶ 11 (S.D.N.Y. July 1, 1994).

[2]Jennings v. C.I.R., T.C. Memo. 1988-521, 1988 WL 117368 (1988) (the broad market is one "in which the work of an artist that is well-known to a broad section of the public is sold").

[Section 2:7]

[1]W. Goebel Porzellanfabrik v. Action Industries, Inc., 589 F. Supp. 763 (S.D. N.Y. 1984) (producer of Hummel figures created by Sister Innocentia Hummel under license by her Order sued unauthorized distributor of Hummel figures in United States, alleging gray market distribution).

[2]W. Goebel Porzellanfabrik v. Action Industries, Inc., 589 F. Supp. 763 at 765 (S.D. N.Y. 1984).

[3]Johnson & Johnson Products, Inc. v. Dal Intern. Trading Co., 798 F.2d 100, 1 U.C.C. Rep. Serv. 2d 1082 (3d Cir. 1986).

[4]Johnson & Johnson Products, Inc. v. Dal Intern. Trading Co., 798 F.2d 100 at 103, 1 U.C.C. Rep. Serv. 2d 1082 (3d Cir. 1986); W. Goebel Porzellanfabrik v. Action Industries, Inc., 589 F. Supp. 763, 767 (S.D. N.Y. 1984).

market exists for stolen, forged, and fraudulent art.[1] The media and the insurance industry report that the black market is a flourishing and lucrative one involving billions of dollars of art, although it is unclear how reliable such estimates are since ordinarily price is not known unless the sale is reported or is part of an undercover operation. The black market resale price or "fence" price, can be 10 percent of estimated value or as little as one percent; art black market prices are discounted to reflect risks, including, inter alia, the country or countries in which transaction(s) occurred, nationality and residence of the buyer, and applicable statutes of limitations.

Traders that knowingly sell both licit and illicit art are dangerous for the unsuspecting because the mix allows legitimacy to mask fraud.[2] Although the black market is linked to criminal conduct, trade of a black market work can unwittingly be made by legitimate participants in the arts community; traders and museums alike agree that even the best can be duped on occasion, and reputable museum exhibitions have been created around fakery. Efforts to report, record, and publicize stolen and counterfeit art are underway domestically and internationally; such registries may expedite notification in the licit market of black or gray goods and reduce illicit trades.[3]

§ 2:9 Financial markets

The art markets are considered to be less secure than and are distinct from financial markets in the eyes of the

---

[Section 2:8]

[1] *See* Ch 11.

[2] *See, e.g.,* U.S. v. Amiel, 995 F.2d 367 (2d Cir. 1993) (affirming denial of defendants' motion to dismiss criminal indictments for art trading under following theories: mail fraud, money laundering, transportation of stolen goods, and RICO violations).

[3] Art Loss Register (New York, London) 126,000 works; Invaluable (London) 100,000 works; Article Classic Identification System (New Scotland Yard); International Foundation for Art Research; *See* Ch 5 (disclosures by traders to clients)

legislatures and the courts.[1] In resolving the estate of Georgia O'Keeffe, the court noted: "A work of art usually does not have intrinsic financial value beyond its desirability as art and lacks external indicia of return prior to resale, such as earnings or investment."[2] Unlike certain turnover sales in capital markets,[3] the purchase of works of art are expressly excluded from many state securities and commodities laws,[4] and have been rejected as "investment contracts" by courts.[5]

§ 2:10 The internet

The Internet has attracted all variants of sellers and buyers. While legal problems relating to internet sales have appeared in the media, few cases have yet been filed and to date none could be found at the precedential level. At least one gallery utilizing eBay had its site suspended after a state attorney general brought suit for deceptive business practices and false advertising on behalf of

---

[Section 2:9]

[1]Mechigian v. Art Capital Corp., 612 F. Supp. 1421 (S.D. N.Y. 1985).

[2]Estate of O'Keeffe v. C.I.R., T.C. Memo. 1992-210, T.C.M. (RIA) ¶ 92210 (1992).

[3]*See, e.g.,* In re Drexel Burnham Lambert Inc., 861 F.2d 1307 (2d Cir. 1988); In re Ivan F. Boesky Securities Litigation, 948 F.2d 1358 (2d Cir. 1991).

[4]For example, Arkansas (Ark. Code Ann. § 19-11-203(5), (14)); Colorado (Colo. Rev. Stat. § 11-53-102); Georgia (Ga. Code Ann. § 10-5A-1); Idaho (Idaho Code § 30-1501); Indiana (Ind. Code § 23-26-4); Iowa (Iowa Code Ann. § 502A-1); Maine (Me. Rev. Stat. T. 32 § 11201); Missouri (Mo. Ann. Stat. § 409.800); Montana (Mont. § 30-10-103); Nebraska (Neb. Rev. Stat. § 8-1705); Nevada (Nev. Rev. Stat. § 91.050); New Mexico (N.M. Stat. Ann. § 58-13A-2); New York (N.Y. Gen. Bus. Law § 359-e); North Carolina (N.C. Gen. Stat. § 78D-1); North Dakota (N.D. Cent. Code, § 51-23-02); Oklahoma (Okla. Stat. T. 71 § 2); Utah (Utah Code Ann. § 61-1-13); Washington (Wash. Rev. Code § 21.30.010).

[5]Mechigian v. Art Capital Corp., 612 F. Supp. 1421 (S.D. N.Y. 1985), cited approvingly in Zion v. Standard Financial Management Corp., 1988 WL 82043 (D. Mass. 1988) (sale of rare coins). The purchase-as-investment issue is distinct from whether or not a collection of art constitutes an "investment" for purposes of the Internal Revenue Code.

numerous buyers claiming the artworks were fake.[1] Bidding schemes to inflate prices of artworks by shill bidding on eBay have been the basis of federal complaints charging conspiracy and mail fraud when United States Postal inspectors traced multiple bids to the same internet protocol [IP] addresses of dealers and collectors hosting the auctions.[2]

D. ART PRODUCT COMPONENTS: THE CROSSAQ FACTOR (CONDITION, RARITY, OWNERSHIP, SIZE, SUBJECT MATTER, AUTHORSHIP, QUALITY)

§ 2:11 Generally

The most basic trade issues about the work of art, in colloquial terms, are: (1) who created it? (authenticity); (2) what's it worth? (valuation and appraisal); and (3) who is selling it? (ownership and title). These questions appear simplistic, but, so stated, they implicate a range of complex issues crucial to the legal viability of any sale: warranty, contract, provenance, authenticity, title, ownership, valuation, and resale value.

What is an artwork in the context of sale? Artwork, unlike widgets, cannot be consensually identified and described by direct examination and physical measurement, as discussed in Ch 1. Art is unique in that many of the components crucial to identification and value are external to the physical object, hence the metier of connoisseurship, which is beyond the scope of a legal treatise. Certain extrinsic elements must be considered by lawyers, however, because they are implicated in art sales.

Basic elements used to evaluate works of art in a sales context include: Condition, Rarity, Ownership, Size,

---

[Section 2:10]

[1]Judith H. Dobryzynski, "Spitzer Sues Gallery Over Fake Art on eBay," New York Times, sec. E (May 26, 2000) (registered domain suspended by eBay pending resolution of case).

[2]Houston Chronicle, p. 4 (Feb. 10, 2002) (defendants arrested for wire fraud in federal criminal complaint alleging shill bidding on Rene LaLique crystal auctioned on eBay).

Subject Matter, Authorship, Quality,[1] referred to for convenience by the acronym CROSSAQ. CROSSAQ establishes a composite profile of the artwork referred to here as the CROSSAQ factor. The CROSSAQ factor contains the basics to assist lawyers in evaluating art sales; connoisseurs, auctioneers, curators, appraisers, insurers, and traders may use additional or alternative traits.

CROSSAQ SUMMARY

(1) Condition (C): What is the condition of the object? Has it been damaged, altered, cleaned, conserved, or restored, and to what degree? (Substantial work by one other than the artist affects authenticity.)

(2) Rarity (R): Is the image typical or unusual for the artist's body of work? Is the object a one-of-a-kind or a multiple? If it is one of a kind, were other similar images made, and if so, how many? If a multiple, what is the size of the edition, and is there more than one edition?[2]

(3) Ownership (O): Has an ownership interest been disclosed? What is the documentation, and what does it recite? Is the object cultural property that might have sovereign ownership?[3] Are there competing, prioritized or superior interests?[4]

(4) Size (S): Size is the measurement of the object; standard recitation is height by width by depth. Seemingly the most objective of components, even size, invites subjectivity: Are the measurements of the object framed or unframed? Is the size based on the object's former placement in a larger

---

[Section 2:11]

[1]When artworks are evaluated under tax matters, some or all of these elements are used. *See, e.g.,* Ferrari v. C.I.R., T.C. Memo. 1989-521, 1989 WL 109420 (1989), judgment aff'd, 931 F.2d 54 (4th Cir. 1991) ("value is determined by the condition, the uniqueness or rarity of the item, authenticity and size, and the market value of comparable objects").

[2]See Ch 12.

[3]See Ch 6.

[4]See Ch 5 and 11.

presentation, like a triptych or an altar piece? Is the size based on rolled or stretched canvas? (Measurements that differ from catalogue entries may raise issues about authenticity.)

(5) Subject matter (S): Subject matter refers to the subject of the work and its presentation, e.g., landscape or still life. Subject matter relates more to value in that certain subjects are considered more saleable to a general public or more unusual in the artist's oeuvre, and thus have greater impact on resale potential. (Subject matter can affect authenticity if the subject matter is considered outside the artist's body of work.)

(6) Authorship (A): Authorship is the core of authenticity, the identification of the relationship of the artist to a particular work. Authorship is the most complicated legal and arts issue, and the terms "authentication," "attribution," and even "appraisal" are often erroneously interchanged.[5] (A forged work could be "authenticated" if the forger were identified as the author, and such forged works have sold for considerable amounts at auction.)

(7) Quality (Q): Quality refers to the execution and composition of the work, usually analyzed in relationship to other works by the artist. Quality thus includes colors, tonalities, lighting, faceting, and other items used in executing the object, the degree to which the work is realized, and sometimes the degree of completion, e.g., a signed and dated drawing compared to an unfinished sketch by the same artist.

The CROSSAQ factor contains intrinsic and extrinsic components, as the following examples show: Signature: The name "Picasso" may appear on the artwork; that is a signature intrinsic to the physical work of art. But that signature is not significant unless the artwork is authored by Picasso; to determine authorship is to authenticate the signature, an extrinsic analysis. Condition: A painting may appear to be in good condition to the naked eye,

---

[5] *See* Ch 3.

termed the "apparent condition,"[6] but the actual condition of the painting may be otherwise; the canvas could have been severely damaged, restored and relined, latent intrinsic factors visible only through scientific testing.

II. MARKET PERFORMANCE AND PLAYERS

A. HISTORICAL EVOLUTION OF ART TRADING

§ 2:12 Generally

Art dealing is traced back to the Roman conquest when Greek works were appropriated for reproduction in Roman workshops. In the early Renaissance, diplomats, emissaries, artists, and advisors purchased and commissioned works from artists on behalf of royal, papal, aristocratic, or merchant-banker procurers. These persons, some referred to as "marchands amateurs," were paid or otherwise remunerated for their efforts. In the seventeenth century, particularly in the low countries, art was sold to a growing prosperous middle class by persons whose occupation primarily involved purchase and sale of art. But it was not until the nineteenth century, when artists rejected the formalities and restrictions of academy rules on artmaking in favor of exploration and invention, that the commercial gallery, as it is known today, appeared. The tradition of dealers as connoisseurs, market-makers, and artist groomers debuts in France in the 1800s and continues to this day.

B. SALES

§ 2:13 Dealers

Dealers almost invariably are involved in mercantile art transactions, and the term is almost universally used in that context.[1] Dealers have been described variously as

---

[6]*See* Ch 14.

[Section 2:13]

[1]For what constitutes selling enough art to satisfy the Commissioner that one is in the business of dealing, *see* Porter v. C. I. R., 437 F.2d 39 (2d Cir. 1970) (taxpayer sold insignificant amounts of art over sixteen year period); custom and usage treat auctioneers separately, and auction sales are covered in Ch 5.

those who trade art[2] with the intent to profit[3] by buying and selling,[4] and those acting as consignors and consignees.[5] Dealers, unlike mercantile gallery owners, may or may not have exhibition spaces open to the public. Several points should here be noted: (1) legal liability attaches to dealer activity well beyond the aforementioned traditional description of dealer conduct; (2) definitions of "art dealer" under state art per se statutes[6] may not comport with definitions of "merchant" under Section 2-104(1) of the Uniform Commercial Code; and (3) art per se definitions of dealers and/or art merchants vary from state to state and even within a state.[7]

Dealers may trade in expectation interests for art not yet in their possession, control, or custodial care. Dealers may acquire by contract future contingent interests to sell art in existence, but not in their possession or control.

---

[2]Courts and statutes tend to restrict dealers to traders who sell so-called "fine" art. *See, e.g.,* McCloud v. Lawrence Gallery, Ltd., 1991 WL 136027 (S.D. N.Y. 1991). But fine art is even more elusive to define than art, and its usage has decreased in the arts. The distinction drawn here, where deemed appropriate, is between retail traders in the mass market, often termed by the trade "commercial," as opposed to others, which may or may not be "fine."

[3]Waitzkin v. C.I.R., T.C. Memo. 1992-216, T.C.M. (RIA) ¶ 92216 (1992) ("commercial galleries whose business is selling art for a profit"); Churchman v. Commission of Internal Revenue, 68 T.C. 696, 701, 1977 WL 3604 (1977).

[4]McCloud v. Lawrence Gallery, Ltd., 1991 WL 136027 (S.D. N.Y. 1991) (dealer "engaged in the business of buying and selling fine art"); Danae Art Intern. Inc. v. Stallone, 163 A.D.2d 81, 557 N.Y.S.2d 338 (1st Dep't 1990) (plaintiff-gallery in dispute over purchase of Francis Bacon painting from celebrity through his art consultant, "plaintiffs are art dealers in the business of selling art").

[5]Matter of Miller, 545 F.2d 916, 20 U.C.C. Rep. Serv. 1314 (5th Cir. 1977) (sculptures and paintings consigned to art gallery for sale). This is not intended to limit the terms by which dealers may hold art, i.e., bailment, entrustment, and trust, discussed in §§ 2:28 to 2:39.

[6]*See* Ch 1.

[7]" 'Merchant' means a person who deals in goods of the kind or otherwise by his occupation holds himself out as having knowledge or skill peculiar to the practices or goods involved in the transaction or to whom such knowledge or skill may be attributed by his employment of an agent or broker or other intermediary who by his occupation holds himself out as having such knowledge or skill." A national survey of state laws defining dealers and their duties is in Appendix 4.

These include preemptive rights, also termed rights of first refusal,[8] and future consignment interests.[9] Both contingent interests have been upheld as valid against challenge under the Rule Against Perpetuities, and common-law unreasonable restraints of alienation.[10]

No governmental licensing procedure, permit application, or registration system exists for dealers.[11] No legal requirements need to be satisfied before denominating an individual or an entity as a dealer, other than the tax laws and those that generally apply to operating a business under the dealer's form of business organization pursuant to state and local law.[12] However, some states impose regional requirements, e.g., a valid sales tax permit, on the definition of "art dealer" under state art per se statutes,[13] or require occupational license taxes under state revenue laws.

§ 2:14 Galleries—Display

Galleries have exhibition spaces regularly open to the public, but, unlike dealers, not all are involved in mercantile transactions. The National Gallery of Fine Art[1] and

---

[8]Wildenstein & Co., Inc. v. Wallis, 79 N.Y.2d 641, 584 N.Y.S.2d 753, 595 N.E.2d 828 (1992) (rights of first refusal also known as preemptive rights).

[9]Wildenstein & Co., Inc. v. Wallis, 79 N.Y.2d 641, 584 N.Y.S.2d 753, 595 N.E.2d 828 (1992) (by settlement agreement executed during lifetime of director-collector Hal B. Wallis, dealer acquired preemptive rights and future consignment interests to portions of Wallis' collection of modern and impressionist art).

[10]Wildenstein & Co., Inc. v. Wallis, 79 N.Y.2d 641, 584 N.Y.S.2d 753, 595 N.E.2d 828 (1992).

[11]State and local laws may require registrations, permits and licenses, e.g., doing business under fictitious names, resale permits, and franchise, use, and license taxes.

[12]For example, fictitious business name statement for d/b/a; incorporated dealers would be subject to state corporate law rules and regulations.

[13]*See, e.g.,* Cal. Civ. Code § 986(c)(3).

[Section 2:14]

[1]Mac'Avoy v. The Smithsonian Inst., 757 F. Supp. 60 (D.D.C. 1991) ("The National Gallery of Fine Art . . . is one of several museums functioning under the auspices of the Smithsonian Institution.").

the Corcoran Gallery of Art, for example, are museums.[2] To the extent galleries are regulated, they are subject to separate laws and practices, i.e., not-for-profit corporate laws, and opinions of the state's attorney general. There are no governmental licensing procedures, permit applications, or registration system for mercantile galleries; no legal requirements need to be satisfied to denominate a business as a "gallery," other than the tax laws and those that generally apply to operating a business under the gallery's form of business organization pursuant to state and local law.

§ 2:15 Galleries—The stable—Representation

The continual and consistent representation of the same living artists by the same gallery that regularly promotes and exhibits their works is occasionally referred to as the stable. Use of the term "stable" indicates a long-term relationship of commitment, support, and sponsorship between dealer and artist, as opposed to occasional sales or episodic exhibitions.

§ 2:16 Galleries—The stable—Artist's removal from stable as interference with contractual relations

A valid cause of action for interference with contractual relations, generally stated, requires a plaintiff to allege the existence of a valid contract; a defendant's knowledge of the contract; a defendant's intentional inducement of a contracting party to breach the contract; and damages arising as a result of breach. A court refused to dismiss a cause of action for intentional breach of contractual relations where one Manhattan gallery alleged another Manhattan gallery induced a critically and commercially recognized artist affiliated with the first gallery to join the second for a $2 million payment.[1]

---

[2] *See also* Mount v. Ormand, 1991 WL 191228 (S.D. N.Y. 1991) ("The Coe-Kerr Gallery is an art auction house").

[Section 2:16]

[1] Sonnabend Gallery v. Halley, No. 12723/92 (N.Y. Sup. 1992).

§ 2:17 Galleries—The stable—Tortious interference with business relations

To allege a valid cause of action for tortious interference with business in some jurisdictions, a plaintiff must allege that a defendant used unlawful means to sever business relations or intended injury. Unlawful in this context involves fraud, misrepresentation, civil suits, or criminal prosecutions and some degree of economic pressure. A competitor is entitled to use lawful methods to induce a party's nonperformance in the interest of business advantage, but it is a question of fact when persuasion becomes economic pressure. Where a plaintiff-gallery alleged this cause of action against a defendant-gallery for taking from the stable one of its artists, the court refused to dismiss, allowing issues to be presented to the fact-finder at trial.[1]

§ 2:18 Galleries—The stable—Conversion

Adequately identified commissions or percentages due a trader upon the sale of art may be converted by another trader where the first trader sells artworks prior to the artist's leaving the stable, if the first trader can identify the buyers and sales from which the commissions were owed. A court refused to dismiss claims for conversion brought by one gallery against another for commissions on sales of paintings made before an artist left the gallery, where the alleged sales were to museums and other galleries.[1] Conversion claims were dismissed where the artist sought return of his photographs from a one-man exhibition at the gallery before it was over, resulting in the dealer's call to police to remove him.[2] Without ruling on whether the facts would sustain conversion, the court dismissed because the artist failed to show compensatory

[Section 2:17]

[1]Sonnabend Gallery v. Halley, No. 12723/92 (N.Y. Sup. 1992).

[Section 2:18]

[1]Sonnabend Gallery v. Halley, No. 12723/92 (N.Y. Sup. 1992).

[2]Koeniges v. Woodward, 183 Misc. 2d 347, 702 N.Y.S.2d 781 (City Civ. Ct. 2000) (summary judgment on replevin of artworks took almost 2 years from time artist demanded gallery to return his art).

or punitive damages.[3] Nor was the artist entitled to attorneys' fees.[4]

§ 2:19 Art consultants, advisers, and agents

Agents, advisers, and art consultants are active in the art markets. Agents may represent artists to the exclusion of other traders and sell their works to third parties, including galleries and dealers, or agents may represent artists in conjunction with dealer or gallery representation. An art agent should not be confused with agency that arises from dealer or gallery representation.

Art agents, unlike those representing talent in entertainment or sports who may be regulated under state laws, do not need to satisfy any legal requirements. The relationships between artists and agents vary; it is a question of fact and circumstance as to when agents fall within the ambit of art dealer definitions under art per se statutes. Agents, like their dealer and gallery counterparts, may hold artworks in trust for artists as a matter of law, and be liable for losses and damages in excess of contractual terms.

Art consultants may represent artists for the purposes of promotion, including obtaining gallery representation, museum exhibition, or corporate acquisition.[1] Common usage, however, refers to those who represent collectors, individual or institutional, to whom they make recommendations regarding purchases of art, for whom they may purchase art in their own name or their client's, and to whom they may offer advice about charitable contribu-

---

[3]Koeniges v. Woodward, 183 Misc. 2d 347, 702 N.Y.S.2d 781 (City Civ. Ct. 2000) (violation of N.Y. Arts & Cult. Aff. Law § 12.01 does not constitute sufficient moral culpability for punitive damages).

[4]Koeniges v. Woodward, 183 Misc. 2d 347, 702 N.Y.S.2d 781 (City Civ. Ct. 2000) (violation of N.Y. Arts & Cult. Aff. Law § 12.01 does not provide for attorneys' fees, punitive or treble damages, civil fines or criminal sanctions).

[Section 2:19]

[1]Waitzkin v. C.I.R., T.C. Memo. 1992-216, T.C.M. (RIA) ¶ 92216 (1992) (artist's sales bolstered by "professional art consultant who frequently recommended that major corporate clients purchase [artist's] works").

tions of art.[2] Fee arrangements vary. Example 4, Journal and Ledger entries, in Appendix 3 illustrates how consultant's remuneration might appear on the books of the trader.

Art consultants may be employed at or affiliated with corporations as in-house consultants charged with acquiring, maintaining, or deaccessioning corporate collections. Art consultants may assist governmental agencies or departments in collecting or displaying art. Art consultants also work independently or on their payrolls, with art sellers, like auctions or galleries, and art museums.

The relationship between consultants and their clients and sources varies, but again, like agents, their relationship to artists may exceed that contracted for under art per se statutes. A consultant's dealings with third parties, who reasonably relied to their detriment on "apparent authority" of the consultant to bind the principal, created agency.[3] Consultant dealing on behalf of individual clients has been the basis for alleging, inter alia, breach of fiduciary duty, breach of contract, negligence and negligent misrepresentation, fraud, and constructive fraud. Under the law of agency, consultants are under duties of loyalty, compelling disclosures to the principal and conduct in its best interest; but under the custom and usage of consultancy trading, secrecy about sources and terms is common and may contravene legal duties.[4] Thus, consultants who are not scrupulous about fee arrangements and client relationships have been vulnerable to claims that they impermissibly serve two masters.

Governmental licensing procedure, permit application, or a registration system does not exist for art agents or

---

[2]Martin S. Ackerman Foundation v. C.I.R., T.C. Memo. 1986-365, 1986 WL 21569 (1986) (status of purported nonprofit corporation and its consultancy role in recommending art donations to institutions in which lawyer served as trustee while he was also president and controlling shareholder in art dealership).

[3]Danae Art Intern. Inc. v. Stallone, 163 A.D.2d 81, 557 N.Y.S.2d 338 (1st Dep't 1990) (consultant as "agent" of collector seeking to sell Francis Bacon painting).

[4]Porter v. Wertz, 56 A.D.2d 570, 392 N.Y.S.2d 10 (1st Dep't 1977) ("in an industry whose transactions cry out for verification of both title to and authenticity of subject matter, it is deemed a poor practice to probe into either").

consultants.[5] In other words, there are no legal requirements to satisfy before denominating oneself an agent or consultant. The field has been further expanded by art brokers who lease artworks to businesses, option art, collect fees and perform related services.

§ 2:20 Trusts and estates

Traders may act as agents to sell artworks from trusts or estates of artists.[1] Representation of estates of artists may arise in these situations: (1) at the behest of the artist while still alive; (2) pursuant to testamentary dispositions; (3) as a result of legal resolution; or (4) at the request of the executors or administrators.[2] Such representation can be divided up by region and/or by body of work, e.g., one trader handles drawings and another paintings. Sales of estate works are carefully controlled for tax reasons and to maintain the integrity of the artist's market; posthumous distribution invariably occurs through various secondary markets.[3]

Trading through trusts or estates appears to create sep-

---

[5]State and local laws may require registrations, permits, and license taxes. Those who resell would be subject to applicable resale laws, which may require licenses, permits, registration, reporting. The Association of Independent Art Consultants is a membership organization.

[Section 2:20]

[1]Licensing agreements that involve creation of future reproductions from artist's oeuvre are also typical. *See, e.g.,* Schlaifer Nance & Co., Inc. v. Estate of Warhol, 764 F. Supp. 43 (S.D. N.Y. 1991); Kudo v. Simels, 1992 WL 80762 (S.D. N.Y. 1992).

[2]Wildenstein & Co. v. Wallis, 756 F. Supp. 158 (S.D. N.Y. 1991), rev'd without opinion, 983 F.2d 1047 (2d Cir. 1992) (art dealer alleges right to sell Hal Wallis collection of Impressionist and modern works of art pursuant to settlement agreement executed by Wallis purporting to give dealer a right of first refusal to sell); *see, e.g.,* Smith's (David) Estate v. Commissioner of Internal Revenue, 57 T.C. 650, 1972 WL 2557 (1972), acq. 1974-2 C.B. and recommendation regarding acquiescence, 1974 WL 36002 (I.R.S. AOD 1974) and aff'd, 510 F.2d 479 (2d Cir. 1975).

[3]Estate of O'Keeffe v. C.I.R., T.C. Memo. 1992-210, T.C.M. (RIA) ¶ 92210 (1992); Smith's (David) Estate v. Commissioner of Internal Revenue, 57 T.C. 650, 1972 WL 2557 (1972), acq. 1974-2 C.B. and recommendation regarding acquiescence, 1974 WL 36002 (I.R.S. AOD 1974) and aff'd, 510 F.2d 479 (2d Cir. 1975); Wildenstein & Co. v. Wallis, 756 F. Supp. 158 (S.D. N.Y. 1991), rev'd without opinion, 983 F.2d

arate standards of care and fiduciary duties above and beyond other trader relations. Failure to properly dispose of, value, or administer the artist's estate has been the basis of lengthy litigation on numerous grounds.[4] Trustees may be liable to third parties for the trading activity of independent dealers who sell art from the trust or trade such art with the trust's knowledge.[5]

§ 2:21 Art fairs

The art fair has become a popular forum for exhibit and sales by both primary and secondary market traders. Many types exist: international expositions, which may prohibit artist-entrants and vet, or purport to vet, trade entrants; invitation-only fairs where artists are selected by panels from their own country or by international jurists; trade fairs; and occasional weekend fairs, these last are often associated with neighborhood or community organizations. Some fairs are operated and managed by families; others are owned my media conglomerates. New York alone has a staggering number of fairs and shows, selectively and alphabetically listed: American Antiques Show, International Art and Design Fair, International Asian Art Fair, International Fine Art and Antique Deal-

---

1047 (2d Cir. 1992) (dealer attempts to enjoin auction house from selling art collection of late Hal B. Wallis).

[4]Estate of Rothko, 84 Misc. 2d 830, 379 N.Y.S.2d 923, 18 U.C.C. Rep. Serv. 1191 (Sur. Ct. 1975), decree modified, 56 A.D.2d 499, 392 N.Y.S.2d 870 (1st Dep't 1977), order aff'd, 43 N.Y.2d 305, 401 N.Y.S.2d 449, 372 N.E.2d 291 (1977) (for costs); Smith's (David) Estate v. Commissioner of Internal Revenue, 57 T.C. 650, 1972 WL 2557 (1972), acq. 1974-2 C.B. and recommendation regarding acquiescence, 1974 WL 36002 (I.R.S. AOD 1974) and aff'd, 510 F.2d 479 (2d Cir. 1975).

[5]Goldman v. Barnett, 793 F. Supp. 28, 18 U.C.C. Rep. Serv. 2d 55 (D. Mass. 1992) (allegations based upon appraisal and valuation of Milton Avery paintings brought by collector against dealer, who allegedly acted as agent for Milton Avery Trust, for conduct which might be imputed to trustee-defendants); *see also* Estate of Rothko, 84 Misc. 2d 830, 379 N.Y.S.2d 923, 18 U.C.C. Rep. Serv. 1191 (Sur. Ct. 1975), decree modified, 56 A.D.2d 499, 392 N.Y.S.2d 870 (1st Dep't 1977), order aff'd, 43 N.Y.2d 305, 401 N.Y.S.2d 449, 372 N.E.2d 291 (1977) (for costs); Smith's (David) Estate v. Commissioner of Internal Revenue, 57 T.C. 650, 1972 WL 2557 (1972), acq. 1974-2 C.B. and recommendation regarding acquiescence, 1974 WL 36002 (I.R.S. AOD 1974) and aff'd, 510 F.2d 479 (2d Cir. 1975).

ers Show, International Fine Art Fair, New York Armory Antiques Show, New York Ceramics Fair, New York Tribal Antiques Show, New York Winter Antiques Show, Outsider Art Fair, Print Fair, Works on Paper. Sales of works exhibited at art fairs have given rise to litigation.[1]

C. SERVICES

§ 2:22 CROSSAQ

Traders generally are cast as transferors of products among disparate purchasers and other traders in one or more markets.[1] In those roles, they have been considered by some courts as the bulwarks of the business, "the foundation stones of the market for fine art."[2] But a review of the markets and the subtext of the cases overwhelmingly support the position that product transfer is but one function. Traders, along with museums and auctions,[3] have diversified their services.[4] The majority of actions against traders claim damages for the services provided involving CROSSAQ.[5] These are dealer authentications, dealer appraisals, dealer certifications, dealer promotional efforts or lack thereof, and dealer disclosures or material omissions regarding prior ownership or possessory interests, restoration, or damage.

Traders, although they technically are distributors for producers in terms of marketing products provided by the producer to wholesale and retail to clients, are unlike com-

---

[Section 2:21]

[1]Greenberg Gallery, Inc. v. Bauman, 817 F. Supp. 167 (D.D.C. 1993), order aff'd, 36 F.3d 127 (D.C. Cir. 1994).

[Section 2:22]

[1]*See* Ch 4 on UCC trading.

[2]Cantor v. Anderson, 639 F. Supp. 364, 367, 2 U.C.C. Rep. Serv. 2d 312 (S.D. N.Y. 1986), judgment aff'd, 833 F.2d 1002 (2d Cir. 1986) ("The acumen and integrity of art dealers are the foundation stones of the market for fine art. Without these pillars the market could not function").

[3]*See* § 2:11 for an explanation of CROSSAQ.

[4]Although this reasoning has never been stated as one which mitigates against utilizing UCC principles for art transactions, it is, in fact, compelling.

[5]*See* § 2:11.

mercial distributors in many pertinent and crucial aspects. In commerce, the manufacturer or producer ordinarily stands behind the chain of distribution as a deep pocket. In art, the "manufacturer" is ordinarily the artist. Unlike other manufacturers, the artist is rarely a deep pocket and almost always an unattractive defendant. Further, the buyer's unhappiness is not usually with the artist's product, i.e., the object itself, but with the dealer's representations or omissions about the product within the sales transaction.

Consumers of general goods can buy products through numerous sources, and obtain product information through consumer guides, store personnel, and advertising. But the nature of the art trade is that an artist may be sold exclusively through only one source, and product information ordinarily does not exist for one-of-a-kind artworks as it does for mass produced goods. "Retail art customers frequently lack expertise in the field of art [and] they do not have the opportunity to have an artwork examined . . . before making a purchase. They are therefore compelled to rely on [trader] representations."[6]

Consumer choice outside the arts is ordinarily a function of price and convenience in instances where the consumer knows he is getting product *x*. If two automobile service stations sell the same brand of gasoline at the same price, purchasers ordinarily will choose the least expensive at the most convenient location. But if two traders sell prints by the same artist *X* from the same edition at the same price, collectors go out of their way to buy artist *X's* print from the dealer they perceive as the most "reputable," "reliable," or "trustworthy," irrespective of location and sometimes even at a higher price.

Thus, the role of the art trader is crucial to the buyer for providing information not publicly accessible, not readily available, and not easily verifiable. If the dealer is sued on CROSSAQ issues, there is ordinarily no other deep pocket behind the dealer,[7] nor are there specification sheets and performance data as an evidentiary base. Trad-

---

[6]In re Austin, 138 B.R. 898 (Bankr. N.D. Ill. 1992).

[7]The issue of insurability of dealer conduct involving CROSSAQ is unsettled. Sometimes the dealer is charged with fraud, and intentional acts are usually outside the scope of insurance. Sometimes, the dealer

ers, in short, are often the first and last chain of defense. The trader, then, is very different from a distributor of most commercial merchandise. Trader services in this regard are separate from those that inhere in contractual warranty or product liability for manufactured products. Attempts thus far to plead trader's representations or omissions about CROSSAQ as separate causes of action apart from contractual warranty, however, have failed in many jurisdictions.[8]

§ 2:23 Special

A trader may offer specific services separate and apart from those already discussed that arise from the sales transaction. The same person can be classified as dealer and historian, dealer and consultant, or dealer and appraiser. These double duties may create conflict of interest claims, fraud, negligence, breaches of trust, and fiduciary duties, in addition to claims based on commercial trading.[1] Some maintain appraisal practices, for which a separate fee arrangement is made independently of any appraisal that accompanies sales of art. Such conduct may contravene professional ethical guidelines of professional appraisal associations, or impact upon federal tax regulations pertaining to proprietary interests in appraised properties.[2] Some dealers act as consultants, for which they charge fees separate and apart from any percentage of sales price they are entitled to receive;[3] some bid at auction on behalf of anonymous clients; some serve as liaisons

---

is charged with negligence; insurance does exist for negligence, through casualty or errors and omissions coverages.

[8]Goldman v. Barnett, 793 F. Supp. 28, 18 U.C.C. Rep. Serv. 2d 55 (D. Mass. 1992).

[Section 2:23]

[1]*See, e.g.,* Goldman v. Barnett, 793 F. Supp. 28, 18 U.C.C. Rep. Serv. 2d 55 (D. Mass. 1992); McNally v. Yarnall, 764 F. Supp. 838, 844 (S.D. N.Y. 1991) (motion for leave to amend complaint to name defense lawyers as parties to defamation action denied because lawyer's statements absolutely privileged under state civil rights law).

[2]*See* Ch 3.

[3]*See* § 2:19.

between collectors and institutions like museums[4] or foundations; others provide finder's services connecting collectors with private sellers.[5]

Traders also function as liaisons between artists and those who wish to: (1) retain artists' services; (2) license their creations;[6] (3) purchase works not yet in existence; or (4) purchase ideas for works not even conceptualized. The category of works not yet in existence or not yet conceptualized involves an act of commissioning.[7] One can commission an artwork or one can commission an artist. In each of these circumstances, traders can charge fees that are separate from the client's costs in obtaining the commission.

§ 2:24 Intellectual property and incorporeal interests

Traders are, ipso facto, involved in transfers of intangible rights[1] and responsibilities that attach to these products. Art product may carry with it "valuable rights, like copyright,"[2] other intellectual property aspects involving trademark and patent, and artist's rights codified in

---

[4]Sammons v. C.I.R., T.C. Memo. 1986-318, 1986 WL 21525 (1986), aff'd in part, rev'd in part on other grounds, 838 F.2d 330 (9th Cir. 1988) (collector provided $140,000 to art dealers for purchase of specific collection of Indian artifacts and delivery to museum, subsequently discovered dealers paid only $60,000 for collection).

[5]Milwaukee Auction Galleries Ltd. v. Chalk, 13 F.3d 1107 (7th Cir. 1994).

[6]Kudo v. Simels, 1992 WL 80762 (S.D. N.Y. 1992) (art dealer retained by estate of John Lennon to "reproduce, sell and license images created by John Lennon and works bearing his visage").

[7]For art commissions, *see* Cook v. U.S., 220 Ct. Cl. 76, 599 F.2d 400 (1979) ("Commissioned sales are ordered in advance by the purchaser and then created 'to order.' "); *accord* Anagnostou v. Stifel, 168 A.D.2d 256, 562 N.Y.S.2d 490 (1st Dep't 1990) (six paintings by Andy Warhol based on Leonardo da Vinci's "Last Supper" were commissioned by art connoisseur); *see also* In re Johnson, 139 B.R. 208 (Bankr. D. Minn. 1992) (defendant commissioned approximately thirty paintings.).

[Section 2:24]

[1]Intangible interests are discussed in Chs 7, 8, and 9.

[2]O'Keeffe v. Snyder, 170 N.J. Super. 75, 405 A.2d 840, 874 (App. Div. 1979), judgment rev'd on other grounds, 83 N.J. 478, 416 A.2d 862 (1980).

federal copyright and extant in some state laws to whatever degree they are not federally preempted.[3] Cases to date have not yet focused on trader representations involving transfers of such intangible rights, but enactment of the Visual Artists Rights Act of 1990 (VARA),[4] now codified in federal copyright[5] and implemented by regulations promulgated thereunder,[6] extends post-sale rights of artists in tangible personal property for certain eligible artworks and imbues artists with incorporeal attribution rights to such properties.[7]

State laws, to the degree they are not preempted by federal law, may extend post-sale rights by rights of survivorship for artist's heirs or designees. State art per se laws compel extensive disclosures by traders about prints, multiples, and other artworks, but with minor exception they are silent about what notice, if any, traders should give their transferees about intangible personal property rights. What disclosures should be, and what circumstances compel them, has not yet been reported.

D. FORMS OF BUSINESS ASSOCIATION

§ 2:25 Generally

Traders may be organized as sole proprietorships,[1] partnerships,[2] or corporations,[3] which can be privately held or publicly traded. The form of business association, however,

---

[3]17 U.S.C.A. § 301.

[4]Pub. L. No. 101-650, 104 Stat. 5089 (1990).

[5]17 U.S.C.A. §§ 101 et seq.

[6]*See* Appendix 18A; 37 CFR §§ 201 et seq., 56 Fed. Reg. 38340 (Aug. 13, 1991).

[7]*See* Ch 9.

[Section 2:25]

[1]Rosen v. Spanierman, 894 F.2d 28, 30, 10 U.C.C. Rep. Serv. 2d 846 (2d Cir. 1990) ("Ira Spanierman is sole owner of the [Spanierman] Gallery"); Duchossois Industries, Inc. v. Stelloh, 1988 WL 2794 (N.D. Ill. 1988) (individual defendant doing business as R.S. Fine Arts); Phillips, Son & Neal, Inc. v. Borghi & Co., 1987 WL 27690 (S.D. N.Y. 1987) (defendant is "a proprietorship dealing in art").

[2]Mount v. Ormand, 1991 WL 191228 (S.D. N.Y. 1991) (defendant was "formerly a partner in the [Coe-Kerr] gallery"); Kudo v. Simels, R.I.C.O. Bus. Disp. Guide (CCH) ¶ 7877, 1991 WL 222165 (S.D. N.Y.

has not defeated criminal or civil RICO claims.[4] It has had varying effect on the ability of parties from other states to allege and obtain jurisdiction over the trader—be it person or entity—irrespective of organizational form or scope of trader activities.[5]

E. TRADER-CLIENT ACTIONS

§ 2:26 Generally

In the late 1980s and early 1990s, perhaps as a result of the fluctuating values realized during that period in the art markets, a number of actions were filed in which prospective purchasers attempted to force dealers to sell them art by specific performance and other remedies.[1] Dealers on occasion sue their clients for monies owed,[2] rescission,[3]

1991) ("Defendant . . . Simels . . . owns and operates art galleries including defendant Marigold Enterprises, Ltd.").

[3]Davis v. Rowe, 1991 WL 181100 (N.D. Ill. 1991) (gallery doing business as The Rowe Company Fine Arts, Inc.); Martin S. Ackerman Foundation v. C.I.R., T.C. Memo. 1986-365, 1986 WL 21569 (1986) (Sovereign American Arts Corp. is a corporation organized as "a private art dealer."); In re Austin, 138 B.R. 898 (Bankr. N.D. Ill. 1992) ("defendant is sole shareholder of several corporations . . . which operate a chain of art galleries in Illinois [and] is responsible for choosing the artwork which is purchased and offered for sale in the galleries and for selecting artwork suppliers"); McCloud v. Lawrence Gallery, Ltd., 1991 WL 136027 (S.D. N.Y. 1991) ("Lawrence Gallery is a New York corporation engaged in the business of buying and selling fine art."); Motion for return of Property Per Rule 41, FRCP, 681 F. Supp. 677 (D. Haw. 1988) (gallery incorporated in 1974 alleged one of "world's largest fine arts galleries").

[4]Kudo v. Simels, R.I.C.O. Bus. Disp. Guide (CCH) ¶ 7877, 1991 WL 222165 (S.D. N.Y. 1991); Galerie Furstenberg v. Coffaro, 697 F. Supp. 1282 (S.D. N.Y. 1988); Hutton v. Klabal, 726 F. Supp. 67 (S.D. N.Y. 1989); Mount v. Ormand, 1991 WL 191228 (S.D. N.Y. 1991).

[5]*See* § 2:48 for jurisdiction.

[Section 2:26]

[1]Hoffmann v. Boone, 708 F. Supp. 78, 9 U.C.C. Rep. Serv. 2d 474 (S.D. N.Y. 1989) (collectors seek specific performance against art dealer/gallery who allegedly agreed to sell them a painting by Brice Marden for $120,000); Jafari v. Wally Findlay Galleries, 741 F. Supp. 64 (S.D.N.Y. 1990).

[2]Boone Associates v. Davidson, 1990 WL 52261 (S.D. N.Y. 1990) (Mary Boone Gallery sues client for tendering check for $215,000 for a

or commissions.[4]

F. TRADER-LANDLORD ACTIONS

§ 2:27 Generally

A landlord's construction of an elevator shaft through a tenant's art gallery, causing diminution of total leasehold space, constituted partial eviction entitling tenant-art gallery and studio to the following: rent abatement and loss of profits from interruption of business.[1]

III. TRADER DUTIES AND OBLIGATIONS

A. STATUTORY DEFINITIONS

§ 2:28 Transactions involving artists

Certain states have enacted art per se statutes[1] which govern sales of "fine art" by "art merchants,"[2] but, with minor exceptions, such laws do not require permits, licenses, or registration. Whether a dealer or other trader is an "art merchant" within the meaning of a particular statute, or a "merchant" within the meaning of Section 2-104 of

---

painting by David Salle and sculpture by Donald Judd refused by bank for insufficient funds).

[3]Feigen v. Weil, No. 13935/90 (N.Y. Sup. May 1992), aff'd, NYLJ, Mar. 18, 1993, at 26, col. 3.

[4]Milwaukee Auction Galleries Ltd. v. Chalk, 13 F.3d 1107 (7th Cir. 1994) (action for, inter alia, promissory estoppel brought by two art dealers against a collector for failure to pay them finder's fee commissions reinstated by appellate court, reversing directed verdict for defendant on that count).

[Section 2:27]

[1]81 Franklin Co. v. Ginaccini, 160 A.D.2d 558, 554 N.Y.S.2d 207 (1st Dep't 1990) (plaintiff landlord initiated nonpayment summary proceedings and defendant-gallery counterclaimed for $200,000 damages for lost revenue based upon breach of lease).

[Section 2:28]

[1]*See* Appendix 4.

[2]The definition of "art merchant" may vary from statute to statute; *see* Ill. Rev. Stat. ch. 121½, ¶ 1401(1) (an art dealer is "a person engaged in the business of selling works of art, other than a person exclusively engaged in the business of selling goods at public auction"), but compare definitions in the various states noted in Appendix 4.

the Uniform Commercial Code,[3] depends upon the applicable facts and circumstances.[4] Judicial interpretations are few. Not only does the definition of an "art dealer" differ from state to state, but within states art per se statutes may define "art dealer" in different ways.[5] For example, a print publisher who produced and distributed lithographs was deemed an "art merchant" for purposes of New York law.[6] The scope of seller conduct and activities should be carefully evaluated within the parameters of the statutory language.

If a trader is deemed an "art merchant," "art dealer," or art per se statutory equivalent, then its activity, or even passivity, by operation of law may create relationships between the trader and the artist that are beyond any contractual committment. Traders may be mere bailees, or become agents or trustees, or both, over property and/or proceeds upon sale, loss, or damage even in the absence of

---

[3]Section 2-104 of the UCC provides, in pertinent part, "(1) 'Merchant' means a person who deals in goods of the kind or otherwise by his occupation holds himself out as having knowledge or skill peculiar to the practices or goods involved in the transaction or to whom such knowledge or skill may be attributed by his employment or an agent or broker or other intermediary who by his occupation holds himself out as having such knowledge or skill." *Cf.* UCC § 1-201(9) (defines buyer in the ordinary as one who buys "in the ordinary course from a person in the business of selling goods of that kind"); *and see* Porter v. Wertz, 56 A.D.2d 570, 392 N.Y.S.2d 10 (1st Dep't 1977).

[4]Davis v. Rowe, 1991 WL 181100 (N.D. Ill. 1991) (court rejected defendant's claim that it was not an art dealer under Illinois consignment statute and that the artist's surviving spouse was not a person who could sue in the artist's name); Eboigbe v. Zoological Soc. of Cincinnati, 96 Ohio App. 3d 102, 644 N.E.2d 693 (1st Dist. Hamilton County 1994) (zoo that exhibited and offered for sale plaintiff's artworks, which were damaged while on display, sued by artist under Ohio art per se consignment statute, in action alleging zoo was an "art dealer" for purposes of the statute).

[5]*Cf.* UCC § 2-104 (definition of merchant).

[6]Wesselmann v. International Images, Inc., 172 Misc. 2d 247, 657 N.Y.S.2d 284 (Sup 1996) (publisher and seller of Pop artist Tom Wesselman fell within definition of "art merchant" under N.Y. Arts & Cult. Aff. Law § 12.01 because he dealt in multiples and supervised printing of limited editions).

the trader's express acquiescence or authorization.[7]

New York, for example, has an art per se statute that governs artist consignments and deliveries to art merchants whereby a trust is created over the property and sales proceeds.[8] Lithographs by Tom Wesselman in the possession of his publisher for sale constituted trust property and sales proceeds therefrom were "trust funds" for the benefit of the artist even when the publisher financed print production.[9]

The statute has been asserted by artists to invalidate purported security interests in artworks claimed by consignee-galleries and to reclaim their artworks from dealers. In one case, a gallery advanced monies to artist Joseph Zucker over a period of years, deducting from sales

---

[7]Hutton v. Klabal, 726 F. Supp. 67, 69 (S.D. N.Y. 1989) (Plaintiff "has asserted that [defendant-art gallery owner and manager had] superior knowledge of art and his representation to her that he is an expert in art as an investment created between them a fiduciary relationship. An expert does not, however, solely by virtue of his expertise, have fiduciary responsibility toward his customers [in the absence of prior dealings] which might create a relationship of trust and confidence."); *but cf.* Lehman v. Lehman, 591 F. Supp. 1523 (S.D. N.Y. 1984) (bailment created when husband leaves art in wife's possession at time of marital separation; wife is liable for conversion when she cannot produce art upon husband's demand); Waller v. Scheer, 175 Ga. App. 1, 332 S.E.2d 293 (1985), cert. dismissed, (July 3, 1985) (no confidential relationship between buyer and seller where buyer was "dealer of valuable art objects" who responded to newspaper advertisement and seller was selling from his home, representing himself as in "dire financial straits"); Struna v. Wolf, 126 Misc. 2d 1031, 484 N.Y.S.2d 392 (Sup 1985) (special relationship between museum, dealer, and consignee-buyer-seller discussed); In re Atlantic Computer Systems Inc., 135 B.R. 463, 16 U.C.C. Rep. Serv. 2d 1204 (Bankr. S.D. N.Y. 1992) ("Bailment is generally defined as 'a delivery of personal property for some particular purpose . . . upon a contract, express or implied, and that after such purpose has been fulfilled it shall be be . . . otherwise dealt with according to directions or kept until . . . reclaim[ed]' "). *See also* Appendix 4.

[8]N.Y. Arts & Cult. Aff. Law § 12.01.

[9]Wesselmann v. International Images, Inc., 172 Misc. 2d 247, 657 N.Y.S.2d 284 (Sup 1996) (financial investment does not negate consignment or trust relationship) *aff'd*, 687 N.Y.S. 2d 339 (1999)(affirming partial summary judgment in favor of artist relating to trust property and ordering mutual accounting).

proceeds art dealer commissions and advances.[10] When the representation ended, the gallery refused to release the artist's artworks unless he repaid the balance of approximately $36,000. When the artist refused, the gallery claimed a security interest in the unsold artworks to cover unpaid loans made to the artist. Section 12.01(a)(v) provides: "no such trust property . . . shall be subject or subordinate to any claims, liens or security interests of any kind or nature whatsoever."[11] The court rejected the gallery's interpretation that the law was intended only to prohibit creation of security interests in favor of an art dealer's creditors, not security interests created in favor of the art dealer for monies loaned to, and owed by, the artist. Such security interests were void.

Where a trader is a trustee over art and proceeds of sale, the payment obligations to the artist are illustrated in Journal and Ledger Entries, Examples 2 and 3.[12] Example 2 explains the trader's obligations to the artist to distribute the proceeds in installment sales. Example 3 explains the trader's obligations to the artist when the buyer defaults on the installment agreement, leaving an unpaid balance.[13] Even in states without art per se statutes, or those where the transaction falls outside the statute, general principles of law and equity may still impose on the trader an agency or a trust and/or a myriad of fiduciary obligations involving hybrids of legal and equitable principles and remedies.[14]

Notwithstanding applicable art per se statutes, artists may experience legal difficulties in reclaiming their works from galleries even after exhibition termination dates. An artist was able to replevy his photographs shown in a gal-

---

[10]Zucker v. Hirschl & Adler Galleries, Inc., 170 Misc. 2d 426, 648 N.Y.S.2d 521, 30 U.C.C. Rep. Serv. 2d 955 (Sup 1996) (artwork as "trust property in the hands of the consignee").

[11]NY Arts & Cult. Aff.Law § 12.01(1)(a)(v).

[12]*See* App. 2.01[2] and [3].

[13]*See* Appendix 3.

[14]Matter of Friedman, 64 A.D.2d 70, 407 N.Y.S.2d 999 (2d Dep't 1978) (estate of artist Arnold Friedman's widow obtained decree ordering dealer to return all artworks to executor because of "inherently fiduciary character of consignment agreement in artist-art dealer relationship").

lery pursuant to an oral agreement but it took almost two years to obtain judicial order.[15] Absent express statutory authority, violations of art per se statutes do not entitle artists to awards of enhanced or punitive damages, costs or attorneys' fees.[16]

Breach of contract actions against galleries for failure to timely return artworks, which do not depend upon art per se statutes, require proof of the agreed-upon consignment term as well as damages.[17] Where the contract is silent, courts have imposed a reasonable time period.[18]

§ 2:29 Transactions involving collectors, traders, and others

Trader conduct as it relates to collectors is more complex.[1] A trader does not, by operation of law, automatically enter into a consignment, an agency, or a trust with a collector when it comes into possession, custody, or care of art from collectors, directly or from others on their behalf.[2] The obligations of the dealer to nonartists and the dealer's standard of care toward art (other than that

---

[15] Koeniges v. Woodward, 183 Misc. 2d 347, 702 N.Y.S.2d 781 (City Civ. Ct. 2000) (N.Y. Arts & Cult. Aff. Law § 12.01 was violated when gallery refused to return consignment of artist's photographs of Willem de Kooning).

[16] Koeniges v. Woodward, 183 Misc. 2d 347, 702 N.Y.S.2d 781 (City Civ. Ct. 2000) (". . . there appears to be a gap in the protections afforded to artists under [N.Y. Arts & Cult. Affairs] section 12.01.")

[17] Koeniges v. Woodward, 183 Misc. 2d 347, 702 N.Y.S.2d 781 (City Civ. Ct. 2000) (artist's breach of contract claim dismissed.

[18] Koeniges v. Woodward, 183 Misc. 2d 347, 702 N.Y.S.2d 781 (City Civ. Ct. 2000).

[Section 2:29]

[1] *See* Ch 3.

[2] Cantor v. Anderson, 639 F. Supp. 364, 368, 2 U.C.C. Rep. Serv. 2d 312 (S.D. N.Y. 1986), judgment aff'd, 833 F.2d 1002 (2d Cir. 1986) (art dealer's consignment of Renoir drawing for resale with private dealer discussed in terms of whether or not effectuated entrustment under UCC); Colnaghi, U.S.A., Ltd. v. Jewelers Protection Services, Ltd., 183 A.D.2d 469, 583 N.Y.S.2d 427 (1st Dep't 1992), appeal granted, reargument denied, 186 A.D.2d 349, 588 N.Y.S.2d 765 (1st Dep't 1992) and order rev'd on other grounds, 81 N.Y.2d 821, 595 N.Y.S.2d 381, 611 N.E.2d 282 (1993).

received from artists)[3] in its possession, control, or custody vary from state to state. The obligations of the collector to the dealer are becoming subject to judicial review.[4]

Courts have discussed, without deciding, whether Section 2-326 of the Uniform Commercial Code "sale on approval/sale or return" provisions apply to art brought to the trader by dealers, collectors, or others for resale.[5] Section 2-326 does not specify when a "sale or return" occurs, but it does define the rights that creditors of a party who purchase goods for resale possess in those goods.[6] Some states specifically exempt art from Section 2-326.[7] Theoretically, art exemption laws should simplify determination of what is consigned and what is a "sale or return."[8] Section 2-327 of the Code imposes risk on the buyer who makes the return to the seller.[9] Article 9 of the Code further complicates determination of rights in such situations. Trader liability for damage or loss under the UCC is

---

[3]Pelletier v. Eisenberg, 177 Cal. App. 3d 558, 223 Cal. Rptr. 84 (4th Dist. 1986) (insured dealer responsible to artist for 100 percent of fair market value of paintings damaged in fire on gallery premises, irrespective of consignment agreement whereby artist only entitled to percentage of sales price; evidence showed dealer pocketed part or all of insurance proceeds instead of paying artist).

[4]Milwaukee Auction Galleries Ltd. v. Chalk, 13 F.3d 1107 (7th Cir. 1994) (collector's obligations to pay two art dealers commissions for sales of paintings by August Renoir and Mary Cassatt sold to persons they referred to collector for purposes of sale).

[5]Cantor v. Anderson, 639 F. Supp. 364, 368, 2 U.C.C. Rep. Serv. 2d 312 (S.D. N.Y. 1986), judgment aff'd, 833 F.2d 1002 (2d Cir. 1986) (art dealer's consignment of Renoir drawing to private dealer for resale discussed in terms of whether a UCC § 2-326 interest effectuated).

[6]*But cf.* U.S. v. One 18th Century Colombian Monstrance, 797 F.2d 1370, 1 U.C.C. Rep. Serv. 2d 1492 (5th Cir. 1986) ("Section 2-326 does not purport . . . to define when a 'sale or return' purchase has been made.").

[7]*See* Appendix 8.

[8]U.S. v. One 18th Century Colombian Monstrance, 797 F.2d 1370, 1 U.C.C. Rep. Serv. 2d 1492 (5th Cir. 1986); Shuttie v. Festa Restaurant, Inc., 566 So. 2d 554, 14 U.C.C. Rep. Serv. 2d 119 (Fla. Dist. Ct. App. 3d Dist. 1990).

[9]UCC § 2-327(2)(b) ("Under a sale or return unless otherwise agreed . . . the return is at the buyer's risk and expense.").

discussed later.[10]

§ 2:30 Bailment

Bailment is variously defined under state laws, but the basics include delivery of subject property by a bailor and acceptance by a bailee, requiring a meeting of the minds, although the contract may be express or implied.[1] In the absence of an express agreement, an implied in fact bailment can be found if it appears from the circumstances that such was the intent of the parties, or where lawful possession arises with a duty to account for the property, regardless of whether the property is entrusted by the true owner or one with a superior possessory right.[2] The bailee does not acquire title to the property but holds it according to the terms of bailment contract, which consign-

---

[10]*See* Ch 4. *See also* Goldman v. Barnett, 793 F. Supp. 28, 18 U.C.C. Rep. Serv. 2d 55 (D. Mass. 1992) ("no duty of care arises from contract between parties for sale of goods"); Colnaghi, U.S.A., Ltd. v. Jewelers Protection Services, Ltd., 183 A.D.2d 469, 583 N.Y.S.2d 427 (1st Dep't 1992), appeal granted, reargument denied, 186 A.D.2d 349, 588 N.Y.S.2d 765 (1st Dep't 1992) and order rev'd, 81 N.Y.2d 821, 595 N.Y.S.2d 381, 611 N.E.2d 282 (1993).

[Section 2:30]

[1]Stellan Holm, Inc. v. Malmberg Intern. Art, 2002 WL 392294 (S.D. N.Y. 2002) (authority of bailee to release Yves Klein painting from storage to plaintiff was question of fact); Nelson v. Sotheby's, Inc., 128 F. Supp. 2d 1172 (N.D. Ill. 2001) (breach of contract claim sustained against auction house that refused to return plaintiff's painting held for appraisal for almost twelve years); Hoelzer v. City of Stamford, Conn., 933 F.2d 1131 (2d Cir. 1991) (declaratory action in which city defending rights to WPA murals claimed plaintiff restorer in possession was mere bailee while the restorer claimed he was akin to good faith purchaser); Mac'Avoy v. The Smithsonian Inst., 757 F. Supp. 60 (D.D.C. 1991) (loan or bailment of art to museum); Reichman v. Warehouse One, Inc., 173 A.D.2d 250, 569 N.Y.S.2d 452 (1st Dep't 1991), appeal dismissed in part, 78 N.Y.2d 1058, 576 N.Y.S.2d 213, 582 N.E.2d 596 (1991) (artist awarded damages for paintings missing from storage under state eviction law protecting consumer bailers).

[2]Pivar v. Graduate School of Figurative Art of the New York Academy of Art, 290 A.D.2d 212, 735 N.Y.S.2d 522 (1st Dep't 2002) (judgment reversed for bailee in replevin action based upon bailor's failure to prove ownership of sculpture casts loaned to art academy for instructional purposes.)

ment agreements can and do create.[3] Interference with the rights of the bailor in contravention of the bailment typically gives rise to a cause of action for any one or more of the following: conversion,[4] breach of contract,[5] or negligence[6] as well as a duty to account,[7] and equitable remedies.[8]

Once a bailment is established, jurisdictions differ on the duty of the bailee to the bailor, and the relief to which the bailor is entitled. The particularities of the bailment, like vehicular bailment, for example, may also effect which

---

[3]Nelson v. Sotheby's, Inc., 128 F. Supp. 2d 1172 (N.D. Ill. 2001) (bailment created by consignment agreement whereby plaintiff delivered painting by Giorgio de Chirico to auction house for appraisal and possible sale); Mucha v. King, 792 F.2d 602 (7th Cir. 1986). *See* Appendix 4.

[4]Stellan Holm, Inc. v. Malmberg Intern. Art, 2002 WL 392294 (S.D. N.Y. 2002) (owner's allegation that storage facility released painting without owner's authorization sufficient to state conversion claim); Pagliai v. Del Re, 2001 WL 220013 (S.D. N.Y. 2001), judgment aff'd as modified, 2002 WL 1000129 (2d Cir. 2002) (New York gallery owner converted painting left in her care when she gave it as collateral for an unrelated debt and it was auctioned to cover the arbitration award but claim barred by statute of limitations); *see* Mucha v. King, 792 F.2d 602 (7th Cir. 1986) (A bailee's unauthorized transfer of bailment goods in breach is an exercise of "ownership, dominion and control" inconsistent with rights of bailee); Mac'Avoy v. The Smithsonian Inst., 757 F. Supp. 60 (D.D.C. 1991).

[5]Nelson v. Sotheby's, Inc., 128 F. Supp. 2d 1172 (N.D. Ill. 2001) (bailment arose from a consignment agreement to evaluate painting that was basis of breach of contract).

[6]Jack Boles Services, Inc. v. Stavely, 906 S.W.2d 185 (Tex. App. Austin 1995), reh'g overruled, (Oct. 11, 1995) and writ denied, (Feb. 9, 1996) (breach of bailment plead in negligence action for value of painting stolen from trunk of automobile, which was valet-parked at country club); Bellis v. Tokio Marine and Fire Ins. Co., Ltd., 2002 WL 193149 (S.D. N.Y. 2002) (prima facie case for negligent bailment when collector showed Tiffany glass delivered in good condition for museum exhibition but returned damaged).

[7]Pagliai v. Del Re, 2001 WL 220013 (S.D. N.Y. 2001), judgment aff'd as modified, 2002 WL 1000129 (2d Cir. 2002) (fifteenth century painting by Cima left in care of New York gallery constituted bailment for which there was a duty to account).

[8]Pagliai v. Del Re, 2001 WL 220013 (S.D. N.Y. 2001), judgment aff'd as modified, 2002 WL 1000129 (2d Cir. 2002) (constructive trust imposed on gallery owner who used painting placed in her care to satisfy her own debts).

rules apply. In some states, a bailee is liable for lost property of which it has actual knowledge as well as property it could reasonably expect to find contained inside bailed items. Notice of the actual contents of a bailed item may not be required to include those contents among the bailee's responsibilities based upon implied acceptance of visible or reasonably anticipated items. Not every breach of bailment, however, entitles the bailee to sue for value of the bailed goods.[9] When a contract of bailment is silent on the date of redelivery, the bailee's obligation to redeliver may be determined by custom and usage.[10]

No bailment existed where the defendant-museum claimed it did not assent to bailment, but was the intended recipient of gifts of approximately twenty paintings and thirty-five drawings of artist Romaine Brooks, over claims of her curator that they belonged to him under a notarized act of sale between the plaintiff and the artist;[11] and no bailment existed in a painting located in automobile trunk unbeknownst to the bailee-valet parking service, where it had no notice of painting and did not accept it as bailed piece of property.[12] Bailment existed in paintings wife retained after separation from her husband.[13] Expenses of art bailment for which a bailee may be liable to a bailor are predictable ones like storage.[14]

---

[9]If breach of bailment contract concerns bailed good *A*, bailor cannot recover damages for conversion of unharmed bailed good *B*.

[10]Nelson v. Sotheby's, Inc., 128 F. Supp. 2d 1172 (N.D. Ill. 2001)) (auction's motion to dismiss breach of contract claim denied where it failed to return plaintiff's painting for almost twelve years even though consignment agreement "for evaluation" did not specify a date).

[11]Mac'Avoy v. The Smithsonian Inst., 757 F. Supp. 60 (D.D.C. 1991).

[12]Jack Boles Services, Inc. v. Stavely, 906 S.W.2d 185 (Tex. App. Austin 1995), reh'g overruled, (Oct. 11, 1995) and writ denied, (Feb. 9, 1996) (reversing judgment against bailee for negligence, court held bailee had no duty of care over painting located in trunk of automobile, which was not in plain view nor reasonably anticipated or foreseeable under the surrounding circumstances when it was valet-parked at country club).

[13]Lehman v. Lehman, 591 F. Supp. 1523 (S.D. N.Y. 1984).

[14]Mucha v. King, 792 F.2d 602 (7th Cir. 1986) (storage expenses of American gallery for art of Czech artist living abroad were expected, not extraordinary).

B. DUTY TO MAINTAIN RECORDS AND ACCOUNT

§ 2:31 Generally

Traders must keep books of account, separate their assets from those of the artists they represent, identify dates of consignment and sales, record terms of sale, insure as applicable, pay artists in a timely fashion, and subscribe to reasonable methods of recordkeeping and accounting.[1] These obligations are variously imposed by state art per se laws,[2] contract,[3] the Internal Revenue Code,[4] and the Bankruptcy Code.[5]

C. INSURANCE

§ 2:32 Duty to insure

Traders are not required by statute to carry property or casualty insurance, but contractual terms in consignment,

---

[Section 2:31]

[1]*See* Ch 1; Rivas v. Jefferson, 412 F.2d 769 (9th Cir. 1969); Kudo v. Simels, R.I.C.O. Bus. Disp. Guide (CCH) ¶ 7877, 1991 WL 222165 (S.D. N.Y. 1991) (dealer's duty to account to artists for royalties/commissions on sales and licensing agreements); Nakian v. DiLaurenti, 673 F. Supp. 699 (S.D. N.Y. 1987); Matter of Friedman, 64 A.D.2d 70, 407 N.Y.S.2d 999 (2d Dep't 1978).

[2]*See* Appendix 4.

[3]Nakian v. DiLaurenti, 673 F. Supp. 699 (S.D. N.Y. 1987) (duty to insure art imposed by contract); Pelletier v. Eisenberg, 177 Cal. App. 3d 558, 223 Cal. Rptr. 84 (4th Dist. 1986) (duty to pay artist insurance proceeds after fire destroyed art interpreted under California art consignment laws); Matter of Friedman, 64 A.D.2d 70, 407 N.Y.S.2d 999 (2d Dep't 1978) (duty to artist's widow to properly administer and account for works of artist); *accord* Davis v. Rowe, 1991 WL 181100 (N.D. Ill. 1991) (duty to account, administer, and pay insurance proceeds to artist's widow for damaged, destroyed artworks under Illinois art consignment laws and contracts).

[4]*See, e.g.*, Andrew Crispo Gallery, Inc. v. C.I.R., T.C. Memo. 1992-106, 1992 WL 31221 (1992), decision aff'd in part and vacated in part, 16 F.3d 1336 (2d Cir. 1994) (release 1994 decision); *see also* Ch 3.

[5]Rivas v. Jefferson, 412 F.2d 769 (9th Cir. 1969) (Ninth Circuit upheld refusal of the bankruptcy court to discharge a dealer's debts based on grounds that he failed to keep, preserve, or produce books of account from which his financial condition and business transactions could be ascertained). *See* § 2:40.

lease, or other agreements can impose the duty.[1] Art per se statutes that impose strict liability upon traders[2] carry an implicit obligation to insure art, but no reported case could be found that has imposed a judicial rule. Those demanding insurance as a term of a contract for representation should assure that their interests are protected by designation as additional insureds[3] evidenced by certificates of insurance. Being named as an additional insured does not, without more, provide that the named insured will be directly paid the proceeds in the event of an insurable loss.[4] Nor does the existence of insurance assure that the amount of proceeds will cover the loss; and an insured should explore the options for determining value of the loss prior to placing coverage.[5]

Terms of payment of the insurance proceeds between an artist and a dealer may be judicially ordered in a way that is contrary to the payment terms of written consignment agreements between the artist and the dealer.[6] For example, a dealer was liable for retail sales prices of consigned artworks damaged in a gallery fire although the terms of the consignment agreement were silent as to loss or damage, and expressly apportioned only a percentage of the retail sales proceeds to the artist.[7]

Art per se statutes do not impose an express duty upon

[Section 2:32]

[1]Nakian v. DiLaurenti, 673 F. Supp. 699 (S.D. N.Y. 1987) (son and executor of sculptor's estate seeks rescission of exclusive agency agreement with gallery where insurance coverage issues existed regarding Reuben Nakian's sculptures).

[2]*See* Appendix 4.

[3]Assured and insured are used interchangeably; *see* Appendix 22.

[4]To obtain direct payment, the named insured would have provided for a certificate of insurance to be transmitted directly to the additional named insured indicating at the minimum the following information: term of insurance; limit of insurance; insured perils and/or property; notice provision to the additional named insured in the event of cancellation, termination, or change in policy.

[5]*See* § 2:33.

[6]*See* Appendix 3.

[7]*See, e.g.*, Pelletier v. Eisenberg, 177 Cal. App. 3d 558, 223 Cal. Rptr. 84 (4th Dist. 1986) (casualty policy for premises liability in force); *accord with respect to paying fair market value*, Davis v. Rowe, 1993 WL 34867 (N.D. Ill. 1993) (business interruption insurance).

traders to maintain insurance, and the courts have not yet directly imposed such duties.[8] Some states impose absolute liability upon the trader in the event of damage or loss to artwork consigned to them by artists. In the event of a casualty loss, courts have held traders are responsible for the full fair market value of the damaged or destroyed artwork, regardless of the trader-artist apportionment of sales proceeds under consignment terms. In such instances, an artist otherwise entitled under consignment terms to 60 percent of the proceeds upon sale would be entitled to 100 percent of the fair market value upon loss or destruction. Some courts have awarded artists future loss of earnings, as well as fair market value, on the theory that a sale would have inured to the benefit of the artist's reputation, but loss of a work undermines the oeuvre.[9]

§ 2:33 Insurance policy claims settlements

Even when insurance is in place, and assuming proper payees, the amount of the proceeds to be paid are frequently disputed.[1] Where an insurance company issued an endorsement for additional coverage for publicly exhibited artworks based upon the artist's price list, it refused to pay $350,000 for a sculpture recited on the price list after the sculpture was damaged.[2] The underwriter testified that he understood "works of art scheduled under any fine arts coverage are given to a maximum value only, meaning that the insurance company could price the art after

---

[8]Davis v. Rowe, 1993 WL 34867 (N.D. Ill. 1993) ("we . . . shall not decide . . . to what extent [the dealer] possessed a duty to maintain insurance proceeds . . . received due to the destruction of art which it held in trust"). *See* Appendix 4.

[9]Pelletier v. Eisenberg, 177 Cal. App. 3d 558, 223 Cal. Rptr. 84 (4th Dist. 1986); *cf.* Karetsos v. Cheung, 670 F. Supp. 111 (S.D. N.Y. 1987) (artist not entitled to lost profits or damages for injury to reputation where gallery failed to exhibit artist's works in a breach of contract action).

[Section 2:33]

[1]Eboigbe v. Zoological Soc. of Cincinnati, 96 Ohio App. 3d 102, 644 N.E.2d 693, 695, (1st Dist. Hamilton County 1994). *See* Ch 3 § 3:67.

[2]Eboigbe v. Zoological Soc. of Cincinnati, 96 Ohio App. 3d 102, 644 N.E.2d 693, 695, (1st Dist. Hamilton County 1994).

any loss."[3] The endorsement that was added to the policy in that case is typical of many, allowing the insurer great latitude in establishing loss.[4]

To ameliorate disputes regarding the value of art after the loss or damage has occurred for purposes of determining the amount of proceeds arising from scheduled items, the insured would be well-advised to explore with the insurer utilizing "agreed-upon" value or "stated" value. Although the verbiage of policies of insurance varies, as do the practices of insurers paying out under such policies, stated value typically signifies that at the time of binding coverage, the insurer is accepting the stated value placed upon the object by the insured. The insured's stated value is generally evidenced by appraisals, which may be required by the insurance company. Stated value applies only where works are scheduled, and ordinarily a stated value must be recited separately for each item on the schedule.

Even single losses can be onerous for the trader and devastating for the artist or other consignor.[5] But in the event of major casualty loss like a fire, few traders can af-

---

[3]Eboigbe v. Zoological Soc. of Cincinnati, 96 Ohio App. 3d 102, 644 N.E.2d 693, 695, (1st Dist. Hamilton County 1994).

[4]Eboigbe v. Zoological Soc. of Cincinnati, 96 Ohio App. 3d 102, 644 N.E.2d 693, 695, (1st Dist. Hamilton County 1994). The endorsement added to the policy by the Cincinnati Insurance Company did not specify the agreed-upon or stated value, reciting as follows:

> Loss settlement. Unless otherwise stated in this policy, the value of the property insured is not agreed upon but shall be determined at the time of loss or damage.
>
> We will not pay more than the least of the following amounts:
>
> (a) the actual cash value of the property at the time of loss or damage;
>
> (b) the amount for which the property could reasonably be expected to be repaired to its condition immediately prior to loss or damage;
>
> (c) the amount for which the article could reasonably be expected to be replaced with one substantially identical to the article; or
>
> (d) the applicable amount of insurance.

[5]*See, e.g.*, Eboigbe v. Zoological Soc. of Cincinnati, 96 Ohio App. 3d 102, 644 N.E.2d 693, 695, (1st Dist. Hamilton County 1994) (single sculpture damaged while on exhibit valued by artist at $350,000); Wool v. Ayres, 283 A.D.2d 299, 724 N.Y.S.2d 612 (1st Dep't, 2001) (award of $1 million damages for artwork destroyed during fire would not be reduced by commissions to galleries because collection was not for sale); see also Clark v. Meyer, 188 F.Supp.2d 416 (S.D.N.Y. 2002) (in

ford to replace an entire art consignment.[6] Moreover, the trader may be judgment proof, even if liable. Insurance is often the artist's sole monetary recourse against a trader for loss of the artist's oeuvre, which could represent many months, or years, of work, for example, if a one-person exhibition were the subject of loss.[7]

§ 2:34 Insurance coverage issues

Traders who do not maintain adequate insurance for consigned artwork under contractual obligations with the artist,[1] or improperly remit to or withhold insurance proceeds from artists have been subject to challenge.[2]

Commercial general liability policies have been the subject of garden variety as well as unusual claims relating to galleries and dealers. An artist sued a gallery and dealer for malicious assault when his eye was injured when the dealer interfered with him taping her as she painted over his mural.[3] The dealer's insurance company denied coverage because the dealer's acts were intentional, not a covered occurrence.

---

breach of contract action for failure to obtain insurance where defendant agreed to insure painting entrusted to her for $200,000.00 but insurance lapsed and painting was destroyed in fire, liability for painting was limited to $8000.00 on testimony of defendant's friend because plaintiff failed to meet burden of proof for value.).

[6]*See* Appendix 3.

[7]*See* Ch. 9 §§ 9:85 to 9:97.

[Section 2:34]

[1]Nakian v. DiLaurenti, 673 F. Supp. 699 (S.D. N.Y. 1987).

[2]Davis v. Rowe, 1991 WL 181100 (N.D. Ill. 1991) (dispute over insurance proceeds owed); Kudo v. Simels, R.I.C.O. Bus. Disp. Guide (CCH) ¶ 7877, 1991 WL 222165 (S.D. N.Y. 1991) (allegation that insurance proceeds not paid); Pelletier v. Eisenberg, 177 Cal. App. 3d 558, 223 Cal. Rptr. 84 (4th Dist. 1986) (insurance proceeds paid but not remitted to artist).

[3]Moncada v. Rubin-Spangle Gallery, Inc., 835 F. Supp. 747 (S.D. N.Y. 1993) (no duty to defend).

D. TRADE APPRAISALS, CERTIFICATIONS, AUTHENTICATIONS

§ 2:35 Generally

Appraisals are judgments about value,[1] authentications are judgments about authorship.[2] While one can impact the other, they are not co-terminous. Traders, and other arts personnel, in the context of trade,[3] who make written or oral statements—or fail to disclose information—about value or authorship, or issue certificates of appraisal or authentication in connection with sales or subsequent to sales, have been held to be engaging in conduct courts deem potentially actionable as follows: fraud,[4] negligence,[5] negligent misrepresentation,[6] breach of contract,[7] RICO,[8]

[Section 2:35]

[1]*See* Ch 3.

[2]*See* Ch 3.

[3]Struna v. Wolf, 126 Misc. 2d 1031, 484 N.Y.S.2d 392 (Sup 1985).

[4]*See* Ch 11; *see also* Michaels v. Wildenstein & Co., Inc., R.I.C.O. Bus. Disp. Guide (CCH) ¶ 8847, 1995 WL 326497 (S.D. N.Y. 1995); Rosen v. Spanierman, 711 F. Supp. 749, 753, 8 U.C.C. Rep. Serv. 2d 713 (S.D. N.Y. 1989), judgment vacated in part on other grounds, 894 F.2d 28, 10 U.C.C. Rep. Serv. 2d 846 (2d Cir. 1990); McCloud v. Lawrence Gallery, Ltd., 1991 WL 136027 (S.D. N.Y. 1991); McKie v. R.H. Love Galleries, Inc., 1990 WL 179797 (N.D. Ill. 1990).

[5]Goldman v. Barnett, 793 F. Supp. 28, 18 U.C.C. Rep. Serv. 2d 55 (D. Mass. 1992); Kremer v. Janet Fleisher Gallery, Inc., 320 Pa. Super. 384, 467 A.2d 377 (1983).

[6]Michaels v. Wildenstein & Co., Inc., R.I.C.O. Bus. Disp. Guide (CCH) P 8847, 1995 WL 326497 (S.D. N.Y. 1995); McKie v. R.H. Love Galleries, Inc., 1990 WL 179797 (N.D. Ill. 1990); Goldman v. Barnett, 793 F. Supp. 28, 18 U.C.C. Rep. Serv. 2d 55 (D. Mass. 1992); California Jury Instructions—Civil. Book of approved jury instructions No. 12.45; Christiansen v. Roddy, 186 Cal. App. 3d 780, 786, 231 Cal. Rptr. 72 (5th Dist. 1986) (implied overruling recognized by, Soderberg v. McKinney, 44 Cal. App. 4th 1760, 52 Cal. Rptr. 2d 635 (2d Dist. 1996)).

[7]Wilson v. Hammer Holdings, Inc., 850 F.2d 3, 6 U.C.C. Rep. Serv. 2d 321 (1st Cir. 1988); Balog v. Center Art Gallery-Hawaii, Inc., 745 F. Supp. 1556, 12 U.C.C. Rep. Serv. 2d 962 (D. Haw. 1990); McKie v. R.H. Love Galleries, Inc., 1990 WL 179797 (N.D. Ill. 1990).

[8]*See* § 11:1; *see also* Michaels v. Wildenstein & Co., Inc., R.I.C.O. Bus. Disp. Guide (CCH) P 8847, 1995 WL 326497 (S.D. N.Y. 1995); McCloud v. Lawrence Gallery, Ltd., 1992 WL 6199 (S.D. N.Y. 1992), aff'd,

and equitable relief.[9]

E. CONSIGNED ART AND RETURNS

§ 2:36 Generally

Duties of traders to release consigned art to artists or their heirs can be upon imposed under the law of agency, under state art per se statutes, and by contract. Where a gallery refused to release to the artist's estate certain artworks from the 300 sculptures it held on consignment under a written exclusive agency agreement, the court issued a mandatory injunction that the art be released for a long planned museum exhibition.[1]

F. SECURITY SYSTEMS ON TRADER PREMISES

§ 2:37 Duty to install and maintain

Traders are not under statutory obligations to install or maintain security systems, but contracts of insurance may be predicated upon the existence of a security system, and may even specify particular qualifications and requirements.

§ 2:38 Security company liability to trader

Security services in some states may exonerate themselves from negligence, but not gross negligence. Where a Manhattan gallery had installed a monitor burglar alarm system, burglars broke in through an unprotected skylight and stole twenty paintings. The plaintiff sued the gallery for ordinary and gross negligence under bailment for two

---

970 F.2d 896 (2d Cir. 1992) (RICO award of $88,000, plus costs and fees, based upon sale of Picasso drawing for $16,000 rejected by Comite Picasso).

[9]Voitier v. Antique Art Gallery, 524 So. 2d 80 (La. Ct. App. 3d Cir. 1988), writ denied, 531 So. 2d 271 (La. 1988) (rescission of contract for sale of painting by George Inness claimed inauthentic).

[Section 2:36]

[1]Nakian v. DiLaurenti, 673 F. Supp. 699 (S.D. N.Y. 1987); *see also* Matter of Friedman, 64 A.D.2d 70, 407 N.Y.S.2d 999 (2d Dep't 1978).

works it had consigned, valued at $2.6 million.[1] The gallery sued the security company for gross negligence under the contract and sought indemnification from the security company if it was found liable to the plaintiff-consignor. The gallery's third-party claim would have been limited to $250 under the liability clause in the installation and service agreement, unless the jury found gross negligence on the installation: "[W]hile a security alarm company may contractually exonerate itself from liability . . . for ordinary negligence, it may not do so with respect to . . . gross negligence." Whether or not failure to protect a skylight was below professional standards and customary practice was an issue of fact for the jury.

§ 2:39 Security company duty to consignor-collector

Consignors to galleries have been considered incidental beneficiaries of the security company contract with the gallery as a matter of law, not third party beneficiaries entitled to sue the security company directly for breach.[1]

IV. BANKRUPTCY

§ 2:40 Generally

Precedential case law on galleries and dealers declaring

[Section 2:38]

[1]Colnaghi, U.S.A., Ltd. v. Jewelers Protection Services, Ltd., 183 A.D.2d 469, 583 N.Y.S.2d 427 (1st Dep't 1992), appeal granted, reargument denied, 186 A.D.2d 349, 588 N.Y.S.2d 765 (1st Dep't 1992) and order rev'd on other grounds, 81 N.Y.2d 821, 595 N.Y.S.2d 381, 611 N.E.2d 282 (1993).

[Section 2:39]

[1]Colnaghi, U.S.A., Ltd. v. Jewelers Protection Services, Ltd., 183 A.D.2d 469, 583 N.Y.S.2d 427 (1st Dep't 1992), appeal granted, reargument denied, 186 A.D.2d 349, 588 N.Y.S.2d 765 (1st Dep't 1992) and order rev'd on other grounds, 81 N.Y.2d 821, 595 N.Y.S.2d 381, 611 N.E.2d 282 (1993). *See also* Bank of New York v. Colnaghi USA, Ltd., 633 N.Y.S. 2d 133 (summary judgment denied to bailor who sued gallery for breach of bailment and damages for diminished value of artwork and cost of restoration after stolen artwork was retrieved in damaged condition because issues of fact existed as to whether it was reasonable for defendant to rely on expertise of security alarm company instead of specifically requesting and checking that skylight was armed).

bankruptcy is limited.[1] The following summarizes common bankruptcy issues that have been adjudicated involving art: art as exempt property under state laws;[2] rights of a trustee in bankruptcy to seize art;[3] equitable doctrine of marshalling assets;[4] standing of governmental agency as creditor of art dealers;[5] a trustee's interests in art on consignment claimed by judgment creditors;[6] transfers of art as fraudulent conveyances;[7] classification of bankrupt's 4000 artworks as tangible personal property subject to state ad valorem taxes or inventory held for sale and

---

[Section 2:40]

[1]*See* Ch 5 for discussion of bankruptcy and auction.

[2]Cal. Civ. Proc. § 704.040 (works of art up to aggregate maximum of $2,500 exempt from the estate of a bankrupt); *see also* In re Leonardo, 102 B.R. 202 (Bankr. E.D. Cal. 1989).

[3]In re Johnson, 139 B.R. 208 (Bankr. D. Minn. 1992) (thirty paintings commissioned by debtor).

[4]Rosenthal, Inc. v. Greenberg Gallery, No. 84-6933, slip op. (S.D.N.Y. 1986) (purpose of the doctrine of marshalling assets is "to prevent the arbitrary action of a senior lienor from destroying the rights of a junior lienor or a creditor having less security").

[5]In re Austin, 138 B.R. 898 (Bankr. N.D. Ill. 1992) (FTC has standing as a "creditor" to assert nondischargeability of art dealer debtor's judgment debt under Section 523(a)(2)(A) of the Bankruptcy Code where FTC had Consent Decree and Permanent Injunction with dealer whereby FTC had right to receive payment of debtor's $1.5 million judgment for deposit into a consumer redress fund for restitution to customers defrauded by the debtor-dealer).

[6]Matter of Miller, 545 F.2d 916, 20 U.C.C. Rep. Serv. 1314 (5th Cir. 1977) (security interest in artwork owned by debtor and held for sale on consignment by art gallery was perfected under UCC § 9-305 despite fact that the debtor had the right to refuse a sale price on any artwork. Retention of control over sale price is reasonable "to avoid a sacrificial sale" and art was placed beyond reach of debtor").

[7]Bernstein v. Hosiery Mfg. Corp. of Morganton, Inc., 850 F. Supp. 176 (E.D. N.Y. 1994); Bayless v. Christie, Manson & Woods Intern., Inc., 2 F.3d 347 (10th Cir. 1993) (directed verdict for auction house on trustee's claim of fraudulent conveyance moot, where judgment for auction reversed on breach of contract claim); In re Charles Weldon, 184 B.R. 710 (D.S.C. 1995) (discharge of debtor under Chapter 7 of Bankruptcy Code denied where debtor failed to disclose significant transactions involving sales and transfers of artwork, the total value of which exceeded $65,000).

exempt from such taxes;[8] failure to keep adequate financial records;[9] and relationship of consigned artwork to bankruptcy estate.[10]

V. ANTITRUST

§ 2:41 Generally

The Sherman Antitrust Act[1] has been pleaded in a variety of art contexts including conspiracy under 15 U.S.C.A. § 1 to terminate distributors;[2] monopolization of artists' markets;[3] and price-fixing.[4] In the most basic of terms, al-

[8]In re Southeast Bank Corp., 97 F.3d 476, 36 Fed. R. Serv. 3d 59 (11th Cir. 1996) (reversed as untimely legal conclusion that artwork in the hands of the Trustee constituted inventory held for sale that did not actually have to be sold on the tax assessment date, and therefore not subject to state tax).

[9]In re Southeast Bank Corp., 97 F.3d 476, 36 Fed. R. Serv. 3d 59 (11th Cir. 1996) (debtor failed to keep minimal recordkeeping requirements of Bankruptcy Code under section 727(a)(3), including failure to document purchase and sale of artworks, failure to keep invoices for artwork sales, and failure to maintain bank records); *see also* Rivas v. Jefferson, 412 F.2d 769 (9th Cir. 1969); Andrew Crispo Gallery, Inc. v. C.I.R., T.C. Memo. 1992-106, 1992 WL 31221 (1992), decision aff'd in part and vacated in part on other grounds, 16 F.3d 1336 (2d Cir. 1994); *see* § 2:31.

[10]Kaufman v. Chalk & Vermilion Fine Arts, LLC, 31 Fed. Appx. 206 (2d Cir. 2002) (unpub. op.) (judgment affirmed for artist in action against debtor-distributor for breach of contract and conversion of consigned artwork).

[Section 2:41]

[1]15 U.S.C.A. §§ 1, 2.

[2]Winn v. Edna Hibel Corp., 858 F.2d 1517 (11th Cir. 1988); *see also* § 2:44.

[3]Vitale v. Marlborough Gallery, 32 U.S.P.Q.2d (BNA) 1283, 1994 WL 654494 (S.D. N.Y. 1994) (dealer alleged gallery and foundation were monopolizing market for paintings by Jackson Pollock).

[4]In re Auction Houses Antitrust Litigation, 135 F. Supp. 2d 438 (S.D. N.Y. 2001), opinion superseded, 138 F. Supp. 2d 548 (S.D. N.Y. 2001) (actions based upon alleged agreement between Sotheby's and Christie's to employ a common rate schedule for premiums charged to buyers, and to use substantially similar rates for sellers' commissions)(indictment and guilty pleas by Sotheby's and former president to criminal price-fixing and conditional amnesty to Christie's and certain personnel for cooperation with the Department of Justice); Kruman v. Christie's Int'l. PLC, 284 F. 3d 384 (2d Cir. 2002) (Sherman Antitrust

legations to support a Sherman Act claim must include the "contract, combination, or conspiracy constituting an unlawful restraint of trade."[5]

The relevant market or submarket must be sufficiently identified to assess the potential antitrust claim. A single product line may qualify as a submarket. In the arts context, an artist's market may constitute a submarket, and the respective oeuvres of Georgia O'Keeffe[6] and Jackson Pollock[7] have been evaluated as submarkets by the courts.

VI. PRODUCER LIABILITY

§ 2:42 Breach of contract

Suppliers of art materials are no different from others when goods contracted for do not arrive or do not conform. Producers have been sued for failure to provide timely and proper raw materials contracted for site specific commissions. Where an artist contracted with a defendant to supply marble for a sculpture in New York, and to transport and cut the marble on site, the artist sued for breach of contract and fraud when the producer failed to take field measurements at the project site to prepare the shop drawings.[1]

§ 2:43 Tort/wrongful death

Site specific installations have caused injury and death

Act applicable to auctions held outside U.S. and to foreign defendants when price-fixing of buyer's premiums and seller's commissions affects domestic worldwide markets); *see also*, Ch 5 §§ 5:26 to 5:30.

[5]In re Auction Houses Antitrust Litigation, 135 F. Supp. 2d 438 (S.D. N.Y. 2001), opinion superseded, 138 F. Supp. 2d 548 (S.D. N.Y. 2001).

[6]Estate of O'Keeffe v. C.I.R., T.C. Memo. 1992-210, T.C.M. (RIA) ¶ 92210 (1992).

[7]Vitale v. Marlborough Gallery, 32 U.S.P.Q.2d (BNA) 1283, 1994 WL 654494 (S.D. N.Y. 1994) (plaintiff alleged "a submarket sufficient to state a claim under 15 U.S.C.A. § 1 or 2," but action time-barred under statute of limitations).

[Section 2:42]

[1]Feigenbaum v. Marble of America, Inc., 735 F. Supp. 79 (S.D. N.Y. 1990).

to workers and viewers. Survivors have sued artists and others.[1]

§ 2:44 Producer-distributor relationship

A producer may independently terminate retailers who do not adhere to price lists. The burden is on the plaintiff to prove conspiracy between the producer and a competing dealer to engage in impermissible concerted action of a manufacturer and its retailers in setting prices; this conduct, if proven, is per se illegal under Section 1 of the Sherman Antitrust Act,[1] and is economically unreasonable, and requires a plaintiff to present evidence which "tends to exclude the possibility" that a producer and competitor acted independently.[2] Concerted action that otherwise has been found reasonable where unique and limited objects like art, purchased for taste and possibly investment value, are not subject to competitive market conditions.[3]

VII. SHIPPERS-TRANSPORTERS

§ 2:45 Carriers

Art is transported intrastate, interstate, and in foreign commerce carriage, invoking many treaties and agreements pertinent to specific types of carriers. A carrier is

---

[Section 2:43]

[1]*See, e.g.*, Johnson v. Serra, 521 F.2d 1289 (8th Cir. 1975) (wrongful death for installation of Serra sculpture brought by widow of workman).

[Section 2:44]

[1]15 U.S.C.A. § 1; *see* § 2:41 for discussion of other claims brought under the Sherman Act.

[2]Winn v. Edna Hibel Corp., 858 F.2d 1517 (11th Cir. 1988) (plaintiff alleged producer of lithographs and collector plates terminated it at urging of competitor for selling artworks at less than suggested retail prices).

[3]Winn v. Edna Hibel Corp., 858 F.2d 1517 (11th Cir. 1988) (To maintain the "image" of art and integrity of the product, is a permissible goal of retail pricing structure. But even if evidence permitted jury to find that producer and competitor conspired to terminate plaintiff-dealer because conduct harmed the "image," this was not a nonprice restraint judged under a rule of reason analysis.). Monopoly profit is more than a "reasonable" profit that can be made in the face of competition.

any entity engaged in the transport of property, i.e., common carriers, contract carriers, private carriers, and freight forwarders.[1] Common carriers hold themselves out to undertake cartage for the public for all goods; contract carriers furnish services only for certain customers and certain goods as they choose. Major revisions to, and repeal of, interstate and foreign commerce statutes, international treaties and conventions have occurred during the recent past that apply to this and following sections. Confirmation of laws and regulations for applicable time periods should be made, including state laws.[2]

Losses of or damage to art in transit are not uncommon and carriers typically assert limitation of liability under the Warsaw Convention[3] or other conventions,[4] or

---

[Section 2:45]

[1]Interstate Commerce Act, 18 U.S.C.A. § 831.

[2]Jane Rini v. United Van Inc., 903 F. Supp. 227 (D. Mass. 1995) (plaintiff awarded treble damages under state law on unfair and deceptive trade practices [Mass. Gen.L. ch. 93A] for artworks lost by common carrier during move of family belongings from Florida to Massachusetts, and carrier's subsequent conduct and actions, including investigation and refusal to pay, after plaintiff filed loss report).

[3]*See* 49 U.S.C.A. § 40105, 49 Stat. 3000, T.S. 876. Substantial changes have been made by Congress regarding international commerce, conventions and treaties; Kesel v. United Parcel Service, Inc., 2002 WL 102606 (N.D. Cal. 2002) (Warsaw Convention inapplicable to claim for loss of seven paintings sent from Russia to the United States because shipment lost after international air transport).

[4]Sotheby's v. Federal Exp. Corp., 97 F. Supp. 2d 491 (S.D. N.Y. 2000) (carrier liable for full value of damage to artwork when it occurred at stopping place not listed on airbill); Kitz Corp. v. Transcon Shipping Specialists, Inc., 89 N.Y.2d 822, 652 N.Y.S.2d 720, 675 N.E.2d 455 (1996) (plaintiff's lamps purchased for $886,000 from Christie's damaged in shipment from New York to Japan); Welliver v. Federal Exp. Corp., 737 F. Supp. 205 (S.D. N.Y. 1990) (painting lost in transit); *cf.* U.S. Gold Corp. v. Federal Exp. Corp., 719 F. Supp. 1217, 11 U.C.C. Rep. Serv. 2d 933 (S.D. N.Y. 1989); Vekris v. Peoples Exp. Airlines, Inc., 707 F. Supp. 675 (S.D. N.Y. 1988) (carrier estopped from asserting paintings valued at $45,000 did not constitute "baggage" under Warsaw Convention); *cf.* Gmurzynska v. United Exposition Service Co., Inc., 1989 WL 27137 (N.D. Ill. 1989); Zucker v. Kid Gloves, Inc., 234 A.D.2d 598, 652 N.Y.S.2d 614 (2d Dep't 1996) (plaintiff's suit against shipper for damage to artwork packed and sent after exhibition would not be dismissed on defendant's theory that artist was not a third party beneficiary of contract between gallery and shipper); Kitz Corp. v. Transcon

contract.[5] Contractual limitation of liability clauses are decided under federal common law. Common carriers may limit their liability on a released valuation basis providing the released value doctrine is satisfied.[6]

§ 2:46 Art transporters

Moving art is like moving grand pianos; it requires skill. Craters, packers, and transporters hold themselves out as specializing in the intrastate and interstate transfer of art from one location to another. Fine art transporters may offer insurance on a per shipment basis; verification of insurance should be made prior to shipment.[1] Those who rely upon the services of these contract carriers should be aware that a common carrier often enters the transport chain unbeknownst to the shipper or receiver until loss or damage occurs.[2] Third party beneficiary theories by artists or collectors arising from contracts between galleries, dealers or others handling the transport of the artwork and shippers or carriers may be available.[3]

§ 2:47 Declared value

The Carmack Amendment to the Interstate Commerce Act governing the liability of motor common carriers in in-

---

Shipping Specialists, Inc., 89 N.Y.2d 822, 652 N.Y.S.2d 720, 675 N.E.2d 455 (1996) (damage) (Warsaw Convention limitation on international cargo carrier).

[5]Kesel v. United Parcel Service, Inc., 2002 WL 102606 (N.D. Cal. 2002) (recovery limited to declared value on the waybill for seven paintings lost in transit).

[6]Kesel v. United Parcel Service, Inc., 2002 WL 102606 (N.D. Cal. 2002) (carrier must provide reasonable notice of limited liability and offer opportunity to purchase higher liability).

[Section 2:46]

[1]Bowling v. United Parcel Service, 1993 WL 76968 (Ohio Ct. App. 2d Dist. Montgomery County 1993) (the art shipper charged Bowling $14 for "what Coast's order form lists as 'insurance' in the amount of $1500").

[2]Bowling v. United Parcel Service, 1993 WL 76968 (Ohio Ct. App. 2d Dist. Montgomery County 1993).

[3]Zucker v. Kid Gloves, Inc., 234 A.D.2d 598, 652 N.Y.S.2d 614 (2d Dep't 1996) (artist filed suit against shipper to recover damages for breach of contract and negligence when his artwork was damaged in transit under contract between gallery and shipper).

terstate shipment of goods recognized the right to limit the carrier's liability to the stipulated value of goods to be shipped. In the absence of declared value, the carrier's limitation on liability ordinarily controlled. The Carmack Amendment's remedies for damages arising from loss of goods during transport do not necessarily limit the total damages award, however, as in instances where Carmack does not preempt relief available under other laws.[1] A plaintiff-gallery sued a carrier for $52,000 based upon the value of two antique tapestries shipped by UPS from Chicago, Illinois, to a gallery in Manhattan. The tapestries were never received because the defendant's driver left the tapestries unattended in a building lobby from which they were stolen and signed the delivery receipt with a fictitious name. The shipper failed to declare the value on the pick up record. The defendant's liability was limited to $100, the presumed value for each tapestry based upon filed tariffs.[2]

The "material deviation" doctrine under admiralty law may apply whereby a material breach of the carriage contract justifies rescission of the entire contract.[3] The doctrine has not been applied to "regulated common carriers because such carriers are governed by an overriding federal policy of uniformity that 'required that the tariffs be applied to all matters arising from the attempted performance of the contract.' "[4] Conversion is a federal common-law exception to the Carmack Amendment. Where a gallery claimed the carrier's misdelivery constituted conversion, the court found none because the carrier did not appropriate the shipped goods for its own benefit,

---

[Section 2:47]

[1]Rini v. United Van Lines, Inc., 903 F. Supp. 224 (D. Mass. 1995), rev'd on other grounds, 104 F.3d 502 (1st Cir. 1997) (plaintiff entitled to treble damages under state unfair trade practices law as well as those under Carmack Amendment, where moving company lost artworks, antiques, and family heirlooms).

[2]Rafaella Gallery, Inc. v. United Parcel Service, Inc., 818 F. Supp. 53 (S.D. N.Y. 1993).

[3]Rafaella Gallery, Inc. v. United Parcel Service, Inc., 818 F. Supp. 53 (S.D. N.Y. 1993).

[4]Rafaella Gallery, Inc. v. United Parcel Service, Inc., 818 F. Supp. 53 (S.D. N.Y. 1993).

stating "mere 'misdelivery is not a conversion which deprives a carrier of the benefit of a tariff provision limiting liability.' "[5]

The declared value is not automatically paid in the event of damage. Where a plaintiff hired fine art transporters to ship a porcelain statue from Los Angeles to Dayton, Ohio, in a box marked "Glass" and "Do not Drop" in large black letters, the company in turn contracted with UPS.[6] The statue arrived broken. UPS offered to pay the plaintiff $328 for cost of repairs and shipping charges based upon a written repair estimate, although the declared value was $1,500. The plaintiff refused and sued in small claims court for $865, which included loss of value as well as repairs. The trial court awarded $363, which was affirmed on appeal.

VIII. STORAGE

§ 2:48 Generally

Facilities exist that specialize in art storage.[1] Premises should be inspected to determine security, construction in approved building materials, and installation of sprinkler systems. Facilities that qualify for AAA fire rating by insurance companies may offer insurance to those leasing space for objects stored on the premises through policies and riders. Art storage facilities are not uncommon parties in disputes where ownership of stored contents is at issue.[2]

---

[5] Rafaella Gallery, Inc. v. United Parcel Service, Inc., 818 F. Supp. 53 (S.D. N.Y. 1993).

[6] Bowling v. United Parcel Service, 1993 WL 76968 (Ohio Ct. App. 2d Dist. Montgomery County 1993).

[Section 2:48]

[1] Werbungs Und Commerz Union Austalt v. LeShufy, 6 U.S.P.Q.2d (BNA) 1153, 1987 WL 33618 (S.D. N.Y. 1987); *see also* Reichman v. Warehouse One, Inc., 173 A.D.2d 250, 569 N.Y.S.2d 452 (1st Dep't 1991), appeal dismissed in part, 78 N.Y.2d 1058, 576 N.Y.S.2d 213, 582 N.E.2d 596 (1991).

[2] Chamberlain v. Cocola Associates, 958 F.2d 282 (9th Cir. 1992); Werbungs Und Commerz Union Austalt v. LeShufy, 6 U.S.P.Q.2d (BNA) 1153, 1987 WL 33618 (S.D. N.Y. 1987); Danae Art Intern. Inc. v. Stallone, 163 A.D.2d 81, 557 N.Y.S.2d 338 (1st Dep't 1990).

IX. JURISDICTION

§ 2:49 Personal jurisdiction: General and specific

Personal jurisdiction may be general (nonforum related)[1] or specific (forum related).[2] Courts asserting specific jurisdiction over nonresident defendants examine the specific acts underlying the plaintiff's claim to determine the propriety of extending jurisdiction. The Supreme Court has approved specific types of acts whereby the defendant "purposefully avails itself" of conducting business within the forum, or "purposefully directs" activities toward forum residents.[3]

§ 2:50 Personal jurisdiction: Minimum contacts

The International Shoe[1] basis for jurisdiction is the defendant's minimum contacts with the forum state and exercise of jurisdiction that would not "offend traditional notions of fair play and substantial justice." The issue is not the general nature and quality of the defendant's art business, but rather the nature and quality of specific business contacts with the forum. Some courts have held that the contacts must be "central to the defendant's business."[2]

Plaintiffs in art cases have attempted to overcome International Shoe by contending that art trading is slithery in jurisdictional terms, as international activity is conducted from, to, and in multi-sited venues. Siting the acts and the injuries is important for a plaintiff because,

---

[Section 2:49]

[1]Where claims are unrelated to or arise from the defendant's contacts with the forum.

[2]Where claims are related to or arise from the defendant's contacts with the forum.

[3]Burger King Corp. v. Rudzewicz, 471 U.S. 462, 474–75, 105 S. Ct. 2174, 85 L. Ed. 2d 528 (1985); World-wide Volkswagen Corp. v. Woodson, 444 U.S. 286, 297, 62 L. Ed. 2d 490 (1980).

[Section 2:50]

[1]International Shoe Co. v. State of Wash., Office of Unemployment Compensation and Placement, 326 U.S. 310, 316, 66 S. Ct. 154, 90 L. Ed. 95, 161 A.L.R. 1057 (1945).

[2]Leonardo Da Vinci's Horse, Inc. v. O'Brien, 761 F. Supp. 1222 (E.D. Pa. 1991).

once a jurisdictional defect is raised, the plaintiff bears the burden of establishing with reasonable particularity sufficient contacts between the defendant and the forum state.[3]

Courts have held requisite minimum contacts were not satisfied where nonresident defendant-traders generally: (1) bought or sold art works outside the forum;[4] (2) bought the art at issue outside the forum;[5] (3) communicated with forum residents regarding a sale transacted outside the forum;[6] or (4) participated in publication of an alleged defamatory exhibition catalogue.[7]

Courts have considered that requisite minimum contacts could be satisfied where traders generally did or had the following:

(1) maintained international offices and clientele in

---

[3]Rosenberg v. Seattle Art Museum, 42 F. Supp. 2d 1029 (W.D. Wash. 1999) (general solicitation of business in forum without solicitation of contract at issue insufficient contact); Gmurzynska v. Hutton, 2003 WL 1193727 (S.D. N.Y. 2003) (no jurisdiction where connections between defendant's activities involving catalogue in Germany and injuries sustained by New York plaintiff were "tenuous"); David Tunick, Inc. v. Kornfeld, 813 F. Supp. 988 (S.D. N.Y. 1993) (plaintiff must make prima facie showing that personal jurisdiction exists when determination is made without a full, evidentiary hearing; where discovery has already occurred on issue of jurisdiction, plaintiff must prove by a preponderance of the evidence that defendant's activities constitute "forum-related" conduct); Foster-Gwin v. Fallwell, 2001 WL 1382069 (N.D. Cal. 2001)(specific jurisdiction lacking over antiques dealer and appraiser where it would be unreasonable, notwithstanding that the claim arose from forum-related activities and defendant might have consummated transactions or "purposely availed" himself of privileges in the forum.).

[4]Leonardo Da Vinci's Horse, Inc. v. O'Brien, 761 F. Supp. 1222 (E.D. Pa. 1991); Buxton v. Wyland Galleries Hawaii, 275 Ill. App. 3d 980, 212 Ill. Dec. 507, 657 N.E.2d 708 (4th Dist. 1995) (no jurisdiction where Hawaiian gallery defendants did not buy or sell art in the forum).

[5]Leonardo Da Vinci's Horse, Inc. v. O'Brien, 761 F. Supp. 1222 (E.D. Pa. 1991).

[6]Rosenberg v. Seattle Art Museum, 42 F. Supp. 2d 1029 (W.D. Wash. 1999) (taking possession of painting in forum, which required mailing letters to forum to finalize deal, was not a solicitation on which to exercise jurisdiction).

[7]Gmurzynska v. Hutton, 2003 WL 1193727 (S.D. N.Y. 2003) (jurisdiction based on "foreseeable effects" must be undertaken with caution, especially in international context).

the forum;[8]

(2) operated out of a personal apartment, rather than a gallery or an office in the forum;[9]

(3) regularly did business and solicited business in the forum;[10]

(4) purchased art for the trader's personal collection in the forum;[11]

(5) sold paintings in the forum that accrued substantial revenues;[12]

(6) engaged in a persistent course of conduct in the forum by undertaking substantial nonbusiness activities, like displaying art in museums located in the forum;[13] and

(7) made a single transaction in the forum involving an uninvited solicitation to sell art, even though the gallery was never physically present in forum.[14]

Intentional conduct in one forum that has an "effect" in a second forum may be a sufficient basis for minimum contacts in the second forum. Where the defendant was a participant in a fraudulent scheme to willfully defraud the plaintiff in connection with the sale of a bronze statue by failing to contact the statue's owner even though the defendant had the name and address of the owner, the court wrote:

> Given plaintiff's assertion of willful and malicious acts by defendant to deprive it of the statue, the apparent state of

---

[8]Leonardo Da Vinci's Horse, Inc. v. O'Brien, 761 F. Supp. 1222 (E.D. Pa. 1991).

[9]Leonardo Da Vinci's Horse, Inc. v. O'Brien, 761 F. Supp. 1222 (E.D. Pa. 1991).

[10]David Tunick, Inc. v. Kornfeld, 813 F. Supp. 988, 990 (S.D. N.Y. 1993).

[11]David Tunick, Inc. v. Kornfeld, 813 F. Supp. 988, 990 (S.D. N.Y. 1993).

[12]David Tunick, Inc. v. Kornfeld, 813 F. Supp. 988, 990 (S.D. N.Y. 1993).

[13]David Tunick, Inc. v. Kornfeld, 813 F. Supp. 988, 990 (S.D. N.Y. 1993).

[14]David Tunick, Inc. v. Kornfeld, 813 F. Supp. 988, 990 (S.D. N.Y. 1993).

> the resale market for art objects, and the Bruton Gallery's inattention and apparent lack of concern for securing concrete proof of authority of defendant . . . , the Court concludes that plaintiff has alleged and carried its burden [of demonstrating Pennsylvania's long arm statute extended jurisdiction over the gallery].[15]

The internet, websites, online auctions like eBay and other internet arts activities raise challenging jurisdictional issues.[16]

X. ABANDONMENT

§ 2:51 Claims and defenses

Abandonment requires a voluntary relinquishment of rights in property, with both intention and action necessary in many jurisdictions before possessory rights will be deemed relinquished; intent will not be presumed and proof must be submitted on both points. The party claiming ownership by default has the burden of proof.[1]

Courts did not find abandonment of artwork in the following circumstances: valuable and historic WPA murals were removed from a city school without any inquiry by the city as to their whereabouts for almost thirty years but the city claimed ownership in declaratory relief action brought by the plaintiff in possession;[2] and renowned "Quo Vadis" painting by Art Nouveau artist Jiri Mucha, consigned for forty years to a gallery, was subsequently claimed by the artist's son who had exchanged letters with the gallery during period when the artist's wife was the

---

[15]Leonardo Da Vinci's Horse, Inc. v. O'Brien, 761 F. Supp. 1222, 1229 (E.D. Pa. 1991).

[16]Foster-Gwin v. Fallwell, 2001 WL 1382069 (N.D. Cal. 2001)(regardless of whether eBay is categorized as a passive forum or an active sales agent, defendant's use of eBay, which resulted in sales totaling less than $1000.00 in the forum, did not satisfy the "fairly high" threshold for general jurisdiction).

[Section 2:51]

[1]Hoelzer v. City of Stamford, Conn., 933 F.2d 1131 (2d Cir. 1991); Mucha v. King, 792 F.2d 602 (7th Cir. 1986).

[2]Hoelzer v. City of Stamford, Conn., 933 F.2d 1131 (2d Cir. 1991).

owner of painting.[3]

§ 2:52 Museum in possession

Although transfers of art to museums have generated litigation—for example, in transfers as loans[1] and transfers as gifts[2]—abandonment claims are typically handled by operation of law in many states having "old loan" laws. Old loan laws repose title in the museum after a period of years if no claimant has come forward.

XI. TORTS

A. DEFAMATION

§ 2:53 Opinion

The U.S. Supreme Court has held that the First Amendment does not protect otherwise defamatory statements on the ground that they "might be labelled 'opinion.' "[1] Although statements of opinion are not automatically immunized from defamation claims under the First Amendment simply because they are opinions, opinions about matters of public concern may enjoy an absolute privilege providing they do not contain provably false, factual connotations. As the Supreme Court stated in Milkovich: "[A] statement on matters of public concern must be provable as false . . . a statement of opinion relating to matters of public concern which does not contain a provably

[3]Mucha v. King, 792 F.2d 602 (7th Cir. 1986).

[Section 2:52]

[1]State "old loan" laws transfer title to a museum by operation of law for art loaned to museums that is unclaimed after a period of years.

[2]Wildenstein & Co. v. Wallis, 756 F. Supp. 158 (S.D. N.Y. 1991), rev'd on other grounds, 983 F.2d 1047 (2d Cir. 1992) (permanent loan of collector to museum terminated by heirs and foundation upon his death; art auctioned when injunction sought by museum denied); Mac'Avoy v. The Smithsonian Inst., 757 F. Supp. 60 (D.D.C. 1991) (plaintiff claimed "gift" to museum was merely loan); Temple v. McCaughen & Burr, Inc., 839 S.W.2d 322 (Mo. Ct. App. E.D. 1992) (museum returns loaned art to dealers instead of owner).

[Section 2:53]

[1]Milkovich v. Lorain Journal Co., 497 U.S. 1, 110 S. Ct. 2695, 2705, 111 L. Ed. 2d 1, 60 Ed. Law Rep. 1061 (1990); Ketcham v. Franklyn Gesner Fine Paintings, Inc., 181 Ga. App. 549, 353 S.E.2d 44 (1987).

false factual connotation will receive full constitutional protection."[2]

§ 2:54 Authenticity as a matter of public concern

The value and authenticity of art are considered matters of public concern, and opinions about art and experts have been protected in these instances: authenticity of stained glass windows purported to be by John LaFarge were challenged by museum personnel in a letter written to prospective buyer-donor and patron of the museum;[1] a magazine article challenging the qualifications of art experts.[2] Statements about the authenticity of artworks displayed at public exhibitions, museums, art fairs and offered for sale to the public have been deemed matters of public concern for purposes of defamation suits even if the market or community affected is limited and does not involve the "population as a whole." Statements about the authenticity of works by Russian Suprematist painter Lazar Khidekel and American stained glass artist John La Farge were considered matters of public concern.[3] Protected opinions have encompassed the following statements: repudiation by artist's heir of catalogue of art exhibition;[4] unprotected opinions include a network and commentator series of broadcasts implying that a dealer had misrepresented the maker, condition, origin, value, and provenance of rare antique silver candelabra sold to a

---

[2]Milkovich v. Lorain Journal Co., 497 U.S. 1, 110 S. Ct. 2695, 2706, 111 L. Ed. 2d 1, 60 Ed. Law Rep. 1061 (1990).

[Section 2:54]

[1]McNally v. Yarnall, 764 F. Supp. 838, 844 (S.D. N.Y. 1991) (defamation action against nonmedia defendants who did not use public medium to disseminate allegedly defamatory material could stand for statements about plaintiff's capacity in trade and business capable of being proven false).

[2]Porcella v. Time, Inc., 300 F.2d 162 (7th Cir. 1962); *cf.* Weller v. American Broadcasting Companies, Inc., 232 Cal. App. 3d 991, 998, 283 Cal. Rptr. 644 (1st Dist. 1991) (fair comment defense in California protects opinions made about artists who place themselves or their works in the public eye).

[3]Boule v. Hutton, 138 F. Supp. 2d 491 (S.D. N.Y. 2001) (Khidekel); McNally v. Yarnall, 764 F. Supp. 838 (S.D. N.Y. 1991).

[4]Boule v. Hutton, 138 F. Supp. 2d 491 (S.D. N.Y. 2001).

San Francisco museum;[5] artist's heirs statements in art magazines and newspapers that certificates of authenticity they executed were fake and that plaintiffs had been told artworks were inauthentic.[6]

§ 2:55 Provable false facts

The plaintiff bears the burden of showing the falsity of factual assertions. What constitutes provable false facts when evaluating authenticity? Generic types of statements in the authenticity context that are incapable of being proven false for purposes of defamation claims are:

(1) particular artwork not recognized as by the artist purported to be by the evaluator;
(2) artwork depicts motif not known in artist's oeuvre;
(3) particular artwork not listed in catalogue raisonne;
(4) unsigned artwork not from particular collection or site; and
(5) artwork does "not seem to be by" artist.

Statements in the art context capable of being proven false for purposes of defamation claims are:

(1) art sold at a "grossly inflated price" (although valuation of antiques is an inexact science, a range of reasonable valuations could have verified objectively whether the purchase was at "grossly inflated price");
(2) statements coupled with comments that art is "ruined in value" and sale is a "sweetheart deal" (although statements could be hyperbolic or out of context they do not negate the impression of defamatory remarks); and
(3) statements of persons denying their own signa-

---

[5]Weller v. American Broadcasting Companies, Inc., 232 Cal. App. 3d 991, 998, 283 Cal. Rptr. 644 (1st Dist. 1991) (jury awards general damages of $1 million, $500,000 for injury to reputation and $500,000 presumed damages to reputation).

[6]Boule v. Hutton, 138 F. Supp. 2d 491 (S.D. N.Y. 2001) (private plaintiff alleging defamation of statements on matters of public concern must prove that the defendant was "grossly irresponsible.")

tures on certificates of authenticity.

In McNally, an action for defamation brought by a dealer against a museum and a museum consultant, the dealer-plaintiff alleged that the consultant stated that the stained glass windows (purportedly) by LaFarge were "irreparably damaged and glass badly shattered due its having been dropped [and] poorly restored." The plaintiff submitted expert evidence showing that the stained glass had deteriorated over time, a process known as "crizzling," and that accepted conservation practices to arrest crizzling could account for the appearance. The court stated, without deciding, that such evidence "could prove false Yarnall's alleged assertion that the glass had been shattered and poorly restored."[1]

§ 2:56 Qualifications of art experts

Libel is based upon written words affecting a person in his professional capacity, trade, or business by imputing incapacity. Statements of a dealer's unfitness or want of necessary qualities to mount an exhibition or prepare a catalogue can constitute libel. For example, where a defendant's letter stated that the plaintiff "has . . . muddled [the history of major works], rendering anything he says about them suspect," the plaintiff's "character and performance" as a professionally competent art dealer was deemed capable of being proved false, but persons "who provide on short notice an oral opinion on the quality of work of art" perform "important functions" which should not be deterred by requiring them to "exhaustive[ly] investigate facts" before issuing opinions.[1] Defamation was dismissed, too, where the dealer counterclaimed against the collector who sought rescission of a sales contract alleging that the painting she bought that had been attributed to famous portrait artist Sir Anthony Van

[Section 2:55]

[1]McNally v. Yarnall, 764 F. Supp. 838, 847 (S.D. N.Y. 1991).

[Section 2:56]

[1]McNally v. Yarnall, 764 F. Supp. 838, 847 (S.D. N.Y. 1991).

Dyck was a fake and had been overvalued by the dealer.[2]

§ 2:57 Specificity of pleading

A claim for defamation must state the particular words which the party contends damages his reputation. Where the statements are not defamatory on their face, as is typical in authentications or valuations, special damages must be pled in New York and other jurisdictions. Failure to plead special damages, along with other pleading defects, can result in dismissal of the complaint.[1] Dismissal for failure to plead was found where an author of books and catalogues on John Singer Sargent sued a gallery, an auction house, and a museum director (who also had written a Sargent book) for defamation for statements that works the plaintiff attributed to Sargent and sold as authentic were actually misattributed. "Mount has not alleged the exact words spoken by [defendants]. He has only asserted that they maintain that certain works attributed to Sargent are not authentic. This is plainly insufficient for a claim of defamation."[2]

B. DISPARAGEMENT

§ 2:58 Elements of tort

Authentications have been the basis of product disparagement actions, which generally require words or conduct reflecting negatively on the quality, condition, or value of a product or property. To prevail on the tort in New York, for example, a plaintiff must establish the following elements: falsity of defendant's statements; publication by defendant to a third person; malice; and special damages, "limited to losses having pecuniary or economic value, and

---

[2]Mennella v. Kurt E. Schon E.A.I., Ltd., 979 F.2d 357 (5th Cir. 1992) (record supported district court's decision that the plaintiff did not make any defamatory comments and that those of her lawyers, presumably referring to the pleadings, could not be attributed to her).

[Section 2:57]

[1]Mount v. Ormand, 1991 WL 191228 (S.D. N.Y. 1991).

[2]Mount v. Ormand, 1991 WL 191228 (S.D. N.Y. 1991).

. . . 'fully and accurately stated.' "[1]

§ 2:59 Publication

An authenticator's solicited statement to an auction house, a cataloguer, and its employees may be adequate to constitute publication for the tort of disparagement.[1] However, even if disclosures to an auction house and others constituted publication, since the persons to whom the disclosures were made were not prospective buyers of the painting and there was no evidence that they circulated statements to outside persons, no effective publication was made.

§ 2:60 Special damages

Owners of art have attempted to claim that persons authenticating artworks have disparaged the works. Where the plaintiff consigned the painting "La Rue de la Paix" by Jean Beraud to Christie's for auction in May 1988, Christie's required as a term of sale that the painting be included in a catalogue raisonne of Beraud, a Wildenstein publication. Wildenstein directly examined the painting in New York, concluding that it might have been "skinned" (removal of paint through overcleaning) or a copy because of its blurred condition. Wildenstein declined to include "La Rue" in the catalogue raisonne, and Christie's withdrew it, believing nonetheless that it was genuine.

Christie's wrote the Paris art dealer whose label was affixed to the back of the painting. The dealer responded

---

[Section 2:58]

[1]Kirby v. Wildenstein, 784 F. Supp. 1112 (S.D. N.Y. 1992); Boule v. Hutton, 138 F. Supp. 2d 491 (S.D. N.Y. 2001) (plaintiffs failed to prove element of product disparagement that defendants' statements about artworks' authenticity were false, where expert testimony on authenticity conflicted.); aff'd in part, vacated in part, 328 F.3d 84, 31 Media L. Rep. (BNA) 1793, 66 U.S.P.Q.2d (BNA) 1659 (2d Cir. 2003) (falsity of statements in two magazines as violation under state unfair competition and disparagement laws).

[Section 2:59]

[1]Kirby v. Wildenstein, 784 F. Supp. 1112 (S.D. N.Y. 1992) (whether such statements constitute publication was not decided because the complaint for disparagement was disposed of by summary judgment).

that it had purchased the painting directly from Beraud in 1907. Christie's sent this documentation to Wildenstein, which agreed to include the painting in the catalogue raisonne, but indicated that a condition notation would recite "an abusive restoration and cleaning" and that Christie's catalogue should contain the same notation. Christie's obtained a report from a conservator regarding the condition of the painting and restoration, and notified Wildenstein that it would not publish the notation, but would make the conservators report available to prospective bidders.

The Beraud was offered for auction in October 1988; the Christie's sales catalogue did not make reference to condition; there were no bidders and the painting did not sell. The plaintiff then sued Wildenstein for product disparagement, alleging $200,000 in damages and that the painting would not sell for more than $50,000 in the present market, but omitting the names of persons who did not bid because of the alleged disparagement. Wildenstein contended that the plaintiff had to name lost customers because special damages consist of lost sales. The district court, relying on a more lenient rule permitting decline in sales to be enough where it is impossible to identify customers, still found that the plaintiff could not show declining sales for the painting. Moreover, since the more lenient rule requires that decline can only be used where other factors have been excluded, the plaintiff's quality and condition problems created factors that could not be excluded.

XII. PROVENANCE

§ 2:61 Definition

Provenance is a chronological history of a work of art traced to the creator by tracking the chain of transfer of ownership and possession, location, publication, reproduction, and display. An analysis of provenance may reveal ownership, prior status, condition, restoration (hence, possible re-attribution or de-attribution), and authenticity.

Provenance can impart information about, inter alia, authenticity and ownership but no uniform guidelines exist to determine it, to document it, or to disclose it. A review of the opinions and art literature indicates that there is neither a standard formulation of the processes to obtain such a history nor consensual methods for investigating it. As to how far back in the chain one ought to go, how to treat gaps in the chain, what ought to be disclosed, and, if disclosed, in what form, by whom, and to whom, there is neither a uniform rule nor custom and usage of the trade.[1]

Prospective buyers who wish to understand more fully what provenance is being obtained should request: (1) the facts revealed by investigating provenance should be disclosed; (2) the disclosure should be reduced to writing; (3) the person(s) responsible for doing the investigation should be identified; (4) the methods and procedures of investigation, as well as the materials and persons referenced, should be recited; (5) the form of the writing should be specified; and (6) the provenance as revealed in the writing should be satisfactory to the purchaser as a condition of sale.

§ 2:62 Background

Courts use provenance[1] to indicate a broad range of meanings about objects, their attributes, and their legal

---

[Section 2:61]

[1]In one state, where there is codified a demand and refusal rule to commence an action for replevin of personal property, the court has opined on who should investigate provenance. *See* Solomon R. Guggenheim Foundation v. Lubell, 153 A.D.2d 143, 550 N.Y.S.2d 618 (1st Dep't 1990), order aff'd, 77 N.Y.2d 311, 567 N.Y.S.2d 623, 569 N.E.2d 426 (1991) ("In our [court of appeals of New York] opinion, the better rules gives the owner [of art] relatively greater protection and places the burden of investigating the provenance of a work of art on the potential purchaser."); *cf.* Mac'Avoy v. The Smithsonian Inst., 757 F. Supp. 60 (D.D.C. 1991) ("plaintiff alleges that the Smithsonian [failed to make] investigation into whether the person from whom they allegedly acquired title had the authority to convey it . . . . However, after extensive discovery, the plaintiff can point to no evidence that the National Gallery of Fine Art . . . had any practice of clarifying issues of title by requiring formal deeds of gift").

[Section 2:62]

[1]Provenance and provenience, meaning "origin or source," derives from the French infinitive provenir (to originate) rooted in the Latin provenire (to come forth). Provenance usually refers to works of art. Provenience usually refers to artifacts, and archaeological, historical, and/or ethnographic objects.

classifications: location[2] and valuation,[3] origin,[4] ownership history,[5] possessory history,[6] capability to transfer ownership,[7] authenticity,[8] certification of authenticity,[9] documen-

---

[2]Klein v. Unidentified Wrecked & Abandoned Sailing Vessel, 758 F.2d 1511 (11th Cir. 1985) ("provenience [is] the exact location at which each item is found in terms of horizontal and vertical coordinates, the extent of burial, water depth and its spatial relationship to other items found"); Golden Budha Corp. v. Canadian Land Co. of America, N.V., 931 F.2d 196, 20 Fed. R. Serv. 3d 388 (2d Cir. 1991) ("The provenance of the Yamashita Treasure is shrouded in mystery [allegedly] 'hidden in The Philippines by the Japanese occupation forces prior to end of World War II' ").

[3]Klein v. Unidentified Wrecked and Abandoned Sailing Vessel, 758 F.2d 1511, 1513 (11th Cir. 1985) ("Archeological provenience is not only important for the historical information . . . but it also adds to the value of the artifacts for donation or sale to interested buyers.").

[4]Klein v. Unidentified Wrecked and Abandoned Sailing Vessel, 758 F.2d 1511, at 1515 (11th Cir. 1985) ("The articles removed from the shipwreck site were not marked or identified so as to preserve their archeological provenience."); Golden Budha Corp. v. Canadian Land Co. of America, N.V., 931 F.2d 196, 20 Fed. R. Serv. 3d 388 (2d Cir. 1991) ("The provenance of the Yamashita Treasure is shrouded in mystery [allegedly] 'hidden in The Philippines by the Japanese occupation forces prior to end of World War II' "); *but cf.* Weller v. American Broadcasting Companies, Inc., 232 Cal. App. 3d 991, 998, 283 Cal. Rptr. 644 (1st Dist. 1991) (distinguishing origin from provenance "misrepresented the maker, condition, origin and provenance of the candelabra"); Jafari v. Wally Findlay Galleries, 1989 WL 116437 (S.D. N.Y. 1989) (provenance equated to authenticity and verification).

[5]Greenberg Gallery, Inc. v. Bauman, 817 F. Supp. 167, 173 (D.D.C. 1993), order aff'd, 36 F.3d 127 (D.C. Cir. 1994) ("provenance" of an Alexander Calder mobile is "the chain of ownership from the original artist to the present owner"). U.S. v. Mount, 896 F.2d 612, 624–25, 29 Fed. R. Evid. Serv. 1026 (1st Cir. 1990) (provenance of historical documents and artist letters as indicia of ownership); DeWeerth v. Baldinger, 836 F.2d 103, 112 (2d Cir. 1987) ("provenance [is] a history of [the work's] ownership, exhibitions in which it has been shown, and published references to it"); *but cf.* Biagiotti v. C.I.R., T.C. Memo. 1986-460, 1986 WL 21685 (1986) (distinguishing history of the work from provenance: "expert began by identifying the history and provenance of each piece").

[6]O'Keeffe v. Snyder, 170 N.J. Super. 75, 405 A.2d 840 (App. Div. 1979), judgment rev'd on other grounds, 83 N.J. 478, 416 A.2d 862, 866 (1980) (owner of paintings by Georgia O'Keeffe does not "trace their provenance, or history of possession of the paintings, back to O'Keeffe").

[7]Autocephalous Greek-Orthodox Church of Cyprus v. Goldberg & Feldman Fine Arts Inc., 717 F. Supp. 1374, 1402 (S.D. Ind. 1989), judg-

tation,[10] and title.[11] Even when similarly defined, application is far from uniform,[12] yet only one court has ever

---

ment aff'd, 917 F.2d 278 (7th Cir. 1990) (distinguishing provenance from authenticity "delivery of all funds contingent on the satisfactory resolution of provenance, authenticity, and restorability") Jafari v. Wally Findlay Galleries, 1989 WL 116437 (S.D. N.Y. 1989) (provenance equated to authenticity and verification; contract terms modified " 'to allow for complete and thorough provenance (expert authentication and verification) of the painting' "); U.S. v. Mount, 896 F.2d 612, 624–25, 29 Fed. R. Evid. Serv. 1026 (1st Cir. 1990) (capability of defendant to transfer ownership of allegedly stolen documents that James Whistler may have handwritten in duplicate); McCloud v. Lawrence Gallery, Ltd., 1991 WL 136027 (S.D. N.Y. 1991); U.S. v. Mount, 896 F.2d 612, 615, 29 Fed. R. Evid. Serv. 1026 (1st Cir. 1990) (distinguishing provenance from ownership: "defense raised . . . questions concerning the ownership and provenance of the documents [by James Whistler]").

[8]Jafari v. Wally Findlay Galleries, 1989 WL 116437 (S.D. N.Y. 1989) (contract terms modified " 'to allow for complete and thorough provenance (expert authentication and verification) of the painting' "); McCloud v. Lawrence Gallery, Ltd., 1991 WL 136027 (S.D. N.Y. 1991) (auction house tells Comite Picasso, a committee that reviews for authenticity works purported to be by Pablo Picasso, that " 'sale is conditional upon receipt of absolute convincing provenance' (i.e., proof of authenticity from the consignor of the drawing"); McNally v. Yarnall, 764 F. Supp. 838, 844 (S.D. N.Y. 1991).

[9]Greenwood v. Koven, 1993 WL 541181 (S.D. N.Y. 1993), on reconsideration in part, 880 F. Supp. 186 (S.D. N.Y. 1995) (authenticity of pastel ascribed to George Braque); Greenberg Gallery, Inc. v. Bauman, 817 F. Supp. 167 (D.D.C. 1993), order aff'd, 36 F.3d 127 (D.C. Cir. 1994) (authenticity of mobile ascribed to Alexander Calder); Peters v. C.I.R., T.C. Memo. 1977-128, 1977 WL 3425 (1977), aff'd, 601 F.2d 603 (9th Cir. 1979); Jafari v. Wally Findlay Galleries, 741 F. Supp. 64 (S.D.N.Y. 1990) ("Before Jafari would agree to buy the painting, he wanted the original certificate of authenticity (the 'provenance').").

[10]Cantor v. Anderson, 639 F. Supp. 364, 367, 2 U.C.C. Rep. Serv. 2d 312 (S.D. N.Y. 1986), judgment aff'd, 833 F.2d 1002 (2d Cir. 1986) ("The provenance of the work did not include a bill of sale since it had been acquired in Europe 10 or 15 years ago"); Duchossois Industries, Inc. v. Stelloh, 1988 WL 2794 (N.D. Ill. 1988) ("Accompanying sale of painting [purportedly by Henry Alken, Sr.] was a document called a 'provenance.' ").

[11]Morgold, Inc. v. Keeler, 891 F. Supp. 1361, 1363, 27 U.C.C. Rep. Serv. 2d 315 (N.D. Cal. 1995) ("The word 'provenance' has developed in the art world as a term for the subject of title to works of art."); *but see* §§ 2:61, 2:63 and §§ 4:9 to 4:17.

[12]Balog v. Center Art Gallery-Hawaii, Inc., 745 F. Supp. 1556, 1566, 12 U.C.C. Rep. Serv. 2d 962 (D. Haw. 1990) ("defendant's failure to

recognized the need to define it as a term of art.[13]

Well-documented provenance affects value because it instills confidence that (1) the object is authentic, and (2) ownership is, and has been, unimpaired. Certain prior

---

have undertaken sufficient investigation in substantiating the provenance of the items . . . would allow for rescission of the transaction with a refund of the purchase price"); Cantor v. Anderson, 639 F. Supp. 364, 367, 2 U.C.C. Rep. Serv. 2d 312 (S.D. N.Y. 1986), judgment aff'd, 833 F.2d 1002 (2d Cir. 1986) ("The provenance of the work did not include a bill of sale."); Biagiotti v. C.I.R., T.C. Memo. 1986-460, 1986 WL 21685 (1986) (appraisal "began [for pre-Colombian art] by identifying the history and provenance of the piece"); Autocephalous Greek-Orthodox Church of Cyprus v. Goldberg & Feldman Fine Arts Inc., 717 F. Supp. 1374, 1566 (S.D. Ind. 1989), judgment aff'd, 917 F.2d 278 (7th Cir. 1990) ("failure to . . . substantiat[e] . . . the provenance"); McNally v. Yarnall, 764 F. Supp. 838, 844 (S.D. N.Y. 1991) ("communication" made in writing regarding "provenance of the [Hollyhocks] Window"); Liebhard v. Square D. Co., 1991 WL 206169 (N.D. Ill. 1991) ("business of selling paintings and in supplying provenances for the paintings it sold"); Shein v. C.I.R, T.C. Memo. 1987-329, 1987 WL 40384 (1987) (expert's inability to "describe the provenance of the work"); Voitier v. Antique Art Gallery, 524 So. 2d 80 (La. Ct. App. 3d Cir. 1988), writ denied, 531 So. 2d 271 (La. 1988) (art auction catalogue recites no responsibility "for the description, genuineness, provenance, or condition of the property."); Weller v. American Broadcasting Companies, Inc., 232 Cal. App. 3d 991, 998, 283 Cal. Rptr. 644 (1st Dist. 1991) (statement by broadcaster that collector misrepresented "the maker, condition, origin and provenance of [silver] candelabra" as basis of defamation suit); Waller v. Scheer, 175 Ga. App. 1, 332 S.E.2d 293 (1985), cert. dismissed, (July 3, 1985) (seller of painting purportedly by Adolf Schreyer "denied he warranted the painting and said he told [buyer] he could not give a provenance and could not give a guarantee as to the painting"); *see also* Solomon R. Guggenheim Foundation v. Lubell, 153 A.D.2d 143, 550 N.Y.S.2d 618 (1st Dep't 1990), order aff'd, 77 N.Y.2d 311, 567 N.Y.S.2d 623, 569 N.E.2d 426 (1991) (purchaser of gouache by Marc Chagall contacts Marc Chagall and his cataloguer to "investigat[e] the provenance" before making the purchase; purchaser should investigate "the provenance of a work of art"); Kunstsammlungen Zu Weimar v. Elicofon, 536 F. Supp. 829 (E.D. N.Y. 1981), aff'd, 678 F.2d 1150 (2d Cir. 1982); Morgold, Inc. v. Keeler, 891 F. Supp. 1361, 27 U.C.C. Rep. Serv. 2d 315 (N.D. Cal. 1995) (defendant in possession of oil painting by Alfred Bricher was deemed titular owner by court where painting was sold in breach of written agreement with coowner plaintiff, where court found defendant had no duty to inquire into provenance); *but see* 891 F. Supp. at 1363 ("The word 'provenance' has developed in the art world as a term for the subject of title to works of art.").

[13]Duchossois Industries, Inc. v. Stelloh, 1988 WL 2794 (N.D. Ill. 1988).

owners or events may effectively enhance value by providing the artworks with a cachet.[14] Ownership may be deliberately falsified to obscure provenance or there may be gaps in the provenance (Nazi cases) or the provenance may be intentionally withheld, a not uncommon business practice in the secondary markets.[15] Gaps in the provenance surrounding World War II for works in public and private collections are now being scrutinized and investigated. Museums and some private entities have formulated web sites dedicated to artworks acquired by museums and others during or after World War II to aid relocation efforts of families, heirs and others listed in Chart 2-1.

Chart 2-1 Nazi Era Stolen and Looted Art: Quick Check for Provenance Web Sites*

Site	Language*
U.S. National Archives & Records Admin. Art Provenance	
http://www.archives.gov/research	English
N.Y. State Banking Dept. Holocaust Claims Proc. Office English	
www.claims.state.ny.us	English
AAM Nazi-era Provenance Portal	
nepip@aam_us.org	
United States Holocaust Memorial Museum English	
www.ushmm.org/assets	English
info@lootedart.com	English
http://www.lostart.ru	Russian

[14]Peters v. C.I.R., T.C. Memo. 1977-128, 1977 WL 3425 (1977), aff'd, 601 F.2d 603 (9th Cir. 1979); Estate of Scull v. C.I.R., T.C. Memo. 1994-211, 1994 WL 179764 (1994) (witness testified that (1) name of collectors generated excitement and resulted in higher prices at auction, and (2) the interest in the collectors themselves raised prices of artworks); see Ch 5, 5:5.

[15]*See, e.g.,* Foxley v. Sotheby's Inc., 893 F. Supp. 1224, 27 U.C.C. Rep. Serv. 2d 1234 (S.D. N.Y. 1995) (summary judgment for auction house on claim of false provenance where name of consignor omitted from provenance list in auction catalogue).

*See App. 25 (Holocaust-era resources for artworks).

*As websites are updated, information may appear in additional languages.

Site	Language*
http://www.restitution.ru	Russian
Lost Art Internet Database	
http://www.lostart.de	German, Russian, English
Art Institute of Chicago	
http://www.artic.edu/aic/provenance/index	English
Cleveland Museum of Art	
http://www.clemusart.com/provintro	English
Harvard University Art Museums	
http://www.artmuseums.harvard.edu/research/provenance/index	English
J. Paul Getty Museum	
http://www.getty.edu/museum/provenance/index	English
Los Angeles County Museum of Art	
http://www.lacma.org/lacma.asp	English
Metropolitan Museum of Art	
http://www.metmuseum.org/collections	English
Provenance Research Project MoMA	
http://www.moma.org/menu/provenance	English
Museum of Fine Arts, Boston	
http://www.mfa.org/research	English
National Gallery of Art	
http://www.nga.gov/resources/ww2res	English
Seattle Art Museum	
http://www.SeattleArtMuseum.org	English

§ 2:63 Clarification of usage

(1) Provenance, as history, is based on primary and secondary sources of which the researcher avails himself. Thus, the reliability of provenance and the degree of its accuracy is, like history, a function of the skills and methodologies of its researchers, availability and accessibility of authoritative sources and materials, and the time and costs allocated to undertake it. Few mercantile traders[1] in the secondary market, unless they are involved

---

[Section 2:63]

[1] *See* §§ 2:28 to 2:39.

in preparing a catalogue raisonne,[2] have the time, money, or scholarship skills to research with any certainty the provenance of objects they sell in the ordinary course of business. Provenance is not static; scholars in different time periods interpret old facts in new ways and discover new documents and information requiring reformulation.

(2) Provenance as history can be oral or written. Documentary sources, like bills of sale, bills of lading, testamentary dispositions, catalogues, and/or catalogues raisonnes, may contain information relevant to provenance. Those who create a document entitling it "provenance," at least within the context of a mercantile transaction, do so at their own peril.[3]

(3) Provenance is not an authentication. Provenance is an history of an object, not an analysis of its genuineness, although provenance is relevant to authenticating objects. Experts who authenticate objects research provenance, but provenance, in and of itself, is not an authentication or a declaration of authenticity.[4] Contention has been made that if a particular provenance traces back to the artist, then it should be equated to an authentication.[5]

(4) Provenance in mercantile transactions is sometimes selective. An attraction of the secondary market is its anonymity. Neither auctioneers nor secondary market traders are obligated generally to disclose names of

---

[2]*See* §§ 2:62, 2:63; *see also* Kirby v. Wildenstein, 784 F. Supp. 1112 (S.D. N.Y. 1992) (mercantile dealer as director of a nonprofit corporation publishing artist catalogues).

[3]Duchossois Industries, Inc. v. Stelloh, 1988 WL 2794 (N.D. Ill. 1988) (negligent misrepresentation, breach of contract, consumer fraud, fraud).

[4]Duchossois Industries, Inc. v. Stelloh, 1988 WL 2794 (N.D. Ill. 1988).

[5]Duchossois Industries, Inc. v. Stelloh, 1988 WL 2794 at ¶ 17 (N.D. Ill. 1988) ("a provenance authenticates a painting only insofar as it traces its 'historical chain of ownership' [to which plaintiff seeking recission of contract based on provenance] agrees . . . but places the historical chain in a different perspective; he says the provenance traces the painting as far as possible 'from the present owner back to the artist' [conceding that the defendant] never physically authenticated the paintings to verify their painter's identity"). Note that even if traced to the artist, the object may have been substituted, damaged, restored, or repainted, or the artist may have repudiated it; *see* § 9:60.

consignors or prior owners.[6]

XIII. CATALOGUE RAISONNE

§ 2:64 Description

A catalogue raisonne is a scholarly published work often prepared in conjunction with foundations or committees,[1] commemorating an artist by recording the artist's oeuvre, or portions of it, encompassing a lifetime or a specified period of time. The catalogue raisonne recites information *known* about works of an artist or purported to be by the artist, including, inter alia, size and/or framed size, medium, year of creation, years of display, exhibition entries, mentions or reproductions in scholarly works and other catalogues, restorations and identities of restorers, identities of owners, and reference to locations. Committees may be composed of, inter alia, museum officials, traders, relatives of the artist, foundation members, and critics. Courts have made varying reference to or mention of catalogues raisonnes,[2] e.g., as "definitive listings" of the

---

[6]*See, e.g.,* Foxley v. Sotheby's Inc., 893 F. Supp. 1224, 27 U.C.C. Rep. Serv. 2d 1234 (S.D. N.Y. 1995) (summary judgment for auction house on claim for false provenance of painting).

[Section 2:64]

[1]Foxley v. Sotheby's Inc., 893 F. Supp. 1224, 27 U.C.C. Rep. Serv. 2d 1234 (S.D. N.Y. (1995)) (Cassatt Committee as evaluator of authenticity of Mary Cassatt paintings); McCloud v. Lawrence Gallery, Ltd., 1991 WL 136027 (S.D. N.Y. 1991) (Comite Picasso determines authenticity of works purported to be by Pablo Picasso); *see also* Kirby v. Wildenstein, 784 F. Supp. 1112 (S.D. N.Y. 1992) (Institut Wildenstein is a nonprofit corporation that engages in art historical research and publishes catalogues of the works of French artists); id. at 1113 ("Patrick Offenstadt, the recognized expert on Jean Beraud, was preparing a 'catalogue raisonne' of the artist's works.").

[2]Rosen v. Spanierman, 894 F.2d 28, 10 U.C.C. Rep. Serv. 2d 846 (2d Cir. 1990); DeWeerth v. Baldinger, 658 F. Supp. 688 (S.D. N.Y. 1987), judgment rev'd on other grounds, 836 F.2d 103 (2d Cir. 1987); Kirby v. Wildenstein, 784 F. Supp. 1112 (S.D. N.Y. 1992); Mount v. Ormand, 1991 WL 191228 (S.D. N.Y. 1991); McNally v. Yarnall, 764 F. Supp. 838, 844 (S.D. N.Y. 1991); Estate of O'Keeffe v. C.I.R., T.C. Memo. 1992-210, T.C.M. (RIA) ¶ 92210 (1992).

works of an artist,[3] a "definitive catalogue" of works of an artist,[4] an "authoritative catalogue,"[5] and "a listing of the 'authentic' works."[6]

Reference to a catalogue raisonne is one step, but only one, in ascertaining provenance.[7] Endorsement of an object in the catalogue raisonne by a cataloguer indicates that the cataloguer believes the work described to be authentic.[8] A catalogue raisonne may include works, by reference, description, or reproduction, that the cataloguer does not believe are authentic, and that belief will be stated.[9] Identification but lack of endorsement in a catalogue raisonne does not mean conclusively that those objects are inauthentic, given the vagaries of authentication.[10] An object omitted from a catalogue raisonne does not mean that the object is not authentic.[11]

---

[3]DeWeerth v. Baldinger, 836 F.2d 103, 112 (2d Cir. 1987) ("A catalogue raisonne is a definitive listing and accounting of the works of an artist.").

[4]Kirby v. Wildenstein, 784 F. Supp. 1112, 1113 (S.D. N.Y. 1992).

[5]Mount v. Ormand, 1991 WL 191228 (S.D. N.Y. 1991).

[6]Mount v. Ormand, 1991 WL 191228 at ¶ 7 (S.D. N.Y. 1991).

[7]DeWeerth v. Baldinger, 658 F. Supp. 688 (S.D. N.Y. 1987), judgment rev'd on other grounds, 836 F.2d 103 (2d Cir. 1987) ("The Monet Catalogue Raisonne depicts each of Monet's works in chronological order and sets forth each work's provenance—a history of its ownership, exhibition in which it has been shown, and published references to it.").

[8]Kirby v. Wildenstein, 784 F. Supp. 1112 (S.D. N.Y. 1992) ("inclusion of a painting in a catalogue raisonne serves to authenticate the work"); *accord* McNally v. Yarnall, 764 F. Supp. 838, 844 (S.D. N.Y. 1991) (museum consultant " 'certainly is not persuaded that [stained glass windows purported to be by John LaFarge] should be included in the [catalogue raisonne] and given the seal of authenticity' ").

[9]Vitale v. Marlborough Gallery, 32 U.S.P.Q.2d (BNA) 1283, 1994 WL 654494 (S.D. N.Y. 1994) (plaintiff's painting categorized as falsely attributed or forged in the Jackson Pollock Catalogue Raisonne published by Yale University).

[10]*See, e.g.,* McNally v. Yarnall, 764 F. Supp. 838, 844 (S.D. N.Y. 1991); Mount v. Ormand, 1991 WL 191228 (S.D. N.Y. 1991).

[11]Kirby v. Wildenstein, 784 F. Supp. 1112 (S.D. N.Y. 1992) ("inclusion of a painting in a catalogue raisonne serves to authenticate the work while non-inclusion *suggests* that the work is not genuine [emphasis added]"); Shaltiel v. Wildenstein, 288 A.D.2d 136, 733 N.Y.S.2d 400 (1st Dep't 2001) (auctioneer removed plaintiff's painting from auction after expert excluded it from Modigliani catalogue in

The realities of tracking an artist's oeuvre do not necessarily comport with the cataloguer's goals of thoroughness, and the evidentiary value of catalogues should be scrutinized by lawyers. First, many artists have not yet had the scholarly review or market scrutiny required to prepare a definitive catalogue; their works are not recorded in a catalogue raisonne because one simply does not exist. Second, some artists have had portions of their oeuvre catalogued, like drawings or paintings, or certain time periods,[12] but not all works. Third, it is often difficult to ascertain how many or what works were created by any one artist. Fourth, the catalogue is no more than the sum of its preparers' skill, research, guess work, expertise, time and cost expenditures, and conclusions.

§ 2:65 Claims

Catalogue raisonnes have been challenged under the Sherman Antitrust Act,[1] the Lanham, Act,[2] disparagement,[3] defamation,[4] tortious interference with contractual

---

preparation at Wildenstein Institute). *But cf.* Grimes, "Who Painted this Picture?," NY Times, Aug. 9, 1992, § 2, at 1, 30 (exclusion of painting by Jackson Pollock from catalogue raisonne inconclusive as to authenticity).

[12]DeWeerth v. Baldinger, 658 F. Supp. 688 (S.D. N.Y. 1987), judgment rev'd on other grounds, 836 F.2d 103 (2d Cir. 1987) (painting by Claude Monet that disappeared during World War II listed as sold in 1974 publication, I Claude Monet: Bibliographie et Catalogue Raisonne 1840–1881), a copy of which was located less than twenty miles from where plaintiff resided).

[Section 2:65]

[1]Vitale v. Marlborough Gallery, 32 U.S.P.Q.2d (BNA) 1283, 1994 WL 654494 (S.D. N.Y. 1994) (anticompetitive conduct of dealers and cataloguers alleged for refusal to authenticate painting, purportedly by Jackson Pollock, owned by plaintiff; failure to use reasonable means to determine authenticity; and recitation in catalogue raisonne of painting as spurious).

[2]15 U.S.C.A. § 43(a); Vitale v. Marlborough Gallery, 32 U.S.P.Q.2d (BNA) 1283, 1994 WL 654494 (S.D. N.Y. 1994) (recitation in catalogue raisonne that painting owned by plaintiff was a spurious Jackson Pollock dismissed as the basis of Section 43(a) action for false advertising and false designation of origin).

[3]Kirby v. Wildenstein, 784 F. Supp. 1112 (S.D. N.Y. 1992) (claims based upon catalogue raisonne recitation that Jean Beraud painting

relations,[5] and copyright infringement.[6]

§ 2:66 Evidentiary significance

A catalogue raisonne may be admitted into evidence under various Federal Rules of Evidence (FRE). The following have been considered: learned treatise rule (collection of works as inadmissible as substantive evidence under FRE 803(18) except to "the extent called to the attention of an expert witness upon cross-examination or relied upon by the expert witness in direct examination");[1] hearsay exception (admissibility under FRE 803(17) permitting "lists, directories, or other published compilations, generally used and relied upon by the public or by persons in particular occupations"). The foundational requirements of Rule 803(17) are satisfied where a dealer or other art professional testifies that the catalogue raisonne is relied upon to locate artworks. If the catalogue is old, out of date, or otherwise considered unreliable, a judge has discretion to allow a jury to evaluate the weight of the catalogue raisonne as proof of ownership on a given date.

---

owned by plaintiff was abusively restored and cleaned was dismissed where painting failed to sell at auction prior to catalogue publication).

[4]McNally v. Yarnall, 764 F. Supp. 838, 844 (S.D. N.Y. 1991) (author of books on artist John La Farge sued cataloguer of La Farge based upon statements made by defendant regarding plaintiff's abilities to authenticate La Farge works); Mount v. Ormand, 1991 WL 191228 (S.D. N.Y. 1991) (action by author of books and catalogue on painter John Singer Sargent dismissed against dealers and authors of Sargent catalogue raisonne where claims based upon defendants' refusal to recite as authentic paintings plaintiff had attributed to Sargent and sold as genuine in catalogue not yet published).

[5]McNally v. Yarnall, 764 F. Supp. 838, 844 (S.D. N.Y. 1991) (author of books on artist John La Farge sued cataloguer of La Farge based upon statements made by defendant to prospective clients of plaintiff regarding authenticity of La Farge stained glass windows offered for sale).

[6]Mount v. Ormand, 1991 WL 191228 (S.D. N.Y. 1991) (action by author of books and catalogue on painter John Singer Sargent dismissed against dealers and authors of Sargent catalogue raisonne where claims based upon their use of historical facts about the artist).

[Section 2:66]

[1]*See* U.S. v. Mount, 896 F.2d 612, 624–25, 29 Fed. R. Evid. Serv. 1026 (1st Cir. 1990).

XIV. DUE DILIGENCE

§ 2:67 Definition

Due diligence is a judicially-created investigative duty of procedural and substantive applications. Due diligence, synthesized from case law, is defined as a fact-sensitive duty to undertake continuous and persistent inquiries through multiple channels of investigation based upon particular facts and circumstances of each case. Among jurisdictions and even within them the opinions are divided; upon whom the duty should be placed, under what circumstances the duty is imposed, and what conduct will satisfy the defining characteristics. The duty has been imposed on various parties in a variety of arts contexts, and may affect both the procedural and substantive posture of the case. Due diligence has been applied to both prospective buyers and dispossessed owners, and involves inquiry into title, warranties, authenticity, provenance, and more.[1] This synthesized definition, under examination of its context in any particular case, seems to require several different forms of conduct and activity along a time continuum:

(1) "Persistent" means that the same notifications and inquiries about the object should be repeatedly directed to the *same* source. In other words, one communication with the same source in a one-year period may not suffice.

(2) "Continuous" means that notifications and inquiries to all sources about the object should be made repeatedly throughout the duration of the object's absence. In other words, fifty communications with one source in a one-year period might satisfy the "persistent" prong, but, if the object were missing for ten years, such communications would not satisfy the "continuous" prong.

(3) "Multiple channels" means that notifications and inquiries should permeate a cross-section of business, government, academia, specialty trades, law enforcement, and world wide web sites, like

---

[Section 2:67]

[1] *See* Ch 6 § 6:130.

those listed in Chart 2-1, where registries and postings are increasing and sites are sometimes linked. Within those areas, they should reach many different institutions, agencies, individuals, and entities. In other words, even fifty communications per year to all sources for ten years would not satisfy the "multiple channels" prong if all such sources were exclusively members of law enforcement and no other source were contacted.

Diligence is "fact-sensitive and must be [determined] on a case by case basis"[2] in the context of the totality of the circumstances. Courts have noted that the standard of due diligence is a fact-specific judgment in each case as to what "a reasonable plaintiff could be expected to do." In art law, that fact-specific judgment is expressly grounded by the courts in the "nature and value of the property."[3] No quantifiable number of sources or contacts or definitive qualitative search that would satisfy due diligence could be found in any opinion, although what would constitute insufficient activity has been.[4]

The following list recites contacts that help establish

---

[2]Autocephalous Greek-Orthodox Church of Cyprus v. Goldberg & Feldman Fine Arts Inc., 717 F. Supp. 1374, 1389 (S.D. Ind. 1989), judgment aff'd, 917 F.2d 278 (7th Cir. 1990).

[3]O'Keeffe v. Snyder, 170 N.J. Super. 75, 405 A.2d 840 (App. Div. 1979), judgment rev'd on other grounds, 83 N.J. 478, 416 A.2d 862, 871 (1980); *accord* Balog v. Center Art Gallery-Hawaii, Inc., 745 F. Supp. 1556, 12 U.C.C. Rep. Serv. 2d 962 (D. Haw. 1990) (in terms of investigating authenticity, not ownership). Ironically, in O'Keeffe, where due diligence debuted in art law, three "small" paintings were, at the time of disappearance, valued at $450.

[4]DeWeerth v. Baldinger, 658 F. Supp. 688 (S.D. N.Y. 1987), judgment rev'd on other grounds, 836 F.2d 103 (2d Cir. 1987); Solomon R. Guggenheim Foundation v. Lubell, 153 A.D.2d 143, 550 N.Y.S.2d 618 (1st Dep't 1990), order aff'd, 77 N.Y.2d 311, 567 N.Y.S.2d 623, 569 N.E.2d 426 (1991); Autocephalous Greek-Orthodox Church of Cyprus v. Goldberg & Feldman Fine Arts Inc., 717 F. Supp. 1374 (S.D. Ind. 1989), judgment aff'd, 917 F.2d 278 (7th Cir. 1990); Greek Orthodox Patriarchate of Jerusalem v. Christie's, Inc., 1999 WL 673347 (S.D. N.Y. 1999); Wertheimer v. Cirker's Hayes Storage Warehouse, Inc., 300 A.D.2d 117, 752 N.Y.S.2d 295 (1st Dep't 2002) (New York gallery advertisement of Nazi-misappropriated painting in art journal in 1951 should have put family residing there on notice to conduct inquiries).

diligence: law enforcement, local, national, and international; museum communities, local, national, and international like INTERPOL, and membership organizations like the International Committee of Museums, the American Association of Museums, academic communities through their departments, archives, and affiliated galleries; mercantile traders and trade associations, appraisers and dealers; scholarly associations; trade, specialty, and scholarly publications; international agencies like UNESCO; embassies and consulates and governments themselves; and stolen art research repositories like the London-based Art Loss Register, now also branched in New York.

Newly established web sites by museums and others provide research opportunities to locate missing and stolen artworks previously unavailable to those seeking recovery. Similarly, sources exist for reporting loss. Some sites specialize in works of World War II provenance, while others provide national lists gathered from state museums. Efforts are being made to link sites, so that broader based information will be more readily available, and loss and recovery reporting will be more centralized. Any contemporary view of diligence will certainly include inquiry about whether or not relevant web searches were initiated.[5]

The duty of due diligence parallels somewhat a commercial good-faith duty of inquiry in the trade under warranty of title in the taking of reasonable steps to ascertain if goods are stolen, converted, or have clouds on title or restrictions on transfer.[6] Some states have attempted to ameliorate the duty of diligence, at least in some circumstances.[7] In some jurisdictions, the inquiry duty is not triggered in the absence of "warnings" or suspicious

[5]See Chart 2-1 and App. 25.

[6]*See* Ch 4 §§ 4:9 to 4:17.

[7]*See, e.g.,* Cal. Civ. Proc. Code § 338(c), Stat. 1982, Ch. 340 § 1 (1982) (three-year statute of limitations for recovery of stolen artwork does not accrue "until the discovery of the whereabouts"; Cal. Civ. Proc. Code § 354.3 (extending statute of limitations for recovery of "Holocaust-era" artworks to Dec. 31, 2010, retroactive, and notwithstanding other limitations); Naftzger v. American Numismatic Society, 42 Cal. App. 4th 421, 49 Cal. Rptr. 2d 784 (2d Dist. 1996), as modified on denial of reh'g, (Mar. 4, 1996) (a prior version of the statute was held as a matter of law to implicitly include a discovery element, ap-

circumstances.

§ 2:68 Party duty imposed upon

Historically, the duty of diligence was imposed upon out-of-possession, theft, or loss victims, seeking return of personal property after the statute of limitations expired. When the defendant pleaded the statute of limitations as a bar to the action, plaintiff's lack of due diligence was invoked by the affirmative defenses.

The duty arose not in actions involving title like declaratory relief or quieting title, but those seeking return of personal property like replevin or claim and delivery. The garden variety case is one where a dispossessed owner discovers that missing artwork, believed to be gone forever, has resurfaced somewhere else, often after a series of interim trades and sales. The plaintiff sues for return of the artwork. Such lawsuits, however, typically occur after the state statute of limitations for return of personal property has expired. The defendant, aside from claiming good title and other substantive defenses, pleads that the statute of limitations bars the lawsuit and affirms the equitable defense of laches, recently revivified as a defense strategy in numerous art dispossession cases.[1]

Interestingly, due diligence is a legal chameleon, taking on different colorations in the defenses of limitations and laches.

The courts, measuring the pull of the rights of former private property owners against commercial favor for finality of contracts, fashioned a rule, originally procedural, with substantive effect: if the plaintiff was duly diligent in pursuing the whereabouts of the lost artwork, and/or the identity of the new "owner" (separate concepts glossed

---

plied retroactively by the court to the theft, which occurred before the 1983 statutory revision).

[Section 2:68]

[1] *See, e.g.,* Solomon R. Guggenheim Foundation v. Lubell, 153 A.D.2d 143, 550 N.Y.S.2d 618 (1st Dep't 1990), order aff'd, 77 N.Y.2d 311, 567 N.Y.S.2d 623, 626–27, 569 N.E.2d 426 (1991); Greek Orthodox Patriarchate of Jerusalem v. Christie's, Inc., 1999 WL 673347 (S.D. N.Y. 1999); Wertheimer v. Cirker's Hayes Storage Warehouse, Inc., 300 A.D.2d 117, 752 N.Y.S.2d 295 (1st Dep't 2002) (unclean hands doctrine was not a bar to laches defense) .

over in many opinions), then the court would create a discovery rule to accrue the action, notwithstanding a state statute of limitations that established the date of theft or loss as the accrual date for the action. Plaintiffs who were not diligent in attempting to locate the property could not bring their actions within a discovery-accrual date, and thus were shut out of court on legal claims under the statute of limitations, regardless of the merits of the suit. Some courts have begun to explore an in-possession defendant's diligence prior to purchase, but this is a separate undertaking, unrelated to the policy and purpose underlying the due diligence rule.[2]

§ 2:69 Origination of duty

Originally, due diligence was a factual affirmation by plaintiffs that arose in the context of invoking the discovery rule to overcome the defense that the statute of limitations had expired and consistent with policies underlying statutes of limitations.[1] The burden of proof to invoke the discovery rule was borne by the plaintiff. If the plaintiff could establish facts "that would justify deferring the beginning of the limitations period," the discovery rule applied and the accrual period recited in the statute of limitations was calculated from the discovery date. California, for example, has a discovery rule specific to art and art-related objects within the general three-year statute of limitations for property.[2] Essentially for many years the duty had this time-stopping discovery rule effect, a recalculation of the limitations clock that could resurrect

---

[2]Autocephalous Greek-Orthodox Church of Cyprus v. Goldberg & Feldman Fine Arts Inc., 717 F. Supp. 1374 (S.D. Ind. 1989), judgment aff'd, 917 F.2d 278 (7th Cir. 1990).

[Section 2:69]

[1]*E.g.,* faded memories, disappearance or death of witnesses, difficulty in gathering evidence, etc.

[2]Cal. Code of Civ. Proc. § 338(c) ("Within three years . . . (c) an action for taking, detaining, or injuring any goods or chattels, including actions for the specific recovery of personal property. The cause of action in the case of theft, as defined in Section 484 of the [California] Penal Code, of any article of historical, interpretive, scientific, or artistic significance is not deemed to have accrued until the discovery of the whereabouts of the article by the aggrieved party . . .").

otherwise dated claims as timely.[3] Traditionally, courts focused upon plaintiff's late arrival at the courthouse when the claim for recovery of personal property would otherwise be stale. Thus, diligence gained prominence as a means to circumvent the time bar to actions after expiration of the statute of limitations.[4]

The doctrine evolved in New York from a demand and refusal rule.[5] Under that rule, an action for return of stolen property from one who innocently purchases it does not begin to run until a demand for return is made and refused; possession by a good faith purchaser is lawful until demand.[6] The demand must be made within a reasonable time from discovery. Federal courts interpreting New York law decided that plaintiffs had a duty of diligence to locate the stolen property, and if they failed to exercise diligence, then a demand made outside the limitations period would not trigger a date from which the limitations period would accrue.

The idea originated in an art case brought by artist Georgia O'Keeffe against an owner of one of her paintings some twenty years after she knew of its "loss" from her husband's gallery, which she never reported to authorities or publicized. The case settled before a substantive judicial

---

[3]Naftzger v. American Numismatic Society, 42 Cal. App. 4th 421, 49 Cal. Rptr. 2d 784 (2d Dist. 1996), as modified on denial of reh'g, (Mar. 4, 1996) (Where a museum did not discover until 1990 that a theft of old coins from its collection had occurred prior to 1970, the court held that the limitations period did not commence until the museum discovered the identity of the person in possession).

[4]*See, e.g.,* Pickett v. American Ordnance Preservation Ass'n, 60 F. Supp. 2d 450 (E.D. Pa. 1999).

[5]N.Y. Civ. Prac. L & R. § 214; Ironically, a New York State court had never made the interpretation of its own statute; since the Second Circuit did not certify the issue, the due diligence doctrine was established and elaborated upon by federal courts assuming what New York courts would do; when the issue reached New York courts through state litigation, New York radically modified the doctrine of due diligence. The issue remains to what degree the doctrine exists in New York today and its effect in analyzing laches. Meanwhile, other jurisdictions that followed federal courts are now in the peculiar legal position of endorsing the New York doctrine that New York does not subscribe to.

[6]Kunstsammlungen Zu Weimar v. Elicofon, 536 F. Supp. 829 (E.D. N.Y. 1981), aff'd, 678 F.2d 1150 (2d Cir. 1982).

rule emerged.[7]

In equity, the time for filing claims is not determined by statutes of limitations timed to specified numbers of years, but claims are bounded by timing considerations under the affirmative defense of laches. Laches requires two prongs: (1) unreasonable delay by the dilatory plaintiff causing; and (2) undue prejudice to the defendant. These two strains of law and equity merged in arts cases to determine the timeliness of actions under an analysis of due diligence.[8]

Diligence has been revisited during the last decade in some highly publicized cases filed in state and federal courts that delineate the different approach to diligence depending upon the legal context. Thus diligence, or lack thereof, is now a viable factor in some jurisdictions for the affirmative equitable defense of laches.[9]

Implicit in the judicially expanded view of diligence is that a party exercising diligence would in fact discover the weak link in the ownership chain, and with discovery would come rejection of the deal. Neither is necessarily true. Parties acting in good faith can exercise diligence but still remain ignorant of a problem; others uncover problems but blunder on. It can be extremely difficult to track artwork through chains of ownership or possession for various reasons, including absence of central registration and recordation procedures and inadequate tracking devices for highly mobile pieces of personal property.

Moreover, while most buyers would refuse to buy a car from a seller who could not produce a "pink slip" for the department of motor vehicles, title taints do not have the same deterrent effect in the art markets, where title itself is a murky concept.[10] Flurries of disclosures about World War II and actual or threatened claims by heirs to

---

[7]O'Keeffe v. Snyder, 170 N.J. Super. 75, 405 A.2d 840 (App. Div. 1979), judgment rev'd, 83 N.J. 478, 416 A.2d 862 (1980).

[8]O'Keeffe v. Snyder, 170 N.J. Super. 75, 405 A.2d 840 (App. Div. 1979), judgment rev'd, 83 N.J. 478, 416 A.2d 862 (1980).

[9]Wertheimer v. Cirker's Hayes Storage Warehouse, Inc., 300 A.D.2d 117, 752 N.Y.S.2d 295 (1st Dep't 2002) (plaintiff's lack of due diligence in seeking return of painting substantially prejudiced defendant from proving prior owners acquired good title).

[10]*See* Ch 4 §§ 4:15 and 4:17.

artworks stolen or removed during the war and now in major institutional collections has led to new sources for art registrations, both private and public. Many museums have posted online objects in their collections that had gaps in provenance for the post-war era so that potential claimants can locate family treasures.[11]

§ 2:70 Duty as issue of fact or conclusion of law

Court have treated diligence variously: as a finding of fact;[1] and as a legal conclusion, subject to review de novo.[2]

§ 2:71 Status of duty

The concept of due diligence remains alive in some case law, even in the absence of a specific judicially perscribed duty.[1]

The status of due diligence as a legal duty has been abrogated in most circumstances in New York; it may still have bearing upon the equitable defense of laches.[2] The rationale for disposing of diligence was premised on New York as an international situs for the art trade.

---

[11]For a list of museum websites, *see* Ch 6 § 6:1.

[Section 2:70]

[1]DeWeerth v. Baldinger, 658 F. Supp. 688 (S.D. N.Y. 1987), judgment rev'd on other grounds, 836 F.2d 103 (2d Cir. 1987); Autocephalous Greek-Orthodox Church of Cyprus v. Goldberg & Feldman Fine Arts Inc., 717 F. Supp. 1374 (S.D. Ind. 1989), judgment aff'd, 917 F.2d 278 (7th Cir. 1990); Pickett v. American Ordnance Preservation Ass'n, 60 F. Supp. 2d 450 (E.D. Pa. 1999) (when the plaintiff should have learned of the fraud through due diligence is a factual determination for the jury to decide regarding what may be considered a reasonable period of time; only where there are undisputed facts that time was unreasonable "may the issue be decided as a matter of law.").

[2]DeWeerth v. Baldinger, 836 F.2d 103 (2d Cir. 1987).

[Section 2:71]

[1]*See, e.g.,* U.S. v. An Original Manuscript Dated November 19, 1778, 1999 WL 97894 (S.D. N.Y. 1999) (innocent ownership defense failed where claimant in forfeiture of defendant-in-rem property pursuant to Cultural Property Implementation Act did not undertake due diligence and was "willfully blind" to suspicious circumstances of sale transaction); *see* Ch 6 §§ 6:77 to 6:115.

[2]Solomon R. Guggenheim Foundation v. Lubell, 153 A.D.2d 143, 550 N.Y.S.2d 618 (1st Dep't 1990), order aff'd, 77 N.Y.2d 311, 567 N.Y.S.2d 623, 569 N.E.2d 426 (1991).

> Our decision today is . . . influenced by . . . New York enjoy[ing] a worldwide reputation as a preeminent cultural center. To place the burden of locating stolen artwork on the true owner and to foreclose the rights of that owner to recover its property if the burden is not met would . . . encourage illicit trafficking in stolen art.[3]

Other jurisdictions that have considered due diligence in art transactions have not yet made reported rulings after New York voided the victim's duty of due diligence to overcome a statute of limitations defense.[4]

§ 2:72 Post-War Considerations

The early twenty-first and late twentieth centuries have seen profound changes in practices and policies involving artworks that have a provenance dating to the Third Reich. A protracted fall-out from the World War II era has occurred for several reasons: investigation and dissemination of information and materials after the break-up of the Soviet Union; the fall of the Berlin Wall and subsequent access to and dispersal of materials located in former East Germany; reconfigured national boundaries and rearranged international alliances resulting in cooperative cultural undertakings; re-evaluation of the concepts of ownership and stewardship.

New trades and old deals with gaps in provenance or suspicious provenance are under scrutiny, as is an extended chain of commerce and transfer: dealers, auctioneers, museums, institutional and individual collectors,

---

[3]Solomon R. Guggenheim Foundation v. Lubell, 153 A.D.2d 143, 550 N.Y.S.2d 618 (1st Dep't 1990), order aff'd, 77 N.Y.2d 311, 567 N.Y.S.2d 623, 569 N.E.2d 426 (1991) ("Underlying [Guggenheim decision] to dispense with the due diligence requirement was an awareness that lost art is extremely difficult to recover, and a policy determination that the burden of proving ownership should not be shifted onto the 'wronged owner' who has already suffered the theft of valuable property.").

[4]Autocephalous Greek-Orthodox Church of Cyprus v. Goldberg & Feldman Fine Arts Inc., 717 F. Supp. 1374 (S.D. Ind. 1989), judgment aff'd, 917 F.2d 278 (7th Cir. 1990); *but cf.* Ryan v. Ford Motor Co., 15 F.3d 1089 (9th Cir. 1994) (lack of due diligence in attempting to uncover facts that would reveal claim for relief does not translate into defendant's active concealment, which could operate to toll statute of limitations).

banks, insurance companies, appraisers, corporations and others. Heightened alert does not necessarily eliminate the cloistered backroom deal. But the human drama behind the military visage of war has attracted the media; front-page features in newspapers and documentary specials on cable and network television increase the likelihood of public exposure.

American museums, governmental agencies, and others have created web sites for public purview of artworks with incompletely documented or suspect provenance.[1] Some institutions are cooperating with heirs and others who claim ownership interests in artworks to return or repatriate them. Statutes of limitations and jurisdictional issues do not necessarily favor defense.[2] The success of extrajudicial solution is a function of the expectation and demands of the parties but it appears to have been effective in certain instances.

Congress has introduced bills and resolutions and passed legislation dealing directly with restitution of Holocaust victims and return of their property.[3]

[Section 2:72]

[1]See Chart 2-1 and App. 25.

[2]Altmann v. Republic of Austria, 142 F. Supp. 2d 1187 (C.D. Cal. 2001) (motion to dismiss for lack of subject matter jurisdiction denied where plaintiff sought recovery of paintings stolen from her family in Austria by the Nazis).

[3]See, e.g., 107 H.R. 3552, 2d. Sess. Dec. 20, 2001 (establishing national foundation for study of holocaust assets); 107 S.Con.Res.49, 1st Sess. June 14, 2001 (restitution of paintings to Auschwitz survivor).

Chapter 3

Valuation and Appraisal*

I. IN GENERAL

II. APPRAISALS

A. INTRODUCTION

B. APPRAISAL COMPONENTS

1. Appraisal Process

2. Appraisal Assignment

3. Identifying Subject Property

4. Visual Inspection of Subject Property

---

*Steven Caudana, a member of the national board of directors of ASA, reviewed and edited Release #1 of this chapter.

IV. TAX APPRAISALS

A. CHARITABLE CONTRIBUTIONS

B. OWNERSHIP AS PREREQUISITE TO CONTRIBUTIONS

C. PROPER VALUATION METHODOLOGIES

1. Market Methods

2. Reproduction Cost Methods

V. PROFESSIONAL APPRAISAL PRACTICE

A. HISTORIC EVENTS

B. PROFESSIONAL MEMBERSHIP ORGANIZATIONS

C. APPRAISER-CLIENT RELATIONSHIP

D. APPRAISER'S COMPETENCE

E. DISINTERESTED APPRAISALS

F. SPECIAL APPRAISALS

I. IN GENERAL

§ 3:1 Generally

Valuation of art is crucial to every aspect of art acquisition, trade, display, gift, donation, and devise. Art appraisal values used by government, financial institutions, and the private sector are integral to administration and disposition of real and personal property. The values assigned to properties in appraisals are stated in numerical terms. The process of determining value is termed "valuation." Valuation is summarily recited in the appraisal based upon: (1) purpose and context of the appraisal assignment; (2) disclosed assumptions and stated limiting conditions; and (3) alternative valuation methodologies.

Lawyers should be aware that appraisals provide valuation *advice,* which is subject to the judgment of the appraiser as the appraiser is informed by knowledge, experience, skill, and training. Competent valuation advice from different appraisers produces different values, a variation even more pronounced for unique objects like art, antiques, and artifacts. If lawyers understand appraisal processes, they will be able to: (1) identify competent valuation; (2) interpret disparities in appraised values; and (3) recognize legal ramifications of incomplete or incorrect appraisals.

The focus of this chapter is the appraisal of personal property (art, artifacts, antiques, architectural pieces) primarily in areas of charitable contributions, estates, trade and appraisal liability. Sections 3:2 to 3:19 considers what an appraisal is and how its preparation is informed and controlled by the context of an appraisal assignment. Sections 3:20 to 3:33 explains the basics of valuation, identification of key terms, and valua tion methodologies. Sections 3:34 to 3:76 is devoted to tax, including Internal Revenue Service appraisal requirements and tax cases involving disputed appraisals of artworks. New legislative proposals affecting estates of artists and their charitable contributions are identified. Sections 3:77 to 3:107 describes the emerging revitalized professional appraisal practice, the Uniform Standards of Professional Appraisal Practice (USPAP),[1] and professional appraisal organizations. USPAP was substantially revised. The original personal property standards are provided in Appendix

[Section 3:1]

[1] *See* Appendix 5.

5. For the updated standards see the USPAP website at: http://www.appraisalfoundation.org/USPAP2001/standard7 and http://www.appraisal foundation.org/USPAP2001/standard8. Sections 3:108 to 3:130 identifies the sources of appraisal litigation, the appraiser's tort exposure for failure to act in accordance with legal duties and obligations. Sections 3:131 to 3:134 focuses upon the appraiser as expert witness and the evidentiary aspects of an appraisal.

II. APPRAISALS

A. INTRODUCTION

§ 3:2 Generally

"In a society [that] not only permits but encourages the private ownership of . . . property . . . there [is] a necessity for [its] appraisal."[1] Art, artifacts, and antiques are no exception. Courts have deemed the appraisal of artworks "a matter of public concern."[2] Although art appraisal is crucial to every aspect of art acquisition, trade, display, gift, donation, and devise,[3] its current status should be examined in the larger context of national reformulations of all appraisal practices and standards.

Virtually every exchange or transfer, regardless of whether it creates profit or loss, involves an appraisal of the property changing hands. When these transfers involve taxable transactions, for example, charitable contributions, estates and gifts, sales of businesses, an appraisal is required for the government to assess the taxable interests. Taxable events are but one aspect of appraisals. In the legal system, the values established in appraisals play a formidable role affecting procedure[4] and serve as the basis for assessing damage claims. The values

[Section 3:2]

[1]ASA, The Principles of Appraisal Practice and Code of Ethics, "Foreword" 1.

[2]Porcella v. Time, Inc., 300 F.2d 162 (7th Cir. 1962).

[3]Porcella v. Time, Inc., 300 F.2d 162 (7th Cir. 1962); McNally v. Yarnall, 764 F. Supp. 838, 844 (S.D. N.Y. 1991).

[4]Burger v. Bartlett, 1990 WL 99025(E.D. Pa. July 11, 1990) (issue of whether art had sufficient value to meet $50,000 predicate for federal

in appraisals are also integral to a capitalistic market economy. Appraisals are regularly used in the American economy:

(1) to structure business transactions, including sales of goods and sales of ongoing concerns;
(2) to obtain policies of insurance;
(3) to adjust insured losses and establish value for uninsured losses;
(4) to administer, distribute, and liquidate estate and corporate assets;
(5) to monitor inventory; and
(6) to inform public decisions and to provide public notice, e.g., charitable contributions, eminent domain, and historical landmarks.

Those who perform valuations and prepare appraisals play critical roles in maintaining the economic and financial infrastructures that affect commerce and culture. Note that the previous sentence uses as its subject the word "those" instead of "appraisers." Under current laws, the critical task of appraising personal property can be performed by anyone who hangs out a shingle or publicly represents that person is an appraiser.[5] Personal property appraisers are not licensed, certified, registered, or directly regulated by government. Effective January 15, 1996, the Internal Revenue Service itself has proactively entered the valuation field by offering taxpayers (for a fee) a Statement of Value for art and artifacts upon which they may rely for federal income tax, estate tax, or gift tax returns that report transfers of artworks.[6]

The lawyer's job, as in many other areas of the arts, is to distinguish the qualified appraiser from others who share the field, and to separate documents that purport to be appraisals from credible appraisals that will comport with Internal Revenue Service requirements and withstand judicial scrutiny. Checklists are provided in this

jurisdiction); U.S. v. Tobin, 576 F.2d 687 (5th Cir. 1978) (issue of whether stolen art had sufficient value to meet $5,000 minimum for goods under the National Stolen Property Act).

[5]Reg. § 1.170A13(c).

[6]IRS Rev. Proc. 96-15, reproduced in Appendix 7; *see also* § 3:47.

chapter to assist the lawyer in doing so.

Events in the capital and financial markets have triggered national investigation into and focus upon professional appraisal practice. Private property values are key to the capitalistic system because investment and distribution are linked to the potential accumulation of capital at each juncture of transfer and exchange. Reinvestment of capital accretion sustains the market system.

Financial transactions purporting to create capital by paper transfer of assets—notably, leveraged buyouts (LBOs) during the 1980s—revealed, however, that such corporate restructuring eventually undermined the market economy. LBOs occurred in tandem with reorganization in financial markets affecting the costs of capital: (1) deregulation; (2) related changes in lending policies; and (3) failures of savings and loans, thrifts, and some banks. Analysts are reevaluating and differentiating the types of transfers and quality of capital accretion that keep the system viable.

Amid the complex recommendations for targeting errors and implementing corrections, one fact became clear: Market economics cannot work if the asset transfers and loan collaterals are improperly valued. But there were no regulatory standards guiding proper valuation. This precipitated a consensus to develop professional appraisal practices, the goals of which would include uniform standards, public notice, and safeguards to deter false and inaccurate valuations of property. These efforts have been spearheaded by appraisal organizations in conjunction with government and nonprofit agencies.

Although real property appraisal has been the major target of regulation, and real property appraisers must be certified under state laws pursuant to federal legislation, personal property appraisal practice has also been scrutinized. As a result, recommended practices, USPAP,[7] were developed, but compliance is voluntary for personal property appraisers. Although no state or federal enforcement mechanism mandates compliance with USPAP, personal property appraisal organizations have generally embraced USPAP among their recommended practices and were instrumental in developing the standards.

---

[7]*See* Appendix 5.

Lawyers should be aware that not all appraisers belong to professional organizations, and, while some personal property appraisers voluntarily subscribe to USPAP, others do not. That is one reason Checklist 3-1 recommends stating whether or not the appraiser will subscribe to USPAP and perform the appraisal in accordance with its standards.

Finally, it should be noted that USPAP and codes of ethics are aspects of a multidimensional appraiser-client relationship involving trust, competence, diligence, communication, and respect. The client-appraiser relationship triggers ethical and moral considerations, as well as legal ones. USPAP alone is not a substitute for the client-appraiser fit, nor a guarantee of a proper appraisal.

B. APPRAISAL COMPONENTS

1. Appraisal Process

§ 3:3 Generally

An appraisal is a summary of processes and judgments applied to a "subject property" in the context of responding to a specific appraisal assignment. The objective of the appraisal is to determine "numerical" value of a subject property responsive to and consistent with the purpose and intended use of the appraisal. In general terms, appraisals seek solutions of specific valuation questions.

General procedures for preparing an appraisal are summarized below, and are detailed in the following sections. This general procedure is not a substitute for preparation of specific appraisal reports required by law for particular types of tax transactions, or for industry reporting requirements for written appraisals recommended by USPAP and professional appraisal organizations.[1]

General Procedures for Preparing an Appraisal

(1) Define the purpose, scope, and intended use of

[Section 3:3]

[1]Discussed in §§ 3:34 to 3:76 and 3:20 to 3:33, respectively. USPAP contains a specific reporting list for written appraisals at Standard II, Rule 2; Rev.Proc. 66-49 contains a specific reporting list for certain tax appraisals (*see* Appendix 7); ASA contains a specific reporting list for appraisal reports.

the appraisal assignment, i.e., specify the valuation question and determine a solution.

(2) Identify the property to be appraised (apparent or absolute identification) and specify how identification will be made (direct physical examination or indirect view of slides, photos).

(3) Disclose limiting conditions and assumptions.

(4) Investigate the property and its placement in the markets.

(5) Select the proper markets to make the valuation.

(6) Apply appropriate methodologies of valuation consistent with purpose and intended use.

(7) Reconcile data to determine final numerical result (single value or range of values).

(8) Form conclusion.

(9) Prepare appraisal document (or oral appraisal), stating the conclusion and summarizing (1) through (8) above.

The process of determining the value of property and preparing an appraisal is termed "valuation."[2] Valuation is not merely a formulaic task. In the words of the courts, valuation is "an inexact science [which] turns on its own particular facts,"[3] and reflects "an approximation derived from all the evidence."[4]

Value thus arises "in context" of facts and circumstances,[5] linked to the context of the appraisal assignment and the purpose of the appraisal. As the appraisal assignment and appraisal purpose vary, so will the estimated values of the subject property. For example, an artwork will be appraised differently depending upon the following purposes for it: insurance, charitable contributions, sales, marital dissolution, and business liquidation. Even if an

---

[2]Some professional appraisal organizations use the verb "determine" value, and define "determine" as "to come to a decision . . . , as the result of investigation, reasoning, etc." ASA, The Principles of Appraisal Practice and Code of Ethics § 1.21(1).

[3]Ashkar v. C. I. R., T.C. Memo. 1991-11, 1991 WL 2056 (1991).

[4]Williford v. C. I. R., T.C. Memo. 1992-450, T.C.M. (RIA) ¶ 92450 (1992).

[5]Babcock, "A Look at Valuation Science," 3, in ASA, *A Handbook on the Appraisal of Personal Property*.

appraisal is prepared for one purpose, i.e., a charitable contribution, more than one value can—and sometimes should—be expressed under different valuation methodologies according to recommended appraisal practices.[6] The courts particularly favor multiple imaginative valuation solutions for art. It is the responsibility of the appraiser to recognize value potential.

The argument has been made that unique objects like art cannot be valued. This concept is not recognized by the courts: "[N]either uniqueness nor a limited market is a barrier to determining value."[7] Unique property can be valued, and has been valued for purposes of contributions and other purposes.[8] But "valuing a unique piece [of art work] is clearly a most difficult task, and the degree of proof . . . require[d] must be tempered by the practicalities of the situation."[9] Thus, the Tax Court accepts that where "the pieces are unique, . . . the appraisers might make chasmal jumps."[10] Art can be valueless,[11] undervalued,[12] or overvalued.[13]

Misstating values in a tax appraisal has severe consequences for the appraiser and the client: In a federal income tax deficiency matter, there may be an assessment of increased interest and penalties against the taxpayer, a civil penalty against the appraiser, and disbarment of the appraiser from federal practice.[14] Misstating values in nontax appraisals may result in a cause of action against the appraiser and potential disciplinary proceedings

---

[6]*See* §§ 3:34 to 3:76.

[7]Estate of Palmer v. C.I.R., 839 F.2d 420, 44 Ed. Law Rep. 1063 (8th Cir. 1988).

[8]Krauskopf v. C.I.R., T.C. Memo. 1984-386, 1984 WL 15036 (1984).

[9]Hawkins v. Comm'r, T.C. Memo 1982-451 n.20 (1982).

[10]Ashkar v. C. I. R., T.C. Memo. 1991-11, 1991 WL 2056 (1991).

[11]*See* § 3:63; *see also* Shuman v. U.S., 891 F.2d 557 (5th Cir. 1990).

[12]Kremer v. Janet Fleisher Gallery, Inc., 320 Pa. Super. 384, 467 A.2d 377 (1983) (action for negligence where plaintiff engaged gallery owner to sell paintings, which were sold at prices below gallery appraisals).

[13]Goldman v. Barnett, 793 F. Supp. 28, 18 U.C.C. Rep. Serv. 2d 55 (D. Mass. 1992) (paintings by Milton Avery allegedly overvalued by appraiser-dealer).

[14]*See* § 3:74; 31 CFR pt. 10.

against the appraiser if he or she belongs to a professional appraisal membership organization.

2. Appraisal Assignment

§ 3:4 Responsive undertaking

An appraisal is a responsive procedure generated for a particular purpose at the behest of a client to provide a value solution to the appraisal assignment. An appraisal is reactive, not proactive. An appraiser prepares an appraisal at the client's request to address the client's particular needs, for the purpose and use of the client. The appraiser is under an obligation, at least where appraisals are prepared for tax purposes, to provide their clients with information and documentation relevant to the appraisal. It is the appraiser's responsibility to understand and clarify the appraisal assignment with the client, and to evaluate information provided, rather than accepting it with blind reliance.

§ 3:5 Purpose of an appraisal

> In developing a personal property appraisal, an appraiser must consider the purpose and intended use of the appraisal and observe the following specific appraisal guidelines: . . . (b) define the purpose . . . of the appraisal.[1]

The appraiser must understand and clarify why he or she is being asked to appraise the subject property. Value is always linked to purpose and intended use: Is the property being liquidated? Is the property being insured? Is the property appraised for an insurance policy? Is the property about to enter probate? Sound appraisal practice is to state clearly the intended purpose of the appraisal. However, a recitation of purpose may not limit the appraiser's liability for values stated in the appraisal if those values are misrepresentations.[2] If the assignment is ambiguous, the valuation process becomes suspect, defeat-

---

[Section 3:5]

[1]USPAP Standards Rule 7-2

[2]*See* Goldman v. Barnett, 793 F. Supp. 28, 18 U.C.C. Rep. Serv. 2d 55 (D. Mass. 1992) (reliance of appraisal recipient not limited to stated purposes of appraisal stating "for insurance purposes"); *see also* Balog

ing a valuation solution.

§ 3:6 Intended use of an appraisal

> In developing a personal property appraisal, an appraiser must consider the purpose and intended use of the appraisal and observe the following specific appraisal guidelines: . . . (b) define the . . . intended use . . . of the appraisal.[1]

In the appraisal assignment, the appraiser should confirm the client's intended use and state it in the appraisal document if one is prepared. An appraiser cannot restrict the client's distribution of the appraisal; in theory, it can be used by anyone who chances upon it. The majority rule in negligence actions against appraisers, however, is that those who do so, rely on the appraisal at their peril unless they are the intended recipients known to the appraiser at the time of preparation.[2] Sound appraisal practice, therefore, is to state clearly the client's intended use.

§ 3:7 Art appraisals—Authentication

The scope of an art appraisal assignment may require an authentication.[1] Some appraisers may have the competence to authenticate; others will refer the client to experts. But the appraiser and the client must decide in

---

v. Center Art Gallery-Hawaii, Inc., 745 F. Supp. 1556, 12 U.C.C. Rep. Serv. 2d 962 (D. Haw. 1990) (values in appraisals would not be limited to insurance purposes, as defendants claimed, but as values inducing plaintiffs to purchase overvalued art).

[Section 3:6]

[1]USPAP Standards Rule 7-2. The USPAP Preamble contained in former drafts broadened the audience, reciting: "It is essential that a professional personal property appraiser . . . communicate his or her analyses . . . to the client, to any third parties involved, to the public or to any other legitimately interested entities." USPAP § A (1987).

[2]Christiansen v. Roddy, 186 Cal. App. 3d 780, 231 Cal. Rptr. 72, 76 (5th Dist. 1986) (implied overruling recognized by, Soderberg v. McKinney, 44 Cal. App. 4th 1760, 52 Cal. Rptr. 2d 635 (2d Dist. 1996)) (no need to know "specific identity").

[Section 3:7]

[1]*See* Foxley v. Sotheby's Inc., 893 F. Supp. 1224, 27 U.C.C. Rep. Serv. 2d 1234 (S.D. N.Y. 1995) (auction house prepared appraisal specifically disclaiming authentication of artwork).

the appraisal assignment whether an authentication will be performed or the appraisal will rely upon an "apparent identification" of the property. An apparent identification means that the property is visually inspected, preferably based upon direct physical examination. An apparent identification, which does not purport to authenticate,[2] ordinarily involves analysis of extrinsic and patent elements of the CROSSAQ factor;[3] scientific testing and laboratory analysis is not performed, and the extent of historical investigation of provenance varies.[4] The art appraiser and the client: (1) should be mindful of how broad and misused the term "authentication" is; (2) should identify the activities that are in order to authenticate or apparently authenticate; and (3) the appraisal assignment should recognize and recite these and specify how they will be treated.

Former tax instructions for preparation of charitable contributions stated "the authenticity of the donated art must be determined by the appraiser."[5] IRS revenue procedures specify criteria for appraising fine art for federal tax purposes, which refers to submission of proof of authenticity by a certificate of authentication or comparable document if one exists.[6] If authenticity is in dispute in a tax related matter, the court can reject the appraisal and the appraiser's testimony, even though the Tax Court does not purport to authenticate works or decide authenticity.[7] Those using appraisals for tax matters should be cognizant of the Tax Court's position that questionable authenticity devalues artworks,[8] and the devaluation may be substantial, as evidenced in Chart

[2]*See* § 3:19.

[3]*See* § 2:11.

[4]*See* §§ 3:10 to 3:12 for identification of property.

[5]U.S. Gov't Printing Office: 1988-2421988-484/80035, at 3.

[6]Rev. Proc. 66-49; *see* Appendix 7.

[7]Peters v. C.I.R., T.C. Memo. 1977-128, 1977 WL 3425 (1977), aff'd, 601 F.2d 603 (9th Cir. 1979).

[8]*See* Mathias v. Commissioner of Internal Revenue, 50 T.C. 994, 1968 WL 1498 (T.C. 1968), acq. 1969-1 C.B. and acq. 1969-2 C.B. and recommendation regarding acquiescence, 1969 WL 20641 (I.R.S. AOD 1969) Vander Hook v. C.I.R., T.C. Memo. 1977-347, 1977 WL 3067 (1977).

3-1, "Comparison of Fake and Genuine Values for Artworks Where Authenticity Questioned."

Chart 3-1: Comparison of Fake and Genuine Values for Artworks

Artist	Case	Artwork	Fake $	Genuine $
Frederic Remington	United States v. Tobin, 576 F.2d 687 (5th Cir. 1978)	BroncoBuster [sculpture]	$3,500 to $7,000	$20,000
Albert Bierstadt	Firestone v. Union League, 672 F. Supp. 819 (E.D. Pa. 1987)	Bombardment Fort Sumter [painting]	$50,000	$500,000
Charles M. Russell	Doherty v. Comm'r, 63 T.C.M. (CCH) 2112 (1992)	Attacking Stagecoach [painting]	$100	$200,000
—	Ferrari v. Comm'r, 58 T.C.M. (CCH) 221 (1989)	[pre-Colombian artifacts]	$500	$18,000
Adolf Schreyer	Waller v. Scheer, 332 S.E.2d 293 (1985)	Arabian Horses [painting]	$6,000 to $8,000	$20,000 to $24,000

Artist	Case	Artwork	Fake $	Genuine $
Ferdinand Keller	Mathias v. Comm'r, 50 T.C. 994 (1968)	Grotto of Love [painting]	$500	$12,750
Gilbert Stuart	Mathias v. Comm'r, 50 T.C. 994 (1968)	Sir John Jervis [painting]	$8,000	$25,000
Berthe Morisot	Peters v. Commissioner, 36 T.C.M. (CCH) 552 (1977)	After the Bath [painting]	$200	$18,500 to $100,000
Bartolome Murillo	Monaghan v. Comm'r, 42 T.C.M. (CCH) 27 (1981)	[painting]	$3,000	$80,000

* Inauthentic by virtue of massive restoration.

Note that a taxpayer who purchases a forged or misattributed painting may be entitled to a theft loss deduction,[9] but not as a matter of course in the absence of proving the seller's fraud. Taxpayers who purchased a landscape attributed to Nicholas Poussin by the dealer and another painting signed by William Merritt Chase auctioned or sold each of them for a loss a few years later after experts authenticating the works found them to be fake: The Poussin was deattributed and the Chase signature was deemed forged.[10] The taxpayer claimed theft loss deductions. The Claims Court held the taxpayer was entitled to a theft loss for the Chase painting as a matter of law because of the forgery, but denied a theft loss deduction for the Poussin in the absence of intentional misrepresentation. The court of appeals reversed the holding for the Chase, stating that a forged painting, without more, was insufficient to prove a theft by false pretenses. "Taxpayer still must prove that the seller defrauded him by knowingly and intentionally misattributing the painting to the artist."[11]

§ 3:8 Art appraisals—Copyright, trademark, moral rights, realty

In addition to physical attributes of tangible property, art contains intangible properties: intellectual property interests, including copyright, trademark, and "moral" rights. Some of these rights are transferable inter vivos and by devise or intestacy, and they have value. The art appraiser and the client should be mindful of these interests and the appraisal assignment should recognize them and specify how they will be treated.[1] Valuing intangible property interests is a specialty unto itself, and may require the competence of appraisal disciplines outside of personal property.

---

[9]Deductions claimed under IRC § 165(c).

[10]Krahmer v. U.S., 810 F.2d 1145, 98 A.L.R. Fed. 221 (Fed. Cir. 1987).

[11]Krahmer v. U.S., 810 F.2d 1145 at 1147, 98 A.L.R. Fed. 221 (Fed. Cir. 1987).

[Section 3:8]

[1]*See* §§ 3:10 to 3:12.

Art can, on occasion, be affixed to or a part of realty, for instance, some murals, mosaics, and stelae. Therefore, transfers of the realty necessarily involve transfers of the artwork; in some states and under federal law, legal responsibilities attach to the owners of such artworks, which cannot be arbitrarily removed or destroyed. These factors affect value, and bear consideration in the appraisal assignment. The art appraiser and the client should be mindful of these interests, and the appraisal assignment should recognize them and specify how they will be treated.

§ 3:9 Art appraisals—Clouds on title

> An appraiser must . . . (b) not commit a substantial error of omission or commission that significantly affects an appraisal; . . . (c) not render appraisal services in a careless or negligent manner.[1]

Artworks are particularly susceptible to ownership claims because: (1) art ownership is rarely registered; (2) ownership documentation can be sparse; (3) art is highly mobile and easily cached; and (4) art is not subject to comprehensive centralized reporting services for dissemination of accurate information. The most common cloud on ownership is a title dispute arising from dispossession of artwork or removal of rights to artwork; the claimant seeking return of the property must prove in court that he is the rightful owner or that his ownership claim is superior to the defendant or other claimants. The claims may result from thefts, will contests, marital dissolution, or importation.

Artwork is also susceptible to impaired title claims where it is composed of, or contains, materials that are unlawfully obtained under federal or state laws. For example, proscriptions exist on the use of certain animal

---

[Section 3:9]

[1]USPAP Standards Rule 7-1(b). Omitted in USPAP 1993 is the following from the USPAP 1987 version: "consider and analyze the effect on value of . . . any damage or imperfections." USPAP Standard I, Rule 2(h)(1).

parts under the Endangered Species Act,[2] use of certain bird materials under the Eagle Protection Act,[3] the Migratory Bird Treaty Act,[4] and the Native American Graves Protection and Repatriation Act.[5] Similarly, title may repose in government as a result of shipwrecks pursuant to maritime law,[6] or archaeological discoveries pursuant to the Archaeological Resources Protection Act (ARPA),[7] the Antiquities Act,[8] the Abandoned Property Act,[9] and comparable state historic preservation laws.[10] The art appraiser and the client should be mindful of title and the appraisal assignment should recognize title issues and specify how they will be treated.

3. *Identifying Subject Property*

§ 3:10 Generally

An appraiser must "adequately identify property to be valued, including the methods of identification."[1] "Each written personal property appraisal must . . . includ[e a] descriptive identification of personal property being appraised."[2]

---

[2]16 U.S.C.A. §§ 1531–1543.

[3]16 U.S.C.A. §§ 668–668d.

[4]16 U.S.C.A. §§ 703–712.

[5]25 U.S.C.A. §§ 3001 et seq.

[6]U.S. v. Steinmetz, 973 F.2d 212 (3d Cir. 1992); Perdue v. C. I. R., T.C. Memo. 1991-478, 1991 WL 188862 (1991).

[7]16 U.S.C.A. §§ 470aa et seq., *see* Ch 13.

[8]16 U.S.C.A. §§ 431 et seq., *see* Ch 13.

[9]40 U.S.C.A. §§ 310 et seq., *see* §§ 13:24 to 13:25.

[10]*See* §§ 14:17 to 14:38.

[Section 3:10]

[1]USPAP Standards Rule 7-2, *see* Appendix 5 for complete text of all USPAP references.

[2]USPAP Standards Rule 8-2. USPAP (1987 Version) Statements on "identification" of subject property: "Adequately identify the objects," Standard I, Rule 2(a). "Consider and analyze the effect on value of: any damage or imperfections," Standard I, Rule 2(h)(1). "Consider and analyze the effect on value of: 'provenance,' " Standard I, Rule 2(h)(3). "Each written appraisal report must . . . identify and describe the personal property being appraised," Standard II, Rule 2(a).

§ 3:11 Tangible personal property

An appraisal has at its core an identifiable interest known as the "subject property." The subject property of an art appraisal is artwork; artwork contains tangible and intangible interests, personalty, and realty. Furthermore, art is not conclusively identified by narrative language, empirical measurements and photographic or other graphic or pictorial reproductions. Even the CROSSAQ factor, a summary of key attributes of the artwork, contains extrinsic and latent elements that cannot be ascertained without independent investigatory techniques and processes.[1]

Sound appraisal practice requires, at a minimum, an apparent identification of the subject property. "Apparent identification" means that the property is visually inspected, preferably based upon direct physical examination.[2] Direct examination permits inspection from all sides and angles, interior and exterior, front (recto) and back (verso), and permits an immediacy of observation regarding patent damage and restoration.[3]

What does an apparent identification in an art appraisal signify? Using as an example a painting by Vincent Van Gogh, the apparent identification recites title, if known, describes the subject matter, indicates any signature and date, measures size, notes condition, and may, if contemplated by the appraisal assignment, compares the work to published works and catalogues and inspects records and documents of sale and prior ownership, loosely termed "provenance."[4]

But this combination of evidentiary support for an appraisal does not mean that the subject property is a genuine Van Gogh. That conclusion, if one can be made, is

---

[Section 3:11]

[1]*See* § 2:11 for definition of the CROSSAQ factor.

[2]*See* § 3:14.

[3]Direct examination is also preferable for an authentication; *see* Kirby v. Wildenstein, 784 F. Supp. 1112 (S.D. N.Y. 1992) (authenticator examined a Jean Beraud painting for twenty minutes, front and back, and at various distances).

[4]*See* §§ 2:53 to 2:60 and § 6:82.

determined by an authentication, not an appraisal.[5] An authentication involves a multiplicity of scientific tests that could include ultraviolet light, x-ray, chemical analyses, and infrared light, as well as historical analysis. An apparent identification ordinarily involves analysis of the extrinsic and patent elements of the CROSSAQ factor.[6] If an apparent identification is used, then the appraiser should clearly disclose that an identification was made, how it was made, and the limiting conditions and stated assumptions.

An apparent identification can reveal that the subject property is not genuine, or has attributes that give notice that further investigation of genuineness is required. In addition to value, visible damage and degree of restoration affect authenticity.[7] For example, surface damage of a painting that exposes a paint-by-number canvas is obviously not the work of a master, regardless of signature or provenance. Another example is artwork that has been more than 50 percent restored; the hand of the artist is considered lost, and the attribution should reflect the subsequent restorations. Most identification-authentication issues are murkier than this hyperbolic example. However, overlooking variables that imply spuriousness in an apparent identification is not uncommon; an appraiser's failure to note apparent conditions in the identification of the subject property is actionable.[8]

§ 3:12 Intangible property and real property

> (g) [I]dentify any real property [and] intangible items that are not personal property but are included in the appraisal.[1]

Art may have many legal interests: tangible personal

---

[5]*See* § 3:7.

[6]*See* § 2:11.

[7]Furstenberg v. U.S., 219 Ct. Cl. 473, 595 F.2d 603 (1979).

[8]Furstenberg v. U. S., 219 Ct. Cl. 473, 595 F.2d 603, 607, 79-1 U.S. Tax Cas. (CCH) P 9280, 43 A.F.T.R.2d 79-908 (1979).

[Section 3:12]

[1]USPAP Standards Rule 7-3. USPAP 1987 version contemplated artworks in its definition of personal property, but omitted intangible and realty interests: "These standards are intended to apply to identifiable portable and tangible objects which are considered by the general public as being 'personal,' e.g., furnishings, artwork, antiques, . . .

property, intangible personal property, real property (a fresco, a mural, a stela). Federal law adds to certain artworks a new interest termed "moral rights," referred to in this work as "inherent rights." Although these interests are increasingly recognized by creators, owners, and courts, garden variety art appraisals ordinarily do not recite values for intangible property rights and inherent rights. To what extent an arts appraiser ought to discuss nontangible property interests with a client has not been directly addressed by the courts and remains a matter of individual discretion in articulating the appraisal assignment.[2]

4. *Visual Inspection of Subject Property*

§ 3:13 Generally

An appraiser's certification of the appraisal must recite: "I have [or have not] made a personal inspection of the property."[1]

§ 3:14 Direct examination

Art has to be subjected to a visual inspection to be appraised, but the key consideration is how that inspection will be made by: (1) direct physical examination; or (2) indirect examination, for example, by slides, photographs, videotape, and transparencies. The CROSSAQ factor[1] indicates the importance of direct examination. Codes of ethics usually promote direct examination, recommending that appraisers "examine[ ] personally . . . or be so noted,"[2] and "good appraisal practice requires adequate inspection

---

collectibles." USPAP § A (1987); *see* http://www.appraisalfoundation.org/USPAP2001/standard7 and http://www.appraisalfoundation.org//USPAP2001/standard8.

[2]*See, e.g.,* ASA Code of Ethics.

[Section 3:13]

[1]USPAP Standards Rule 8-3. USPAP (1987) permitted identification without physical inspection if "the method of identification [is disclosed] if other than or in addition to a personal physical inspection." Standard I, Rule 2(a).

[Section 3:14]

[1]*See* § 2:11.

[2]AAA Code of Ethics.

and investigation to determine" physical condition.[3]

At a minimum, sound appraisal practice requires that limiting conditions disclose whether the property was inspected by direct physical examination or other means, and specifying those means. Failure to disclose the type of inspection in the limiting conditions may undermine the validity of the appraisal.

§ 3:15 Indirect examination

The appraiser's failure to conduct direct examination of the subject property is not always considered by the courts a "defect in . . . appraisal technique."[1] Reliance upon a photographic record has ordinarily satisfied the Tax Court because "photographs serve as the basis for appraisals by the [IRS] Art Advisory Panel."[2] The photographic evidence, however, must be "reliable."[3] But even that may not be enough. In Johnson,[4] the court rejected appraisals based upon photographs on the ground that "independent" and "objective" visual examination of some of 140 native American artifacts donated to a museum was "essential." And,

---

[3]Monaghan v. C.I.R., T.C. Memo. 1981-280, 1981 WL 10597 (1981) (appraisal based solely on photographs rather than painting did not reveal poor condition and restorations); *see also,* ASA, Principles of Appraisal Practice and Code of Ethics § 6.9.

[Section 3:15]

[1]Lightman v. C.I.R., T.C. Memo. 1985-315, 1985 WL 14942 (1985) (court did not consider an appraisal based upon indirect examination a "defect in appraisal technique, stating, 'reliance on photographs is not unusual in appraising paintings'."); *but cf.* Ashkar v. C. I. R., T.C. Memo. 1991-11, 1991 WL 2056 (1991); In re Lisser, 90-2 U.S. Tax Cas. (CCH) ¶ 50,352 (N.D. Tex. 1990); Johnson v. C.I.R., 85 T.C. 469, 1985 WL 15393 (1985).

[2]Lightman v. C.I.R., T.C. Memo. 1985-315, 1985 WL 14942 (1985) (court did not consider an appraisal based upon indirect examination a "defect in appraisal technique, stating, 'reliance on photographs is not unusual in appraising paintings'."); *but cf.* Ashkar v. C. I. R., T.C. Memo. 1991-11, 1991 WL 2056 (1991); In re Lisser, 90-2 U.S. Tax Cas. (CCH) ¶ 50,352 (N.D. Tex. 1990); Johnson v. C.I.R., 85 T.C. 469, 1985 WL 15393 (1985); Greenberg Gallery, Inc. v. Bauman, 817 F. Supp. 167 (D.D.C. 1993), order aff'd, 36 F.3d 127 (D.C. Cir. 1994) (challenged use of photographs in contract and breach of warranty suit to authenticate three-dimensional mobile by Alexander Calder).

[3]Johnson v. C.I.R., 85 T.C. 469, 1985 WL 15393 (1985).

[4]Johnson v. C.I.R., 85 T.C. 469, 1985 WL 15393 (1985).

in Shein,[5] the failure to disclose how inspection was made caused the court to discount the weight of appraiser's evidence, stating: "There is no indication in [the] appraisals whether he inspected the actual works in question."

5. *Appraisal Values Are Expressed in Numerical Terms*

§ 3:16 Generally

An appraiser's certification of the appraisal must recite:

> [M]y compensation is not contingent upon the reporting of a predetermined value or direction in value that favors the cause of the client.[1]

The objective of an appraisal is to reach a "numerical result." The numerical result is a judgment based upon the appraiser's choice of methodologies, stated assumptions, and limiting conditions under which the appraisal is rendered in response to the appraisal assignment. The numerical result is not an empirical measurement that can be objectively compared to a universal standard.

The numerical result may be expressed as a single value, i.e., $10,000, or a range of values, usually stated from low to high, i.e., $10,000 to $20,000, termed a "two-figure estimate" of value.[2] The IRS has accepted range of values for federal tax purposes,[3] but some appraisers contend that range of values is inappropriate for appraisals. The numerical result should be reached independently by the appraiser without reference to the result oriented objectives of others, including the client and/or

---

[5]Shein v. C.I.R, T.C. Memo. 1987-329, 1987 WL 40384 (1987); *see also* "Fed. income tax charitable deductions: property fair market value determinations," 90 A.L.R. Fed. 402 § 13.

[Section 3:16]

[1]*See* Appendix 5, USPAP Standards Rule 8-3.

[2]Ferrari v. C.I.R., T.C. Memo. 1989-521, 1989 WL 109420 (1989), judgment aff'd, 931 F.2d 54 (4th Cir. 1991) (range of values may be required by court if retail prices of same or comparable objects vary among retail sales); *see also* Shein v. C.I.R, T.C. Memo. 1987-329, 1987 WL 40384 (1987).

[3]*See* §§ 3:34 to 3:76.

counsel.[4] If the appraiser is informed in advance of the desired numerical result, the appraisal loses its impartiality and undermines the integrity of the appraiser's judgment. Sound appraisal practice requires open-ended values, not predetermined results.

6. *Appraisals Can Be Written or Oral*

§ 3:17 Generally

> [E]ach oral personal property appraisal report . . . must address the substantive matters set forth [for written reports].[1]

The appraisal is a summary of process and methodology, including assumptions and conditions, research and theory, and methodologies of valuation utilized to produce the numerical results. Codes of ethics generally favor written appraisals, although oral appraisals are an accepted practice. Oral statements about art may constitute an appraisal even where specific numerical values were not stated and the speaker did not purport to be an appraiser or issuing an appraisal.[2] Although some appraisal assignments may request oral appraisal, ordinarily, the complexity of an appraisal warrants reduction to writing. The evidentiary value of a written appraisal in a court of law is also considered of greater weight than an oral appraisal,[3] the role of a writing is also considered more weighty in a statute of frauds defense.

The form of the writing varies; that a variety of writings have constituted appraisals should not be surprising in an unregulated field. For specific appraisals, e.g., charitable contributions of artworks, the Internal Revenue Service

---

[4]ASA, Principles of Appraisal Practice and Code of Ethics 3. Appraisers do not consider themselves agents of their clients in determining value, but their codes of ethics are structured around agency principles. These oft-time contradictory and inconsistent obligations have not been directly addressed in the case law. *See* §§ 3:77 to 3:107.

[Section 3:17]

[1]*See* Appendix 5, USPAP Standards Rule 8-4; *see also* id. at Rule 8-1. USPAP 1987 version contemplated oral appraisals, and referred to written or oral "appraisal report[s]." Standard II, Rule 1.

[2]Struna v. Wolf, 126 Misc. 2d 1031, 484 N.Y.S.2d 392 (Sup 1985).

[3]Kremer v. Janet Fleisher Gallery, Inc., 320 Pa. Super. 384, 467 A.2d 377 (1983).

prescribes the title, form, and terms of the appraisal document,[4] and uses published criteria for appraising art and representing its authenticity in an appraisal.[5]

In trade cases, the title, form, and terms of the appraisal do not control: A document may constitute an appraisal even though the words "appraisal" or "valuation" do not appear in the title or in the text.[6] A document may constitute an appraisal even though the title identifies it as something other than an appraisal, i.e., a certificate of authenticity.[7] A document may constitute an appraisal for any purpose and be used as the basis of a negligence, fraud, or breach of contract action against the appraiser even though the appraisal states "for insurance purposes."[8]

7. *Limiting Conditions and Assumptions*

§ 3:18 Generally

> (b) . . . [I]nclude all general and specific limiting conditions. Each written personal property appraisal must include (c) . . . any extraordinary assumption or limiting condition that directly affects the appraisal.
>
> Each written personal property appraisal must include (g) all assumptions and limiting conditions.[1]

Limiting conditions and assumptions establish the crucial context for the valuation conclusion in the

---

[4]IRS Form 8283 is reproduced in Appendix 6.

[5]Rev. Proc. 66-49, *see* Appendix 7.

[6]*See, e.g.,* Rosen v. Spanierman, 894 F.2d 28, 10 U.C.C. Rep. Serv. 2d 846 (2d Cir. 1990); Goldman v. Barnett, 793 F. Supp. 28, 18 U.C.C. Rep. Serv. 2d 55 (D. Mass. 1992); Balog v. Center Art Gallery-Hawaii, Inc., 745 F. Supp. 1556, 12 U.C.C. Rep. Serv. 2d 962 (D. Haw. 1990).

[7]Balog v. Center Art Gallery-Hawaii, Inc., 745 F. Supp. 1556, 12 U.C.C. Rep. Serv. 2d 962 (D. Haw. 1990).

[8]Goldman v. Barnett, 793 F. Supp. 28, 18 U.C.C. Rep. Serv. 2d 55 (D. Mass. 1992) (reliance of appraisal recipient not limited to stated purposes of appraisal stating "for insurance purposes"); *see also* Balog v. Center Art Gallery-Hawaii, Inc., 745 F. Supp. 1556, 12 U.C.C. Rep. Serv. 2d 962 (D. Haw. 1990) (values in appraisals would not be limited to insurance purposes as defendants claimed but as values inducing plaintiffs to purchase overvalued art).

[Section 3:18]

[1]USPAP Standards Rules 7-2, 8-1, and 8-2, respectively. *See* Appendix 5.

appraisal. An appraisal cannot analyze every aspect of the subject property and markets. The limiting conditions and assumptions notify and communicate what the appraiser has done and what the appraiser has relied upon in preparing the appraisal. Sound appraisal practice requires disclosing the limiting conditions.

C. COMPARISON OF APPRAISAL AND AUTHENTICATION

§ 3:19 Generally

There is a good deal of controversy within and without appraisal practice about the separation of authentication from appraisal. Authentication and appraisal are two distinct processes, which has been recognized by some courts,[1] and has been hopelessly confused by others.[2] However, there is a convergence of authentication and appraisal for appraisals done for federal tax purposes. Before explaining the overlap of the processes in the tax context, the lawyer should understand what the two processes are:

(1) Appraisal valuation is ordinarily based upon ap-

[Section 3:19]

[1]Ashkar v. C. I. R., T.C. Memo. 1991-11, 1991 WL 2056 (1991). (professors presented "academic rather than commercial valuations [as] scholars not professional appraisers of ancient documents. They convinced us of the authenticity of the Ashkar-Gilson collection, but not of the [appraised] financial value."); Foxley v. Sotheby's Inc., 893 F. Supp. 1224, 27 U.C.C. Rep. Serv. 2d 1234 (S.D. N.Y. 1995) (auction house appraisal of artwork does not necessarily need to include authentication).

[2]*See* Dubin v. C.I.R., T.C. Memo. 1986-433, 1986 WL 21643 (1986); Monaghan v. C.I.R., T.C. Memo. 1981-280, 1981 WL 10597 (1981); Rupke v. C. I. R., T.C. Memo. 1973-234, 1973 WL 2413 (1973), recommendation regarding acquiescence, 1974 WL 35958 (I.R.S. AOD 1974); *see also* Vander Hook v. C.I.R., T.C. Memo. 1977-347, 1977 WL 3067 (1977) (for resolution of authenticity); *and see* Holtzman v. C.I.R., T.C. Memo. 1980-174, 1980 WL 4020 (1980); Peters v. C.I.R., T.C. Memo. 1977-128, 1977 WL 3425 (1977), aff'd, 601 F.2d 603 (9th Cir. 1979); Gordon v. C.I.R., T.C. Memo. 1976-274, 1976 WL 3456 (1976); Farber v. Comm'r, T.C. Memo 1974-155, aff'd in unpublished opinion (2d Cir. Nov. 20, 1975); Mathias v. Commissioner of Internal Revenue, 50 T.C. 994, 1968 WL 1498 (T.C. 1968), acq. 1969-1 C.B. and acq. 1969-2 C.B. and recommendation regarding acquiescence, 1969 WL 20641 (I.R.S. AOD 1969).

parent identification of the subject property; the appraisal refers to authenticity through the stated assumptions and limiting conditions but does not purport to be an independent authentication.[3]

(2) Authentication is a function of belief in the genuineness or spuriousness of the subject property based upon a process of determining the absolute identity, rather than the apparent identity, of the property. Absolute analysis includes evaluation of extrinsic and latent elements that comprise the CROSSAQ factor,[4] which requires scientific testing (e.g., ultraviolet light, infrared light, X-ray, chemical testing), physical inspection of latent structural components (i.e., age and type of stretcher bars), and historical analysis.[5]

Authentications and appraisals produce very different results: Appraisals are directed to financial and economic considerations; authentications are concerned with the historical accuracy and integrity of an artist's body of work. They thus inform the market about different aspects of artworks and are guided by different principles, practices, theories, and doctrines.

The federal tax practice for personal property appraisal, which is in flux, has converged appraisal and authentication to a certain degree. Revenue Procedure 66-49, which is applicable to art appraisals used for federal income tax purposes, requires that appraisals include: "A history of the item including proof of authenticity such as a certificate of authentication, if such exists."[6]

This requirement is confusing on both factual and interpretative grounds. First, certificates of authenticity issued by retailers in the decorative market and by some other sellers of art are red flags to appraisers that the art

---

[3] *But cf.* Farber v. Comm'r, T.C. Memo 1974-155, aff'd in unpublished opinion (2d Cir. Nov. 20, 1975) (appraiser as authenticator of Tintoretto painting).

[4] *See* § 2:11.

[5] *See* Ch 2 §§ 2:11, 2:22 to 2:24.

[6] Rev. Proc. 66-49, § 3.03(3)

is fake. This belief has been supported by such certificates.[7] Sound appraisal practice requires the appraiser to differentiate the legitimate certification from that which is intended to deceive. Second, even legitimate certificates do not mean that the artwork is authentic; the certificate is a function of precisely what research and activity was done by the person purporting to authenticate, information which should be disclosed. Third, Revenue Procedure 66-49 does not speak directly to the appraiser's independent requirement to authenticate: It can be reasonably interpreted to mean that the appraiser must consider authenticity in the analysis, i.e., if certificates or other documents exist.

Sound appraisal practice also requires that authenticity issues be considered, regardless of statements in limiting conditions or assumptions about authentication. That the appraiser ordinarily cannot verify authenticity or perform an independent authentication does not mean that he or she has no duty to investigate or recommend further investigation based upon an apparent identification.[8] The paint-by-number example[9] would have indicated an authenticity problem by examining the condition of the canvas. An appraiser cannot simply ignore facts relevant to authenticity revealed by condition. Other factors evident even by apparent identification may raise authenticity questions: massive restoration; labels or certificates attached to the art; indicia of former ownership that is inconsistent with provenance; and discrepancies in, for example, size, between the artwork and references to the artwork in publications.

The degree to which investigation of these aspects, especially an analysis of provenance and disclosure about findings, is required by the appraiser is a matter determined under negligence standards.[10] If a court finds that an appraiser reasonably should have known on the date of valuation about questionable authenticity, then the valuation

[7] *See* Chs 11 and 12.

[8] *See* discussion of due diligence in § 6:130; *see also* Luper Auction Galleries, Inc. v. Judge (William), No. 3:92cv556 (D.C. Va. March 16, 1993).

[9] *See* §§ 3:10 to 3:12.

[10] *See* §§ 6.26 and 6.27.

is suspect. In negligence actions, this can result in undervaluation because authentic art is unknowingly sold at grossly undervalued prices.[11] In tax matters, this can result in overvaluation as the "shadow cast . . . acts as a depressant on value."[12]

As a practical matter, fee structures for appraisals do not include the costs and expenses of lengthy procedures and tests involved in authentication. Even if appraisers were gratuitously willing to include authentication as part of the services rendered, there are serious ethical and legal considerations regarding the appraiser's authority to do so without the permission of the owner. Nor can appraisers compel reimbursement for authentication costs incurred by them absent contractual arrangements or authorization. Appraisers can refuse appraisal assignments if they believe the work is fake, or recite values for objects assuming their spuriousness.

III. VALUATION

A. FAIR MARKET VALUE (FMV)

§ 3:20 Tax matters—General tax definition

The talismanic term for value in appraisal practice relating to tax matters is "fair market value" (FMV).[1] FMV informs all tax appraisals and affects virtually all appraisal practice. FMV is commonly defined by all tax regulations as follows: "The fair market value is the price at which the property would change hands between a willing buyer and a willing seller, neither being under any

---

[11]Estate of Querbach v. A & B Appraisal Serv., No. cv. L-089362-85 (N.J. Super. 1987) (painting by Hudson River Valley School artist J.F. Cropsey sold for defendant's appraised value of $50 instead of expert's value of $14,800 because defendant-appraiser failed to notice artist's signature and date on painting and label on verso reciting the artist's studio and address).

[12]Doherty v. C.I.R., T.C. Memo. 1992-98, 1992 WL 26049 (1992), judgment aff'd, 16 F.3d 338 (9th Cir. 1994); Mathias v. Commissioner of Internal Revenue, 50 T.C. 994, 998, 1968 WL 1498 (T.C. 1968), acq. 1969-1 C.B. and acq. 1969-2 C.B. and recommendation regarding acquiescence, 1969 WL 20641 (I.R.S. AOD 1969).

[Section 3:20]

[1]*See* 90 A.L.R. Fed. 402 § 17, for discussion of FMV for charitable contributions.

compulsion to buy or sell and both having reasonable knowledge of relevant facts."[2] The definitional origin of FMV is codified in the tax laws, but judicial interpretation has expanded and elaborated its meaning. Further, tax regulations for gift tax, estate tax, and charitable contributions may qualify the meaning of the general FMV definition, therefore, the regulations should be reviewed for specific transactions.[3] Chart 3-2 identifies value mentioned in IRS materials.

Chart 3-2: Value Identified in IRS Materials

Document	Topic
Reg. § 1.170A-1(c)(2)	Charitable Contributions
Reg. § 20.2031-1	Estates
Reg. § 25.2512-1	Gifts
Rev.Proc. 66-49 1965-2 C.B. 1002	Charitable Contributions (Appendix 7)
IRS Form 8283	Charitable Contributions (Appendix 6)
Publication 561	Value of Donated Property
Publication 547	Nonbusiness Disasters, Casualties and Thefts
IRS Form 4684	Casualties and Thefts
Publication 584	Nonbusiness Disaster, Casualty and Theft Loss Workbook (App. 7)
1966-2 C.B. 1257, 1258 Rev. Proc. 65-19	Estate Tax
IRS Form 706	Estate Tax Return

Courts hold that there is only one FMV for each valuation question. The most probative evidence of fair market value of art is the actual price paid in a bona fide sale if the sales transaction occurs at or near the time of

[2]*See generally* U.S. v. Cartwright, 411 U.S. 546, 93 S. Ct. 1713, 36 L. Ed. 2d 528 (1973). For additional qualifying language that may affect FMV in particular cases, the applicable tax, gift, or estate regulation should be reviewed.

[3]Reg. § 1.170A-1(c); *see* McGuire v. C. I. R., 44 T.C. 801, 806, 1965 WL 1207 (T.C. 1965), acq. in result 1966-1 C.B. and acq. in result 1966-2 C.B..

contribution.[4] But fair market value will vary depending upon the valuation methodology, the proper market for the property, and the specific tax transaction contemplated.[5] Actual sales price information is not always available for unique objects held in collections or only episodically offered on the market.[6]

§ 3:21 Tax matters—Determination of FMV is finding of fact by tax court

Where more than one value is offered, the rule of thumb is: Appraisers *estimate* FMV, courts *establish* FMV. The courts, not the parties, determine "fair market value [FMV] [a]s a question of fact to be determined by an examination of the entire record."[1] All relevant evidence is considered and weighed by the trial court before it makes its determination of FMV as a finding of fact.

Determining FMV is a "question of judgment rather than mathematics."[2] A court regularly substitutes its judgment for that of appraisers. A court is under no obligation to reach a "middle of the road compromise" between the FMV urged by the taxpayer and the FMV contended by the IRS.[3] Thus, the court's final result may prove a "significant financial defeat for [the taxpayer] or [the

---

[4]Hunter v. Comm'r, T.C. Memo. (P2-H) ¶ 86-308 (1986).

[5]*See* §§ 3:34 to 3:76.

[6]Reg. § 1.170A0-1(c)(1). Where the property is other than money, "the amount of the contribution is generally the fair market value of the property at the time of the contribution" ("reduced as provided in [IRC] section 170(e)(1) regarding ordinary income and capital gain").

[Section 3:21]

[1]Anselmo v. Commissioner of Internal Revenue, 80 T.C. 872, 1983 WL 14829 (1983), decision aff'd, 757 F.2d 1208 (11th Cir. 1985); Doherty v. C.I.R., T.C. Memo. 1992-98, 1992 WL 26049 (1992), judgment aff'd, 16 F.3d 338 (9th Cir. 1994); Goldstein (Joel H., Elaine P.) v. Commissioner of Internal Revenue, 89 T.C. 535, 544, 1987 WL 45157 (1987); Biagiotti v. C.I.R., T.C. Memo. 1986-460, 1986 WL 21685 (1986).

[2]Williford v. C. I. R., T.C. Memo. 1992-450, T.C.M. (RIA) ¶ 92450 (1992).

[3]Murphy v. C. I. R., T.C. Memo. 1991-276, 1991 WL 104312 (1991), rev'd on other grounds, 8 F.3d 28 (9th Cir. 1993).

government]."[4] Chart 3-3 demonstrates how the court resolved claims of divergent FMVs urged by the taxpayer and the government through their respective appraisers.

---

[4]Murphy v. C. I. R., T.C. Memo. 1991-276, 1991 WL 104312 (1991), rev'd on other grounds, 8 F.3d 28 (9th Cir. 1993).

Chart 3–3: Comparison of Disputed FMVs Prior to and After Adjudication

	FMV	FMV	FMV	FMV	FMV	FMV	FMV	FMV	FMV	FMV	FMV
Case:	*Ashkar*	*Koftinow*	*Hunter*	*Monaghan*	*Murphy*	*Lightman*	*Williford*	*Doherty*	*Shein**	*Shein***	*Warhol****
Taxpayer	700,000	750,000	29,625	80,000	500,000	25,000	500,000	200,000	45,000	17,000	103,353,738 [estate]
IRS	25,000	275,000	<7,549	1,000	30,000	9,000	150,000	100	15,000–25,000	3,000–5,000	708,000,000 [lawyer]
Court	337,500	600,000	7,459	3,000	30,000	18,360	375,000	30,000	25,000	5,000	390,979,278
Average	354,167	541,667	14,878	28,000	18,667	17,453	341,667	76,700	28,333–31,667	8,333–9,000	405,676,869

* Values obtained for work by one artist.

** Values obtained for work by another artist.

*** Values obtained for artist's works in estate determined in an action by executor's attorney against estate in a county surrogate court, and not in a tax proceeding involving taxpayer claim with the government.

§ 3:22 Tax matters—Burden of proof for FMV

The IRS determination of FMV in a notice of deficiency to a taxpayer is presumptively correct.[1] The taxpayer bears the burden of proving by a preponderance of the evidence that the IRS determination of FMV is erroneous.[2] This same burden and level of proof applies to the taxpayer's showing that his FMV is correct.[3] However, if the IRS determination of FMV in a notice of deficiency is "zero," courts have mitigated the taxpayer's burden of proof, not by "shifting" the burden, but by "somewhat lighten[ing]" it.[4] When the deficiency is litigated in the Tax Court, the IRS bears the burden of proof for new government claims or newly raised issues. But the burden of proof may be on either the taxpayer or the IRS if new issues are raised in the Claims Court or a district court.

§ 3:23 Tax matters—Standard of review

The applicable standard of review for findings of fact is the clearly erroneous standard, held to be the applicable standard for reviewing FMV findings made by the court. However, there is a major qualification of the standard pertinent to value disputes. The question of what criteria the appraiser used to determine value is considered a question of law. The appraiser's methodology is thus subject to a de novo standard of review.[1]

[Section 3:22]

[1]Welch v. Helvering, 290 U.S. 111, 115, 54 S. Ct. 8, 78 L. Ed. 212 (1933); Rule 142(a); *see also* Shein v. C.I.R, T.C. Memo. 1987-329, 1987 WL 40384 (1987) (arts context).

[2]Rule 142(a); *see* Biagiotti v. C.I.R., T.C. Memo. 1986-460, 1986 WL 21685 (1986); Lightman v. C.I.R., T.C. Memo. 1985-315, 1985 WL 14942 (1985).

[3]*See, e.g.,* Reynolds v. C.I.R., T.C. Memo. 1981-714, 1981 WL 11092 (1981) (taxpayers failed to bear their burden of proof on FMV for four watercolor paintings by J. Mammen).

[4]Engel v. Comm'r, T.C. Memo 1993-362 (1993).

[Section 3:23]

[1]Estate of Palmer v. C.I.R., 839 F.2d 420, 44 Ed. Law Rep. 1063 (8th Cir. 1988) (result unchanged by Tax Reform Act of 1986).

§ 3:24 Nontax matters

FMV is the tax standard for value, but appraisers estimate values for purposes other than tax.[1] These include sales, insurance policies, uninsured losses, and marital dissolution. Each purpose and situation may have its own policies, terms, and guidelines for establishing value, e.g., actual cash value, or replacement cost minus depreciation, which should be discussed by the appraiser and the client. Thus, where a fire destroyed artworks in a gallery, a federal district court found that the value of consigned artworks should be determined at its fair market value at the time of the fire and that value was an issue of fact to be determined by the jury.[2]

B. METHODOLOGIES OF VALUATION

§ 3:25 Generally

There are basically three methods of valuing property: (1) market;[1] (2) income; and (3) cost.[2] Market is the most common for art, cost is occasionally used. Within each of these, more than one valuation method exists. The choice of method for determining value is within the appraiser's discretion. Sound appraisal practice may require several different methodologies. Tax courts favor appraisals that rely upon multiple analyses and imaginative and precise

---

[Section 3:24]

[1]Babcock, "A Look at Valuation Science," ASA, *A Handbook on the Appraisal of Personal Property* 3.

[2]Davis v. Rowe, 1991 WL 181100 (N.D. Ill. 1991), later proceeding, 1992 WL 5905 (N.D. Ill. 1992), summary judgment denied, 1992 WL 112237 (N.D. Ill. 1992), later proceeding, 1993 WL 34867 (N.D. Ill. 1993)(fair market value required notwithstanding policies of insurance for art, proceeds of which consignor to gallery claimed were not paid to her under terms of gallery consignment agreement).

[Section 3:25]

[1]USPAP (1993) uses term "sales" method.

[2]Cost methods for art have been used: Koftinow v. C.I.R., T.C. Memo. 1986-396, 1986 WL 21606 (1986), recommendation regarding acquiescence, AOD- 1987-23, 1987 WL 430249 (I.R.S. AOD 1987) (reconstruction costs of art determined by cost of building replicas); *see also* Estate of Palmer v. C.I.R., 839 F.2d 420, 44 Ed. Law Rep. 1063 (8th Cir. 1988) (reproduction cost of renovating Victorian mansion).

solutions to the valuation question of "unique" artworks. Depending upon data available, the following methodologies and data have been given weight in determining fair market value:

(1) Market: acquisition costs,[3] price lists,[4] median prices,[5] weighted prices,[6] auction prices,[7] private sales,[8] future uses,[9] insured values,[10] blockage discounts,[11] and bona fide market offers.[12]

---

[3]Furstenberg v. U.S., 219 Ct. Cl. 473, 595 F.2d 603 (1979); Williford v. C. I. R., T.C. Memo. 1992-450, T.C.M. (RIA) ¶ 92450 (1992) ("comparable sales of similar properties that are reasonably proximate in time represent the best evidence of fair market value"); Biagiotti v. C.I.R., T.C. Memo. 1986-460, 1986 WL 21685 (1986); Peterson v. C.I.R., T.C. Memo. 1982-438, 1982 WL 10730 (1982); Farber v. Comm'r, T.C. Memo 1974-155, aff'd in unpublished opinion (2d Cir. Nov. 20, 1975).

[4]Hunter v. Comm'r, T.C. Memo (P2-H) ¶ 86-308 (1986); *see also* Rev. Proc. 66-49 in Appendix 7.

[5]Ferrari v. C.I.R., T.C. Memo. 1989-521, 1989 WL 109420 (1989), judgment aff'd, 931 F.2d 54 (4th Cir. 1991).

[6]Ferrari v. C.I.R., T.C. Memo. 1989-521, 1989 WL 109420 (1989), judgment aff'd, 931 F.2d 54 (4th Cir. 1991).

[7]Furstenberg v. U.S., 219 Ct. Cl. 473, 595 F.2d 603 (1979); Williford v. C. I. R., T.C. Memo. 1992-450, T.C.M. (RIA) ¶ 92450 (1992); Mathias v. Commissioner of Internal Revenue, 50 T.C. 994, 998, 1968 WL 1498 (T.C. 1968), acq. 1969-1 C.B. and acq. 1969-2 C.B. and recommendation regarding acquiescence, 1969 WL 20641 (I.R.S. AOD 1969).

[8]Furstenberg v. U.S., 219 Ct. Cl. 473, 595 F.2d 603 (1979); Williford v. C. I. R., T.C. Memo. 1992-450, T.C.M. (RIA) ¶ 92450 (1992); Mathias v. Commissioner of Internal Revenue, 50 T.C. 994, 998, 1968 WL 1498 (T.C. 1968), acq. 1969-1 C.B. and acq. 1969-2 C.B. and recommendation regarding acquiescence, 1969 WL 20641 (I.R.S. AOD 1969).

[9]Dubin v. C.I.R., T.C. Memo. 1986-433, 1986 WL 21643 (1986) (uncut stones donated at value of $1.2 million based upon future sale in jewelry stores after cutting into gemstones rejected).

[10]*See, e.g.,* Angell v. C.I.R., T.C. Memo. 1986-528, 1986 WL 21740 (1986), aff'd, 861 F.2d 723 (7th Cir. 1988); Lightman v. C.I.R., T.C. Memo. 1985-315, 1985 WL 14942 (1985); Lio v. C.I.R., 85 T.C. 56 (1985), aff'd sub nom., Orth v. Comm'r, 813 F.2d 837 (7th Cir. 1987), Skripak v. Commissioner of Internal Revenue, 84 T.C. 285, 1985 WL 15315 (1985).

[11]Hunter v. Comm'r, T.C. Memo (P2-H) ¶ 86-308 (1986); Skripak v. Commissioner of Internal Revenue, 84 T.C. 285, 1985 WL 15315 (1985); *see also* Smith's (David) Estate v. Commissioner of Internal Revenue, 57 T.C. 650, 1972 WL 2557 (1972), acq. 1974-2 C.B. and recommenda-

(2) Cost: reproduction cost,[13] and replacement cost under the "french point system."[14]

Examples of each of these methods of valuation are beyond the scope of this treatise, however, some are discussed in context.

C. SELECTING THE PROPER MARKET

§ 3:26 Market selection is a question of fact

The FMV of property varies depending upon the market in which the property is sold.[1] To determine FMV, the proper market (termed the "relevant" market) must be identified for the property. Determination of the proper market is a question of fact for the trier of fact,[2] that is reviewed for clear error.[3] The Tax Court can reject as improper the relevant market selected by either the IRS or the taxpayer,[4] and can disregard valuations made in improper markets.[5] The "selection of the relevant market at a given time for appraisal purposes is tantamount to

---

tion regarding acquiescence, 1974 WL 36002 (I.R.S. AOD 1974) and aff'd, 510 F.2d 479 (2d Cir. 1975) (blockage discount first applied to estate works of art).

[12]Ashkar v. C. I. R., T.C. Memo. 1991-11, 1991 WL 2056 (1991).

[13]Estate of Palmer v. C.I.R., 839 F.2d 420, 44 Ed. Law Rep. 1063 (8th Cir. 1988).

[14]The French Point System establishes prices by calculating a square inch unit price of a given artwork by the artist based on a recorded sale and multiplying the size of subject property of the same artist by the unit price. *See* Williford v. C. I. R., T.C. Memo. 1992-450, T.C.M. (RIA) ¶ 92450 (1992); Harken v. C.I.R., T.C. Memo. 1985-468, 1985 WL 15096 (1985); Cukor v. Comm'r, 27 T.C.M. (CCH) 90 (1968).

[Section 3:26]

[1]Biagiotti v. C.I.R., T.C. Memo. 1986-460, 1986 WL 21685 (1986).

[2]Anselmo v. Commissioner of Internal Revenue, 80 T.C. 872, 1983 WL 14829 (1983), decision aff'd, 757 F.2d 1208, 1213 (11th Cir. 1985).

[3]Sammons v. C.I.R., T.C. Memo. 1986-318, 1986 WL 21525 (1986), aff'd in part, rev'd in part, 838 F.2d 330 (9th Cir. 1988).

[4]Koftinow v. Comm'r, T.C. Memo (P2-H) ¶ 86,396 (1986) (statue valued in improper market makes appraisal report erroneous).

[5]Koftinow v. Comm'r, T.C. Memo (P2-H) ¶ 86,396 (1986) (offered by IRS); Goldman v. C.I.R., 388 F.2d 476, 478 (6th Cir. 1967); Lio v. Comm'r, 85 T.C. 56 (1985), aff'd sub nom., Orth v. Comm'r, 813 F.2d 837 (7th Cir. 1987); Skripak v. Commissioner of Internal Revenue, 84 T.C. 285, 1985 WL 15315 (1985); Anselmo v. Commissioner of Internal

selecting the price."[6]

Section 170 of the Internal Revenue Code (IRC) for charitable contributions and the regulations thereunder are silent about how to select the relevant market. It is well established that estate and gift tax regulations for market selection are applied to Section 170 charitable contributions.[7] Guidelines for relevant market selection are:

> [T]he [FMV] of an item of property to be determined by the *sale price of the item in a market . . . in which such item is most commonly sold to the public,* taking into account the location of the item wherever appropriate. Thus, in the case of an item . . . which is generally obtained by the public in the retail market, the [FMV] of such an item of property is the price at which the item or comparable item would be sold at retail.[8]

Even though property may be unique, a market exists for valuing the property.[9] Where there are persons willing to purchase, "[t]he fact that a piece of property is unique does not . . . establish that there is no market."[10] Similarly, even if the property is unlawfully obtained and available for likely sale in an illicit market, there exists a market for valuation purposes.[11] "(b) [P]ersonal property has several measurable marketplaces and the appraisal must

---

Revenue, 80 T.C. 872, 1983 WL 14829 (1983), decision aff'd, 757 F.2d 1208 (11th Cir. 1985).

[6]Anselmo v. Commissioner of Internal Revenue, 80 T.C. 872, 1983 WL 14829 (1983), decision aff'd, 757 F.2d 1208 (11th Cir. 1985).

[7]Anselmo v. Commissioner of Internal Revenue, 80 T.C. 872, 1983 WL 14829 (1983), decision aff'd, 757 F.2d 1208 (11th Cir. 1985).

[8]Reg. §§ 20.2031-1(b), 25.2512-1 (emphasis added); *see also* 26 CFR § 601.105; Rev. Proc. 65-19 (in Appendix 7) (retail sales of tangible personal property at auction).

[9]Publicker v. C.I.R., 206 F.2d 250, 60 A.L.R.2d 1295 (3d Cir. 1953) (evaluating FMV for gift tax purposes of unique jewels).

[10]Publicker v. C.I.R., 206 F.2d 250, 60 A.L.R.2d 1295 (3d Cir. 1953).

[11]*See, e.g.,* Jones v. Comm'r, T.C. Memo 1991-28 (street market for cocaine); Caffery v. Comm'r, T.C. Memo 1990-498 (retail street market for low quality marijuana); Priv. Ltr. Rul. 9152005 (Aug. 30, 1991) (document may not be used or cited as precedent) (for stolen property that can only be sold in an illicit market, IRS position is that there is still a "market" for estate tax purposes; the relevant illicit market is the particular illicit market in which such property is generally sold; this is the "discreet retail markets of the international network of traf-

identify, define, and analyze the appropriate market consistent with the purpose of the appraisal."[12]

§ 3:27 Key to market selection—Market of ultimate consumers

Fair market value of an item of property is determined in the market where such items are "most commonly sold to the public,"[1] [or] to a "retail customer who is the ultimate consumer of the property."[2] Every retail sale is not co-terminous with a sale to the ultimate consumer. "[A] sale to the ultimate consumer is any sale to . . . persons who do not hold the item for subsequent resale."[3]

The inquiry into proper market selection does not terminate based upon presentation of retail sales for purposes of determining FMV; the specifics of the transaction and the location of the sale to the taxpayers in various markets is examined.[4] In Skripak v. Commissioner,[5] the court found that scholarly reprint books are ordinarily

---

fickers in stolen art as well as the legitimate retail art markets consisting of international auction firms" where the price would be the "highest price that would have been paid at that time").

[12]USPAP Standards Rule 7-3.

[Section 3:27]

[1]Reg. §§ 20.2031-1b, 25.2512-1; *see* Goldman v. C.I.R., 388 F.2d 476, 478 (6th Cir. 1967); Lio v. C.I.R., 85 T.C. 56 (1985), aff'd sub nom., Orth v. Comm'r, 813 F.2d 837 (7th Cir. 1987), Skripak v. Commissioner of Internal Revenue, 84 T.C. 285, 1985 WL 15315 (1985); Anselmo v. Commissioner of Internal Revenue, 80 T.C. 872, 1983 WL 14829 (1983), decision aff'd, 757 F.2d 1208 (11th Cir. 1985).

[2]Goldstein (Joel H., Elaine P.) v. Commissioner of Internal Revenue, 89 T.C. 535, 544, 1987 WL 45157 (1987); Anselmo v. Commissioner of Internal Revenue, 80 T.C. 872, 882, 1983 WL 14829 (1983), decision aff'd, 757 F.2d 1208 (11th Cir. 1985); Ashkar v. C. I. R., T.C. Memo. 1991-11, 1991 WL 2056 (1991).

[3]Goldman v. C.I.R., 388 F.2d 476, 478 (6th Cir. 1967); Lio v. Comm'r, 85 T.C. 56 (1985), 1985 WL 15372, (1985)aff'd sub nom., Orth v. Comm'r, 813 F.2d 837 (7th Cir. 1987)..

[4]Lightman v. C.I.R., T.C. Memo. 1985-315, 1985 WL 14942 (1985) (taxpayers contend that only relevant retail prices are those from the "orderly private market" which constitutes private treaty sales or gallery sales to collectors or museums but not public auction sales). For definition of these terms *see* Auction Ch 5.

[5]Skripak v. Commissioner of Internal Revenue, 84 T.C. 285, 1985 WL 15315 (1985).

sold to the ultimate consumer in a "retail market place, comprised largely of institutional buyers (libraries) and, to a minor extent, of individuals seeking a specific scholarly text." But, the court rejected the taxpayer's evidence of publisher's retail prices. Similarly, retail sales made at auction are not necessarily sales to the ultimate consumer.[6] A dealer's retail sale to collectors just days before the donation was rejected as a sale to ultimate consumers because the dealer had purchased the artworks in bulk for bulk resale.[7] Where a consumer has a choice of several sources for an item, the most expensive retail source is not necessarily the proper retail market.[8]

§ 3:28 Key to market selection—Bona fide sales

The most probative evidence of fair market value of donated art is the actual price paid in a bona fide sale if the sales transaction occurs at or near the time of contribution.[1] In Orth v. Commissioner,[2] the Seventh Circuit stated that purchase price accurately reflects FMV where there is only a brief interval between the purchase and the donation. In Hunter,[3] the purchase price of prints one year prior to donation was deemed fair market value of the prints even though the price reflected a discount

---

[6]Ferrari v. C.I.R., T.C. Memo. 1989-521, 1989 WL 109420 (1989), judgment aff'd, 931 F.2d 54 (4th Cir. 1991).

[7]Goldstein (Joel H., Elaine P.) v. Commissioner of Internal Revenue, 89 T.C. 535, 1987 WL 45157 (1987); *see also* Lio v. C.I.R., 85 T.C. 56 (1985), aff'd sub nom., Orth v. Comm'r, 813 F.2d 837 (7th Cir. 1987).

[8]Lio v. C.I.R., 85 T.C. 56 (1985), aff'd sub nom., Orth v. Comm'r, 813 F.2d 837 (7th Cir. 1987); *but cf.* Priv. Ltr. Rul. 9152005 (Aug. 30, 1991) (document may not be used or cited as precedent) (for property that can only be sold in an illicit market, there is still a market for estate tax purposes; the relevant illicit market is the particular illicit market in which such property is generally sold; this is the "discreet retail markets of the international network of traffickers in stolen art as well as the legitimate retail art markets consisting of international auction firms" where the price would be the "highest price that would have been paid at that time").

[Section 3:28]

[1]In re Lisser, 90-2 U.S. Tax Cas. (CCH) ¶ 50,352 (N.D. Tex. 1990); Hunter v. Comm'r, T.C. Memo (P2-H) ¶ 86-308 (1986).

[2]Orth v. C.I.R., 813 F.2d 837, 842 (7th Cir. 1987).

[3]Hunter v. Comm'r, T.C. Memo (P2-H) ¶ 86-308 (1986).

below price lists or comparable prices.[4] And, in In re Lisser,[5] the purchase price of a graphics collection twelve months before donation was held the best indication of value.

But if a contemporaneous sale cannot be established, markets must be chosen where sales would or could occur. The general rule for proper market selection is the market of "ultimate consumers," associated with, but not always located in a retail market.

§ 3:29 Key to market selection—Bona fide offers

The next best indicator after actual sales is bona fide offers to purchase. In Ashkar,[1] the taxpayers donated to Duke University religious center some Judaica (religious holy manuscript fragments from the Torah) ordinarily not offered in the retail market because of rarity and specialty. In determining who the ultimate consumers would be for such materials, the court found collectors of like antiquities, and decided that the relevant market in those circumstances was a collector's market. The court found there had been bona fide offers to purchase the Judaica approximately one year prior to taxpayer's donation of the collection because the person making the offer was a knowledgeable collector of like antiquities and had the financial capability to pay the $337,000 if the offer had been accepted.

§ 3:30 Key to market selection—Most active markets

The most appropriate market for an item among ultimate consumers is "the most active marketplace for the

---

[4]Hunter v. Comm'r, T.C. Memo (P2-H) ¶ 86-308 (1986) (reductions in prices of publisher's retail price list for prints that constituted excess inventory).

[5]In re Lisser, 1990 WL 105824 (N.D. Tex. 1990).

[Section 3:29]

[1]Ashkar v. C. I. R., T.C. Memo. 1991-11, 1991 WL 2056 (1991).

particular item involved."[1] The way to establish an active market is to provide examples of comparable sales prices within that market.[2]

Where taxpayers purchased dozens of prints from a corporation that exclusively made sales in contemplation of donations it arranged with qualified institutions, the court determined that the most active market at the time of the donation was a market for sale qua donation specially established by the corporation as a basis of its business.[3] The taxpayers were not able to convince the court that retail galleries in a tourist area of San Francisco constituted the most active market for batiks and hand carvings they had collected in Thailand and subsequently donated to museums in the United States.[4]

§ 3:31 Key to market selection—Auction markets

Auction is an undifferentiated mixed market of wholesalers and retail customers. Since traders and ultimate consumers both buy at auction, auction generally is not recognized by the tax courts as a distinct market in terms of proper market selection for charitable contributions.[1] In Biagiotti,[2] the court explained why auction is not an appropriate market of ultimate consumers for charitable contributions:

> Prices at auction depend to a large extent on the level of bidding, and it is difficult to label prices as wholesale or retail since collectors, dealers, and occasionally buyers for museums all acquire pieces there. As a result, items purchased may or may not be resold at a later dates.

However, tax courts have accepted auction as the relevant

[Section 3:30]

[1]Ashkar v. C. I. R., T.C. Memo. 1991-11, 1991 WL 2056 (1991); Lio v. C.I.R., 85 T.C. 56 (1985), aff'd sub nom., Orth v. Comm'r, 813 F.2d 837 (7th Cir. 1987); Biagiotti v. C.I.R., T.C. Memo. 1986-460, 1986 WL 21685 (1986).

[2]Jennings v. C.I.R., T.C. Memo. 1988-521, 1988 WL 117368 (1988).

[3]Hunter v. Comm'r, T. C. Memo (P2-H) ¶ 86-308 (1986).

[4]Jennings v. C.I.R., T.C. Memo. 1988-521, 1988 WL 117368 (1988).

[Section 3:31]

[1]Jennings v. C.I.R., T.C. Memo. 1988-521, 1988 WL 117368 (1988).

[2]Biagiotti v. C.I.R., T.C. Memo. 1986-460, 1986 WL 21685 (1986).

market where taxpayers presented no comparables from retail markets and no retail market for the artworks could be found by IRS appraisers because the artists were from other countries, were unknown in the United States, and had no following.[3]

Even if auction is not the proper market, auction prices have been occasionally considered legitimate comparables among other evidence to establish FMV.[4] (For estate tax purposes, auctions have been specially designated as appropriate for establishing retail sales prices of tangible personal property in decedent's estate.)[5] But some courts disregard auction prices as comparables because "auctions sales [prices] can only be characterized as a mixture of wholesale and retail prices."[6]

Even outside tax courts, auction sales prices have been considered "idiosyncratic rather than accurate reflections" of the market.[7] Auction sales prices were not considered determinative of the amount in controversy to satisfy diversity jurisdiction in federal court.[8] Where the property converted consists of unique goods like artworks, the appropriate measure of damages is the value of the item at trial.[9]

---

[3]Jennings v. C.I.R., T.C. Memo. 1988-521, 1988 WL 117368 (1988).

[4]Furstenberg v. U.S., 219 Ct. Cl. 473, 595 F.2d 603 (1979); Mathias v. Commissioner of Internal Revenue, 50 T.C. 994, 1968 WL 1498 (T.C. 1968), acq. 1969-1 C.B. and acq. 1969-2 C.B. and recommendation regarding acquiescence, 1969 WL 20641 (I.R.S. AOD 1969).

[5]Rev. Proc. 65-19 (§ 3: "Where . . . there is a bona fide sale of an item of tangible personal property at a public auction, the price for which it is sold will be presumed to be the retail sales price of the item at the time of sale.").

[6]Biagiotti v. C.I.R., T.C. Memo. 1986-460, 1986 WL 21685 (1986).

[7]Pagliai v. Del Re, 2000 WL 122142 (S.D. N.Y. 2000) (citations omitted) (action for replevin and conversion of fifteenth century painting).

[8]Pagliai v. Del Re, 2000 WL 122142 (S.D. N.Y. 2000) (sale price of $74,000 at auction in January 1997 would not be sufficient to dismiss complaint for conversion of painting on ground that amount in controversy was less than jurisdictional $75,000).

[9]Pagliai v. Del Re, 2000 WL 122142 (S.D. N.Y. 2000) (auction price does not establish damage amount for conversion).

§ 3:32 Key to market selection—International markets

Some courts focus upon markets in the taxpayer's environs or that of the donee-institution,[1] presumably relying upon the language of Section 20.2031-1(b) of the Regulations, which states that market selection should "tak[e] into account the location of the item." Some courts accept a broader market, particularly where the market is "thin" for the particular item of donation,[2] or has international significance.[3] As O'Keeffe[4] explains, selecting comparables from relevant markets and choosing the relevant market may require broad-based analysis in terms of geography. The appraiser must "distinguish between the markets for European and American artists." Acceptance of expanding markets implicitly incorporates recognition of global retail price flattening, international art pricing, international franchising, and trade agreements.[5]

§ 3:33 Key to market selection—Miscellaneous markets

The courts, sometimes on their own or through the parties involved, have identified a variety of specialty markets (numismatic) and markets not commonly recognized by appraisers or the trade (glamour market; celebrity market; collector's market). The IRS has also identified a market for stolen art, which it calls the "illicit market" or,

[Section 3:32]

[1]Harken v. C.I.R., T.C. Memo. 1985-468, 1985 WL 15096 (1985).

[2]Estate of O'Keeffe v. C.I.R., T.C. Memo. 1992-210, T.C.M. (RIA) ¶ 92210 (1992); Williford v. C. I. R., T.C. Memo. 1992-450, T.C.M. (RIA) ¶ 92450 (1992).

[3]Priv. Ltr. Rul. 9152005 (Aug. 30, 1991) (document may not be used or cited as precedent; an international market of collectors for certain types of stolen art).

[4]Estate of O'Keeffe v. C.I.R., T.C. Memo. 1992-210, T.C.M. (RIA) ¶ 92210 (1992).

[5]Estate of O'Keeffe v. C.I.R., T.C. Memo. 1992-210, T.C.M. (RIA) ¶ 92210 (1992); Krauskopf v. C.I.R., T.C. Memo. 1984-386, 1984 WL 15036 (1984).

euphemistically, the "discreet retail market."[1] Nothing in the Code or the Regulations prohibits identification of a new market, but it must be supported objectively as the "relevant" market pursuant to the foregoing principles.

IV. TAX APPRAISALS

A. CHARITABLE CONTRIBUTIONS

§ 3:34 Internal Revenue Service (IRS) Rule 170 and Regulations

Section 170(a) of the Internal Revenue Code (IRC) allows as deductions on federal income tax all or part of the appraised value of contributions or gifts to a Section 170(c) entity within the taxable year, reduced as provided in Section 170(e)(1). Section 170(a)(1) provides, in pertinent part: "There shall be allowed as a deduction any charitable contribution . . . payment of which is made within the taxable year." A charitable contribution is defined as a "contribution or gift to or for the use of" any of the designated entities.[1] Section 170(c) allows the contribution to made to the following entities: "A corporation, trust, . . . fund or foundation. . . organized and operated exclusively for . . . educational purposes."[2]

Section 170 refers to tax-exempt organizations under Section 501(c)(3).[3] Most museums qualify as Section 501(c)(3) entities under the "operational test" based upon their organization and operation for educational purposes under Section 1.501(c)(3)3-(1)(c) of the Regulations, but all arts foundations and organizations do not; eligibility

---

[Section 3:33]

[1]Priv. Ltr. Rul. 9152005 (Aug. 30, 1991) (document may not be used or cited as precedent; FMV for stolen art in the estate for purposes of valuing the decedent's estate is the highest price that would have been paid in the discreet market or legitimate art market at the time of death).

[Section 3:34]

[1]IRC § 170(c) (education is among the purposes exempt from taxation under IRC § 501(c)(3); *see also* Reg. § 1.501(c)(3)3-1(d)(1)(i)(f), 1.501(c)(3)3-1(d)(3)(i).

[2]IRC § 170(c)(2).

[3]*See* IRS Pub. 78, "Cumulative List of Organizations" 328, for list of recognized educational institutions qualifying under IRC § 170.

should be investigated for organizations qualified to receive Section 170 contributions.[4]

The contribution covers various types of property; this discussion focuses upon individual taxpayer[5] donations of tangible personal property.[6] Section 170A0-1(c)(1) of the Regulations provides that the amount of charitable contributions made in property other than money is generally the fair market value of the property at the time of contribution.

The IRS recognizes that personal property contributions include art, antiques, and artifacts (art objects). Art is described by the IRS as "paintings, sculptures, watercolors, prints, drawings, ceramics, antique furniture, decorative arts, textiles, carpets, silver, rare manuscripts, historical memorabilia, and other similar objects."[7] The IRS description is not restrictive; other unique objects have been donated and successfully claimed as deductions on tax returns.[8]

Section 170 can act as a federal tax incentive to donors who make charitable contributions of arts objects to

---

[4]*See* St. Louis Science Fiction Ltd. v. C.I.R., T.C. Memo. 1985-162, 1985 WL 14791 (1985) (arts organization not qualifying under IRC § 501(c)(3); *see also* Martin S. Ackerman Foundation v. C.I.R., T.C. Memo. 1986-365, 1986 WL 21569 (1986) (private arts foundation involved in arranging donations of art to museums supported with nonpublic sources did not qualify under IRC § 501(c)(3)).

[5]For contested corporate donations of art, *see* Hanrahan v. Kruidenier, 473 N.W.2d 184 (Iowa 1991) (minority shareholders suit contesting corporate donation of artworks valued at $250,000 to art museum prior to corporate liquidation); Kahn v. Sullivan, 594 A.2d 48 (Del. 1991) (shareholder litigation involving Occidental Petroleum Corporation whose Chair, Armand Hammer, acquired personal art collection, and whose outside directors purported to make a charitable contribution to "construct and fund an art museum" for the collection).

[6]For architecture, *see* § 3:61.

[7]IRS Form 8283, § B, pt. 1, reproduced in Appendix 6; Rev. Proc. 96-15, § 4.01, reproduced in Appendix 7.

[8]*See, e.g.,* Williford v. C. I. R., T.C. Memo. 1992-450, T.C.M. (RIA) ¶ 92450 (1992) (architectural frieze); Goldstein (Joel H., Elaine P.) v. Commissioner of Internal Revenue, 89 T.C. 535, 1987 WL 45157 (1987) (warehouse receipts); *see also* Isaacs v. C. I. R., T.C. Memo. 1991-473, 1991 WL 187966 (1991) (tapestries and book).

museums and other qualified institutions.[9] The incentive lies in allowing the taxpayer to deduct on federal income tax returns a dollar-for-dollar deduction for all or part of the FMV of the donation at or near the date of donation, subject to qualifications and conditions relating to percentage limitations.[10] An individual taxpayer, for example, ordinarily may only deduct charitable contributions to the extent that they do not exceed 50 percent of adjusted gross income; for capital gain property, the taxpayer may ordinarily deduct up to 30 percent of adjusted gross income; and for capital gain property, the taxpayer may ordinarily deduct up to 30 percent of adjusted gross income; for capital gain property, the taxpayer may ordinarily deduct up to 30 percent of adjusted gross income.[11] Excess charitable contributions may be carried forward over five successive years following the contribution and are deductible subject to limitations.[12]

Charitable contributions comprise a significant portion of appraisal practice. Appraisers are regularly retained by both government and taxpayers to appraise artworks under Section 170. The IRS has its own Art Advisory Panel that screens the values claimed for charitable contributions.[13] Until 1996, the Art Advisory panel reviewed art values claimed by taxpayers in tax returns already filed when the contribution, gift, or devise had already occurred. Effective 1996, taxpayers reporting transfers of art by contribution, gift, or devise may seek a Statement of Value *prior* to filing by requesting such a statement from the IRS after January 15, 1996.[14]

There have been many revisions to tax laws affecting charitable giving during the last decade, including new laws passed in 1993. The current status of contributions should be investigated through the most current legal materials. Major legislation affecting charitable contributions of art from 1984 to 1993 includes the following:

---

[9]IRC § 170(c).

[10]*See* IRC § 170(b)(1)(A)–(B), 170(b)(2).

[11]IRC § 170(b)(1)(C)(i).

[12]IRC § 170(d)(1) (individuals); 170(d)(2) (corporations).

[13]*See* § 3:46.

[14]IRS Rev. Proc. 96-15, reproduced in Appendix 7.

(1) Deficit Reduction Act of 1984[15] whereby the IRS added substantiation requirements to the regulations for Section 170, effective January 1, 1985. The concept of qualified appraisers and qualified appraisals was created and applied to any charitable contribution of more than $5,000 made after December 31, 1984.[16]

(2) The Tax Reform Act of 1986 whereby the tax benefits of charitable contributions of artwork to qualified institutions were effectively eliminated by treating the amount of appreciation of capital gain personal property, i.e., art, as a tax preference item in computing alternative minimum taxable income (AMT). A tax preference item means the amount is deductible for regular tax, but not for AMT. Since AMT generally affects only higher income taxpayers, who are often the owners of valuable artworks, the 1986 law was viewed as discouraging art donations to museums. Whether a donation of appreciated artworks would subject a particular taxpayer to AMT depends upon the individual taxpayer, the amount of appreciation, other tax preferences, classification of income as ordinary income or capital gains or combination and other factors.

(3) Omnibus Budget Reconciliation Act of 1989 whereby Congress revised and repealed sections on tax deficiency, interest, and penalty sections involving valuations, overvaluations, undervaluations, and negligence.[17]

(4) The Revenue Reconciliation Act of 1990[18] effective January 1, 1991 to December 31, 1991 (time period called the window), whereby the appreciated value of charitable contributions of personal property (for taxpayers whose adjusted gross income exceeds $100,000) would no longer be included in the definition of capital gain property

---

[15]Pub. L. No. 98-369, § 155, 98 Stat. 494, 691.

[16]Temp. Reg. § 1.170A-13 (for "qualified appraisers" and "qualified appraisals"), now 26 CFR § 1.170A-13.

[17]*See* §§ 3:64 to 3:73.

[18]Pub. L. No. 101-508, §§ 11001–11901, amending IRC § 57(a)(6)(B).

and the appreciation on such property is not a line item tax preference. The taxpayer is entitled to claim FMV deduction for donated artworks under both regular tax and AMT.

(5) The Tax Extension Act of 1991[19] extended the window, effective December 11, 1991, by adding to Section 57(a)(6) the following language: "In the case of a contribution made before July 1, 1992, in a taxable year beginning in 1992, such term shall not include any tangible personal property."[20] In 1992, Congress reexamined the effects of the appreciated property charitable contribution on museums and the arts and issued a joint report.[21]

(6) The Revenue Reconciliation Act of 1993 repealed Section 57(a)(6).[22]

§ 3:35 Significance of Section 170 for the arts

Congress crafted Section 170 of the Internal Revenue Code to stimulate and reward charitable contributions; Section 170 is considered by the arts community to be a government sanctioned method to transfer unique and valuable works from private collectors to institutions. The incentive to donate art from the private sector to the museum sector is central to America's position on the role of the arts in a democratic culture: art publicly accessible through geographic and socioeconomic dispersal. The museum system in America reflects this position, but contends it could not exist as a public repository of exhibition objects without tax induced patronage. When the tax incentive for charitable contributions was removed by the Tax Reform Act of 1986, patronage was curtailed. According to the Association of American Museums, the 1986 Act resulted in a 40 percent decrease in art donations.

The 1992 congressional joint committee report presents

---

[19]Pub. L. No. 102-227, § 112, 105 Stat. 1686, 1689.

[20]Pub. L. No. 102-486, § 1915, continued extension effective for tax years beginning after December 31, 1992.

[21]Joint Comm. Report, H.R. 2264, 102d Cong. 2d Sess. (Jan. 27, 1992).

[22]Pub. L. No. 103-66, §§ 13171(a), 13172 (repeals IRC § 57(a)(6)).

an alternative interpretation of the tax law effect, pointing out that although the art donation may be curtailed during the lifetime of the taxpayer, there is no data to indicate that art would not be bequeathed upon death. In other words, the Tax Reform Act of 1986 may have slowed up the gift giving process, but did not extinguish it. The Joint Committee further analyzed the AMT effect on art donations as follows:

> The . . . data on charitable donations also present a mixed picture of the effect of tax deductions on gifts of appreciated property. Although gifts of appreciated property declined [since 1986], the total value of gifts to charity has continued to grow [t]he decline [of appreciated property gifts] has been largely offset by increases in cash gifts.
>
> The decline in . . . contributions received by . . . museums, may be due in part to factors other than the AMT treatment of donated appreciated property. Such factors include . . . increased investment in art and higher art prices during the mid-1980s, tougher appraisal rules and penalties enacted in 1984, and competition . . . from other non-profit organizations.[1]

The market data supports the conclusion that instead of giving, after 1986 art collectors began selling art, heightening the art boom and exacerbating the art bust. The influx of privately held art that flowed into the auction markets remained privatized because the bidding was largely done by other private interests, many, if not most, inexperienced as to art and auction. Initially, the abundant supply of artworks as a result of privately held works being disposed of by auction instead of donation did not cause prices to drop. During the boom period, "increased market activity and competition drove up the prices of works of art."[2]

Few museums had acquisition budgets to compete in these bidding wars, a financial reality that obfuscated robust debate on what role institutions could and should have in market situations where art is selling for distorted

---

[Section 3:35]

[1]Jt. Comm. Report, H.R. 2264, 102d Cong., 2d Sess. (Jan. 27, 1992).

[2]Estate of O'Keeffe v. C.I.R., T.C. Memo. 1992-210, T.C.M. (RIA) ¶ 92210 (1992).

values—and, in retrospect, false values.[3] Some works, given charitable contribution amendments,[4] will be donated to museums, creating ethical and moral questions regarding institutional acquiescence to valuations made by the donor and the appraiser on the requisite IRS forms. The consequences of overpriced artworks affect not just the art market, but also the arts as a whole.

The following sections describe how arts contributions are documented and valued by appraisers according to IRS requirements, and identify the types of litigated issues that arise when the taxpayer and the IRS disagree upon value.

§ 3:36 IRS Form 8283: Donor-donee tax filing obligations

The taxpayer whose donation of art is valued at an amount less than or equal to $500 does not need to provide the IRS with information or documentation other than the regular federal income tax return; for individual taxpayers, this ordinarily means filing Form 1040.

A taxpayer seeking a deduction for donated art valued at more than $500 must attach to the federal income tax return Form 8283, entitled "Noncash Charitable Contributions."[1] Form 8283 basically establishes a valuation hierarchy: as the value claimed for the work rises, the appraisal reporting requirement increases. Form 8283 uses the following "value points" based upon the amount of deduction claimed to determine the degree and extent of appraisal reporting: summarized in Chart 3-4 as follows:

---

[3] *See* §§ 3:77 to 3:107.

[4] *See* § 3:34.

[Section 3:36]

[1] *See* Appendix 6 for Form 8283 and its instructions.

Chart 3-4: Form 8283 Submission Requirements *

Value of Deduction Claimed	Form 8283 Submission Requirements
(1) Individual items worth $500 or less	No appraisal requirement for items less than $500, but see Section B, Part II re: identifying artworks under $500 that are part of larger total values
(2) Individual items or groups of similar items of property** worth more than $500, but less than or equal to $5,000	Section A, Part I Appraisal from a qualified appraiser (appraisal does not have to be submitted with form)
(3) Individual items or groups of similar items worth more than $5,000, but less than $20,000	Section B Qualified Appraisal Appraisal Summary
(4) Individual items worth $20,000 or more [if donated after 1987]	Qualified Appraisal (a) Sign and attach to Form 8283 a qualified appraisal for each object valued at more than $20,000. (b) Obtain 8″ × 10″ color photograph or 4″ × 5″ color transparency prior to donation. (submit photo/transparency upon request) (c) Groups of similar items where total deduction is $20,000 or more also require qualified appraisals.

* *See* Appendix 6.

** "[S]imilar items of property" means "property of the same generic category or type, such as . . . lithographs, paintings, photographs."

§ 3:37 Appraisal documentation—Introduction

Appraisals relied upon for tax purposes must comply with minimum guidelines provided in Section 1.170A-13 of the Regulations and Revenue Procedure 66-49, subsequently modified by IRS Revenue Procedure 96-15.[1] Although Revenue Procedure 66-49 involves valuation of unique objects in general, its "significant section" was intended to be charitable contributions under Section 170. In fact, Revenue Procedure 66-49 has become a veritable standard for all art appraisals, regardless of tax purpose, pursuant to Section 3, the minimum procedural formatting standards for "appraisal reports."[2] Those standards are beefed up for taxpayers who seek a pre-transfer Statement of Value from the IRS for artworks whose appraised value is $50,000 or more.[3]

Appraisal reports contain basic information pertaining to the artwork, the artist, and the market. Appraisals prepared for taxpayers to determine FMV, but not submitted with tax returns should be supported by appraisal reports. The IRS can impose additional requirements for particular appraisals, and it has done so through the "qualified appraisal."[4] The qualified appraisal must be submitted with Form 8283 for donations valued at more than $20,000; for donations between $5,000 and $20,000, the IRS requires an "Appraisal Summary," which is a summary of a "qualified appraisal." For items appraised at $50,000 or more, taxpayers seeking a prefiling Statement of Value under new revenue procedures effective in 1996 must submit, along with their request to the IRS, a quali-

---

[Section 3:37]

[1] *See* Appendix 7 for Rev. Proc. 66-49 and Rev. Proc. 96-15.

[2] Estate of Querbach v. A & B Appraisal Serv., No. cv. L-089362-85 (N.J. Super. 1987) (Rev. Proc. 66-49 sets the standard for negligence in case involving estate tax).

[3] Rev. Proc. 96-15, §§ 3, 6, reproduced in Appendix 7; items appraised at less than $50,000 may also be reviewed under this procedure at the taxpayer's request if one item meets the $50,000 threshhold and the IRS agrees the Statement of Value would be "in the best interest of efficient tax administration." Rev. Proc. 96-15, §§ 3, reproduced in Appendix 7.

[4] Reg. § 170A-13(c)(3).

fied appraisal[5] that meets additional, specified guidelines,[6] a completed appraisal summary,[7] and payment of a prescribed fee.[8] Finally, USPAP and applicable codes of ethics may recommend or require disclosure of additional information in the appraisal.

§ 3:38 Appraisal documentation—Appraisal report—Contents

The appraisal report requirements are specified in Section 3.02 of Revenue Procedure 66-49, and the report must satisfy Rule 143(f). These include the appraiser's qualifications; statements of value and definition of value; basis of appraisal; date property was valued; signature of appraiser; and date; complete description of the property, including subject matter, medium, artist, creation date, and interest transfered; cost, date, and manner of acquisition, history of the art, including proof of authenticity, if available; photographs of the art under IRS Form 8283 (not required for submission unless requested); statement of factors upon which the appraisal is based, including comparable sales prices and dealers' catalogue prices; state of the art market; exhibition record; and the standing of the artist among his peers and with critics.

Failure to provide the appraiser's qualifications contrary to Revenue Procedure 66-49 has not been grounds to reject an appraisal, but appraisals that do not meet the "minimum guidelines for appraisal formats suggested by . . . Rev. Proc 66-49 " have been rejected.[1]

---

[5]*See* § 3:40.

[6]*See* Rev. Proc. 96-15, § 6, reproduced in Appendix 7.

[7]*See* § 3:41.

[8]*See* Rev. Proc. 96-15, § 5.01(2), reproduced in Appendix 7.

[Section 3:38]

[1]In re Lisser, 1990 WL 105824 (N.D. Tex. 1990) (debtor's surviving spouse disputed IRS reevaluation of charitable contribution of silkscreens to Goucher College from $39,000 to $6,700, but court disallowed her submitted appraisal because it did not conform to Rev. Proc. 66-49).

§ 3:39 Appraisal documentation—Appraisal report—Evidentiary effect

An appraisal report is an expert report, and constitutes the expert's direct testimony.[1] An expert report must be submitted to the court and an opposing party not later than thirty days prior to trial. The court has discretion to allow additional direct testimony regarding an appraisal report but is not obligated to do so.[2]

§ 3:40 Appraisal documentation—Qualified appraisal

A "qualified appraisal," for purposes of Section 170(c), is a document that "relates to an appraisal . . . made not earlier than sixty days prior to the date of contribution . . . ; is prepared, signed and dated by a qualified appraiser . . . ; does not involve a prohibited appraisal fee, and includes a precise statement of detailed information recited in Tax. Reg. 1.170A-13(c)(3)(ii)." The taxpayer must submit a qualified appraisal attached to Form 8283 for each artwork valued at more than $20,000, or art whose aggregate value is more than $20,000 donated after December 31, 1987. The taxpayer must submit a qualified appraisal if a Statement of Value is sought.[1]

§ 3:41 Appraisal documentation—Appraisal summary

An "appraisal summary" is a "summary of a qualified appraisal" made on an IRS prescribed form, signed and dated by the donee and the qualified appraiser, and includes a precise statement of detailed information recited in Section 1.170A-13(c)(4)(ii) of the Regulations. For each item of art donated after December 31, 1987, valued at less than $20,000 but more than $5,000, the taxpayer or appraiser must complete an "Appraisal Sum-

---

[Section 3:39]

[1]Tax Rule 143(f).

[2]Estate of Scull v. C.I.R., T.C. Memo. 1994-211, 1994 WL 179764 (1994).

[Section 3:40]

[1]Rev. Proc. 96-15, § 6, reproduced in Appendix 7; *see also* § 3:46.

mary" currently prescribed on Form 8283, Part I.

The appraisal summary, specified in Section 1.170A-13(c)(4) of the Regulations and required by Revenue Procedure 96-15, generally requires the following:

Checklist 3-1: Checklist for Appraisal Summary

(1) Description of property in detail
(2) Summary of overall condition
(3) Manner of acquisition and date of acquisition by donor
(4) Donor's cost or adjusted basis
(5) Date the donee received property
(6) Statement regarding bargain sale and amount of any consideration received from the donee for the contribution (for contributions after June 6, 1988)
(7) FMV of property on date of contribution
(8) Declarations of appraiser
(9) Signature or acknowledgment of donee
(10) Signature or certification of appraiser
(11) Signature of donor
(12) All necessary tax identification information, i.e., addresses, phone numbers, etc.

§ 3:42 Appraisal documentation—Qualified appraiser

A "qualified appraiser" is an individual who declares in the appraisal summary that he holds himself out the public as an appraiser, is qualified to value the subject property, is not a donee, donor, or employee or relative, and understands the penalty for false or fraudulent overstatements of value in the qualified appraisal or appraisal summary. A precise statement of detailed information regarding the qualified appraiser is recited in Section 1.170A-13(c)(5) of the Regulations.

§ 3:43 Appraisal documentation—Appraiser certifications and donee acknowledgments—Certification

An appraiser whose appraisals are used to support Form

8283 values must sign the Form 8283 Certification. The appraisal must be made by a qualified appraiser, defined in Section 1.170A-13(c)(5) of the Regulations. The Regulations are detailed and specific. A few examples are listed here. Parties to the donation and their employees and relatives are not qualified appraisers, and cannot sign the certification. Persons who sold, exchanged, or gave the property to the donor may sign the certification if the property is donated within two months of the donor's date of acquisition and the appraised value does not exceed the acquisition price.

§ 3:44 Appraisal documentation—Appraiser certifications and donee acknowledgments—Acknowledgment

Part IV of Form 8283 requires the donee to acknowledge its qualification under section 170(c) and its receipt of the donated property, and requires an authorized individual to sign the acknowledgment on behalf of the donee. However, Form 8283 states that the "donee not represent concurrence in the claimed market value." If the donee sells, exchanges, or otherwise disposes of the donation or any portion of it within two years after the date of receipt, the donee must file IRS Form 8282, "Donee Information Return," and furnish a copy to the donor.

§ 3:45 IRS office of art appraisal services

The IRS office of Art Appraisal Services (AAS) employs fulltime art appraisers who review FMV claims for charitable contributions, gift and estate taxes. The IRS district offices refer charitable contribution claims to the AAS on returns selected for audit when the taxpayer claims a deduction greater than $20,000. AAS reviews the valuations in conjunction with consultations by the Art Advisory Panel (the Panel). Determinations of value by the Panel in conjunction with AAS represent the position of the IRS to the taxpayer. AAS assists government counsel in explaining and supporting its values at examination and litigation.

§ 3:46 Art advisory panel

The Art Advisory Panel, authorized by the Treasury

Department, is a federal advisory committee chartered by Congress. The Panel, established in 1968, was rechartered by Congress in 1992.[1] The Panel assists the IRS by reviewing and evaluating personal property appraisals submitted to support FMV deduction on taxpayers' federal income, estate, or gift taxes.[2]

Chaired by an IRS employee from AAS, the Panel is a "voluntary group of distinguished art experts who advise the IRS about the value of particular works of art."[3] Panelists include dealers, critics, curators, museum directors, and historians appointed by the Commissioner of the IRS for rotating terms of tenure.[4] From 1968 to 1984 the Panel had twelve members, and subsequently expanded to twenty-five. Meeting once or twice a year in Washington, D.C., panelists are reimbursed for travel expenses under government rates, but receive no compensation and agree to refrain from making appraisals for federal tax purposes during their tenure.

The Panel is charged with independent determination of valuation at meetings closed to the public. The Panel initially reviews the taxpayer's documentation in conjunction with relying upon its own investigation, which may include requests for photographic documentation and/or a direct examination of the art. Panel conclusions are reviewed by the AAS. The recommendations of FMV are sent to the IRS office with a report explaining the determination. Taxpayers may request a reconsideration of an adjusted value if they provide additional new information. If AAS deems the information has probative value, it submits it to the Panel for reconsideration.

§ 3:47 Statement of value

Taxpayers may seek review after January 15, 1996, of

[Section 3:46]

[1]57 Fed. Reg. 3243 (1992).

[2]57 Fed. Reg. 3243 (1992).

[3]Williford v. C. I. R., T.C. Memo. 1992-450, T.C.M. (RIA) ¶ 92450 (1992).

[4]Furstenberg v. U.S., 219 Ct. Cl. 473, 595 F.2d 603 (1979) (ability of former members of Panel to fairly appraise same artworks before them as Panel members on prior occasions).

the value of artworks appraised at a value of $50,000 or more at a pretransfer, prefiling stage through a new IRS Revenue Procedure 96-15, enabling taxpayers to request a Statement of Value, for a fee.[1] The Statement of Value does not replace the appraisal process in any way; taxpayers must still comply with tax requirements for appraisals, and then some, given that the Statement of Value imposes additional—not substituted—requirements upon the taxpayer and appraiser. The list is long and specific for contributions, and estate and gift taxes,[2] and includes items like provenance, authentication, and photographic documentation.[3] A taxpayer's executed declaration in support of the request is also required.[4]

In short, the taxpayer is paying the IRS a fee to vet an appraisal for which he has also paid, a function the IRS currently performs for no additional fee under existing regulations. If the IRS issues a Statement of Value that confirms the appraisal value, it may be relied upon by the taxpayer in his return, without resort to further administrative or judicial review. However, if the Statement of Value differs from the taxpayer's appraisal value, the taxpayer is still required to submit the Statement with his return, and may submit additional information to support the different value. In other words, he is in no better, and is perhaps in a worse, position than if he had gone forward under existing procedures. As a practical matter, absent newly discovered or inadvertently omitted information, the likelihood that the taxpayer will convince the IRS to reinstate his appraised value seems slight, after the time-consuming and costly request to vet, and presumably, time and costs of the vet itself. Moreover, nowhere in the new procedures is it spelled out just how the vetting is done, or precisely who will do it. The taxpayer will have to weigh

---

[Section 3:47]

[1]Rev. Proc. 96-15, reproduced at Appendix 7; note that items under $50,000 may also be included if a request includes at least one item that satisfies the threshold.

[2]*See* Rev. Proc. 96-15, §§ 6 and 8, respectively, reproduced in Appendix 7.

[3]*See* Rev. Proc. 96-15, §§ 6 and 8, respectively, reproduced in Appendix 7.

[4]*See* Rev. Proc. 96-15, § 9.

the benefits, if any, of providing, in advance, notice to the governing of his "giving" portfolio, in the context of his donative obligations, tax and estate planning, and the individual particularities of the affected tax returns.

B. OWNERSHIP AS PREREQUISITE TO CONTRIBUTIONS

§ 3:48 Elements of ownership

A taxpayer must own the property he purports to transfer before he is entitled to make a deductible charitable contribution.[1] To determine the existence of ownership and timing of the charitable contribution, the court applies the same six-part analysis used to determine the existence and timing of an inter vivos gift, summarized as follows:

(1) competent donor;
(2) capable donee;
(3) clear and unmistakable intent on donor's part to divest himself irrevocably and absolutely of title, dominion, and control of the gift, in praesenti;
(4) irrevocable transfer of present legal title and dominion and control of entire gift to donee;
(5) delivery by donor to donee of gift or of most effectual means of commanding dominion of it; and
(6) donee's acceptance of gift.[2]

§ 3:49 Possession not required

Ownership is determined by the "right to beneficial enjoyment of the property, rather than the possession of the property."[1] In Hunter v. Commissioner, the date the donor executed a check for partial payment of the prints and signed a promissory note evidencing the balance was deemed to be the date title passed for purposes of a

[Section 3:48]

[1]Hunter v. Comm'r, T.C. Memo (P2-H) ¶ 86-308 (1986).

[2]Murphy v. C. I. R., T.C. Memo. 1991-276, 1991 WL 104312 (1991), rev'd on other grounds, 8 F.3d 28 (9th Cir. 1993) (citations omitted).

[Section 3:49]

[1]Hunter v. Comm'r, T.C. Memo (P-H) ¶ 86-308 (1986).

charitable contribution of art, notwithstanding that the donor never obtained possession of the art.[2]

In Murphy v. Commissioner,[3] a rock sculpture was never physically delivered to the donee-university. The donor, at his expense, placed it in storage and paid the fees. The court held that actual delivery is not necessary "where the donor and donee both acknowledge the gift and no third party is involved in the transaction."

§ 3:50 Formal documents of title unnecessary

Title does not have to be formally conveyed.[1] The date the donor executed a check for partial payment of prints and a promissory note for the balance has been deemed the date title passed for purposes of evaluating a charitable contribution of art.[2]

§ 3:51 Clouds on title

Art objects are particularly troublesome to appraisers in the area of title; a common practice is to place the issue of client ownership under the assumptions in the appraisal. Sometimes, the ownership is so questionable that the appraiser assumes the art is stolen property, and must decide how to proceed in a personally and professionally ethical manner.[1] In certain instances, the art may have a cloud on title even in the absence of theft.

---

[2]Hunter v. Comm'r, T.C. Memo (P-H) ¶ 86-308 (1986); Goldstein (Joel H., Elaine P.) v. Commissioner of Internal Revenue, 89 T.C. 535, 1987 WL 45157 (1987) (donors never obtained possession of posters donated to religious institution, but their contribution of warehouse receipts signifying posters in storage was sufficient).

[3]Murphy v. C. I. R., T.C. Memo. 1991-276, 1991 WL 104312 (1991), rev'd on other grounds, 8 F.3d 28 (9th Cir. 1993).

[Section 3:50]

[1]Hunter v. Comm'r, T.C. Memo (P-H) ¶ 86-308 (1986); *see also* Chamberlain v. Cocola Associates, 958 F.2d 282 (9th Cir. 1992).

[2]Hunter v. Comm'r, T.C. Memo (P-H) ¶ 86-308 (1986).

[Section 3:51]

[1]*See* §§ 3:108 to 3:130.

In Sammons v. Commissioner,[2] taxpayers donated to a museum Native American artifacts that contained feathers, bird claws, and other bird parts that were arguably in violation of the Eagle Protection Act,[3] the Migratory Bird Treaty Act,[4] and the Endangered Species Act.[5] The IRS argued that because the artifacts may have violated federal law subject to criminal and civil penalties, the taxpayers lacked title. The Tax Court rejected the argument, affirmed on appeal stating: "We conclude that the Sammons had a sufficient ownership interest in the [artifacts] to contribute them to the museum."

§ 3:52 Delivery and dominion

Charitable contribution deductions are possible only after delivery of the gift and upon the donor's parting with dominion and control of it.[1] In Murphy v. Commissioner,[2] where a deed of gift contained a restriction that the donee-university not dispose of the contribution of massive rock sculpture for a two-year period, the IRS argued that the donor was "not divested of dominion and control." After the donor testified that he did not intend for the art to revert back to him and the donee testified that it did not intend to sell the rock within the two-year period, the deduction was allowable under an interpretation of Section 1.170A0-1(e) of the Regulations. The court stated: "If an interest in property passes to, or is vested in, a charitable organization on the date of the gift, and the interest would be defeated by the subsequent performance of some act, . . . the possibility of occurrence of which appears on the date of the gift to be so remote as to be

---

[2]Sammons v. C.I.R., T.C. Memo. 1986-318, 1986 WL 21525 (1986), aff'd in part, rev'd in part, 838 F.2d 330 (9th Cir. 1988).

[3]16 U.S.C.A. §§ 668–668d.

[4]16 U.S.C.A. §§ 703–712.

[5]16 U.S.C.A. §§ 1531–1543.

[Section 3:52]

[1]Hunter v. Comm'r, T.C. Memo (P-H) ¶ 86-308 (1986).

[2]Murphy v. C. I. R., T.C. Memo. 1991-276, 1991 WL 104312 (1991), rev'd on other grounds, 8 F.3d 28 (9th Cir. 1993).

negligible, the deduction is allowable."[3]

§ 3:53 Duration of ownership: Capital gains and ordinary income

Section 170(e) distinguishes between contributions of property classified as ordinary income[1] and long-term capital gain. The contributed property must be held long enough to receive long-term capital gains treatment if it is sold.[2] Donations of ordinary income property are subject to further reductions.[3]

In Hunter v. Commissioner,[4] the IRS argued that donors who purchased prints for the purpose of donating them to qualified institutions became "art dealers" whose charitable contributions should be calculated as ordinary income property. Ordinary income property includes property held by the donor primarily for sale to customers in the ordinary course of a trade or business.[5] The Tax Court disagreed stating that art buyers "are not converted into art dealers by virtue of their donations. . . . The purchase of art should be viewed no differently than the purchase of stocks, stamps, gold, paintings, sculpture, or any other investment properties;"[6] sale of such properties produces long-term capital gain.

---

[3]Murphy v. C. I. R., T.C. Memo. 1991-276, 1991 WL 104312 (1991), rev'd on other grounds, 8 F.3d 28 (9th Cir. 1993).

[Section 3:53]

[1]*See* Andrew Crispo Gallery, Inc. v. C.I.R., T.C. Memo. 1992-106, 1992 WL 31221 (1992), decision aff'd in part and vacated in part, 16 F.3d 1336 (2d Cir. 1994), for a general discussion of tax consequences of selling art inventory and the comparison of sales of art as investment property or inventory.

[2]Biagiotti v. C.I.R., T.C. Memo. 1986-460, 1986 WL 21685 (1986) (property held sufficiently long); note that IRC § 57(a) was repealed in 1993.

[3]IRC § 170(e)(1).

[4]Hunter v. Comm'r, T.C. Memo (P-H) ¶ 86-308 (1986).

[5]*See* Williford v. C. I. R., T.C. Memo. 1992-450, T.C.M. (RIA) ¶ 92450 (1992), for a discussion of what constitutes a collection of art held primarily for sale in the ordinary course of business and held for investment.

[6]Hunter v. Comm'r, T.C. Memo (P-H) ¶ 86-308 (1986), *referring to* Anselmo v. Commissioner of Internal Revenue, 80 T.C. 872, 1983 WL 14829 (1983), decision aff'd, 757 F.2d 1208 (11th Cir. 1985).

C. PROPER VALUATION METHODOLOGIES

1. *Market Methods*

§ 3:54 Comparable sales prices

Comparable sales prices are perhaps the most common method used for artworks, and are given the greatest weight in determining FMV under a market methodology.[1] A comparable sales price is the "actual sales price" of properties similar to the subject property, which are then related to prices for the subject property.[2] "[C]omparable sales of similar properties that are reasonably proximate in time represent the best evidence of fair market value."[3] Comparability is based upon numerous characteristics encompassed in CROSSAQ,[4] with no one factor (aside from authenticity) being determinative. Among comparables, retail sales prices at galleries, if available and relevant to the type of property, provide the most significant criteria for FMV.[5]

Evaluating comparable sales at or near the time of contribution is a proper valuation technique providing that the "properties that provide the market benchmark have qualities substantially similar to the property for which a value is sought."[6] Sometimes, sales prior to the donation are valuable indicators of FMV because they reveal mar-

---

[Section 3:54]

[1]Estate of Andy Warhol, N.Y.L.J., Apr. 18, 1994, at 29 (Surrogate's Ct., NY County) ("No better indicator of [FMV] exists than the price a buyer has actually paid for a comparable work of art.").

[2]Estate of Palmer v. C.I.R., 839 F.2d 420, 423, 44 Ed. Law Rep. 1063 (8th Cir. 1988).

[3]Williford v. C. I. R., T.C. Memo. 1992-450, T.C.M. (RIA) ¶ 92450 (1992); *see also* Perdue v. C. I. R., T.C. Memo. 1991-478, 1991 WL 188862 (1991).

[4]Condition, rarity, ownership, size, subject matter, authenticity, quality; *see* § 2:11 for a complete definition.

[5]Ferrari v. C.I.R., T.C. Memo. 1989-521, 1989 WL 109420 (1989), judgment aff'd, 931 F.2d 54 (4th Cir. 1991) (retail sales of commercial galleries proper comparables); Biagiotti v. C.I.R., T.C. Memo. 1986-460, 1986 WL 21685 (1986) (retail sales prices in galleries are most reliable indicators of fair market value for pre-Columbian artifacts).

[6]Estate of Palmer v. C.I.R., 839 F.2d 420, 423, 44 Ed. Law Rep. 1063 (8th Cir. 1988).

ket trends.[7] Post-donation sales may also provide valuable comparables "if there are no uncertain probabilities or contingencies which affect the value of the property."[8]

In Koftinow v. Commissioner,[9] the court accepted evidence of comparable sale prices of large-scale sculptures and site specific sculptures made by other famous artists located in the same state as the creator to determine FMV of a unique, site-specific, seventy-two foot high sculpture by the artist whose work was the subject of the donation. In Murphy v. Commissioner,[10] where the artist who created a rock sculpture had few verifiable sales, the IRS expert provided comparable sales of sculptures by other artists. Sample testimony on comparable sales prices of sculptures demonstrates how an appraiser researched market, auction, and private sales to create comparable sales prices for the donated sculpture.

Chart 3-5: Expert Testimony in Murphy v. Commissioner[11] Based on Comparables

Artist	Price	Year	Reserve
Eduardo Paoluzzi	$10,540	1985	na
Francois Brochet	b.i.**	1983	$2,000–3,000
Frank Gallo	b.i.	1985	4,000–6,000
Buckminster Fuller	b.i.	1985	10,000–15,000
Red Grooms	4,400	1984	na
Sandro Chia	46,750	1984	na

[7] Isaacs v. C. I. R., T.C. Memo. 1991-473, 1991 WL 187966 (1991).

[8] Isaacs v. C. I. R., T.C. Memo. 1991-473, 1991 WL 187966 (1991); Perdue v. C. I. R., T.C. Memo. 1991-478, 1991 WL 188862 (1991).

[9] Koftinow v. C.I.R., T.C. Memo. 1986-396, 1986 WL 21606 (1986), recommendation regarding acquiescence, AOD- 1987-23, 1987 WL 430249 (I.R.S. AOD 1987).

[10] Murphy v. C. I. R., T.C. Memo. 1991-276, 1991 WL 104312 (1991), rev'd on other grounds, 8 F.3d 28 (9th Cir. 1993).

[11] Murphy v. C. I. R., T.C. Memo. 1991-276, 1991 WL 104312 (1991), rev'd on other grounds, 8 F.3d 28 (9th Cir. 1993) (testimony by Charles D. Peavy, valuation expert for IRS, as reported in opinion).

Chart 3-5: Expert Testimony in Murphy v. Commissioner[11] Based on Comparables*			
Artist	Price	Year	Reserve
Seiji Kunishima	100,000		commission
Strong	>100,000		commission

* Testimony by IRS expert to challenge taxpayer's claimed FMV for donated artwork by artist Strong.

** b.i. means bought-in. *See* § 5:22.

Interestingly, the appraiser included potential auction prices among the comparables, which are not accepted by all tax courts, as the following section makes clear. More noteworthy is the recitation of bought-ins among the comparables;[12] a bought-in cannot be a comparable sales price because a bought-in is not a sale: bought-in means no sale occurred at auction.

§ 3:55 Auction prices

Although gallery sales prices have virtually unanimous acceptance, there is a split in the tax opinions as to the propriety of sales at auction as reliable indicators of comparable values for purposes of FMV.[1] Courts are divided as to whether art auction sales provide appropriate comparables because auction buyers cannot easily be seg-

[12] *See* Ch 5.

[Section 3:55]

[1] Biagiotti v. C.I.R., T.C. Memo. 1986-460, 1986 WL 21685 (1986) (auction sales rejected where prices cannot be segregated into wholesale and retail components which depend upon the bidding); Ferrari v. C.I.R., T.C. Memo. 1989-521, 1989 WL 109420 (1989), judgment aff'd, 931 F.2d 54 (4th Cir. 1991) (auction prices not acceptable); *but cf.* Estate of Andy Warhol, N.Y.L.J., Apr. 18, 1994, at 29, (Surrogates Ct., N.Y. County) (auctions as an important market for contemporary art sales, providing that comparable auction sales are examined from more than one auction house). Auction prices may be relied upon by the tax courts in other circumstances, *see, e.g.,* Mathias v. Commissioner of Internal Revenue, 50 T.C. 994, 999, 1968 WL 1498 (T.C. 1968), acq. 1969-1 C.B. and acq. 1969-2 C.B. and recommendation regarding acquiescence, 1969 WL 20641 (I.R.S. AOD 1969). For use of auction sales prices in non-tax cases, *see* §§ 3:60 to 3:62.

regated into wholesale and retail categories,[2] thus blurring the market of the ultimate consumer. Common at auction are sales to the trade for resale in the secondary market; these are obviously not sales to the ultimate consumer in the retail market, and thus would not be appropriate comparables for determining value in the contribution context.

Auction prices have been deemed appropriate for determining fair market value in some cases.[3] In Lightman v. Commissioner,[4] the IRS used auction sales prices of works by the donated artists to support its appraisal. The effect was to devalue the FMV of taxpayers' donation of nineteen paintings donated to the El Paso Museum of Art in 1978. Although the taxpayer argued that public auction sales constituted a "disorderly" market of wholesale values, the Tax Court disagreed, stating: "auction sales prices are relevant to the determination of fair market value in this case. The controlling question is whether art auction sales represent sales to the ultimate consumer, not whether identical 'consumer' prices are also available to dealers."[5]

That "a significant number of auction sales [were] to consumers" persuaded the Tax Court that auction prices could constitute proper comparables for a determination of fair market value even though both the taxpayers and the IRS estimated that only 40 to 50 percent of auction mar-

---

[2]Biagiotti v. C.I.R., T.C. Memo. 1986-460, 1986 WL 21685 (1986); McGuire v. C. I. R., 44 T.C. 801, 1965 WL 1207 (T.C. 1965), acq. in result 1966-1 C.B. and acq. in result 1966-2 C.B.; Peterson v. Comm'r, T.C. Memo 1982-438 (1982); Mathias v. Commissioner of Internal Revenue, 50 T.C. 994, 999, 1968 WL 1498 (T.C. 1968), acq. 1969-1 C.B. and acq. 1969-2 C.B. and recommendation regarding acquiescence, 1969 WL 20641 (I.R.S. AOD 1969).

[3]Smith's (David) Estate v. Commissioner of Internal Revenue, 57 T.C. 650, 1972 WL 2557 (1972), acq. 1974-2 C.B. and recommendation regarding acquiescence, 1974 WL 36002 (I.R.S. AOD 1974) and aff'd, 510 F.2d 479 (2d Cir. 1975); Peterson v. Comm'r, T.C. Memo 1982-438 (1982); Farber v. Comm'r, T.C. Memo 1974-155, aff'd in unpublished opinion (2d Cir. Nov. 20, 1975).

[4]Lightman v. C.I.R., T.C. Memo. 1985-315, 1985 WL 14942 (1985).

[5]Lightman v. C.I.R., T.C. Memo. 1985-315, 1985 WL 14942 (1985).

ket sales were made to private consumers.[6] The court rejected expert testimony urging that comparable sales prices should be restricted to the "orderly private market," defined as private treaty sales by auction[7] or gallery sales to art collectors or museums.

§ 3:56 Bulk sales and distress sales

Bulk sales are sales made in "lots" or large numbers of artworks purchased or sold simultaneously.[1] The purchaser may or may not receive a discount from the seller for the bulk purchase. If the taxpayer can prove a true bargain has been made, he or she may be able to claim FMV at an amount higher than the bulk purchase price.[2] However, the fact that the art was purchased from a dealer who sells in bulk does not mean that every purchase made from him reflects a discounted bulk price. In Lightman,[3] the Tax Court found that for some taxpayers the purchase prices from a bulk dealer were the same as retail prices from other sources; therefore, their FMV was limited to purchase price. In Rimmer v. Commissioner,[4] the court applied the concept of a bulk discount in connection with a charitable contribution, the FMV of which it evaluated in combination with a modified blockage discount and other valuations.

Bulk sales should not be confused with forced or distress sale rates. A distress sale is a sale where one party is

---

[6]Lightman v. C.I.R., T.C. Memo. 1985-315, 1985 WL 14942 (1985).

[7]*See* § 5:23.

[Section 3:56]

[1]Lightman v. C.I.R., T.C. Memo. 1985-315, 1985 WL 14942 (1985); Anselmo v. Commissioner of Internal Revenue, 80 T.C. 872, 884, 1983 WL 14829 (1983), decision aff'd, 757 F.2d 1208 (11th Cir. 1985); Chiu v. Commissioner of Internal Revenue, 84 T.C. 722, 1985 WL 15340 (1985).

[2]Lightman v. C.I.R., T.C. Memo. 1985-315, 1985 WL 14942 (1985) (paintings purchased in bulk, where it could be shown that bulk purchase was made with adjusted discount, did not limit taxpayer's claim of FMV to bulk cost of artworks).

[3]Lightman v. C.I.R., T.C. Memo. 1985-315, 1985 WL 14942 (1985).

[4]Rimmer v. C.I.R., T.C. Memo. 1995-215, T.C.M. (RIA) ¶ 95215 (1995) (contribution to a book center en masse of 85,000 pieces of Yiddish sheet music that contained 650 separate titles).

"desperate for funds."[5] "The [FMV] of a particular item of property . . . is not to be determined by a forced sale price."[6] However, a bulk liquidation of substantial numbers of paintings does not necessarily indicate distress sale prices.[7]

§ 3:57 Blockage discounts

A blockage discount, which originated for artworks in the context of estate taxation,[1] has, on occasion, been applied to charitable contributions. In summary, a blockage discount simply means that in appraisal terms, the whole can be less than the sum of the parts.[2] A block is the total of the separate units of art. If a large block is sold at once, those sales would not garner the sum of the FMV for each of the artworks in the block. In short, abundant supply would depress market prices for each work. To account for this, courts consider value from the perspective of a series of staggered sales of artworks over sufficient time periods to achieve maximum, or at least reasonable, value, offset by carrying, inventory, marketing, interest, selling costs, promotion, maintenance insurance, and other costs.

The analysis further includes evaluating the effects of inflation against present value, with some, but not all, courts willing to offset one against the other for a "wash" in the interests of judicial economy.[3] Thus, the FMV of a block is not merely the total of each unit value in the block, but a discounted amount referred to as the "blockage discount."

Is the blockage discount a particular figure, like 10

---

[5]Perdue v. C. I. R., T.C. Memo. 1991-478, 1991 WL 188862 (1991) (acquisition cost of sunken treasure at distress sale rates does not establish FMV of charitable contribution).

[6]Reg. § 20.2031-1(b); *see also* Perdue v. Comm'r, 1991 WL 188862(1991).

[7]Lightman v. C.I.R., T.C. Memo. 1985-315, 1985 WL 14942 (1985).

[Section 3:57]

[1]*See* §§ 3:75 to 3:76.

[2]*See* §§ 3:75 to 3:76, for a detailed analysis of blockage discounts.

[3]Estate of Andy Warhol, N.Y.L.J., Apr. 18, 1994, at 29 (Surrogate's Ct., N.Y. County) (Surrogate's Court offset inflation and present value in proceeding to fix the compensation of counsel to the estate executor for Andy Warhol).

percent, or a variable tied to some objective number like the prevailing prime rate, or some other specified numerical amount? A blockage discount rate is a unique number arrived at on a case-by-case basis by the court. Invariably, the parties propose different discount rates, and experts on the same side typically use and apply different discount rates. The strength or weakness of a proposed rate is not the varied approaches to calculating discount rates; on the contrary, the courts seem grateful for multiple perspectives. The key is to justify the proposed discount on the facts for the particular artist and the potential and actual markets for distribution of the artworks.

In Skripak v. Commissioner,[4] the court applied a blockage discount to charitable contributions of reprint books purchased en masse for donation to qualified rural libraries. In Rimmer v. Commissioner,[5] the court utilized a modified blockage discount and other valuations in valuing a large charitable contribution of sheet music. In Hunter v. Commissioner,[6] the Tax Court found a blockage discount was not proper where the prints purchased by the taxpayer represented a small portion of the total number in each edition, and an even smaller portion of the total work produced and unsold by each artist.

§ 3:58 Median sales prices

Use of median sales prices to provide comparables has been upheld in instances where experts obtained high and low values for pre-Columbian artifacts, and then provided the median as the proper value.[1]

---

[4]Skripak v. Commissioner of Internal Revenue, 84 T.C. 285, 1985 WL 15315 (1985) (150,000 books purchased through contribution program).

[5]Rimmer v. C.I.R., T.C. Memo. 1995-215, T.C.M. (RIA) ¶ 95215 (1995) (contribution to a book center en masse of 85,000 pieces of Yiddish sheet music that contained 650 separate titles).

[6]Hunter v. Comm'r, T.C. Memo (P-H) ¶ 86-308 (1986) (marginal increase in supply by sale of taxpayers prints would "not have seriously affected the prices of these prints").

[Section 3:58]

[1]Ferrari v. C.I.R., T.C. Memo. 1989-521, 1989 WL 109420 (1989), judgment aff'd, 931 F.2d 54 (4th Cir. 1991) (unpublished disposition).

§ 3:59 Insurance policy values

Insured values do not necessarily provide comparables. In Ashkar v. Commissioner,[1] the court refused to consider a $1 million insurance policy on ancient artifacts as a comparable because the appraisal for insurance was prepared without direct examination. In Lightman v. Commissioner,[2] the taxpayers offered the value at which paintings were insured by the El Paso Museum of Art as "objective estimates of fair market value of donated artworks." The court disagreed, finding that the insured amounts "had no probative value" since the taxpayers determined the amounts for which the paintings were initially insured by the museum. In Chou v. Commissioner,[3] where taxpayers claimed a FMV for an opal at more than ten times the amount they insured it for in shipping the donation to the American Museum of Natural History, a negligence penalty imposed by the IRS was upheld on appeal.

Insurance policies can contribute to tax deficiencies, especially when they are fraudulently obtained. A taxpayer obtained an insurance policy for paintings by a Ghirlandaio and Piero della Francesca.[4] For hundreds of years the paintings have been, and remain, in the collection of the Vatican. The insured then claimed a theft occurred and recovered under the new policy. After an FBI raid, he admitted the theft was bogus, the insurance claim was fraudulent, and plead guilty to mail fraud. He did not, however, report the insurance proceeds on his federal income tax returns. The IRS determined income tax deficiencies and fraud penalties of $200,000.

[Section 3:59]

[1]Ashkar v. C. I. R., T.C. Memo. 1991-11, 1991 WL 2056 (1991); *but cf.* Lightman v. C.I.R., T.C. Memo. 1985-315, 1985 WL 14942 (1985) (court did not consider an appraisal based upon indirect examination a "defect in appraisal technique," stating, "reliance on photographs is not unusual in appraising paintings").

[2]Lightman v. C.I.R., T.C. Memo. 1985-315, 1985 WL 14942 (1985).

[3]Chou v. C. I. R., T.C. Memo. 1990-90, 1990 WL 16342 (1990), aff'd, 937 F.2d 611 (9th Cir. 1991) (appeal later opinion not for publication or citation except as provided by Ninth Circuit Rule 36-3).

[4]Ambroselli v. IRS, T.C. Memo 1999-158 (May 11, 1999).

2. *Reproduction Cost Methods*

§ 3:60 Generally

Reproduction cost or replacement cost is appropriate where there is "total lack of market."[1] The Eighth Circuit, for example, has accepted reproduction cost for determination of FMV, stating: "Reproduction cost is a relevant measure of fair market value when the property to be valued is unique, its market limited, and when there is no evidence of sales of comparable properties." For a cost method to be used as a measure of FMV, there must be a "probative correlation" between the cost of reproduction and FMV.[2]

§ 3:61 Architecture

Reproduction cost has also been used to value contributions of historic homes, where the property value on the real estate market would be inapt because it was not a viable sale property. The children of Dr. Palmer, the founder of chiropractic medicine, donated to the chiropractic college he founded a Victorian mansion located in the center of and surrounded by the campus.[1] Although Dr. Palmer and his family originally lived in the mansion, for many years prior to the donation it was used as a faculty center and dormitory, and had been subsequently renovated as an exhibition space to display chiropractic memorabilia.

The Tax Court used the market approach of comparable sales to determine the "highest and best use" of the mansion as a single family residence. The Eighth Circuit reversed, deciding that the Tax Court's findings were clearly erroneous, and remanded the case to the Tax Court for determination of FMV under the reproduction cost of the mansion with improvements, adjusted for depreciation.

[Section 3:60]

[1]Engel v. Comm'r, T.C. Memo 1993-362 (1993) (court used both market and replacement cost valuation methods).

[2]Estate of Palmer v. Comm'r, 420, 424 (8th Cir. 1988). Rev. Proc. 66-49 is reproduced in Appendix 7.

[Section 3:61]

[1]Estate of Palmer v. C.I.R., 839 F.2d 420, 424, 44 Ed. Law Rep. 1063 (8th Cir. 1988).

§ 3:62 Artworks

In Koftinow v. Commissioner,[1] a French Point System[2] approach was used to determine the value of a unique, site-specific, seventy-two foot high sculpture created and installed in 1969, but donated in 1979. The court found proper a method of extrapolating the value of the site-specific sculpture by taking the fair market values of smaller sculptures by the same artist, based upon sale prices,[3] and calculating reproduction costs based upon the costs of reconstructing a full-scale replica.

D. VALUELESS ART OBJECTS

§ 3:63 Generally

Do certain arts objects have no worth? In Shuman v. Commissioner,[1] investors sought deductions for depreciation and investment tax credits for lithographic master plates from which they had no intention of producing prints. The IRS appraiser found that the plates had no value, thus, no valuation method (cost, income, reproduction) was offered. The trial court granted summary judgment for the taxpayer, finding that the appraiser was unable to value the plates. The Fifth Circuit reversed and remanded, finding a genuine factual issue as to whether the plates were "valueless" as the IRS contended.[2] The appellate court found the appraiser's affidavit did not indicate he could not value the property but that his opinion was the property had no value. The appraiser's affidavit recited:

The term "master plate" is . . . misleading and . . . atypi-

[Section 3:62]

[1]Koftinow v. Comm'r, 1986 WL 21606.

[2]A French Point System establishes prices by calculating a square inch unit price of a given artwork by the artist based on a recorded sale and multiplying the size of subject property of the same artist by the unit price.

[3]Koftinow v. Comm'r, 1986 WL 21606. *Accord* Brown, *Ink, Paper, Metal, Wood: How to Recognize Contemporary Artists' Prints.*

[Section 3:63]

[1]Shuman v. U.S., 891 F.2d 557 (5th Cir. 1990).

[2]Shuman v. U.S., 891 F.2d 557 (5th Cir. 1990).

> cal to the legitimate art printing industry [and that] even if the [purchase] agreements had conveyed normal rights to reproduce, [those] rights would have little or no value . . . because . . . the quantity of reproductions and ancillary products which must be sold in order to recoup the cost of manufacture, distribution, promotion, advertisement and sale of these products would far outstrip demand. Therefore, neither the right to exploit those images nor even the so-called "master plates" has any value.[3]

Similarly, in Rose v. Commissioner,[4] the Sixth Circuit affirmed the tax court's refusal to allow taxpayers depreciation, miscellaneous deductions, or investment credits on reproduction masters of works by Pablo Picasso. The taxpayers reported zero income and depreciation expenses in the amount of $125,776 under an art business that had no activity. The "reproduction master" was a four by five inch color transparency taken from a thirty-five millimeter slide of a Picasso work. The cost of the creating the transparency was $200; the taxpayers paid $545,000. The Sixth Circuit, affirming the holding that the taxpayers did not have an actual and honest profit objective and the transactions were devoid of economic substance, wrote:

> Without investigation of the highly sophisticated art market into which they were entering, the taxpayers paid a total of $550,000. [T]he taxpayes [sic] did not receive or have available any independent appraisals of the value of the Picasso packages . . . . At trial, the taxpayers had two highly inflated appraisals . . . but neither appraiser could provide any data to support their assertions as to the sales potential of the reproductions.[5]

In Mast v. Commissioner,[6] the IRS initially contended an entire collection of nineteenth century glass stereoscopic negatives taxpayers donated to the University of California had a value of zero,[7] in contrast to the claimed charitable contribution of more than $1.5 million FMV. The court, rejecting the IRS expert, determined $1.25 mil-

---

[3]Shuman v. U.S., 891 F.2d 557 at 559 (5th Cir. 1990).

[4]Rose v. C.I.R., 868 F.2d 851 (6th Cir. 1989).

[5]Rose v. C.I.R., 868 F.2d 851 at 852 (6th Cir. 1989).

[6]Mast v. C.I.R., T.C. Memo. 1989-119, 1989 WL 26716 (1989).

[7]The IRS subsequently retained another appraiser who raised the FMV to just under $500,000.

lion FMV because the collections the expert had relied upon were not comparable collections to the donation. The IRS was charged with unreasonable conduct for its zero valuation and, in a subsequent opinion, it was required to pay the Masts' attorney fees.[8]

E. TAXPAYER LIABILITY: DEFICIENCIES, PENALTIES, AND INTEREST

1. *Additions to Tax for Negligence: Section 6653*

§ 3:64 Law before 1990

Section 6653(a)(1) of the Code imposed an addition to tax equal to 5 percent of the underpayment of tax "if any part of the underpayment of income tax is due to negligence or intentional disregard of rules or regulations."[1] Section 6653(a)(2) imposed an additional liability in the amount of 50 percent of the interest due "on that portion of the underpayment attributable to the negligence or intentional disregard."[2] Negligence in this context was defined as "lack of due care or failure to do what a reasonable and ordinarily prudent person would do under the circumstances."[3] Honesty, good faith, and disclosure by the taxpayer do "not always negate negligence.[4]

The IRS determined negligence under Section 6653 based upon the following: the taxpayers' acceptance of appraisals they should have known contained inflated values compared to other appraisals in their possession;[5] the taxpayers' failure to maintain records of prices paid for

---

[8]Mast v. C.I.R., T.C. Memo. 1989-438, 1989 WL 91729 (1989).

[Section 3:64]

[1]Engel v. Comm'r, T.C. Memo 1993-362 (1993) (underpayment not negligent where taxpayer went to one of the few available appraisers to perform appraisals for that type of property and sought highest possible valuation).

[2]Engel v. Comm'r, T.C. Memo 1993-362 (1993).

[3]Neely v. C.I.R., 85 T.C. 934, 947, 1985 WL 15422 (1985); Isaacs v. C. I. R., T.C. Memo. 1991-473, 1991 WL 187966 (1991).

[4]Isaacs v. C. I. R., T.C. Memo. 1991-473, 1991 WL 187966 (1991).

[5]Biagiotti v. C.I.R., T.C. Memo. 1986-460, 1986 WL 21685 (1986) (held not negligent).

art subsequently contributed;[6] the taxpayers' erroneous inclusion of artworks as charitable donations although the art was not actually donated;[7] and the sophisticated taxpayers' reliance upon appraisers whose valuations at the time of donation ($548,000) grossly exceeded the purchase price paid a few months prior ($140,000).[8]

If the IRS determined that a Section 6653 addition to tax was applicable, taxpayers "have the burden of disproving [the government's] determination,"[9] which is presumptively correct, and "must be sustained unless the taxpayer can establish that he or she was not negligent."[10] The taxpayer bore the burden of proof that the underpayment of tax was not due to negligence or intentional disregard[11] by showing that he or she acted "reasonably and prudently and exercised due care."[12]

Good faith reliance upon advice of competent, independent appraisers, lawyers, or accountants, "possessed of all the information," or appraisal reports attached to income tax returns might have provided relief from the imposition of Section 6653 additions to tax. Taxpayers had the burden of proving "that they acted reasonably and prudently and exercised due care in obtaining the appraisals of FMV which they use[ ] on . . . tax returns."[13] Taxpayers were required to present "some proof" in support of the FMV to

---

[6]Biagiotti v. C.I.R., T.C. Memo. 1986-460, 1986 WL 21685 (1986).

[7]Hunter v. Comm'r, T.C. Memo (P-H) ¶ 86-308 (1986) (held not negligent).

[8]Sammons v. C.I.R., T.C. Memo. 1986-318, 1986 WL 21525 (1986), aff'd in part, rev'd in part, 838 F.2d 330 (9th Cir. 1988).

[9]Biagiotti v. C.I.R., T.C. Memo. 1986-460, 1986 WL 21685 (1986).

[10]Biagiotti v. C.I.R., T.C. Memo. 1986-460, 1986 WL 21685 (1986).

[11]Rule 142(a); *see* Isaacs v. C. I. R., T.C. Memo. 1991-473, 1991 WL 187966 (1991).

[12]Rule 142(a); *see* Isaacs v. C. I. R., T.C. Memo. 1991-473, 1991 WL 187966 (1991).

[13]Rule 142(a); Biagiotti v. Comm'r, 52 T.C.M (CCH) 588 (1986); *but cf.* Hunter v. Comm'r, T.C. Memo (P-H) ¶ 86-308 (1986) (where Commissioner adds addition to tax under Section 6653(a) by amended answer, bears burden of showing taxpayer's underpayment was due to overvaluation of donated property).

show they had reasonably relied on it.[14] Demonstrating good faith reliance on appraisal reports had mixed results: additions to tax because of negligence,[15] and no additions to tax.[16] In Biagiotti,[17] the Tax Court did not accord any probative weight to the taxpayer's appraiser's report in determining the FMV of pre-Columbian artifacts, but did not find a negligence penalty was appropriate because the taxpayers had no reason to question the appraiser's ability.

§ 3:65 Law effective January 1, 1990

The Omnibus Budget Reconciliation Act of 1989[1] amended Section 6653, effective January 1, 1990, which no longer applies for purposes of charitable contributions. These provisions are now recited at Section 6662, and new definitions and special rules are provided at Section 6664.[2]

---

[14]Sammons v. C.I.R., T.C. Memo. 1986-318, 1986 WL 21525 (1986), aff'd in part, rev'd in part, 838 F.2d 330 (9th Cir. 1988).

[15]Goldstein (Joel H., Elaine P.) v. Commissioner of Internal Revenue, 89 T.C. 535, 1987 WL 45157 (1987) ("well-educated" taxpayers should have been aware that the present value of their purchase price of posters to a temple for small cash payment and four promissory notes "was far below the $20,000 claimed by them" as FMV of the posters); Murphy v. C. I. R., T.C. Memo. 1991-276, 1991 WL 104312 (1991), rev'd on other grounds, 8 F.3d 28 (9th Cir. 1993) (taxpayer who promoted site specific sculpture and provided appraiser with information for appraisal knew or should have known it would lead to overvaluation, thus, his reliance on appraisal was not reasonable and prudent).

[16]Williford v. C. I. R., T.C. Memo. 1992-450, T.C.M. (RIA) ¶ 92450 (1992) ($10,000 cost basis for architectural frieze reported in taxpayer's returns instead of $1,800 blamed on accountant who had relied upon appraisal—court found reliance justified because of reputation of appraiser); Isaacs v. C. I. R., T.C. Memo. 1991-473, 1991 WL 187966 (1991) (appraiser's failure to recite credentials in appraisal did not constitute grounds for taxpayer's unreasonable reliance on his appraisals); Sammons v. C.I.R., T.C. Memo. 1986-318, 1986 WL 21525 (1986), aff'd in part, rev'd in part, 838 F.2d 330 (9th Cir. 1988).

[17]Biagiotti v. C.I.R., T.C. Memo. 1986-460, 1986 WL 21685 (1986).

[Section 3:65]

[1]Pub. L. 101-239, § 7721, 103 Stat. 2106 (hereinafter cited as the 1989 Revenue Act).

[2]*See* § 3:72.

2. *Valuation Overstatement: Section 6659*

§ 3:66 Law before 1990

Overvalued artworks for purposes of obtaining distorted deductions for charitable contributions have been used as specific examples in legislative histories.[1] Additions to tax were imposed under Section 6659 because of underpayments attributable to valuation overstatements. A "valuation overstatement" was defined in Section 6659(c) as a "claim on a return that the value of any property is 150 percent or more of the amount determined to be the correct value."

If a valuation overstatement existed, the addition to tax for charitable contributions claimed in returns filed after December 31, 1984 was an amount equal to 30 percent of the underpayment attributable to the valuation overstatement.[2] Valuation overstatements involving charitable contributions have been assessed and liability has been found for additions to tax under section 6659;[3] in other cases, no additional tax liability was imposed.[4]

§ 3:67 Law effective January 1, 1990

The 1989 Revenue Act[1] repealed Section 6659, effective for returns due on or after January 1, 1990. The provisions are now recited at Section 6662, and revised definitions and special rules are provided at Section 6664.

[Section 3:66]

[1] *See, e.g.,* Joint Comm. on Tax'n, 97th Cong., 1st Sess, General Explanation of Econ. Recovery Act of 1981, 334 (1981).

[2] IRC § 6659(f)(1).

[3] Murphy v. C. I. R., T.C. Memo. 1991-276, 1991 WL 104312 (1991), rev'd on other grounds, 8 F.3d 28 (9th Cir. 1993) (site-specific sculpture); In re Lisser, 1990 WL 105824 (N.D. Tex. 1990) (graphics collection); Frates v. C.I.R., T.C. Memo. 1987-79, 1987 WL 40138 (1987) (paintings); Engel v. Comm'r, T.C. Memo 1993-362 (1993) (game mounts).

[4] Williford v. C. I. R., T.C. Memo. 1992-450, T.C.M. (RIA) ¶ 92450 (1992) (architectural frieze); Perdue v. C. I. R., T.C. Memo. 1991-478, 1991 WL 188862 (1991) (artifacts, coins and gold from sunken ship).

[Section 3:67]

[1] 1989 Revenue Act § 7721(c)(2).

3. *Substantial Understatement: IRC Section 6661(a)*

§ 3:68 Law before 1990

Section 6661(a) imposed an addition to tax where there was a substantial understatement of income tax in any given year.[1] Section 6661(a) provided: "if there is a substantial understatement of income tax for any taxable year, there shall be added to the tax an amount equal to 25 percent of the amount of any underpayment attributable to such understatement."[2] The Omnibus Budget Reconciliation Act of 1986 increased the penalty to 25 percent for penalties incurred after October 21, 1986[3] and the Omnibus Budget Reconciliation Act of 1989 repealed IRC Section 6661.

An understatement was determined "if there is an excess of the amount of tax required to be shown on the return over the amount of tax imposed which is shown on the return."[4] Section 6661(b) provided that a substantial understatement existed if the amount of the understatement exceeded the greater of 10 percent of the tax required to be shown on the return or $5,000.[5] The amount of the addition to tax assessed under Section 6661(a) was determined without regard to penalties imposed under Section 6659.[6]

[Section 3:68]

[1]*See, e.g.,* Isaacs v. C. I. R., T.C. Memo. 1991-473, 1991 WL 187966 (1991) (no understatement found).

[2]The Tax Reform Act of 1986 raised the penalty to 20 percent from 10 percent, effective January 1987.

[3]Pub. L. Nos. 99-514, 100 Stat. 2085; Pub. L. No. 100-203, 101 Stat. 1330; and Pub. L. No. 100-647, 102 Stat. 3342, respectively.

[4]Engel v. Comm'r, T.C. Memo 1993-362 (1993), *citing* IRC § 6661(b)(2)(a).

[5]IRC § 6661(b)(1)(A).

[6]IRC § 6661(b)(3); *see also* Murphy v. C. I. R., T.C. Memo. 1991-276, 1991 WL 104312 (1991), rev'd and remanded, 8 F.3d 28 (9th Cir. 1993) (no addition under IRC § 6661 because of effect of IRC § 6661(b)).

§ 3:69 Law effective January 1, 1990

The 1989 Revenue Act[1] repealed Section 6661, effective for returns the due date for which was January 1, 1990. These provisions are now recited at Section 6662, and revised definitions and special rules are provided at Section 6664.

4. *Increased Rates of Interest: Section 6621*

§ 3:70 Law before 1990

Increased rates of interest were upheld in cases involving "blatant misuse of the charitable donation provisions."[1] An increased rate of interest on tax liability was provided for in Section 6621(c): "interest accru[ing] after December 31, 1984 on a substantial underpayment attributable to a tax motivated transaction shall be 120 percent of the otherwise applicable rate." The increased interest was effective as to interest accruing after December 31, 1984 even if the tax motivated transaction was entered into before that date and "regardless of the date the return was filed."[2]

A tax motivated transaction included, inter alia, any valuation overstatement.[3] A "valuation overstatement" was defined in Section 6659(c) as a claim on a return that the value of any property is 150 percent or more of the amount determined to be the correct value.

The Tax Court raised a taxpayer's liability for increased interest under Section 6621 sua sponte.[4] Where tax motivated transactions resulted in underpayments of more than $1,000 based upon overvaluations of charitable contributions of artworks, increased rates of interest were

---

[Section 3:69]

[1] 1989 Revenue Act at § 7721(c)(2).

[Section 3:70]

[1] Williford v. C. I. R., T.C. Memo. 1992-450, T.C.M. (RIA) ¶ 92450 (1992) (underpayment of tax to be recalculated).

[2] Williford v. C. I. R., T.C. Memo. 1992-450, T.C.M. (RIA) ¶ 92450 (1992), *citing* H.R. Rep. 861, 98th Cong., 2d Sess., 1984-3 C.B. (Vol. 2) 1, 239.

[3] IRC § 6621(d)(3)(A)(i).

[4] Frates v. C.I.R., T.C. Memo. 1987-79, 1987 WL 40138 (1987).

applied to back taxes and imposed against taxpayers.[5]

§ 3:71 Law effective January 1, 1990

The 1989 Revenue Act,[1] repealed Section 6621(c), effective for returns the due date for which is January 1, 1990. These provisions are now recited at Section 6662, and revised definitions and special rules are provided at Section 6664.

5. *Law Effective January 1, 1990: Sections 6662 and 6664*

§ 3:72 Generally

Section 6662, "Imposition of Accuracy-related Penalty," provides penalties for understatements, negligence, substantial valuation misstatements, and substantial estate or gift tax valuation understatements, formerly covered in the separate (repealed or amended) Sections discussed above. Understatements and overstatements, as well as negligence, are redefined and categorized; Section 6662 is comprehensive and should be consulted for particulars. Section 6664, "Definitions and special rules," redefines underpayments and makes special rules for charitable contributions. No cases under the new laws involving artworks have been found. Presumably, the courts will continue to apply the tax principles that have evolved over the years in the context of the revised rules.

6. *Tax Shelters: Section 6700*

§ 3:73 Generally

Section 6700 is intended to discourage promoters of overvalued investments known as tax shelters. In a tax shelter, taxpayers typically overstate their cost basis in an

---

[5]Johnson v. C.I.R., 85 T.C. 469, 477, 1985 WL 15393 (1985) (addition upheld); Frates v. C.I.R., T.C. Memo. 1987-79, 1987 WL 40138 (1987) (addition imposed); Hunter v. Comm'r, T.C. Memo (P-H) ¶ 86-308 (1986); Engel v. Comm'r, T.C. Memo 1993-362 (1993) (addition upheld for game mounts); *but cf.* Perdue v. C. I. R., T.C. Memo. 1991-478, 1991 WL 188862 (1991) (no addition).

[Section 3:71]

[1]1989 Revenue Act at § 7721(b).

attempt to obtain deductions for depreciation and investment tax credits which are "unreal and produce distortions." Art has been the subject of tax shelter schemes.[1]

Section 6700 imposes penalties upon persons who participate, plan, arrange, or promote tax shelters as a means to obtain tax benefits known to be false or fraudulent, or a "gross valuation overstatement as to any material matter." "Gross valuation overstatement" is defined in Section 6700(b)(1) as a statement which "exceeds 200% of the amount determined to be the correct valuation."

In Shuman,[2] the Fifth Circuit reversed and remanded a Section 6700 case where the taxpayers claimed unrealistic deductions for depreciation and investment tax credits based upon their purchase of lithographic master plates. Their cash payment was $5,000, with an $80,000 balance recited in long-term promissory notes. The cost of the plates was unrealistic because $85,000 was not representative of the fair market value of the plates, compounded by the fact that the plates were purchased with long-term promissory notes. An IRS expert testified that the plates had no value, since the taxpayers had no intention of producing prints from them, stating: "The value of the rights implied by the terms 'masters' or 'master-plates' would be the net income from the sale of the prints produced after the recapture of all expenses other than the price of the rights."[3] Since no prints were being produced, the plates had no value.

In Skripak v. Commissioner,[4] the taxpayers participated in a charitable tax contributions tax shelter program involving scholarly reprint books. They signed documents evidencing purchase of the books at a cost of one-third of the publisher's catalogue retail list prices and waited the applicable capital gains holding period before donating the

---

[Section 3:73]

[1]Shuman v. U.S., 891 F.2d 557 (5th Cir. 1990); U.S. v. Petrelli, 704 F. Supp. 122 (N.D. Ohio 1986); Skripak v. Commissioner of Internal Revenue, 84 T.C. 285, 1985 WL 15315 (1985).

[2]Shuman v. U.S., 891 F.2d 557 (5th Cir. 1990).

[3]Shuman v. U.S., 891 F.2d 557 (5th Cir. 1990).

[4]Skripak v. Commissioner of Internal Revenue, 84 T.C. 285, 1985 WL 15315 (1985).

books to qualified libraries. They claimed deductions for the retail list prices, instead of the discounted prices. The Tax Court held the transaction was not a sham, but limited the amount of the contribution by reducing the FMV of the books to no more than 20 percent of the retail list prices.

The 1989 Revenue Act[5] amended Section 6700, effective for activities on or after January 1, 1990. Tax shelter cases may also be affected by Section 6662(d)(2)(C), "Special rules in cases involving tax shelters." Tax shelters involving the sale of valueless photographic plates of artwork have also been the predicate for injunctive action.[6]

F. APPRAISER LIABILITY UNDER THE INTERNAL REVENUE CODE

§ 3:74 Generally

Appraisers may be subject to civil penalties under Section 6701(a) for aiding and abetting an understatement of tax liability in their preparation of tax appraisals. The appraiser must know or have reason to believe that the appraisal will be used "in connection with any material matter" and, if used, would result in an understatement of tax liability.[1] The penalty is $1,000 per appraiser per period, or $10,000 if the return relates to tax liability of a corporation.[2] In addition to penalties, the Regulations provide for disqualifying the appraiser from federal practice.[3]

Whenever the IRS Director of Practice becomes aware that a penalty has been assessed after 1984, the Director can reprimand the appraiser or institute a disbarment of

---

[5] 1989 Revenue Act at § 7734.

[6] *See, e.g.*, U.S. v. Petrelli, 704 F. Supp. 122 (N.D. Ohio 1986) (federal government enjoins defendants from selling tax shelters whose subject was artwork plates from which prints were never published).

[Section 3:74]

[1] IRC § 6701(a).

[2] IRC § 6701(b).

[3] 1 CFR pt. 10.

the appraiser.[4] If an appraiser is disbarred, federal tax appraisals made by the appraiser on or after the effective date of disbarment are disregarded.[5] This means that during the term of disbarment, none of those appraisals can be used for any purpose or any taxpayer, other than as evidence that the taxpayer relied upon the appraisal in good faith.[6] The appraiser is also barred during the same period from presenting evidence or giving testimony.[7] The appraiser may be subject to discipline from the appraiser's professional appraisal organization,[8] and subject to suit.[9]

G. ESTATE AND GIFT TAXES

§ 3:75 Estates of artists: Blockage discount

Property in the decedent's gross estate is ordinarily valued at the FMV on the date of decedent's death.[1] Section 20.2031-1(b) of the Regulations defines FMV.[2] When an artist is the decedent, there typically exists a body of unsold works. For a prolific artist or an artist whose works did not consistently sell during his lifetime, the number can be considerable. A legislative proposal would amend the IRC to exclude the value of certain artworks created by the decedent from the gross estate.[3] Large numbers of artwork by a single artist cannot simultaneously be readily disposed of in the market without affecting the artworks' value.

Estates of artists raise unique market considerations because of the potential flooding of the market all at once with the artist's work. The FMV of individual works of art

---

[4]31 CFR § 10.78.

[5]31 U.S.C.A. § 330; 31 CFR pt. 10 ff.

[6]31 CFR § 10.77(b)(2); *see also* Biagiotti v. C.I.R., T.C. Memo. 1986-460, 1986 WL 21685 (1986) (appraiser disbarred under settlement agreement with Commissioner).

[7]31 CFR § 10.77(b)(2).

[8]Deficit Reduction Act of 1984, Pub. L. No. 98-369, 98 Stat. 494.

[9]*See* §§ 3:77 to 3:107.

[Section 3:75]

[1]IRC § 2031(a).

[2]*See* §§ 3:20 to 3:24.

[3]2001 H.R. 467, 107th Cong. 1st. Sess.

in the estate may be high; but if the works were simultaneously offered for sale on the artist's death, the availability of "such a large block . . . would . . . depress . . . price[s] . . . of each . . . individual work."[4] To determine FMV, the appraiser has to posit a hypothetical en bloc purchaser who buys for resale. Applying the concept of an en bloc purchaser as one who buys in bulk at a discount, and holds and resells piece by piece, or as slowly as the market will absorb the work without depressing prices, courts have accepted that for estate tax purposes, the FMV of the aggregate works of art in an estate are substantially less than the total FMV of each artwork. This has given rise to a discount on FMV known as "blockage," which originated in securities sales.[5]

The blockage discount was first applied to artworks in the Estate of Smith case.[6] That case does not establish a specific standard percentage to use as the discount factor. The amount of the blockage discount depends on the market for the work, the type of work, the number of works, general carrying costs, inventory, maintenance and insurance, marketing and other promotion costs, interest expense, general selling costs, the general art markets, the artist's submarket, predictability of future sales, present and future relationship between submarket and general art markets, and a reasonable time estimate required to sell the entire quantity of work in small lots.[7] Factors to be considered in determining the propriety of applying a blockage discount are established in the *IRS Valuation*

---

[4]Estate of O'Keeffe v. C.I.R., T.C. Memo. 1992-210, T.C.M. (RIA) ¶ 92210 (1992).

[5]Maytag v. C.I.R., 187 F.2d 962, 965 (10th Cir. 1951).

[6]Smith's (David) Estate v. Commissioner of Internal Revenue, 57 T.C. 650, 1972 WL 2557 (1972), acq. 1974-2 C.B. and recommendation regarding acquiescence, 1974 WL 36002 (I.R.S. AOD 1974) and aff'd, 510 F.2d 479 (2d Cir. 1975).

[7]Estate of O'Keeffe v. C.I.R., T.C. Memo. 1992-210, T.C.M. (RIA) ¶ 92210 (1992); *accord* Rimmer v. C.I.R., T.C. Memo. 1995-215, T.C.M. (RIA) ¶ 95215 (1995) ("When property is being valued, the number of items of which such property consists, and not simply the value determined for each item, is a relevant consideration."); Estate of Andy Warhol, N.Y.L.J., Apr. 18, 1994, at 29 (Surrogate's Ct., N.Y. County).

Guide for Income, Estate and Gift Taxes,[8] and can be summarized as follows: opportunity cost of holding the inventory; carrying costs of the inventory; expected period of time to dispose of the inventory; and quantity and quality of art.

In Estate of Smith,[9] the Tax Court had to determine the FMV of 425 abstract metal sculptures created by artist David Smith. The IRS determined the FMV of each artwork as if sold separately in the retail market one-by-one. The estate applied a 75 percent discount. The Smith court concluded:

> We think that a museum or individual collector of art objects would not completely ignore the resale value of a given item, although it obviously has far less significance than in the case of a dealer. . . . the amount which an en bloc purchaser for resale would pay and the aggregate of the separate one-at-a-time values . . . in the "retail market" would be the same.

The court concluded that the FMV of the 425 sculptures was $2,700,000. That conclusion has been interpreted to mean that the appropriate blockage discount is 37 percent, derived from viewing the court's determination as a percentage of the individual values of the Smith sculptures at $4,284,000. But the Tax Court did not indicate that it was applying a particular percentage discount, as it subsequently clarified in Estate of O'Keeffe: "[N]othing in the [Smith] opinion explains the conclusion of value by application of a particular percentage to the total."[10]

In Estate of O'Keeffe,[11] the Tax Court applied a mixed percentage blockage discount by segmenting the works in the artist's estate by "quality, uniqueness and salability,"

[8]Fed. Est. & Gift Tax Rep. (CCH) No. 115, at 30 (Oct. 14, 1985); Estate of O'Keeffe v. C.I.R., T.C. Memo. 1992-210, T.C.M. (RIA) ¶ 92210 (1992); Estate of Andy Warhol, N.Y.L.J., Apr. 18, 1994, at 29 (Surrogate's Ct., N.Y. County).

[9]Smith's (David) Estate v. Commissioner of Internal Revenue, 57 T.C. 650, 1972 WL 2557 (1972), acq. 1974-2 C.B. and recommendation regarding acquiescence, 1974 WL 36002 (I.R.S. AOD 1974) and aff'd, 510 F.2d 479 (2d Cir. 1975).

[10]Estate of O'Keeffe v. C.I.R., T.C. Memo. 1992-210, T.C.M. (RIA) ¶ 92210 (1992).

[11]Estate of O'Keeffe v. C.I.R., T.C. Memo. 1992-210, T.C.M. (RIA) ¶ 92210 (1992).

based upon short-term and long-term sales. Rejecting FMVs urged by both the IRS and the estate as incorrect because of improper assumptions about and choice of the relevant market, the court divided the estate into equal halves based upon the segmentation, and applied a 75 percent discount urged by the estate to half of the segment and a 25 percent discount urged by the IRS to the other half.[12] In Estate of Andy Warhol, where the amount of the executor's attorney fees was linked to estate value, the Surrogate's Court for the County of New York applied different discount rates to different types of artworks, contrary to the single rate applied by the auction house that prepared the appraisal on behalf of the estate.[13]

§ 3:76 Gifts

Section 2512 provides that if a gift is made in property, its value on the date of the gift will be the amount of the gift. Section 25.2512-1 of the Regulations establishes valuation for gifts in terms that are comparable to Section 20.2031-1(b) of the Regulations.[1] The elements necessary for making a gift have been discussed.[2]

In Calder v. Commissioner,[3] a blockage discount was applied to gifts of art made by the widow of artist Alexander Calder to her children. Responding to the parties' focus upon the length of time to liquidate the art, the Tax Court calculated the blockage discount by reducing to present value the stream of income from sales based upon the

---

[12]For penalties involving estate tax understatements, *see* IRC § 6662(g).

[13]Estate of Andy Warhol, N.Y.L.J., Apr. 18, 1994, at 29 (Surrogate's Ct., N.Y. County) (an FMV on May 1, 1995, yielded estate claim of value at $103,353,738.00, after discount; lawyer claim of value at $708,000,000.00, with no discount; court determined value at $390,979,278.00, applying varying discounts); *see also* Chart 3-3.

[Section 3:76]

[1]*See* §§ 3:26 to 3:33.

[2]*See* § 3:48; *Cf.* Cartier v. Jackson, 1991 WL 28026 (Conn. Super. Ct. 1991) (summary judgment denied on motion of children bringing suit against father for wrongful conversion of paintings allegedly "gifts" to them, discussing elements necessary for showing donative intent).

[3]Calder v. C.I.R., 85 T.C. 713, 1985 WL 15408 (1985).

artist's average annual sales.[4]

V. PROFESSIONAL APPRAISAL PRACTICE

A. HISTORIC EVENTS

§ 3:77 Savings and loan failures

The practice of appraisal "is an emerging profession."[1] It is redefining itself as a result of internal reassessment, federal scrutiny, and public demand for accountability. Although these factors existed for some time, restructuring was accelerated in the 1980s after disclosures about the role of appraisals in the savings and loan debacle, failed thrifts, misvalued realty, undervalued collateral, and spurious lending practices. False or fraudulent real estate appraisals were viewed as a source of these problems.

§ 3:78 FIRREA—Generally

In response to public outrage at nationwide failures of savings and loans and thrifts, Congress passed the Financial Institutions Reform, Recovery and Enforcement Act of 1989 (FIRREA)[1] to restructure financial institutions and regulate their activities. FIRREA requires that real property appraisers be certified and licensed by states[2] in accordance with federal standards. Section 1122 of title XI of FIRREA mandated a feasibility study to determine if FIRREA requirements for real property appraisal should be extended to personal property appraisal. In response, a Personal Property Appraisal Study (the Study) was submitted to Congress in March 1991.[3] The Study concluded that regulation of personal property appraisal under FIRREA was not feasible or desirable, and personal

---

[4]For penalties involving gift tax understatements, *see* IRC § 6662(g).

[Section 3:77]

[1]ASA, Principles of Valuation 4.

[Section 3:78]

[1]Pub. L. No. 101-73, 103 Stat 183, codified throughout U.S. Code.

[2]*See, e.g.,* Cal. Bus. & Prof. Code §§ 11300 et seq., "Licensing and Certification of Real Estate Appraisers."

[3]*See* Federal Financial Institutions Examination Council, Appraisal Subcommittee, "Personal Property Appraisal Study" (March 1991).

property apprais ers do not have to be certified or licensed under state or federal law.

FIRREA authorizes the Federal Deposit Insurance Corporation (FDIC) to dispose of assets owned by failed financial institutions and thrifts. As unlikely as it may seem for deposit organizations, their assets included art collections they had purchased—often with the aid of consultants and auction houses—during the heydays of the late 1980s.[4] FIRREA requires that appraisals for art (and other personal property) valued at more than $100,000 awaiting FDIC disposal be prepared according to uniform appraisal instructions.

§ 3:79 FIRREA—FIRREA and FDIC

When the FDIC began disposing of art, disputes arose over appraised values of art and ownership access. In Gosnell,[1] an art collector tried to purchase a collection of maritime paintings controlled by the FDIC after the Seamen's Bank for Savings was placed in receivership. The collection was appraised at under $3.5 million. The South Street Seaport Museum in Manhattan offered to buy the collection at the appraised value.

While the FDIC was deciding, plaintiff offered to buy the collection for $100,000 more than the museum bid, and he sent an irrevocable letter of credit to support his offer. When the FDIC accepted the museum's offer, he sued in district court to enjoin consummation of the sale on the ground that the FDIC had not placed the collection on the open market for competitive bids and his price provided a greater monetary return for the public. The district court granted summary judgment in favor of the FDIC on the ground that it lacked subject matter jurisdiction. The Second Circuit affirmed, holding that disappointed bidders lack standing under FIRREA to challenge an FDIC distribution of assets.

§ 3:80 Appraisal foundation

Redefinition of appraisal practice has taken multiple

---

[4] *See* Ch 1.

[Section 3:79]

[1] Gosnell v. F.D.I.C., 1991 WL 533637 (W.D. N.Y. 1991), judgment aff'd, 938 F.2d 372 (2d Cir. 1991).

forms. The Appraisal Foundation, a nonprofit organization incorporated in Illinois in 1987, with offices in Washington, D.C., was formed by eight leading appraisal organizations to develop national professional appraisal standards and to oversee entry of qualified appraisers to the practice.

§ 3:81 Appraisal standards board (ASB)

The Appraisal Foundation is the parent entity for the Appraisal Standards Board created in 1989. Although the Appraisal Foundation originally issued USPAP, the Appraisal Standards Board was established to publish, review, interpret, and amend USPAP, and to issue Advisory Opinions thereunder.

§ 3:82 Uniform standards of professional appraisal practice (USPAP)

In 1986 an ad hoc committee of nationally recognized Canadian and American professional organizations developed the Uniform Standards of Professional Appraisal Practice (USPAP) to guide appraisal practice. Although USPAP is substantially devoted to real property appraisal, Standards 7 and 8 are devoted to the personal property appraisal practice.[1]

USPAP, which guides professional appraisal practice and its oral and written recitation of values, has been adopted by major appraisal organizations and its standards are recognized by state and federal agencies as the generally accepted standards for practice.[2] USPAP may not apply to all transactions as a matter of law; nonetheless, adoption of USPAP by professional appraisal organizations has made such standards virtually part of the appraisal practice, either directly or through codes of ethics. Some organizations require their members to complete a curriculum in USPAP.

[Section 3:82]

[1]USPAP Standards Rules 7 and 8 have been updated in 1999. The original is reproduced in Appendix 5.

[2]Appraisal Foundation Subscription Service; Uniform Commercial and Industrial Appraisal Report Manuals.

B. PROFESSIONAL MEMBERSHIP ORGANIZATIONS

§ 3:83 Organizational requirements and codes of ethics

Even before FIRREA and the Appraisal Foundation, professional appraisal membership organizations existed. The major national appraisal associations in the United States whose members include personal property appraisers are the American Society of Appraisers (ASA) (membership includes appraisers from other disciplines), the Appraisers Association of America (AAA) (exclusively personal property appraisers), and the International Society of Appraisers (ISA) (exclusively personal property appraisers).[1] Approximately 62,500 of an estimated 250,000 appraisers belong to the major professional appraisal organizations.[2] Members of some organizations are tested under nationally administered examinations; some organizations require all members to continue educational training through ongoing accredited programs.

Appraisal organizations vet their membership; criteria for eligibility and mechanisms for monitoring compliance vary. Guidelines of practice and sanctions for misconduct

---

[Section 3:83]

[1]Following is a list of appraisal organizations and the disciplines they represent:

American Society of Appraisers (ASA)	Appraisers Association of America (AAA)	International Society of Appraisers (ISA)
Real Property	Personal Property	Personal Property
Personal Property		
Business Valuation		
Machinery and Equipment		
Appraisal Administration		
Appraisal Education		
Technical Valuation		

[2]ASA, Principles of Appraisal Practice and Code of Ethics.

are published in organizational codes of ethics.[3] In response to concerns reflected in FIRREA, such organizations are revising their codes of ethics and organizational guidelines to impose duties and obligations on subscribing members that will meet or exceed USPAP's.

§ 3:84 Unaffiliated appraisers

If the estimates are correct, only one in four appraisers belongs to a professional appraisal organization. That means that 75 percent of appraisals are done by unregulated, unlicensed persons who are not subject to organizational ethical guidelines. They are not under mandate to comply with USPAP and are not required to take continuing education.

Duties involving appraisals have been ascribed to persons whether or not they call themselves appraisers: dealers have been found liable for sales of art in which they established inflated appraised values,[1] even where the fee structure was for the sale price, not the appraisal; dealers may be liable for fraud for unsolicited post-sale appraisals;[2] curators have been sued for their evaluation of artworks, even though no numerical values were expressed.[3]

---

[3]*See* Appendix 15A to Appendix 15D for excerpts from the ASA, AAA, and ISA Codes of Ethics.

[Section 3:84]

[1]Goldman v. Barnett, 793 F. Supp. 28, 18 U.C.C. Rep. Serv. 2d 55 (D. Mass. 1992) (summary judgment improper against trustees who appeared to ratify inflated appraisal prices of art sold and appraised by dealer who obtained artworks from trust); *see also* Voitier v. Antique Art Gallery, 524 So. 2d 80 (La. Ct. App. 3d Cir. 1988), writ denied, 531 So. 2d 271 (La. 1988); Balog v. Center Art Gallery-Hawaii, Inc., 745 F. Supp. 1556, 12 U.C.C. Rep. Serv. 2d 962 (D. Haw. 1990) (inflated prices of art in appraisals actionable under contract theories); *and see* In re Grand Jury Proceedings, 707 F. Supp. 1207 (D. Haw. 1989) (criminal proceedings against Center Gallery defendants in Balog case).

[2]Rosen v. Spanierman, 894 F.2d 28, 10 U.C.C. Rep. Serv. 2d 846 (2d Cir. 1990).

[3]*See* McNally v. Yarnall, 764 F. Supp. 838, 844 (S.D. N.Y. 1991); Struna v. Wolf, 126 Misc. 2d 1031, 484 N.Y.S.2d 392 (Sup 1985).

C. APPRAISER-CLIENT RELATIONSHIP

§ 3:85 Generally

Regardless of the appraiser's status or affiliation, the appraiser-client relationship and the appraiser's obligations to the public at large are being scrutinized as a result of the savings and loan disaster and its aftermath. USPAP and revised codes of ethics are attempts to guide the practicing appraiser and educate the public. But the appraiser-client relationship establishes the terms of the appraisal.

In any given appraiser-client relationship, the context of preparing the appraisal is a factually specific undertaking in a particular working relationship. The terms of that relationship may be better understood prospectively by the parties if they are reduced to writing. The appraiser must understand what the client needs, define the scope and purpose of the appraisal assignment consistent with its client's needs, and present the valuation question. Appraisers often use standard retainer agreements, letter agreements, and contracts, revised by assignment to reflect the subject appraisal.

Parties to an appraisal agreement should be mindful of the following Checklist 3-2:

Checklist 3-2: Appraiser-Client General Checklist

(1) Is the appraiser a member in good standing of a professional appraisal organization? Are there categories of membership, i.e., junior/senior? Does the organization publish the methods used to vet members and the meaning of membership categories? (*See* §§ 3:83 to 3:84.)

(2) Is the appraiser a specialist in the subject property? How many years experience does the appraiser have with such types of property and what is the nature of the experience? Is a certification available for the specialty from an appraisal organization, and if so, does the appraiser have it? (*See* §§ 3:86 to 3:87.)

(3) What is the appraiser's educational background? Does it include training applicable to the subject

property? (*See* §§ 3:86 to 3:87.)

(4) Has the appraiser served as an expert witness in a court of law? If so, which courts and for what type of property did the appraiser qualify as an expert? (*See* §§ 3:131 to 3:134.)

(5) Can the appraiser provide institutional references from museums, foundations, auctions?

(6) Is the subject property available for physical inspection and direct examination by the appraiser? If not, why not? What visual documentation is the appraiser expected to review? (*See* §§ 3:10 to 3:12.)

(7) Where will the property be maintained for appraisal? If travel or shipping is contemplated, schedule timing, destination and location, and identify and allocate costs, expenses, insurance responsibilities and terms. (*See* §§ 3:4 to 3:9.)

(8) How will authentication be handled, by whom, and at whose time and expense? Is the client authorizing transport of the artwork to authenticators? Who is responsible for making such arrangements and who bears risks associated with authentication testing? (*See* §§ 3:7 to 3:9 and 3:19.)

(9) Will intangible interests and inherent rights interests be valued? If so, by whom? (*See* §§ 3:10 to 3:12.)

(10) Will the client provide all relevant information in its possession regarding the subject property? If not, why not? (*See* §§ 3:34 to 3:76.)

(11) To whom will the appraisal be made/delivered? If the client wants others to receive appraisal, identify them. Obtain authorizations from client for release of appraisals. (*See* §§ 3:105 to 3:107.)

(12) Will the client have access to work in progress during the appraisal and/or work product after the appraisal is complete? (*See* § 3:104.)

(13) If litigation is contemplated, what are fee arrangements for depositions, discovery, court testimony? (*See* §§ 3:100 to 3:103.)

(14) Specify fee arrangements for appraisal, timing

of appraisal preparation, and completion and timing of payments. (*See* §§ 3:100 to 3:103.)

(15) Specify arrangements for receipt of work if services terminate prior to preparation of appraisal. (*See* § 3:104.)

(16) Confirm appraiser's disinterest in subject property. (*See* §§ 3:88 to 3:93.)

(17) For tax purposes, especially charitable contributions, confirm appraiser is "qualified appraiser" who can prepare a "qualified appraisal." (*See* §§ 3:34 to 3:76.)

(18) Has the appraiser ever been disbarred from federal tax practice? If so, during what period? Has the appraiser been reinstated? (*See* §§ 3:34 to 3:76.)

(19) Will the appraisal be prepared in compliance with USPAP? federal tax procedures? other? Include recitation in the appraisal assignment of what standards are being applied.

(20) If appraisal is not for tax purposes, specify if retention of appraiser is one of agency and include a recitation clause that appraiser is not acting, or purporting to act, as agent for others with respect to subject property.

D. APPRAISER'S COMPETENCE

§ 3:86 Appraisal performance

Checklist 3-2 above contains queries relating to the competence of the appraiser. Codes of ethics of professional appraisal organizations impose upon appraisers an obligation to accept assignments that are consistent with their training. The ASA permits appraisers to associate themselves with appraisers having the proper qualifications or to disclose their own limitations to the client.[1] The AAA states the appraiser is "to contract for appraisal work only within the areas of his professional competence and expertise," or to recommend a qualified appraiser for the

---

[Section 3:86]

[1]ASA; Principles of Appraisal Practice and Code of Ethics § 4.2 (1989).

portion of the appraisal not within his expertise.[2]

The IRS has its own requirements for "qualified appraisers" who prepare tax appraisals for charitable contributions,[3] and valuations for estate and gift tax.[4]

USPAP competency provision in the 1995 edition recites the following:

> Prior to accepting an assignment or entering into an agreement to perform any assignment, an appraiser must properly identify the problem to be addressed and have the knowledge and experience to complete the assignment competently; or alternatively
>
> 1. disclose the lack of knowledge and/or experience to the client before accepting the assignment; and
> 2. take all steps necessary or appropriate to complete the assignment competently; and
> 3. describe the lack of knowledge and/or experience and the steps taken to complete the assignment competently in the report.[5]

§ 3:87 Court testimony

Persons who seek appraisals in contemplation of litigation should consider the appraiser's qualifications as an expert witness. An appraiser's competence in performing appraisals does not automatically confer expert witness

---

[2]AAA, By Laws and Code of Ethics 15.

[3]IRS Form 8283, reproduced in Appendix 6.

[4]Reg. § 20.2031-6(d) ("care should be taken to see that [appraisers] are reputable and of recognized competency to appraise the particular class of property involved"). *See* §§ 3:131 to 3:134.

[5]*See also* 1987 USPAP § B. USPAP 1987 recites the following:

> Prior to agreeing to perform a personal property appraisal, the appraiser must carefully consider the knowledge, training and experience that will be required to complete the appraisal competently, and either:
>
> 1. has been tested and certified in the field . . .
> 2. assume personal responsibility . . . that he or she has the specialized knowledge . . . or
> 3. immediately disclose the lack of required knowledge . . . to the client . . . or, with the client's approval, take all steps necessary and appropriate to complete the appraisal competently, such as use of necessary experts.

status in a court of law.[1] If the appraiser does not qualify as an expert witness, opinion testimony as a lay witness may be admissible if it is relevant to value and is "weighed in light of the qualifications of the witness" and all other relevant evidence.[2] Even as lay witnesses, appraisers ought to be sanguine about the following:

(1) an understanding of purpose and scope of valuation sought;
(2) a consideration of all the relevant factors which bear upon the valuation;
(3) a facility with methodology, facts and research, analysis and conclusions appropriate to purpose and scope of valuation; and
(4) an ability to select the proper market based upon (3).[3]

Courts have made a substantial record articulating their views about the role of appraisal experts in valuation litigation.[4]

"[E]ach oral personal property appraisal report (including expert testimony) must [comply with USPAP standards for written appraisals]."[5]

E. DISINTERESTED APPRAISALS

§ 3:88 Introduction

To maintain public confidence in appraisal practice and to instill integrity in the appraisal profession, appraisers are discouraged from obtaining or expecting any pecuniary or nonpecuniary interest in the property being appraised, or as a result of the appraisal, other than a reasonable fee for services.

[Section 3:87]

[1]Engel v. Comm'r, T.C. Memo 1993-362 (1993).

[2]Biagiotti v. C.I.R., T.C. Memo. 1986-460, 1986 WL 21685 (1986).

[3]*See also* USPAP App. 5.

[4]*See* §§ 3:131 to 3:134.

[5]USPAP Standards Rule 8.4.

§ 3:89 Legal requirements—Federal (internal revenue code (IRC))

The IRS requires an appraiser's disinterest[1] in the property appraised for specified federal tax transactions. Form 8283 for Non Cash Charitable Contributions contains a Certification of Appraiser section, which must be signed by the appraiser, and states:

> I . . . am not . . . a party to the transaction in which the donor acquired the property, employed by, married to, or related to any of the [donors or donees], or an appraiser regularly used by any of the foregoing persons and who does not perform a majority of appraisals during the taxable year for other persons.

§ 3:90 Legal requirements—State (insurance laws)

Policies of insurance governed by codes of civil procedure, insurance codes, and interpretative judicial cases under state law may require appraisal enforcement proceedings for appraising losses where values are disputed by the insurer and the insured. In California, for example, standard fire insurance policy forms must contain a standard appraisal clause which allows the insured who contests the insurer's determination of actual cash value to have an appraisal enforcement proceeding.[1]

The insured and the insurance company each select a "disinterested" appraiser; these two appraisers in turn select a third, and all three evaluate the loss.[2] Under these circumstances, the appraiser is not an agent of either party, and is not subject to control and direction.[3]

In Figi,[4] the California Court of Appeals reversed a judgment confirming such an arbitration award where undis-

---

[Section 3:89]

[1]26 CFR § 1.170A0-13(iv).

[Section 3:90]

[1]Cal. Ins. Code § 2070-71.

[2]Cal. Ins. Code § 2070-71.

[3]Figi v. New Hampshire Ins. Co., 108 Cal. App. 3d 772, 777, 166 Cal. Rptr. 774 (4th Dist. 1980).

[4]Figi v. New Hampshire Ins. Co., 108 Cal. App. 3d 772, 777, 166 Cal. Rptr. 774 (4th Dist. 1980).

closed business relationships existed between the neutral appraiser, the insurance company, and the insurance company's appraiser. The court stated:

> We believe that [the] duty [an insurance company has to its insured, good faith and fair dealing, which specifically includes conduct of the insurance company during an appraisal procedure] compels the conclusion that despite the appraiser's more limited function [of evaluating loss and not considering questions of policy scope] he is held to a higher standard of impartiality than . . . arbitrators generally.

The California Court of Appeal held that an appraiser who did business with the insurance company's appraiser while the appraisal procedure for that company was pending cannot be "neutral." The appraiser was not "disinterested" as a matter of law.[5]

Appraisers who sit on statutory appraisal enforcement proceedings as a result of disputed contracts of insurance must determine a single specific factual question: the "actual cash value of insured [object]."[6] Appraisers are not authorized to test the credibility of the insured or to reevaluate the claim. Although the value or amount of loss is a question of fact ordinarily not reviewable on appeal, the court may examine the record to ascertain what the appraisers considered to be the factual issues before them.[7]

In Sharma,[8] appraisers who made a factual determination that the insured's artwork had not been stolen, as he claimed, were held to be acting beyond the scope of their appraisal authority. The insured challenged the actual

---

[5]Figi v. New Hampshire Ins. Co., 108 Cal. App. 3d 772, 777, 166 Cal. Rptr. 774 (4th Dist. 1980) (insured may be able to waive his right to disinterested appraiser under state law if full disclosure of appraiser's interest; appraisers held to higher standard of "disinterest" than arbitrators, whose "ordinary and insubstantial business dealings" with insurance companies do not require disclosure).

[6]Safeco Ins. Co. v. Sharma, 160 Cal. App. 3d 1060, 207 Cal. Rptr. 104 (2d Dist. 1984) (appraisers are unlike arbitrators, who consider questions of policy, interpretation, or scope of coverage).

[7]Safeco Ins. Co. v. Sharma, 160 Cal. App. 3d 1060, 207 Cal. Rptr. 104 (2d Dist. 1984).

[8]Safeco Ins. Co. v. Sharma, 160 Cal. App. 3d 1060, 207 Cal. Rptr. 104 (2d Dist. 1984).

cash value the insurance company was willing to pay for his stolen matched "set of 36 Rajput miniature paintings, Bundi School, India." But the appraisers issued their award based upon "36 unmatched paintings," a significantly lower value than for a "set." Their award was rejected by the California court because unmatched paintings were not the basis of the insured's claim.

§ 3:91 USPAP requirements

Each appraisal certification must include the following language: "I have no (or the specified) present or prospective interest in the property . . . and I have no (or the specified) personal interest or bias with respect to the parties involved."[1]

§ 3:92 Codes of ethics

Certain codes of ethics permit appraisers to have interests in the subject property, providing that (1) full disclosure of the interest is made to the client, (2) acceptance by the client of such interests, and (3) recitation of the "nature and extent of the interest [is recited] in the appraisal report."[1] "Interest" is defined as "ownership of the subject property, acting or having some expectation of acting, as agent in the purchase, sale or financing of the subject property; and managing, or having some expectation of managing the subject property." An appraiser's statement of disinterest may be requested in the appraisal report.[2] Other association standards differ and contain less stringent disclosure obligations.[3]

[Section 3:91]

[1]USPAP Standards Rule 8-3.

[Section 3:92]

[1]ASA, Principles of Appraisal Practice and Code of Ethics § 7.3.

[2]ASA, Principles of Appraisal Practice and Code of Ethics § 8.5.

[3]Estate of Andy Warhol, N.Y.L.J., Apr. 18, 1994, at 29 (Surrogate's Ct., N.Y. County) ("Appraisers Association of America . . . acknowledged that the [AAA] Code of Ethics . . . requires that an appraiser maintain standards of objectivity and that the appraiser should not disclose any desire to act as the exclusive sales agent until after the appraisal has been completed.").

§ 3:93 Judicial opinions

Courts may, and on occasion do, disregard expert testimony of an appraiser if bias or collusion exists between the appraiser and the taxpayer.[1] Where an auction house hired by the executor to conduct appraisals for Andy Warhol's estate met with the president of the Andy Warhol Foundation prior to submitting its appraisal to discuss payment and availability of works for sale, the court found no collusion, but did find "a conflict on the part of Christie's in seeking future business from the Foundation the same time it was retained to render an impartial appraisal."[2]

F. SPECIAL APPRAISALS

§ 3:94 Restored or damaged art

Authenticity, and intrinsic value, are affected by damage and restoration. The appraiser's role in authenticating should be specified in the appraisal assignment, and stated in the limiting conditions and assumptions. But the appraiser's role, at a minimum, is to make an apparent identification, which includes examining condition. Sound appraisal practice requires noting damage and visible restoration as elements of condition.

Damaged art depresses its value, whether or not the damage has been or will be restored. The Tax Court devalues donated art if damage is identified. A portrait rock sculpture missing significant facial features was considered sufficient damage for the tax court to devalue a contribution claim from $500,000 to $30,000.[1] And, where a sole appraiser of a painting among many expert appraisers who offered FMV was the only person to identify the

---

[Section 3:93]

[1]*See* §§ 3:121 to 3:122.

[2]Estate of Andy Warhol, N.Y.L.J., Apr. 18, 1994, at 29 (Surrogate's Ct., N.Y. County).

[Section 3:94]

[1]Murphy v. C. I. R., T.C. Memo. 1991-276, 1991 WL 104312 (1991), rev'd on other grounds, 8 F.3d 28 (9th Cir. 1993).

damage,[2] the court accepted that appraisal over all others.

Damage can be minimized or exacerbated depending upon the quality of restoration.[3] Restoration, like damage, affects value.[4] A piece that is more than 50 percent restored is susceptible to reattribution, i.e., its authenticity is impaired. Reattribution means that the work is deattributed to the original or purported artist and is reattributed to another artist, school, studio, or style, or to an anonymous source.

Restoration can dramatically depress value because of potential deattribution.[5] In Monaghan v. Commissioner,[6] the taxpayer, in 1974, donated a portrait to the Detroit Institute of Arts that was attributed to Spanish painter Bartolomo Esteban Murillo and claimed an $80,000 deduction as a charitable contribution under Section 170 of the Code. When the portrait was stripped, i.e., overpainting was removed, only 40 percent of the original painting existed. Experts deattributed the work and the Tax Court accepted their decision, valuing the work at only $3,000.[7] Appraisers should also be careful about categorizing an object from one period when substantial restoration occurs in another.[8]

§ 3:95 Ownership issues and title impairments

Ownership and title are murky areas in art law; appraisers ordinarily do not have all the relevant facts needed to assess title or ownership, nor do they have the

---

[2]Lightman v. C.I.R., T.C. Memo. 1985-315, 1985 WL 14942 (1985).

[3]Furstenberg v. U.S., 219 Ct. Cl. 473, 595 F.2d 603 (1979) (the "Helfer restoration" of a painting by Jean Baptiste Camille Corot was "a disaster . . . the restorer did a considerable amount of overpainting").

[4]Rupke v. C. I. R., T.C. Memo. 1973-234, 1973 WL 2413 (1973), recommendation regarding acquiescence, 1974 WL 35958 (I.R.S. AOD 1974) (appraiser contended he would not change valuation of restored painting even if it were in perfect condition).

[5]Furstenberg v. U.S., 219 Ct. Cl. 473, 595 F.2d 603 (1979); Farber v. Comm'r, T.C. Memo 1974-155 (1974), aff'd in unpublished opinion (2d Cir. Nov. 20, 1975).

[6]Monaghan v. C.I.R., T.C. Memo. 1981-280, 1981 WL 10597 (1981).

[7]*See* Chart 3-3.

[8]Ferrari v. C.I.R., T.C. Memo. 1989-521, 1989 WL 109420 (1989), judgment aff'd, 931 F.2d 54 (4th Cir. 1991). *See* Chart 3-1.

background to evaluate the viability of legal claims or defenses. For charitable contributions, the property owner is supposed to inform the appraiser how he obtained possession and title, usually documented by bills of sale, invoices, and similar memoranda. As a practical matter, appraisers ordinarily assume the client has title and information about title is assumed.

However, appraisers' assumptions don't absolve appraisers of fulfilling duties. Duties of skill and competence compel appraisers to consult available governmental and private resources that publish stolen art bulletins and reports. Failure to consult such sources and disclose the findings to clients is actionable under theories of tort. It should be emphasized that the fact of publication by such reporting services does not mean the art is "stolen" as a matter of law. A legal classification requires an adjudication under procedural safeguards. And art sourced to unauthorized archaeological sites or from questionable importations, which also might impair title, are rarely reported. Thus, even after investigation, the appraiser is confronted with acting upon his or her reasonable belief that the artwork may be the object of criminal or unlawful activity.

What is the recommended course of action for an appraiser who suspects that the client is holding art from tainted sources? Neither USPAP nor appraisal organizations have squarely addressed how the practice should respond to these thorny issues. The general rule is that appraisers are under no legal obligation to report discovery of art from suspicious sources in their client's possession to law enforcement, unless their conduct rises to the level of accessory status or aiding and abetting pursuant to the provisions of particular statutes. While knowledge could be imputed to appraisers under accessory statutes, the knowing participation of the principal is also required.

Common practice is to report such concerns to the clients; codes of ethics arguably recommend appraiser disclosure to clients under duties of skill and competence. USPAP's requirements of communication and disclosure would also compel that result. Cases involving similar situations reveal that appraisers notified clients of suspicions and refused to accept, or withdrew from, the representation.[1] The appraiser is thus removed from participating in any wrongdoing but the suspected artwork remains in the market unreported,[2] a disturbing fact to law enforcement. Certain codes of ethics implicitly support the appraiser's silence by their requirements of confidentiality.[3]

§ 3:96 Appraised value for purposes of jurisdiction—Diversity jurisdiction

If the value of art is challenged as the basis of a court's jurisdiction, the appraisal not made by a disinterested independent appraiser can be challenged. This has occurred for civil and criminal matters establishing value as jurisdictional predicates. District courts have original jurisdiction where complete diversity is met and the matter in controversy exceeds $50,000.[1] To justify dismissal of a complaint, it must appear "to a legal certainty" that the claim is for less than the jurisdictional minimum.

[Section 3:95]

[1]U.S. v. Hollinshead, 495 F.2d 1154 (9th Cir. 1974) (many appraisers viewed artifacts without reporting through dealer's repeated attempts to sell them); U.S. v. McClain, 545 F.2d 988 (5th Cir. 1977) (artifacts viewed under suspicious circumstances without reporting); *but cf.* Autocephalous Greek-Orthodox Church of Cyprus v. Goldberg & Feldman Fine Arts Inc., 717 F. Supp. 1374 (S.D. Ind. 1989), judgment aff'd, 917 F.2d 278 (7th Cir. 1990) (museum curator from J. Paul Getty Museum contacts officials of Cyprus who claimed ownership of Byzantine mosaics when dealer offered to sell them to her museum); *see also* Priv. Ltr. Rul. 9152005 (Aug. 30, 1991) (document may not be used or cited as precedent; many appraisers shown Carolingian treasures stolen from German church notified residual heirs of estate that treasures were stolen).

[2]Priv. Ltr. Rul. 9152005 (document may not be used or cited as precedent; stolen art is includable in the decedent's gross estate under IRC § 2033 in that 2033 is based upon economic perquisites of ownership rather than legal title; since decedent had enjoyed art and could have disposed of art during his life before it passed to residual heirs, and since heirs used art as collateral for loans, the necessary degree of ownership existed under Texas state law).

[3]Imprudent, inaccurate, wrongful disclosures might under certain circumstances constitute a basis for defamation or other torts. *See* §§ 10:63 to 10:71.

[Section 3:96]

[1]28 U.S.C.A. § 1332.

In Burger v. Bartlett,[2] the artist Jennifer Bartlett argued a federal district court lacked jurisdiction in a diversity action brought by collectors under Section 1332 of title 28 of the U.S. Code for declaratory relief to determine title to one of her paintings in which she also claimed an interest. The artist notified an auction house of her claim to title and it refused to auction the painting until title was resolved. The artist contended her painting was not worth the federal jurisdictional minimum of $50,000. She filed her dealer's affidavit that the painting was worth less than $50,000, and had "little or no value."

The court disregarded the dealer's appraisal, emphasizing that the artwork had not been independently appraised and that Bartlett's paintings regularly sold for more than $50,000. The test for dismissing a federal case for lack of jurisdiction based upon insufficient monetary minimum, explained the Pennsylvania district court, has a "legal standard . . . more stringent. Unless it appears to a legal certainty that the claim set forth in the complaint is for less than [$50,000], the amount in controversy . . . is met."[3]

But, in Dajon Corp. v. Hartman,[4] a diversity action alleging misrepresentation and fraud in the sale of a silver tankard for $13,000 that the buyer subsequently learned was fake, the court concluded that it appeared to a legal certainty that the plaintiff's claim could not meet the $50,000 threshold.[5]

§ 3:97 Appraised value for purposes of jurisdiction—National Stolen Property Act

Federal jurisdiction over the substantive offense of transportation of stolen goods in interstate commerce under the National Stolen Property Act (NSPA) is predicated on the goods having a value of at least $5,000. The

---

[2]Burger v. Bartlett, 1990 WL 99025 (E.D. Pa. 1990) (transferring case to New York district court for venue).

[3]Burger v. Bartlett, 1990 WL 99025 (E.D. Pa. 1990).

[4]Dajon Corp. of Mississippi v. Hartman, 1991 WL 121214 (E.D. La. 1991).

[5]*Cf.* U.S. v. Tobin, 576 F.2d 687 (5th Cir. 1978) (stolen art determined to be fake did not undermine the $5,000 minimum value for goods under the National Stolen Property Act.

government has the burden of proof that the art is worth a minimum of $5,000 for substantive violations; but proof is unnecessary where the charge is conspiracy to violate NSPA.[1]

Courts have accepted as evidence of the $5,000 a gallery owner's testimony on market value of gallery prices arrived at by gallery-artist negotiation,[2] a defendant's belief it would profit $2 million from sale of stolen art,[3] and docent testimony on value based upon other documentation. NSPA valuations can be made at the time and place the goods were stolen or at any time during their receipt and concealment.[4] In United States v. Tobin,[5] the appellate court upheld a conviction under NSPA over defendant's argument that since one of the sculptures was actually a fake, the value of the goods did not equal $5,000 and therefore the NSPA did not apply.

§ 3:98 Appraised value for purposes of bankruptcy

In United States v. Grant,[1] a debtor under chapter 7 of the Bankruptcy Code appealed a felony conviction for concealing artwork belonging to an estate in violation of Section 152 of title 18 of the U.S. Code.[2] At issue was the value of a dozen or more remarqued maritime prints by John Stobart purchased by the debtor from the Stobart

---

[Section 3:97]

[1]U.S. v. Sarro, 742 F.2d 1286, 16 Fed. R. Evid. Serv. 971 (11th Cir. 1984); U.S. v. Lehning, 742 F.2d 1113 (7th Cir. 1984).

[2]U.S. v. Lehning, 742 F.2d 1113 (7th Cir. 1984) ($5,000 minimum for NSPA upheld on appeal based on testimony of gallery owner in case charging conspiracy of NSPA where defendants went from Illinois to Indiana to steal bronze sculptures from gallery but could not transport all of them at once).

[3]U.S. v. Sarro, 742 F.2d 1286, 16 Fed. R. Evid. Serv. 971 (11th Cir. 1984) (in NSPA conspiracy charge, conspirator's belief that stealing paintings for resale would yield more than $5,000 was enough).

[4]U.S. v. Lehning, 742 F.2d 1113 (7th Cir. 1984).

[5]U.S. v. Tobin, 576 F.2d 687 (5th Cir. 1978).

[Section 3:98]

[1]U.S. v. Grant, 971 F.2d 799 (1st Cir. 1992).

[2]18 U.S.C.A. § 152, as amended by the Bankruptcy Reform Act of 1978 ("Whoever knowingly and fraudulently conceals from a . . . trustee . . . , any property belonging to the estate of a debtor . . . shall

Gallery in the early 1980s for between $1,500 to $3,000 each. Included among inventory, the prints were surreptitiously removed from the debtor's offices and replaced by inexpensive photographs prior to the arrival of the trustee. The debtor was indicted for " 'concealing at least six Stobart prints with an approximate value of $12,000.' "[3]

At trial, the debtor provided appraisals of $50 each for two Stobart prints found at his residence; the gallery invoices for the two prints had a combined value of $3,600. On appeal, the debtor argued that the combined value of $100 under his appraisals was "too insubstantial a value, as a matter of law, in relation to a debtor estate of $3,000,000 to $4,000,000."[4] The First Circuit found no authority for the "substantiality" requirement of the property concealed under Section 152. Although the district court did not require the government to prove that the concealed property was worth $12,000—the indictment estimate—the First Circuit cast doubt upon the debtor's appraiser, a general auctioneer who had only appraised artwork three or four times in seventeen years. That appraiser used a liquidation value based upon a general auction of residence contents.

The government offered evidence that the prints were part of a valuable limited series, and if sold through an art gallery they would have commanded a substantially higher price. The government offered market value and cost value for the prints. The appellate court concluded that the record supported a finding of $12,000 value as stated in the indictment.

§ 3:99 Appraised value for purposes of U.S. customs

U.S. Customs is authorized to seize, inter alia, art and antiques imported in violation of the customs laws. Seizure and forfeiture depend upon the value of the works; U.S.

---

be fined not more than $5,000 or imprisoned not more than five years, or both."].

[3]U.S. v. Grant, 971 F.2d 799, 802 (1st Cir. 1992).

[4]U.S. v. Grant, 971 F.2d 799, 808–809 (1st Cir. 1992).

Customs is required to appraise such imports.[1]

G. APPRAISAL FEES

§ 3:100 For service

Sound appraisal practice supports a fee for service arrangement; the charge for the appraisal can be a flat fee or an hourly rate. In both situations, the appraiser may require a retainer prior to commencing work. Fee arrangements should be specified in the appraisal agreement. However, where an appraiser received approximately $440,000 from a single dealer in appraisal fees for preparing postsale appraisals for 2,400 "master plates," which he examined only from photographs,[1] a federal district court assessed punitive damages of $250,000 in a fraud claim against the appraiser.[2]

§ 3:101 Contingent

Contingent fees are simply fees that relate to conditions external to appraisal services. The fee may be contingent upon the following: percentage of the value established; based upon awards made in property settlements or court actions where the appraiser made the valuations; the amount of tax reduction obtained as a result of the appraisal; or linked to consummation of sale or financing of property. That these situations encourage biased results and create conflicts of interest is obvious.

The IRS prohibits contingent fee arrangements based upon percentages of appraised values.[1] IRS Form 8283[2] requires the appraiser to sign a certification that recites, in pertinent part: "I certify that the appraisal fees were

---

[Section 3:99]

[1] *See* §§ 6:54 to 6:63.

[Section 3:100]

[1] *See* Ch 11.

[2] Ross v. Jackie Fine Arts, Inc., 1991 WL 213815 (D.S.C. 1991) (a RICO judgment existed against the same appraiser, who obtained a $50 "kickback" from the dealer on each appraisal).

[Section 3:101]

[1] Reg. § 1.170A0-13(c)(6). Exceptions exist for fees paid to nonprofit organizations that regulate appraisers. Reg. § 1.170A0-13(c) at (6)(ii).

not based upon a percentage of the appraised property value."

Codes of ethics may consider contingency arrangements unethical. The ASA, for example, "declares it . . . unethical and unprofessional for an appraiser . . . to contract for or accept compensation for appraisal services in the form of a commission, rebate, division of brokerage commissions, or any similar forms,"[3] and "to do work for a fixed percentage of the amount of value."[4] Each appraisal certification must include the statement: "my fee is not contingent."[5]

§ 3:102 Deductibility—Charitable contributions

Amounts paid as appraisal fees to determine the FMV of charitable contribution deductions are not deductible as charitable contributions, but individual taxpayers may deduct them for income tax purposes under Section 212(3) of the Code, which provides: "In the case of an individual, there shall be allowed as a deduction all the ordinary and necessary expenses paid or incurred during the taxable year . . . (3) in connection with the determination, collection, or refund of any tax."[1]

Appraisal expenses may be entered as miscellaneous deductions subject to a 2 percent limit on IRS Form 1040, Schedule A, which permits as deductions expenses paid in connection with determination of income tax liability.[2] The taxpayer can only deduct the costs of appraisals actually relied upon and attached to the tax returns, not on all the appraisals obtained for purposes of deciding which pieces

---

[2]Form 8283, along with IRS instructions, is reproduced in Appendix 6.

[3]ASA Code of Ethics § 7.1.

[4]ASA Code of Ethics § 7.2.

[5]USPAP Standards Rule 8-3.

[Section 3:102]

[1]*See also* Reg. § 1.212-1(1); Rev. Rul. 67-461, 1967-2 C.B. 125.

[2]Biagiotti v. C.I.R., T.C. Memo. 1986-460, 1986 WL 21685 (1986), *citing* Neely v. C.I.R., 85 T.C. 934, 950, 1985 WL 15422 (1985).

to donate.[3]

§ 3:103 Deductibility—Estates

The deductibility of appraisal fees to determine FMV of property in the decedent's gross estate is provided in Section 20-2053 of the Regulations which provides for deduction of "administration expenses."[1] "Administration expenses include . . . (3) miscellaneous expenses."[2] Appraisal fees are expressly classified as "miscellaneous administration expenses."[3]

H. OWNERSHIP OF APPRAISALS

§ 3:104 Generally

Who owns the written appraisal? The appraisal document, whatever its denomination, is the property of the client. Although appraisers intend for the appraisal to be used only for specified purposes stated in the written appraisal, the appraiser cannot control the client's use or distribution of the appraisal.

The appraiser is entitled to maintain copies of the document, and sound appraisal practice dictates that the appraiser should do so. But the appraiser's use or distribution of an appraisal is circumscribed by confidentiality requirements recited in codes of ethics. The duties may run to persons other than those signing the retainer agreement and paying the fees.

The person retaining the appraiser is not necessarily the person for whom the appraisal will be used. Bankers, accountants, and attorneys, among others, regularly retain appraisers. In an attorney-client relationship, rules of professional responsibility and rules of evidence respect the attorney-client relationship, regardless of who is the financially responsible party. Counterpart principles do not exist for appraisers. Appraisers should be cognizant of

---

[3]Biagiotti v. C.I.R., T.C. Memo. 1986-460, 1986 WL 21685 (1986); Reg § 1.170A0-13(d)(2)(v).

[Section 3:103]

[1]Reg. §§ 20.2053-1 and 20.2053-3.

[2]Reg. § 20.2053-3(a).

[3]Reg. § 20.2053-3(d)(1).

their duties and to whom the duties flow, and should obtain authorizations to release data where ambiguity exists.

These considerations must be dealt with on a case-by-case basis under the particular facts and circumstances of the retainer agreement. Aside from ethical controls on unauthorized use of appraisals, improprieties in this area by the appraiser may be actionable.[1]

In the event the client terminates the services of the appraiser prior to preparation of the appraisal document, who owns the appraiser's work product? Although this is a common question among appraisers, no dispositive case could be found in the appraisal context. Absent contractual agreement, it would appear that the appraiser is entitled to keep the work product and that there is no obligation to provide it to the client.

If no written appraisal exists at the time of the termination, but a written appraisal was contracted for, is the client entitled to some documentation? The appraiser's thoughts, research, drafts, and so forth, are ordinarily not part of the appraiser-client bargain, other than their final expression in the written appraisal document. Clients who wish to obtain documentation short of a written appraisal should contract for it, and specify arrangements for document transfer if services are terminated prior to completion of an appraisal. USPAP does not mention appraisal ownership; it does refer to "field notes" and contains a section on recordkeeping.[2]

I. CONFIDENTIALITY OF APPRAISALS

§ 3:105 Duties during representation

The contents of the appraisal and the fact of retention to prepare an appraisal require confidentiality under

[Section 3:104]

[1]For example, interference with contract, disparagement, or privacy/publicity issues.

[2]*See* USPAP Ethics Provisions, Record Keeping.

certain codes of ethics.[1] Appraisers should obtain written authorization from the client in the form of an informed consent to disclose any aspect of the appraisal, and the scope of disclosure should be explicitly recited in the retainer agreement. Contractual terms in the retainer agreement may contain clauses reciting specific requirements in this area, particularly where the appraiser is not retained by the owner of the subject property. USPAP does not mention or refer to confidentiality.

§ 3:106 Duties after representation

If, during the course of representation, the appraiser is required by codes of ethics to maintain confidentiality surrounding the appraisal, the duty should not terminate after the representation ends. Appraisal documents prepared for clients are not acceptable as evidence of professional qualifications for application to or promotion in professional societies because of confidentiality nor should written appraisals be published in identifiable form without the express, written informed consent of the client and/or relevant parties.

§ 3:107 Due process exception

Codes of ethics make an express exception for disclosure of appraisals demanded under "due process of law."[1] What does "due process" mean in this context? The codes do not specify, and no case could be found. Does due process, for purposes of interpreting the codes, arise from a discovery motion, a subpoena, a court order? The appraiser who is asked to release client appraisals should be mindful of potential legal interests as well as ethical ones.

The prudent course of action for appraisers who have been asked to release client appraisal information in the context of litigation is to obtain the written permission of

---

[Section 3:105]

[1]The ASA mentions both; the AA states: "to keep all appraisals confidential, unless required by the owner . . . to release such appraisal."

[Section 3:107]

[1]AAA Code of Ethics at 15; ASA Code of Ethics at 5.

the client (and others as necessary) for the specific purpose of the request. Where authorization is not made or is ambiguous, the appraiser should consider applying to the applicable court for a protective order or comparable relief coupled with judicial instruction as to document release. So far, no reported case could be found that has dealt with these issues.

VI. APPRAISAL TORT LIABILITY

A. PROFESSIONAL APPRAISAL MALPRACTICE

§ 3:108 Generally

Hornbook law provides that the standard of care in a negligence action imposes a duty upon the defendant to act as a reasonable person of ordinary prudence to avoid foreseeable injury to others.[1] However, where a person has special knowledge, skill, and training and undertakes to use that superior ability in performing services for others, the law requires that the person act not only with reasonable care, but also consistently with that special skill. The higher duty applies to anyone qualifying by virtue of special skill, but is often expressed as one of a professional rendering services to a client in the context of a contractual relationship. In such cases, the standard of care is the requirements of the profession, and liability attaches for failure to exercise reasonable care and skill consistent with those requirements. Some courts have held real property appraisers to the same standards of care as other professionals.[2]

No opinions could be found where a cause of action for professional personal property appraisal malpractice was

---

[Section 3:108]

[1]Prosser and Keeton on the Law of Torts § 32; *see* Federal Sav. and Loan Ins. Corp. v. Texas Real Estate Counselors, Inc., 955 F.2d 261 (5th Cir. 1992).

[2]Federal Sav. and Loan Ins. Corp. v. Texas Real Estate Counselors, Inc., 955 F.2d 261 (5th Cir. 1992) (real property appraiser negligence upheld on one count, remanded on another); Federal Sav. & Loan Ins. Corp. v. Derbes, 731 F. Supp. 755 (E.D. La. 1990); Hoffman v. Greenberg, 159 Ariz. 377, 767 P.2d 725 (Ct. App. Div. 2 1988).

upheld.[3] Some courts have used the term "appraisal malpractice" or "professional appraisal negligence" in evaluating claims made for valuations and authentications of art in the context of personal property appraisal, but none relied on a professional malpractice cause of action or recognized accepted professional standards of care. A federal district court has considered a somewhat analogous situation of computer experts providing services to their clients. In an action alleging computer malpractice, the court found no cause of action for professional malpractice or professional computer negligence because computer experts did not fit the following description:

> Professionals may be sued for malpractice because the higher standards of care imposed on them by their profession and by state licensing requirements engenders trust in them by clients that is not the norm in the marketplace. When no such higher code of ethics binds a person such trust is unwarranted. Hence, no duties independent of those created by contract or under ordinary tort principles are imposed.[4]

Personal property appraisers are not licensed, certified, regulated, or admitted to practice. Those who belong to professional organizations voluntarily agree to follow guidelines in codes of ethics, as well as USPAP, if the appraisal organization has adopted it, which excludes the estimated 75 percent of appraisers who do not belong to such organizations. Although USPAP Standards 7 and 8[5] add a provocative element to the evaluation of appraisers as a professional class in that they purport to professionalize and standardize the practice, personal property appraisal malpractice has yet to be a recognized cause of

---

[3]*See, e.g.,* Goldman v. Barnett, 793 F. Supp. 28, 18 U.C.C. Rep. Serv. 2d 55 (D. Mass. 1992) (negligent misrepresentation claim substituted for appraisal malpractice); Rosen v. Spanierman, 711 F. Supp. 749, 8 U.C.C. Rep. Serv. 2d 713 (S.D. N.Y. 1989), judgment vacated in part on other grounds and remanded, 894 F.2d 28, 10 U.C.C. Rep. Serv. 2d 846 (2d Cir. 1990) (rejecting professional malpractice claims against art dealer for sale of art); Struna v. Wolf, 126 Misc. 2d 1031, 484 N.Y.S.2d 392 (Sup 1985) (rejecting professional malpractice regarding allegedly improper appraisal of sculpture).

[4]Hospital Computer Systems, Inc. v. Staten Island Hosp., 788 F. Supp. 1351, 1361, 18 U.C.C. Rep. Serv. 2d 140 (D.N.J. 1992).

[5]*See* Appendix 5.

action. That appraisers have not been subject to professional malpractice actions does not mean that they operate without legal exposure. The cases make clear that appraisers are subject to tort claims, but the murky issue is the standard of care that will be applied.

B. NEGLIGENT MISREPRESENTATION

§ 3:109 Elements of tort

Courts have concluded that a cause of action for appraisal malpractice is "in essence" a claim for negligent misrepresentation.[1] While the court may be making such a substitution of claims based on the pleadings, the claims are not coterminous.

In a professional malpractice action, the standard of care is still reasonable, but the ante is raised to a higher requisite standard of care owed by professionals to their clients; the duty is created by virtue of professional stature and is measured according to established recognized professional standards. Professional malpractice can be based on commission or omission of an act or conduct, and the parties ordinarily are client-plaintiffs, or their surrogates, and the professional-defendant. This is not the posture of a negligent misrepresentation claim.

Negligent misrepresentation is not contingent upon hierarchical duties of care arising from superior skills measured by applicable professional standards of care. Negligent misrepresentation requires as one of its elements commission of a statement, not mere omission. Negligent misrepresentation is not limited to plaintiff-clients and defendant-professionals; in some jurisdictions, defendants and plaintiffs under certain circumstances may not necessarily have engaged in client-adviser relationship. Whether or not malpractice is a viable claim against appraisers remains an issue, but it is inaccurate to presume that negligent misrepresentation provides a substitutible remedy.

Negligent misrepresentation is evaluated under state law; each jurisdiction should be checked for the precise

---

[Section 3:109]

[1]Struna v. Wolf, 126 Misc. 2d 1031, 484 N.Y.S.2d 392 (Sup 1985).

recitation of the elements.[2] Basically, the tort includes a false representation of a material fact made without any reasonable ground for believing it to be true with the intent to induce plaintiff's reliance, causing a plaintiff to act in justifiable reliance upon the truth of representation to his damage.[3]

The majority rule is that where the representation is made by a defendant directly to a plaintiff, in the course of dealings with the defendant, or is made to him with knowledge that he intends to rely upon it, a duty of reasonable care is imposed.[4] A client relationship is not required. Some jurisdictions require a special relationship of "closer trust" between the parties, which can be based upon previous or continuing relations.[5]

§ 3:110 Appraisals made to plaintiff for purpose of selling artworks to plaintiff

In Goldman v. Barnett,[1] the plaintiff brought, inter alia, negligent misrepresentation claims against trustees of the Milton Avery Trust and a dealer-appraiser who allegedly made overvalued appraisals of Avery paintings consigned to him by the trust. Relying on the appraisals, plaintiff bought more than $1 million of Avery paintings from the dealer, who remitted a portion of the profits to the trust. The independent experts deemed the paintings to be

---

[2]Illinois, for example, defines the context of one, "who in the course of his business or profession, supplies information for the guidance of others in their business transactions." McKie v. R.H. Love Galleries, Inc., 1990 WL 179797 (N.D. Ill. 1990) (denying summary judgment to defendants on negligent misrepresentation because pleadings sufficient to allege facts for jury).

[3]Christiansen v. Roddy, 183 Cal. App. 3d 780, 231 Cal. Rptr. 72 (1986) overruled in part by Soderberg v. McKinney, 44 Cal. App. 4th 1760, 52 Cal. Rptr 2d 635 (1996).

[4]*But cf.* Goldman v. Barnett, 793 F. Supp. 28, 18 U.C.C. Rep. Serv. 2d 55 (D. Mass. 1992).

[5]*See* Rosen v. Spanierman, 711 F. Supp. 749, 8 U.C.C. Rep. Serv. 2d 713 (S.D. N.Y. 1989), judgment vacated in part on other grounds and remanded, 894 F.2d 28, 10 U.C.C. Rep. Serv. 2d 846 (2d Cir. 1990); Struna v. Wolf, 126 Misc. 2d 1031, 484 N.Y.S.2d 392 (Sup 1985).

[Section 3:110]

[1]Goldman v. Barnett, 793 F. Supp. 28, 18 U.C.C. Rep. Serv. 2d 55 (D. Mass. 1992).

overvalued more than fourfold.

The court, denying summary judgment to the trustees, found a material question of fact existed as to whether the dealer's alleged misrepresentations of value could be attributed to them. The facts the court considered to support attribution were based on the relationship as follows: The trustees consigned Avery artworks to the dealer, and the dealer gave the plaintiff oral and written appraisals in contemplation of sale and communicated the appraised prices to the trustees. The appraisals were prepared on gallery letterhead identifying the dealer as an appraiser, reciting his membership in a national appraisal association, and indicating the trustees' knowledge of prices.

In Struna v. Wolf,[2] the Supreme Court of New York granted summary judgment to the Metropolitan Museum in a negligent appraisal action brought by a plaintiff-owner who alleged he relied on a museum curator's appraisal to purchase a sculpture. The court found that the plaintiff failed to show that the defendant had knowledge that the plaintiff would act upon the curator's statements since it believed the plaintiff already owned the sculpture.

§ 3:111 Appraisals relied upon by third persons—Appraiser's duty of care to others—Duty where knowledge and inducement to specific plaintiff

The majority rule is that appraisers have no duty of care to the public or to unidentified unknown third persons. However, a duty of reasonable care may be found where a representation is made to a third person with knowledge that he intends to communicate it to the specific plaintiff for purposes of inducing him to act.

§ 3:112 Appraisals relied upon by third persons—Appraiser's duty of care to others—No duty where unspecified persons rely

The majority rule is that reasonable anticipation or even knowledge that the recipient of the representation intends to make commercial use of the representation in dealing with unspecified persons is not sufficient to create a duty

---

[2] Struna v. Wolf, 126 Misc. 2d 1031, 484 N.Y.S.2d 392 (Sup 1985).

of care toward them.[1] A minority view extends the duty of care in limited circumstances.[2]

These rules have been applied to appraisers who prepared appraisals relied upon by unknown persons. In Christiansen v. Roddy,[3] a real property appraiser named Files valued a meat packing plant for the owner, who intended to use the property as collateral for a loan from the defendant-loan brokerage firm. The appraiser valued the property at $230,000, using only one method of valuation and omitting an encroachment on the property. He submitted the appraisal to the loan applicant. The defendant-investment counselor, Roddy, who had initially contacted him to do the appraisal, obtained a copy and used it in a loan brochure distributed to prospective investors.

The plaintiffs loaned money against the property and the owner defaulted. When the property was revalued for a forced sale, it was appraised by others under two methods of valuation at $51,000. The plaintiffs sued the appraiser and the investment counselor for negligent misrepresentation.

The trial court found that Files, the appraiser, had negligently misrepresented the value of the realty to the plaintiffs, but the appellate court reversed, deciding as a matter of law that the appraiser had no duty of care to the plaintiffs based upon two grounds: (1) he did not know them; and (2) he did not know his appraisal would be used by them to decide whether or not to loan money secured by the property. The appellate court affirmed that the investment counselor, negligently misrepresented value: "Roddy [had] no reasonable ground for believing the valuation to be accurate. [He] did not review the appraisal, but

---

[Section 3:112]

[1]Christiansen v. Roddy, 186 Cal. App. 3d 780, 231 Cal. Rptr. 72 (5th Dist. 1986) (implied overruling recognized by, Soderberg v. McKinney, 44 Cal. App. 4th 1760, 52 Cal. Rptr. 2d 635 (2d Dist. 1996)).

[2]Prosser and Keeton on the Law of Torts § 107 (the test is not "foreseeability" (as in Michigan law) but whether the plaintiff is the person for whose use the representation was intended).

[3]Christiansen v. Roddy, 186 Cal. App. 3d 780, 231 Cal. Rptr. 72 (5th Dist. 1986) (implied overruling recognized by, Soderberg v. McKinney, 44 Cal. App. 4th 1760, 52 Cal. Rptr. 2d 635 (2d Dist. 1996)).

merely 'glanced at it one time.' "[4]

§ 3:113 Appraisals relied upon by third persons—Appraiser's duty of care to others—Duty to unspecified persons where category is identifiable

The California courts have disapproved Christianson and the protection it afforded appraisers, although supporting its result on the facts. In Soderberg v. McKinney,[1] the appellate court reversed summary adjudication on a negligent misrepresentation claim brought by an investor against a realty appraiser who prepared an appraisal report for a brokerage firm. The California Court of Appeals held, in seriatim, that third party liability formulated for public accountants performing audits extended to real property appraisers and all "information-supplying professionals," and that such persons are under a duty to third persons regardless of whether the plaintiff's identity is specifically known. The Soderberg opinion explained the Restatement Second of Torts[2] and the California Supreme Court's Bily holding[3] as follows:

> . . . a professional supplier of information need not know the third party's name or specific identity; it is sufficient that the third party belongs to a particular group or class which the information was intended to benefit.[4]

The Soderberg appraiser had not established as a matter of law that he believed the appraisal would be used

---

[4]Christiansen v. Roddy, 186 Cal. App. 3d 780, 231 Cal. Rptr. 72 (5th Dist. 1986) (implied overruling recognized by, Soderberg v. McKinney, 44 Cal. App. 4th 1760, 52 Cal. Rptr. 2d 635 (2d Dist. 1996)).

[Section 3:113]

[1]Christiansen v. Roddy, 186 Cal. App. 3d 780, 231 Cal. Rptr. 72 (5th Dist. 1986) (implied overruling recognized by, Soderberg v. McKinney, 44 Cal. App. 4th 1760, 52 Cal. Rptr. 2d 635 (2d Dist. 1996)).

[2]Restatement 2d Torts, sec. 552, Comment h.

[3]Bily v. Arthur Young & Co., 3 Cal. 4th 370, 11 Cal. Rptr. 2d 51, 834 P.2d 745, 48 A.L.R.5th 835 (1992), as modified, (Nov. 12, 1992) (auditor may be liable to a third party non-client who relies on an audit report containing negligent misrepresentations, provided the auditor intended that the third party use the report).

[4]Soderberg v. McKinney, 44 Cal. App. 4th 1760, 52 Cal. Rptr. 2d 635 (2d Dist. 1996).

solely by the mortgage brokers:

> [T]he [defendant-appraiser] knows that a particular group or class of persons to which plaintiffs belonged—potential investors contacted by Home Loans—would rely on his report in the course of a specific type of transaction he contemplated: investing in a deed of trust secured by the appraised property. . . . It does not matter that Home Loans (instead of [defendant]) transmitted the appraisal report to plaintiffs. *An appraiser may be liable if he knew that his client would forward the report to a particular class of persons* (emphasis added)[5]

§ 3:114 Appraisals relied upon by third persons—Special relationship between appraiser and plaintiff may create duty of care

The rule for extending the duty of care also changes when a special relationship exists between the appraiser and the relying party that would create a duty of care, entitling a plaintiff to rely upon a defendant's representations. The existence of the special relationship is determined based upon the facts and circumstances of each case and the rules of the jurisdiction, which may include existence of a prior or ongoing relationship of business or trust.

In Struna v. Wolf,[1] a curator employed by a museum favorably commented about a contemporary sculpture purportedly by Elie Nadelman that was offered for sale to his department by the plaintiff, who was believed to be the owner. Through the curator's contacts, a museum patron was identified to buy the sculpture. Subsequent questions about authenticity and condition caused the patron to stop paying the seller by instalment.

The seller turned out to be a mere consignee who himself immediately purchased the sculpture for quick resale to

---

[5]Soderberg v. McKinney, 44 Cal. App. 4th 1760, 52 Cal. Rptr. 2d 635 (2d Dist. 1996), *accord,* Robert H. Sorosky M.D. Defined Benefit Pension Plan v. Hamill, 56 Cal. Rptr. 2d 313 (App. 4th Dist. 1996), review denied and ordered not to be officially published, (Nov. 20, 1996) (liability of appraisers to third person who belong to "class of persons" for whom appraisal is intended).

[Section 3:114]

[1]Struna v. Wolf, 126 Misc. 2d 1031, 484 N.Y.S.2d 392 (Sup 1985).

the patrons after the curator's comments. He sued the museum and the curator for, among other causes, negligent misrepresentation, and the museum moved for summary judgment. The court found that no special relationship existed between the museum and the plaintiff, stating, "it appears that the plaintiff was acting at arm's length in attempt to achieve a sale of the sculpture to the museum." The sale was thus an arm's length transaction that is "an antithesis of the 'special relationship' . . . required [to] support holding the defendant to a higher duty of care."

C. NEGLIGENCE

§ 3:115 General elements of tort

Everyone has a duty to act as a reasonable person of ordinary prudence to avoid foreseeable injury to others.[1] The duty must exist, the injury must be foreseeable, and the harm must be proximately caused. Persons of special knowledge, skill, and training who undertake to use such superior ability in performing services for others must act not only with reasonable care, but also in a manner that is consistent with that special skill.

Whether or not a particular defendant owes a legal duty to the plaintiff is a question of law for the court. Whether the defendant failed to adhere to the applicable standard of care is a question of fact for the finder of fact.

§ 3:116 Appraisals made to plaintiff for purpose of selling artworks owned by plaintiff

In Kremer v. Janet Fleisher Gallery,[1] Kremer sued the dealer for negligence for selling paintings consigned to her at prices far below the dealer's appraised values. After a year elapsed with no sales, the parties agreed to auction a

---

[Section 3:115]

[1]Prosser and Keeton on the Law of Torts § 32; *see* Federal Sav. and Loan Ins. Corp. v. Texas Real Estate Counselors, Inc., 955 F.2d 261 (5th Cir. 1992).

[Section 3:116]

[1]Kremer v. Janet Fleisher Gallery, Inc., 320 Pa. Super. 384, 467 A.2d 377 (1983).

few paintings at a particular auction that sold works with comparable prices to those of the appraised paintings. The auction sales were used to test the market, and the proceeds were applied to unpaid bills for storage and appraisal fees. The gallery owner instead auctioned them elsewhere, "where lower quality artwork was sold."

The trial court awarded judgment for the gallery on its counterclaim and Kremer appealed, arguing that the trial court erroneously charged the jury by omitting applicable principles of agency. Given the dealer-client relationship, the "jury should have been informed of an agent's duty to his principal, the standard of care owed, the agent's liability for breach, and that an agent is responsible to the principal for the actions of the agent's servant."[2] The Superior Court of Pennsylvania, vacating the judgment, ordered a new trial stating: "Nowhere [in the jury instructions] were the concepts of 'duty' or 'negligence' defined. We don't see how the jury could possibly have gleaned from this charge the standard by which it was supposed to measure the facts."

Trade cases do not unconditionally support the proposition that client-dealer relations establish agency or that art sellers have a duty as agents to nonartist consignors.[3] The requisite duty has been found in a sales transaction without relying upon agency in circumstances where the appraiser was hired to value a decedent's estate for federal tax purposes. In Estate of Querbach v. A & B Appraisal Service,[4] a New Jersey court considered the standard of care a personal property appraiser must exercise when valuing artwork that is part of an estate. The estate executor hired the defendant to appraise the decedent's houseful of art and antiques; a museum, one of the residuary legatees, wanted to acquire some of the art and antiques, crediting value against its future interest.

The defendant, who represented himself as an expert in fine art and recited his affiliation with a professional ap-

[2]Kremer v. Janet Fleisher Gallery, Inc., 320 Pa. Super. 384, 467 A.2d 377 (1983), *citing* Restatement (Second) of Agency §§ 379, 401, 405.

[3]*See* Chs 2 and 6.

[4]Estate of Querbach v. A & B Appraisal Serv., Civ. No. L-089362-85 (N.J. Super. Ct. 1987).

praisal organization in a solicitation letter, made a room-by-room household inspection. His appraisal listed "three (3) small unframed oil paintings, $50 ea. $150" located on a living room bookshelf. Based upon the appraisal, the estate sold one of the paintings. When the buyer took the painting for framing an appraisal was recommended. Subsequent appraisals determined the painting was by a famous American artist of the Hudson River Valley School; in fact, the signature "J.F. Cropsey 1882" appeared on the face of the painting. The painting was valued at $14,800.

The plaintiff sued the appraiser for negligence and damages. The court, finding "no cases stating the professional standards and procedures for identifying and evaluating fine art," relied upon criteria recited in Revenue Procedure 66-49[5] since the appraiser was told the purpose of the appraisal was for federal tax purposes. Since the appraiser failed to apply any of the criteria of Revenue Procedure 66-49, and offered no contrary evidence to the plaintiff's authentications of the Cropsey, the court found the appraiser negligent and awarded $14,700 in damages plus prejudgment interest.

§ 3:117 Appraisals made to plaintiff for purpose of selling artworks to plaintiff

In the Goldman case,[1] the trustees sought summary judgment on negligence claims, arguing that no duty of care existed between the dealer and the plaintiff-buyer regarding the appraisals because the underlying contract was for a sale of goods, not for an appraisal. If the dealer owed no duty, the trustees argued, neither did they.

Without deciding whether a duty of care existed between the appraiser and the buyer or whether the trustees had a duty to plaintiff, the federal district court, granting summary judgment found the trustees could not have been

---

[5] *See* Appendix 7.

[Section 3:117]

[1] Goldman v. Barnett, 793 F. Supp. 28, 18 U.C.C. Rep. Serv. 2d 55 (D. Mass. 1992); Michaels v. Wildenstein & Co., Inc., R.I.C.O. Bus. Disp. Guide (CCH) ¶ 8847, 1995 WL 326497 (S.D. N.Y. 1995) (negligent mispresentation and RICO claims against independent appraiser for allegedly overvaluing paintings sold by defendant over a period of years to plaintiff).

negligent as a matter of law because: (1) they made no appraisals; (2) they lacked qualifications to make appraisals; (3) they were not members of a professional appraisal organization; (4) they derived no revenue from appraisals; and (5) they did not sign the appraisals.

The Goldman court further found the trustees could not be negligent even if they had directly appraised and sold the Avery paintings to the plaintiff, stating that "a seller has no duty to set a fair price." That unqualified statement, in view of the significant number of trade cases[2] holding otherwise, is unsupported and does not appear to reflect current market practices.

§ 3:118 Author's comment

The negligence cases reveal the outcome when there is an initial failure to understand what an appraisal is, who the appraiser is, and how the appraiser stands in relation to his client and the subject property. The problem is exacerbated when secondarily there is a failure to distinguish between the appraisal prepared for purposes of government use—be it the IRS or a state—and the appraisal prepared for private uses and market purposes.

An appraiser retained by a client for purposes of preparing valuations used for federal or state taxes is neither an agent of the government or the client. This comports with enunciated principles in USPAP and most codes of ethics. The Querbach[1] court adopted as a standard of care IRS revenue procedures—published, established, and accepted federal procedures—for preparing art appraisals even though the case was based upon a sales transaction. The court positioned its use because the appraiser was retained to prepare an estate appraisal, the effects of which ultimately impact the government through state and estate taxes. What is novel about Querbach, but ultimately

[2]*See* Ch 2.

[Section 3:118]

[1]Estate of Querbach v. A & B Appraisal Serv., Civ. No. L-089362-85 (N.J. Super. 1987) (painting by Hudson River Valley School artist J.F. Cropsey sold for defendant's appraised value of $50 instead of expert's value of $14,800 because defendant-appraiser failed to notice artist's signature and date on painting and label verso reciting the artist's studio and address).

sound under the facts, is that rigorous federal tax standards controlled.

Many appraisals fall outside the Querbach rationale. Appraisers ordinarily are retained to prepare appraisals in conjunction with trade activities, where the appraisal is linked to sale, usually involving remuneration from sales proceeds to the person making the appraisal. These are the facts of Kremer, Goldman, and Rosen[2] (based on fraud), but the courts fail to make this important distinction. Such cases should not stand or fall on the existence of an underlying agency. USPAP eliminates agency between client and appraiser. The fact of the appraisal should be enough to trigger the requisite duty and support a claim of negligence. Agency should not be read into a cause of action for appraisal negligence.

In Kremer, the dealer was the client's agent and represented her vis-a-vis others, so in that case agency happened to exist, but negligence claims should have been actionable even without agency. In Goldman, it was unclear for whom the dealer was acting as agent. On the facts presented, the seller-appraiser was arguably acting in a conflict of interest with trustees on the one hand, and the buyer on the other. In fact, the court concluded that if the dealer were agent for the trust, all the plaintiff's claims would fail, because the duties would run exclusively to the trust.

The Goldman reasoning is even more perplexing because whether or not an appraisal has been made is considered by some courts a question of fact for the jury, not a matter of law for summary disposition by the court. Yet the court never addressed the issue of whether the trustees themselves made and presented an appraisal to the plaintiff; instead, it concluded circuitously that because the trustees were not qualified to appraise, ipso facto, they did not appraise. That is not the issue: The issue is whether without qualifications the trustees nonetheless did appraise the art for the plaintiff and invited the plaintiff's

---

[2]Goldman v. Barnett, 793 F. Supp. 28, 18 U.C.C. Rep. Serv. 2d 55 (D. Mass. 1992); Rosen v. Spanierman, 711 F. Supp. 749, 8 U.C.C. Rep. Serv. 2d 713 (S.D. N.Y. 1989), judgment vacated in part and remanded, 894 F.2d 28, 10 U.C.C. Rep. Serv. 2d 846 (2d Cir. 1990); Kremer v. Janet Fleisher Gallery, Inc., 320 Pa. Super. 384, 467 A.2d 377, 380 (1983).

reliance by virtue of their exclusive and perhaps monopolistic relationship with and control over the Avery oeuvre. Moreover, the trust did receive revenues from sales, and the degree of income appears to have had a direct relationship under consignment arrangements to the allegedly misstated higher values.

Finally, Goldman raises the provocative issue, not addressed by the court, of what obligation is imposed on trustees to fairly and honestly value art in a trust, given the recognized societal goal of preserving the reputation of the deceased artist and maintaining the integrity of the oeuvre for the public. Fiduciary obligations acquire significance in situations where the trust res comprises the single or substantial source of the artist's works for market. False values undermine the integrity of the artist's oeuvre, and have consequences for institutional and private collections as well as the market.

Persons using appraisers should be mindful that trade appraisers are not considered agents absent contractual arrangements that support that relationship. Goldman makes clear that the defendant may be able to assert agency against the appraisal recipient. Where the appraisal is commingled with other trade functions, cases do not support finding a duty of care. Contractual recitation of the capacity in which the appraiser is being retained, for whose benefit, and by what standards will, at a minimum, ameliorate misunderstanding. Reciting that the person making the trade appraisal will comply with USPAP is one way to clarify the trade appraisal assignment and establish a standard by which a duty will be measured.

D. FRAUD

§ 3:119 Generally

The elements of fraud, basically stated, require false representation of material fact made with knowledge of falsity for the purpose of inducing the plaintiff to rely, plus actual justifiable reliance upon the false representation by plaintiff to plaintiff's damage. This section presents examples of civil cases, but the fraudulent appraisal generated as a part of criminal scam has been the subject of government enforcement actions under federal statutes.[1] Law enforcement and Federal Trade Commission actions handle unsolicited appraisals prepared in the context of scams quite differently from courts dealing with appraisals, often client-solicited, in regular commercial trade.

In Goldman v. Barnett,[2] the plaintiff sued an appraiser-dealer and the trustees of the estate of Milton Avery for fraud, alleging overvalued appraisals induced him to purchase Avery paintings in an amount in excess of $1 million. The dealer was consigned works by the estate, confirmed selling prices with trustees, made appraisals for the purpose of selling to the plaintiff, and actually made sales to the plaintiff.

On the motion of trustees for summary judgment, the federal district court found sufficient evidence in the record to prove the dealer's fraudulent appraisal and that his fraud could be attributed to the trustees based on his activities "within the scope of his authority as agent for the Trust." The court concluded letters written reciting the trustees' knowledge of appraised values could indicate ratification of the misrepresentation, and that a jury could find the trustees vested the dealer with authority to negotiate prices and to consummate sales.

The defendants argued that the appraisals could not support fraud because appraised value is mere opinion, falling short of the misrepresentation of material fact that is required. The court did not directly address that contention, but it decided that a jury could find that one who held himself out as an expert appraiser could be found to possess knowledge of market value. This principle has been applied to auction appraisals made under certain circumstances.[3]

[Section 3:119]

[1] *See* Ch 11.

[2] Goldman v. Barnett, 793 F. Supp. 28, 18 U.C.C. Rep. Serv. 2d 55 (D. Mass. 1992).

[3] *See, e.g.,* Pasternack v. Esskay Art Galleries, Inc., 90 F. Supp. 849 (W.D. Ark. 1950) and Ch 5.

In Rosen v. Spanierman,[4] the defendant-gallery provided the plaintiffs with a series of appraisals for a painting by John Singer Sargent from 1968, when the gallery owner sold it, through 1986. Some of the appraisals were used by the plaintiffs for insurance policies. The plaintiffs received higher appraisal values from others, but when they placed the painting at auction many years later, it was withdrawn as inauthentic.

The plaintiffs sued the gallery and its owner for, inter alia, fraud. The trial court dismissed the case, finding that the alleged fraudulent misrepresentations would have occurred in the underlying transaction of sale of the painting, paid for by the plaintiffs' in-laws; since the painting was a gift in a transaction to which they were not a party, the court found that the plaintiffs could not have relied. The Second Circuit reversed and remanded on the fraud claim, concluding that a fraud could have been perpetuated irrespective of source of payment.

E. EVIDENTIARY ASPECTS OF APPRAISAL

§ 3:120 Appraisal as finding of fact or conclusion of law

Is the query as to whether statements constitute an appraisal an issue of fact for the trier of fact[1] or a conclusion of law for the court? In Struna,[2] a case on point, a Metropolitan Museum of Art curator made oral statements relating to the quality and value of a sculpture by artist Elie Nadelman shown to him by a dealer representing the plaintiff-owner. A sale was arranged through the curator and the dealer to museum patrons, who paid the owner by installments. The patrons stopped paying when they became concerned about the authenticity of the sculpture.

The plaintiff-owner sued the curator and the Metropolitan Museum of Art for negligent misrepresentation, stating that he had been a mere consignee of the sculpture at

[4]Rosen v. Spanierman, 894 F.2d 28, 10 U.C.C. Rep. Serv. 2d 846 (2d Cir. 1990) (appraisals held time-barred as contractual warranties under the UCC statute of limitations).

[Section 3:120]

[1]Struna v. Wolf, 126 Misc. 2d 1031, 484 N.Y.S.2d 392 (Sup 1985).

[2]Struna v. Wolf, 126 Misc. 2d 1031, 484 N.Y.S.2d 392 (Sup 1985).

the time of showing and would not have purchased it for resale without the curator's statements, which he argued constituted an appraisal. The defendant-museum argued that even if the statements had been made, they did not constitute an appraisal.

A federal district court in New York granted the museum's motion for summary judgment because it found no relationship between the parties that would give rise to a duty of care. If the issue of whether an appraisal was made had been the sole basis for the summary judgment, the court emphasized that it would have denied the motion because conflicting affidavits raised factual issues as to "whether or not the Museum appraised the sculpture."[3]

§ 3:121 Admissibility of appraisal—Generally

The admissibility of the appraisal, and its relevance, weight, and value are a function of the facts and circumstances of the particular claims and the applicable rules of evidence and procedure, which obviously should be examined in the context of the litigation. As noted in the following section, art appraisals have been evaluated as evidence.

§ 3:122 Admissibility of appraisal—Settlement offers and negotiations

Rule 408 of the Federal Rules of Civil Procedure makes inadmissible evidence of offers, acceptances, conduct, or statements made during settlement negotiations that are presented to prove a party's liability for a claim or its amount.[1] Rule 408 does not require exclusion when the evidence is offered for other purposes, for instance, proving bias or witness prejudice.[2] The objection to the admission

---

[3]Struna v. Wolf, 126 Misc. 2d 1031, 484 N.Y.S.2d 392 (Sup 1985).

[Section 3:122]

[1]The scope of settlement offers has been circumscribed by judicial rulings that a claim must be in actual dispute at the time the statement was made or the document was prepared. A dispute has been held to exist even though no claims were yet filed and the parties disputed the validity of a claim.

[2]Fed. R. Civ. Proc. 408.

can be made by motion in limine.[3]

In Davis v. Rowe,[4] written and oral statements about the value of artwork made by a gallery owner to his insurance company were held inadmissible under Rule 408 in an action brought under the Illinois art consignment statute by an artist's widow. A fire occurred in the gallery and paintings by the plaintiff's late husband were destroyed. The owner's communications with the insurer to settle the claim consisted of: a letter to the insurance carrier that the "value of the collection [burned] was $4,635,000," subsequently affirmed under oath; and a letter to the artist's widow that the value of the destroyed works exceeded the insurance proceeds and that the consigned artwork exceeded $250,000, the limit on the amount of insurance he had agreed to obtain under the consignment agreement with the widow. The court granted the owner's motion in limine to exclude the letters for purposes of proving the value of the art.

§ 3:123 Admissibility of evidence of value to prove appraiser negligence

In Kremer v. Janet Fleisher Gallery,[1] Kremer sued the dealer for negligence for selling paintings consigned to the gallery at prices far below their value. The dealer appraised some of the consigned paintings and subsequently agreed to auction a few paintings at a particular auction to test the market and apply the proceeds to an unpaid bill for appraisals and storage. The gallery owner instead auctioned them from a different gallery, "where lower quality artwork was sold."

The trial court did not allow the plaintiff to introduce evidence on value based on a finding that she had authorized the sales, and value was only relevant to damages. The appellate court, vacating the judgment and ordering a new trial based upon exclusion of evidence, stated:

> Evidence establishing a discrepancy between the value of

---

[3]Davis v. Rowe, 1993 WL 34867 (N.D. Ill. 1993).

[4]Davis v. Rowe, 1993 WL 34867 (N.D. Ill. 1993).

[Section 3:123]

[1]Kremer v. Janet Fleisher Gallery, Inc., 320 Pa. Super. 384, 467 A.2d 377 (1983).

> the paintings and the price they commanded was . . . relevant to . . . damages, but before that, it was relevant to the issue of liability, specifically, to whether appellants had as a result of appellee's negligence suffered an injury.[2]

The type of evidence held admissible and relevant to liability was the gallery owner's written appraisals of works of art by the same artists as those who had done the plaintiff's paintings, to which she had testified in court. The appellate court found the documentary evidence would have had "extra weight" with the jury, especially because the gallery owner's expert testified that written appraisals have more "authority" than oral appraisals. Furthermore, the appraisals constituted an admission of a party-opponent, an exception to the hearsay rule.

The appellate court also found as error that justified a new trial the court's exclusion of testimony by an expert in the art business who owned paintings by the same artists as Kremer; he would have testified to the prices he paid and the appreciation of the paintings over time. The appellate court stated: "The question of whether evidence of a prior purchase price is admissible on the issue of current value depends upon whether the prior sale was too remote in time to be relevant. . . . The prior sale was not too remote."[3]

§ 3:124 Codes of ethics as standards of care—Introduction

What is the evidentiary value of a code of ethics on standards of care for preparing personal property appraisals? Although professional personal property appraisal organizations are regularly identified in cases involving personal property negligence, personal property organizational codes of ethics are not mentioned in the opinions, nor have they mentioned the applicable USPAP Standards 7 to 8, perhaps because USPAP is so new.

However, offering into evidence codes of ethics to establish standards of care has been attempted in real property

[2] Kremer v. Janet Fleisher Gallery, Inc., 320 Pa. Super. 384, 467 A.2d 377 (1983).

[3] Kremer v. Janet Fleisher Gallery, Inc., 320 Pa. Super. 384, 467 A.2d 377 at 380 (1983).

appraisal negligence actions, as well as other professional undertakings, for example, engineering and computer science. The results provide interesting analogies for personal property appraisal.

Even if the evidentiary value of personal property codes of ethics and standards is clarified by future judicial decisions, appraisers should be aware that ethical codes are aspects of the appraiser-client relationship, but are not its absolute determinant. The totality of the appraiser-client relationship turns upon the exercise of personal and professional judgment and ethics in the context of each appraisal assignment.

§ 3:125 Codes of ethics as standards of care—Codes of ethics as material evidence

Codes of ethics are admitted as a clear enunciation of the specific standard of care applicable to a particular defendant where licensure exists for the professional group and the defendant is a member. In such cases, e.g., doctors and lawyers, courts have held that codes of ethics establish specific standards for purposes of professional malpractice and negligence.

Codes of ethics for licensed engineers have been deemed admissible and relevant at trial over objection to show related industry standards of conduct for the unlicensed. The trial court found the codes relevant because they provided guidance in determining what conduct is appropriate for an unlicensed engineer.[1] The Tenth Circuit, upholding the ruling on appeal, agreed that such codes of ethics may be limited to examples of standards, but cannot be the sole standard of care because professional licensure existed but did not apply to the particular defendant (e.g., an engineering license was required, but not for

---

[Section 3:125]

[1]The Post Office v. Portec, Inc., 913 F.2d 802 (10th Cir. 1990), cert. granted, judgment vacated, 499 U.S. 915, 111 S. Ct. 1299, 113 L. Ed. 2d 235 (1991) and decision vacated, appeal dismissed as moot, 935 F.2d 1105 (10th Cir. 1991).

the type of engineering practiced by defendant).[2] Codes of ethics for real property appraisers were also admitted in negligence action against real property appraisers and used as the standard of care against those defendants.

§ 3:126 Codes of ethics as standards of care—Admissibility of testimony about code of ethics provisions as establishing standard of care

The codes constitute material evidence regarding standards of care. Testimony about the codes may also be admissible and relevant, even in instances where the codes are for licensed professionals, but the defendants themselves are unlicensed.

In the engineering field, testimony about violations of specific provisions of codes of ethics as breaches of duty of care has been held admissible even though the codes applied to licensed engineers but the action involved unlicensed engineers. In Portec, the court allowed the testimony because the defendant failed to object at trial to the admission of the testimony, after objecting and being overruled on admission of the code itself.

If testimony is admitted over an objection, the objector can still try to limit the testimony by seeking to restrict its use or weight.[1] If the testimony is admitted over objection, the objector can request limiting jury instructions reciting that the code of ethics and testimony about the code is but one example of comparable conduct, but is not an enunciation of the single standard of care owed by defendant.[2]

---

[2]The Post Office v. Portec, Inc., 913 F.2d 802 (10th Cir. 1990), cert. granted, judgment vacated, 499 U.S. 915, 111 S. Ct. 1299, 113 L. Ed. 2d 235 (1991) and decision vacated, appeal dismissed as moot, 935 F.2d 1105 (10th Cir. 1991).

[Section 3:126]

[1]The Post Office v. Portec, Inc., 913 F.2d 802 (10th Cir. 1990), cert. granted, judgment vacated, 499 U.S. 915, 111 S. Ct. 1299, 113 L. Ed. 2d 235 (1991) and decision vacated, appeal dismissed as moot, 935 F.2d 1105 (10th Cir. 1991).

[2]The Post Office v. Portec, Inc., 913 F.2d 802 (10th Cir. 1990), cert. granted, judgment vacated, 499 U.S. 915, 111 S. Ct. 1299, 113 L. Ed.

§ 3:127 Codes of ethics as standards of care—Federal appraisal standards of care—USPAP and real property appraisal

Does USPAP create a federal appraisal standard enunciating the standard of care for appraisers in negligence actions, at least for licensed appraisers? Notwithstanding FIRREA requirements for real property appraisers, and acceptance of USPAP as the applicable standards through state testing for licensure and certification of real property appraisers pursuant to FIRREA, the Fifth Circuit declined to accept a "a federalized standard of care" for real property appraisers in a prelicensure appraisal negligence action brought by Federal Savings and Loan Insurance Corp., as plaintiff, and the FDIC, as plaintiff-appellee, the successors in interest to failed savings and loans.[1]

In Federal Savings, the defendant-real estate appraisers challenged the district court's finding that its failure to verify completion of alleged improvements of property constituted negligence. They asserted that industry standards permitted limited scope appraisals, referred to as "windshield" appraisals, in which verification is not necessary, and that they fully disclosed in their reports that they had performed only limited scope appraisals. There was no absolute duty to verify because industry standards do not require verification; therefore, the defendants contended they were not negligent.

The federal district court in Texas made no explicit holding on a federal specific standard of care that is applicable to real property appraisers, finding them negligent under various organizational codes of ethics, which both parties had offered: the codes of ethics and standards of practice from the American Institute of Real Estate Appraisers and the Society of Real Estate Appraisers. USPAP, published after the defendants completed the conduct constituting the negligence action, does not appear to have

---

2d 235 (1991) and decision vacated, appeal dismissed as moot, 935 F.2d 1105 (10th Cir. 1991).

[Section 3:127]

[1]Federal Sav. and Loan Ins. Corp. v. Texas Real Estate Counselors, Inc., 955 F.2d 261 (5th Cir. 1992).

been offered into evidence, although the organizational codes and practices contained provisions similar to some adopted by USPAP.

Appraisal institutes and professional organizations filed as amici curiae, asking the appellate court to reverse and remand. The Fifth Circuit, finding that there was no evidence of federalized standards below and none on appeal, declined to reach the issue of whether a federalized standard of care existed and upheld negligence for failure to verify completion of the improvements.[2]

§ 3:128 Codes of ethics as standards of care—Federal appraisal standards of care—USPAP and personal property appraisal

Whether USPAP will be evidentiary of a sole standard of care or limited to one example among many appraisal standards for personal property appraisers is a question of first impression for the courts. To date, no reported case could be found that relied upon USPAP's personal property standards rules as an independent standard for liability in a negligence action.[1] Material and testimonial evidence on USPAP, as well as trade practice not covered in codes of ethics or USPAP, should be admissible pursuant to general rules of evidence and relevant for other purposes in addition to standards.

§ 3:129 IRS rules and procedures as standards of care

One state court relied upon IRS Revenue Procedures for art appraisal to establish the standard of care for fine art and antique personal property appraisal in a negligence

---

[2]Federal Sav. and Loan Ins. Corp. v. Texas Real Estate Counselors, Inc., 955 F.2d 261 (5th Cir. 1992) (case remanded on issue of whether accepting a limited scope appraisal assignment constituted negligence).

[Section 3:128]

[1]Reference has been made by courts that USPAP might provide a federal standard of liability as it applies to real property appraisers, who are licensed and certified under state laws pursuant to FIRREA mandate. No ruling could be found that actually held USPAP is the federal standard in realty appraisal cases.

action against the appraiser.[1] He represented himself to the executor of the estate as an expert, a fine art appraiser qualified to do a household inspection of the decedent's art and antiques[2] Since the appraiser was told the purpose of the appraisal was for state and federal income tax purposes, the court decided that the Revenue Procedures for appraising fine art were properly applied.[3] If Revenue Procedures serve as standards, other IRS issuances may also be offered as evidence to demonstrate standards and the appraiser's failure to follow established protocols for art appraisal.

F. APPRAISER AS PUBLIC OFFICIAL

§ 3:130 Generally

Depending upon the type of appraisal assignment, an appraiser may be deemed a public official. In United States v. Madeoy,[1] a Veterans Administration fee appraiser was convicted of bribery for performing appraisals on real property for which the appraiser rendered inflated values. This caused the VA, in reliance, to issue certificates which the Federal Housing Administration relied upon in issuing insurance commitments.

The appraiser argued on appeal that he could not be convicted of bribery counts because he was not a "public official" under the bribery charging statute,[2] and that the trial court had erroneously charged the jury that his status was a matter of law. Holding that whether an individual is a public official is a question of law for judicial resolution, the Court of Appeals for the District of Columbia emphasized responsibilities of appraisers in performing

---

[Section 3:129]

[1]Estate of Querbach v. A & B Appraisal Serv., Civ. No. L-089362-85 (N.J. Super. 1987). *See* Appendix 7.

[2]Estate of Querbach v. A & B Appraisal Serv., Civ. No. L-089362-85 (N.J. Super. 1987).

[3]Estate of Querbach v. A & B Appraisal Serv., Civ. No. L-089362-85 (N.J. Super. 1987).

[Section 3:130]

[1]U.S. v. Madeoy, 912 F.2d 1486 (D.C. Cir. 1990).

[2]18 U.S.C.A. § 201(a)(1).

public duties, which are significant for federal appraisal tax practice and all appraisals in an interdependent market economy:

> [T]he [U.S.] Supreme Court has interpreted the term "public official" to mean a person who "occupies a position of public trust with official federal responsibilities." [A] fee appraiser must certify that he knows the applicable regulations and must promise not to accept any assignment for which he has a conflict of interest or to take any payment other than the appraiser's set fee.[3]

VII. APPRAISER AS EXPERT IN COURT

§ 3:131 Qualifications of expert witnesses

Expert opinion is admissible evidence relevant to issues of value.[1] " 'The determination of the qualification of an expert is largely a matter for the discretion of the trial court.' "[2] In determining admissibility of expert testimony, the court may exclude an expert's analysis that is inadequate or incomplete.[3] The court may take judicial notice of expert qualifications based upon prior opinions.[4]

The opinion is never more important than the underlying facts, and the facts must "corroborate" the opinion, or the court can discount or reject it. To be persuasive, "the

---

[3]U.S. v. Madeoy, 912 F.2d 1486, 1494 (D.C. Cir. 1990).

[Section 3:131]

[1]Rule 702 of the Federal Rules of Evidence provides: "If scientific, technical, or other specialized knowledge will assist the trier of fact to understand the evidence or to determine a fact in issue, a witness qualified as an expert by knowledge, skill, experience, training, or education, may testify thereto in the form of an opinion or otherwise." "The proponent of the testimony bears the burden of [proof] that their (sic) proffered testimony meets these requirements [FRE 702]." Frey v. Chicago Conservation Center, 119 F. Supp. 2d 794, 55 Fed. R. Evid. Serv. 1237 (N.D. Ill. 2000). *See also* Ch 11 § 11:42, and Biagiotti v. C.I.R., T.C. Memo. 1986-460, 1986 WL 21685 (1986).

[2]State v. Kennedy, 20 Conn. App. 354, 567 A.2d 841 (1989) (citations omitted).

[3]Frey v. Chicago Conservation Center, 119 F. Supp. 2d 794, 55 Fed. R. Evid. Serv. 1237 (N.D. Ill. 2000) (appraiser's expert testimony on ozone damage to art excluded under FRE 702, admitting witness' limited lay opinion under FRE 701).

[4]Ferrari v. C.I.R., T.C. Memo. 1989-521, 1989 WL 109420 (1989), judgment aff'd, 931 F.2d 54 (4th Cir. 1991) (unpublished disposition).

opinion should be expressed by a person qualified in background, experience, intelligence, familiarity with the property, and with the valuation problem involved."[5] Expert valuations that provide "no convincing reasons in support of . . . determinations" are deemed unpersuasive.[6] In examining the competence of appraisers as expert witnesses, courts have considered the following: scholarly background;[7] teaching experience;[8] publications;[9] membership in professional appraisal organization;[10] membership in the Art Advisory Panel;[11] direct market experience;[12] museum employment;[13] sales experience with the type of art appraised;[14] sales experience with the art appraised;[15] direct physical examination or visual inspection by photo-

[5]Reynolds v. C.I.R., T.C. Memo. 1981-714, 1981 WL 11092 (1981).

[6]Koftinow v. Comm'r, 1986 WL 21606.

[7]Frates v. C.I.R., T.C. Memo. 1987-79, 1987 WL 40138 (1987) (scholarly education of appraiser but appraiser's opinion rejected on other grounds).

[8]Monaghan v. C.I.R., T.C. Memo. 1981-280, 1981 WL 10597 (1981) (appraiser as professor who received awards for academic work).

[9]Monaghan v. C.I.R., T.C. Memo. 1981-280, 1981 WL 10597 (1981).

[10]Ferrari v. C.I.R., T.C. Memo. 1989-521, 1989 WL 109420 (1989), judgment aff'd, 931 F.2d 54 (4th Cir. 1991) (unpublished).

[11]Ferrari v. C.I.R., T.C. Memo. 1989-521, 1989 WL 109420 (1989), judgment aff'd, 931 F.2d 54 (4th Cir. 1991); *see also* Furstenberg v. U.S., 219 Ct. Cl. 473, 595 F.2d 603 (1979).

[12]Furstenberg v. U.S., 219 Ct. Cl. 473, 595 F.2d 603 (1979) (sales experience); Frates v. C.I.R., T.C. Memo. 1987-79, 1987 WL 40138 (1987) (gallery owner with direct market experience expert witness for FMV).

[13]Frates v. C.I.R., T.C. Memo. 1987-79, 1987 WL 40138 (1987) (deputy director of National Gallery of Art qualified as expert witness).

[14]Shein v. C.I.R, T.C. Memo. 1987-329, 1987 WL 40384 (1987); *see also* Furstenberg v. U.S., 219 Ct. Cl. 473, 595 F.2d 603 (1979) (sales experience with artist); Reynolds v. C.I.R., T.C. Memo. 1981-714, 1981 WL 11092 (1981) (art dealer involved in purchase of many works by same artist and seller of same works); Rupke v. C. I. R., T.C. Memo. 1973-234, 1973 WL 2413 (1973), recommendation regarding acquiescence, 1974 WL 35958 (I.R.S. AOD 1974) (taxpayer's appraiser had never bought or sold paintings by Gerolamo Bassano whose work was donated).

[15]Shein v. C.I.R, T.C. Memo. 1987-329, 1987 WL 40384 (1987).

graph;[16] familiarity with sales prices of comparable artworks and their sources;[17] familiarity with the CROSSAQ factor for comparables;[18] familiarity with provenance of the artwork;[19] degree to which the appraisal is objectively supported by data;[20] appraiser bias;[21] and general acceptance of methodology by other experts in the field.[22]

§ 3:132 Testimony

Value is ordinarily determined by expert testimony,[1] and virtually always by experts in tax matters. The opinions of experts are "weighed according to their

---

[16]In re Lisser, 1990 WL 105824 (visuals of artworks relied upon by appraiser did not match actual artworks donated); Lightman v. C.I.R., T.C. Memo. 1985-315, 1985 WL 14942 (1985) (probative value of physical examination "weighed heavily" by court); Monaghan v. C.I.R., T.C. Memo. 1981-280, 1981 WL 10597 (1981) (appraiser examined work by photographs, not direct examination).

[17]*See* Ch 3 §§ 3:54 to 3:59.

[18]Frates v. C.I.R., T.C. Memo. 1987-79, 1987 WL 40138 (1987) (subject matter, quality of execution).

[19]Furstenberg v. U.S., 219 Ct. Cl. 473, 595 F.2d 603 (1979); Peters v. C.I.R., T.C. Memo. 1977-128, 1977 WL 3425 (1977), aff'd, 601 F.2d 603 (9th Cir. 1979) (provenance completely lacking in appraisals).

[20]Reynolds v. C.I.R., T.C. Memo. 1981-714, 1981 WL 11092 (1981) (expert opinions without factual support).

[21]Furstenberg v. U.S., 219 Ct. Cl. 473, 595 F.2d 603 (1979) (government appraiser found to be biased because of his position on Art Advisory Panel, adopting trial court's findings of fact except for bias of appraiser); Frates v. C.I.R., T.C. Memo. 1987-79, 1987 WL 40138 (1987) (appraisal based on race or gender of artists not objectively supported by data); Reynolds v. C.I.R., T.C. Memo. 1981-714, 1981 WL 11092 (1981).

[22]Frey v. Chicago Conservation Center, 119 F. Supp. 2d 794, 55 Fed. R. Evid. Serv. 1237 (N.D. Ill. 2000) (expert's conclusion that ozone damaged plaintiffs' artworks was not supported by evidence that processes used were deemed by others appraisers and conservators to "yield reliable results.").

[Section 3:132]

[1]U.S. v. Tobin, 576 F.2d 687 (5th Cir. 1978); *but cf.* Kremer v. Janet Fleisher Gallery, Inc., 320 Pa. Super. 384, 467 A.2d 377, 380 (1983) (in a civil case, "The owner of personalty traditionally has been permitted to testify to its value in civil cases." The presumption that the owner knows the value of his or her things can be overcome by defendant's evidence.).

qualifications and other relevant evidence."[2] Expert witness opinions aid the court in areas requiring "specialized training, knowledge, or judgment."[3]

However, the court is not bound by expert opinions.[4] The court may accept the expert opinion "in entirety," "be selective as to the portions . . . utilize[d],"[5] weight the testimony,[6] or categorically reject it in totality. Thus, courts have rejected expert witness testimony where it was based upon exaggerated values;[7] the wrong artworks;[8] defied common sense;[9] excluded bequeathed art;[10] ignored relevant facts;[11] contravened the interests of hypothetical sellers;[12] selected the wrong market;[13] or the testimony provided no convincing reasons.[14] or no documented methodology of general acceptance by other experts in the

---

[2]Johnson v. C.I.R., 85 T.C. 469, 477, 1985 WL 15393 (1985).

[3]Williford v. C. I. R., T.C. Memo. 1992-450, T.C.M. (RIA) ¶ 92450 (1992).

[4]Williford v. C. I. R., T.C. Memo. 1992-450, T.C.M. (RIA) ¶ 92450 (1992); Engel v. Comm'r, T.C. Memo 1993-362 (1993).

[5]Engel v. Comm'r, T.C. Memo 1993-362 (1993).

[6]Shein v. C.I.R, T.C. Memo. 1987-329, 1987 WL 40384 (1987).

[7]Chiu v. Commissioner of Internal Revenue, 84 T.C. 722, 734–35, 1985 WL 15340 (1985).

[8]In re Lisser, 1990 WL 105824.

[9]Estate of O'Keeffe v. C.I.R., T.C. Memo. 1992-210, T.C.M. (RIA) ¶ 92210 (1992).

[10]Estate of O'Keeffe v. C.I.R., T.C. Memo. 1992-210, T.C.M. (RIA) ¶ 92210 (1992).

[11]Estate of Palmer v. C.I.R., 839 F.2d 420, 44 Ed. Law Rep. 1063 (8th Cir. 1988); Estate of O'Keeffe v. C.I.R., T.C. Memo. 1992-210, T.C.M. (RIA) ¶ 92210 (1992).

[12]Estate of O'Keeffe v. C.I.R., T.C. Memo. 1992-210, T.C.M. (RIA) ¶ 92210 (1992).

[13]Anselmo v. Commissioner of Internal Revenue, 80 T.C. 872, 1983 WL 14829 (1983), decision aff'd, 757 F.2d 1208 (11th Cir. 1985) (gemstones); Estate of O'Keeffe v. C.I.R., T.C. Memo. 1992-210, T.C.M. (RIA) ¶ 92210 (1992) (paintings); Koftinow v. C.I.R., T.C. Memo. 1986-396, 1986 WL 21606 (1986), recommendation regarding acquiescence, AOD- 1987-23, 1987 WL 430249 (I.R.S. AOD 1987) (sculpture).

[14]Koftinow v. C.I.R., T.C. Memo. 1986-396, 1986 WL 21606 (1986), recommendation regarding acquiescence, AOD- 1987-23, 1987 WL 430249 (I.R.S. AOD 1987).

field.[15]

The inadmissibility of the underlying basis for the opinion, however, may not defeat admissibility of the expert opinion, although objection can and should be directed to the weight of opinion.[16] In State v. Kennedy,[17] the appellate court ruled: "an expert may testify to value, though his knowledge of details is simply derived from inadmissible sources." The court concluded a museum docent familiar with a stolen collection of netsuke on which she had given weekly lectures had sufficient general education and personal knowledge to "render a competent opinion as to the value of . . . missing artifacts despite the fact that she had never previously evaluated collections."[18]

Expert appraisal reports are often supported by "clarifying [court] testimony."[19] Appraisal reports that are unsupported by direct testimony have been held to have "no probative value."[20] In most, but not all cases, courts consider together the material and testimonial evidence.[21] Rule 143(f) permits expert appraisal opinion through admission into evidence of expert reports, and tax opinions

---

[15]Frey v. Chicago Conservation Center, 119 F. Supp. 2d 794, 55 Fed. R. Evid. Serv. 1237 (N.D. Ill. 2000) (expert's conclusion that ozone damaged plaintiffs' artworks was not supported by evidence that processes used were deemed by others appraisers and conservators to "yield reliable results.").

[16]State v. Kennedy, 20 Conn. App. 354, 567 A.2d 841 (1989).

[17]State v. Kennedy, 20 Conn. App. 354, 567 A.2d 841 (1989) (citations omitted).

[18]State v. Kennedy, 20 Conn. App. 354, 567 A.2d 841 (1989) (citations omitted).

[19]Koftinow v. C.I.R., T.C. Memo. 1986-396, 1986 WL 21606 (1986), recommendation regarding acquiescence, AOD- 1987-23, 1987 WL 430249 (I.R.S. AOD 1987).

[20]Lightman v. C.I.R., T.C. Memo. 1985-315, 1985 WL 14942 (1985) (appraisal accorded no probative weight where appraiser not called to testify); Mathias v. Commissioner of Internal Revenue, 50 T.C. 994, 999, 1968 WL 1498 (T.C. 1968), acq. 1969-1 C.B. and acq. 1969-2 C.B. and recommendation regarding acquiescence, 1969 WL 20641 (I.R.S. AOD 1969).

[21]Biagiotti v. C.I.R., T.C. Memo. 1986-460, 1986 WL 21685 (1986) (both); Shein v. C.I.R, T.C. Memo. 1987-329, 1987 WL 40384 (1987) (both).

may rely upon appraisal reports alone.[22]

§ 3:133 Sources of appraisal litigation—Tax

Tax litigation involving appraisal is based upon sections of the Internal Revenue Code and Regulations promulgated thereunder for charitable contributions of art, estate and gift taxes.[1]

§ 3:134 Sources of appraisal litigation—Civil

Civil litigation involving appraisals is based upon negligence, negligent misrepresentation and fraud, and other claims filed in state and federal courts.[1]

---

[22] Engel v. Comm'r, T.C. Memo 1993-362 (1993) (court rejected written appraisal as an "expert report" under Tax Rules of Practice and Procedure Rule 143(f) and disregarded appraisal as direct testimony of appraiser because it offered "little assistance").

[Section 3:133]

[1] *See* §§ 3:34 to 3:76.

[Section 3:134]

[1] *See* §§ 3:77 to 3:107.

Chapter 4

Uniform Commercial Code (UCC)

I. INTRODUCTION

II. UCC Article 2: SALES

A. APPLICATION OF ARTICLE 2 TO ART

B. TITLE

C. EXPRESS WARRANTY

D. IMPLIED WARRANTIES

E. STATUTE OF LIMITATIONS

F. ORAL CONTRACTS TO PURCHASE ARTWORKS

KeyCite®: Cases and other legal materials listed in KeyCite Scope can be researched through West's KeyCite service on Westlaw®. Use KeyCite to check citations for form, parallel references, prior and later history, and comprehensive citator information, including citations to other decisions and secondary materials.

I. INTRODUCTION

§ 4:1 Generally

Attempts have been made to use the Uniform Commercial Code (UCC) to resolve art purchase and sale disputes under article 2, "Sales," and to prioritize interests among creditors claiming consignment interests in art from those claiming it as collateral under article 9, "Secured Transactions."

Under article 2, the two primary areas of art disputes involving purchase and sale are title and authenticity. Although many actions are filed under article 2 alleging breach of warranty provisions based upon improper authentications or misattributions, most of them have been summarily adjudicated because they were barred by the UCC statute of limitations. The breach of warranty claims, rarely examined, are evaluated here.

A predicate issue for article 2 claims is UCC applicability to artworks. Although commentators and opinions have historically expressed concerns about applying commercial law to art, many courts today appear willing to use UCC principles, and some expressly discuss the propriety of UCC application. By the time the matter becomes a creditor dispute within the reach of article 9, or a creditor demand on consigned goods under article 2, the courts have no problem treating art as the type of goods that are attachable, collateralized, and secured for debt. Article 9 cases involve artists, dealers, creditors, and, sometimes, the trustee in bankruptcy, alleging competing interests under various theories.

The art deal is often bound by a handshake and a promise. Such oral agreements are vulnerable under the UCC statute of frauds, and the statute has been an effective defense for all types of buyers. The parol evidence rule is also a common evidentiary issue in art trading cases.

This chapter contains many, but not all, the UCC statutes and cases discussed in this treatise. In the interests of space, UCC matters discussed in other chapters because of their relevance to that chapter cannot be repeated here. Please note that Ch 2 §§ 2:28 to 2:39, Ch 5 §§ 5:2 to 5:11 and 5:50 to 5:79, and Ch 9 §§ 9:2 to 9:4 and 9:52 to 9:118 include important UCC materials. Where practical, UCC cases cited elsewhere are also footnoted throughout this chapter for the convenience of the reader.

II. UCC Article 2: SALES

A. APPLICATION OF ARTICLE 2 TO ART

§ 4:2 Art as "goods"

UCC article 2 contains different types of warranties: warranty of title[1] and against infringement;[2] express war-

---

[Section 4:2]

[1]UCC § 2-312; *see also* Porter v. Wertz, 68 A.D.2d 141, 416 N.Y.S.2d 254, 26 U.C.C. Rep. Serv. 876 (1st Dep't 1979), judgment aff'd, 53 N.Y.2d 696, 439 N.Y.S.2d 105, 421 N.E.2d 500, 30 U.C.C. Rep. Serv.

ranties by affirmation, promise, and description;[3] and implied warranties of merchantability[4] and fitness for a particular purpose.[5] Article 2 applies to sales transactions of goods, as well as to certain transfers involving a mix of goods and services. Are artworks classified as UCC goods? If they are UCC goods, is the sale a "transaction in goods" within the meaning of the UCC?

Art itself is difficult to classify as has been made clear in the courts: "[T]he case law which [sic] pinpoints the definition of 'art' [is] scarce."[6] The party that wants a transaction classified under article 2 has the burden of proving that the art dispute involves a sale of goods within the meaning of the UCC. Whether the transaction is within the meaning of the UCC is decided as a matter of statutory construction by the court.[7]

§ 4:3 Definition of "goods"

Section 2-102 of the UCC states article 2 "applies to transactions in goods." Section 2-105(1) defines "goods" as

---

1582 (1981) (title dispute involving entrustment of goods under UCC Section 2-403); Solomon R. Guggenheim Foundation v. Lubell, 153 A.D.2d 143, 550 N.Y.S.2d 618 (1st Dep't 1990), order aff'd, 77 N.Y.2d 311, 567 N.Y.S.2d 623, 569 N.E.2d 426 (1991) (potential voidable title claims under UCC Section 2-403(1) for good faith purchaser regarding mysterious disappearance of Marc Chagall painting); *cf.* Menzel v. List, 22 A.D.2d 647, 253 N.Y.S.2d 43 (1st Dep't 1964) (title case based in replevin).

[2]UCC § 2-312.

[3]UCC § 2-313.

[4]UCC § 2-314; Balog v. Center Art Gallery-Hawaii, Inc., 745 F. Supp. 1556, 1563 n.16, 12 U.C.C. Rep. Serv. 2d 962 (D. Haw. 1990) (rejecting implied warranties of UCC §§ 2-314 and 2-315 as applied to art).

[5]UCC § 2-315.

[6]In re Leonardo, 102 B.R. 202 (Bankr. E.D. Cal. 1989).

[7]*See, e.g.,* First Comics, Inc. v. World Color Press, Inc., 884 F.2d 1033, 1036 (7th Cir. 1989); Botello v. Shell Oil Co., 229 Cal. App. 3d 1130, 280 Cal. Rptr. 535 (2d Dist. 1991) (whether or not a mural is a "painting" for purposes of state arts preservation statute is a matter of law); F.T.C. v. Magui Publishers, Inc., 1991-1 Trade Cas. (CCH) ¶ 69425, 1991 WL 90895 (C.D. Cal. 1991), aff'd, 9 F.3d 1551 (9th Cir. 1993) (crossover of conclusions of law and findings of fact in case involving false representations of values and authorship of prints by Salvador Dali and others).

"all things (including specially manufactured goods) which are movable at the time of identification to the contract for sale". Chart 4-1[1] summarizes how courts have handled the art as "goods" issue. Recent courts reviewing garden variety purchase and sale transactions of art objects like paintings and sculptures have had no difficulty classifying them as sales of goods under the U.C.C.[2]

[Section 4:3]

[1]*See* Chart 4-1.

[2]Foxley v. Sotheby's Inc., 893 F. Supp. 1224, 27 U.C.C. Rep. Serv. 2d 1234 (S.D. N.Y. 1995) (Article 2 applies to sale of painting at auction even if purchase price combines goods and services).

Chart 4-1: Courts' Classification of Art as "Goods"

Decision	Case	Court's Statement
Artwork not considered "goods" under UCC.	Fink v. DeClassis, 745 F. Supp. 509 (E.D.Ill. 1990); accord Insul-Mark Midwest, Inc. v. Modern Materials, 612 N.E.2d 550 (Ind. 1993) (works commissioned from artists are not "goods")	"[A]rtwork [is an] asset [that] cannot be legitimately characterized as goods, and [no] authority . . . suggests that such assets fall within the scope of Article 2."
Art works classified as "goods."	(1) Balog v. Center Art Gallery-Haw., Inc., 745 F.Supp. 1556, 1562 & n.14 (D. Haw. 1990) (2) Firestone & Parson, Inc. v. Union League, 672 F.Supp. 819, 821–22 (E.D. Pa. 1987), aff'd, 833 F.2d 304 (3d Cir. 1987)	(1) "Paintings, prints and sculpture . . . fall within the [UCC] definition of goods." (2) "[A] painting is a 'good' within the meaning of the U[CC]."

Decision	Case	Court's Statement
Article 2 warranty theory discussed without expressly addressing whether or not art as "goods"	(1) Rosen v. Spanierman, 894 F.2d 28 (2d Cir. 1990) (2) Wilson v. Hammer Holdings, Inc., 850 F.2d 3 (1st Cir. 1988) (3) Sundlun v. Shoemaker, 671 A.2d 1330 (1992)	(1) Dismissal of breach of warranty action based on sale of John Singer Sargent painting upheld because barred by UCC statute of limitations. (2) Breach of warranty action based on sale of Albert Bierstadt painting barred by statute of limitations. (3) Sales transaction of antique "occurred in a commercial context, and is governed by . . . UCC."
Art as services outside the reach of article 2. [3]	(1) Cook v. United States, 599 F.2d 400, 405 n.8 (Ct. Cl. 1979) (2) Tobey v. Comm'r, 60 T.C. 227 (1973)	(1) "[The IRS] . . . assumes [incorrectly] that, if the artist's products are 'personal property' under tax sourcing rules, such products are also 'goods' covered by Article 2 of the U[CC]," for purposes of determining federal income tax.

Decision	Case	Court's Statement
Purchase and sale agreements for art involving financing not considered transaction for "goods."	McCulley Fine Arts Gallery, Inc. v. "X" Partners, 860 S.W.2d 473 (1993)	Sale of Van Gogh painting "Roadway in a Paris Park" not a sale of goods under UCC, and an agreement to fund its purchase outside the scope of the UCC ("defendants' contention that . . . agreement to purchase [Van Gogh painting] was a 'sale of goods' in excess of $500 and that a written contract was . . . required" overturned on appeal where court held case represents a "failure to fund."
Secured transactions under Article 9 where collateral is artwork, art is considered "goods."	Fortune Finans AB v. Andersson, 192 A.D.2d 124 (N.Y. 1992)	Art is goods in which security interest can attach under UCC § 9-103.
Consignment interests under article 2 where consigned goods are art, art is considered "goods."	Shuttie v. Festa Restaurant, Inc., 566 So.2d 554 (1990)	Creditor-bank with rights in inventory has rights in consigned artworks, even though not part of owner inventory and artist's creditor exemption existed in that state.

[3] 1 R. Anderson, *On the* Uniform Commercial Code § 2-105(1) ("Article 2 does not apply to 'service' contracts), *cited with approval in* Cook v. United States, 599 F.2d 400, 405 (Ct. Cl. 1979).

§ 4:4 Mixed transfers of goods and other interests—Tests

"Many modern commercial transactions cannot be classified as transactions purely for goods . . . but are 'mixed.' "[1] If the transaction is mixed, the court must determine as a matter of statutory construction whether the mix falls within or without the UCC. Various tests have been offered to determine whether the sale is a "transaction of goods" within Section 2-102; the test of any particular jurisdiction should be checked, but the following tests are commonly used:

(1) "Predominant thrust" test[2] (also termed the "dominant" test,[3] and the "predominant factor" test[4] Is the transaction's "predominant factor . . . rendition of a service, with goods incidentally involved . . . or . . . a transaction of sale, with labor incidentally involved?"[5] Result: A contract that predominantly involves sale of goods is subject to the UCC in its entirety; other contracts are not subject to the UCC at all.

(2) Bifurcated Test: Divide the contract into goods portions and nongoods portions. Result: The portion of the transaction involving goods is governed by the UCC, and other portions are treated under common law or applicable statutes.

§ 4:5 Mixed transfers of goods and other interests—Burden of proof

The burden of proof is on the party seeking to locate the

[Section 4:4]

[1]Insul-Mark Midwest, Inc. v. Modern Materials, Inc., 612 N.E.2d 550, 21 U.C.C. Rep. Serv. 2d 219 (Ind. 1993).

[2]Annot., Applicability of UCC Article 2 to Mixed Contracts for Sale of Goods and Services, 5 A.L.R. 4th 501.

[3]Fink v. DeClassis, 745 F. Supp. 509, 13 U.C.C. Rep. Serv. 2d 693 (N.D. Ill. 1990).

[4]United States, ex rel., Bartec Indus., Inc. v. Union Pac. Co., 976 F.2d 1274 (10th Cir. 1992).

[5]Insul-Mark Midwest, Inc. v. Modern Materials, Inc., 612 N.E.2d 550, 554, 21 U.C.C. Rep. Serv. 2d 219 (Ind. 1993).

transaction under the UCC to prove that the thrust of the transaction is predominantly for goods. The court determines as a matter of law whether the test has been satisfied.

The language of the contract must be examined in light of the situation of the parties and the surrounding circumstances, especially terms describing performance and words used to describe the relationship between the parties. Beyond contractual terms, consideration must be given to the final product the purchaser bargained to receive. If the cost of the goods is but a "small portion of the overall contract price" the likelihood increases that services predominate over goods.[1]

Artwork commissioned from artists has not been considered a "transfer of goods" under the predominant thrust test.[2] Commissioned art is also subject to special treatment by the IRS depending upon the Code rule or regulation that is being applied.[3] If art is an irreconcilable hybrid of product and service at the creation stage in terms of the artist's labor input for tax purposes, does art become more goods-like by the time it reaches the market? The artist's services have dropped out of the transfer by the time the art is realized, but courts have still been reluctant to apply article 2 to compel artists to provide or deliver completed artworks under contract. Such contracts are ultimately considered personal and creative service contracts, rather than contracts for product.

If the art is valued more for its copyright interests than its value as a discrete object, the mix shifts to nongoods. A contract transferring corporate assets of tangible and intangible assets, where the intangible assets were valued higher than the tangible, was held not to be a contract transferring goods.[4]

[Section 4:5]

[1]Insul-Mark Midwest, Inc. v. Modern Materials, Inc., 612 N.E.2d 550, 554, 21 U.C.C. Rep. Serv. 2d 219 (Ind. 1993).

[2]Insul-Mark Midwest, Inc. v. Modern Materials, Inc., 612 N.E.2d 550, 554, 21 U.C.C. Rep. Serv. 2d 219 (Ind. 1993).

[3]*See, e.g.,* Cook v. U.S., 220 Ct. Cl. 76, 599 F.2d 400, 405 (1979).

[4]Fink v. DeClassis, 745 F. Supp. 509, 13 U.C.C. Rep. Serv. 2d 693 (N.D. Ill. 1990).

§ 4:6 Objections to art as goods—Views of others

The UCC statutory structure and definitions seem broad enough to include artworks, but traditionally courts and commentators have been reticent to classify art as goods.[1] Although the basis for reluctance is not always expressly stated in the comment or opinion, the concerns can be summarized as follows: broad-based philosophical objections;[2] availability of alternative remedies under general common-law principles,[3] or specific art statutes; and art as a unique object that is inappropriate for the UCC.

§ 4:7 Objections to art as goods—Author's comment—Issue oriented approach

UCC Section 1-102(1) provides that the UCC "shall be liberally construed and applied to promote its underlying purposes and policies." Throughout this chapter there are indications that the policies and purposes of the UCC are not well suited to artworks. In general, however, the UCC is more suited to some arts disputes than others. Rather than make a global affirmation or denial of the propriety of UCC application to art, an issue-by-issue approach is presented through basic categories: goods, title, and warranties.

§ 4:8 Objections to art as goods—Author's comment—Goods

At the outset, art objects rarely garner legal consensus regarding their classification: realty or personalty, good or service, idea or object. As the software and other technology cases indicate, the UCC was not constructed for boisterous litigation on the predicate issue of whether or not an object can or should be classified as a UCC good.

[Section 4:6]

[1]Cook v. U.S., 220 Ct. Cl. 76, 599 F.2d 400, 405 (1979) ("it is far from clear that commissioned or noncommissioned art works were intended to fall within the definition of 'goods' ").

[2]Balog v. Center Art Gallery-Hawaii, Inc., 745 F. Supp. 1556, 1562, 12 U.C.C. Rep. Serv. 2d 962 (D. Haw. 1990) ("there has been considerable scholarly disagreement regarding the adequacy of the protection afforded the purchaser of artwork by the UCC").

[3]Dawson v. G. Malina, Inc., 463 F. Supp. 461, 467 (S.D. N.Y. 1978).

The drafters in mid-century were oriented towards industrial manufacture, not artificial intelligence and the internet.

Nonetheless, garden variety artwork does exist, the painting, drawing, sculpture; other statutory schemes for art are intermittent and generally unsatisfactory. The UCC has an internal integrity which often allows for creative as well as equitable resolutions which are appropriate in the arts. Therefore, the author recommends a preliminary analysis on a case-by-case basis to determine article 2 applicability to the particular transaction.

First: Is the artwork a "good" under the UCC definition of goods? If a sale does not involve goods "movable at the time of identification to the contract for sale," the artwork is not an article 2 good and the UCC does not apply, placing the transaction outside the UCC and under common law, other applicable statutes, or other legal or equitable remedy.

Second: Assuming the artwork is a "good," is the sale a "transaction in goods" under article 2? Art is often a mix of goods and services, goods and intangible interests, or goods and realty. If the nongoods aspect of the deal weighs too heavily in the mix, the "goods" status may be jeopardized.[1]

A UCC good is not a consensual product, and the sale of art is not consistently considered a "transaction of goods." For example, courts hold that commissioned artworks cannot be the basis of article 2 actions because they are not "transfers of goods." Some courts have found that other art sales contain impermissible mixes of services and goods or intangible interests or realty that require disposition outside the UCC. If the artworks are goods, but the sale is not a pure "transaction in goods" because of its nongoods aspects, article 2 may or may not apply, depending upon the test applied by the jurisdiction for mixed contracts.

Even after art as goods issues are resolved under article 2, what does the UCC offer? Is article 2 configured to accommodate aspects of the deal unique to art that trigger

---

[Section 4:8]

[1] *See* Ch 9.

warranty, like provenance and authenticity? Do risks of commercial trading that the UCC allocates between buyers and sellers embody comparable counterparts that can be equitably apportioned in the art marketplace?

B. TITLE

§ 4:9 When title passes in sale of commercial goods

UCC Section 2-106 provides, "A 'sale' consists in the passing of title from the seller to the buyer for a price." Section 2-106 cross-references Section 2-401. Section 2-401 establishes general principles of title, reciting in pertinent part: "[T]itle to goods passes from the seller to the buyer in any manner and on any conditions explicitly agreed on by the parties."[1] Parties to art contracts have established when title will pass in a purchase and sale agreement,[2] and how title will pass from an artist's agent to third persons in a consignment agreement.[3]

However, title is not always a stated term or condition in contracts for the sale or consignment of art, a circumstance generally recognized by UCC Section 2-401(2), which provides that "title passes to the buyer at the time and place at which the seller completes his performance with reference to the physical delivery of the goods." Section 2-401(2) also provides for title passage in the instances of shipments and deliveries. The simplicity of title transfers under Section 2-401 is complicated by Section 2-403, which involves commercial expectations regarding title of those who buy from persons in trade.

[Section 4:9]

[1]UCC § 2-401(1), subject to other provisos in that subparagraph.

[2]*See, e.g.*, Andrew Crispo Gallery, Inc. v. Maroney, 187 A.D.2d 251, 589 N.Y.S.2d 445 (1st Dep't 1992) (where written sales agreement between buyer and seller stated title remained with seller until artwork fully paid for, which plaintiff failed to do, seller not obligated to buyer for profits from resale of a painting under UCC § 2-706(6)).

[3]Matter of Miller, 545 F.2d 916, 20 U.C.C. Rep. Serv. 1314 (5th Cir. 1977) (consignment of paintings to dealer under written consignment agreement gave dealer "full power . . . to convey title to each of the paintings to third parties").

§ 4:10 Warranty of title

UCC Section 2-312(1) provides that "there is in a contract for sale a warranty by the seller that (a) the title conveyed shall be good, and its transfer rightful." Subsection (1) is modified by subsection (2) which excludes such warranties "only by specific language or by circumstances which give the buyer reason to know that the person selling does not claim title in himself or that he is purporting to sell only such right or title as he or a third person may have." A UCC Section 2-312(1) warranty of title was not violated where a painting was exported unlawfully from a country having export controls, although such facts support a cloud on title in the market.[1]

§ 4:11 Entruster provision: UCC Section 2-403(2)—Entrustment

Under common law, property that finds its way from the owner's transferee into the hands of a third party may be legally owned by the third party.[1] UCC Section 2-403(2) extends the common-law rule, providing: "[A]ny entrusting of possession of goods to a merchant who deals in goods of that kind gives him power to transfer all rights of the entruster to a buyer in the ordinary course of business." The entruster provision is "designed to enhance the reliability of commercial sales by merchants . . . while shifting the risk of loss through fraudulent transfer to the owner of goods, who can select the merchant to whom he entrusts his property." Protection is deemed to extend

---

[Section 4:10]

[1]Jeanneret v. Vichey, 693 F.2d 259, 35 U.C.C. Rep. Serv. 75 (2d Cir. 1982) (reversing trial court award of $938,000 to plaintiff and remanding case where Swiss art dealer bought painting by Henri Matisse from American defendants, who inherited it in Italy and possibly exported it illegally from Italy to Switzerland, considering but not deciding that no breach of warranty of title occurred).

[Section 4:11]

[1]Equitable estoppel or estoppel in pais is the principle by which a party is precluded at law and in equity from denying any material fact which, by words or conduct, affirmative or negative, intentionally or through culpable negligence, induced another ignorant of the true facts, who had a right to rely and who did rely, to change his position to his detriment.

only to those who buy from merchants to whom the property was entrusted in the ordinary course of business.[2] Whether an entrustment has been made is ordinarily a question of fact.[3]Section 2-403(2) has protected original owners in the arts context because of its "ordinary course of business" and "merchant" conditions.

§ 4:12 Entruster provision: UCC Section 2-403(2)—Buyer in the ordinary course

A "buyer in the ordinary course," defined in UCC Section 1-201(9), is "a person who in good faith and without knowledge that the sale to him is in violation of the ownership rights or security interest of a third party in the goods buys in ordinary course from a person in the business of selling goods of that kind." ". . . . [B]uying . . . does not include a transfer . . . in total or partial satisfaction of a money debt."[1] One does not qualify as a buyer in the ordinary course under an entrustment theory if the purchase was made before the time of entrustment or the interests acquired constitute forgiveness of prior debt.[2]

In Cantor v. Anderson,[3] Wildenstein, a dealer, consigned an Auguste Renoir drawing valued at $160,000 to the defendant, a private dealer. The private dealer delivered the

---

[2]Cantor v. Anderson, 639 F. Supp. 364, 2 U.C.C. Rep. Serv. 2d 312 (S.D. N.Y. 1986), judgment aff'd, 833 F.2d 1002 (2d Cir. 1986); Porter v. Wertz, 53 N.Y.2d 696, 439 N.Y.S.2d 105, 421 N.E.2d 500, 30 U.C.C. Rep. Serv. 1582 (1981); see also Spainerman Gallery, Profit Sharing Plan v. Merritt, 49 U.C.C. Rep. Serv. 2d 809 (S.D. N.Y. 2003) (declaratory judgment sought for good title to an Arthur Wesley Dow painting under UCC 2-403)..

[3]Stellan Holm, Inc. v. Malmberg Intern. Art, 2002 WL 392294 (S.D. N.Y. 2002) (plaintiff had no title in Yves Klein painting under entrustment theory); see also Spainerman Gallery, Profit Sharing Plan v. Merritt, 49 U.C.C. Rep. Serv. 2d 809 (S.D. N.Y. 2003) (summary judgment denied regarding title to painting under UCC 2-403 because questions of fact on whether entrustee was "merchant" and sale was in the ordinary course)..

[Section 4:12]

[1]UCC Section 1-209(9).

[2]Stellan Holm, Inc. v. Malmberg Intern. Art, 2002 WL 392294 (S.D. N.Y. 2002) (no entrustment where no "buy" occurred).

[3]Cantor v. Anderson, 639 F. Supp. 364, 2 U.C.C. Rep. Serv. 2d 312 (S.D. N.Y. 1986), judgment aff'd, 833 F.2d 1002 (2d Cir. 1986).

Renoir to the plaintiff's doorstep in response to demand letters from Cantor's lawyers to pay Cantor for debts that arose through art deals Cantor and the private dealer had had over the years. Cantor refused to accept the Renoir, but the private dealer instructed the delivery company to leave it at the door.

Cantor sued the dealer, and Wildenstein intervened, asserting title to the Renoir and seeking return of personal property or damages. Cantor claimed the Renoir through the entruster provision. The district court, affirmed by the Second Circuit, held that "a buyer in the ordinary course" excludes persons who receive goods "in total or partial satisfaction of a money debt." Since Cantor admitted the private dealer owed him money from prior dealings, the court disqualified him as a buyer in the ordinary course, and found the entrustment provision inapplicable. Wildenstein was entitled to return of the Renoir or damages.

In Porter v. Wertz,[4] the plaintiff-art collector entrusted a painting by Maurice Utrillo to Von Maker for the purpose of contemplating its purchase while it hung in Von Maker's home. Von Maker delivered the Utrillo to Wertz, whom the court described as a "delicatessen" salesman. Wertz sold the painting to Feigen Gallery, whom Porter also sued for damages and to recover the painting.

Feigen defended on the entruster provision, contending that when he bought from Wertz he assumed Wertz was an art dealer, and therefore the purchase was from a merchant in the ordinary course of business. The New York Court of Appeals, affirming the Appellate Division, found on the evidence that Wertz dealt in pastrami, not paintings—the requisite "goods of that kind" under UCC Section 1-201(9). Therefore, the sale was not in the ordinary course of his business.[5] The court further concluded that Section 2-403(2) did not bar plaintiff's recovery because Porter did not entrust the Utrillo to Wertz, but to Von Maker.

---

[4]Porter v. Wertz, 56 A.D.2d 570, 392 N.Y.S.2d 10 (1st Dep't 1977).

[5]Porter v. Wertz, 53 N.Y.2d 696, 439 N.Y.S.2d 105, 421 N.E.2d 500, 30 U.C.C. Rep. Serv. 1582 (1981).

§ 4:13 Entruster provision: UCC Section 2-403(2)—Statutory estoppel[1]—Reliance upon plaintiff's agent

Under common law, an original owner may be estopped to assert title against a third party. UCC Section 2-403(2) incorporates common-law principles of estoppel and agency. In Porter v. Wertz,[2] the New York Court of Appeals considered whether the facts could be interpreted to support Feigen's defense of estoppel to protect his defective title: Had Porter "clothed" Wertz with authority to sell the Utrillo, which authority Feigen relied upon when he purchased the painting?

The court found no reliance since "nothing Porter did influenced the Feigen Gallery's decision" and rejected the defense of estoppel as inappropriate. The Court of Appeals declined to rule upon the appellate division's decision to reject statutory estoppel, based upon its conclusion that Feigen was not in good faith, a requirement under UCC Section 1-201(9), which defines "buyer in the ordinary course" as one "in good faith and without knowledge" that the sale is in violation of others' ownership rights.

[Section 4:13]

[1]Promissory estoppel can be treated as a doctrine of contract law or in some states as an alternative theory to breach of contract. *See, e.g.,* Milwaukee Auction Galleries, Ltd. v. Chalk, 13 F.3d 1107 (7th Cir. 1994) (directed verdict for defendant reversed on promissory estoppel claims in action based upon sale of paintings brought by dealers against collector). A claim of promissory estoppel was stated where plaintiffs alleged "'[a] clear and unambiguous promise; a reasonable and foreseeable reliance by the party to whom the promise was made; and an injury sustained by the party asserting the estoppel by reason of his reliance.'" Granat v. Center Art Galleries--Hawaii Inc., R.I.C.O. Bus. Disp. Guide (CCH) ¶ 8425, 1993 WL 403977 (S.D. N.Y. 1993), *citing* City of Yonkers v. Otis Elevator Co., 844 F.2d 42, 48, 10 Fed. R. Serv. 3d 1088 (2d Cir. 1988) (defendants' motion to dismiss promissory estoppel action denied where plaintiff-buyers alleged that they purchased more than $5 million of artworks from defendant gallery based upon defendant's promises to resell the artworks and its failure to take steps to make the resales).

[2]Porter v. Wertz, 53 N.Y.2d 696, 439 N.Y.S.2d 105, 421 N.E.2d 500, 30 U.C.C. Rep. Serv. 1582 (1981).

§ 4:14 Entruster provision: UCC Section 2-403(2)—Statutory estoppel—Good faith purchase from merchant in ordinary course

UCC Section 2-103(1)(b) defines the good faith under UCC 1-201(9) required for merchants as "honesty in fact and the observance of reasonable commercial standards of fair dealing in the trade." In Porter v. Wertz, the New York Court of Appeals declined to opine on the issue of whether good faith among art dealers requires them to inquire into prior ownership of an artwork before purchasing it since it found estoppel.

The appellate division, however, concluded that the failure of Feigen to investigate and inquire about title to the Utrillo was a departure from reasonable commercial standards, eviscerating his good faith status under the UCC and preventing him from relying upon statutory estoppel.[1] The appellate division wrote: "[UCC 2-103(1)(b)] cannot . . . be interpreted to permit, countenance or condone commercial standards of sharp trade practice or indifference as to the 'provenance,' i.e., history of ownership or the right to possessor sell an object d'art."[2]

A federal district court has affirmed in principle under California commercial law the inquiry duty that Porter imposed upon art dealers, but only where "warnings" exist to trigger the duty.[3] The court found no warnings existed, even though the price of the Alfred Bricher painting—"Marlton's Cove, Grand Manan, Maine"—at issue in a title

---

[Section 4:14]

[1]Porter v. Wertz, 68 A.D.2d 141, 145, 416 N.Y.S.2d 254, 26 U.C.C. Rep. Serv. 876 (1st Dep't 1979), judgment aff'd, 53 N.Y.2d 696, 439 N.Y.S.2d 105, 421 N.E.2d 500, 30 U.C.C. Rep. Serv. 1582 (1981).

[2]Porter v. Wertz, 68 A.D.2d 141, 145, 416 N.Y.S.2d 254, 26 U.C.C. Rep. Serv. 876 (1st Dep't 1979), judgment aff'd, 53 N.Y.2d 696, 439 N.Y.S.2d 105, 421 N.E.2d 500, 30 U.C.C. Rep. Serv. 1582 (1981). *See also* Johnson & Johnson Products, Inc. v. Dal Intern. Trading Co., 798 F.2d 100, 1 U.C.C. Rep. Serv. 2d 1082 (3d Cir. 1986) (gray market sale was conducted under suspicious circumstances that "cried out for inquiry" which would have uncovered voidable title).

[3]Morgold, Inc. v. Keeler, 891 F. Supp. 1361, 27 U.C.C. Rep. Serv. 2d 315 (N.D. Cal. 1995); *but see* Ch 2 §§ 2:67 to 2:71, and Ch 6 § 6:130 (discussion on the investigatory duty of due diligence applicable to out-of-possession plaintiffs seeking return of personal property after expiration of the statute of limitations).

dispute dropped to approximately one-half the asking price in a short time period, and a prior possessor in the chain obtained the painting in exchange for forgiveness of outstanding debt.[4] The court found that lack of inquiries by prospective buyers, even dealers subject to the observance of reasonable commercial standards of fair dealing, was not significant if those contacted did not disclose or reveal "telling" information.[5] Nor did the court classify the commercial propriety of the contacts themselves.[6]

The reach of the inquiry rule, reasonable in commercial arts transactions, has been foreshortened by a judicial overlay in some jurisdictions that warnings must exist to trigger the duty. The inquiry rule is eviscerated if courts fail to understand the facts, and the pattern of facts and circumstances, that constitute warnings in the context of an art transaction.[7] The Porter court has also offered a variation on dealer's obligations in the context of mutual mistake.[8]

§ 4:15 Voidable title

At common law, innocent purchasers who gave valuable consideration were protected against true owners under certain circumstances. That principle is encompassed expressly within the good faith purchaser exception of UCC Section 2-403(1), which recites: "A person with voidable title has power to transfer a good title to a good faith purchaser for value." This has been referred to as the good faith purchaser exception. The good faith purchaser exception is intended to promote commerce by reducing transaction costs and encouraging persons to buy and sell goods without costly investigation of the rights of all previous possessors in the chain of distribution.

What is voidable title in an art sales context? New York

---

[4]Morgold, Inc. v. Keeler, 891 F. Supp. 1361, 27 U.C.C. Rep. Serv. 2d 315 (N.D. Cal. 1995); *but see* § 4:17.

[5]Morgold, Inc. v. Keeler, 891 F. Supp. 1361, 27 U.C.C. Rep. Serv. 2d 315 (N.D. Cal. 1995).

[6]Morgold, Inc. v. Keeler, 891 F. Supp. 1361, 27 U.C.C. Rep. Serv. 2d 315 (N.D. Cal. 1995).

[7]*See* § 4:17.

[8]*See* § 4:52.

courts have examined this issue in a famous case, ultimately settled, brought by the Guggenheim Museum against a collector for recovery of a painting, the gouache "Le Marchand de Bestiaux" by Marc Chagall.[1] Le Marchand hung in the plaintiff's living room for more than twenty years, and had been loaned intermittently for public exhibitions. She and her husband had bought it in 1967 from a New York gallery, consulting with Chagall and his cataloguer at the time of purchase. When an auction employee happened upon a transparency of the painting in the late 1980s, he recognized it from his tenure at the Guggenheim, where it had been deemed mysteriously missing from storage since the 1970s. He notified his former employers, and the museum sued Mrs. Lubell in 1989 for recovery.

Mrs. Lubell moved for summary judgment on the ground, inter alia, that if she were a good faith purchaser for value and the Chagall had not been stolen, her title was superior to the Guggenheim's. The gallery from which the painting was purchased would have had to have voidable title,[2] as recited in UCC Section 2-403(1): "When goods have been delivered under a transaction of purchase the purchaser has such power [to transfer] even though . . . . (d) The delivery was procured through fraud punishable as larcenous under the criminal law."

UCC Section 2-403(1)(d) is defined differently by various courts, but generally applies only where a person delivers goods to a subsequent seller with the intention, however misguided, that the seller become the owner of the goods. Voidable title can arise by fraud if delivery is made through a transaction of purchase, i.e., goods sold and paid for with a forged check. But, in New York and most other jurisdictions, a thief acquires no title and can pass

---

[Section 4:15]

[1]Solomon R. Guggenheim Foundation v. Lubell, 153 A.D.2d 143, 550 N.Y.S.2d 618 (1st Dep't 1990), order aff'd, 77 N.Y.2d 311, 567 N.Y.S.2d 623, 569 N.E.2d 426 (1991); *see also* U.S. v. Lavin, 942 F.2d 177, 20 Fed. R. Serv. 3d 969 (3d Cir. 1991) (voidable title).

[2]Johnson & Johnson Products, Inc. v. Dal Intern. Trading Co., 798 F.2d 100, 1 U.C.C. Rep. Serv. 2d 1082 (3d Cir. 1986) (seller with voidable title such as that acquired by common-law fraud can transfer good title to a good faith purchaser).

no title. Theft does not qualify as a type of voidable title fraud referred to in Section 2-403(1)(d) because stolen goods are not obtained through a "transaction of purchase."

The key issue in the Lubell case for purposes of a UCC voidable title defense was whether or not the Chagall was stolen from the Guggenheim; if a theft had occurred, the chain of sale was tainted and title could not pass. Refusing to grant Mrs. Lubell's motion for summary judgment because of unresolved facts about theft, the appellate division, affirmed by the Court of Appeals of New York, placed the "onerous" burden of disproving theft on Mrs. Lubell.[3]

§ 4:16 Title in art purchase and sale contracts outside UCC

Louisiana, which did not adopt article 2, has nonetheless examined passage of title in an art sales contract where authenticity was at issue. In Mennella v. Kurt E. Schon E.A.I., Ltd.,[1] the Fifth Circuit applied Louisiana law to an aborted sale of a portrait by Sir Anthony Van Dyck priced at $350,000 that the plaintiff initially agreed to buy from the defendant-gallery in April 1988. Her down payment was $50,000, and she made some installments that were applied to the balance. The gallery maintained possession of the Van Dyck. Six months after the due date for the balance, the plaintiff requested from the gallery an authentication to secure a loan she needed to pay the balance. The gallery sent an "expert's appraisal,"[2] reciting that the portrait was "one of five copies by Sir Anthony Van Dyck," subsequently sending her another authentication by a retired art history professor.

Sometime after December 1988, the plaintiff became

---

[3]Solomon R. Guggenheim Foundation v. Lubell, 153 A.D.2d 143, 152, 550 N.Y.S.2d 618 (1st Dep't 1990), order aff'd, 77 N.Y.2d 311, 567 N.Y.S.2d 623, 569 N.E.2d 426 (1991). The settlement, like the facts, was odd. Plaintiff reportedly paid virtually the full fair market value alleged for the artwork during the boom, although, by the time of trial, the market had substantially declined. What recovery, if any, she obtained from the sellers is not known.

[Section 4:16]

[1]Mennella v. Kurt E. Schon E.A.I., Ltd., 979 F.2d 357 (5th Cir. 1992).

[2]*See* § 3:19 for comparison of appraisals and authentications.

concerned that the portrait might be a fake, and instructed her lawyer to demand full refund from the gallery of $140,000. In April 1989, the gallery demanded full performance by payment within five days or advised it would sell the painting. The plaintiff did not enforce her rights or seek an authentication. In May 1989, the gallery wrote that plaintiff's inaction constituted default and the sale was cancelled. In September 1989 the gallery offered to refund plaintiff $95,000, her payment minus commissions and costs of authentication, or give her $140,000 in gallery credit. She rejected both offers.

In November 1989, the gallery auctioned the painting at Christie's in London, where it sold for more than $1.4 million. Unaware of the sale, plaintiff filed a suit for rescission of the sale and damages in December 1989, alleging that the painting was an overvalued fake. When the plaintiff received the answer, she moved to amend her complaint, alleging a completed sale and that the gallery converted her painting by auctioning it. The trial court awarded the plaintiff her payments and interest from the day of demand, finding that the sale was conditional upon full payment and delivery, and rejecting conversion claims. The Fifth Circuit, reversing, decided that title did pass to the plaintiff on the date of sale, notwithstanding the credit sale; however, by refusing to perform, the Fifth Circuit found that the plaintiff had repudiated the contract and deemed the contract dissolved, upholding the district court's award of damages.

§ 4:17 Author's comment

UCC warranty of title is appropriate for art transactions, provided that the role of the merchant and the good faith purchaser is understood in an art market context. Some courts interpret the UCC and common law as imposing upon buyers, most notably dealer-merchants, a duty of inquiry consistent with commercial reasonableness and custom and usage, prior to sale.

The reach of the inquiry rule has been foreshortened by a judicial overlay in some jurisdictions that warnings must exist to trigger the duty. The inquiry rule is eviscerated if courts fail to understand the type of facts, and the patterns of facts and circumstances, that constitute warnings in the context of an art transaction. Given the complexity of secondary markets,[1] virtually all transactions require investigation; the nature and character of trading in the secondary market itself constitutes warning. Certain dealers routinely investigate, knowing that attention must be paid regardless of any specific fact or circumstance. By interposing a higher threshold to trigger the duty in art transactions courts are generally undermining the concept of the UCC good faith purchaser as well as specifically eroding the UCC Section 1-201(9) good faith merchant, thus affecting Section 2-403 voidable title transactions. This wider blanket of judicially interpreted reasonableness can harm the secondary market and further fractionalize it.

Assuming, arguendo, that warning flags must fly in order for the inquiry duty to arise, the failure to understand the nature of the duty enables self-deluded buyers greater operating power with impunity in the secondary market. In practice, this interferes with the rights of prior, and rightful, owners, and weakens the integrity of the market.

The Morgold opinion reveals in part such surely unintended results.[2] First, by failing to differentiate types of experts that should be contacted, the court merges issues of authenticity and title.[3] Typically, different experts are needed to inquire into different aspects of sale—authenticity and title. Experts on art history, artist biography, or authenticity, for example, are not necessarily knowledgeable about ownership, let alone title. Even cataloguers are not always aware of "who owns what" for transactions that occur after catalogue production or publications.[4] Furthermore, such experts ordinarily are not privy to the type of financial information pertinent to title, like debt swaps, subordinated or shared interests, and loan

---

[Section 4:17]

[1]*See* Ch 2 §§ 2:4 to 2:10.

[2]Morgold, Inc. v. Keeler, 891 F. Supp. 1361, 27 U.C.C. Rep. Serv. 2d 315 (N.D. Cal. 1995).

[3]*See* Ch 2 §§ 2:53 to 2:60 and 2:64 to 2:66, and Ch 3 §§ 3:3 to 3:18.

[4]*See, e.g.,* Solomon R. Guggenheim Foundation v. Lubell, 77 N.Y.2d 311, 567 N.Y.S.2d 623, 569 N.E.2d 426 (1991) (contact with cataloguer of Marc Chagall by prospective private purchaser did not reveal defects in chain of ownership of painting offered for sale).

forgiveness.

The second point exemplified in Morgold relates to the reasonableness of what queries a dealer should be making to ascertain if warnings exist. If the proper questions are not asked, answers obtaining information that provides warning become serendipitous and random. The UCC, and the common law before that, either expressly or implicitly require reasonable duties of commercial conduct that inform allocation of loss and assignment of risk. Courts should not be discouraging such duties in the art trade.

The quality of inquiry is part and parcel of the information sought. The buyer who doesn't want to know is being judicially excused from the underlying duty of inquiry, which may or may not trigger the relevant warnings. Contrary to judicial assumption, where disclosure of debt financing occurs, information that is ordinarily difficult to ascertain becomes a warning that further inquiry is indicated.

By posing the buyer as a passive recipient of information, and by endorsing a practice of contacting sources unlikely to be knowledgeable on key points, courts are abrogating the implicit investigatory duties in the arts context of a UCC merchant engaged in reasonable practices.

C. EXPRESS WARRANTY

§ 4:18 UCC Section 2-313

Although art buyers claim various warranties under article 2, the predominant challenge is that the art is inauthentic, a claim often framed as a breach of express warranty under UCC Section 2-313, which provides as follows:

> (1) Express warranties by the seller are created as follows:
>
> (a) Any affirmation of fact or promise made by the seller to the buyer which relates to the goods and becomes part of the basis of the bargain creates an express warranty that the goods shall conform to the affirmation or promise.
>
> (b) Any description of the goods which is made part of the basis of the bargain creates an express warranty that the goods shall conform to the description.

. . .

(2) [A]n affirmation merely of the value of the goods or a statement purporting to be merely the seller's opinion or commendation of the goods does not create a warranty.

How do the UCC Section 2-313 affirmations apply to authenticating works of art sold in commercial transactions?[1] Few cases have actually tackled these issues directly. The following sections, [b][i] and [b][ii], examine the conceptual conundrums of Section 2-313 in an analytically "pure" art trading context, assuming an uncontaminated trade, where buyer and seller both reasonably believe that the object is genuine. Sections [b][iii]–[v] evaluate actual trades that have been subjected to judicial scrutiny, including those where the seller had knowledge of authenticity problems, or evidence was available indicating authenticity was in question.

Authentication in the trade context generally is the dealer's representation of authorship, i.e., "This painting is by Van Gogh."[2] The problem with authenticity is that it can be interpreted simultaneously as guarantee under UCC Section 2-313(1), and as opinion under UCC Section 2-313(2).

§ 4:19 Authenticity as guarantee or guess—Guarantee

What is warranted in an art sale?[1] Art gets sold because dealers tell buyers that the work is by Artist *X*, e.g.: "This picture ["The Misses Wertheimer"] is fully guaranteed by the undersigned to be an original work by John Singer

[Section 4:18]

[1] *See* Ch 5 for contractual warranties at auction.

[2] *See* Ch 3.

[Section 4:19]

[1] This discussion excludes the sui generis market of auctions, unless expressly specified, discussed at Ch 5, primary market traders, discussed at Ch 2 and artist sales, discussed at Ch 9 §§ 9:72 to 9:123.

Sargent."[2] Does such language brings the deal within UCC Section 2-313 ? "The foundation of every express warranty provision is the core description . . . the core description is non-disclaimable by a seller . . . . However, the coverage of the express warranty is limited to the extent that statements used by the seller in describing his products become the 'basis of the bargain.' "[3] Whether they are the basis of the bargain "rest[s] [on] 'dickered' aspects of the individual bargain."[4] Occasional collectors whose purchases totalled under $50,000 were held not to have dickered away the "express warranty . . . that all pieces of art sold to them were Dali originals."[5]

Care must be taken to determine whether buyers have dickered away attribution.[6] Except in very limited circumstances, parties do not "dicker" away authorship. If on occasion authorship drops out of the bargain, a huge and palpable price differential would be apparent. For example, the dealer who says "This painting is by Van Gogh" offers the work at prices the market commands. The dealer who says "This might or might not be by Van Gogh" rarely can command the same price,[7] except to very limited number of buyers. This is one reason artworks of questionable authenticity are auctioned.[8] Art of consensual questionable authenticity often goes to auction, where caveat emptor historically prevails, within the auction entity's obliga-

---

[2]Rosen v. Spanierman, 894 F.2d 28, 30, 10 U.C.C. Rep. Serv. 2d 846 (2d Cir. 1990).

[3]Balog v. Center Art Gallery-Hawaii, Inc., 745 F. Supp. 1556, 12 U.C.C. Rep. Serv. 2d 962 (D. Haw. 1990).

[4]UCC § 2-313, Official Comment 1.

[5]Balog v. Center Art Gallery-Hawaii, Inc., 745 F. Supp. 1556, 1563, 12 U.C.C. Rep. Serv. 2d 962 (D. Haw. 1990).

[6]Balog v. Center Art Gallery-Hawaii, Inc., 745 F. Supp. 1556, 1563 at n.17, 12 U.C.C. Rep. Serv. 2d 962 (D. Haw. 1990).

[7]*See* Ch 3, particularly Chart 3-1; *see also* Firestone & Parson, Inc. v. Union League of Philadelphia, 672 F. Supp. 819, 3 U.C.C. Rep. Serv. 2d 449 (E.D. Pa. 1987), judgment aff'd, 833 F.2d 304 (3d Cir. 1987) (painting by Albert Bierstadt would be worth $500,000, but if the work was painted by John Key it would be worth $50,000). When the work is not reattributed to another recognized artist, but is simply a copy or is by an unknown, disparities in price are even greater, sometimes reducing the value to decorative art.

[8]*See* Ch 5.

tions to comply with trade practices regarding authorship.[9] When doubt about authorship enters a good faith sale, the sale dissolves or the price structure weakens; outside the auction market, business reality dictates that dealers not hedge on authenticity.

§ 4:20 Authenticity as guarantee or guess—Guess

If the dealers' statements about authorship are the basis of the bargain under UCC Section 2-313(1), how does UCC Section 2-313(2) alter the warranty? "[T]he fact that a warranty was offered does not end the matter, since Section 2-313(2) provides that 'any affirmation merely of the value of the goods or a statement . . . merely the seller's opinion . . . does not create a warranty.' "[1] Authorship is a judgment: "A dealer's statement that a work is the product of a particular artist can never be more than an educated guess or opinion";[2] "proper attribution for [art] is to a substantial extent a subjective judgment based upon whether an expert finds a given piece to be aesthetically consistent with other works of the period on the basis of . . . elusive characteristics . . . . [F]or these reasons, such . . . attempt[s] must necessarily be imprecise."[3]

The crucial point is that make-or-break claims of authorship, which form the basis of the bargain, are rarely more than opinion, judgment, or subjective evaluation. If authorship is opinion based, then why don't dealers just hedge by stating "I think it is Van Gogh," or "It might be a Rembrandt [van Rijn]." Except at auction and in certain other very limited instances, sellers who do not warrant authorship would not be long in business as dealers. Compare statements declaring authorship of a painting of sunflowers as "by Van Gogh" with "this could be a Van Gogh." As a practical matter, the dealer of name brand art is compelled to announce authorship, that troublesome hybrid of guess and guarantee.

---

[9] *See* Ch 5.

[Section 4:20]

[1] Balog v. Center Art Gallery-Haw., Inc., 745 F. Supp. at 1556–68 and 1564 n.17.

[2] Balog v. Center Art Gallery-Haw., Inc., 745 F. Supp. at 1564.

[3] Dawson v. G. Malina, Inc., 463 F. Supp. 461 (S.D. N.Y. 1978).

When that dichotomy of dealmaking is relocated under the UCC, it becomes apparent that express warranty under article 2 imposes on art sellers simultaneous, contradictory legal obligations: As a matter of law, art sellers are deemed to warrant the unwarrantable; they must in essence guarantee opinion, or, under some tests, the prevailing opinion as reconstructed by experts at the time of trial.[4] Furthermore, art buyers, unlike goods buyers, face different substantive standards to prove breach of warranty: those suing before the UCC statute of limitations has expired, and those suing after.[5]

§ 4:21 Authenticity as guarantee or guess—Judicial resolution

No court has squarely resolved the guess/guarantee conundrum by deciding authorship classification under UCC express warranty.[1] Few courts have actually subjected the issue of art authorship to proof in any context.[2] A few courts have offered standards of proof, although

---

[4]*See* § 4:21.

[5]*See* §§ 4:35 to 4:41.

[Section 4:21]

[1]Foxley v. Sotheby's Inc., 893 F. Supp. 1224, 27 U.C.C. Rep. Serv. 2d 1234 (S.D. N.Y. 1995) (challenge to authentication of Mary Cassatt painting time-barred by U.C.C. statute of limitations); Balog v. Center Art Gallery-Hawaii, Inc., 745 F. Supp. 1556, 12 U.C.C. Rep. Serv. 2d 962 (D. Haw. 1990) (defendants' motion for judgment on the pleadings denied without determining whether artwork authentic or not).

[2]Estate of Querbach v. A & B Appraisal Serv., No. cv. L-0893622-85 (N.J. Super. 1987); Weisz v. Parke-Bernet Galleries, Inc., 67 Misc. 2d 1077, 325 N.Y.S.2d 576, 10 U.C.C. Rep. Serv. 292 (City Civ. Ct. 1971), judgment rev'd on other grounds, 77 Misc. 2d 80, 351 N.Y.S.2d 911, 14 U.C.C. Rep. Serv. 358 (App. Term 1974) (no ruling of authenticity in case decided under New York sales law where extent and effect of auction catalogue listings and disclaimers were at issue involving paintings by Raoul Dufy subsequently claimed to be fakes); *see also* Rosen v. Spanierman, 894 F.2d 28, 34, 10 U.C.C. Rep. Serv. 2d 846 (2d Cir. 1990) ("We assume for purposes of discussion that the painting is not an authentic work of John Singer Sargent . . . . The district court did not reach this issue and it is not presented on appeal."); Lawson v. London Arts Group, 708 F.2d 226, 36 U.C.C. Rep. Serv. 561 (6th Cir. 1983) (state discovery statute for state fine art statute on warranty of quality applied to calculate statute of limitations in case where Frederick Remington pastel certified as "an original work as described" by

trial application has not been made in the UCC context. Some courts have favored the reasonable basis-in-fact test.[3] Has plaintiff established "by a fair preponderance of the evidence that the [defendant's] representations . . . were without a reasonable basis in fact at the time [they] were made?"[4] "[T]o the extent that the evidence indicates that such representations [regarding art authorship] do not possess a reasonable basis in fact, at the time the[y] were made, this court finds that the party offering those representations will have violated the express warranties provided for under [UCC Section] 2-313."[5]

§ 4:22 Authenticity as guarantee or guess—Seller warranties where authentication contested—General

The warranty formulation changes when the seller knows, or has reason to know, that authenticity of a work is contested, but still makes a warranty of authenticity. The court decided a breach of warranty under UCC 2-313(a) had occurred where the bill of sale recited: "I . . . make the following warranties . . . that the seller has no knowledge of any challenge to . . . authenticity of the Painting . . . ." The facts showed the seller had been advised by gallery owners and auction houses of several

---

dealer was demonstrated at trial as a "copy"); Dawson v. G. Malina, Inc., 463 F. Supp. 461, 467 (S.D. N.Y. 1978) (inauthenticity of antique porcelain declared under former New York general business law); Greenberg Gallery, Inc. v. Bauman, 817 F. Supp. 167 (D.D.C. 1993), order aff'd, 36 F.3d 127 (D.C. Cir. 1994) (authentication of mobile purportedly by Alexander Calder in contract and breach of warranty suit made by finder of fact according to a preponderance of evidence).

[3]Rogath v. Siebenmann, 941 F. Supp. 416, 31 U.C.C. Rep. Serv. 2d 345 (S.D. N.Y. 1996), vacated, 129 F.3d 261, 34 U.C.C. Rep. Serv. 2d 63 (2d Cir. 1997) (plaintiff's motion for partial summary judgment on a breach of warranty claim regarding authenticity of a painting purportedly by Francis Bacon under Bill of Sale warranties granted).

[4]Dawson v. G. Malina, Inc., 463 F. Supp. 461, 467 (S.D. N.Y. 1978).

[5]Weber v. Peck, 1999 WL 493383 (S.D. N.Y. 1999) (seller's failure to provide letters of authentication for painting per sales contract grounds for breach of warranty action); Balog v. Center Art Gallery-Hawaii, Inc., 745 F. Supp. 1556, 12 U.C.C. Rep. Serv. 2d 962 (D. Haw. 1990).

specific authentication problems.[1] Similarly, an authenticity disclaimer in an appraisal may not be valid where the appraiser is aware of facts that cloud authenticity.[2]

§ 4:23 Authenticity as guarantee or guess—Seller warranties where authentication contested—Written contract

An unusual fact circumstance worth noting because of a district court's holding that a breach of provenance warranty could stand under New York 2-313 involved a preauction contract and bill of sale for a painting purportedly by Jacob van Ruisdael.[1] Denying recission of the sale, but ordering summary judgment for plaintiff on the issue of breach of provenance, the court concluded that as a matter of law, the provision stating "the . . . painting is authentic [as herein] described," which recited, "Artist: Jacob Van Ruisdael," and to which attached by reference a list of the painting's provenance, constituted a "warranty of the painting's provenance." The court wrote, "Defendant has conceded that the provenance was inaccurate. Sotheby's 'eliminated references to owners . . . ' because it was unable to verify these references . . . [S]otheby's added that the painting had previously sold as 'attributed to Ruisdael,' a lesser degree of certainty than an authenticated work. Defendant, therefore, breached his warranty

---

[Section 4:22]

[1]Rogath v. Siebenmann, 941 F. Supp. 416, 31 U.C.C. Rep. Serv. 2d 345 (S.D. N.Y. 1996), vacated and remanded, 129 F.3d 261, 34 U.C.C. Rep. Serv. 2d 63 (2d Cir. 1997) (plaintiff's motion for partial summary judgment on a breach of warranty claim regarding authenticity of a painting, purportedly by Francis Bacon, under Bill of Sale warranties granted).

[2]Foxley v. Sotheby's Inc., 893 F. Supp. 1224, 27 U.C.C. Rep. Serv. 2d 1234 (S.D. N.Y. 1995) (court refused to dismiss a complaint alleging bad faith and gross negligence against auction house notwithstanding that its appraisal disclaimed authentication, where pleading recited sufficient facts for fraudulent appraisal).

[Section 4:23]

[1]Weber v. Peck, 1999 WL 493383 (S.D. N.Y. 1999) (denying summary judgment for both parties on breach of warranty based upon authenticating letters).

of the provenance's accuracy."[2]

This is one of the first cases, if not the first reported case, endorsing a cause of action for breach of provenance under the UCC, and ordering judgment for its breach.

§ 4:24 Authenticity as guarantee or guess—Burden of proof on authorship in breach of warranty

The burden of proof is on the plaintiff to establish breach of warranty. In some jurisdictions, the plaintiff must also prove by a preponderance of the evidence that the artwork is not as it had been represented.[1] An art collector sued a dealer for rescission and damages under breach of warranty in connection with some Chinese art objects he had purchased for more than $100,000; when he received them, he doubted the authenticity of a $35,000 vase attributed to the Sung Dynasty.[2] The court established a standard of proof based upon whether the representations about authenticity were made with "a reasonable basis in fact," that basis being evaluated in conjunction with expert testimony at trial. Finding the buyer had failed to substantiate that the seller's statements were made without reasonable basis in fact, the court rejected the breach of warranty claim, allowing rescission and a refund of the purchase price, plus interest.

The reasonable basis in fact standard was chosen as appropriate, but was never applied, for a UCC express warranty action where dealers assured plaintiffs that works were by Salvador Dali and repeatedly mailed certificates of authenticity to them.[3] The court relied upon the price [too low to justify plaintiff's investigation of authenticity],

---

[2]Weber v. Peck, 1999 WL 493383 (S.D. N.Y. 1999) (factual issues involving the amount of damages based upon the painting's loss of value were reserved for trial).

[Section 4:24]

[1]Greenberg Gallery, Inc. v. Bauman, 817 F. Supp. 167 (D.D.C. 1993), order aff'd, 36 F.3d 127 (D.C. Cir. 1994) (breach of contract action dismissed where plaintiffs could not prove by preponderance of evidence that art was fake).

[2]Dawson v. G. Malina, Inc., 463 F. Supp. 461 (S.D. N.Y. 1978).

[3]Balog v. Center Art Gallery-Hawaii, Inc., 745 F. Supp. 1556, 12 U.C.C. Rep. Serv. 2d 962 (D. Haw. 1990).

disparity between buyers and sellers regarding access to information about authenticity [sellers were professional dealers] to decide that ". . . fairness dictates that representations offered by one party with the expectation that they be relied upon by another have some reasonable basis in fact."

§ 4:25 Authenticity as guarantee or guess—Author's comment

No uniform methodology or standard set of procedures is accepted to authenticate a work of art. The process of authenticating may involve one or multiple tests; no one test appears to be dispositive as Chart 4-2 indicates.

Chart 4-2: Examples of Scientific Tests for Authenticating

Some examples of current scientific tests and methodologies used in conservation to aid in the authentication of a work of art, progressing from the general to the minute, in conjunction with art historical connoisseurship:

(1) Detailed observation and identification of structure and materials

(2) Visual examination under ultraviolet light, raking light, transmitted light, and microscopy

(3) Further visual examination enhanced by infrared photography, infrared vidicon, photomicrographs, x-radiography, and ultraviolet light microscopy

(4) Analysis of cross-sections, staining of cross-sections, x-ray diffraction, gas chromatography, x-ray fluorescence

(5) Scanning electron microscopy and infrared reflectography

(6) Comparison with known samples

Although there are relatively inexpensive standard preliminary procedures for beginning the process—i.e., historical analysis and investigation of provenance, and referral to catalogue raisonne, exhibition catalogues and publications—dealers operate under no industry standard to undertake even these measures.

Breach of express warranty under the UCC in connection with representations of authorship should consider the following: (1) the methods and means used to determine the spectrum of authenticity are not consensual or standardized, being highly subjective, idiosyncratic, and subject to time and money constraints; (2) where the spurious work cannot be conclusively identified, no clear line exists between what is authentic and what might be authentic; and (3) the buyer is suing on a statement of artist identification that is at one and the same time the seller's guess and guarantee.

Like the term appraisal, the term authentication has little meaning without clarification of its terms and specification of the precise processes used to form its conclusions. Unfortunately, statements purporting to authenticate do not necessarily disclose their methodologies or their sources. The phrase, "I guarantee the painting *X* as genuine and authentic work by artist *Y*, signed and dated by seller *Z*," is not uncommon. Such statements should be challenged by those who intend to rely upon them.

Authentication marries art and science in an uncertain union. Historical evaluation, laboratory testing, forensic analysis, and a large splatter of intuition enter into tenuous conclusions. An authentication can involve coordinated efforts of many specialists, yet the same analyses can yield contradictory conclusions, often at great cost and expense and well publicized in the art world.[1]

How should authentication be analyzed under UCC Section 2-313? In express warranty terms, authorship is often the core description of the garden variety art deal.[2] The collector who wants to buy a painting by Vincent Van Gogh will not, at any price, purchase in its stead a painting

---

[Section 4:25]

[1]Boule v. Hutton, 138 F. Supp. 2d 491 (S.D. N.Y. 2001) (detailed and conflicting expert evidence by art historians, forensic microscopists and artist's heir on authenticity of artworks by Lazar Khidekel); P. Landesman, "A Crisis of Fakes," N.Y.Times Mag., Sec. 6 at p.37 (March 18, 2001); Konstandarus, "Meeting Casts Further Doubt on Statue's Authenticity," May 28, 1992 (AP) (statue at J. Paul Getty Museum).

[2]Auction, a sui generis art market, is excluded from this discussion, except where indicated.

represented as not by Van Gogh.[3] In short, authorship is often a singular deal-maker/deal-breaker item, impervious to price elasticity or product substitution.[4] Unlike other goods where functionally comparable look-alike objects are acceptable substitutes, neither a direct copy nor a painting that resembles Van Gogh's work will do.

§ 4:26 Authenticity as static or fluid

Authenticity is often inconclusive and evolutionary. Changes and developments in scholarship, methodologies, and technologies, as well as newly discovered documentary materials, factor into the equation. One era's Rembrandt is another's studio attribution; one scholar's premillenia sculpture is another's twentieth century reconstruction. Bands of itinerant authenticators exist who circumnavigate the globe "de-attributing" works of certain famous artists. Some courts have recognized this: "[M]y ruling that plaintiffs' claims are time-barred should not be interpreted as suggesting that [they are] valid: in the arcane world of high-priced art, market value is affected by market perceptions; the market value of a painting is determined by the prevailing views of the marketplace concerning its attribution."[1]

---

[3]But an experienced collector might buy a painting that is not represented as "by Van Gogh," if the price is right and the collector believes it to be by Van Gogh or has it authenticated.

[4]This does not apply to auction, where mediated risk of authenticity is part of the process, *see* Ch 5. *But see* Weber v. Peck, 1999 WL 493383 (S.D. N.Y. 1999) (denying summary judgment for both parties on breach of warranty for authenticating letters but ordering summary judgment for plaintiff on breach of provenance warranty where the parties entered into a multitiered preauction sales agreement linking payment to a percentage of the resale price notwithstanding irregularities regarding authenticity and provenance apparent prior to auction).

[Section 4:26]

[1]Firestone & Parson, Inc. v. Union League of Philadelphia, 672 F. Supp. 819, 3 U.C.C. Rep. Serv. 2d 449 (E.D. Pa. 1987), judgment aff'd, 833 F.2d 304 (3d Cir. 1987); *but cf.*, id. ("the fact that [expert's] article [questioning Bierstadt attribution] did not appear until February 1986 does not readily translate into the conclusion that plaintiffs could not reasonably have learned of the alleged error in attribution long before that date"). This conclusion is odd since the Firestone court repeatedly emphasized that attributions change over time, raising questions as to

§ 4:27 Business practices

The authorship that dealers of art in the ordinary course of business offer for art works does not ordinarily reach the level of intensive investigatory processes, extensive scientific testing, and copious international review. Nor could it; dealers do not have the time or money to send art out for extensive and expensive analysis. Few museums subject acquisitions to such outside analyses, and even when they do, the results can be inconclusive.

In general, absent a request from a buyer, dealers do not spend the time or the money to shopwalk their art works through these or other world's experts. The dealer's authorship at point of sale is rarely, in fact, co-terminous with an authentication such as those performed by groups of experts and often supported by documentation. This point has not been clarified in the cases, and is crucial in terms of UCC Section 2-313. Sometimes, works will be sold subject to conditions, i.e., based upon issuance of a certificate of authenticity from authenticators who can be self-designated or artist-designated: cataloguers,[1] surviving family members,[2] trusts,[3] or committees.[4]

Like other works of art discussed throughout this and other chapters, irresoluble disputes may exist regarding authenticity. A recent case highlights how authenticity ir-

---

what the court considered would have been recognizeable by a second opinion.

[Section 4:27]

[1]*See, e.g.,* McNally v. Yarnall, 764 F. Supp. 838, 844, (S.D. N.Y. 1991); Mount v. Ormand, 1991 WL 191228 (S.D. N.Y. 1991).

[2]Family members sometimes sit on committees, e.g., the Comite Picasso. Under French law, heirs or designates by will are given authority of the artist's droit moral, including the right to authenticate. *See* Greenwood v. Koven, 880 F. Supp. 186 (S.D. N.Y. 1995) ("Claude Laurens holds the droit moral for George Braque").

[3]Goldman v. Barnett, 793 F. Supp. 28, 18 U.C.C. Rep. Serv. 2d 55 (D. Mass. 1992) (Milton Avery trust).

[4]McCloud v. Lawrence Gallery, Ltd., 1991 WL 136027 (S.D. N.Y. 1991) (Comite Picasso rejects drawing of Pablo Picasso as inauthentic); Vitale v. Marlborough Gallery, 32 U.S.P.Q.2d (BNA) 1283, 1994 WL 654494 (S.D. N.Y. 1994) ("Pollock- Krasner Authentication Board," "Krasner Committee" identified as entities that authenticate works by Jackson Pollock (Lee Krasner, the widow of Pollock, being deceased since 1984)).

regularities sometimes do not dissuade a purchase and sale, and the consequences. Plaintiff and defendant entered into a sales agreement regarding a painting purportedly by Jacob van Ruisdael, where unsubstantiated references and gaps in the provenance[5] as well as a prior sale by attribution,[6] raised a flag on authenticity.[7] Plaintiff contracted to pay defendant almost $400,000 and a percentage of proceeds from resale at auction. The auction house examined the painting and reportedly thought it authentic, but prior to auction, its catalogue disclosed its discovery that the painting had previously sold as "attributed" to the artist, and could not confirm the provenance. The auction catalogue recited a two-figure estimate between $300,000 and $400,000, and "stated the painting was authentic."[8] A bid of $300,000 was accepted, but payment was never made, and the parties cross-claimed for summary judgment.[9] Authenticity could not be decided at law and motion, and may never be satisfactorily judicially resolved.

§ 4:28 How authenticity has been construed under express warranty—Elements of breach of warranty on authenticity

Although express warranty under UCC Section 2-313 is often alleged in arts cases, its application to authenticity disputes rarely has been analyzed by the courts because such lawsuits have been held barred as a matter of law under the UCC four-year statute of limitations under Section 2-725.[1] The elements of what constitutes the warranty, or the breach thereof, have not been elaborated on

---

[5]*See* Ch 2.

[6]*See* Ch 5.

[7]Weber v. Peck, 1999 WL 493383 (S.D. N.Y. 1999) (denying summary judgment for both parties on breach of warranty for authenticating letters but ordering summary judgment for plaintiff on breach of provenance warranty).

[8]Weber v. Peck, 1999 WL 493383 (S.D. N.Y. 1999).

[9]Weber v. Peck, 1999 WL 493383 (S.D. N.Y. 1999) (plaintiff's claim for recission was dismissed).

[Section 4:28]

[1]Wilson v. Hammer Holdings, Inc., 850 F.2d 3, 6 U.C.C. Rep. Serv. 2d 321 (1st Cir. 1988); Firestone & Parson, Inc. v. Union League of

in an adjudicatory setting.

The artwork remains the same visibly and intrinsically, before and after breach, unlike utilitarian goods whose defects are visible, or cause palpable effects elsewhere. The only thing that is different about artwork is the perception of it, and perception about art is 99 percent of value. The breach is ordinarily not inherent in or innate to the artwork itself,[2] but in the seller's statements about the artwork. The few courts examining the seller's statements have required as a standard that the statements of authorship be made with a reasonable basis in fact.

§ 4:29 How authenticity has been construed under express warranty—Timing of discovering breach

What has not been properly recognized is that express warranty cases based upon authenticity, or lack thereof, fall into two distinct categories: those that accrue within the four-year limitations period (or the permissible period set by contract) or after. Each has its own substantive standards.

Philadelphia, 672 F. Supp. 819, 822–23, 3 U.C.C. Rep. Serv. 2d 449 (E.D. Pa. 1987), judgment aff'd, 833 F.2d 304 (3d Cir. 1987); *but cf.,* Balog v. Center Art Gallery-Hawaii, Inc., 745 F. Supp. 1556, 12 U.C.C. Rep. Serv. 2d 962 (D. Haw. 1990) (express warranty claim valid for art misrepresented as to authorship); Solomon R. Guggenheim Foundation v. Lubell, 153 A.D.2d 143, 550 N.Y.S.2d 618 (1st Dep't 1990), order aff'd, 77 N.Y.2d 311, 567 N.Y.S.2d 623, 569 N.E.2d 426 (1991) (UCC Section 2-725 defense rejected in action by museum asserting ownership of collector's artwork owned by collector for twenty-five years or more, where museum did all that was reasonably required under common practices at the time of mysterious disappearance of the artwork); Foxley v. Sotheby's Inc., 893 F. Supp. 1224, 27 U.C.C. Rep. Serv. 2d 1234 (S.D. N.Y. 1995) (U.C.C. Section 2-725 barred action for breach of warranty where guarantee of authenticity five years from date of sale was not warranty of future performance but a limited warranty.).

[2]*But see* Estate of Querbach v. A & B Appraisal Serv., No. cv. L-089362-85 (N.J. Super. 1987) (painting signed on face, "J.Cropsey" is a painting by Jasper Francis Cropsey, a Hudson Valley painter whose work is worth thousands of dollars, not a $50 household item in appraisal negligence action).

§ 4:30 How authenticity has been construed under express warranty—Timing of discovering breach—Within four years

Few are contract claims of authenticity brought within the four-year UCC period.[1] The reason for that presumably falls within the realities of art trading and the attributes of art. The authenticity or spuriousness of many artworks is not known until well after four years of purchase, when the artwork is publicly displayed, e.g., at auction, a catalogue raisonne is published on the artist, or the art is seen by an expert. When an authenticity issue arises within four years, some dealers agree to accept return or credit of works if authorship is in legitimate dispute, and some will so state in purchase and sale agreements, which may specify a shorter period for return.[2]

§ 4:31 How authenticity has been construed under express warranty—Timing of discovering breach—After four years

After four years, UCC Section 2-725(2) is triggered.[1] Section 2-725 is an effective shield for defendants, shifting virtually insurmountable burdens to plaintiffs because of its requirement for "performance." By literally construing the language of Section 2-725, courts have effectively converted a procedural rule into a substantive one for art. This is the crucial point at which the UCC policies of commercial trading and art dealing collide.

Nothing under express warranty UCC Section 2-313 requires art to "perform" as UCC Section 2-725 does. If courts had analyzed breach of express warranty claims in

---

[Section 4:30]

[1]Ketcham v. Franklyn Gesner Fine Paintings, Inc., 181 Ga. App. 549, 353 S.E.2d 44 (1987) (action for breach of contract brought within four years of purchase of painting by Martin Johnson Heade deemed to be inauthentic; fraud action dismissed by directed verdict in favor of seller and breach of contract issue not before jury).

[2]UCC § 2-725(1) (statute of limitations for sale of contract by original agreement may be reduced to not less than one year, but not extended).

[Section 4:31]

[1]*See* §§ 4:35–4:41.

connection with authenticity, it would be clear that:

(1) the buyer is suing on something extrinsic to the good which does not alter the good itself, but affects market perception about the good;
(2) in many cases, no clear lines separate the authentic from the spurious, the potentially authentic from the potentially spurious;
(3) the methods and means to determine the spectrum of authenticity are not consensual or standardized, but are highly subjective, idiosyncratic, and subject to time and money constraints; and
(4) no consensus exists as to who is responsible for authenticating, the buyer or the seller.

§ 4:32 Recission

UCC Section 2-607 provides for recission of the contract as follows: "Acceptance of goods . . . with knowledge of a non-conformity cannot be revoked because of it unless the acceptance was on the reasonable assumption that the non-conformity would be seasonably cured."[1] If the cure is not effected, then the buyer may revoke the acceptance[2] within a reasonable time.[3]

Plaintiff was not entitled to rescind a contract of sale for a painting where he failed to timely notify seller of revocation and acted inconsistently with the seller's ownership by attempting to resell the painting at auction, even though he was aware of authentication and provenance problems.[4]

[Section 4:32]

[1]UCC § 2-607(2).

[2]UCC § 2-608(1)(a).

[3]UCC § 2-608(2).

[4]Foxley v. Sotheby's Inc., 893 F. Supp. 1224, 27 U.C.C. Rep. Serv. 2d 1234 (S.D. N.Y. 1995) (recission claim based upon unilateral or mutual mistake of painting authenticity time barred because action filed more than six years after auction); Weber v. Peck, 1999 WL 493383 (S.D. N.Y. 1999) (recission claim dismissed by district court applying New York law).

D. IMPLIED WARRANTIES

§ 4:33 Breach of warranty of merchantability

Courts are divided on potential actionability of implied warranties for art authentications under the UCC.[1] UCC Section 2-314 provides, inter alia:

> (1) [A] warranty that the goods shall be merchantable is implied in a contract for their sale if the seller is a merchant with respect to goods of that kind . . . .
>
> (2) Goods to be merchantable must be at least such as (a) Pass without objection in the trade under the contract description . . . (f) Conform to the promises or affirmations of fact made on the container or label if any.[2]

Courts that have found that an implied warranty of merchantability applies to art, allowing claims under UCC Section 2-314 were for: (1) an Authentication and Appraisal Report for a painting by William Merritt Chase made by a trader in connection with its sale for $370,000 is classified as a "promise . . . made on the container or label" within the meaning of UCC Section 2-314(2)(f);[3] and (2) if a painting does not conform to affirmations in an authentication, it could not pass under that description and would be unmerchantable under UCC Section

---

[Section 4:33]

[1]Balog v. Center Art Gallery-Hawaii, Inc., 745 F. Supp. 1556, 12 U.C.C. Rep. Serv. 2d 962 (D. Haw. 1990) (rejecting applicability of implied warranties to authentication actions); McCloud v. Lawrence Gallery, Ltd., 1991 WL 136027 (S.D. N.Y. 1991) (action against dealer for breach of implied and express warranties under Ohio law for sale of Picasso drawing by dealer rejected by Comite Picasso); *see also* McCloud v. Lawrence Gallery, Ltd., 1992 WL 6199 (S.D. N.Y. 1992), aff'd, 970 F.2d 896 (2d Cir. 1992); McKie v. R.H. Love Galleries, Inc., 1990 WL 179797 (N.D. Ill. 1990) (breach of warranty of merchantability and breach of warranty for a particular purpose upheld against motion to dismiss for failure to state a claim in connection with certificate of authenticity for purchase of painting by William Merritt Chase).

[2]UCC § 2-314.

[3]McKie v. R.H. Love Galleries, Inc., 1990 WL 179797 (N.D. Ill. 1990).

2-314(2)(a).[4] A court found that an implied warranty of merchantability does not apply to art, disallowing claims under UCC Section 2-314 where they found that counterfeit art is as merchantable as authentic art since its primary purpose is display for aesthetic appeal.[5]

§ 4:34 Breach of warranty of fitness for a particular purpose

UCC Section 2-315 provides: "[W]here the seller at the time of contracting has reason to know any particular purpose for which the goods are required and that the buyer is relying on the seller's skill or judgment to select or furnish suitable goods, there is . . . an implied warranty that the goods shall be fit for such purpose."[1] A particular purpose differs from ordinary purpose "in that it envisages a specific use by the buyer which is peculiar to the nature of his business whereas the ordinary purposes for which goods are used are those envisaged in concept of merchantability."[2]

In McKie, the court found that an implied warranty of fitness for a particular purpose does apply to art, allowing claims under UCC Section 2-315. The plaintiff-buyers alleged that they informed the trader-sellers they desired high quality works with potential for price appreciation. This was sufficient pleading to withstand a motion to dismiss for failure to state a claim, where the plaintiffs relied on incorrect information the defendant provided.[3] In Balog, the court found that an implied warranty of fitness for a particular purpose does not apply to art, disallowing claims under UCC section 2-315; museums and collectors cannot use this warranty because the customary use of artwork is display, and art has no particular use that is

---

[4]McKie v. R.H. Love Galleries, Inc., 1990 WL 179797 (N.D. Ill. 1990).

[5]Balog v. Center Art Gallery-Hawaii, Inc., 745 F. Supp. 1556, 12 U.C.C. Rep. Serv. 2d 962 (D. Haw. 1990).

[Section 4:34]

[1]UCC § 2-315.

[2]UCC § 2-315, Official Comment 2.

[3]McKie v. R.H. Love Galleries, Inc., 1990 WL 179797 (N.D. Ill. 1990).

different from ordinary purpose.[4]

E. STATUTE OF LIMITATIONS[5]

§ 4:35 Four-year rule: UCC Section 2-725(1)

UCC Section 2-725(1) provides: "An action for breach of any contract for sale must be commenced within four years after the cause of action has accrued." Section 2-725(2) mandates commencing the accrual period even before knowledge of the breach: "A cause of action accrues when the breach occurs, regardless of the aggrieved party's lack of knowledge of the breach." Section 2-725(2) establishes accrual for breach of warranty even more specifically: "A breach of warranty occurs when tender of delivery is made." If more than four years has elapsed since delivery, UCC Section 2-725 generally bars the claim unless the plaintiff can fit within the exceptions under Section 2-725(2).

Once UCC Section 2-725 runs, the allegation of breach of express warranty for authenticity changes: Buyers must now prove that the seller offered a warranty and breached the warranty,[1] *but also* that the breach could not have been discovered until future performance and that the seller expressly and explicitly intended for the warranty to carry forward to that future date. The courts have imposed "performance" upon art; art is now required to "do" things that it innately does not do, i.e., perform. The result is that a procedural statute of limitations of UCC Section 2-725(2) operates as a substantive rule of law for art.

§ 4:36 Discovery rule: UCC Section 2-725(2)

The UCC Section 2-725(2) discovery rule is a two-part

---

[4]Balog v. Center Art Gallery-Hawaii, Inc., 745 F. Supp. 1556, 12 U.C.C. Rep. Serv. 2d 962 (D. Haw. 1990).

[5]For a discussion of statutes of limitations under replevin and other claims for return of property, see due diligence discussion in § 6:130, provenance in § 6:82, and auctions in §§ 5:66 to 5:67. This section focuses upon the UCC and the UCC statute of limitations.

[Section 4:35]

[1]That the representations about the art constitute an express warranty and that the warranty was breached has been difficult to prove.

test requiring: (1) a warranty explicitly extending to future performance; and (2) discovery of the breach must await future performance. UCC Section 2-725(2) provides, in pertinent part, as follows: "A breach of warranty occurs when tender of delivery is made except where a warranty explicitly extends to future performance of the goods *and* discovery of the breach must await the time of such performance [emphasis added]."

Firestone & Parson, Inc. v. Union League,[1] was an action brought by dealers for lost profits based upon their claim that an Albert Bierstadt painting purchased from the defendant in 1981 had been reattributed in 1986. None of the parties claimed an authentication had been made prior to or at the time of sale of the painting, "Bombardment of Fort Sumter." The reattribution was reportedly sourced to one article published in 1986 by an art historian and its subsequent acceptance by art experts at the time of suit in 1987.[2]

The court, rather than the parties, recast the lawsuit for rescission based upon mutual mistake as a UCC action, contending that no mutual mistake could have occurred since both parties believed the prevailing market attribution to Bierstadt was correct. The plaintiffs were, according to the court, not rescinding for mistake, but were revoking acceptance. The breach occurred in 1981 at the time of delivery under UCC Section 2-725(2), irrespective of when the plaintiff's gained knowledge of the breach. The district court held that contract claims were timed-barred since the suit was filed more than four years after delivery date.[3] Without discussing the merits of the claim, the court dismissed the plaintiffs' argument that a

---

[Section 4:36]

[1]Firestone & Parson, Inc. v. Union League of Philadelphia, 672 F. Supp. 819, 822–23, 3 U.C.C. Rep. Serv. 2d 449 (E.D. Pa. 1987), judgment aff'd, 833 F.2d 304 (3d Cir. 1987).

[2]In general, a one-year period is not a sufficient time for a reattribution to garner consensus among art experts; it barely allows time for scholarly public debate or published response to the new attribution.

[3]Firestone & Parson, Inc. v. Union League of Philadelphia, 672 F. Supp. 819, 3 U.C.C. Rep. Serv. 2d 449 (E.D. Pa. 1987), judgment aff'd, 833 F.2d 304 (3d Cir. 1987) (deciding the same rule would apply under another Pennsylvania limitations statute; *accord* Shaheen v. Stephen Hahn, Inc., 1994 WL 854659 (S.D. N.Y. 1994) (breach of warranty ac-

discovery rule should apply; UCC Section 2-725(2) precluded the action and state law did not otherwise allow it.

§ 4:37 Performance of an artwork—Discovery of breach must await future performance

Since art does not "perform" like other commercial goods, application of Section 2-725 to artworks is problematic. Some courts interpret "performance" of art under UCC Section 2-725 to mean that art "performs" if it is authentic;[1] others suggest that spurious art does not impair an owner's use and enjoyment.[2] Germane to the inquiry is whether art "performs" at all within the meaning of UCC Section 2-725.[3]

The First Circuit has assumed without deciding that "a painting 'perform[s]' by being genuine." There, the plaintiffs, who were not traders like the Firestone plaintiffs, purchased a painting by Edouard Vuillard in 1961 from the defendant-gallery. The sale was accompanied by a written express guarantee of authenticity. When the plaintiffs prepared to sell the painting some twenty-four years later, they were informed it was a fake; they returned the painting to the gallery, and in 1987 filed suit

---

tion in connection with sale of pastel by Mary Cassatt brought under UCC and state arts law dismissed as untimely after four-year limitations period because, although equitable estoppel applied to negligent misrepresentation claim, court refused to expand doctrine under UCC 2-725(2)).

[Section 4:37]

[1]Wilson v. Hammer Holdings, Inc., 850 F.2d 3, 6 U.C.C. Rep. Serv. 2d 321 (1st Cir. 1988); Balog v. Center Art Gallery-Hawaii, Inc., 745 F. Supp. 1556, 1571, 12 U.C.C. Rep. Serv. 2d 962 (D. Haw. 1990) ("artwork does not 'perform' in the traditional sense of goods covered in the U.C.C., and since the authenticity of a work of art, i.e., its 'performance' would not change over time, . . . [the] warranty necessarily guaranteed the present and future existence of the art as authentic"); Firestone & Parson, Inc. v. Union League of Philadelphia, 672 F. Supp. 819, 3 U.C.C. Rep. Serv. 2d 449 (E.D. Pa. 1987), judgment aff'd, 833 F.2d 304 (3d Cir. 1987).

[2]Solomon R. Guggenheim Foundation v. Lubell, 153 A.D.2d 143, 550 N.Y.S.2d 618 (1st Dep't 1990), order aff'd, 77 N.Y.2d 311, 567 N.Y.S.2d 623, 569 N.E.2d 426 (1991).

[3]*See* "Author's Comment," § 4:41.

for, inter alia, breach of express warranty under the UCC.[4]

On appeal, the court wrote:

> Because of the static nature of authenticity, the Wilsons were no less capable of discovering that "Femme Debout" was a fake at the time of purchase than they were at a later time . . . . [T]he product's performance never changed. The painting failed to exist as a Vuillard as much at the time of purchase in 1961 as at the time the Wilsons discovered its true nature.[5]

The plaintiffs contended that a "warranty of authenticity of a painting necessarily relates to the future condition of the artwork." Since authenticity of a painting does not change over time according to the plaintiffs, the warranty protects present authentication as well as future authentication, and any express language as to future extension in a warranty would be superfluous. The First Circuit, affirming the district court, "did not decide th[e] issue" of whether the gallery's authentication satisfied the prospective warranty requirement of UCC Section 2-725(2) because it concluded that the action was time-barred under the second prong requiring that discovery "must await" future performance.[6] The only case applying a discovery rule analysis is Balog v. Center Art Gallery-Hawaii, Inc.[7]

---

[4]Wilson v. Hammer Holdings, Inc., 850 F.2d 3, 6 U.C.C. Rep. Serv. 2d 321 (1st Cir. 1988); *see also* Lawson v. London Arts Group, 708 F.2d 226, 36 U.C.C. Rep. Serv. 561 (6th Cir. 1983) (specific statute of limitations under Michigan's art per se laws on warranty (not UCC), which provided for a discovery rule of the breach at the time of discovery or at the time the defect should have reasonably been discovered).

[5]Wilson v. Hammer Holdings, Inc., 850 F.2d 3, 6-7, 6 U.C.C. Rep. Serv. 2d 321 (1st Cir. 1988); *see also* Lawson v. London Arts Group, 708 F.2d 226, 36 U.C.C. Rep. Serv. 561 (6th Cir. 1983).

[6]Wilson v. Hammer Holdings, Inc., 850 F.2d 3, 6, 6 U.C.C. Rep. Serv. 2d 321 (1st Cir. 1988); *see also* Rosen v. Spanierman, 894 F.2d 28, 32, 10 U.C.C. Rep. Serv. 2d 846 (2d Cir. 1990) ("[The buyers'] discovery of the alleged lack of authenticity did not, as required by [UCC § 2-725(2)], necessarily await future performance because [the buyers] could have discovered the defect immediately after sale [citation omitted]. [A] painting's lack of authenticity is readily apparent to the trained eye of an art expert.").

[7]Balog v. Center Art Gallery-Hawaii, Inc., 745 F. Supp. 1556, 12 U.C.C. Rep. Serv. 2d 962 (D. Haw. 1990), discussed in § 4:38.

§ 4:38 Performance of an artwork—Warranty explicitly extending to future performance

In Rosen v. Spanierman,[1] a seemingly satisfactory guarantee of authenticity was held not to extend to future performance under UCC Section 2-725(2). The buyers brought, inter alia, UCC breach of warranty and fraud claims based upon disputed authenticity of a painting by John Singer Sargent twenty years after they purchased it from the dealer-defendant. The dealer had provided a written guarantee of authenticity and subsequent insurance appraisals from 1975 to 1986, the last one valuing the painting at $130,000.

The district court accepted that performance of art means "it [the painting] is [as] purported to be, i.e., an authentic work of the artist."[2] But the warranty had run because the gallery's warranty did not explicitly extend to future performance.[3] The warranty recited: "This picture is fully guaranteed by the undersigned to be an original work by John Singer Sargent." The plaintiffs argued that a warranty of authenticity stating the painting is authentic "for its lifetime" would be superfluous language in an express guarantee of authenticity. The court was not

[Section 4:38]

[1]Rosen v. Spanierman, 711 F. Supp. 749, 8 U.C.C. Rep. Serv. 2d 713 (S.D. N.Y. 1989), judgment vacated in part on other grounds, 894 F.2d 28, 10 U.C.C. Rep. Serv. 2d 846 (2d Cir. 1990). *See* Ch 3 regarding appraisals made by sellers in the trade and appraisals prepared by independent appraisers.

[2]Rosen v. Spanierman, 711 F. Supp. 749, 753, 8 U.C.C. Rep. Serv. 2d 713 (S.D. N.Y. 1989), judgment vacated in part on other grounds, 894 F.2d 28, 10 U.C.C. Rep. Serv. 2d 846 (2d Cir. 1990), *citing with approval* Lawson v. London Arts Group, 708 F.2d 226, 228, 36 U.C.C. Rep. Serv. 561 (6th Cir. 1983) (discovery of nonauthenticity of painting does not necessarily await future performance); *accord* Shaheen v. Stephen Hahn, Inc., 1994 WL 854659 (S.D. N.Y. 1994) (summary judgment in favor of dealer defendants, dismissing cause of action for breach of warranty as time-barred under UCC Section 2-725(2) because the representations about authenticity of a pastel purportedly by Mary Cassatt did not explicitly extend to future performance, citing approvingly Rosen v. Spanierman.

[3]Rosen v. Spanierman, 894 F.2d 28, 33, 10 U.C.C. Rep. Serv. 2d 846 (2d Cir. 1990) (court also held that discovery of the defect in the painting did not necessarily await future performance under UCC § 2-725(2)).

persuaded: "this does not present a reason for ignoring the plain language of Section 2-725(2). The fact that a warranty of authenticity does not fit neatly within the statute as written does not justify judicial modification of the statute's requirements."[4]

But in Balog,[5] the only case that allowed a UCC breach of warranty action based upon an authenticity dispute after four years, a district court held that a certificate of authenticity "should be understood to provide what it said . . . an explicit warranty that the work was, and would be in the future, a Dali original."[6] The court's position was unequivocal: "this court holds that in the case of artwork which is certified authentic by an expert in the field or a merchant dealing in goods of that type, such a certification of authenticity constitutes an explicit warranty of future performance."[7]

The defendants, also convicted in criminal charges relating to sale of overvalued or misrepresented art, issued a series of certificates of authenticity over several years for Salvador Dali prints, as they continued to solicit sales from the plaintiffs. The court found these certificates, "guarantee the present and future existence of the art as authentic." That warranties should extend to the future was appropriate, stated the court, because "artwork does not 'perform' in the traditional sense of goods . . . and . . . authenticity of a work of art, i.e., its 'performance' would not change over time."[8]

The court disposed of the need to obtain an independent authentication by linking the "defect must await future performance" prong, with the "explicit future guarantee"

---

[4]Rosen v. Spanierman, 894 F.2d 28, 32, 10 U.C.C. Rep. Serv. 2d 846 (2d Cir. 1990) (court also held that discovery of the defect in the painting did not necessarily await future performance under UCC § 2-725(2)); *see also* Shaheen v. Stephen Hahn, Inc., 1994 WL 854659 (S.D. N.Y. 1994).

[5]Balog v. Center Art Gallery-Hawaii, Inc., 745 F. Supp. 1556, 12 U.C.C. Rep. Serv. 2d 962 (D. Haw. 1990).

[6]Balog v. Center Art Gallery-Hawaii, Inc., 745 F. Supp. 1556, 1571, 12 U.C.C. Rep. Serv. 2d 962 (D. Haw. 1990).

[7]Balog v. Center Art Gallery-Hawaii, Inc., 745 F. Supp. 1556, 1570, 12 U.C.C. Rep. Serv. 2d 962 (D. Haw. 1990).

[8]Balog v. Center Art Gallery-Hawaii, Inc., 745 F. Supp. 1556, 1571. 12 U.C.C. Rep. Serv. 2d 962 (D. Haw. 1990).

prong: "This court will not require art purchasers to hire a second expert to verify the purported work of the first in order to preserve their rights under a future breach of warranty claim. . . . Based on such an explicit warranty of future performance, that statute [of limitations] is tolled until such time as the defect in the product was, or reasonably should have been, discovered."[9]

Balog is a minority rule, and several caveats should be noted. First, only sales by dealers or experts, not necessarily other sellers, would trigger the liberal construction of UCC Section 2-725; second, Hawaii's commercial code allows tolling the statute of limitations, which the court relied on to backstop its opinion; third, the amount of money involved was, in the court's mind, insufficient to warrant plaintiffs to undertake a costly independent authentication; and fourth, plaintiffs were tourists, Hawaii's economy is heavily dependent upon tourism, and tourists are known to frequent island galleries for purchases they might not otherwise make at home, a regional subtext among the nation's national efforts to punish sellers or impose costs on them.[10]

§ 4:39 Performance of an artwork—Continuing conduct

Where the defendants made repeated mailings of certificates of authenticity to the plaintiffs over a course of years, the date of the last mailing was the date set as the time from which the UCC Section 2-725 four-year period should be calculated.[1]

§ 4:40 Performance of an artwork—Fraudulent concealment

Some jurisdictions allow plaintiffs to avoid the four-year

---

[9]Balog v. Center Art Gallery-Hawaii, Inc., 745 F. Supp. 1556 at 1571, 12 U.C.C. Rep. Serv. 2d 962 (D. Haw. 1990).

[10]Query whether these efforts actually penalize sellers or simply are incorporated as a cost of doing business (*see* Chs 12 and 11) or whether they focus buyers' attention upon dangers of uneducated purchases in the print market, effectively shifting the burden to buyers.

[Section 4:39]

[1]Balog v. Center Art Gallery-Hawaii, Inc., 745 F. Supp. 1556, 12 U.C.C. Rep. Serv. 2d 962 (D. Haw. 1990).

time-bar of the statute of limitations if certain forms of fraud induce the plaintiff to refrain from timely filing. Where the defendants engaged in affirmative conduct by mailing certificates of authenticity to the plaintiffs, thereby "lulling" the plaintiffs into believing the work was authentic, such conduct was held to constitute fraudulent concealment, whereby UCC Section 2-725 was tolled.[1]

§ 4:41 Author's comment

The inadequacy of the UCC for art disputes is rooted not so much in its construction as in its express linkage to productivity cycles based upon "performing" goods and its related warranty scheme based upon efficient market entry and exit of goods from inventory or order for special manufacture to obsolescence. The UCC four-year statute of limitations contemplates expeditious commercial turnover of goods. The production system is predicated upon speedy performance and identifiable misperformance within a specified period. Breach of warranty under article 2 is based on the assumption that defects in goods can be identified, and that four years is enough time to identify them. Historically, art is not turned over for resale within four-year periods,[1] and authorship is not a typical "defect," neither apparent on the good, nor discoverable through "use." Public display and publication of art are the standard ways authenticity issues arise, through auction, cataloguing, and retrospectives. Absent public scrutiny by knowledgeable experts, questions about authorship typi-

[Section 4:40]

[1] Balog v. Center Art Gallery-Hawaii, Inc., 745 F. Supp. 1556, 12 U.C.C. Rep. Serv. 2d 962 (D. Haw. 1990); *cf.* Shaheen v. Stephen Hahn, Inc., 1994 WL 854659 (S.D. N.Y. 1994), where the court refused to find the defendant was equitably estopped from pleading Section 2-725(2) in a breach of warranty claim involving sale of a pastel purportedly by Mary Cassatt, although it found defendant was equitably estopped to plead the statute of frauds in a cause of action for negligent representation filed more than six years after purchase, beyond the limitations period of New York law.

[Section 4:41]

[1] Exceptions occurred for speculation during the boom, undermining the integrity of the market and precipitating price decline and sales stagnation for some types of art.

cally occur after the limitations period has run.

The legal frailties of considering art "goods" under the UCC have already been raised; but discovery of authenticity questions after four years raises the particularly troublesome issues of whether art "performs" within the meaning of UCC Section 2-725. If art cannot satisfy the performance requirements to trigger the discovery rule under the statute of limitations, then the breach of warranty claim, no matter how meritorious, is never reached.

The UCC world of goods is based upon widgets, objects with intrinsic components, parts, and elements, and warranty law is based upon representations and disclaimers about them. Within four years of use, the "performance" of the goods can be evaluated against the representations and disclaimers. After four years of use, common experience, objective and scientific testing, and so forth, determines whether or not discovery of defects had to await future performance.

Art is an anomoly in the world of goods in that it is essentially "use"-less under commercial utilitarian standards, and its value relating to authorship in certain circumstances is based upon extrinsic factors, opinions and judgments. The representations and disclaimers are not about "use" of the art or its performance, but about perception of the artwork and its author. Depending upon who is making the judgment, the basis for it, and how it is obtained, the range of meaning in representations about authorship is boundless. Few but the cognescenti know how to interpret representations about authorship, and even they are fooled or misled on occasion.

Once the limitations period has run, the breach of warranty claim for art changes and the performance difference between art and widgets is crystallized: Buyers must now not only prove that the seller breached warranty, but also that the defect—nebulous and indefinable as it may be—could not have been discovered until the future date. Common experience, and objective and scientific testing are not as readily available to make these determinations for art as they are for widgets.

The UCC world of goods is based upon use-and-performance product life, scheduled for market exit through obsolescence and depreciation. Goods move out of UCC warranties after four years and commercial expectations about goods are consistent with the warranty period. Art is a perpetual product, with an indeterminate useful life and a potentially infinite life. Art does not become obsolete and exit the market like widgets; art returns to the market for resale, often at appreciating prices, at regular intervals, i.e., after death or divorce, with new warranties and new expectations.[2]

The trade stream metaphor for commercial products, with its unilinear direction tied to production cycles from market entrance to market exit, is inapt for art. Art moves in a trade tide, back and forth, ebbing and flowing through financial and economic cycles. Unlike "used" goods, buyers expect new warranties to issue for art at each point of sale in the trade tides. Art warranties issue and re-issue on the same objects at points in time farther and farther from the date of creation and initial market entry, and deeper and deeper along a lengthening chain of sale or ownership.

F. ORAL CONTRACTS TO PURCHASE ARTWORKS

§ 4:42 Statute of frauds: General requirements for a writing

Oral contracts for the sale of goods valued at more than $500 are governed by the UCC statute of frauds, Section 2-201(1), which provides in pertinent part: "Except as otherwise provided . . . a contract for the sale of goods at a price of $500 or more is not enforceable by way of action or defense unless there is some writing sufficient to indicate that a contract has been made between the parties and signed by the party against whom enforcement is sought."[1]

By requiring a written contract to be signed, the statute

---

[2]*Accord* Simon v. C.I.R., 103 T.C. 247, 1994 WL 450480 (1994), aff'd, 68 F.3d 41 (2d Cir. 1995), nonacq., 1996-29 I.R.B. 41996-29 I.R.B. 4 and recommendation regarding acquiescence, 1996-29 I.R.B. 4AOD-1996-9, 1996 WL 390088 (I.R.S. AOD 1996) and nonacq., 1996-29 I.R.B. 4 (July 15, 1996) and nonacq., 1996-2 C.B. 1 (Jan. 6, 1997) ("a 'work of art' retains its character . . . because it does not have a determinable useful life and generally does not decline in value over a predictable period").

[Section 4:42]

[1]UCC § 2-201(1).

of frauds serves to authenticate the information contained in the writing. But signature is broadly defined to include any authentication "which identifies the party to be charged."[2] UCC Section 2-201 is generally broad based; it contemplates writings that fall short of contracts, and incorporates as applicable course of dealing between the parties.[3] Vagueness or incompleteness do not necessarily negate the existence of a contract under the UCC, Section 2-201, providing that quantity is expressly stated in writing,[4] although bits-and-pieces agreements become vulnerable, under certain circumstances, to parol evidence rule challenge.[5]

The art trade largely operates on words and faith, although that long-established modus operandi may be changing as art litigation increases. Recordation historically is sparse for transfer in any of the art markets. As a result, there has been confusion about what interests are being transferred—tangible or intangible—and which statutes of frauds apply. Those seeking to negate agreements have invoked the applicable statute of frauds that suited their claims, i.e., UCC or copyright, by blending the tangible and intangible characteristics of the art object.[6] Trader-client agreements and trader-artist agreements for the purchase and sale of art not evidenced by the requisite Section 2-201 writing do not always result in dismissal of claims.

---

[2]UCC § 2-201, Official Comment ¶ 1.

[3]Rosenfeld v. Basquiat, 78 F.3d 84, 43 Fed. R. Evid. Serv. 983, 29 U.C.C. Rep. Serv. 2d 104 (2d Cir. 1996) (crayon-scrawled writing signed by artist and buyer that specified price, date, and paintings to be sold was sufficient to prevent invalidating contract for sale based upon statute of frauds).

[4]UCC 2-201, Official Comment 1 (". . . All that is required is that the writing afford a basis for believing that the offered oral evidence rests on a real transaction.")

[5]The differences in the requisite writings between the UCC statute of frauds and the copyright statute of frauds are clear. Federal copyright has its own formalities, modified after the Berne Convention. Artists should assure that the specific copyright interest be expressly recited, as well as the intended scope and purpose of its use. *See* Chs 7 and 9.

[6]*See, e.g.,* Chamberlain v. Cocola Associates, 958 F.2d 282 (9th Cir. 1992).

§ 4:43 Dealer-artist agreements

Dealers should be cognizant of the statute of frauds, reducing to writing agreements with artists for the purchase and sale of artworks. For example, a plaintiff-gallery alleged it had a general right pursuant to oral agreements with Peter Halley to purchase his works.[1] The gallery did not purchase a particular artwork based on an oral "understanding" that Halley would supply another at dealer prices. The artist then terminated his relationship with the plaintiff, joined another dealer, and refused to supply additional artworks to the plaintiff. Since the understanding was not documented by a writing, the claim was dismissed by the trial court as an unenforceable agreement under UCC Section 2-201(1).

A dealer sued the estate of Jean-Michel Basquiat, alleging he had agreed to a sale of three identified paintings, for which she paid a cash deposit, and received a crayon contract, dated and signed. Delivery was delayed, and in the interim the artist died, the paintings disappeared, and the estate refused to pay. The Second Circuit rejected the estates's contention that the statute of frauds barred enforcement of the contract.[2]

§ 4:44 Dealer-collector agreements—Dealer asserting statute of frauds

A statute of frauds defense was accepted in the following: an action by collectors against a gallery to compel specific performance of sale of a painting by Brice Marden, dismissed by a federal district court under UCC Section 2-201[1] although the gallery clients alleged they had "bought" the Marden pursuant to oral agreement, conduct, trade practice, and course of dealing; and an action by a

---

[Section 4:43]

[1] Sonnabend Gallery v. Halley, No. 12723/92 (N.Y. Sup. 1992).

[2] Rosenfeld v. Basquiat, 78 F.3d 84, 43 Fed. R. Evid. Serv. 983, 29 U.C.C. Rep. Serv. 2d 104 (2d Cir. 1996) (reversing and remanding with instruction to bar plaintiff's testimony under state Dead Man's Statute).

[Section 4:44]

[1] Hoffmann v. Boone, 708 F. Supp. 78, 9 U.C.C. Rep. Serv. 2d 474 (S.D. N.Y. 1989) (oral agreement to purchase art barred by statute of frauds under Uniform Commercial Code).

collector against a gallery to enforce an oral agreement to exchange artwork for another artwork, dismissed by a federal district court under state statute of frauds where the agreement was deemed a "lifetime return policy" of the gallery that could not have been fully performed within one year.[2] A statute of frauds defense was not accepted where the dealer initialed handwritten terms for price and title on letterhead, although he did not sign the contract.[3] The statute initially defeated a claim for breach of oral contract alleged by the collector that he could exchange a pastel by Mary Cassatt purchased from the dealer for works of comparable or greater value.[4] The collector argued that the understanding was enforceable because he could have returned the pastel to the dealer within one year under the applicable state statute of frauds.[5] The court dismissed the claim, characterizing the agreement as a "lifetime return policy" that could apply to any painting the collector had bought from the gallery, continuing until the death of the plaintiff or defendant. The claim was reinstated on rehearing by characterizing the oral contract as one for a series of separate prospective purchases, which would permit exchange of a single purchase like the pastel within one year of purchase.[6]

§ 4:45 Dealer-collector agreements—Collector-buyer asserting statute of frauds

Sellers should obtain writings documenting sales; buyers' defenses under the statute of frauds are ordinarily successful. A dealer sued a buyer for breach of oral contract based upon the defendant's failure to purchase

---

[2]Shaheen v. Stephen Hahn, Inc., 1994 WL 854659 (S.D. N.Y. 1994) (cause of action dismissed under N.Y. Gen. Oblig. Law § 5-701).

[3]Jafari v. Wally Findlay Galleries, 1989 WL 116437 (S.D. N.Y. 1989) (motion to dismiss statute of frauds claim denied), *later proceeding,* Jafari v. Wally Findlay Galleries, 714 F. Supp. 64 (S.D.N.Y. 1990).

[4]Shaheen v. Stephen Hahn, Inc., 1994 WL 854659 (S.D. N.Y. 1994) (pastel titled "Mother About to Kiss Her Baby" by Mary Cassatt purchased in 1978 by collector from New York dealer could be exchanged for more expensive works, provided that collector paid the difference in value).

[5]N.Y. Gen. Oblig. Law § 5-701.

[6]Shaheen v. Stephen Hahn, Inc., 1994 WL 854659 (S.D. N.Y. 1994).

two sculptures made by artists the dealer represented. The court stated: "As for [oral breach of contract claim], even if it is accepted at face value, it describes a contract rendered unenforceable by . . . (the UCC version of the Statute of Frauds). . . . [U]nless Robin admits . . . that a contract for sale was made, [the] breach of contract claims will have to be dismissed."[1]

The plaintiff sued a museum and collectors, inter alia, for breach of contract based on the collectors' failure to pay the balance owed for a sculpture, "La Femme Assise," purportedly by Elie Nadelman, sold to the collectors through the good offices of a museum curator.[2] The court found that no contract action could be sustained against the museum because there was no writing indicating a purchase agreement by the museum for the sculpture as required by UCC Section 2-201.

A partnership asked a plaintiff-gallery to buy art on its behalf, paying commissions on purchase.[3] In 1989, the gallery obtained an option on a Van Gogh painting and offered it to the partnership-defendants for $3.5 million, of which $500,000 reflected its commission. Over a course of meetings, the partnership asked the plaintiff to withhold his commission until resale of the Van Gogh, and promised he would get his commission, plus 10 percent of the profits over $3.5 million. The partnership never paid for the Van Gogh and the option expired. The gallery sued, inter alia, for breach of contract. The defense was that the UCC statute of frauds barred the action because no writing supported the agreement, which involved a sale of goods in excess of $500. Reversing the trial court, the Court of Appeals of Texas found the agreement was "to purchase from a third party seller, in the nature of an agreement to fund" outside the scope of the UCC and Section 2-201.

[Section 4:45]

[1]MHR Corp. v. Robin, 1988 WL 58502 (N.D. Ill. 1988) (an account stated is not created by an invoice sent to a prospective purchaser of two sculptures where nothing but an unenforceable oral promise to pay represents the buyer's part of the bargain).

[2]Struna v. Wolf, 126 Misc. 2d 1031, 484 N.Y.S.2d 392 (Sup 1985).

[3]McCulley Fine Arts Gallery, Inc. v. X Partners, 860 S.W.2d 473, 23 U.C.C. Rep. Serv. 2d 350 (Tex. App. El Paso 1993).

§ 4:46 Art per se laws that impose writing requirements for conveying interests in artworks

Do state art per se laws containing provisions that ownership of an artwork is not automatically conveyed when certain rights in art are also conveyed—unless a specific writing exists signed by the artist or agent expressly reciting the transfer—operate as statutes of frauds? In Chamberlain v. Cocola Associates,[1] an artist sought to assert ownership in his valuable sculpture that had been in the possession of, and on display in, the defendant's restaurant, which also claimed ownership. The artist relied on Section 988 of the California Civil Code,[2] which contains provisions and verbiage typical of many state statutes, and created a statute of frauds requiring a writing for *any* transfer of art ownership, and claimed that his transfer to the defendant-restaurant was merely a loan. Both parties agreed that no written contract existed specifically transferring ownership interest from the artist to the restaurant under the terms of Section 988, but the restaurant contended that a transfer of 50 percent stock ownership in the restaurant was made to the artist's son based upon acquisition of the sculpture in lieu of cash payment.

The district court ruled that Section 988 created a statute of frauds and that its strict terms of transfer had to be satisfied to enforce ownership interests in artworks. The Ninth Circuit reversed and remanded, holding that Section 988 does not require a writing to transfer ownership rights each time physical possession of an artwork is transferred. Relying upon the legislative history of the state law and referring to federal copyright concerning transfers of intangible personal property, the court restricted application of Section 988 to intangible property interest transfers: "[W]here there is an express, written conveyance of one or more of the limited rights listed in [Section 988], there can be no accompanying transfer of

---

[Section 4:46]

[1]Chamberlain v. Cocola Associates, 958 F.2d 282 (9th Cir. 1992). For a list of states with art per se laws, *see* Appendix 20.

[2]*See* Ch 9 §§ 9:62 to 9:63.

ownership unless the transfer of ownership is also in writing."[3]

§ 4:47 Exceptions to statute of frauds—Admission in pleadings or testimony

Clients of a gallery claimed they had an oral agreement to purchase a contemporary painting by Brice Marden. When the gallery did not sell them the painting, they brought an action for specific performance, and the gallery defended under the statute of frauds. The collectors claimed that the exception to the statute of frauds applied under UCC Section 2-201(3)(b), which provides that oral contracts are enforceable if the party against whom enforcement is sought admits the contract in court pleadings or testimony.[1] But the gallery owner averred by affidavit that no contract was entered into with the collectors, and the court refused to apply the exception.

§ 4:48 Exceptions to statute of frauds—Doctrine of promissory estoppel

The basic elements of promissory estoppel are a clear and unambiguous promise, reasonable and foreseeable reliance on the promise, and resultant injury, the requisite degree of injury varying among jurisdictions.[1] The viability of a separate estoppel depends upon the law of the state, some merging it within breach of contract, others treating it as an alternative theory to breach of contract. In the UCC context, federal courts applying state law have ap-

---

[3]Chamberlain v. Cocola Associates, 958 F.2d 282 at 285 (9th Cir. 1992) (although the Ninth Circuit did not reach the preemption issue, query whether Section 988 is preempted under federal copyright, 17 U.S.C.A. § 301); *cf.* Hoffmann v. Boone, 708 F. Supp. 78, 9 U.C.C. Rep. Serv. 2d 474 (S.D. N.Y. 1989) (collectors' action against gallery to enforce putative oral agreement to purchase a painting by Brice Marden for $125,000 barred by statute of frauds in the absence of documentation or invoice, notwithstanding that they had purchased other artworks from the gallery based upon oral agreements).

[Section 4:47]

[1]Hoffmann v. Boone, 708 F. Supp. 78, 9 U.C.C. Rep. Serv. 2d 474 (S.D. N.Y. 1989).

[Section 4:48]

[1]*See also* §§ 4:13 to 4:14.

plied estoppel to contracts for the sale of goods. The party seeking to deny the contract is estopped from denying the existence of the oral contract, the estoppel doctrine satisfying proof considerations embodied in the statute of frauds. In evaluating promissory estoppel as grounds for an exception to the statute of frauds in an action based upon an oral contract to purchase a painting from a gallery, the following did not constitute sufficient injury to satisfy an estoppel: (1) plaintiff's out-of-pocket expenses for three round trips from New York to Florida; (2) recitation of the painting as owned by plaintiffs in documents relating to a museum exhibition; and (3) special characteristics of the painting absent in other paintings by the same artist. The court stated, "[The collector's] failure to purchase another Marden and their embarrassment in connection with the show at the Chicago museum are nothing more than part of the usual disappointment that attends a failed deal. [T]hat the . . . deal involved art rather than [other goods] and . . . engaged esthetic and perhaps egoistic considerations in addition to crass economic ones, is legally irrelevant."[2]

The elements of promissory estoppel were sufficiently pled to survive a motion to dismiss, where plaintiff-purchasers alleged they agreed to buy artworks based on defendant-gallery's promise to resell the paintings in the future, that the paintings were purchased for an amount exceeding $5 million, and that they were thereby damaged.[3]

§ 4:49 Omission of authenticity in an oral contract to purchase art (general principles of oral contract)

If an oral contract omits material terms, there can be no meeting of the minds and no binding contract is ordinarily found. Where defendant-partnerships alleged that no contract had been made because an oral agreement for sale of a $3.5 million painting by Van Gogh did not specify

---

[2]Hoffmann v. Boone, 708 F. Supp. 78, at 82 (S.D. N.Y. 1989).

[3]Granat v. Center Art Galleries--Hawaii Inc., R.I.C.O. Bus. Disp. Guide (CCH) ¶ 8425, 1993 WL 403977 (S.D. N.Y. 1993).

terms or duties regarding authenticity,[1] the court found that authenticity is an implied condition precedent to performance of an art sales contract. The court rejected the claim that since authenticity was unstated, it was an essential term left open for future negotiation and thus no binding contract existed.

§ 4:50 Particular works of art

Where the plaintiff-gallery alleged a contract right to purchase a diptych (a painting depicted on two panels) under an oral agreement with a former gallery artist who left the plaintiff to join the stable of another gallery, the court dismissed the claim in the absence of a writing under UCC Section 2-201(1). The court noted the policy against compelling specific performance of personal and creative services, e.g., ordering an artist to paint artwork.

§ 4:51 Solo exhibitions

Gallery owners and artists ordinarily engage in a series of oral communications regarding the solo exhibition of the artist at the gallery.[1] In preparation for the exhibition, gallery owners typically promote and presell artworks, arrange advertising, print announcements, and so forth.

Where the defendant-artist relocated from one gallery to another prior to an allegedly scheduled solo exhibition at the first under an oral contract, the artist contended that no agreement had been reached regarding number of artworks and promotional details, and therefore the essential terms were lacking for an enforceable agreement. The court refused to dismiss the plaintiff's claim for breach of oral contract.[2]

[Section 4:49]

[1]McCulley Fine Arts Gallery, Inc. v. X Partners, 860 S.W.2d 473, 23 U.C.C. Rep. Serv. 2d 350 (Tex. App. El Paso 1993).

[Section 4:51]

[1]*See* § 4:53.

[2]Sonnabend Gallery v. Halley, No. 12723/92 (N.Y. Sup. 1992).

G. MUTUAL MISTAKE

§ 4:52 Generally

If the parties to a contract both make a mistake about material facts in existence at the time of contracting, the equitable doctrine of mutual mistake allows rescission of the contract on the ground that the requisite "meeting of the minds" is lacking.[1] The philosophy underlying the doctrine is to prevent injustice that would arise by enforcing a contract neither party intended; rescission of unintended contracts allows the parties to return to the status quo.

In Firestone & Parson, Inc. v. Union League,[2] the dealers brought an action to rescind a contract for sale of an Albert Bierstadt painting they bought from the defendant in 1981 at a price of $50,000. Some years later, an article suggested the Bierstadt was a fake. The district court contended no mutual mistake occurred since both parties believed the painting was by Bierstadt. This was supported by the price, reflecting belief on both sides that the painting was by Bierstadt. The court's rationale supports a finding that a mutual mistake occurred. When the court recast the mutual mistake claim under the UCC, the plaintiffs' right to recovery was barred by the UCC four-year statute of limitations.

In Feigen v. Weil,[3] which was affirmed on appeal, the court found the doctrine applicable to the purchase and sale of an ink drawing by Matisse consigned for resale to the plaintiff-dealer by the defendant-collector. Feigen sold the Matisse to a third party for $165,000 and remitted $100,000 to Weil. One year later, the Matisse estate declared it a forgery, a "clever forgery" according to a curator at the Museum of Modern Art who examined it. Feigen notified Weil that he had returned to his client the $165,000, plus interest, and demanded that Weil reim-

---

[Section 4:52]

[1]Feigen v. Weil, No. 13935/90 (N.Y. Sup. May 1992), aff'd, 595 N.Y.S.2d 683.

[2]Firestone & Parson, Inc. v. Union League of Philadelphia, 672 F. Supp. 819, 822–23, 3 U.C.C. Rep. Serv. 2d 449 (E.D. Pa. 1987), judgment aff'd, 833 F.2d 304 (3d Cir. 1987).

[3]Feigen v. Weil, No. 13935/90 (N.Y. May 1992), aff'd, 595 N.Y.S.2d 683.

burse Feigen for the $100,000. After the demand was refused, the dealer brought the action, inter alia, to rescind the contract and moved for summary judgment.

Like the defendant in Firestone, the Weil defendant effectively agreed that both parties mistakenly believed the artwork was authentic. But Weil argued that Feigen was consciously ignorant. The conscious ignorance exception to the doctrine of mutual mistake can be traced to Wood v. Boynton[4] where a seller, uncertain of the identity of an uncut stone, presented it to the defendant-jeweler who expressed the view it that it could be a topaz and purchased it for $1. The stone turned out to be a diamond worth $700. Wood tendered the $1 and demanded return of the stone. The court refused rescission because the price had been fixed while the seller was aware that the stone might be something other than topaz.

But in the Feigen case, the court found that Feigen was not uncertain as to a crucial fact, ignored it, and contracted notwithstanding the uncertainty. The court found that even though Feigen had limited knowledge about the authenticity of the Matisse, both parties assumed the Matisse was authentic. Rejecting Weil's equitable argument that dealers should bear the risk of authenticity because they are experts, the court found no authority for the proposition that mutual mistake is not available to an expert in rescinding a contract between an expert and a nonexpert. The court refused to find that art dealers are under a duty to authenticate artwork. In the absence of providing Weil with a certificate of authenticity, permitted but not required under New York law, which Weil did not request, the court found Feigen had no independent duty to authenticate. The court also rejected Weil's claim that Feigen's cursory observation of the drawing constituted bad faith. The court held that Feigen, as consignee, did not have a substantive or legal obligation to go beyond a "cursory inquiry" as to authenticity.

In Luper Auction Galleries,[5] a federal district court again examined applicability of the doctrine to a contract between an auction house and consignors of a painting,

---

[4]Wood v. Boynton 64 Wis. 265, 25 N.W. 42 (1885).

[5]Luper Auction Galleries, Inc. v. Judge (William), No. 3:92cv556 (D. Va. Mar. 16, 1993).

"Femme Accoudee," purportedly by Pablo Picasso. The plaintiff-auction house sued the defendants to enforce an auction contract providing for reimbursement for advertising and other fees based upon a withdrawal fee clause. The Picasso painting, which defendants had consigned to the auction, was withdrawn by the auction house when it received the painting and began investigating its authenticity. The defendants claimed the auction contract was unenforceable based upon mutual mistake, that they and the auctioneers believed the Picasso to be authentic. Holding the contract valid and enforceable, the court rejected mutual mistake because the evidence showed that the defendants knew of authenticity problems because the painting was rejected by other auction entities, which they had failed to disclose to the plaintiff.

The mutual mistake doctrine was again the basis of a rescission claim based upon an underlying sale of artwork in Herstand & Co. v. Gertrude Stein Gallery.[6] There, the pencil drawing "Colette in Profile," by Balthazar Klossowski de Rola, known as Balthus, was purchased by the defendant-gallery who—after photographing it—obtained a certificate of authenticity from the seller who had lived with Balthus for many years. In 1988, the drawing and certificate of authenticity were given to the plaintiff in the context of a consignment, the drawing was sold with the invoice reciting it as a "Balthus Drawing," and the plaintiff paid the Gertrude Stein Gallery $40,000.

In 1989, the plaintiff resold the drawing to the Claude Bernard Gallery for $51,000 and delivered with it the certificate of authenticity. In 1990, the Bernard Gallery notified plaintiff the drawing was a fake by virtue of Balthus' repudiation. The plaintiff submitted affidavits from Balthus declaring the drawing a fake based upon his review of three photographs. The plaintiff refunded Bernard's money, retook possession, and notified Stein, who refused demands to refund plaintiff's money. The plaintiff sued, inter alia, for rescission based upon mutual mistake that both parties believed the drawing was by

[6]Herstand & Co. v. Gertrude Stein Gallery, Inc., 1A Part 14 (Justice M. Altman) (Apr. 22, 1993), reversed, 626 N.Y.S.2d 74 (App. Div. 1995) (reversing summary judgment in favor of plaintiff on ground of mutual mistake).

Balthus.

Unlike the defendants in the aforementioned mutual mistake cases, the Stein Gallery claimed that there was no mutual mistake because the drawing was, in fact, by Balthus, refusing to accept Balthus' repudiation of his own artwork. The court found otherwise, stating, "plaintiff has proffered a prima facie case that the 'Colette in Profile' is a fake and defendant has failed to come forward with sufficient probative evidence to rebut plaintiff's proof. I therefore find that the parties entered into their contract under a mutual mistake of fact and the proper remedy . . . is rescission."

Two years later, however, the Appellate Division held the remedy of rescission unavailable to plaintiff as a matter of law.[7] The court held that the certificates of falsity by Balthus were hearsay, offered for the truth of the matter asserted therein, and noted they were not subject to exclusionary exception. In addition, Balthus had not been deposed or cross-examined. Defendant's witness, a curator at a major museum, rebutted plaintiff's claim, attesting to the authenticity of the drawing based upon his knowledge of original Balthus works and a meeting in 1980 at which a catalogue containing the contested drawing was discussed by the artist with the curator without mention of falsity or attribution problems. Stein Gallery had thus raised a triable issue of fact, "fully rebutt[ing] any notion of mistake, mutual or otherwise," precluding summary disposal of the claims.[8]

§ 4:53 Parol evidence rule

The parol evidence rule recited in UCC Section 2-202 provides, in pertinent part:

> Terms with respect to which the confirmatory memoranda of the parties agree or which are otherwise set forth in a

---

[7]Herstand & Co. v. Gertrude Stein Gallery, Inc., 1A Part 14 (Justice M. Altman) (Apr. 22, 1993), reversed, 6262 N.Y.S.2d 774 (App. Div. 1995). (reversing summary judgment in favor of plaintiff on ground of mutual mistake).

[8]Herstand & Co. v. Gertrude Stein Gallery, Inc., 1A Part 14 (Justice M. Altman) (Apr. 22, 1993), reversed, 6262 N.Y.S.2d 774 (App. Div. 1995). (reversing summary judgment in favor of plaintiff on ground of mutual mistake). *See* § 9:10 for a discussion of repudiation.

> writing intended by the parties as a final expression . . . may not be contradicted by the evidence of any prior agreement or of a contemporaneous oral agreement but may be explained or supplemented:
> 1. By course of dealing or usage of trade [1-205] . . . or by course of performance [2-208]; and
> 2. By evidence of consistent additional terms unless the court finds the writing to have been intended also as a complete and exclusive statement of the terms of the agreement.[1]

The admission of parol evidence is within the sound discretion of the trial court, which can deny motions in limine to exclude parol evidence, not reversible on appeal absent clear abuse of discretion.

A court has examined the UCC parol evidence rule in the context of a written purchase agreement for an antique clock.[2] The parties examined and discussed the clock on several occasions, wherein the seller-defendant, an antique dealer, told the buyer the clock feet were original. The seller warranted the authenticity of a rare "Thomas Mendenhall Cherry Tall Case Clock, circa 1774," in the sales agreement by attaching to it an exhibit describing the clock. The exhibit was a six-page horologist report certifying the clock was made between 1773 and 1774 and mentioning that "ogee [s-shaped curved] feet carry the case."

After purchasing the clock for $97,500, the antiques broker who bought it discovered that the clock feet were not the original ones. The buyer and the seller both agreed the value was diminished by this fact. When the buyer was unable to resell the clock at various prices, he demanded the seller accept it on return under another paragraph of the sales agreement, which provided: "Seller herein personally guarantees the authenticity of the Clock and if it is determined that the Clock is not as described, Seller shall purchase back from Buyer the Clock for the purchase price plus interest." The clause terminated after one year or resale.

[Section 4:53]

[1]*See also* § 4:51.

[2]Sundlun v. Shoemaker, 421 Pa. Super. 353, 617 A.2d 1330, 20 U.C.C. Rep. Serv. 2d 432 (1992).

The seller, however, refused to repurchase the clock on the ground that the written agreement warranted only that the clock was "as described" in the horologist report, and that the replacement feet did not affect the clock's authenticity as described in that report. Admitting that he told the buyer the feet were original, the seller contended that his oral representations were not part of the warranted description in the writing memorializing the sales agreement. The buyer sold the clock at auction for $22,000 and sued the seller for breach of contract and breach of warranty; a jury awarded the buyer $75,500, the difference between the purchase price and the auction price. The seller appealed on the ground that the UCC parol evidence rule barred the oral representations about the clock feet. His oral comments modified the unambiguous language of the written contract and therefore should not have been considered. The trial court considered the oral statements "consistent additional terms" which did not contradict the written sales agreement, but rather explained the meaning of its terms, thus supplementing it.

On appeal, the court agreed with the trial court that the oral statements about the clock feet were properly admitted into evidence as "consistent additional terms," and further concluded that nothing in the written sales agreement, notably the absence of an integration clause, supported the seller's contention that it was the complete and final agreement. Referencing the official comment to Section 2-202, the appellate court noted that the UCC parol evidence rule allows the jury to consider consistent parol evidence in discerning the meaning of a written contract. Since the seller's oral comments were made in the course of dealing, they became an element of the meaning of the words used in the writing, unless he negated them by written terms. The court, noting that the seller had changed other terms in the contract, explained that the seller could have excluded from warranty his oral representations by changing the provision to read: "as described in the Wood report attached hereto."

III. ARTICLE 9: SECURED TRANSACTIONS

§ 4:54 Creating a security agreement in artwork

Article 9 of the UCC applies to "any transaction . . .

which is intended to create a security interest in personal property."[1] The principal test is whether "the transaction [is] intended to have effect as security."[2] A security interest is defined in UCC Section 1-201(37) as "an interest in personal property . . . which secures payment or performance of an obligation."[3] No formal wording is required and several documents, considered together, can constitute a security agreement.[4]

UCC Section 9-113 recognizes that a security interest may arise under article 2; if it does and the goods are not in the possession of the debtor, no security agreement is required under article 9. If the debtor defaults, the rights of the secured party are governed by article 2. However, if the debtor obtains possession and defaults, then the requirements of article 9 apply to the secured creditor.

Unlike security interests in proceeds, which require perfection by filing a financing statement, security interests in goods under Article 9 can be perfected in other ways.[5] UCC Section 9-305 provides:

> A security interest in . . . goods . . . may be perfected by the secured party's taking possession of the collateral. . . . A security interest is perfected by possession from the time possession is taken without relation back, and continues only so long as possession is retained, unless otherwise specified in this article."[6]

Possession of secured goods . . . obviate[s] the need to have a written security agreement describing the collateral and the need to file a financing statement in order to perfect a security interest [under] UCC 9-203(1)(a), Comment 1."[7]

If the collateral is in the possession of a bailee or con-

[Section 4:54]

[1]UCC § 9-102(1)(a).

[2]UCC § 9-102(1)(a), Comment 1.

[3]UCC § 1-201(37).

[4]Matter of Miller, 545 F.2d 916, 20 U.C.C. Rep. Serv. 1314 (5th Cir. 1977).

[5]UCC § 9-305.

[6]UCC § 9-305.

[7]Cantor v. Anderson, 639 F. Supp. 364, 367, 2 U.C.C. Rep. Serv. 2d 312 (S.D. N.Y. 1986), judgment aff'd, 833 F.2d 1002 (2d Cir. 1986).

signee, however, the security interest is perfected by notifying the bailee or consignee of the secured party's interest, whereby the secured party is deemed to be in possession.[8]

§ 4:55 Collateral

Courts have examined whether a consignment agreement for art and assignment of proceeds from the sale of art create security interests.[1] Courts have found a debtor-consignor's letter to the consignee-gallery informing it of the creditor's rights in the artwork and assignment of proceeds constituted the requisite notice of the creditor's interest in the collateral.

When a party in possession obtains art collateral in circumstances that impose a duty to inquire about the ownership of the art and "to investigate the transaction scrupulously to insure its legitimacy," failure to do so "may cast doubt on whether the parties 'intended to create a security interest in [the art].' "[2] A collector, aware of financial problems of a dealer who owed him money, received a painting by Auguste Renoir in lieu of payment, which was delivered without the collector's solicitation. When he asserted the painting was collateral, the court held the collector was obligated to make further inquiry as to ownership of the Renoir, given his familiarity with the dealer's

---

[8]Matter of Miller, 545 F.2d 916, 20 U.C.C. Rep. Serv. 1314 (5th Cir. 1977) (security interest in artwork owned by debtor and held for sale on consignment by an art gallery was perfected under UCC § 9-305 despite the fact that the debtor had the right to refuse a sale price on any artwork. Retention of control over sale price was reasonable "to avoid a sacrificial sale" and art was placed beyond reach of debtor).

[Section 4:55]

[1]Matter of Miller, 545 F.2d 916, 20 U.C.C. Rep. Serv. 1314 (5th Cir. 1977).

[2]Cantor v. Anderson, 639 F. Supp. 364, 367, 2 U.C.C. Rep. Serv. 2d 312 (S.D. N.Y. 1986), judgment aff'd, 833 F.2d 1002 (2d Cir. 1986) (defendant-art dealer held liable to plaintiff for converting his lithograph, which he had purchased from a thief who represented himself as plaintiff's nephew; the court found circumstances surrounding purchase obligated dealer to investigate transaction scrupulously to insure legitimacy).

practice of selling works on consignment.[3]

§ 4:56 Perfecting a security interest—Attachment

A security interest cannot attach until the debtor has "rights in the collateral" pursuant to UCC Sections 9-203(1)(c) and 9-204(1). A dealer was held not to have rights in art collateral under a theory of entrustment where the dealer obtained the art from another dealer and then delivered it to the collector.[1] The court relied upon UCC Section 2-403(2), which provides: "Any entrusting of possession of goods to a merchant who deals in goods of that kind gives him power to transfer all rights of the entruster to a buyer in the ordinary course of business."

UCC Section 1-201(g) defines "buyer in the ordinary course of business" as "a person who in good faith and without knowledge that the sale to him is in violation of the ownership rights or security interest of a third party in the goods buys in ordinary course from a person in the business of selling goods of that kind." Where a collector was owed money by a dealer for prior sales, receipt by the collector of artworks from the dealer subsequent to the debts was not a receipt by a buyer in the ordinary course;[2] the UCC definition, by its terms, excludes persons who receive goods "in total or partial satisfaction of a money debt."[3]

§ 4:57 Perfecting a security interest—Multiple jurisdictions

UCC Section 9-103(1) prescribes how to determine perfection of security interests when the goods pass through multiple jurisdictions, which is not uncommon for

---

[3]Cantor v. Anderson, 639 F. Supp. 364, 368, 2 U.C.C. Rep. Serv. 2d 312 (S.D. N.Y. 1986), judgment aff'd, 833 F.2d 1002 (2d Cir. 1986).

[Section 4:56]

[1]Cantor v. Anderson, 639 F. Supp. 364, 2 U.C.C. Rep. Serv. 2d 312 (S.D. N.Y. 1986), judgment aff'd, 833 F.2d 1002 (2d Cir. 1986).

[2]Cantor v. Anderson, 639 F. Supp. 364, 2 U.C.C. Rep. Serv. 2d 312 (S.D. N.Y. 1986), judgment aff'd, 833 F.2d 1002 (2d Cir. 1986).

[3]UCC § 1-201(g).

art in international trade.[1] UCC Section 9-103(1)(c) provides:

> If the parties to a transaction creating a purchase money security interest in goods in one jurisdiction understand at the time that the security interest attaches that the goods will be kept in another jurisdiction, then the law of the other jurisdiction governs the perfection and the effect of perfection or nonperfection of the security interest from the time it attaches until 30 days after the debtor receives possession of the goods and thereafter if the goods are taken to the other jurisdiction before the end of the 30 day period.

Section 9-103(1)(d) provides:

> When collateral is brought into and kept in [the] state while subject to a security interest perfected under the law of the jurisdiction from which the collateral was removed, the security interest remains perfected, but if action is required by Part 3 of the Article to perfect the security interest:
>
> (i) if the action is not taken before the expiration of the period of perfection in the other jurisdiction or the end of four months after the collateral is brought into [the] state, whichever period first expires, the security interest becomes unperfected at the end of that period and is thereafter deemed to have been unperfected as against a person whom became a purchaser after removal.

Courts have considered the priority interests of creditors in artwork under these statutes. The Fortune case involved the painting, "Die Landschaft Mit Dem Regenbogem," by Peter Paul Rubens.[2] The plaintiff, a Swedish finance company, loaned the defendant-art dealer $4.7 million to purchase artworks. The art dealer subsequently obtained a $1 million loan from other respondents to purchase the Rubens for resale. The dealer executed promissory notes in favor of the respondents and granted them a security interest in the Rubens.

On March 16, 1990, the dealer purchased the Rubens, located in Switzerland, which was picked up at the dealer's instructions by another person charged with making the transfer. According to the evidence, the transferor was

---

[Section 4:57]

[1]*See* Ch 6.

[2]Fortune Finans AB v. Andersson, 192 A.D.2d 124, 600 N.Y.S.2d 460, 21 U.C.C. Rep. Serv. 2d 352 (1st Dep't 1993).

told of the security interests of the dealer and secured parties. The transferor gave the Rubens to a transport company without relaying the interests, from which it was shipped SwissAir to a trucker who delivered it to a warehouse in New York that took it without notice of the security interests.

The dealer defaulted on his loans to the plaintiff, who sought to enjoin the warehouse from disposing of artworks in which it claimed a security interest; those works did not include the Rubens. However, to secure assets to pay the $4.7 million debt, the plaintiff obtained an order of attachment over the dealer's others assets in New York, and the Rubens, among other art, was levied upon by the sheriff.

The respondents moved to exclude the Rubens from the order, alleging that they had perfected a security interest under Swiss law, and that, since they were unaware the painting was removed to New York, the security interest was still in effect for four months following arrival of the painting in New York pursuant to UCC Section 9-103(d). In July, within the four months, the respondents filed financing statements in New York perfecting a security interest in the Rubens under New York law.

The trial court found that (1) the respondents were unaware the Rubens was being shipped to New York, and (2) their security interests were perfected for the four-month period under UCC Section 9-103(d)(i), therefore, the Rubens was ordered removed from the attachment. The appellate division held that while UCC Section 9-103 measured the grace period to perfect a security interest in New York once the Rubens was moved from Switzerland, it did not automatically provide a four-month period to do so. The appellate division found dispositive the issue of when "the expiration of the period of perfection in the other jurisdiction" would occur. To determine the time when the creditor is required to reperfect its security interest in the new jurisdiction, "it is necessary to determine the remaining duration of perfection in the original jurisdiction."

Under the facts of the Fortune case, the critical test became when the security interest expired under Swiss law, since UCC Section 9-103(1)(d)(i) refers to "whichever period first expires." According to respondents' expert, under Swiss law, the security interest in the Rubens was extinguished at the point when the secured party ceases to have possession and cannot demand it back from third parties in possession without notice. The court cut off the respondent's grace period to reperfect at the time of the transfer of the Rubens to the New York warehouse. The attachment order excluding the Rubens was reversed.

§ 4:58 Art on consignment—Consignment under UCC Section 2-326

Generally, a consignment agreement does not protect consigned goods against the claims of the consignee's secured creditors. UCC Section 2-326 allows limited exceptions if it:

> "[C]omplies with applicable law providing for a consignor's interest or the like to be evidenced by a sign, or
>
> "establishes that the person conducting the business is generally known by his or her creditors to be substantially engaged in selling the goods of others, or
>
> . . .
>
> "delivers a work of art subject to the Artists' Consignment Act.[1]

The burden of proof is on the consignor to prove by a preponderance of the evidence that the transaction falls within one of the exceptions to UCC Section 2-326. Although Section 2-326 does not specify when a "sale or return" occurs, it does describe the rights of the creditors where the seller receives, through consignment or purchase, goods for resale.[2]

A bankruptcy court considered whether retail jewelers asserted a superior lien position to that of an equity security holder bank by their consignors' interest in goods held

---

[Section 4:58]

[1]Tex. Bus. & Com. Code Ann. § 2-326(c); for states expressly amending UCC § 2-326 to signify creditor exemption for artworks, *see* Appendix 8.

[2]U.S. v. One 18th Century Colombian Monstrance, 797 F.2d 1370, 1 U.C.C. Rep. Serv. 2d 1492 (5th Cir. 1986) ("[UCC] Section 2-326 does not purport . . . to define when a "sale or return" purchase has been made.").

by the debtor at the time of bankruptcy.[3] The bank had filed financing statements under Texas law describing its interest in collateral as "all inventory . . . used or consumed in debtor's business whether now owned or hereafter acquired." The bank and the debtor signed a security agreement covering "all inventory . . . including all goods held for sale." The jewelers did not file financing statements nor post signage on the premises of the debtor regarding consignment interests. The jewelers delivered goods to the debtor, reserving title under consignment terms.

Initially, the jewelers claimed under the Texas Artist Consignment Act, which, on its face, exempts creditors of art dealers from works consigned by artists.[4] Texas is one of several states that specifically exempt from UCC Section 2-326 the rights of general trade creditors to interests in artworks consigned by artists. Even if the jewelry were considered "unique" like art, the court refused to apply the Act: "I find that plaintiffs' deliveries did not constitute 'art,' [the plaintiffs are corporations that] do not appear to meet the definition of 'artists' in said Act . . . and the debtor, . . . a jewelry retail store, does not meet the criteria of 'art dealer.' "

The seminal issue under UCC Section 2-326(3)(b)[5] is whether or not the debtor was "generally known by his or her creditors to be substantially engaged in the selling the goods of others." The creditors must prove by a preponderance of the evidence that the debtor was so known by his creditors.[6] Paragraph 2 of the Official Comment states that the exception will be made where "the buyer is known to be engaged *primarily* in selling the goods of others

---

[3]In re Arthur A. Everts Co., 35 B.R. 706, 37 U.C.C. Rep. Serv. 1537 (Bankr. N.D. Tex. 1984).

[4]*But cf.* Shuttie v. Festa Restaurant, Inc., 566 So. 2d 554, 14 U.C.C. Rep. Serv. 2d 119 (Fla. Dist. Ct. App. 3d Dist. 1990), where the Florida court interpreted comparable provisions in a Florida artist's consignment law differently, finding that the artist failed to take the necessary steps to perfect an interest in her own artwork which her dealer used as a collateral for a loan from a third party unbeknownst to her. *See* Appendix 8.

[5]*See, e.g.,* Cal. Com. Code § 2-326(3)(b).

[6]In re Arthur A. Everts Co., 35 B.R. 706, 37 U.C.C. Rep. Serv. 1537 (Bankr. N.D. Tex. 1984).

[emphasis added].” Judicial interpretation holds that the “plain wording” of “substantially” under UCC Section 2-326(3) is not limited to situations where the seller is “primarily” engaged in selling goods of others.[7]

Evidence that consigned goods equalled $75,000 in a total inventory equal to $690,000 was not enough to prove that the debtor was primarily or substantially engaged in selling the goods of others. Even if the amount were enough, the fact must be “generally known.” Testimony of other creditors did not demonstrate that it was generally known that the retail jeweler sold consigned goods. Where trade creditors showed ten of fifty-five creditors knew another debtor sold goods on consignment, the court found the evidence insufficient to prove that his consigned interests were generally known.[8] Trade creditors’ goods were found to be for “sale or return” under UCC Section 2-326(3), and the bank was given priority in the inventory as a secured creditor pursuant to its financing statement and security agreement.

§ 4:59 Art on consignment—Consignment under art consignment laws

Some states attempt to override UCC Section 2-326 by expressly exempting from the reach of a dealer’s creditors artworks consigned by artists to dealers.[1] The artist-consignor can protect art from creditor claims under the following methods available in the UCC:

(1) comply with law providing for a consignor’s interest to be evidenced by signage or posting;
(2) establish that a trader conducting business is generally known by his creditors to be substantially engaged in selling the goods of others; or
(3) comply with the filing provisions on secured

---

[7] In re Arthur A. Everts Co., 35 B.R. 706, 37 U.C.C. Rep. Serv. 1537 (Bankr. N.D. Tex. 1984) (citation omitted).

[8] In re Arthur A. Everts Co., 35 B.R. 706, 37 U.C.C. Rep. Serv. 1537 (Bankr. N.D. Tex. 1984) (citation omitted).

[Section 4:59]

[1] *See* Appendix 8.

transactions in UCC division 9.[2]

In states that have amended the UCC to protect artist-consignors from creditors under certain circumstances, a fourth means of protection may exist under a state art per se consignment statute, but artists who do not comply with other state law noticing provisions may still not be able to take advantage of the artist-consignor protection.[3]

In Shuttie, a replevin action brought by an artist against a restaurant to recover sixteen paintings in its possession, the debtor was an art dealer to whom the artist had consigned the art, and then disappeared. Florida has an Art Consignment Act that, on its face, purports to exempt artworks in such circumstances from a dealer's trade creditors. The dealer had represented to the defendant-restaurant that the paintings were from his private collection, loaning them for display and sale, and obtaining from the restaurant a $25,000 loan secured by the paintings.

The court affirmed the trial court judgment, denying replevin to the artist on the grounds that the artist had ample means to notify third persons of the consignment arrangement under the Act. The artist admitted that, contrary to Florida mandatory public notice provisions,[4] he did not label his artworks to give notice to third parties of his consigned interest and provided no signage to the gallery indicating such interests. But the artist argued he was protected under another section, which provides "a priority in favor of the artist over the claims, liens, or security interest of the creditors of the art dealer, notwithstanding any provision of the U.C.C."[5]

The artist was estopped from using the artist's creditor exemption section because he ignored the mandatory consignment notice requirements under Florida law. The legislation, explained the court, was intended to protect the artistic community only with co-extensive statutory notice to the public. The court would not allow the artist to pick and choose selective sections of a comprehensive

---

[2]UCC § 2-326.

[3]*See* Shuttie v. Festa Restaurant, Inc., 566 So. 2d 554, 14 U.C.C. Rep. Serv. 2d 119 (Fla. Dist. Ct. App. 3d Dist. 1990).

[4]Fla. Stat. Ann. § 686.502(2).

[5]Fla. Stat. Ann. § 686.503(5).

statutory whole to make his case, holding as follows:

> We hold that as a matter of law when an artist fails to avail himself of the provisions of the Artist's Consignment Act . . . and places in commerce paintings of art with no notation as to ownership thereon, an innocent third party who takes a security position in these paintings has a superior possessory interest, vis a vis the artist[,] under the long established principle of law that as between two innocent parties, the one that created the situation causing the loss, will not be held to have superior position to the completely innocent party.[6]

§ 4:60 Art on consignment—Interests of judgment creditor and trustee in bankruptcy in art on consignment

In In re Miller,[1] the debtor placed several paintings for sale on consignment at an art gallery to obtain proceeds to pay off a debt evidenced by a note. The debtor executed an irrevocable consignment in favor of the creditor, terminable only by the creditor, assigning the proceeds of art sales to the creditor, and providing written notice to the gallery of the arrangement. When the debt was not repaid after one year, the creditor obtained final judgment on the underlying note. The debtor filed for bankruptcy and the creditor attempted in state court to foreclose. The state court proceeding was stayed when the trustee in bankruptcy claimed that the consignment was a mere executory agreement because the debtor retained the right to control sales prices of the art. The trustee's interest as a hypothetical lien creditor takes priority over all other security interests in the debtor's property except for those perfected under state law prior to the filing date of the petition in bankruptcy. The court ordered a turnover order, from which the creditor appealed. The Fifth Circuit held a security interest in consigned art was perfected under UCC Section 9-305 despite the fact that the debtor had the right to refuse offering prices; retention of control over the sale price was reasonable "to avoid a sacrificial sale."

---

[6] 566 So. 2d at 558.

[Section 4:60]

[1] Matter of Miller, 545 F.2d 916, 20 U.C.C. Rep. Serv. 1314 (5th Cir. 1977).

Chapter 5

Auction

I. INTRODUCTION

II. LAWS OF AUCTION

A. PUBLIC AUCTION

B. AUCTION BUSINESS: PAST AND PRESENT

C. UNIFORM COMMERCIAL CODE (UCC)

D. ART PER SE AUCTIONEERING LAWS

III. MECHANICS OF AUCTION

A. TERMS AND CONDITIONS

E. FRAUD

F. REMEDIES

V. LIABILITY: RELATIONSHIP WITH BUYERS

A. IN GENERAL

B. AUTHENTICATION

C. GUARANTEES OF LOT CONTENTS

D. CONSUMER FRAUD

E. VALUE

F. TIME LIMITATIONS FOR SUIT

G. Racketeer Influenced and Corrupt Organizations Act (RICO)

H. PERSONAL LIABILITY OF AUCTIONEER

I. DAMAGES

J. TITLE CLAIMS

VI. THIRD-PARTY ACTIONS AND OTHER ACTIONS

VII. AUCTION AS PLAINTIFF

KeyCite®: Cases and other legal materials listed in KeyCite Scope can be researched through West's KeyCite service on Westlaw®. Use KeyCite to check citations for form, parallel references, prior and later history, and comprehensive citator information, including citations to other decisions and secondary materials.

I. INTRODUCTION

§ 5:1 Generally

Auction is the largest single secondary art market, whereby billions of dollars of art are sold annually. Historically considered a mere conduit between seller and buyer, auctions today regularly obtain proprietary or financial interests in the deal, or otherwise participate as principals in the sale. Traditional auction law, which resided in common-law agency for sellers and caveat emptor for buyers, no longer adequately encompasses auction activity in the markets.

Issues of title, value and authenticity have brought new causes of action against auctions, including RICO, breach of contract, breach of warranty, and breach of consumer protection statutes; indemnity and interpleader actions bring in additional parties. Recent claims and charges brought by private parties and government against Christie's and Sotheby's, which together control ninety percent of the worldwide auction market,[1] allege violations of federal antitrust laws and federal criminal investigations are proceeding. The Chairman of the Board and the President at Sotheby's, a publicly-held company, resigned, and the chief executive at Christie's, a private company purchased in 1998 by Francois Pinault, resigned. In 2000 Sotheby's former president plead guilty to criminal price-fixing,[2] and Christie's was offered conditional amnesty for cooperation with the Department of Justice. Sotheby's plead guilty,[3] and the court sentenced it to pay a

[Section 5:1]

[1]NY Times, Files of Ex-Christie's Chief Fuel Inquiry into Art Auction, Frantz, D., Oct. 6, 2000 at 1, 28.

[2]United States v. Diana D. Brooks, 00 Crim 1084 (RMB).

[3]N.Y. slipop United States v. Sotheby's Holdings, Inc. 00 Crim. 1081 (LAK).

$45 million fine.[4] The two houses agreed to pay $512 million to resolve lawsuits by shareholders, with an option of paying $125 million in coupons to future sellers that could be used for commission fees. Three lawsuits by buyers at foreign auctions were dismissed in 2001 because the auctions were abroad without direct or substantial impact in the United States. In March 2002, the Second Circuit Court of Appeals reinstated the foreign-based price-fixing actions against Sotheby's and Christie's.[5] The European Commission Union fined Sotheby's $20 million in 2002 for colluding with Christie's to fix commission fees under its ban of cartels and other business practices.

Whatever longterm effect the proceedings and pleas have on auction, the public revelations about auction practices from the litigation is itself market-educating. Other auction houses have forayed into the market with mixed results as the two major historical rivals reposition.

The internet as virtual showroom has not gone unnoticed.[6] eBay is the largest online auction service, and over time it has absorbed or ventured with established auction houses. In 2001 eBay Premier was created to auction art and high-end collectibles.

Meanwhile, Sotheby's launched its own web site in 1999. By 2000 Sotheby's and Amazon.com agreed to operate a joint web site called Sothebys.amazon.com. to challenge eBay. But by 2002, eBay Inc. and Sotheby's had created a new Sothebys.com site, replacing Sotheby's existing internet presence and eBay Premier. Christie's had announced plans for Internet Auctions but subsequently abandoned them. In the late 1990s, dozens of sites registered domain names to auction art online. Nor is America the only place for online auction fever. In Ger-

---

[4]In re Auction Houses Antitrust Litigation, 135 F. Supp. 2d 438 (S.D. N.Y. 2001), opinion superseded, 138 F. Supp. 2d 548 (S.D. N.Y. 2001).

[5]Kruman v. Christie's Int'l. PLC, 284 F. 3d 384 (2d Cir. 2002) (Sherman Antitrust Act applicable to auctions held outside U.S. and to foreign defendants where price-fixing of buyer's premiums and seller's commissions affected domestic worldwide markets.).

[6]Sotheby's web site is www.sothebys.com. Christie's web site is www.christies.com. Phillips de Pury web site is www.phillips.auction.com. Butterfield Bonham's web site is www.Butterfields.com. Bonham's web site is www.Bonhams.com.

many, Artnet.com, listed on Neuer Markt, sells art.

The viability of online art auction auctioneering under existing configurations is questionable. eBay's online art auctions, for example, have resulted in criminal charges against sellers for shill bidding and forgery. The market will determine the efficacy and enforceability of safeguards reportedly being implemented.

Although authenticity and ownership are common grounds for suit against all traders and sellers, this chapter focuses on the auction entity, the auctioneer, and the auction process—terms and conditions of auction contracts, criminal and civil liability of auctioneers, state and local art auction laws, auction catalogues, and practices, customs and usage unique to auction. There is a dearth of precedential case law, notable when one considers the number of annual auction sales. Provisions on authenticity and ownership discussed in chapters on traders and the UCC should be consulted to recognize the scope and context of claims and defenses that arise outside the auction setting.

Sections 5:2 to 5:11 discusses general state and local auction laws, focusing on art auction, licensing, suspension and revocation, and registration.

Sections 5:12 to 5:30 covers the mechanics of auction, including a description of commonly used terms and conditions and an explanation of auction remuneration through premiums, commissions and charges, including the premium issues from the antitrust litigation.

Sections 5:31 to 5:49 identifies sources of auction liability to sellers, duties to value and promote sale, supported by cases and principles on agency and indemnification, damages.

Sections 5:50 to 5:79 identifies sources of auction liability to buyers, including the various remedies plead for disputes on authenticity, title, and lot contents, supported by cases and statutes.

Section 5:80 to 5:83 describes various third party actions brought by sellers and buyers against persons other than auction for conduct that relates to artwork auctioned or offered at auction. Sections 5:84 to 5:88 contains the auction-as-plaintiff cases.

Charts and appendixes, including sample auction agreements and composites of commissions and charges, support the chapter.

II. LAWS OF AUCTION

A. PUBLIC AUCTION

§ 5:2 Generally

The focus of these sections is "public" auction, where property is sold in a public sale to the highest bidder by one licensed under state and/or local law.[1] Auctions are held by itinerant auctioneers or by auction houses, corporate or other entities with offices and perhaps galleries in fixed locations. Auction houses may be publicly or privately owned; the term "public" auction is unrelated to the form of ownership of the auction house.

Public refers to legal requirements of public notice,[2] public access,[3] and the notion that "the business of an auctioneer . . . has always been affected with a public interest."[4] The hours of public auction as well as the form of public announcement of the auction are regulated by law. Attendance is open to the public, but admission can be limited by ticketing or other systems. A bidder ordinarily must register and establish credit under the rules and policies of the auction house prior to participation at auction. Bidders who attend with regularity sometimes are issued a client card by the auction house to expedite the registration system.

The potential of Internet trading has not been lost on auctioneers. Established auction houses have established online presences. New start-up ventures on the Internet, like eBay, have captured large unexploited markets of consumers who are not, or at least have not been, typical paddlers in the traditional houses. Virtual auction has not

---

[Section 5:2]

[1]*See* Appendix 9. English bids are incrementally higher.

[2]*See, e.g.,* Appendix 11, at Appendix 11-2 to Appendix 11-3.

[3]Barrett v. U.S. Banknote Corp., 806 F. Supp. 1094 (S.D. N.Y. 1992) ("Christie's . . . is a New York corporation that conducts public auctions of works of art.").

[4]Cristallina S.A. v. Christie, Manson & Woods Intern., Inc., 117 A.D.2d 284, 295, 502 N.Y.S.2d 165 (1st Dep't 1986).

escaped problems, like fraud and authenticity, that beset the auction markets. Such claims will test jurisdictional concepts in the legal system, invoke new case law and perhaps precipitate legislative response.

Reported litigation in the arts centers around public auction, and unless otherwise specified herein, public auction (excluding forced sales) and state auction laws are discussed.

B. AUCTION BUSINESS: PAST AND PRESENT

§ 5:3 Market data

Auction is a multibillion-dollar business,[1] the impact of which is felt in interstate and international commerce—a trend that no doubt will continue given European Community (EC) regulations and directives on art effective in 1993, redefining the trade of art within the EC and beyond.[2] Christie's, a United Kingdom corporation, and Sotheby's, now domestic, control ninety-seven percent of the world market for sales of art, antiques and collectibles.[3] Phillips, another established London house under new ownership, had ventured a greater presence in the American market but that is reportedly retracting as ownership interests continue to change.

Auction is invariably regarded as a secondary market transaction in terms of sales practices,[4] associated with greater risk to the buyer and reduced legal exposure to

---

[Section 5:3]

[1]Usborne, D., *"Sotheby's Pay Pounds 170M to Settle Price-Fixing Case,"* The Independent, Sept. 26, 2000, at 13 (5 billion dollar-a-year global auction market); Frantz, D., *Files of Ex-Christie's Chief Fuel Inquiry into Art Auction,* N.Y. Times, Oct. 6, 2000, at 1, 28 (4 billion dollars-a-year as of 2000); Watson, *From Manet to Manhattan* (1992); "Survey of the World Art Markets," The Economist Dec. 22, 1990.

[2]*See* Ch 6 §§ 6:77 to 6:115.

[3]Kruman v. Christie's Int'l PLC, 284 F.3d 384 (2d Cir. 2002) (antitrust action by foreign buyers and sellers alleging price-fixing).

[4]Jennings v. C.I.R., T.C. Memo. 1988-521, 1988 WL 117368 (1988) ("The secondary market is characterized by auction sales.").

the auctioneer.[5] Auctioneers are ordinarily expressly excluded from the definitions of "art merchants" or "art dealers" under state art per se statutes and other state art laws, and are not required to make the same disclosures regarding authorship recited in those laws.[6]

Auction is a particularly visible secondary market, and unlike other aspects of the arts, substantial financial and sales information is available. The public nature of auction involves publications in general trade and specialty press. Auctions, particularly those involving collections of famous persons or famous artworks, receive advance publicity in the media and in the market through press releases and catalogues. Sales prices realized at auction are reprinted in recognized sales indexes.[7] These sources serve as measures for appraisers, collectors and others to value works by the same artists, as well as to compare works by other artists.

§ 5:4 Diversified services

Auction houses historically were viewed as market intermediaries, primarily selling consigned works on behalf of others, for whom they acted in the capacity of limited agents. The auction entity did not obtain a financial, equity or proprietary interest in the objects it sold; remuneration was limited to premiums, commissions, and recoupment of costs and expenses. Until the 1970s, auction houses generally sold in that capacity to other traders, collectors, museums, or arts professionals.[1]

---

[5]*See* Ch 2 § 2:4 on comparison of primary and secondary market traders.

[6]*See* Appendix 4-2.

[7]See Chart 5-1.

[Section 5:4]

[1]"A Survey of the World Art Markets," The Economist, Dec. 22, 1990, at 11.

Chart 5-1: Selected Publications * ** on Auction Sales Indexes

Author/Editor	Title
Acatos Publ.	Mayer International Auction Records
ADEC Diffusion	Int'l Art Price Annual (L'annuaire des Cotes)
Franklin & James	American Artists at Auction
Gordon & Lawrence, Inc.	Gordon's Print Price Annual
Hislop, Duncan (ed.)	Annual Art Sales Index
Theran, Susan	Leonard's Annual Price Index of Prints, Posters and Photographs
Zanatta, J. (ed.)	Contemporary Print Portfolio: A Guide to Auction Prices 1987–1994

* Some publications include premiums in sales results.

** Dr. Stefan W. Klima, Fine Arts Librarian, City of Beverly Hills Library, contributed to the preparation of this chart.

Auction houses, like museums, expanded their constituencies and services, performing an array of functions in addition to sales: appraisals,[2] promotional services,[3] loan and price guarantee programs,[4] consultancy services, catalogues, or itinerant worldwide exhibitions. These ef-

[2]Nelson v. Sotheby's, Inc., 128 F. Supp. 2d 1172 (N.D. Ill. 2001) (motion to dismiss breach of contract claim denied where auction house unreasonably withheld return of bailed painting to plaintiff for twelve years); see also Sotheby's Inc. v. Dumba, 1992 WL 27043 (S.D. N.Y. 1992) (auction evaluation that painting by Mary Cassatt was in good condition and worth between $1,300,000.00 and $1,700,000.00 could not be basis for fraud claim for defendant's nonpayment of promissory note secured by painting) and Ch 2 § 2:30.

[3]Ravenna v. Christie's Inc., 289 A.D.2d 15, 734 N.Y.S.2d 21 (1st Dep't 2001) (gratuitous authentication provided at walk-in inquiry).

[4]Sotheby's Inc. v. Dumba, 1992 WL 27043 (S.D. N.Y. 1992) (loan by auction house affiliate to defendant secured by painting appraised by auction house; Christie's, Inc. v. Croce, 5 F. Supp. 2d 206 (S.D. N.Y. 1998) (debtor's counterclaim for negligent misrepresentation successful

forts popularized auction for private buyers and encouraged new market entrants to auction, ironically leading to more auction litigation. And in the 1980s at least one auction house became an owner and principal in a substantial art inventory of a mercantile gallery,[5] and obtained a collateralized interest in a museum collection.

The role of the auction house in bringing art to market is now multidimensional. Defining auctioneers as sellers and auction sales as only public sales does not encompass the actual activities of art auctions from the 1980s to the present. The auctioneer as mere consignor's agent is no longer a business reality or a legal limitation: Today the role of the auction entity can be as principal, secured or unsecured creditor, primary or secondary market trader and as specialist site for appraisal and authentication.[6] Practices like minimum guaranteed prices,[7] lien[8] and loan policies[9] place the auction house directly in the deal.

Although case law has not yet caught up with the expanded role of auction entities, substantial litigation has developed over the years about how and upon whom the risks of art auction should be allocated before the diversification of auction activity. Even when the auction entity was considered the seller's agent,[10] risks litigated

---

against plaintiff-creditor in suit to recover shortfall of $600,000 on loan of $3.1 million secured by Old Master paintings and drawings); Christie's Inc. v. Davis, 247 F. Supp. 2d 414, 49 U.C.C. Rep. Serv. 2d 684 (S.D. N.Y. 2002) (loans by auction house to collectors secured by artworks that auction house appraised).

[5]Sotheby's purchased inventory of modern and contemporary art from Pierre Matisse Gallery under joint venture with dealer William Acquavella.

[6]Ravenna v. Christie's Inc., 289 A.D.2d 15, 734 N.Y.S.2d 21 (1st Dep't 2001) (action for negligent misrepresentation based on misstatement of art specialist regarding origin of painting dismissed notwithstanding plaintiff's reliance where consultation lacked requisite special relationship of trust and confidence).

[7]*See* App. 11, N.Y. Admin. Code, Reg. II, #11.

[8]*See* App. 11, N.Y. Admin. Code, Reg. II, #15.

[9]*See* App. 11, N.Y. Admin. Code, Reg. II, #15.

[10]*See generally* Auction Sales under UCC Section 2-328, 44 A.L.R. 4th 110; Wildenstein & Co. v. Wallis, 756 F. Supp. 158 (S.D. N.Y. 1991), rev'd without opinion, 983 F.2d 1047 (2d Cir. 1992) (rights of first refusal in estate collection set for auction and the rule against perpetu-

include authenticity,[11] title disputes,[12] custodianship,[13] valuation,[14] and legal fees and costs of litigation,[15] discussed below. Some of these issues, like valuation, have

---

ities failed); Voitier v. Antique Art Gallery, 524 So. 2d 80 (La. Ct. App. 3d Cir. 1988), writ denied, 531 So. 2d 271 (La. 1988) (effect of disclosures in auction catalogue); McNally v. Yarnall, 764 F. Supp. 838, 844 (S.D. N.Y. 1991) (role of auction house in authenticating art works); Weisz v. Parke-Bernet Galleries, Inc., 67 Misc. 2d 1077, 325 N.Y.S.2d 576, 10 U.C.C. Rep. Serv. 292 (City Civ. Ct. 1971), judgment rev'd, 77 Misc. 2d 80, 351 N.Y.S.2d 911, 14 U.C.C. Rep. Serv. 358 (App. Term 1974) (auction catalogue authentications); U.S. v. Von Cseh, 354 F. Supp. 315 (S.D. Tex. 1972); Stein v. Annenberg Research Institute, 1991 WL 143400 (S.D. N.Y. 1991) (collector consigns Roman Jewish liturgical manuscript for sale at auction); Kirby v. Wildenstein, 784 F. Supp. 1112 (S.D. N.Y. 1992) (auction house's role in authenticating painting); Estate of O'Keeffe v. C.I.R., T.C. Memo. 1992-210, T.C.M. (RIA) ¶ 92210 (1992) (auction values realized for Georgia O'Keeffe from 1979 to 1991); Ichiyasu v. Christie, Manson & Woods Intern., Inc., 630 F. Supp. 340 (N.D. Ill. 1986) (dealer's attempt to enjoin disposition of auction proceeds by client for whom it consigned art to auction).

[11]Ernst v. Ernst, 722 F. Supp. 61 (S.D. N.Y. 1989) (dispute between heir of Max Ernst and his fourth wife over disposition of his sculptures, including sales at auction of allegedly unauthorized castings); Waller v. Scheer, 175 Ga. App. 1, 332 S.E.2d 293 (1985), cert. dismissed, (July 3, 1985) (buyer of artwork brought action against seller for fraud, breach of warranty and violation of Fair Business Practice Act because auction house rejected painting purportedly by Adolf Schreyer, whereupon buyer attempted to rescind sale); Dajon Corp. of Mississippi v. Hartman, 1991 WL 121214 (E.D. La. 1991) (buyer of silver tankard, represented as by Benjamin Burt in auction catalogue by auctioneer to whom defendant consigned it, sued seller for fraud and misrepresentation after learning it was fake); McCloud v. Lawrence Gallery, Ltd., 970 F.2d 896 (2d Cir. 1992) (auction house offered drawing by Pablo Picasso as authentic, although aware that its authenticity was in dispute, and the drawing ultimately was rejected by Comite Picasso as not authentic); Weisz v. Parke-Bernet Galleries, Inc., 67 Misc. 2d 1077, 325 N.Y.S.2d 576, 10 U.C.C. Rep. Serv. 292 (City Civ. Ct. 1971), judgment rev'd, 77 Misc. 2d 80, 351 N.Y.S.2d 911, 14 U.C.C. Rep. Serv. 358 (App. Term 1974); *cf.* McNally v. Yarnall, 764 F. Supp. 838, 844 (S.D. N.Y. 1991) (role of auction house employees on authenticating art works, in action where auction was not a party); Kohler v. Leslie Hindman, Inc., 1994 WL 233801 (N.D. Ill. 1994) (summary judgment in favor of auction house where it agreed, under a side agreement with a buyer, to rescind sale of painting "Plains of Meudon," attributed to Theodore Rousseau and consigned for auction by plaintiffs, after authenticity was challenged by buyer's expert); *see also,* Kohler v. Leslie Hindman, Inc., 1995 WL 250427 (N.D. Ill. 1995) (auction house sought attorney fees and costs from consignors arising from consignment of their painting, subsequently deemed inauthentic by a prospective buyer's expert).

been revisited in the context of the more tangled relation-

[12]Cartier v. Jackson, 1991 WL 28026 (Conn. Super. Ct. 1991) (CUTPA violations arising from defendant's representation of ownership of paintings, and delivery of same for sale to auction house); Burger v. Bartlett, 1990 WL 99025 (E.D. Pa. 1990) (auction house dismissed as defendant by agreement of parties, but refused to relinquish possession of painting by Jennifer Bartlett that it had withdrawn because of ownership dispute, until court ordered declaration of ownership); Ichiyasu v. Christie, Manson & Woods Intern., Inc., 637 F. Supp. 187 (N.D. Ill. 1986) (auction house, in possession of etching and aquatint purportedly by Pablo Picasso that sold for $95,000, refused to return it to owner after sale was rescinded when owner advised that work was stolen); Walt Disney Productions v. Basmajian, 600 F. Supp. 439 (S.D. N.Y. 1984) (animation studio unsuccessful in obtaining a preliminary injunction against a former employee to stop an auction of a collection of studio's celluloid art work); Clyde v. Sotheby Parke Bernet, Int'l, CA No. 80-4235, slip op. (E.D. Pa. 1980) (motion to remand to state court granted by art gallery and museum that auction house, as agent of others, took possession of and converted paintings from a trust)

[13]Burger v. Bartlett, 1990 WL 99025 (E.D. Pa. July 13, 1990). State v. Childs, 242 N.J. Super. 121, 576 A.2d 42 (App. Div. 1990) (auction house dismissed as defendant by agreement of parties, but refused to relinquish possession of painting by Jennifer Bartlett that it had withdrawn because of ownership dispute, until court ordered declaration of ownership); Ichiyasu v. Christie, Manson & Woods Intern., Inc., 630 F. Supp. 340 (N.D. Ill. 1986) (auction house, in possession of etching and aquatint purportedly by Pablo Picasso that sold for $95,000, refused to return it to owner after sale was rescinded because owner advised that work was stolen); In re Bobroff, 1990 WL 178557 (E.D. Pa. 1990) (Bankruptcy Court issued order directing trustee to seize debtor's property, which included forty paintings and antiques stored by Continental Bank at an auction house); Stein v. Annenberg Research Institute, 1991 WL 143400 (S.D. N.Y. 1991) (Sotheby's maintained possession of Roman-Jewish liturgical manuscript after withdrawing it from auction when litigation was filed regarding ownership).

[14]Cristallina S.A. v. Christie, Manson & Woods Intern., Inc., 117 A.D.2d 284, 502 N.Y.S.2d 165 (1st Dep't 1986); Pasternack v. Esskay Art Galleries, Inc., 90 F. Supp. 849 (W.D. Ark. 1950).

[15]Basmajian v. Christie, Manson & Woods Intern., Inc., 629 F. Supp. 995 (S.D. N.Y. 1986) (auction house deduction of legal fees from seller's sale proceeds); Kohler v. Leslie Hindman, Inc., 1995 WL 250427 (N.D. Ill. 1995) (auction house sought attorney fees and costs from consignors arising from consignment of their painting "Plains of Meudon" attributed to Theodore Rousseau, subsequently deemed inauthentic by a prospective buyer's expert).

ships between auction and client.[16]

C. UNIFORM COMMERCIAL CODE (UCC)[*]

§ 5:5 UCC Section 2-328

Auctions for arts and auctions for other objects are bound in theory by Section 2-328 of the Uniform Commercial Code, whose intended purpose is to harmonize internal provisions, state and common laws.[1] However, whether a particular claim arising from goods sent to auction will fall within the UCC depends upon the particular facts and circumstances, as well as, the terms of the auction contracts.[2] The consignment for sale of artwork to an auction house under the terms of its consignment agreement was held not to constitute a contract of sale under UCC § 2-106 in that title did not pass from the seller to the buyer for a price, and the artwork was not sold under UCC § 2-328(2).[3]

Notwithstanding the harmonizing intent of the UCC, some state and local legislatures, such as Illinois and New York City, have enacted art auctioneering laws.[4] The scope of state and local laws governing auction licensing and

---

[16]Christie's Inc. v. Davis, 247 F. Supp. 2d 414, 49 U.C.C. Rep. Serv. 2d 684 (S.D. N.Y. 2002) (claims that foreclosure valuations of collateralized artworks by auction house after defendants defaulted on loans were "lowball estimates" to obtain more lots and increase seller's premiums not supported by specific facts for purposes of summary judgment).

[*]For an in-depth discussion of the UCC, *see* Ch 4.

[Section 5:5]

[1]Annot., Auction Sales under UCC Section 2-328, 44 A.L.R. 4th 110 § 2b.

[2]Christie's Inc. v. Davis, 247 F. Supp. 2d 414, 49 U.C.C. Rep. Serv. 2d 684 (S.D. N.Y. 2002) (secured promissory note for loan of $15.5 million to collectors gave auction house foreclosure rights under UCC § 9-601).

[3]Pilliard v. Sotheby's, Inc., motion for recon., 1998 WL 126060 (S.D.N.Y. Mar. 19, 1998); Private Letter Ruling, PLR 9728005, 1997 WL 381975 (I.R.S. PLR 1997) (since title did not pass for consigned jar purportedly by Paul Gaugin and was not sold within the meaning of UCC § 2-328(2), then UCC § 2-725 four-year statute of limitations did not apply); *see* Ch 4 §§ 4:35 to 4:41.

[4]Foreign auctions are sometimes state-operated, e.g., People's Republic of China (Chinese antiques, jewelry, paintings, books and cal-

auction entities generally vary tremendously.[5]

§ 5:6 Article 2 warranties

Judicial application of UCC warranty provisions to art auction entities has been limited.[1] In fact, the interaction of all types of art trading with UCC commercial trading is patchwork, state and federal courts variously interpreting and applying the UCC.[2]

Unhappy buyers ordinarily allege that art sold at auction was not authentic; the UCC issue is whether or not warranty existed on authenticity under the fact-opinion conundrum,[3] and if so, did the auction entity properly disclaim. State laws vary as to what art merchants in general must disclose about authorship of objects and what may be disclaimed, but almost all those laws expressly exclude auctioneers from disclosure requirements.[4] In general, UCC warranty may have limited application to auction buyers for garden variety bids and sales; auction is viewed as a secondary market where caveat emptor plays an important, if not prevailing role. Some auction houses, as a matter of practice or policy, will refund money to buyers for legitimate post-sale authenticity concerns for a period of time coterminous with the UCC statute of limitations (four years), or a shorter time period specified in the conditions of sale agreement or bill of sale.[5] The auction, in turn, seeks to protect itself by demanding warranties and indemnifications from sellers-consignors under the

---

ligraphy auctioned at the Beijing International Auction). For an extensive contemporary discussion of art auctions, *see generally* Watson, From Manet to Manhattan (1992).

[5]*See* Appendix 9.

[Section 5:6]

[1]Giusti v. Sotheby Parke Bernet, Inc., No. 6843/76 (NY Sup. 1982) (UCC § 2-316(3) "as is" in auction catalogue constitutes sufficient attention to "the buyer's attention to the exclusion of warranties").

[2]*See* Ch 4.

[3]*See* §§ 4:18 to 4:32.

[4]*See* Appendix 2.

[5]*See* §§ 5:80 to 5:83.

terms and conditions of consignment agreements.[6]

D. ART PER SE AUCTIONEERING LAWS

§ 5:7 City of New York

In New York City, where Sotheby's and Christie's regularly conduct arts auctions, local rules and regulations, revised in 1987[1] in response to complaints and improprieties, purport to govern auction practice. Although the new laws were codified in the New York Administrative Code after a study of art auctions by the Department of Consumer Affairs, those revisions were still not satisfactory to some state legislators; bills have been proposed at the state level in New York to reform art auctioneering practices.[2]

§ 5:8 State of Illinois

Illinois is the only state to enact an Art Auction House Act.[1] An art auction house is defined in the Illinois code as "any person, partnership, corporation, association or group engaged for profit primarily in the business of conducting auctions at which it acts as agent for any seller of works of art, antiques."[2]

Under Illinois law, the house is required to register annually with the Secretary of State and to file bank or savings statements identifying the institutions where it

---

[6]Kohler v. Leslie Hindman, Inc., 1994 WL 233801 (N.D. Ill. 1994), aff'd, 80 F.3d 1181 (7th Cir. 1996) (conversion claim dismissed against auction house where it agreed, under a side agreement with a buyer, to rescind sale of painting consigned for auction by plaintiffs, the "Plains of Meudon" purportedly by Theodore Rousseau, after authenticity was challenged by buyer's expert). *See also, e.g.,* Appendix 10.

[Section 5:7]

[1]*See* App. 11, N.Y. Admin. Code.

[2]Committee on Oversight, Analysis and Investigation and Committee on Tourism, Sports and Arts, New York State Assembly, proposed by Assemb. Richard Brodsky (D-Westchester), chairman of Oversight Committee; hearings held January 1991. NY Admin. Code auction provisions are contained in Appendix 11.

[Section 5:8]

[1]Ill. Rev. Stat. ch. 121½, ¶ 1100, reproduced in Appendix 11.

[2]Ill. Rev. Stat. ch. 121½, ¶ 1101.

maintains separate accounts for customer funds.[3] Funds must be segregated upon receipt and disbursed to sellers thirty days thereafter.[4] Violations trigger class 4 felonies and fines of not less than $25,000, penalties stricter than any other state, or even the City of New York auction law.[5]

§ 5:9 State auctioneering laws—Licensing required

States have enacted auctioneer laws establishing licensing requirements for engaging in auction, and providing penalties for failure to comply. The laws that pertain to auctions for personal property are summarized in Appendix 9.

As a general summary of the laws, auctions are conducted by auctioneers in the employ of auction houses or auction entities, or by independent auctioneers. Auctioneers are the individuals authorized to sell goods at public sale, pursuant to state law licensing requirements and/or registration with governmental bodies.[1] Auctioneers may be required to post bonds prior to auction in accordance with state requirements.

The auctioneer's license is held by the individual, not the entity for whom auctioneering services are performed, although it also may be subject to registration or license under the law of the jurisdiction.[2] The auctioneer may be assisted for sales purposes by unlicensed persons; others employed by the auction house, or independently associated with it, are not regulated by auctioneering laws.

§ 5:10 State auctioneering laws—Suspension and revocation

The auctioneer's license may be revoked or suspended

---

[3]Ill. Rev. Stat. ch. 121½, ¶ 1103.

[4]Ill. Rev. Stat. ch. 121½, ¶ 1102.

[5]Ill. Rev. Stat. ch. 121½, ¶ 1104.

[Section 5:9]

[1]*See, e.g.,* Cal. Bus. & Prof. Code §§ 5701 et seq. and N.Y. Admin. Code, App. 11.

[2]*See, e.g.,* Ill. Art Auction House Act, at Appendix 11 (house must register with secretary of state).

under the terms of the state or local licensing law. Auction licenses have been suspended for irregularities regarding representations of value made to the seller,[1] and revoked where an auctioneer admitted bid pooling at auction.[2] Laws that authorize auction boards of examiners to commingle prosecutorial and adjudicatory functions in reviewing sus pensions and revocations may violate due process.[3]

§ 5:11 State auctioneering laws—Criminal violations

In addition to civil suits, conduct of the auctioneer and/or auction house may trigger charges of criminal fraud and/or statutory felonies or misdemeanors.[1]

[Section 5:10]

[1]Cristallina S.A. v. Christie, Manson & Woods Intern., Inc., 117 A.D.2d 284, 502 N.Y.S.2d 165 (1st Dep't 1986) (consent judgment against Christie's resulted in $80,000 fine and suspension of two auctioneer's licenses in connection with issuance of false press releases).

[2]Bunch v. Com., State Bd. of Auctioneer Examiners, 152 Pa. Commw. 616, 620 A.2d 578 (1993) (auctioneer's protest that he was not acting as an auctioneer when he engaged in bid pooling was rejected because conviction for bid pooling occurred during the term of his licensure as auctioneer).

[3]Bunch v. Com., State Bd. of Auctioneer Examiners, 152 Pa. Commw. 616, 620 A.2d 578 (1993) (order of board of auctioneer examiners requiring auctioneer to show cause why his license should not be suspended or revoked was reversed and remanded with instructions to the board to devise "a non-commingled [adjudicatory and prosecutorial] approach").

[Section 5:11]

[1]*See, e.g.,* Cal. Penal Code § 436 ("Every person who acts as an auctioneer in violation of the laws of this state relating to auctions and auctioneers is guilty of a misdemeanor."); Cal. Penal Code § 536 ("Every merchant, broker, agent . . . or consignee, who shall wilfully and corruptly make or cause to be made, to the principal or consignor. . . . a false statement as to the price obtained for any property consigned or entrusted for sale or as to the quality or quantity of any property so consigned or entrusted . . . shall be deemed guilty of a misdemeanor and on conviction thereof, shall be punished by fine not exceeding. . . . $1000 and not less than . . . $200, or by imprisonment in the county jail not exceeding six months and not less than 10 days, or by both such fine and imprisonment."); N.Y. Admin. Code § 20-288 ("Any auctioneer who shall have knowledge of any false or fraudulent representations . . . in respect to the character of any sale . . . or the quality,

III. MECHANICS OF AUCTION

A. TERMS AND CONDITIONS

§ 5:12 English auction: Lots on the block

Art auctions are ordinarily English auctions based upon sales made to the highest bidder.[1] Such "auction is a . . . sale of lots by competitive bidding to the highest bidder," where "the bid is the offer" and the auctioneer's acceptance—historically marked by the "fall of the hammer" over the object "on the block"—constitutes formation of the contract.[2]

Goods sold at auction, including art, are sold by lots. A "lot" is "a parcel [of articles] or a single article which is the subject matter of a separate sale."[3] In other words, a lot is single object or a group of objects offered together for sale as one unit.

§ 5:13 Hammer prices

The UCC states: "A sale by auction is complete when the auctioneer so announces by the fall of the hammer or

condition, ownership, situation or value of any property, real or personal . . . put up, or offered by him or her for sale at public auction, shall be deemed guilty of a misdemeanor, and, upon conviction thereof shall be punished by imprisonment not exceeding one year or by a fine not exceeding one thousand dollars."); United States v. Diana D. Brooks, 284 F.3d 384 (guilty plea by former president of Sotheby's on felony count of criminal pricefixing); United States v. Sotheby's Holdings, Inc., 284 F.3d 384 (former chair of Sotheby's convicted on felony count of criminal pricefixing and corporation fined $45 million); In re Auction Houses Antitrust Litigation, 135 F. Supp. 2d 438 (S.D. N.Y. 2001), opinion superseded, 138 F. Supp. 2d 548 (S.D. N.Y. 2001) (related civil case).

[Section 5:12]

[1]A Dutch auction is a "public offer of [goods] at a price beyond [their] value . . . gradually lowering the price until someone becomes the purchaser." Black's Law Dictionary (6th ed.) p 130.

[2]Annot., Auction Sales under UCC Section 2-328, 44 A.L.R. 4th 110.

[3]UCC § 2-105(5).

in other customary manner."[1] A gavel is ordinarily used. Prices realized at auction are thus referred to as "hammer" prices, "knock down" prices or "struck down" prices.[2] The auctioneer in practice calls the lot "sold" or "knocked down" at a particular price.

The hammer price is not the total sales price, nor does it necessarily reflect fair market value[3] or even actual price,[4] as a result of financing arrangements, guaranteed minimum prices, financial participation of the auction

---

[Section 5:13]

[1]UCC § 2-328(2) continues tradition that "sale is complete as a matter of law even though payment has not yet been made." Exceptions exist where goods knocked down are subject to confirmation by a trustee in bankruptcy. Joseph E. DeMarco, Inc. v. Campo, 163 B.R. 49 (S.D. N.Y. 1994) ("A sale is not final until the trustee [in bankruptcy] confirms the bid. . . . the the fact that the sale may have been final under state law does not make the sale final for bankruptcy purposes. . . [UCC] section [2-328] should not be read to preclude the imposition of fair and reasonable conditions on the auction of sale goods . . . .").

[2]Annot., Auction Sales under UCC Section 2-328, 44 A.L.R. 4th 110. The object offered for sale is considered "knocked down" to the bidder by the fall of the hammer. The sales price owed by the successful bidder to the auction exceeds the hammer price.

[3]Biagiotti v. C.I.R., T.C. Memo. 1986-460, 1986 WL 21685 (1986) (Some tax courts reject auction prices as comparable sales prices for determining fair market value of art, because (1) auction sales do not represent a significant portion of the market for sales of art of that kind in the United States during relevant years; (2) auction prices do not accurately represent average sales prices of art in the United States; and (3) auction prices cannot be segregated into wholesale and retail prices, as no definitive way exists to separate "ultimate consumers" from other buyers.); *but cf.* Adam A. Weschler & Son, Inc. v. Klank, 561 A.2d 1003 (D.C. 1989) (auction, as sale to consumer, is based upon "nature of purchaser"; if purchaser is not in regular business of "retail sale of antiques," he is a consumer for purposes of protection under the consumer protection act). Some courts are willing to accept unsubstantiated estimates of the percentages of persons at auction believed to be wholesalers and retailers. These undocumented figures are not reliable in the opinion of the author.

[4]The most publicized instance of a "sales price" not being the actual price paid is the $50 million-plus sale of the painting *Irises* by Vincent Van Gogh. Australian industrialist Alan Bond purchased it, but never paid that amount; Sotheby's loaned him $27 million against the price. Sotheby's subsequently resold *Irises* for an undisclosed sum to the J. Paul Getty Museum in Malibu, California.

house in the sale, or other proprietary interests in the object. Local laws may govern disclosures of these factors and their effects.[5] The sale may be reopened for further bidding after the knock down only in limited circumstances.[6] Auctioneers issue "fair warning" announcements after the final bid before they announce the knock down, which as a matter of practice prevents post-knock down bids.

Bidding is ordinarily done in increments not exceeding 10 percent of the previous bid, or as established by the house. Bidding may be done by telephone, order bid or in person by the buyer or buyer's designate in the public salesroom at the auction house. The salesroom is occasionally referred to as the "gallery."

§ 5:14 Paddler bids

Bidding may be indicated by calling out, prearranged visual signals, or raising of numbered paddles provided by the auction house. Bidders are thus sometimes called "paddlers." Bids may be retracted until the announcement that the sale is complete "but a bidder's retraction does not revive any previous bid."[1]

§ 5:15 Absentee bids—Order bids and telecommunication bids

Bidding may also be accepted by the auction entity through prearrangement: (1) by telephone; or (2) in writing; absentee bidders must be registered with the house prior to auction. Absentee bidding in writing is termed an "order bid;" the order recites the maximum purchase price the absentee bidder authorizes. Order bids are recognized by the auctioneer, sometimes indicated by the phrase, "the bid is with me," "order bid," "my bid," "in the book," or "absentee bidder" (which also applies to telephone bids).

---

[5]*See, e.g.,* N.Y. Admin. Code, tit. 20, Ch. 2, subchapter 13, and regulations thereto, and Illinois Art Auction House Law, reproduced in Appendix 11.

[6]Marx v. Sotheby Parke Bernet, Inc., 102 A.D.2d 729, 476 N.Y.S.2d 482 (1st Dep't 1984).

[Section 5:14]

[1]UCC § 2-328(3).

Order bids are accepted in sequence against paddler bids from the gallery. The order bid is executed at the lowest price and is bid incrementally until the bid is successful or the maximum is exceeded by other bidders. Out of state bidders may be bound by completed sales transacted by telephonic means under jurisdictional statutes of the state where the auction occurs.[1]

§ 5:16 Absentee bids—Jurisdiction

Absentee bidding has not defeated jurisdictional claims over such bidders in actions to enforce sales contracts.[1] In Parke-Bernet Galleries, Inc. v. Franklyn,[2] the New York Court of Appeals held that a person in New York who notified a bidder in California by telephone of the progress of a New York auction, relaying California bids to the auctioneer, was a bidder's agent for purposes of New York's jurisdictional statute.

[Section 5:15]

[1]*See, e.g.,* Parke-Bernet Galleries, Inc. v. Franklyn, 26 N.Y.2d 13, 308 N.Y.S.2d 337, 256 N.E.2d 506 (1970) (action against defendant bidder, relating to contract to purchase art executed by bidding via telephone from California to New York auction, constitutional because bidder was transacting business within the state through the agent relaying bids); *but cf.* Zakaria v. Safani, 741 F. Supp. 1263 (S.D. Miss. 1990) (single telephone call, and mailing of check for ancient stone head by Manhattan gallery to Mississippi, did not constitute sufficient contacts for in personam jurisdiction over nonresident gallery under Mississippi long-arm statute, in action where plaintiff alleged that defendant auctioned bust at Sotheby's for $22,000 but only paid plaintiff $5,200 from a private sale, claiming Sotheby's would not accept it).

[Section 5:16]

[1]*See, e.g.,* Parke-Bernet Galleries, Inc. v. Franklyn, 26 N.Y.2d 13, 308 N.Y.S.2d 337, 256 N.E.2d 506 (1970); *but cf.* Zakaria v. Safani, 741 F. Supp. 1263 (S.D. Miss. 1990) (single telephone call, and mailing of check for ancient stone head by Manhattan gallery to Mississippi, did not constitute sufficient contacts for in personam jurisdiction over nonresident gallery under Mississippi long-arm statute, in action where plaintiff alleged defendant auctioned head at Sotheby's for $22,000 but only paid plaintiff $5,200 from a private sale, claiming Sotheby's would not accept head).

[2]Parke-Bernet Galleries, Inc. v. Franklyn, 26 N.Y.2d 13, 308 N.Y.S.2d 337, 256 N.E.2d 506 (1970).

§ 5:17 Absentee bids—Statute of frauds

Nor is the absence of the bidder's written acceptance fatal under the UCC statute of frauds. This intermediary role of "relay station" suffices for jurisdictional purposes.[1] The auctioneer is deemed to act as the buyer's agent when he memorializes the sale in his memorandum; in some states acceptance of the auctioneer's notation of sale as a writing is codified to prevent avoidance of the contract under a statute of frauds defense.[2]

§ 5:18 Chandelier bids

Auctioneer bids on behalf of the seller until the reserve is met, without identifying the type of bid, are termed "chandelier bids." Chandelier bidding is prohibited by law above the reserve.[1] A chandelier bid is also called a "consecutive bid," or "puffing."[2] Chandelier bidding can occur where bids are made by a designated individual known as a "plant" or a "shill," who artificially bids up the price, or by the auctioneer, who uses a euphemism to indicate creation of a bid.

The term "chandelier bid" reportedly originates from the auctioneer's proverbial gaze upward at the chandelier,

---

[Section 5:17]

[1]*See* Mayer v. Josiah Wedgwood & Sons, Ltd., 601 F. Supp. 1523 (S.D. N.Y. 1985) (relay station role by agent acting in New York for British defendant enough for jurisdiction under New York state law).

[2]UCC § 2-201 ("a contract for the sale of goods for the price of five hundred dollars ($500) or more is not enforceable by way of action or defense unless there is some writing sufficient to indicate that a contract for sale has been made between the parties and signed by the party against whom enforcement is sought or by his or her authorized agent or broker"); Cal. Civ. Code § 2363 empowers auctioneers to make such designations ("An auctioneer has authority from a bidder at the auction, as well as from the seller, to bind both by a memorandum of the contract"); *see also* N.Y. Gen. Oblig. Law § 5-701a6.

[Section 5:18]

[1]N.Y. Admin.Code, tit. 20, Ch. 2, subchapter 13, §§ 20-278 et seq., reg. III, # 22(a) ("After bidding has reached the reserve price . . . the auctioneer may not bid on behalf of the consignor or the auction house.").

[2]"Secret bidding" at auction is termed "puffing"; *see* 46 A.L.R. 122 for the effects of puffing on auction sales.

instead of toward the gallery. If the auctioneer were genuinely seeking independent bids, he would have to look at the gallery to see bidders' cues, but since he is creating the bid he looks upward. "Consecutive" refers to the auctioneer's repeated, consecutive and incremental bids (in the absence of independent competitive bidders) until the reserve is met. The auctioneer is not permitted to continue bidding on the seller's behalf after the reserve has been satisfied.

UCC Section 2-328(4) states that buyers may at their option void the sale or "take the goods at the price of the last good faith bid prior to the completion of the sale . . . [i]f the auctioneer knowingly receives a bid on the seller's behalf or the seller makes or procures such a bid . . . and . . . notice has not been given that liberty for such bidding is reserved."[3]

Auction houses explain that consecutive bids are made "on behalf of the consignor"; such bidding is defended as a way of protecting the seller's interests, precipitating genuine bidding and triggering the reserve. But as discussed below, complicated loan, lien and guarantee arrangements raise questions about for whom the auctioneer is acting, the house or the seller, and the propriety of such bids.

The legal proscription on chandelier bidding above the reserve is considered ineffective, because "chandelier bidding [above the reserve] is irrelevant" in that the bidder's risk is focused not on "the entire price he is bidding, only the incremental bid over the last one, because he believes his cushion is a ready, willing and able underbidder."[4] This is not the case with a chandelier bid, where no actual underbidder exists.

§ 5:19 Chill bidding

Chill bidding occurs when two or more persons, often in collusion with the auctioneer, refrain from competitive

[3]UCC § 2-328(4).

[4]Feigen, "Beware of the Chandelier," Newsday, Feb. 28, 1991, at 56.

bidding to reduce the hammer price.[1] Chill bidding, sometimes called bid pooling, stifles open competitive sales. Any act by auctioneers or others "which prevents a fair, free and open sale, or which diminishes competition and stifles or chills the sale, is contrary to public policy and vitiates the sale."[2] Chill bidding may constitute a federal violation of Section 1 of the Sherman Antitrust Act and be grounds for revocation of the auctioneer's license under state law.[3]

§ 5:20 Estimates

What the bids mean, however, is not patently clear from activities in the gallery without reference to auction catalogues or other materials that recite sales price estimates.

The values an auction house assigns to goods for auction are termed presale estimates, sometimes referred to as "two-figure" estimates[1] because two figures, i.e., a high and low, are often used to indicate a range of values. Presale estimates from low to high, e.g., $10,000–$15,000, appear in auction catalogues or other auction materials or statements. That the presale estimates are available to the bidder may not be enough under the law of the jurisdiction; some local laws specify the terms of disclosing the

---

[Section 5:19]

[1]A chill bid is an "act of bidders or others who combine or conspire to suppress fair competition at a sale for the purpose of acquiring the property at less than its fair value." Bunch v. Com., State Bd. of Auctioneer Examiners, 152 Pa. Commw. 616, 620 A.2d 578 (1993) ("Bid pooling is a conspiracy among art or antique dealers to refrain from bidding against each other to obtain items at artificially low prices.").

[2]Gainesville Oil & Gas Co., Inc. v. Farm Credit Bank of Texas, 847 S.W.2d 655 (Tex. App. Texarkana 1993) (citations omitted).

[3]Bunch v. Com., State Bd. of Auctioneer Examiners, 152 Pa. Commw. 616, 620 A.2d 578 (1993) (auctioneer plead guilty to violation of § 1 of the Sherman Antitrust Act, 15 U.S.C.A. § 1, for bid pooling).

[Section 5:20]

[1]Two-figure estimates are accepted by the tax courts. *See, e.g.,* Andrew Crispo Gallery, Inc. v. C.I.R., T.C. Memo. 1992-106, 1992 WL 31221 (1992), decision aff'd in part and vacated in part on other grounds, 16 F.3d 1336 (2d Cir. 1994).

meaning of the estimates.[2] In New York, "a general description of the estimate and its meaning and function must be included in such printed material."[3]

Estimates of sales prices are based upon the opinion of the auction house, but the basis for the opinion is not disclosed.[4] Auction estimates ordinarily take into account the CROSSAQ factor[5] or portions of it, focusing upon marketability of the object itself in terms of its appeal and condition, as well as market conditions at the time of auction. The process is subjective, "predicting and accounting for [various] mutable . . . [economic and aesthetic] factors."[6]

Presale estimates do not reflect valuation methodologies used in the preparation of independent appraisals pursuant to federal tax laws, under uniform standard practices, or by appraisers following standards and guidelines adopted by professional appraisal organizations.[7] Objects sell at auction above the high estimate, or not at all[8] if no bids are made or the bids are not high enough to meet the reserve.[9]

§ 5:21 Reserves

The normal procedure for auction is sale with reserve.[1] The UCC states that "a sale is with reserve unless the

---

[2]*See, e.g.,* App. 11, N.Y. Admin. Code, Reg. II, # 17.

[3]*See, e.g.,* App. 11, N.Y. Admin. Code, Reg. II, # 17.

[4]Cristallina S.A. v. Christie, Manson & Woods Intern., Inc., 117 A.D.2d 284, 502 N.Y.S.2d 165 (1st Dep't 1986).

[5]*See* discussion of CROSSAQ factor, § 2:22.

[6]Christie's Inc. v. Davis, 247 F. Supp. 2d 414, 49 U.C.C. Rep. Serv. 2d 684 (S.D. N.Y. 2002) (that dealer's valuations were higher than those of auction house was not probative of unreasonableness or bad faith).

[7]*See* Ch 3; Appendix 5.

[8]Auction may have the right to sell the work after the auction by private sale. *See* § 5:23.

[9]Cristallina S.A. v. Christie, Manson & Woods Intern., Inc., 117 A.D.2d 284, 502 N.Y.S.2d 165 (1st Dep't 1986) (auction house liable to consignor where only one of eight paintings sold at auction, in circumstances where reserves were set higher than high presale estimates).

[Section 5:21]

[1]UCC § 2-328, Official Comment ¶ 1.

goods are in explicit terms put up without reserve."[2] Local laws may require that the existence of reserves be expressly affirmed. Art auctioned "without reserve" may still have other sale restrictions.[3] The reserve is an undisclosed minimum price below which the auctioneer does not have to sell the object to bidders at public auction. The confidential reserve is normally agreed upon by the seller and the auction house. If the seller-consignor and the auction house do not mutually agree upon a reserve, confirmed in writing by the seller, an auction may establish its own reserve. Regardless of who sets the reserve, catalogues and contracts recite the term "seller's reserve" or "subject to the seller's reserve."

Even if the amount of the reserve is confidential, the relationship of the reserve to the presale estimates may not be, as established under law. In New York City the reserve, whatever its amount, may not "exceed the maximum estimated value . . . as published in any catalogue or other printed material distributed by the auctioneer."[4] Christie's stated practice is that the reserve "will not exceed the low of the presale estimate."[5] This practice means the confidentiality of the precise amount of the reserve is maintained, but the public is notified of a price floor.

There is no single formula for establishing the reserve;[6] it depends upon the auction house, its internal policies

---

[2]UCC § 2-328(2).

[3]U.S. v. Von Cseh, 354 F. Supp. 315 (S.D. Tex. 1972) (in government action to foreclose a tax lien on a painting, a federal district court concluded that the phrase "without reserve" was a term of art meaning that (1) the property would go to the highest bidder; and (2) the property would not be withdrawn from the sale before the acceptance of a bid; "without reserve" was therefore not equivalent to a term of sale "without restriction").

[4]N.Y. Admin. Code, Reg. III, # 23 (App. 11).

[5]"Bidding at Christie's" 3 (1993) (brochure published by auction house).

[6]Shein v. C.I.R, T.C. Memo. 1987-329, 1987 WL 40384 (1987) (" 'reserve' is usually a figure which is two-thirds of the low estimate."); Kirby v. Wildenstein, 784 F. Supp. 1112 (S.D. N.Y. 1992) (reserve set by Christie's for 1988 auction at low estimate); Cristallina S.A. v. Christie, Manson & Woods Intern., Inc., 117 A.D.2d 284, 502 N.Y.S.2d 165 (1st Dep't 1986) (reserves set above high estimates).

and practices, and perception of the marketability of the object at the time of auction. Reserves have been set at low presale estimates,[7] at or above high estimates,[8] at a percentage of the estimate.[9] A "floating reserve" is an established undisclosed amount the auctioneer can use to increase the reserve on any work of art he or she deems appropriate. Adding a floating reserve on works already overvalued decreases the likelihood of sale.[10] If the reserve is not met by the bidding, the object may be withdrawn from auction or sold after auction by a private treaty sale.

§ 5:22 Withdrawn, pass, bought-in

If the reserve of any lot is not met by the bidding, the auctioneer notifies the gallery that the work will not be sold at auction through terminology like "withdrawn," "passed," "returned to owner," or "bought-in."[1]

The term "bought-in," sometimes abbreviated b.i., implies that the auction house itself is "buying in" the piece, but it simply means that the work is removed from auction on behalf of the seller, and will be returned to the owner absent other sales arrangements.

§ 5:23 Private treaty sales

A private treaty sale is a private sale made by the auction entity if the work does not sell at public auction; by contract auction entities may retain rights to sell by private treaty for limited time periods. Private treaty sales may be below the reserve. The contract governs what the seller is entitled to receive for such sales; e.g., the seller may be paid the net reserve, which is the reserve minus

---

[7]Kirby v. Wildenstein, 784 F. Supp. 1112 (S.D. N.Y. 1992).

[8]Cristallina S.A. v. Christie, Manson & Woods Intern., Inc., 117 A.D.2d 284, 502 N.Y.S.2d 165 (1st Dep't 1986) ("in violation of normal practice").

[9]Shein v. C.I.R, T.C. Memo. 1987-329, 1987 WL 40384 (1987) ("'reserve' is usually a figure which is two-thirds of the low estimate.").

[10]Cristallina S.A. v. Christie, Manson & Woods Intern., Inc., 117 A.D.2d 284, 502 N.Y.S.2d 165 (1st Dep't 1986) (auctioneer testimony on use of floating reserve and effect on sales).

[Section 5:22]

[1]N.Y. Admin. Code, Reg III, # 20 (App. 11).

costs, fees, and other expenses. The auction for various reasons may sell art by private sale without ever offering it at auction. Some houses publish private treaty sales as well as public auction sales.[1]

§ 5:24 Withdrawal

Prior to auction the auction house may withdraw the work for reasons recited in the consignment agreement, e.g., authenticity, impaired title, seller's warranties, breaches of contract, etc. The UCC position is "that goods may be withdrawn before they are 'put up' regardless of whether the auction is advertised as one without reserve, without liability on the part of the auction announcer."[1] The auction may still be entitled to commissions and charges.[2]

§ 5:25 Burned art

Art that does not sell at auction is sometimes referred to as "burned." (Burned art also refers to art unsold on the market for a long period of time.) "Burn" is a term derived from fire sale terminology for goods sold below market prices when businesses are liquidated substantially below market value.[1]

Art that is "bought in" is arguably considered to decrease in value.[2] Because an object does not sell on a particular date amongst particular lots offered to specific bidders should not diminish value. Recent auctions dem-

---

[Section 5:23]

[1]For 1992 Christie's reported private treaty sales totaled $45 million; Sotheby's did not release total private treaty sales.

[Section 5:24]

[1]UCC § 2-328, Official Comment 2.

[2]*See* Appendix 4 and chart 5-3, at § 5:27.

[Section 5:25]

[1]Christie's Inc. v. Davis, 247 F. Supp. 2d 414, 49 U.C.C. Rep. Serv. 2d 684 (S.D. N.Y. 2002) (sale of artworks at foreclosure prices below earlier presale estimates would not necessarily be a commercially unreasonable "fire sale").

[2]Cristallina S.A. v. Christie, Manson & Woods Intern., Inc., 117 A.D.2d 284, 502 N.Y.S.2d 165 (1st Dep't 1986).

onstrate that art sold shortly after being bought-in did not suffer a burn; in fact, sales prices were higher than high presale estimates from the first auction. However, the value of art is based upon perception, and bought-in art can create a negative public perception. Publicity surrounding auction means that subsequent buyers interested in the work are aware, or easily made aware, of the fact that it was bought-in, and of the amount of the minimum presale estimate.

B. PREMIUMS, COMMISSIONS, CHARGES

§ 5:26 Generally

The hammer price is not the total sales price the successful bidder owes the auction or the sole source of revenue for the auctioneer. The auction house collects commissions for its services, known as buyer's premiums and auctioneer's or seller's commissions. The auction may charge and collect both a buyer's premium and an auctioneer's commission. These premiums and commissions are the revenue-generators for the auction houses; their usage and implementation is the subject of criminal and civil antitrust litigation.[1] The auction may also collect fees and charges for services and arrangements.

§ 5:27 Auctioneer's commission

The auctioneer's commission, sometimes referred to as the seller's commission,[1] is a charge to the seller-consignor based upon a percentage of the hammer price, deducted from the sale proceeds the auction house pays to the seller. The auctioneer's commission was based on a sliding scale at Christie's and Sotheby's, subject to negotiation at some

---

[Section 5:26]

[1]In re Auction Houses Antitrust Litigation, 193 F.R.D. 162 (S.D. N.Y. 2000) (consolidated class actions seeking damages and other relief for price fixing settled); Kruman v. Christie's Int'l PLC, 284 F.3d 384 (2d Cir. 2002) (antitrust action by foreign buyers and sellers alleging price-fixing); United States v. Diana D. Brooks, 00 CRIM. 1084 (RMB); U.S. v. Sotheby's Holdings, Inc., 2001 WL 77055 (S.D. N.Y. 2001).

[Section 5:27]

[1]In re Auction Houses Antitrust Litigation, 193 F.R.D. 162 (S.D. N.Y. 2000).

auction houses for preferred clients, at least prior to the deal between Christie's and Sotheby's on commissions, a practice the 1995 changes were intended to stop. Other auction houses have other arrangements. In the absence of a negotiated agreement, the auctioneer's commission at one auction house in 1993 was as follows:

Chart 5-3: Auctioneer's Commission at Christie's (1993)[2]

Percentage	Hammer Price
20%	<$2,000
15%	≥ $2,000 <$7,500
10%	≥ $7,500
Pass	~ 5% reserve

Sotheby's had a substantially similar commission structure. By Spring 1995, both Christie's and Sotheby's announced an identical new pricing structure, introducing a sliding scale that ranged from two to twenty per cent, depending on the value of the item. Both auction houses further declared that seller's commissions were no longer negotiable. The antitrust litigation alleged that Sotheby's and Christie's conspired to manipulate prices by agreeing to employ a common rate schedule for charges and commissions, even exchanging preferred customer lists for those not charged a seller's commission.[3]

The lockstep commission rate changes of the two auction houses was too coincidental for their clients and federal prosecutors. A criminal investigation for pricefixing in violation of the antitrust laws and civil class action for collusion to fix commission rates yielded resignations of top executives from Christie's and Sotheby's, a conditional amnesty for the former for its government cooperation, and a settlement in the civil action. The settlement terms included $512 million, divided between the two houses, in conjunction with their providing discount coupons to reduce seller's commissions on future sales.

---

[2]Source: Christie's (1993). Commissions change and prevailing rates should be checked.

[3]In re Auction Houses Antitrust Litigation, 193 F.R.D. 162 (S.D. N.Y. 2000) (certification of consolidated class actions seeking damages and other relief for price fixing); *see* Ch 5 § 5:1.

Renewed viability of the antitrust class action for foreign claims may have an additional impact.[4] As of May 2002 the 130,000 victims of the price-fixing scheme had not been paid, reportedly because of the unresolved overseas transactions.

Sotheby's was assessed penalties of $45 million and its former chair was convicted in federal court for criminal conspiracy and pricefixing. He was sentenced to one year and a day in prison, which made him eligible for a 15% percent term reduction and fined $7.5 million. He was ordered to pay for his incarceration. The former chair of Christie's was indicted but refused to leave Britain and was not subject to extradition. Sotheby's president plead guilty on a felony count and was sentenced to three years probation including six months house arrest, fined $350,000.00 and ordered to perform 1000 hours community service.

Regardless of the amount of the commission, the seller also has contractual obligations under consignment agreements for various costs, fees and expenses, like packing, shipping, insurance, restoration, framing, and photography.[5]

The components of sales proceeds are:

Hammer Price
Less: Auctioneer's Commission
Less: Out-of-Pocket Costs (e.g., insurance, packing, shipping, photography, catalogue illustrations)
Less: Authentications, other services, etc.

Total Net Proceeds

§ 5:28 Buyer's premium

The buyer's premium is a charge to the buyer based upon a percentage of the hammer price on each item sold; the premium is added to the sales price and paid directly

---

[4]Kruman v. Christie's Int'l PLC, 284 F.3d 384 (2d Cir. 2002); Glovin, D, "Sotheby's, Christie's Must Defend Overseas Lawsuits," Bloomberg News, March 13, 2002).

[5]*See* Appendix 10.

to the auctioneer.[1] Buyer's premiums, standard practice in the auction industry, were initiated in the United States by Christie's in 1977, followed by Sotheby's in 1979.

Like auctioneer's commissions, buyer's premiums were also the subject of a federal investigation surrounding the antitrust litigation against Sotheby's and Christie's.[2] In November 1992, Sotheby's increased the buyer's premium from 10 to 15 percent of the hammer price up to and including a hammer price of $50,000; above $50,000, the buyer's premium was 10 percent. In December 1992, Christie's announced an identical premium increase, effective March 1, 1993.

Responding to the antitrust litigation, which is examined in preceding sections, both auction houses announced changes in the buyer's premium. In February 2000 Christie's raised its charges to buyers to 17.5% on the first $80,000 of the hammer price and 10% above that, effective March 31st. In March 2000 Sotheby's raised its buyer's premiums to 20% on the first $15,000 of the hammer price, 15% between $15,000 and $100,000, and 10% above $100,000.

The new 2002 post-litigation buyer's premiums announced by the two houses in Spring 2002 raise questions about the efficacy of the prosecution and litigation. In March, Sotheby's announced buyer's premiums would be raised to 19.5% on the first $100,000 of the hammer price and 10% above that, effective April 1st. In April 2002, Christie's announced an identical premium raise, effective April 15th. The two auction houses contended the return to lockstep premium rates was not collusive but market-driven. Sotheby's again raised the buyer's premium to 20 percent for the first $100,000 and 12 percent above that, effective November 2003. Christie's buyer's premium effective March 30, 2004 was 19.5% for the first $100,000 and 12% above. The Introduction at § 5:1 lists auction web sites where current buyer's premium rates can be confirmed. After the antitrust litigation against Sotheby's and Christie's for manipulating prices by agreeing to a

---

[Section 5:28]

[1]In re Rossmiller, 148 B.R. 326 (D. Colo. 1992).

[2]*See* Ch 5 § 5:27.

common rate schedule for premiums, auction commissions undoubtedly will be scrutinized.[3]

The buyer's premium is considered integral to and a component part of the sales price, and published listed sales prices for auction ordinarily include the premium. The Internal Revenue Service has taken the position that since the buyer's premium is a recognized part of the sales price, it should be included in determining fair market value of artworks for purposes of estate tax and gift tax.[4]

Components of purchase price are:

Hammer Price
Plus: Buyer's Premium
Plus: Taxes
Plus: Transport, Shipping, Insurance, Miscellaneous

Total Sales Price

Note, however, that delays in prompt payment (three to seven days from sale) may trigger delivery, storage, and insurance costs, due and payable before an object will be released.

§ 5:29 Buyer's premium for sales made under bankruptcy

Auctioneers selling art through bankruptcy proceedings should be mindful of disclosing to the trustee and the court the existence and amount of buyer's premiums, and their intentions regarding collecting and retaining them. In In

---

[3]In re Auction Houses Antitrust Litigation, 193 F.R.D. 162 (S.D. N.Y. 2000) (certification of consolidated class actions seeking damages and other relief for price fixing); Kruman v. Christie's Int'l Plc, 284 F.3d 384 (2d Cir. 2002) (antitrust action by foreign buyers and sellers alleging price-fixing).

[4]*See, e.g.,* Priv. Letter Ruling 9235005 (May 27, 1992), which although it may not be used or cited as precedent, is based upon Publicker v. C.I.R., 206 F.2d 250, 60 A.L.R.2d 1295 (3d Cir. 1953); Smith's (David) Estate v. Commissioner of Internal Revenue, 57 T.C. 650, 659 n.10, 1972 WL 2557 (1972), acq. 1974-2 C.B. and recommendation regarding acquiescence, 1974 WL 36002 (I.R.S. AOD 1974) and aff'd, 510 F.2d 479 (2d Cir. 1975); Guggenheim v. Rasquin, 312 U.S. 254, 61 S. Ct. 507, 85 L. Ed. 813 (1941).

re Rossmiller,[1] the bankruptcy court denied an auctioneer all compensation on sales of art auctioned under a judicially approved trustee's agreement, including an approved 20 percent auctioneer's commission on the art. The court refused to authorize payment of any compensation to the auctioneer because he had failed to disclose to the court or trustee that he was collecting an additional 10 percent buyer's premium. Although the bankruptcy court found the auctioneer in "egregious" violation of Bankruptcy Rule 11,[2] the district court remanded the case to the bankruptcy court to reconsider whether denial of all compensation was an appropriate sanction under Rule 11.

§ 5:30 Minimum price guarantee

In the 1970s some auctions implemented a controversial practice of guaranteeing the seller a minimum price, irrespective of performance at auction or by treaty sale. The auction pays the consignor a specified amount for the lot whether or not the minimum price guarantee (MPG) is realized at auction. This means that if the reserve is not met the auction house itself becomes the purchaser. In other words, the lot is not bought-in for the seller-consignor, but on behalf of the auction house, which acquires a proprietary interest in the lot and is obligated to pay the seller the net MPG.

If bids exceed the MPG at auction, the seller-consignor is entitled to the MPG plus any overages. The auction house may demand a higher auctioneer's commission for MPG sales.

MPG sales differ from post-auction private treaty sales for several reasons:

(1) Post-b.i. sales do not inhere ownership interest in the auction house, but unsold MPG art does;

(2) MPGs are not necessarily a function of the relationship of reserve prices to estimates, but instead reflect the power and/or idiosyncrasies of particular sellers over particular lots vis-a-vis

[Section 5:29]

[1] In re Rossmiller, 148 B.R. 326 (D. Colo. 1992).

[2] Fed. R. Bankr. Rule 9011(a).

the auction house;

(3) MPGs, unlike reserves, which may float throughout the auction, are determined prior to acceptance of the consignment relationship to induce sellers to use the services of one auction house over another.

Failure to realize the minimum price at the bidding triggers the auction house's: (1) immediate right to purchase; and (2) postpurchase rights to sell for its own account, presumably at any price or at a negotiated price. Auction catalogues designate property sold with MPG. Guaranteed collections that don't sell for anticipated estimates can severely undermine profitability. Phillips strategy to increase its market share while Christie's and Sotheby's defended antitrust litigation reportedly was to guarantee enormous sums for collections that did not sell well at auction.[1]

IV. AUCTION LIABILITY: RELATIONSHIP WITH SELLERS

A. IN GENERAL

§ 5:31 Checklist; Potential causes of action by seller

(1) Breach of contract

(2) Breach of fiduciary duty

(3) Breach of covenant of good faith and fair dealing or honest practices

(4) Breach of agency

(5) Negligence

(6) Negligent misrepresentation

(7) Fraud

(8) Fraudulent or reckless misrepresentation

[Section 5:30]

[1]T. Thornycroft, "A Saleroom Goes for a Song," Financial Times (London ed.), Feb. 23, 2002, at 13 (Phillips reportedly guaranteed $100 million to Heinz Berggruen for post-Impressionist paintings that realized only $71 million and $185 million for the Smooke collection of 20th century art that realized only $86 million).

(9) Lanham Act[1]

(10) Conversion

(11) Declaratory relief or injunctive relief

B. AGENCY

§ 5:32 General

The primary relationship of the seller-consignor and the auction entity-consignee in a straightforward consignment is one of agency.[1] But courts have interpreted that relationship in the context of general auction practices, the particular consignment agreement entered into by the auction house, and the seller and the specific written conditions of sale.[2] Generally, all duties of the agent apply to the auction; the duties discussed in this Section are those that have been litigated in reported cases.

§ 5:33 Fiduciary duty—Pleading

The fiduciary relationship exists as a matter of law between principal and agent where the agent acts within the scope of the agency.[1] The auctioneer as agent of the consignor has a "fiduciary duty to act in the utmost good faith and in the interest of . . . its principal throughout their

---

[Section 5:31]

[1]*See* Ch 11.

[Section 5:32]

[1]Kohler v. Leslie Hindman, Inc., 80 F.3d 1181, 34 Fed. R. Serv. 3d 1342 (7th Cir. 1996) (auction house relationship to consignor as agent-principal); Pilliard v. Sotheby's, Inc., motion for recon., 1998 WL 126060 (S.D.N.Y. Mar. 19, 1998); Private Letter Ruling, PLR 9728005, 1997 WL 381975 (I.R.S. PLR 1997) (consignment agreement constituted agency agreement for auction services); Cristallina S.A. v. Christie, Manson & Woods Intern., Inc., 117 A.D.2d 284, 502 N.Y.S.2d 165 (1st Dep't 1986) ("Christie's concedes, as it must, that an auction house acts as an agent on behalf of its consignors. The auctioneer is the agent of the consignor.").

[2]Cristallina S.A. v. Christie, Manson & Woods Intern., Inc., 117 A.D.2d 284, 502 N.Y.S.2d 165 (1st Dep't 1986).

[Section 5:33]

[1]Restatement (Second) of Agency § 13.

relationship."[2] The fiduciary duties of the agency may be modified by agreement of the principal and agent.[3] Although prudent pleading would allege the existence of the fiduciary relationship, failure to do so by consignors-sellers in a complaint against an auction house was not grounds for a motion to dismiss for failure to state a claim.[4] Auctioneer's unconditional rescission clauses and sole discretion clauses in consignment agreements have been upheld against consignor's claims that such acts constitute breach of fiduciary duty.[5]

Entering into a verbal side agreement with a bidder regarding authenticity of the consigned artwork; providing a bidder with oral warranty of authenticity; and allowing a bidder to take possession of artwork without payment did not constitute breach of fiduciary duty where consignment agreement granted auctioneer sole discretionary powers.[6]

Failure to disclose material facts to a principal can sustain such a breach of fiduciary duty. Failure by an auction house to inform consignors that it had discovered an

[2]Mickle v. Christie's, Inc., 207 F. Supp. 2d 237 (S.D. N.Y. 2002) ("under some circumstances an agent may be required to act in a fiduciary capacity in carrying out the duties entrusted by the principal"); Cristallina S.A. v. Christie, Manson & Woods Intern., Inc., 117 A.D.2d 284, 502 N.Y.S.2d 165 (1st Dep't 1986).

[3]Mickle v. Christie's, Inc., 207 F. Supp. 2d 237 (S.D. N.Y. 2002) (consignment agreement permitted auction house to "serve dual loyalties" to buyers and sellers and to prioritize its interest before that of consignor).

[4]Kohler v. Leslie Hindman, Inc., 1994 WL 233801 (N.D. Ill. 1994), aff'd, 80 F.3d 1181 (7th Cir. 1996) (where auction acted in good faith within scope of its authority, no breach of consignment agreement or fiduciary duty); Granat v. Center Art Galleries—Hawaii Inc., R.I.C.O. Bus. Disp. Guide (CCH) ¶ 8425, 1993 WL 403977 (S.D. N.Y. 1993) (breach of fiduciary duty claim dismissed in an action where gallery sold plaintiffs $1.8 million worth of artworks subsequently valued at only $250,000 because commercial transaction did not create fiduciary relationship).

[5]Mickle v. Christie's, Inc., 207 F. Supp. 2d 237 (S.D. N.Y. 2002) (unconditional authority to cancel sale in the event of non-payment); Kohler v. Leslie Hindman, Inc., 80 F.3d 1181, 34 Fed. R. Serv. 3d 1342 (7th Cir. 1996) (sole discretion rescissionary clause for sales affects liability under warranty of authenticity).

[6]Kohler v. Leslie Hindman, Inc., 1995 WL 89015 (N.D. Ill. 1995), judgment aff'd, 80 F.3d 1181, 34 Fed. R. Serv. 3d 1342 (7th Cir. 1996).

authenticity problem, and as a result had entered into an oral side agreement with a buyer prior to auction, allowing rescission if authenticity could not be assured, was not deemed such a breach. The court concluded that the facts were not material. Relying upon a jurisdictional definition that material facts are "those . . . which the agent should realize have or are likely to have a bearing upon the desirability of the transaction from the viewpoint of the principal[,]"[7] the court decided that the consignors would have been in the same position whether or not the auction had disclosed the problem, since either they or the auction house could have withdrawn the painting, and the auction could have rescinded the sale.

§ 5:34 Duty to use best efforts to promote

One of the auction's "'implied good faith obligation[s is that the agent] . . . use his best efforts to promote the principal's product.'"[1] That has been interpreted in the auction context as, at a minimum, reasonably valuing the art by preparing estimates and setting reserves that will promote sale, and communicating the information to the seller so that he may have the opportunity to sell at auction or remove the artwork before it incurs a potential burn.

§ 5:35 Duty to value—Compliance with auction policies and practices

Value is not precise, and auctions often use two-figure presale estimates to give public notice of a price range and their belief in the price marketability of a particular work. What relationship should those estimates have with market conditions? At a minimum, an auction has a duty to value the presale estimates and set the reserves in accordance with its own policies, practices and guidelines.

---

[7]Kohler v. Leslie Hindman, Inc., 1995 WL 89015 at ¶ 19–20 (N.D. Ill. 1995), judgment aff'd, 80 F.3d 1181, 34 Fed. R. Serv. 3d 1342 (7th Cir. 1996) (citation omitted).

[Section 5:34]

[1]Kohler v. Leslie Hindman, Inc., 1995 WL 89015 (N.D. Ill. 1995); Kremer v. Janet Fleisher Gallery, Inc., 320 Pa. Super. 384, 467 A.2d 377 (1983).

In Cristallina S.A. v. Christie, Manson & Woods, Int'l, Inc.,[1] the appellate division of the New York Supreme Court reversed summary judgment dismissing a seller's complaint against Christie's for fraudulent misrepresentation, negligence, breach of contract and breach of fiduciary duty. Christie's actively solicited the seller; an auctioneer flew to Switzerland and convinced the owner to use auction instead of private sale, made a memorandum emphasizing high presale estimates totaling $12,600,000 for eight paintings, and negotiated reduced commissions and other deal points.

When the eight paintings arrived at Christie's in New York, another employee decided the paintings had limited appeal and decided his colleague's presale estimates were "unobtainable." The auction then dropped the presale estimates by a couple of million dollars without informing the seller, thus making the reserves higher than high presale estimates. Only one painting sold at auction. Since the auction house contravened its own practices regarding the reserves, the court found it owed a duty to set values and reserves reasonably and in accordance with its own practices.

§ 5:36 Duty to value—Reliance on special skills and knowledge

A principal is entitled to rely on the agent's judgment and integrity. While an auction is not required to guarantee that art will sell at presale estimates, or sell at all, it is required to set the estimates with a standard of care commensurate with the special skill which is the norm in the locality for that kind of work.

The auction house has a duty to the seller-consignor to formulate presale estimates within the demands of the

---

[Section 5:35]

[1]Cristallina S.A. v. Christie, Manson & Woods Intern., Inc., 117 A.D.2d 284, 291, 502 N.Y.S.2d 165 (1st Dep't 1986); *see also* McKie v. R.H. Love Galleries, Inc., 1990 WL 179797 (N.D. Ill. 1990).

market,[1] to recommend a reserve geared to triggering bidding on any given lot, and to disclose the meaning and effect of the reserve upon potential sales to the consignor. The duty is applicable to agency relationships where the agent, which does not itself auction, allows the consignor's paintings to be auctioned at prices below appraised values.[2] Failure to comply with the duty in certain circumstances can be actionable.[3] New or revised laws impose increasing duties on auctioneers in New York to improve the clarity of auctioneer's disclosures and disclaimers.[4]

§ 5:37 Statements of value as fact or opinion

Whether statements regarding value of property are expressions of opinion or representations of material fact to support a negligent or fraudulent misrepresentation claim depends upon the person making the statement, the relationship of the parties, and the circumstances of the

---

[Section 5:36]

[1]Kremer v. Janet Fleisher Gallery, Inc., 320 Pa. Super. 384, 467 A.2d 377 (1983) (dealer's obligations to sell art at auction at prices reflecting true and fair value).

[2]Kremer v. Janet Fleisher Gallery, Inc., 320 Pa. Super. 384, 467 A.2d 377 (1983) (dismissal not appropriate in action where dealer had works sold at auction below their appraised values. Consignor-seller was held entitled to new trial on negligence against the dealer; refusal to admit evidence on value constituted clear error).

[3]Cristallina S.A. v. Christie, Manson & Woods Intern., Inc., 117 A.D.2d 284, 502 N.Y.S.2d 165 (1st Dep't 1986) (summary judgment not appropriate where there was a triable issue of fact as to whether auction house acted with skill in setting estimates and reserves); *see also* Kremer v. Janet Fleisher Gallery, Inc., 320 Pa. Super. 384, 467 A.2d 377 (1983) (reversing judgment against seller-consignor, whose works were sold at auction below prices appraised by the dealer who had arranged for their auction at a particular house).

[4]NY Arts & Cult. Aff. art. 13; *cf.* U.S. v. Von Cseh, 354 F. Supp. 315 (S.D. Tex. 1972) (in government action to foreclose a tax lien on a painting, the federal district court concluded that the phrase "without reserve" was a term of art meaning that: (1) the property would go to the highest bidder; and (2) the property would not be withdrawn from the sale before the acceptance of a bid; "without reserve" was therefore not equivalent to a term of sale "without restriction").

valuation.[1] Statements of value have been regarded as representations of fact actionable under misrepresentation claims in the context of the consignor-auction relationship. In Esskay,[2] a federal district court considering fraud claims brought by buyers against auctioneers for sale of overvalued jewelry decided that an oral appraisal of value, combined with other factual statements made by an auctioneer to a prospective bidder, constituted material representations of fact. Since statements of value were made about specialized goods "peculiarly within [the auctioneer's] knowledge . . . coupled with statements of other facts which affect . . . value . . . to an innocent and unwitting purchaser,"[3] such statements were held to constitute material facts to support fraud. In awarding the difference between the appraised price and the purchase price to plaintiffs, the court observed:

> While statements relative to the value of property are ordinarily mere expressions of opinion, the statements made by the [auctioneer] were made as a fact . . . and concerned a subject . . . peculiarly within his knowledge. Furthermore, the representations of value were coupled with statements of other facts which affected value and satisfactorily explained, especially to the innocent and unwitting purchaser, the reason for the sale so far below represented value. Therefore, the statements . . . as to the value of the jewelry were statements of material fact.[4]

In Cristallina,[5] where auctioneers induced a seller to sell art at auction by providing unrealistically high values, failing to disclose risks of auction, and setting the reserves

---

[Section 5:37]

[1] *See* McNally v. Yarnall, 764 F. Supp. 838, 844 (S.D. N.Y. 1991); Struna v. Wolf, 126 Misc. 2d 1031, 484 N.Y.S.2d 392 (Sup 1985); McKie v. R.H. Love Galleries, Inc., 1990 WL 179797 (N.D. Ill. 1990).

[2] Pasternack v. Esskay Art Galleries, Inc., 90 F. Supp. 849 (W.D. Ark. 1950).

[3] Pasternack v. Esskay Art Galleries, Inc., 90 F. Supp. 849 (W.D. Ark. 1950) (auctioneer's statements to buyer that jewelry purchased for $16,000 would be a good value and could be sold separately for substantially greater amounts constituted material fact).

[4] Pasternack v. Esskay Art Galleries, Inc., 90 F. Supp. 849 (W.D. Ark. 1950).

[5] Cristallina S.A. v. Christie, Manson & Woods Intern., Inc., 117 A.D.2d 284, 502 N.Y.S.2d 165 (1st Dep't 1986).

at amounts higher than presale estimates, the court found statements of value could support misrepresentation claims. The court concluded that the auctioneer "had an obligation to render such opinion [about value and marketability of paintings] truthfully." The court further stated that when the opinion predicts some future event, known by the author to be false or made despite the anticipation that the event will not occur, the opinion constitutes a statement of material fact sufficient to support fraud.

Statements of value may constitute facts for purposes of other claims, e.g., defamation.[6]

§ 5:38 Duty to use reasonable efforts to communicate

Restatement (Second) of Agency[1] describes an agent's duty to communicate: "[A]gent is subject to a duty to use reasonable efforts to give his principal information which is relevant to affairs entrusted to him and which, as the agent has notice, the principal would desire to have and which can be communicated without violating a superior duty." In Cristallina,[2] the court held that auctioneers have duties to keep consignors apprised of their conduct and activities. Specifically, the auctioneers had a duty to communicate that they disagreed amongst themselves as to the marketability of the paintings, that presale estimates originally quoted were in question, and that reserves were set higher than or equal to high presale estimates. But in Kohler,[3] failure of the auctioneer to communicate to the consignors: (1) that the authenticity of a painting they had

---

[6]*See, e.g.,* McNally v. Yarnall, 764 F. Supp. 838, 844 (S.D. N.Y. 1991); Milkovich v. Lorain Journal Co., 497 U.S. 1, 110 S. Ct. 2695, 2705, 111 L. Ed. 2d 1, 60 Ed. Law Rep. 1061 (1990); McKie v. R.H. Love Galleries, Inc., 1990 WL 179797 (N.D. Ill. 1990); Struna v. Wolf, 126 Misc. 2d 1031, 484 N.Y.S.2d 392 (Sup 1985).

[Section 5:38]

[1]Restatement (Second) of Agency § 381.

[2]Cristallina S.A. v. Christie, Manson & Woods Intern., Inc., 117 A.D.2d 284, 502 N.Y.S.2d 165 (1st Dep't 1986).

[3]Kohler v. Leslie Hindman, Inc., 1995 WL 89015 (N.D. Ill. 1995), aff'd, 80 F.3d 1181, 34 Fed. R. Serv. 3d 1342 (7th Cir. 1996); *cf.* Nelson v. Sotheby's, Inc., 128 F. Supp. 2d 1172 (N.D. Ill. 2001) (defendant's motion to dismiss denied on breach of contract and granted on breach

consigned for auction was at issue; and (2) the existence of an oral side agreement with a prospective buyer regarding authenticating the painting and rescinding the sale, were not considered actionable.[4]

§ 5:39 Duty not to undertake the impossible or impracticable

Restatement (Second) of Agency[1] defines as an agent's duty "not to continue to render service which subjects the principal to risk of expense if it reasonably appears to him to be impossible or impracticable for him to accomplish the objects of the principal." Where an auctioneer knows of problems in selling paintings at auction, it may have a duty not to pursue the sale under the duty not to attempt the impossible or impracticable.[2]

C. CONTRACT

§ 5:40 Consignment agreement

The written consignment agreement between the auction entity and the consignor is ordinarily drafted by the auction and, except in rare circumstances, is not negotiable.[1] Ambiguities in the contract may be resolved against the drafter of the contract under general principles interpreting contracts of adhesion,[2] but some courts have imputed to participants a certain level of knowledge about

---

of fiduciary duty when auction house, to whom plaintiff consigned painting by Giorgio de Chirico for appraisal, failed to communicate resolution of disputed ownership or return painting).

[4]Kohler v. Leslie Hindman, Inc., 1995 WL 89015 (N.D. Ill. 1995), aff'd, 80 F.3d 1181, 34 Fed. R. Serv. 3d 1342 (7th Cir. 1996) (auction house had no obligation to enforce sale of painting or pursue buyer for payment where it had unconditional authority to cancel).

[Section 5:39]

[1]Restatement (Second) of Agency § 384.

[2]Cristallina S.A. v. Christie, Manson & Woods Intern., Inc., 117 A.D.2d 284, 502 N.Y.S.2d 165 (1st Dep't 1986).

[Section 5:40]

[1]*See* Appendix 10, pp. 10-2 to 10-4; *see also* § 5:32.

[2]Walt Disney Productions v. Basmajian, 600 F. Supp. 439 (S.D. N.Y. 1984); Basmajian v. Christie, Manson & Woods Intern., Inc., 629 F. Supp. 995, 998 (S.D. N.Y. 1986).

the risks of art auction.

§ 5:41 Relationship between consignment agreement and conditions of sale agreement

The auction entity's obligations under the consignment agreement are not necessarily the sole contractual obligations that affect the seller-consignor relationship. Conditions of sale agreements entered into between the auction and the buyer may affect the auction house's contractual duties to the seller.[1] Where the auction house's consignment agreement expressly incorporates by reference the conditions of sale, the courts have utilized both contracts in determining claims. In Kohler v. Leslie Hindman, Inc.,[2] consignors sued the Chicago-based auction house on a sale of their painting the "Plains of Meudon," purportedly by Theodore Rousseau. The painting sported papers and documentation, which were provided to the auction. The auction catalogue recited that the painting was "by" Rousseau, which indicated for that house that it believed the painting to be by the artist.[3]

A prospective bidder raised authenticity questions in 1991 on the eve of auction. Rather than withdrawing the painting from auction, a right the parties agreed the auction had under language of the consignment agreement allowing withdrawal "before sale if the [auction house] deem[s] it unsuitable for auction for any reason whatsoever," the auction house permitted the bidder to take the work for authentication to an agreed-upon expert. No payment was required in advance. When the expert decided it was not by Rousseau, the auction house rescinded the sale, relying upon the following powers conferred by the consignment agreement: "[R]escission was permitted [i]f [auction] at any time in [its] sole discretion determined that the offering for sale of the property . . . subjected [it

[Section 5:41]

[1]*See* § 5:53; *see also* Appendix 10, pp. 10-5 to 10-6 for a sample conditions of sale agreement.

[2]Kohler v. Leslie Hindman, Inc., 1995 WL 89015 (N.D. Ill. 1995), judgment aff'd, 80 F.3d 1181, 34 Fed. R. Serv. 3d 1342 (7th Cir. 1996).

[3]*See* Chart 5-6 for examples of other auction catalogue recitations regarding authenticity of works.

or consignors] to any liability under a warranty of authenticity."

The consignors sued for breach of contract alleging that the auction house had made an unauthorized warranty of authenticity to the buyer, relying upon an "as is" provision in the conditions of sale agreement, contained in the auction catalogue and incorporated by reference into the consignment agreement: "All lots are sold 'AS IS' and neither Hindman nor the Consignor makes any warranties or representations, express or implied, with respect to such lots."[4] Initially, the court denied the auction house's motion to dismiss for failure to state a contract claim.[5] Granting summary judgment in favor of the auction house on a subsequent motion, the court concluded that the "as is" provisions in the sales agreement did not abrogate the auction house's broad rights to rescind under the consignment agreement.[6] Rejecting the consignors' argument that the auction house was precluded from acting under the consignment agreement after it altered its warranty exclusions in the "as is" provision of the sales agreement, the court concluded that recitation of the "by" in the catalogue could have constituted a warranty of title, subjecting it and the Kohlers to liability, and therefore additional grounds to rescind.[7]

Thus, a breach of contract claim against an auction house for rescinding to a third-party buyer a sale of a painting, "Plains of Meudon," purportedly by Theodore Rousseau, was disposed of by summary judgment in favor of the auction house, based upon terms of the consignment agreement. Although the defendant auction house without the knowledge of the consignors, had entered into a separate oral side agreement with the buyer regarding the painting's authenticity and allowing him time to authenticate it, the court concluded that neither the consignment

---

[4]Kohler v. Leslie Hindman, Inc., 1995 WL 89015 (N.D. Ill. 1995), judgment aff'd, 80 F.3d 1181, 34 Fed. R. Serv. 3d 1342 (7th Cir. 1996).

[5]Kohler v. Leslie Hindman, Inc., 1994 WL 233801 (N.D. Ill. 1994).

[6]Kohler v. Leslie Hindman, Inc., 1995 WL 89015 (N.D. Ill. 1995), judgment aff'd, 80 F.3d 1181, 34 Fed. R. Serv. 3d 1342 (7th Cir. 1996).

[7]Kohler v. Leslie Hindman, Inc., 1994 WL 233801 at ¶¶ 14–15 (N.D. Ill. 1994).

agreement nor the sales agreement had been breached.[8]

D. INDEMNIFICATION

§ 5:42 Generally

Restatement (Second) of Agency establishes a duty of the principal, unless otherwise agreed, to indemnify the agent for, inter alia, authorized payments made on his behalf, payments upon obligations arising from possession of goods which the agent is authorized to hold on account of the principal, and expenses of defending actions by third persons brought because of the agent's authorized conduct.[1]

Typical of auction consignment contracts is a broad provision whereby the seller-consignor agrees to indemnify and hold harmless the auction for "any and all losses, damages, liabilities, claims and all fees, costs and expenses of any kind" relating to the sale of the consigned artwork.[2]

§ 5:43 Warranty of title

Duties of the consignor to indemnify for clear title may be brought by the auction house against the consignor before or after auction. In Ichiyasu v. Christie, Manson & Woods, International, Inc.,[1] the auction house filed a third-party complaint against a dealer-consignor for breach of

---

[8]Kohler v. Leslie Hindman, Inc., 1995 WL 89015 (N.D. Ill. 1995), judgment aff'd, 80 F.3d 1181, 34 Fed. R. Serv. 3d 1342 (7th Cir. 1996); *but see* Kohler v. Leslie Hindman, Inc., 1995 WL 250427 (N.D. Ill. 1995) (denying attorney fees and costs to defendant auction house under consignment agreement provision for same because the action for which fees were sought arose from verbal side agreement made by defendant with third-party buyer that was unrelated to breach of consignors' warranty under the consignment agreement that triggered the attorney fees provision).

[Section 5:42]

[1]*See generally* Restatement of (Second) Agency §§ 438, 439.

[2]*See* Appendix 10 for an example of an indemnity clause in a consignment agreement.

[Section 5:43]

[1]Ichiyasu v. Christie, Manson & Woods Intern., Inc., 630 F. Supp. 340 (N.D. Ill. 1986).

the implied and express warranties of good title based on the consignment agreement. Christie's had auctioned a lithograph, La Femme Au Tambourin, by Pablo Picasso, and paid the dealer $88,150, who in turn paid the alleged thief. The dealer in turn filed a cross-claim against its consignor, alleging that it had acted within the scope of its authority vis-a-vis Christie's, and that the consignor owed the dealer a duty of indemnity.

§ 5:44 Legal fees

The propriety of an auction house deducting legal fees from proceeds paid to consignors pursuant to indemnification was considered under both contractual terms and common law in Basmajian v. Christie's, Manson & Woods, International, Inc.[1] There the contract incorporated the common law of agency, reciting that the auction house as agent was allowed to deduct "any expenses due it."

The consignor, a former animator and employee at Walt Disney Studios, amassed, with Disney's permission, celluloids, sketches and drawings otherwise designated for the trash heap forty years prior to auction. Over the years, he had them matted, framed, and inventoried, and in time they increased in value. When Disney discovered Basmajian was auctioning the materials, it sued the animator for damages and injunctive relief. Christie's voluntarily entered that litigation with its own counsel, and did not pay for Basmajian's counsel. Basmajian was declared the prima facie owner at a hearing, and Disney later voluntarily dismissed the underlying lawsuit.

After Christie's auctioned the art, it withheld attorney's fees relating to that lawsuit from the auction proceeds remitted to Basmajian, and he sued the auction for conversion. On summary judgment motion, the district court awarded Basmajian the amount of attorney's fees withheld, plus interest and costs, holding that Christie's was not entitled to legal fees under principles of agency.

Christie's contract provided that the consignor was responsible for "claims, loss, liabilities and expenses

---

[Section 5:44]

[1]Basmajian v. Christie, Manson & Woods Intern., Inc., 629 F. Supp. 995 (S.D. N.Y. 1986).

(including reasonable attorney's fees) relating to the claims of buyers or persons claiming for buyers." The court found that Disney was a third party claimant, not a "buyer" or a "person claiming for a buyer" under the terms of the consignment contract.

Christie's contract also authorized it to deduct "any expenses due it," interpreted by the court as common law indemnification of agency. But where "the principal defends himself, the agent is not eligible for indemnification unless the principal's defense leaves the agent's interests unprotected." Finding that Basmajian's counsel protected the position of the auction house, the federal district court wrote: "[T]he defense of [Basmajian's] title necessarily protected Christie's ability to proceed with the auction . . . [t]he Disney suit was not a post hoc damages action [following the agency] but an ex ante equity action. The distinction . . . alters the relationship between principal and agent at the time the legal fees are incurred."[2]

Another contractual provision in Christie's consignment agreement provided that the auction house could deduct "any expenses incurred for seller's account." The court concluded that meant payments made on the seller's behalf. Since Basmajian retained and paid for his own lawyers in the Disney action, and Christie's did not retain counsel on his behalf, the court found the "causal nexus" did not transform Christie's expenditure of legal fees into "expenses incurred for seller's account."

In Kohler,[3] an auction house sought attorney fees and costs pursuant to an indemnification clause in the consignment agreement. The court had previously ordered summary judgment in favor of the auction house on a breach of contract claim arising from the consignment agreement, where the plaintiffs had unsuccessfully contested the auction house's rescission of a sale involving their consigned painting. The indemnity clause, in pertinent part, provided that the auction house was entitled to fees and costs "relating to claims of purchasers arising out of [consignor] breach or alleged breach of any representation or warran-

---

[2]Basmajian v. Christie, Manson & Woods Intern., Inc., 629 F. Supp. 995 at 1000 (S.D. N.Y. 1986).

[3]Kohler v. Leslie Hindman, Inc., 1995 WL 250427 (N.D. Ill. 1995).

ties resulting from the offer for sale by us of any property consigned under this Agreement." Since the underlying litigation was not based upon the consignors' representations about the authenticity of their painting, but upon the auction house's oral side agreement relating to authenticity with a prospective seller, the court denied the motion for fees and costs.

E. FRAUD

§ 5:45 Constructive fraud

Constructive fraud is variously defined under state laws as a breach of legal or equitable duty deemed fraudulent because of its tendency to deceive others, although ordinarily it does not require actual dishonesty or intent to deceive. Pleading the context of the duty and the specific elements for the fraud should be examined under the laws of the particular jurisdiction.

In Kohler v. Leslie Hindman, Inc., an action for constructive fraud brought by consignors against an auction house arising from a rescinded sale of a painting, the court applied the definition as follows: "any act, statement or omission which amounts to positive fraud or which is construed as a fraud by the courts because of its detrimental effect upon public interest and public or private confidence."[1] The consignor testified that he wanted the sale enforced regardless of whether or not the painting was authentic, and he expected his share of the proceeds from the $90,000 bid even if the painting were forged. Granting summary judgment in favor of the auction house, the court noted, "As we see it, it was the [consignors], and not [the auction house], that sought to perpetrate a fraud against public interests and public confidence."[2]

F. REMEDIES

§ 5:46 Damages—Contract

When a breach of the agent's duty occurs, the auction as

[Section 5:45]

[1] Kohler v. Leslie Hindman, Inc., 1995 WL 89015 (N.D. Ill. 1995), judgment aff'd, 80 F.3d 1181, 34 Fed. R. Serv. 3d 1342 (7th Cir. 1996).

[2] Kohler v. Leslie Hindman, Inc., 1995 WL 89015 at ¶ 22 (N.D. Ill. 1995).

agent is liable to the principal for damages, whether the cause of action is based on contract or in tort.[1] The measure of damages depends upon the underlying action and the circumstances.

Restatement (Second) of Agency, noting that the law of contract damages is "sometimes unique when applied to agency situations," states that the agent is generally liable for harm, for loss of profits reasonably anticipated and which would have been made but for the agent's failure, and excludes remote or avoidable consequences.[2]

§ 5:47 Damages—Tort

Tort damages seek to make the plaintiff whole, or in the same condition he was in before the tort. Thus, courts have measured damages as the difference between the value of the artwork pre-auction and post-auction, where the work did not sell at auction and allegedly declined in price afterward as a result of burn.[1] Pre-auction values may be established by presale estimates, insured values, appraisals and bona fide sales, and "may serve as the basis of a damage award."[2] Post-sale values may be established by appraisals.

§ 5:48 Damages—Punitive

Punitive damages, not available in contract actions, may be awarded where authorized by law depending upon facts and circumstances, which are presented to the trier of

---

[Section 5:46]

[1]Cristallina S.A. v. Christie, Manson & Woods Intern., Inc., 117 A.D.2d 284, 502 N.Y.S.2d 165 (1st Dep't 1986).

[2]Restatement (Second) of Agency § 400; *see also* Restatement of Contracts § 330.

[Section 5:47]

[1]Cristallina S.A. v. Christie, Manson & Woods Intern., Inc., 117 A.D.2d 284, 502 N.Y.S.2d 165 (1st Dep't 1986).

[2]Cristallina S.A. v. Christie, Manson & Woods Intern., Inc., 117 A.D.2d 284, 502 N.Y.S.2d 165 (1st Dep't 1986).

fact.[1]

V. LIABILITY: RELATIONSHIP WITH BUYERS

A. IN GENERAL

§ 5:49 Checklist: Potential causes of action by buyer

(1) Breach of contract

(2) Breach of warranty

(3) Negligent misrepresentation

(4) Fraud

(5) Fraudulent misrepresentation

(6) Breach of the duty of good faith and fair dealing, unfair consumer practices

(7) Breach of consumer warranties

(8) Consumer fraud

(9) Rescission

B. AUTHENTICATION

§ 5:50 Generally

Establishing authorship in the arts is a process known as authentication. The courts are divided as to whether authentication in art trading is a fact or opinion, giving rise to either express or implied warranties.[1] Auction, however, is a special art trading forum, among the riskiest secondary market transactions. Buyers are assumed to know the risks, and those risks are recognized in the auction process:

[Section 5:48]

[1]Cristallina S.A. v. Christie, Manson & Woods Intern., Inc., 117 A.D.2d 284, 502 N.Y.S.2d 165 (1st Dep't 1986); *but cf.* Jeanneret v. Vichey, 693 F.2d 259, 35 U.C.C. Rep. Serv. 75 (2d Cir. 1982).

[Section 5:50]

[1]*See* Ch 4; *see also* Pilliard v. Sotheby's, Inc., motion for recon., 1998 WL 126060 (S.D.N.Y. MAr. 19, 1998). Private Letter Ruling, PLR 9728005, 1997 WL 381975 (I.R.S. PLR 1997) (issues of authenticity and value exist also between consignors and auction houses); *see also* §§ 5:31 to 5:49.

(1) Bidders ordinarily have an opportunity prior to auction to visually inspect the art, and retain their own experts to evaluate it;

(2) The hammer price is one indicia of market reaction to the work, including the CROSSAQ factor. As the court stated in Weisz, "a . . . factor entering into competition among bidders at the public auction [i]s the variable value of the paintings depending upon the degree of certainty with which they could be authenticated and established as the works of the ascribed artist."[2]

Auctions do not establish authenticity vis-a-vis the public, whatever their internal practices,[3] nor has any reported opinion considered them guarantors of authenticity in the absence of fraud or sharp trade practices, providing the terms of auction are adequately disclosed and warranties are disclaimed. The auction, however, that represents by affirmation or omission that a work is authentic, when it knows or should know authenticity is in dispute, exposes itself to liability.[4]

Buyers are ordinarily given opportunities before auction to inspect and investigate the authenticity of particular artworks in the auction showroom. Even after auction a buyer with a legitimate authenticity challenge may obtain a refund or a net refund within the limitation terms of the sales contract as a matter of the house's practice or policy. And where buyers still question authenticity in post-sale circumstances, the auction house may rescind the contract

---

[2]Weisz v. Parke-Bernet Galleries, Inc., 67 Misc. 2d 1077, 325 N.Y.S.2d 576, 10 U.C.C. Rep. Serv. 292 (City Civ. Ct. 1971), judgment rev'd, 77 Misc. 2d 80, 351 N.Y.S.2d 911, 912, 14 U.C.C. Rep. Serv. 358 (App. Term 1974) (buyer's could not complain after making bad bargain). *See* § 2:22 for discussion of CROSSAQ.

[3]Greenwood v. Koven, 1993 WL 541181 (S.D. N.Y. 1993), on reconsideration in part, 880 F. Supp. 186 (S.D. N.Y. 1995).

[4]McCloud v. Lawrence Gallery, Ltd., 1991 WL 136027 (S.D. N.Y. 1991); McCloud v. Lawrence Gallery, Ltd., 1992 WL 6199 (S.D. N.Y. 1992), aff'd, 970 F.2d 896 (2d Cir. 1992) (auction house offered a Pablo Picasso drawing with knowledge that its authenticity was in dispute; Comite Picasso subsequently rejected the drawing as inauthentic).

and refund the purchase price upon tender of the art.[5]

An authentication generally identifies authorship of the object, discussed under the CROSSAQ factor.[6] In common parlance, this is referred to as attributing an artist to an object. At auction, the term "attribution" takes on a different meaning, i.e., it functions as a term of art. An attribution to an artist made by an auction means that authenticity is uncertain; the auction believes it could be by the artist named in the attribution but is not sure. This auction trade practice contrasts with noncommercial definitions of attribution used in the field of authentication.[7] Example: Painting *X* is by Pablo Picasso. (This attribution ordinarily constitutes an authentication in private trade.) Compare Painting *X* is "attributed to" Pablo Picasso. (This attribution does *not* constitute an authentication at auction.)

Duties of auctioneers do not coincide with duties of other traders in authenticating artworks, and primary and secondary market transactions are associated with different terms and different levels of risk. The opinions reflect *caveat emptor,* a buyer who comes to an art auction is expected to know the risks.

§ 5:51 Catalogues

Auction houses have been sued for the accuracy of their representations or omissions about authorship and provenance. Claims for breach of warranties, misrepresentation (fraudulent, reckless and negligent), breach of the duty of good faith and fair dealing, fraud, unfair consumer practices, or breach of consumer warranties, false provenance and others have been claimed.

The contractual relationship typically examined by the courts is one or all of the following: Condition of sale agreements, catalogue warranties and disclaimers, and "as is"

[5]Greenwood v. Koven, 1993 WL 541181 (S.D. N.Y. 1993), on reconsideration in part, 880 F. Supp. 186 (S.D. N.Y. 1995) (pastel by Braque that was auctioned by Christie's, and subsequently could not be authenticated by successors of George Braque in France, was grounds for voluntary rescission of the purchase and sale contract, and refund of the purchase price).

[6]*See* Ch 3 § 3:19.

[7]*See* Ch 10.

clauses. Catalogues usually contain the aforementioned provisions as well as encoded notification systems. The "attribution" referred to above is but one of many codes contained in art auction catalogues. A review of the limited number of relevant opinions leads to the conclusion that the uninitiated who buy without understanding the meaning of the codes and the clauses are generally unprotected by the courts.

Auction catalogues use a multiple notification system using terms and fonts to put bidders on inquiry notice about the authenticity of the work. The term-and-font system is intended to alert prospective bidders to potential authenticity problems.[1] Each auction may use its own code system; a sample of what some auctions have used follows:

Chart 5-4: Sample Auction Catalogue Codes

FONTS:	For Paintings	All capital letters [PABLO PICASSO]:	In the opinion of the auction, a work by the artist.

[Section 5:51]

[1]*See, e.g.,* Weisz v. Parke-Bernet Galleries, Inc., 67 Misc. 2d 1077, 325 N.Y.S.2d 576, 10 U.C.C. Rep. Serv. 292 (City Civ. Ct. 1971), judgment rev'd on other grounds, 77 Misc. 2d 80, 351 N.Y.S.2d 911, 14 U.C.C. Rep. Serv. 358 (App. Term 1974); *see* Ch 12 § 12:24 (linguistic conventions, terms and usages generally accepted in the trade where authorship is in doubt).

	For Sculptures	All capital letters [DAVID SMITH]:	(1) In the opinion of the auction, a work by the artist. (2) For multiples, means work has been cast with artist's or estate's consent. (3) For marble, wood, or other hand carved medium, means work has been carved by artist or his studio under his supervision.
<u>TERMS:</u>	For Paintings, Drawings, Prints, and Miniatures, unless Sculptures are indicated parenthetically		
	"signed"		In the opinion of the auction, it is the signature of the artist.
	"bears a signature"		In the opinion of the auction, it might be the signature of the artist.
	"dated"		Is so dated and in the opinion of the auction was executed at about that date.

"bears date"		Is so dated and in the opinion of the auction may have been executed at about that date.
"attributed to"	(painting, et al.)	In the opinion of auction, work made during period of artist which may be in whole or in part work by the artist
"attributed to"	(sculpture)	In the opinion of the auction, a work of the period of the artist which may be work of the artist
"after"	(painting, et al.)	In the opinion of auction, a copy of work of the artist
"after"	(sculpture)	In the opinion of the auction, a later unauthorized copy after a work by the artist and not directly connected with the artist, studio, or estate.

Auction catalogues reciting express disclaimers regarding provenance have been upheld as valid against actions for false provenance.[2]

---

[2]Foxley v. Sotheby's Inc., 893 F. Supp. 1224, 27 U.C.C. Rep. Serv. 2d 1234 (S.D. N.Y. 1995) (catalogue recited ". . . neither [the auction] nor the Consignor make any warranties or representations of the cor-

§ 5:52 Conditions of sale contracts

Bills of sale, conditions of sale contracts, and other sales memoranda further recite limitations, often also included in the auction catalogues, such as, "any statement of the auction is opinion"; "artworks are sold as is"; "no warranties are made for title, authenticity, attribution, provenance, condition, or restoration." A sample auction conditions of sales contract is contained in Appendix 10. Absent fraud, "as is" clauses have been held enforceable in most jurisdictions if they are clear and brought to the attention of the buyer, either through text location, font size, or signature acknowledgment.[1]

Sales memoranda and catalogues ordinarily include express disclaimers by the auction regarding warranties of authenticity, attribution, provenance, and the like. Many auctions require the buyer to acknowledge the disclaimer by signing it.

§ 5:53 Oral authentications

Actions for fraud have been brought by buyers against auctioneers when the auctioneer—in the absence of written descriptions—made oral representations about authenticity. In Plimpton v. Friedberg,[1] a buyer purchased English paintings asserted by the auctioneer to be genuine prior to sale, and supported by authenticating docu-

---

rectness of the catalogue or other description [including] . . . provenance . . . .").

[Section 5:52]

[1]Weisz v. Parke-Bernet Galleries, Inc., 67 Misc. 2d 1077, 325 N.Y.S.2d 576, 10 U.C.C. Rep. Serv. 292 (City Civ. Ct. 1971), judgment rev'd, 77 Misc. 2d 80, 351 N.Y.S.2d 911, 14 U.C.C. Rep. Serv. 358 (App. Term 1974) (catalogue disclaimed any representation of genuineness, and disclaimed warranty that paintings were products of artists listed in catalogues); *but cf.* Kohler v. Leslie Hindman, Inc., 1994 WL 233801 (N.D. Ill. 1994); and Kohler v. Leslie Hindman, Inc., 1995 WL 89015 (N.D. Ill. 1995), judgment aff'd, 80 F.3d 1181, 34 Fed. R. Serv. 3d 1342 (7th Cir. 1996) (oral side agreement with bidder overrode warranty disclaimers recited in the "as is" provisions in the conditions of sales agreement); *see* §§ 5:43 to 5:45.

[Section 5:53]

[1]Plimpton v. Friedberg, 110 N.J.L. 427, 166 A. 295 (N.J. Ct. Err. & App. 1933).

ments after sale. When the paintings were subsequently determined to be fakes, the buyer sued for fraud.

The trial court entered judgment of nonsuit for the auctioneer. The appellate court reversed and ordered a new trial,[2] based upon the auctioneer's testimony. He had represented that the paintings were authentic, although: (1) he lacked personal knowledge as to the authorship of the paintings; (2) he lacked any information on the genuineness of the paintings; and (3) he had no direct communication with the consignor regarding authenticity.[3]

In Phillips,[4] which was based not on authenticity but on completeness of lot contents, the buyer claimed that the auction made oral representations that a particular lot constituted the entire amount of Rudolf Bauer drawings from a specific estate. He purchased the lot. Within one year, the buyer discovered the same auction house was auctioning additional drawings by the same artist from the same estate. A federal district court denied a motion for a temporary restraining order to stop the second auction because the conditions of sale in the contract "preclude[d] any oral statement from binding" the auctioneer.

§ 5:54 Misrepresentations: Negligence and fraud

Plaintiffs have alleged negligent, reckless and fraudulent representation by the auction with respect to authenticity.[1] There is little precedential authority interpreting such claims.[2]

---

[2]Plimpton v. Friedberg, 110 N.J.L. 427, 166 A. 295 at 297 (N.J. Ct. Err. & App. 1933).

[3]Plimpton v. Friedberg, 110 N.J.L. 427, 166 A. 295 at 297 (N.J. Ct. Err. & App. 1933).

[4]Phillips, Son & Neal, Inc. v. Borghi & Co., 1987 WL 27690 (S.D. N.Y. 1987).

[Section 5:54]

[1]*See* §§ 5:32 to 5:40 for negligent and fraudulent misrepresentation based upon value of objects auctioned.

[2]Plimpton v. Friedberg, 110 N.J.L. 427, 166 A. 295 (N.J. Ct. Err. & App. 1933) (fraud upheld against auction based on oral representations); Pasternack v. Esskay Art Galleries, Inc., 90 F. Supp. 849 (W.D. Ark. 1950) (fraud upheld in auction of jewelry); *see also* Barrett v. U.S.

§ 5:55 Warranty

In Weisz v. Parke-Bernet Galleries,[1] one buyer purchased at auction a painting by Raoul Dufy for $3300 and another purchased a Dufy at a subsequent auction for $9300. The paintings were subsequently determined to be fakes. The buyers sued the auction house for breach of express warranty. Both auction catalogues contained an alphabetical "List of Artists" cross-referenced to page numbers; on the relevant pages the name "RAOUL DUFY" appeared in "large black print," followed by smaller print reciting "French 1880–1953."

The "Conditions of Sale" in the catalogues stated that the art was sold "as is" and that "neither the [auction house] nor the [consignor] warrants or represents . . . the correctness . . . of genuineness [or] authorship . . . and no statement contained in the catalogue . . . shall be deemed to be such a warranty or representation."

The trial court found that the first buyer was not aware of the catalogue disclaimer, and could not be bound by it in the absence of the auction house doing "considerably

---

Banknote Corp., 806 F. Supp. 1094 (S.D. N.Y. 1992) (action for fraud based upon contents of lots); Ravenna v. Christie's Inc., 289 A.D.2d 15, 734 N.Y.S.2d 21 (1st Dep't 2001) (judgment dismissing complaint for negligent misrepresentation of origin of painting by auction house affirmed where no special relationship); Foxley v. Sotheby's Inc., 893 F. Supp. 1224, 27 U.C.C. Rep. Serv. 2d 1234 (S.D. N.Y. 1995) (claim for negligent misrepresentation arising from sale by auction house of painting purportedly by Mary Cassatt dismissed notwithstanding ongoing relationship because contacts did not establish fiduciary duty); Kelly v. Brooks, 1993 WL 88259 (S.D. N.Y. 1993) (fraud dismissed against auction where buyers had no reason to rely on authenticity, obtained their own expert opinions on authenticity, and auctioneer disclaimed authenticity); *cf.* McKie v. R.H. Love Galleries, Inc., 1990 WL 179797 (N.D. Ill. 1990) (denial of motion to dismiss fraud, negligent misrepresentation, and consumer fraud charges brought against gallery for sale of painting).

[Section 5:55]

[1]Weisz v. Parke-Bernet Galleries, Inc., 67 Misc. 2d 1077, 1079, 325 N.Y.S.2d 576, 10 U.C.C. Rep. Serv. 292 (City Civ. Ct. 1971), judgment rev'd, 77 Misc. 2d 80, 351 N.Y.S.2d 911, 14 U.C.C. Rep. Serv. 358 (App. Term 1974).

more . . . to call those conditions of sale to his attention."[2] The second buyer knew the conditions of sale, but for him the court found the disclaimer legally defective where "well-known [auction houses], linked in the minds of people with the handling, exhibition and sale of valuable artistic works and invested with an aura of expertness and reliability . . . inspire confidence that [works it sells are] genuine and that the listed artist in fact [is] the creator of the work."[3]

The appellate court reversed on the grounds that neither statutory nor common law "recognized the expressed opinion of the seller as giving rise to any implied warranty of authenticity of authorship,"[4] and that the prefatory terms of sale in the catalogue gave "a clear and unequivocal disclaimer of any express or implied warranty" of authenticity.

In Phillips,[5] no warranty was found to cover auction lot contents where the auction catalogue made no representations about what the lots contained.

§ 5:56 Disclaimers

Disclaimers relating to authentications have to be clearly indicated to prospective buyers and appear on documents that constitute recitations of the sale. Auctions do disclaim authenticity in their catalogues and sales agreements, and such disclaimers are ordinarily upheld in the absence of sharp practices or bad faith. Weisz found the "as is" and "conditions" clauses in the auction cata-

[2]Weisz v. Parke-Bernet Galleries, Inc., 67 Misc. 2d 1077, 1079, 325 N.Y.S.2d 576, 10 U.C.C. Rep. Serv. 292 (City Civ. Ct. 1971), judgment rev'd, 77 Misc. 2d 80, 351 N.Y.S.2d 911, 14 U.C.C. Rep. Serv. 358 (App. Term 1974), 67 Misc. 2d. at 1081, 325 N.Y.S.2d. at 580.

[3]Weisz v. Parke-Bernet Galleries, Inc., 67 Misc. 2d 1077, 1079, 325 N.Y.S.2d 576, 10 U.C.C. Rep. Serv. 292 (City Civ. Ct. 1971), judgment rev'd, 77 Misc. 2d 80, 351 N.Y.S.2d 911, 14 U.C.C. Rep. Serv. 358 (App. Term 1974), 67 Misc. 2d. at 1082, 325 N.Y.S.2d at 581.

[4]Weisz v. Parke-Bernet Galleries, Inc., 67 Misc. 2d 1077, 1079, 325 N.Y.S.2d 576, 10 U.C.C. Rep. Serv. 292 (City Civ. Ct. 1971), judgment rev'd, 77 Misc. 2d 80, 351 N.Y.S.2d 911, 14 U.C.C. Rep. Serv. 358 (App. Term 1974).

[5]Phillips, Son & Neal, Inc. v. Borghi & Co., 1987 WL 27690 (S.D. N.Y. 1987) (denying buyer a temporary restraining order to enjoin a second auction of drawings).

logue valid and enforceable disclaimers. The Weisz court found the prefatory terms of sale in the catalogue were a "clear, unequivocal disclaimer" about the genuineness of the paintings.[1]

In Kelly v. Brooks,[2] a federal district court dismissed a complaint brought by buyers against an auctioneer for breach of warranty, fraud, and misrepresentation, based upon paintings bought at auction to start their own art business. They subsequently claimed the paintings had questionable authenticity. One of the plaintiffs, a lawyer, had signed a bill of sale containing a written disclaimer, which included an "as is" clause. The disclaimer expressly excluded "genuineness, authorship, attribution, provenance," reciting as follows:

> All property is sold 'AS IS', and neither [auction] nor the Consignor make any guarantees, warranties or representations, expressed or implied, with respect to property purchased, and in no event shall the seller nor the consignor be responsible for genuineness, nor deemed to have made any representation of genuineness, authorship, attribution, provenance, period, culture, source, origin, or condition of the purchased property . . . . The purchase, by signing this Bill of Sale agrees to the above stated terms and conditions without exceptions.

The court found the disclaimer "clear and unequivocal." Since plaintiffs signed the disclaimer the court dismissed the argument that the disclaimer was not brought to their attention.

In Voitier v. Antique Art Gallery,[3] an appellate state court ordered rescission of a contract for sale of a painting, purportedly by George Inness, that the plaintiff purchased at auction by telephonic bid. When the painting arrived, it lacked the auction house's promised letter of

---

[Section 5:56]

[1]Weisz v. Parke-Bernet Galleries, Inc., 67 Misc. 2d 1077, 325 N.Y.S.2d 576, 10 U.C.C. Rep. Serv. 292 (City Civ. Ct. 1971), judgment rev'd, 77 Misc. 2d 80, 351 N.Y.S.2d 911, 912, 14 U.C.C. Rep. Serv. 358 (App. Term 1974).

[2]Kelly v. Brooks, 1993 WL 88259 (S.D. N.Y. 1993).

[3]Voitier v. Antique Art Gallery, 524 So. 2d 80 (La. Ct. App. 3d Cir. 1988), writ denied, 531 So. 2d 271 (La. 1988) (decided under Louisiana law, which did not adopt UCC Article 2).

authenticity. Authentications subsequently provided to the buyer were unsatisfactory, and the painting was determined to be fake.

The defendants did not argue that the Inness was genuine; they claimed no warranty of authenticity attached to the sale since the auction catalogue contained "as is" clauses. The catalogue further recited that neither the auction house nor its consignor was liable for description, genuineness, or provenance, and that no statement constituted warranty. The court found the auctioneer's disclaimer ineffective, since it did not appear anywhere on bills of sale or invoices presented to the buyer; that the terms were not brought to the buyer's attention nor explained to him; and that contrary to the catalogue disclaimer, the auction house had assured the buyer when he viewed the painting that the Inness was genuine, as well as advertising the painting as created by George Inness.

The circumstances are more complicated where a written appraisal, prepared by an auction house rather than an independent appraiser,[4] contains a disclaimer reciting that the auction is not authenticating the artwork. Even disclaiming, the appraiser may be liable if the appraisal is performed in bad faith or with gross negligence, particularly where facts casting doubt on authenticity are known to appraiser.[5]

§ 5:57 Breach of duty of honesty and fair dealing

In Kelly,[1] a federal district court dismissed a complaint for breach of the duty of honesty and fair dealing based upon an allegedly false authentication. Some jurisdictions uphold a requirement that the auctioneer engage in "fair dealing where there is a relationship between parties in which there is a basic inequality of knowledge, expertness

---

[4] *See* Ch 3 §§ 3:7 to 3:9 and 3:19.

[5] Foxley v. Sotheby's Inc., 893 F. Supp. 1224, 27 U.C.C. Rep. Serv. 2d 1234 (S.D. N.Y. 1995) (court refused to dismiss a complaint alleging bad faith and gross negligence against auction house, notwithstanding that its appraisal disclaimed authentication where pleading recited sufficient facts for fraudulent appraisal).

[Section 5:57]

[1] Kelly v. Brooks, 1993 WL 88259 (S.D. N.Y. 1993).

or economic power."[2] But it is not clear that buyers who come to auction can establish the requisite disparity of knowledge and reliance upon superior skill to establish the duty. In Kelly, the court found no reliance on expertise where the plaintiffs did independent research and had the paintings authenticated by experts prior to sale. If in fact the plaintiffs relied, said the court, the reliance was unreasonable, since they did not know the auctioneer when they purchased the paintings with which they planned to embark on a business making "large profit[s] on . . . resale."

§ 5:58 Mistake

The equitable doctrine of mistake is discussed in detail in Ch 4. The doctrine has been alleged by buyers against auctions.

In Voitier,[1] the court granted rescission of a sales contract by which plaintiff bought at auction a George Inness painting subsequently determined to be fake. Under Louisiana law, a contract may be invalidated for "unilateral error as to a fact which was the principle cause for making the contract, where the other party knew or should have known it was the principle cause. [citations omitted] Error as the nature or object may be with regard to either the substance or the object of the agreement, or substantial quality of the object, or some other quality of the object if such quality is the principle cause of making the contract."[2] Since before the auction defendant represented the painting as an Inness to plaintiff and advertised it as by Inness, the court found the buyer was entitled to rescission

---

[2]Weisz v. Parke-Bernet Galleries, Inc., 67 Misc. 2d 1077, 325 N.Y.S.2d 576, 10 U.C.C. Rep. Serv. 292 (City Civ. Ct. 1971), judgment rev'd on other grounds, 77 Misc. 2d 80, 351 N.Y.S.2d 911, 14 U.C.C. Rep. Serv. 358 (App. Term 1974).

[Section 5:58]

[1]Voitier v. Antique Art Gallery, 524 So. 2d 80 (La. Ct. App. 3d Cir. 1988), writ denied, 531 So. 2d 271 (La. 1988).

[2]Voitier v. Antique Art Gallery, 524 So. 2d 80 (La. Ct. App. 3d Cir. 1988), writ denied, 531 So. 2d 271 (La. 1988). 524 So. 2d at 83.

under unilateral mistake.[3]

§ 5:59 Remedies—Revocation by buyer: UCC Section 2-608

UCC Section 2-608 allows buyers to revoke acceptance of nonconforming goods, and to obtain by revocation all rights and duties as if they had rejected them. Section 2-608 provides:

> (1) The buyer may revoke his acceptance of a lot . . . whose nonconformity substantially impairs its value to him if he has accepted it:
>
> (a) On the reasonable assumption that its nonconformity would be cured and it has not been seasonably cured; or
>
> (b) Without discovery of such nonconformity if his acceptance was reasonably induced either by the difficulty of discovery before acceptance or by the seller's assurances.
>
> (2) Revocation of acceptance must occur within a reasonable time after the buyer discovers or should have discovered the ground for it and before any substantial change in condition of the goods which is not caused by their own defects. It is not effective until the buyer notifies the seller of it.
>
> (3) A buyer who so revokes has the same rights and duties with regard to the goods involved as if he had rejected them.[1]

This section has only recently been used by buyers claiming art is not authentic,[2] and no case has raised the provocative issue of whether the reasonable time period recited in Section 2-608 provides an alternative position for buyers frustrated by the four-year statute of limitations in Section 2-725.[3] Recovery of damages is still available to the buyer, since revocation does not require the buyer to elect.[4]

---

[3]Voitier v. Antique Art Gallery, 524 So. 2d 80 (La. Ct. App. 3d Cir. 1988), writ denied, 531 So. 2d 271 (La. 1988). *See also* §§ 5:85 to 5:86 regarding Mutual Mistake.

[Section 5:59]

[1]UCC § 2-608(1)–(3).

[2]David Tunick, Inc. v. Kornfeld, 813 F. Supp. 988 (S.D. N.Y. 1993).

[3]*See* UCC § 2-608, Official Comment ¶ 4.

[4]*See* UCC § 2-608, Official Comment ¶ 1.

In Tunick, Inc. v. Kornfeld,[5] the buyer promptly notified the gallery and owner that a Pablo Picasso print he bought at auction had a forged signature, tendered the print and demanded rescission of the contract. The court found these acts constituted revocation under Section 2-608.

§ 5:60 Remedies—Cure by seller: UCC Section 2-508

A revocation under UCC Section 2-608 triggers the seller's right to cure under UCC Section 2-508, which provides:

> (1) Where any tender or delivery by the seller is rejected because nonconforming and the time for performance has not yet expired, the seller may seasonably notify the buyer of his intention to cure and may then within the contract time make a conforming delivery.
>
> (2) Where the buyer rejects a nonconforming tender which the seller had reasonable grounds to believe would be acceptable with or without money allowance the seller may if he seasonably notifies the buyer have a further reasonable time to substitute a conforming tender.[1]

Conformance is discussed at Section 2-106: "Goods . . . are 'conforming' or conform to the contract when they are in accordance with the obligations under the contract."[2]

The degree to which an art seller can cure under UCC Section 2-508 is unclear. One-of-a-kind artworks should not be considered curable absent buyer agreement. Multiples pose different considerations. Multiples can be produced in many different ways.[3] Hand-made multiples are more like one-of-a-kinds than mass-produced multiples, and there are many multiples that fall in between. Some multiples may have more attributes of fungible goods, which should be eligible for cure under the UCC, than unique goods, which may or may not be curable. A court has held UCC Section 2-508 "is not applicable to prints . . . . Prints are inherently unique and are pur-

---

[5]David Tunick, Inc. v. Kornfeld, 813 F. Supp. 988 (S.D. N.Y. 1993).

[Section 5:60]

[1]UCC § 2-508(1)–(2).

[2]UCC § 2-106(2).

[3]*See* Ch 12.

chased for their aesthetic qualities and investment value. Such value is dictated by those attributed common only to the specific print purchased."[4]

In Tunick, Inc. v. Kornfeld,[5] a buyer was not required to accept as a UCC Section 2-508 cure a signed Pablo Picasso print from the same series as the print purchased at auction, which he claimed was not signed by Picasso. A district court decided that prints from a series by Picasso were not interchangeable conforming goods for purposes of cure under Section 2-508. Instead of relying on, or even utilizing UCC Section 2-106 on fungible goods, the court stated, "No court in this Circuit or in New York appears to have been presented with the question of whether a non-conforming tender of a work of art may be cured by an offer of a different but similar work."[6] The court concluded that the seller's offer of a replacement print, purportedly signed by Picasso, of Le Minotaurmachie was not interchangeable, and denied the dealer summary judgment.

The conclusion begs the question of whether or not the offered replacement was, or could be, interchangeable. The characterization of "different but similar" is problematic. Section 1-201 states, "fungible with respect to goods . . . means goods . . . of which any unit is, by nature or usage of trade, the equivalent of any other like unit. Goods which are not fungible shall be deemed fungible for the purposes of this code to the extent that under a particular agreement or document unlike units are treated as equivalents."[7]

§ 5:61 Remedies—Damages

UCC Section 2-714 provides, in pertinent part:

(2) The measure of damages for breach of warranty is the

---

[4]David Tunick, Inc. v. Kornfeld, 813 F. Supp. 988 (S.D. N.Y. 1993).

[5]David Tunick, Inc. v. Kornfeld, 813 F. Supp. 988 (S.D. N.Y. 1993).

[6]David Tunick, Inc. v. Kornfeld, 813 F. Supp. 988 (S.D. N.Y. 1993). The court supported its conclusion by referring to UCC § 2-716, the right to specific performance or replevin, although that claim was not alleged by plaintiff. Relying upon the official comment to § 2-716, the court found that specific performance is available for unique works of art, and that New York courts would find that prints are "intrinsically unique."

[7]UCC § 1-201(17).

difference at the time and place of acceptance between the value of the goods accepted and the value they would have had if they been as warranted, unless special circumstances show proximate damages of a different amount.
(3) In a proper case any incidental and consequential damages under the next section [2-715] may also be recovered.[1]

Damages have been recovered by buyers at auction, but the underlying claims were in tort rather than contract.[2]

C. GUARANTEES OF LOT CONTENTS

§ 5:62 Generally

Auction houses do not have a duty to specify to buyers that lots are unique or contain only certain works, but when they choose to do so the representations must be accurate under the information available to them from the consignor and/or others. In Barrett v. Banknote Corp.,[1] a buyer sued an auction house for intentional misrepresentation when it purchased old, rare bank notes, allegedly assured by the auction that there were no other specimens being sold by the defendant-seller-note printer. The auction occurred in November 1990; by June 1991 similar banknotes from the same archive of the same defendant were auctioned by the same auction house.

D. CONSUMER FRAUD

§ 5:63 Generally

Many states have consumer fraud and/or warranty laws that provide private rights of action. Whether consign-

---

[Section 5:61]

[1]UCC § 2-714(1)–(2).

[2]*Cf.* Balog v. Center Art Gallery-Hawaii, Inc., 745 F. Supp. 1556, 12 U.C.C. Rep. Serv. 2d 962 (D. Haw. 1990) (buyers from gallery entitled to breach of contract for sales of fake art); *see also* Menzel v. List, 22 A.D.2d 647, 253 N.Y.S.2d 43 (1st Dep't 1964) (damages from gallery for breach of warranty of title in sale of painting claimed by deportees after World War II decided on law prior to UCC).

[Section 5:62]

[1]Barrett v. U.S. Banknote Corp., 806 F. Supp. 1094 (S.D. N.Y. 1992) (plaintiff sued bank note printer for breach of contract, misrepresentation and breach of warranty).

ment and sale agreements constitute consumer transactions within the meaning of state consumer protection laws is determined by state law. A consignment agreement for sale of a painting by an auction house was held not to be a consumer transaction "primarily for personal, family or household purposes" in New York. A "unique, one-of-a-kind painting [is not] a typical consumer good, nor [is] an agreement governing the consignment for auction sale of . . . art[work] a consumer transaction within the meaning of [the statute]."[1] Similarly, a consignment agreement and secured promissory note whereby an auction house advanced funds secured by consignor's artwork was not a consumer contract.[2] Buyers have challenged sales made at auction under state consumer statutes based upon authenticity,[3] and value.[4] In Nataros v. Fine Arts Gallery, Inc.,[5] the Court of Appeals of Arizona, conceding that a misled consumer could use a state consumer fraud statute to sue an auctioneer for damages for concealing the provenance of art and misrepresenting its value, found

---

[Section 5:63]

[1]Mickle v. Christie's, Inc., 214 F. Supp. 2d 430 (S.D. N.Y. 2002) (statute establishing evidentiary requirements for typeface size in printed form consumer contracts inapplicable to auction house contracts).

[2]Christie's, Inc. v. Croce, 5 F. Supp. 2d 206 (S.D. N.Y. 1998) (auction house's advance of funds secured by paintings and drawings to refinance consignor's loan to another auction and for his speculative investment was not a consumer transaction under New York law).

[3]Adam A. Weschler & Son, Inc. v. Klank, 561 A.2d 1003 (D.C. 1989) (action by auction entity to recover monies from buyer, dismissed where buyer filed consumer complaint under District of Columbia law claiming chest was inauthentic and not as described in auction catalogue); Kohler v. Leslie Hindman, Inc., 1995 WL 89015 (N.D. Ill. 1995), judgment aff'd, 80 F.3d 1181, 34 Fed. R. Serv. 3d 1342 (7th Cir. 1996) (seller who rescinded sale of painting cross-claimed against auction house for breach of contract, fraud, promissory estoppel, and violations of Illinois Consumer Fraud and Deceptive Business Practices, 815 Ill. Comp. Stat. § 505/2).

[4]Nataros v. Fine Arts Gallery of Scottsdale, Inc., 126 Ariz. 44, 612 P.2d 500 (buyers at auction brought consumer fraud action against auctioneer under Arizona law, alleging values and appraisals were false).

[5]Nataros v. Fine Arts Gallery of Scottsdale, Inc., 126 Ariz. 44, 612 P.2d 500.

that plaintiffs did not prove the requisite injury was caused by the alleged misrepresentations. Upholding a directed verdict for the defendants, the court stated, "[e]ven indulging in this assumption [that the art purchased was from an advertised estate within the meaning of A.R.S. 44-1522], no evidence was introduced . . . that such a misrepresentation resulted in any damage . . . There is no evidence to show that if the items purchased . . . [were from the Estate] they would have a greater value than if purchased [elsewhere]."[6]

In Wechsler v. Klank,[7] where the buyer refused to pay the auction after bidding several thousand dollars above the high presale estimate, the auctioneer's suit to recover monies owed was dismissed by the District of Columbia court because the buyer filed a consumer complaint against the auction.

E. VALUE

§ 5:64 Generally

Buyers have sued the auction entity, auctioneers, and owners of the auction for negligent misrepresentation and fraud based upon false representations of value, even where authenticity was not challenged.[1] In the absence of a sham transaction, chandelier bidding, or other sharp practices, a directed verdict for defendants was upheld where estimated market values they provided were within the range of values established by free and open bidding at auction. The auction process itself was considered an open market establishing the best evidence of market value; testimony by others about what prices should have been realized on that auction day did not raise a triable issue of fact as to the value actually established.[2]

---

[6]Nataros v. Fine Arts Gallery of Scottsdale, Inc., 126 Ariz. 44, 612 P.2d 500 at 503.

[7]Adam A. Weschler & Son, Inc. v. Klank, 561 A.2d 1003 (D.C. 1989).

[Section 5:64]

[1]Nataros v. Fine Arts Gallery of Scottsdale, Inc., 126 Ariz. 44, 612 P.2d 500 (Ct. App. Div. 1 1980).

[2]Nataros v. Fine Arts Gallery of Scottsdale, Inc., 126 Ariz. 44, 612 P.2d 500 (Ct. App. Div. 1 1980) at 504 (distinguishing Pasternack v.

F. TIME LIMITATIONS FOR SUIT

§ 5:65 UCC

Timing of contract warranty actions based upon authenticity of artwork brought against auction houses is determined by UCC Section 2-725, absent other contractual terms.[1] UCC Section 2-725(1) provides a four-year statute of limitations for contracts of sale, absent agreement.[2] Auction contracts often include conditions of sale that reduce the UCC time period; such limitations are in accord with UCC Section 2-725(1), which states: "By the original agreement, the parties may reduce the period of limitation to not less than one year."

§ 5:66 Contractual limitations

In Tunick, Inc. v. Kornfeld,[1] a buyer who purchased at auction a print, "Le Minotauromachie," signed by Pablo Picasso, sued the auction house for fraud, misrepresentation, breach of duty of honesty and good faith in fair dealing, and breach of fiduciary duty, when its forensic expert claimed the signature was a forgery.

The auction moved to dismiss because the terms and conditions of sale agreement specified that any "protest" involving the auction sale had to be made four weeks from the date of auction. Denying the motion, the trial court stated, "[a]s a matter of public policy, contractual provisions that purport to shorten otherwise applicable limitations periods will be enforced only if reasonable [and such

---

Esskay Art Galleries, Inc., 90 F. Supp. 849 (W.D. Ark. 1950), where the auction was a sham and the quality of the jewelry was misrepresented).

[Section 5:65]

[1]*See, e.g.,* Pita v. Sotheby's, Inc., 1991 WL 183351 (S.D. N.Y. 1991) (in the absence of judicial interpretation of how UCC § 2-725 applied to authenticity claims, a lawsuit based on such claims filed more than four years after sale was not frivolous).

[2]*See* Ch 4 §§ 4:35 to 4:41, for a detailed discussion of the UCC statute of limitations.

[Section 5:66]

[1]David Tunick, Inc. v. Kornfeld, 813 F. Supp. 988 (S.D. N.Y. 1993).

agreements are] strictly construed."[2]

G. Racketeer Influenced and Corrupt Organizations Act (RICO)

§ 5:67 Generally

RICO is a comprehensive and complex statute judicially expanded to apply to circumstances and defendants beyond those of classic racketeering schemes, including sales of fake art and overvalued art.[1] RICO has had mixed reception in the courts as a statutory predicate to remedy art trading claims generally, and RICO may be even less suitable for auction claims.[2] RICO claims against auction entities are summarized below.

§ 5:68 Elements of pattern—Time period too short

In Barrett v. Banknote Corp.,[1] defendants bought archival material at auction after being told they were buying the only available works; a few months later, the same auction offered more works. A federal district court denied the buyers leave to add RICO to a complaint for breach of contract, breach of warranty and intentional misrepresentation against the auction house and the bank note publisher. "Plaintiff and other buyers at the November auction were defrauded when [auction and other defendants] represented that duplicates of the items sold did not exist and would not be sold, when in fact such duplicates existed and were sold by Defendants in June 1991 and . . . in September 1991. . . . [T]he claims are based on the November [1991] auction. This is too short a time to constitute a pattern of continuing criminal activity."[2]

---

[2]David Tunick, Inc. v. Kornfeld, 813 F. Supp. 988 (S.D. N.Y. 1993).

[Section 5:67]

[1]*See* §§ 11:15 to 11:21.

[2]*See* Ch 10 §§ 10:37 to 10:71.

[Section 5:68]

[1]Barrett v. U.S. Banknote Corp., 806 F. Supp. 1094 (S.D. N.Y. 1992).

[2]Barrett v. U.S. Banknote Corp., 806 F. Supp. 1094 at 1100 (S.D. N.Y. 1992).

§ 5:69 Elements of pattern—Limited objective insufficient

A single fraudulent goal in some jurisdictions will not support a RICO claim. In Barrett,[1] the auction contract between Christie's and the consignor had an expiration date after which the auction house did not associate with the other defendants. The court held the "objective [of auction] too limited to constitute a pattern of *continuing* fraud."[2]

In Ichiyasu v. Christie, Manson & Woods, International, Inc.,[3] a purported theft victim sued defendants (other than the auction house) under RICO for stealing his artworks, transporting them in interstate commerce, and consigning them to Christie's for auction. The district court, dismissing the RICO claims, wrote: "[T]he allegations of transportation and sale of stolen goods seem to be part and parcel of a single alleged criminal episode. The same criminal act is being broken up into its component parts for pleading purposes."[4]

§ 5:70 Damages

Where defendants sold work by Pablo Picasso knowing about authenticity problems, an Ohio state court awarded compensatory treble damages and punitive damages under RICO, plus fees and costs totaling $88,154, as well as attorney's fees.[1]

[Section 5:69]

[1]Barrett v. U.S. Banknote Corp., 806 F. Supp. 1094 (S.D. N.Y. 1992).

[2]Barrett v. U.S. Banknote Corp., 806 F. Supp. 1094 at 1100 (S.D. N.Y. 1992).

[3]Ichiyasu v. Christie, Manson & Woods Intern., Inc., 630 F. Supp. 340 (N.D. Ill. 1986).

[4]Ichiyasu v. Christie, Manson & Woods Intern., Inc., 630 F. Supp. 340 (N.D. Ill. 1986).

[Section 5:70]

[1]McCloud v. Lawrence Gallery, Ltd., 1992 WL 6199(S.D.N.Y. Jan. 9, 1992), aff'd in unpublished op., 970 F.2d 896 (2d Cir. 1992) (enforcement of default judgment action in New York for judgment obtained in Ohio on RICO claims for sale of inauthentic art).

H. PERSONAL LIABILITY OF AUCTIONEER

§ 5:71 Generally

A buyer may sue the auctioneer and auction owner in their individual capacities as well as naming the corporate entity.[1] Suit has been upheld against both the auction entity and the auction owner for torts committed in the latter's individual capacity.[2]

I. DAMAGES

§ 5:72 Generally

In Esskay,[1] a fraud action based upon works sold at auction for an overvalued price, the measure of damages for the buyer was the difference between the post-sale appraisal value and the auction price. In Barrett,[2] the court allowed punitive damages to be plead in misrepresentation action where the plaintiff alleged auction representations were false and the auction house "knew they were false or was recklessly indifferent" to falsity.

J. TITLE CLAIMS

§ 5:73 Duty to buyer

Artwork scheduled for public auction receives public at-

[Section 5:71]

[1]Cristallina S.A. v. Christie, Manson & Woods Intern., Inc., 117 A.D.2d 284, 502 N.Y.S.2d 165 (1st Dep't 1986) (auctioneers and auction house sued for misrepresentation); David Tunick, Inc. v. Kornfeld, 813 F. Supp. 988 (S.D. N.Y. 1993).

[2]David Tunick, Inc. v. Kornfeld, 813 F. Supp. 988 (S.D. N.Y. 1993) (federal district court rejected the argument that an unlimited partner of a limited partnership cannot be sued personally for a debt incurred by the partnership until it is dissolved or until after an unsuccessful effort to execute a judgment against the partnership).

[Section 5:72]

[1]Pasternack v. Esskay Art Galleries, Inc., 90 F. Supp. 849 (W.D. Ark. 1950).

[2]Barrett v. U.S. Banknote Corp., 806 F. Supp. 1094 (S.D. N.Y. 1992).

tention,[1] making auction fertile ground for title disputes.[2] The "long lost" artwork suddenly reappears on the auction market after disappearance by theft or mysterious circumstances years, or even decades, earlier. Depiction in an auction catalogue or news item garners one or more putative owners who claim title against the consignor. That the artwork is sourced to a museum enhances its provenance, but does not necessarily assure unimpaired ownership and clear title.[3] Auction houses have taken significant steps to address these issues. Some have supplemented catalogue provenance disclosures with "provenance" sections in the Conditions of Sale Agreement as well as entered into agreements with stolen art registries that issue certification to prospective buyers that a search has been made.[4]

The auction entity requires as a matter of course that the consignor warrant clear title, and indemnify it and hold it harmless for title disputes.[5] One or two trial courts have held that an auction entity is obligated to investigate title "scrupulously," and have held sales of art without such investigation grounds for conversion.[6] No precedential opinion could be found declaring auction entities respon-

[Section 5:73]

[1]Solomon R. Guggenheim Foundation v. Lubell, 153 A.D.2d 143, 550 N.Y.S.2d 618 (1st Dep't 1990), order aff'd, 77 N.Y.2d 311, 567 N.Y.S.2d 623, 569 N.E.2d 426 (1991) (Marc Chagall painting missing from Guggenheim Museum for more than twenty-five years discovered when owner sent visuals of painting to auction house).

[2]For title disputes, *see generally* Annot., "Liability of Auctioneer . . . to Buyer as to Title,", 80 A.L.R. 2d 1237 § 6; *see also* Stein v. Annenberg Research Inst., 1991 WL 143400 (S.D.N.Y. July 19, 1991) (collector consigned Roman Jewish liturgical manuscript to auction).

[3]Wildenstein & Co. v. Wallis, 756 F. Supp. 158 (S.D. N.Y. 1991), rev'd without opinion, 983 F.2d 1047 (2d Cir. 1992) (paintings on "permanent" loan to museum auctioned when heirs of collector-lender removed them for auction; court denied injunctive relief);

[4]See App. 10.

[5]*See* Appendix 9.

[6]Howley v. Sotheby's, Inc., N.Y.L.J., Feb. 20, 1986 Civ. Ct. NY County (action for conversion of lithograph sold at auction without dealer-buyer inquiry into circumstances, where the thief represented himself as plaintiff's nephew); *see also* Clyde v. Sotheby Parke Bernet, Int'l, CV 80-4235 slip op. (E.D. Pa. 1980) (state action for assumpsit, trespass and replevin, denying Sotheby's motion to remove to federal

sible for "scrupulously" investigating title in all instances; where suspicious circumstances exist, then the auction, like other traders, is placed on inquiry notice that further investigation is necessary.[7]

§ 5:74 Export-import licenses and permits

Federal customs laws and recent cultural property laws implicitly impose a legal obligation upon the auction entity to verify export permits and export licenses, and to confirm import documents for art from international sources before selling or offering for sale such goods in the United States.[1] Such works may be prohibited imports as a matter of law.[2]

§ 5:75 Auction options

For title disputes that emerge prior to the time of auction, the auction entity may withdraw the work, sue the consignor and recover expenses. The auction entity may also withdraw the work,[1] retain possession, and seek interpleader, or join the underlying litigation.[2] The auction entity is not authorized to decide title among competing parties; in such circumstances, the purported owner and consignor may seek declaratory relief or the auction entity may seek interpleader.

---

court for diversity jurisdiction where plaintiffs and certain defendants were both citizens of same state and claims were not separate and independent because they all involved unauthorized sale of the paintings).

[7] *See* Ch 2.

[Section 5:74]

[1] *See* § 11:22.

[2] Cernuda v. Heavey, 720 F. Supp. 1544 (S.D. Fla. 1989) (government allowed others to sell Cuban art without valid licenses required under Trading with the Enemy Act, but prohibited Cuban Art Museum from selling similar artworks for failure to obtain licenses).

[Section 5:75]

[1] John v. Sotheby's, Inc., 141 F.R.D. 29 (S.D. N.Y. 1992) (consignment contract permits auction to withdraw the painting for breach of consignor's assurance that painting is free of all claims, liens and encumbrances).

[2] *See, e.g.,* Walt Disney Productions v. Basmajian, 600 F. Supp. 439 (S.D. N.Y. 1984) (Disney sued consignor, claiming ownership of celluloids consigned to Christie's by defendant for auction, and Christie's entered the lawsuit).

§ 5:76 Declaratory relief

If title is put in question prior to auction, the auction entity may withdraw the work and refuse to relinquish the art to the consignor or claimant without a court order. Consignors in such situations have sought declaratory relief against the putative owner.[1] In Burger v. Bartlett,[2] the artist Jennifer Bartlett contacted Sotheby's regarding a painting in the auction catalogue whose provenance was "the artist." She claimed the painting belonged to her. The consignors sued the artist in federal district court for declaratory relief, and the auction house was dismissed from the action by agreement of the parties.

§ 5:77 Statutory interpleader

Two types of interpleader have been used in the auction context—statutory and rule interpleader. Section 1335 of title 28 of the U.S. Code provides a district court with jurisdiction over any civil action of interpleader involving property worth $500 or more, if two or more adverse claimants of diverse citizenship "are claiming or may claim to be entitled to such . . . property." Statutory interpleader also requires that the asset[s] be deposited with the court as a jurisdictional prerequisite.

In Phillips, Son & Neal, Inc. v. Borghi & Co.,[1] the auction house-plaintiff filed a statutory interpleader action under Section 1335 against a dealer-buyer and an estate-consignor after it auctioned a set of Bauer drawings from the estate to the dealer, who refused to pay for them. The auction paid the estate-consignor the amount it was owed

---

[Section 5:76]

[1]Burger v. Bartlett, 1990 WL 99025 (E.D. Pa. 1990) (consignor sued Jennifer Bartlett over Bartlett painting consigned to auction by plaintiff); *see also* Walt Disney Productions v. Basmajian, 600 F. Supp. 439 (S.D. N.Y. 1984) (Disney sued consignor, claiming ownership of animated art consigned to Christie's by defendant for auction); *see also* Basmajian v. Christie, Manson & Woods Intern., Inc., 629 F. Supp. 995 (S.D. N.Y. 1986).

[2]Burger v. Bartlett, 1990 WL 99025 (E.D. Pa. 1990).

[Section 5:77]

[1]Phillips, Son & Neal, Inc. v. Borghi & Co., 1987 WL 27690 (S.D. N.Y. 1987).

and sought a determination of title to the drawings, which it retained in its possession.

The dealer, who bought estate drawings by Rudolf Bauer auctioned in a single lot for $40,000 from the auction in 1985, allegedly was told by the auctioneer that the Bauer lot constituted all the Bauer works in the estate. But in 1986 plaintiff auctioned additional Bauer drawings from the same estate. At the second auction the same dealer bought the second set of drawings for $20,000, but refused to pay the auction entity.

The auction entity's interpleader action was dismissed for lack of jurisdiction on the grounds that: (1) it had not deposited a res with the court's registry in the form of either the Bauer drawings or a bond, and (2) two or more adverse claimants of diverse citizenship were lacking, since the defendant-estate did not claim the drawings. The court noted that for interpleader the auction entity had to have, as a predicate ground, "a bona fide fear of multiple liability." In the Phillips case, since only the dealer claimed title to the Bauer drawings and the estate made no claim, there was no fear of multiple liability.

§ 5:78 Rule interpleader

Federal Rules of Civil Procedure Rule 22(1) provides that "persons having claims against the plaintiff may be joined as defendants and required to interplead when their claims are such that the plaintiff is or may be exposed to double or multiple liability . . . . [I]nterpleader may be obtained by way of cross-claim or counterclaim," providing that the action has some "nexus" with the party. Rule 22 interpleader is proper if the party seeking it "is or may be exposed to double or multiple liability."[1]

[Section 5:78]

[1]Koons v. Christie, Manson & Woods Intern. Inc., 1999 Copr. L. Dec. ¶ 27867, 1999 WL 38195 (S.D. N.Y. 1999) (citations omitted) (Fed.R.Civ.P.Rule 22 interpleader proper where auction house consignee in possession of sculpture by well-known contemporary artist who stated it was fake and summary judgment granted for auction on artist's copyright claim and for consignor on conversion and breach of contract).

In John v. Sotheby's, Inc.,[2] the federal district court found rule interpleader appropriate against a third party because defendant auction did not know to whom the painting in its possession, Christus by Rembrandt Van Rijn, should be returned, the plaintiff-consignor or the third party, Dr. Julian Nava. Sotheby's withdrew the painting, consigned by the former wife of a friend of Dr. Nava pursuant to a marital settlement, after Dr. Nava informed Sotheby's that he owned the painting and produced a bill of sale. The district court granted Nava's motion to intervene,[3] but subsequently denied Nava's motion for summary judgment against John on the ownership issue. Nava's motion was supported by a state court judgment awarding the Rembrandt painting to Nava in an action between Nava and John's former spouse, but the federal court did not accord it preclusive effect under the full Faith and Credit Clause[4] because the state court lacked personal jurisdiction over Ms. John and was incompetent to adjudicate her rights in the painting.[5]

Deposit of property with the court is not a jurisdictional prerequisite for rule interpleader the way it is for statutory interpleader under Section 1335 of title 28 of the U.S. Code. Thus, the Rembrandt painting, unlike the Bauer drawings, did not have to be deposited with the court.

However, under Rule 67 a party, with notice and by leave of the court, "may deposit" with the court all or part of the property.[6] Rule 67 is intended to "relieve the depositor of responsibility for a fund in dispute" and the "burden of administering an asset." The court denied Sotheby's deposit motion since Sotheby's remained in the underlying conversion action, and the Rembrandt would be safer at

---

[2]John v. Sotheby's, Inc., 141 F.R.D. 29 (S.D. N.Y. 1992).

[3]John v. Sotheby's, Inc., 141 F.R.D. 29 at 37 (S.D. N.Y. 1992).

[4]U.S. Const. art. IV., § 1.

[5]John v. Sotheby's, Inc., 1994 WL 88614 (S.D. N.Y. 1994) (court rules plaintiff and intervenor in title dispute involving Rembrandt painting each entitled to a 50 percent interest in net proceeds from sale of painting, by auction, private sale, or other arrangement).

[6]Koons v. Christie, Manson & Woods Intern. Inc., 1999 Copr. L. Dec. ¶ 27867, 1999 WL 38195 (S.D. N.Y. 1999) (interpleader auction house in possession of sculpture to retain custody until judgment entered, at which time auction to dispose of it in accordance with terms, costs of insurance to be borne by plaintiff and defendant).

Sotheby's facilities.

VI. THIRD-PARTY ACTIONS AND OTHER ACTIONS

§ 5:79 Checklist: Actions against third parties by consignors

(1) Conversion

(2) Tortious interference with contract or prospective contractual relations

(3) Defamation and disparagement

(4) Declaratory and injunctive relief

§ 5:80 Consignor actions against third persons—Consignor actions against seller

Consignors have sued sellers from whom they purchased art when the art was rejected by auction as inauthentic. In Ketcham v. Gesner Fine Paintings, Inc.,[1] plaintiff bought a painting purportedly by American painter Martin Johnson Heade, subsequently offering it at auction. After the auction entity withdrew it prior to sale because of authenticity problems, he sued the person from whom he had purchased it, alleging fraud, rescission and breach of contract. In Ichiyasu,[2] the dealer who consigned a Picasso to Christie's sued the person who consigned the artwork to him.

§ 5:81 Consignor actions against third persons—Consignor actions against buyers

Sales rescinded by auction are a source of consignor suits against prospective or actual buyers. In Greenwood

---

[Section 5:80]

[1]Ketcham v. Franklyn Gesner Fine Paintings, Inc., 181 Ga. App. 549, 353 S.E.2d 44 (1987).

[2]Ichiyasu v. Christie, Manson & Woods Intern., Inc., 630 F. Supp. 340 (N.D. Ill. 1986).

v. Koven,[1] the consignor to Christie's of a pastel by Georges Braque sued the buyer for breach of contract for failing to return the purchase price of $660,000 to Christie's after Christie's rescinded the sale. Braque's successors refused to authenticate the pastel. The district court ordered summary judgment for the buyer on the grounds that (1) the complaint did not state a claim for relief because the sale was rescinded, relieving the buyer of any obligation to pay Christie's the sale price; and (2) even if the allegations stated a cause of action, no proof was offered to support allegation that the buyer acted in bad faith, raising authenticity as a means to escape a bad deal.

In Kohler v. Leslie Hindman, Inc.,[2] consignors sought damages or, in the alternative, specific performance, against a buyer who did not consummate sale of a painting they had auctioned after his expert deemed it inauthentic subsequent to auction. The court granted summary judgment in favor of the buyer, rejecting the argument that the auction house's secret oral side agreement with the prospective buyer rescinding the sale was invalid because the consignors had not authorized it.

§ 5:82 Buyer actions against consignors

Buyers have sued consignors for representations made in connection with auction sales. Where an auction house sold substantially similar bank notes from the same archive of the consignor at two separate auctions, allegedly representing at the first auction that the objects were the only available specimens,[1] the buyer sued the consignor and the auction for breach of contract and breach of

[Section 5:81]

[1]Greenwood v. Koven, 1993 WL 541181 (S.D. N.Y. 1993), on reconsideration in part, 880 F. Supp. 186 (S.D. N.Y. 1995).

[2]Kohler v. Leslie Hindman, Inc., 1995 WL 89015 (N.D. Ill. 1995), judgment aff'd, 80 F.3d 1181, 34 Fed. R. Serv. 3d 1342 (7th Cir. 1996); see also Kohler v. Leslie Hindman, Inc., 80 F.3d 1181, 34 Fed. R. Serv. 3d 1342 (7th Cir. 1996) (where auction had "sole discretion" to rescind sale held, recission held not to breach consignment agreement even where recission effectuated a contractually excluded warranty of authenticity).

[Section 5:82]

[1]Barrett v. U.S. Banknote Corp., 806 F. Supp. 1094 (S.D. N.Y. 1992).

warranty.

VII. AUCTION AS PLAINTIFF

§ 5:83 Checklist; Causes of actions by the auction

(1) Action for monies owed (e.g., breach of contract, account stated)

(2) Breach of warranty

(3) Breach of contract

(4) Interpleader

(5) Declaratory relief

§ 5:84 Auction actions against buyers—Monies owed

The auction entity is entitled to monies owed based upon the hammer price and the premiums and other charges; when such monies are not paid, various remedies exist to enforce the purchase agreement.[1]

In Wechsler & Son, Inc. v. Klank,[2] an auctioneer sued a bidder, who had purchased an eighteenth century blanket chest described in the auction catalog as "circa 1791," for monies owed ($21,000). After auction the bidder filed a complaint with District of Columbia Consumer Affairs alleging that the bid should be disregarded because the chest was not authentic. The representation in the catalog, he contended, constituted an unfair trade practice by the auctioneer under consumer protection law. The appellate court affirmed dismissal of the auctioneer's complaint.

§ 5:85 Auction actions against buyers—Consumer warranty law

Art auction has been held to be outside the scope of consumer protection laws in New York and some other

---

[Section 5:84]

[1] Parke-Bernet Galleries, Inc. v. Franklyn, 26 N.Y.2d 13, 308 N.Y.S.2d 337, 256 N.E.2d 506 (1970) (auction action against defendant bidder who failed to pay for purchase of art by telephonic bidding).

[2] Adam A. Weschler & Son, Inc. v. Klank, 561 A.2d 1003 (D.C. 1989).

jurisdictions.[1] But in Wechsler & Son, Inc. v. Klank,[2] the District of Columbia allowed consumer protection statutes to be used as a defense by an auction bidder who did not pay for an antique blanket chest he bought at auction. Buying on behalf of a principal, the bidder alleged the blanket chest was not "circa 1781" as described in the catalogue.

Wechsler argued he was not a "merchant" under the District of Columbia Code. "Merchant" is defined as "a person who does or would sell, lease, or transfer, either directly or indirectly, consumer goods or services, or a person who does or would supply the goods or services which are or would be the subject matter of a trade practice."[3] Judicial interpretation expanded "merchant" to include sellers "connected with the supply side" of goods. The Court of Appeals for the District of Columbia decided the auctioneer was a merchant.

The auctioneer argued that an antique blanket chest sold for $21,000 was not a consumer good offered in a consumer transaction. The Court of Appeals responded: "Many persons display valuable antiques in their homes or offices and such use falls squarely within the broad 'personal, household or family use' definition given by the Act."[4] Finally, the auctioneer argued that since the bidder was acting on behalf of a principal, and was not buying the chest for his own use, he was not a consumer within

---

[Section 5:85]

[1]Waller v. Scheer, 175 Ga. App. 1, 332 S.E.2d 293 (1985), cert. dismissed, (July 3, 1985); *but cf.* McKie v. R.H. Love Galleries, Inc., 1990 WL 179797 (N.D. Ill. 1990) (court denied motion for dismissal for failure to state claims on plaintiffs' claim for violation of Illinois Consumer Fraud and Deceptive Business Practices Act, Ill. Rev. Stat. § 2, ch. 121½, in complaint based upon sale of painting by William Merrit Chase which they bought from defendant gallery for $370,000); Kohler v. Leslie Hindman, Inc., 1995 WL 250427 (N.D. Ill. 1995) (highest bidder, who returned painting to auction entity because his expert deemed it inauthentic, was sued by consignors, and cross-claimed against auction for, inter alia, violations of Illinois Consumer Fraud and Deceptive Business Practices, 815 Ill. Comp. Stat. § 505/2).

[2]Adam A. Weschler & Son, Inc. v. Klank, 561 A.2d 1003 (D.C. 1989).

[3]D.C. Code § 28-3901(a)(3).

[4]Adam A. Weschler & Son, Inc. v. Klank, 561 A.2d at 1003, 1004 (App. D.C. 1989).

the meaning of the statute, but a purchaser for resale. The court responded:

> [The Act seeks to reach] the ultimate retail transaction between the final distributor and the individual member of the consuming public . . . Accordingly, it is not the use to which the purchaser ultimately puts the goods or services, but rather the nature of the purchaser that determines the nature of the transaction . . . . If . . . the purchaser is not engaged in the regular business of purchasing this type of goods or service and reselling it, then the transaction will usually fall within the Act.[5]

§ 5:86 Auction actions against consignors—Monies owed

In Luper Auction Galleries, Inc. v. Judge,[1] an auction entity sued consignors to enforce an auction contract providing for reimbursement for advertising and other fees, based upon defendants' consignment of the painting *Femme Accoudee,* purportedly by Pablo Picasso. The auction entity sought to enforce a withdrawal fee clause after it withdrew the Picasso because of questionable authenticity.

The defendants claimed the auction contract was unenforceable, based upon the equitable doctrine of mutual mistake. Holding the contract valid and enforceable, the court rejected mutual mistake because the evidence showed that defendants knew of the authenticity problems when the painting was rejected from other auctions, yet they failed to disclose the information to plaintiff.

§ 5:87 Auction actions against consignors—Attorney fees and costs

Auction entity sought attorney fees and costs from consignors arising from consignment for auction of their painting "Plains of Meudon," purportedly by Theodore

---

[5]Adam A. Weschler & Son, Inc. v. Klank, 561 A.2d at 1003, 1004 (App. D.C. 1989).

[Section 5:86]

[1]Luper Auction Galleries, Inc. v. Judge (William), No. 3:92cv556, Mar. 16, 1993 (D. Va. 1993).

Rousseau, subsequently deemed inauthentic. Although summary judgment was entered in favor of auction based upon the terms of the consignment agreement, attorney fees were not awarded. The consignment agreement provided for fees if the action arose from consignors' representations and warranties. But the consignors had not made such representations; the underlying action involved the auction house's separate side agreement warranty to a prospective buyer, an agreement made without the knowledge of the consignors.[1]

[Section 5:87]

[1]Kohler v. Leslie Hindman, Inc., 1994 WL 233801 (N.D. Ill. 1994), Kohler v. Leslie Hindman, Inc., 1995 WL 89015 (N.D. Ill. 1995), judgment aff'd, 80 F.3d 1181, 34 Fed. R. Serv. 3d 1342 (7th Cir. 1996), and Kohler v. Leslie Hindman, Inc., 1995 WL 250427 (N.D. Ill. 1995) (denying attorney fees and costs to auction defendant in suit brought pursuant to consignment agreement provision for same because the action for which fees were sought arose from verbal side agreement made by defendant with third-party buyer, unrelated to breach of consignors' warranty under the consignment agreement that triggered the attorney fees provision).

Chapter 6

International Trade

I. IMPORT-EXPORT

A. OVERVIEW

B. U.S. CUSTOMS SERVICE

1. In General

2. Distinguishing Dutiable Art from Duty-Free Art

3. Duty

4. Customs Review and Examination

C. IMPORTATION: ART DUTY RATES

1. Introduction

2. Paintings

3. Drawings

4. Photography

5. Collages and Assemblages

6. Engravings, Prints, and Lithographs

7. Sculptures and Statuary

8. Antiques

G. ADDITIONAL IMPORT RESTRICTIONS

II. ART EXPORTS

III. CULTURAL PROPERTY

A. IN GENERAL

B. FEDERAL LAW

C. ART AS UNIVERSAL HERITAGE

D. UNESCO CONVENTION

E. Cultural Property Implementation Act

F. DIFFERENTIAL IMPORT RESTRICTIONS: Section 12.104a of title 19 of the Code of Federal Regulations CATEGORIES

G. STOLEN CULTURAL PROPERTY IMPORT CONTROLS

H. ARCHAEOLOGICAL AND ETHNOLOGICAL MATERIALS IMPORT RESTRICTIONS

I. IMPORT EXEMPTIONS: Section 312

F. MISCELLANEOUS ISSUES

I. IMPORT-EXPORT

A. OVERVIEW

§ 6:1 Generally

A sophisticated international art market makes art a universal export. The export flow is typically to countries with wealth to acquire art, the United States prominent among them. American policy favors the importation of art and antiques, and its customs laws reflect this policy.

Sections 6:1 to 6:76 provides a practice guide for importing art into the United States. United States Customs (U.S. Customs) regulations and guidelines for importing sculpture, drawings, paintings, prints, and photography are identified and described. Generally art is treated like other imports in that it is scheduled in tariffs from which duties are levied by U.S. Customs. Customs agents, often in conjunction with customs brokers, assess art shipments on a case-by-case basis to determine if duty is owed and the amount of duty.

A how-to guide is provided for preparation of the U.S. Customs required commercial invoice, and checklists are provided to qualify for U.S. Customs Binding Ruling Classification (BRC) for art regularly imported into the United States. Interpretative guidelines, cases, charts and for detailed reference, tariff schedules, are also provided here.

Legitimate documentation of art imports, and understanding the terms of the tariff art classifications, are key factors to assure orderly and expeditious import. Where the documentation is counterfeit, the declaration false, or the importation improper, U.S. Customs has the right to detain, seize, and forfeit property. The administrative procedures for doing so, and the defenses, are contained in these sections. Judicial hearing and judicial forfeiture are also included.

The U.S. Customs is also the first line of domestic regulation for importation of obscene material and unlawful merchandise, as well as pirated copyright material and trademark violations. Sections 6:1 to 6:76 contain the applicable laws and regulations. That goods pass customs and enter the United States does not immunize them from search or seizure if the import is subsequently determined unlawful.

The international art trade necessarily involves consideration of whether the import is cultural property.[1] However, even for general import-export purposes, persons importing art should be prepared to have export licenses, permits, and documents where necessary, and should be aware that third parties, including sovereign states, can seek U.S. Customs assistance where an ownership dispute exists.[2]

Sections 6:71 to 6:76 also focus upon an area of virtually nonexistent regulation, the export of art for commercial purposes from the United States. Unlike other nations that attempt to restrict export of so-called national treasures through licensing or to prohibit export by export bans, the United States, with minor exception for certain artifacts under federal archaeological protection laws, does not control cultural export.

Also included is a summary of art exports and imports for cultural exchange and/or exhibition; these exhibitions and exchanges are outside commercial trade and are regulated by separate federal laws.

A caveat to readers: other than the tariff schedules and the Code of Federal Regulations (CFR), few judicial interpretations augment the administrative policies and guidelines for art importation. The importer should be prepared to demonstrate and document that the work

---

[Section 6:1]

[1] *See* §§ 6:77 to 6:133.

[2] *See* §§ 6:71 to 6:76.

conforms to the description of duty-free art under the applicable tariff.

CFR expanded its cultural property controls; for convenience, full text regulations are included.[3]

During the last ten years, there has been increased focus upon the distribution of artworks that "disappeared" during World War II. Some works have never been located; others taken from Jewish and other owners are in private and public collections. Litigation to recover such works has been patchwork, and the results have been mixed.[4] As a result of the collapse of the Soviet Union and the reunification of Germany, archives, libraries, documents, private papers, and other materials that were heretofore unavailable to scholars, historians, and writers have been reviewed and scrutinized, a process that continues as this is written. The provenance of some artworks has been clarified through the documentation process. As a result of this and other factors, artworks on loan from European institutions and displayed here, as well as works in the permanent collections of American museums and private hands, have become subjects of reclamation claims and, in some instances, lawsuits.

The issue of war booty and "repatriation" has been kept on the political agenda and front pages of the nation's press by newly revealed activities of the Swiss banks during and after World War II, involving their policies and practices in handling deposits of war victims as well as their role in financing Nazi enterprises.

The American polity has responded, as have some American museums that have developed web sites listing works in collections that have gaps in the provenance during the 1930s and 1940s.[5] The precipitating legislation was the U.S. Holocaust Assets Commission Act of 1998, which

---

[3]*See* Appendix 14B; *see also* §§ 6:77 to 6:115.

[4]*See* §§ 6:77 to 6:133. *See also,* U.S. v. Portrait of Wally, 105 F. Supp. 2d 288 (S.D. N.Y. 2000) (heirs of Nazi victims claimed ownership of painting by Egon Schiele loaned by Austrian museum to Museum of Modern Art for exhibition).

[5]Art Institute of Chicago http://www.artic.edu/aic/provenance/index; Cleveland Museum of Art http://www.clemusart.com/provintro; Harvard University Art Museums http://www.artmuseums.harvard.edu/research/provenance/index; J. Paul Getty Museum http://www.getty.edu/museum/provenance/index; Los Angeles County

established the Presidential Advisory Commission on Holocaust Assets [PCHA].[6] The primary goal of PCHA was to conduct research on the status of assets of Holocaust victims that were collected by, or in the possession of, the federal government. On December 15, 2000, the Commission issued its Report. The U.S. National Archives & Records Administration implemented its own research base and website, the National Archives and Records Administration Art Provenance and Claims Research Project.[7] Federal legislation supplemented renewed interest in unaccounted for artworks and assets. The Stolen Artwork Restitution Act of 1998 is one such measure.[8] The Holocaust Victims Redress Act is another.[9]

On April 30, 2001, the Association of Art Museum Directors [AAMD] responded to the Report by issuing an Addendum to its own "*Task Force Report on the Spoliation of Art during the Nazi/World War II Era* (1933-1945)," urging members "to make full disclosure of their ongoing provenance research" for such works of art, especially those created before 1946, transferred after 1932 and before 1946 and which were, or could have been, in continental Europe.[10] AAMD developed guidelines regarding provenance research and disclosures. Some AAMD members began posting their research online, available on the websites listed here. Some states have enacted legislation dealing with art specifically, like the New York State Banking Department Holocaust Claims Processing Office

---

Museum of Art http://www.lacma.org/lacma.asp; Metropolitan Museum of Art http://www.metmuseum.org/collections/Provenance Research Project; MoMA http://www.moma.org/menu/provenance; Museum of Fine Arts, Boston http://www.mfa.org/research; National Gallery of Art http://www.nga.gov/resources/ww2res; Seattle Art Museum http://www.SeattleArtMuseum.org.; American Association of Museums: Nazi-era Provenance Internet Portal [2003]; nepip@aam_us.org; see also Chart 2-1 and App. 25.

[6]Pub. L. No. 105-186.

[7]See App. 25.

[8]H.R. Rep. 4138, 105th Cong., 2d Sess.; *see also* Cal. Code Civ. Proc. § 354.3 (extending claims period until Dec. 31, 2010 for "Holocaust era" works).

[9]S. 1390, 105th Cong., 1st Sess., H.R. Rep. 2591, 105th Cong., 1st Sess. (references artworks).

[10]See App. 25.

for Art Claims.[11] Other laws were intended to rectify unpaid proceeds from life insurance policies of war victims.[12]

The international community has also responded. The Russian Ministry of Culture established two web sites containing 10,000 items from many different Russian museums.[13] Germany created a Lost Art Internet Database.[14] The Commission for Looted Art in Europe has a Central Registry containing two databases.[15]

Cultural property law beginning at § 6:77 has also rapidly expanded. The United States has entered into agreements with many countries regarding protection of cultural properties, and many new federal regulations have been promulgated.[16] The arts community recognizes the importance of cultural property oversight. Cultural property claims affect acquisition and collection policies, integrity in the market as well as in museums, and as an important aspect of their public missions. Member organizations have implemented new guidelines or revised ethical codes, including the Archaeological Institute of America guidelines,[17] the International Council of Museums' [ICOM] amended provisions on the Return and Restitution of Cultural Property,[18] the American Association of Museums' [AAM] Code of Ethics,[19] newly issued statement on cultural property.[20]

---

[11]See App. 25 (Art Claim Form).

[12]American Ins. Ass'n v. Garamendi, 539 U.S. 396, 123 S. Ct. 2374, 156 L. Ed. 2d 376 (2003) (California Holocaust Victim Insurance Relief Act preempted by federal law because of impermissible interference with presidential conduct of foreign affairs).

[13]http://www.lostart.ru and http://www.restitution.ru [Russian only].

[14]http://www.lostart.de [German, Russian, English].

[15]http://info@lootedart.com.

[16]See App. 14B.

[17]*See* Appendix 15C.

[18]See App. 15A(i) and (ii).

[19]See App.15B and AAM's.

[20]App.15D

§ 6:2 International regulation of art imports-exports

All international commerce involves economic, legal, and political controls in today's web of global interdependent trade networks. But art has been particularly singled out for special handling under various agreements:

(1) the General Agreement on Tariffs and Trade (GATT);[1]

(2) international treaties to which the United States is a party or member by congressional ratification, e.g., the UNESCO Convention on Cultural Property;[2]

(3) bilateral cultural property treaties executed by the executive branch;[3]

(4) international treaties and unions to which the United States is not a party or a member but nonetheless is affected as a trading partner, e.g., the European Union Treaty;[4]

(5) international treaties and unions to which the United States is not a party or a member but is nonetheless potentially affected through United Nations or other undertakings, e.g., the Gulf War, the Hague Convention on Cultural Property in the Event of Armed Conflict of 1954 and Second Protocol[5] and the UNIDROIT Convention

---

[Section 6:2]

[1]The General Agreement on Tariffs and Trade Act, 1 BDIEL at 9.

[2]19 U.S.C.A. §§ 2601 et seq.

[3]*See* Chart 6-8.

[4]European Union Treaty, Feb. 7, 1992, European Report No. 1746 (Feb. 22, 1992) (also referred to as the Treaty of Maastricht); Single European Act, 25 ILM 506 (1986) (not ratified as of writing). *See also* 1993 O.J. (L.74) (Mar. 15, 1993) (The Council of the European Communities adopted a Directive pursuant to Article 36 of the Treaty regarding return of cultural property to Member States, which each Member was allowed to define and to protect after 1992 within the perimeter of the Community.); *see also* Bull. EC 11-1992, 1.3.20–1.3.21 (Regulation EEC No. 3911/92 (conditions for return of cultural property in absence of formal controls at intra-Community frontiers and export licenses for export beyond the Community customs territory).

[5]*See* Appendix 16A and 16B.

on Stolen or Illegally Exported Cultural Objects;[6] and

(6) foreign laws[7] of exporting and transshipment countries, inter alia, patrimony laws, licensing laws, commercial laws.

Obviously, choice of laws as well as conflicts affect determination of the proper situs of a sales transaction, export requirements, and resolution of ownership disputes in domestic courts; depending upon the export, such resolution may also affect importation. Further import-export documents often play an important evidentiary role in international ownership disputes.

§ 6:3 American policy

America has a "historical policy of encouraging the importation of art [and antiques]."[1] To facilitate this policy, there have been few restrictions on the importation of art. Since the 1980s some import restrictions were enacted by treaties, statutes, and implementing regulations affecting import of art,[2] artifacts,[3] and cultural properties.[4] This regulation of art importation has political as well as economic considerations as the following spectrum of legal

---

[6]See App. 16C.

[7]*See, e.g.,* Autocephalous Greek-Orthodox Church of Cyprus v. Goldberg & Feldman Fine Arts Inc., 717 F. Supp. 1374 (S.D. Ind. 1989), judgment aff'd, 917 F.2d 278 (7th Cir. 1990) (Cyprus, Turkey, and Switzerland); U.S. v. McClain, 545 F.2d 988 (5th Cir. 1977) (Mexico); Jeanneret v. Vichey, 693 F.2d 259, 35 U.C.C. Rep. Serv. 75 (2d Cir. 1982) (Switzerland); Republic of Turkey v. Metropolitan Museum of Art, 762 F. Supp. 44 (S.D. N.Y. 1990) (Turkey).

[Section 6:3]

[1]U.S. v. McClain, 545 F.2d 988 (5th Cir. 1977) (United States encourages importation of art more than 100 years old).

[2]*See* Appendix 12. Harmonized Tariff Schedule of the United States (1992), § XXI, Ch. 97, Explanatory Notes on "Works of Art, Collectors' Pieces and Antiques."

[3]Harmonized Tariff Schedule of the United States (1992), § XXI, Ch. 97, Explanatory Notes on "Works of Art, Collectors' Pieces and Antiques".

[4]Customs Directive Policies & Procedures Manual, Customs Directive Re: Detention and Seizure of Cultural Property (Apr. 18, 1991) (U.S. Customs Pub.)

vehicles indicate:

(1) economic (U.S. Customs laws, Uniform Harmonized Tax Schedules);
(2) political (Cultural Property Protection Implementation Act; Trading with the Enemy Act, bilateral and multilateral treaties); and
(3) educational (scientific and cultural exchange programs and international exhibitions; Mutual Educational and Cultural Exchange Acts).

§ 6:4 Federal regulation

Art importation is controlled by Congress and the executive branch through legislation and executive orders, which empower various departments and agencies of government to implement trading policies and guidelines by regulating the import of artworks.

The entity that has the greatest impact upon art importation is the U.S. Customs, its powers derive from the federal Constitution[1] and its establishment originates with the First Acts of Congress.[2] The scope of these powers broadly affects the current import tariff schedules.

B. U.S. CUSTOMS SERVICE

1. In General

§ 6:5 Checklist; Basics on how to import artworks

(1) obtain export permits and licenses, if necessary, and bills of sale, consignment or broker agreements, transfer documents, et cetera.

(2) prepare or obtain shipping documents, bills of lading;[1]

[Section 6:4]

[1]U.S. Const. art I, § 8.

[2]1 Stat. 24 (Tariff Act (July 4, 1789)); 1 Stat. 27 (Duties on Tonnage (July 20, 1789)); 1 Stat. 29 (Duties on Tonnage and Establishment of Customs Districts (July 31, 1789)).

[Section 6:5]

[1]19 CFR § 10.48(a).

(3) prepare artist declaration, if applicable;[2]

(4) prepare seller or shipper declaration, if (3) not available;[3]

(5) prepare commercial invoice, identifying artist, and whether work is original, replica, reproduction or copy;[4]

(6) insure shipment and obtain insurance policy or rider;

(7) identify recipient;

(8) prepare declaration of importer;[5]

(9) designate customs broker;[6]

(10) provide all documentation to customs broker;[7]

(11) provide Binding Ruling Classification (BRC) to customs broker, as applicable, or artist credentials, for sculpture;[8] and

(12) upon request of U.S. Customs Service, provide proof of character of article from curators or recognized art authorities.[9]

§ 6:6 Art and antique specialty

The U.S. Customs Service, part of the Department of Treasury, is responsible for classifying art imports and determining duty.[1] The U.S. Customs maintains an Office of National Import Specialists for Art and Antiques in New York City, and employs field specialists in customs offices located around the country to assist and evaluate art importation. An import occurs for purposes of this discussion each time art enters U.S. Customs after cross-

---

[2]19 CFR § 10.48(b) (waivable).

[3]19 CFR § 10.48(b)(2) (waivable).

[4]*See* §§ 6:16 to 6:17.

[5]19 CFR § 10.48(c).

[6]*See* § 6:14.

[7]*See* § 6:14.

[8]*See* §§ 6:19 to 6:49.

[9]19 CFR § 10.48(e).

[Section 6:6]

[1]Prince & Keller, U.S. Customs: A Bicentennial History.

ing a territorial border of a sovereign[2] in contemplation of sale. Art imports, whether hand-carried or separately shipped, must be declared to U.S. Customs if valued at or above the minimum declaration value. Declaring the art does not mean duty is owed; artworks that conform to tariff schedule classifications may qualify as duty-free imports.

2. *Distinguishing Dutiable Art from Duty-Free Art*

§ 6:7 Definition of "free fine art"

To be duty free, "a work of art must be of the free fine arts."[1] "Free fine arts" is not a term of common usage or universal meaning, and it has been variously defined as follows: "the artist creating the object is able to put something of his own into the work";[2] "rare and special genius usually attributed to works of the free fine arts";[3] "originality of conception, execution and design."[4]

The free fine art holdings are only applied to sculpture,[5] based upon a policy of excluding commercial statuary from duty-free imports. A sculptor can copy a work and still meet the definition, providing that the artist's hand is apparent on the sculpture,[6] or the sculpture is made under his supervision and direction. "[A]n artist's copies of antique master-pieces are works of art of as high a (sic)

---

[2]Autocephalous Greek-Orthodox Church of Cyprus v. Goldberg & Feldman Fine Arts Inc., 717 F. Supp. 1374 (S.D. Ind. 1989), judgment aff'd, 917 F.2d 278 (7th Cir. 1990) (treatment by U.S. courts under rules of sovereignty of laws re military occupying power not recognized by world community).

[Section 6:7]

[1]19 CFR § 10.48(e).

[2]Seibert v. U.S., 65 Cust. Ct. 380, 382, 1970 WL 15458 (Cust. Ct. 3 Div. 1970).

[3]H.H. Elder & Co. v. U.S., 53 Cust. Ct. 116, 1964 WL 9758 (Cust. Ct. 3 Div. 1964); Seibert v. U.S., 65 Cust. Ct. 380, 384, 1970 WL 15458 (Cust. Ct. 3 Div. 1970).

[4]65 Cust. Ct. at 382; *see also* 53 Cust. Ct. at 116.

[5]*See* §§ 6:33 to 6:40.

[6]B. Altman & Co. v. U.S., 224 U.S. 583, 32 S. Ct. 593, 56 L. Ed. 894 (1912) (importation of a bronze bust dutiable because it "was not wrought by hand from metal . . . cast . . . by artisans . . . and . . .

grade as those executed by the same hand from the original models of modern sculptors."[7]

§ 6:8 Factors supporting free fine art

Factors demonstrating that the work is fine art include display at art exhibitions and galleries, the status of the artist, the reputation of the artist as a professional,[1] and the value of the work.[2] An artist's signature on the work does not guarantee a finding that the work will be fine art. In Merritt v. Tiffany,[3] the Supreme Court explained:

> [W]hat productions are deemed professional productions of a . . . sculptor [ ] is difficult to state in general terms . . . . It is sufficiently accurate . . . to say the definition embraces such works of art as are the result of the artist's own creation, or are copies of them, made under his direction and supervision, or copies of works of other artists, made under the like direction and supervision, as distinguished from the productions of the manufacturer or machine.

§ 6:9 Decorative and industrial art exclusions

A work of free fine art excludes decorative or industrial arts. Industrial and decorative artworks include "works performed by potters, glassmakers, goldsmiths, weavers, woodworkers, jewelers and other artisans and craftsmen." Tariff schedules exclude "works of conventional craftsmanship of a commercial character such as ornaments, religious effigies, articles of personal adornment."[1]

---

very little touched, if at all, in its finishing, by the professional designer.").

[7]Tutton v. Viti, 108 U.S. 312, 313, 2 S. Ct. 687, 27 L. Ed. 737 (1883).

[Section 6:8]

[1]*See* §§ 6:19 to 6:49.

[2]1992 U.S. Custom HQ LEXIS 1109 (Aug. 6, 1992) (customs ruling in LEXIS does not constitute publication of ruling under 19 CFR § 177.10(b)) (under $10 invoice price for hand-carved ostrich egg does not support "fine art").

[3]Merritt v. Tiffany, 132 U.S. 167, 10 S. Ct. 52, 33 L. Ed. 299 (1889).

[Section 6:9]

[1]*See* Appendix 1.

In William S. Pitcairn Corp. v. United States,[2] the court determined that although decorative works may be artistic and beautiful, "it can hardly be seriously contended that it was the legislative purpose to include such things [decorative and industrial arts] . . . in a provision which . . . was intended to favor that particular kind of art of which painting and sculpture are the types."[3] A hand-carved ostrich egg shell signed by the artist intended for year-round display was not a work of the free fine arts where there was no evidence that the artist had exhibited in galleries or museums, or of his skill or stature, and the invoice price was under $10.[4]

3. *Duty*

§ 6:10 Point of entry

Duty is owed at the point of entry, also known as the point of importation. The point of importation is the first territorial location the art has contact with in the United States, whether it is arriving by air, sea, or land.

§ 6:11 Tariff schedules

Since January 1, 1988, the U.S. Customs Service has been classifying art objects according to the Uniform Harmonized Tax Schedules (UHTS), which replaces the former Tariff Schedules of the United States (TSUS) used since the 1960s[1] to determine duty. The UHTS derives from the Harmonized Commodity Description and Coding System, an internationally developed system of uniform goods nomenclature produced by the Customs Cooperation Council based in Brussels, Belgium. As adapted by the United States the UHTS, with certain reservations, is referred to by U.S. Customs as the Harmonized Schedules

---

[2]Wm S Pitcairn Corp v. U S, 39 C.C.P.A. 15, C.A.D. 458, 1951 WL 5335 (1951).

[3]U.S. v. Olivotti & Co., T.D. 36309 (Ct. Cust. App. 1916); Headquarters Ruling Ltr. 063320 (Sept. 29, 1979).

[4]1992 U.S. Custom HQ LEXIS 1109 (Aug. 6, 1992).

[Section 6:11]

[1]19 U.S.C.A. § 1202.

(HS).[2] HS maintains some prior TSUS art categories, broadens other categories, and eliminates duty-free rates for "works of art which (sic) were products of American artists temporarily residing abroad."[3]

§ 6:12 Decisions under TSUS apply to HS

Judicial interpretations involving art imports under TSUS are equally applicable to successor provisions under chapter 97 of HS.[1]

§ 6:13 Customs custody

At the point of importation, the object has not yet formally entered the United States; it has merely entered customs custody where U.S. Customs classifies property. A commercial invoice is required for formal entry. Merchandise ordinarily cannot be admitted without bond.

§ 6:14 Customs brokers

Customs brokers are authorized to administer customs importation on behalf of importers.[1] As a practical matter, customs brokers actually make many of the classifications for art based upon documentation provided by the importer and shipper; thus, bills of lading, bills of sale, documents of transfer, et cetera, are critical for importing art, and should be provided to the customs broker or the importer to facilitate admission of the goods into the United States. Customs brokers typically prepare import documentation

---

[2]*The Harmonized Commodity Description and Coding System and the United States Tariff* (1989), Introduction, W. Von Raab, Commissioner of Customs, at 3.

[3]The Tariff Schedules of the United States, sched. 7, pt. 11, § 765.30 (1982).

[Section 6:12]

[1]Wm S Pitcairn Corp v. U S, 39 C.C.P.A. 15, C.A.D. 458, 1951 WL 5335 (1951) (inclusion of customs ruling does not constitute publication of ruling under 19 CFR § 177.10(b)); *see* Appendix 12.

[Section 6:14]

[1]19 CFR § 111; U.S. v. An Antique Platter of Gold, 991 F. Supp. 222 (S.D. N.Y. 1997), aff'd, 184 F.3d 131 (2d Cir. 1999), cert. denied, 528 U.S. 1136, 120 S. Ct. 978, 145 L. Ed. 2d 929 (2000) (role of customs broker in preparing customs forms).

and obtain any necessary bonds for formal entry.

§ 6:15 Bonds

A bond is necessary for importation.[1] Art may be "admitted temporarily free of duty under bond" under certain circumstances.[2]

§ 6:16 Commercial invoice—Contents of invoice

A commercial invoice is required to make formal entry.[1] The customs broker relies upon a commercial invoice provided by the shipper to make HS classifications. The commercial invoice (CI), which must be provided by the shipper whether or not the work has ever been sold as a commercial good, is a crucial document. The CI must be typed and signed by the shipper.

Checklist 6-2: Preparation of Commercial Invoices

(1) shippers' name, address, telephone and/or facsimile numbers;
(2) recipient's name, address, telephone and/or facsimile numbers;
(3) artist(s) name(s);
(4) title(s) of each work;
(5) quantity of each work;
(6) medium of each work;
(7) size of each work (height x width x depth);
(8) component materials;
(9) for multiples

(a) edition number, e.g., edition of 50;

[Section 6:15]

[1]19 CFR §§ 113.61 et seq. *See also* Appendix 2.

[2]*See* § 6:76 and Appendix 12.

[Section 6:16]

[1]19 CFR § 142.3(a)(3); U.S. v. An Antique Platter of Gold, 991 F. Supp. 222 (S.D. N.Y. 1997), aff'd, 184 F.3d 131 (2d Cir. 1999), cert. denied, 528 U.S. 1136, 120 S. Ct. 978, 145 L. Ed. 2d 929 (2000) (preparation of customs forms by broker based upon false commercial invoice).

(b) number of the work in the edition, e.g., 9/10;[2]

(10) declared value of each work based upon transactional[3] value, i.e., purchase price or payable price (see (11) if no purchase price); and

(11) if no price, declared value should be fair market value (discrepancies in fair market value and insured value may present problems for the importer and may indicate irregularities with the shipment).[4]

§ 6:17 Commercial invoice—Merchandise processing fee

All articles imported under chapter 97 are subject to a merchandise processing fee (MPF). The MPF at the time of writing is 0.17 percent of the price entered in the commercial invoice (or declared FMV); minimum MPF is $21, and maximum MPF is $400.

4. *Customs Review and Examination*

§ 6:18 Generally

After the customs broker presents the initial classification on the import papers, and the bond issues, the proposed formal entry is reviewed by U.S. Customs which in its discretion may do any of the following:

(1) open the shipment at the point of importation, e.g., a pier;

(2) open the shipment at a devanning station, e.g., a warehouse;

(3) open the shipment by outside examination, e.g., artist's studio or gallery, in the presence of U.S. Customs and/or the artist, dealer, or designate; or

(4) release shipment from custody for formal entry

---

[2]*See* Ch 12 for definition of multiples fraction and print fraction.

[3]19 U.S.C.A. § 1401a(b)(1).

[4]*See, e.g.,* Autocephalous Greek-Orthodox Church of Cyprus v. Goldberg & Feldman Fine Arts Inc., 717 F. Supp. 1374 (S.D. Ind. 1989), judgment aff'd, 917 F.2d 278 (7th Cir. 1990).

without examination.

C. IMPORTATION: ART DUTY RATES

1. Introduction

§ 6:19 Generally

Art is not imported into the United States duty free unless it qualifies as a duty-free import under the terms of HS classifications under Section 9700 or Section 9800.[1] The U.S. Customs exercises discretion to classify artworks under HS since art does not easily conform to standard classifications. Certain works of art and antiques that are deemed proper under the HS classification system may enter the United States under a free rate of duty, duty free.[2]

Paintings typically pass duty free, providing the painting satisfies the HS classification, but sculptures, multiples and some mixed media, technological or experimental works might not. Even museum quality artworks—like bronze sculptures by Edgar Degas—are subject to duty if the edition number exceeds the HS cap for free duty, which is an original plus twelve copies.[3]

2. Paintings

§ 6:20 All hand limitations

Paintings, certain drawings and pastels, "whether ancient or modern,"[1] irrespective of artistic merit or aes-

---

[Section 6:19]

[1] 19 CFR pt. 10; *see also* Angel v. Seattle-First Nat. Bank, 653 F.2d 1293 (9th Cir. 1981) (although paintings were smuggled into the United States, "no duty would have been due had the goods been declared (under 19 U.S.C.A. § 1202, sched. 7, pt. 11].").

[2] Harmonized Tariff Schedule of the United States, § XXI, ch. 97, Explanatory Notes on "Works of Art, Collectors' Pieces and Antiques" (1992); *see* Appendix 12.

[3] *See* §§ 6:33 to 6:40 and Appendix 12.

[Section 6:20]

[1] Harmonized Tariff Schedule of the United States, § XXI, ch. 97, Explanatory Notes on "Works of Art, Collectors' Pieces and Antiques," § 97.01A, at 1616 (1992); *see* Appendix 12.

thetic value, "executed entirely by hand" are duty free.[2] Paintings that "wholly or partly" contain any process other than that applied "entirely by hand" are excluded, and duty applies. Paintings that are dripped or swabbed or airbrushed are considered executed "entirely by hand," providing that they do not include in whole or in part any process not applied entirely by hand.

§ 6:21 Media and support

Paintings can be done in any medium:[1] oil, wax, tempera, acrylic, watercolor, or gouache. The medium can be applied to any support, i.e., canvas, linen, or board.[2] Paintings include illuminated manuscripts.

§ 6:22 Exclusions

The following elements in a painting will defeat duty-free entry under HS painting classification:

(1) paintings . . . obtained by photomechanical processes;

(2) paintings executed by hand on an outline or on a drawing obtained by ordinary engraving or printing processes;

(3) so-called " 'authentic copies' of paintings, obtained by means of a number of masks or stencils, even if [such] copies are certified authentic by

---

[2]Harmonized Tariff Schedule of the United States, § XXI, ch. 97, Explanatory Notes on "Works of Art, Collectors' Pieces and Antiques," § 97.01.

[Section 6:21]

[1]Harmonized Tariff Schedule Harmonized Tariff Schedule of the United States, § XXI, ch. 97, Explanatory Notes on "Works of Art, Collectors' Pieces and Antiques," at § 97.01.10.00.00.1.

[2]Excluded are hand decorated or hand painted manufactured articles. harmonized tariff schedule Harmonized Tariff Schedule of the United States, § XXI, ch. 97, Explanatory Notes on "Works of Art, Collectors' Pieces and Antiques," at 97.01; *see also* Madison Galleries, Ltd. v. U.S., 12 Ct. Int 485688 F. Supp. 1544 (1988), judgment aff'd, 7 Fed. Cir. (T) 56, 870 F.2d 627 (1989).

the artist."[1]

(4) paintings on canvas, even if executed entirely by hand and without the proscribed processes if used as "theatrical scenery [or] studio back-cloths"[2]

Note that "originality" is not required for paintings.

§ 6:23 Frames

Frames, if any, around the paintings, drawings, or pastels are treated as "part of those articles and classified with them . . . *only* if they are of a kind and of a value normal thereto."[1]

3. *Drawings*

§ 6:24 All hand limitation

Drawings must be executed entirely by hand. Drawings, like paintings, may not incorporate in part or in whole any other process.[1]

§ 6:25 Media and support

Drawings can be done in pencil, conte, charcoal, or pen, and executed on any support, i.e., paper, vellum, et cetera.[1]

[Section 6:22]

[1]Harmonized Tariff Schedule of the United States, § XXI, ch. 97, Explanatory Notes on "Works of Art, Collectors' Pieces and Antiques," § 9701.10, at 1616 (1992); *see* Appendix 12.

[2]Harmonized Tariff Schedule of the United States, § XXI, ch. 97, Explanatory Notes on "Works of Art, Collectors' Pieces and Antiques," § 9701.10, at 1616 (1992).

[Section 6:23]

[1]Harmonized Tariff Schedule of the United States, § XXI, ch. 97, Explanatory Notes on "Works of Art, Collectors' Pieces and Antiques," § 97.01B, at 1616 (1992) (emphasis in original); *see* Appendix 12.

[Section 6:24]

[1]See §§ 6:24 to 6:26.

[Section 6:25]

[1]Harmonized Tariff Schedule of the United States, § XXI, ch. 97, Explanatory Notes on "Works of Art, Collectors' Pieces and Antiques," § 9701.10, at 1616 (1992); *see* Appendix 12.

§ 6:26 Exclusions

Excluded are plans and drawings "for industrial, architectural or engineering purposes . . . fashion models, jewellery (sic), wallpaper, fabrics furniture, [even if] originals drawn by hand."[1]

Note that "originality" is not required for drawings.

4. *Photography*

§ 6:27 Generally

Printed photographs and photographic negatives or positives on transparent bases are treated differently in HS.[1] Photographs more than twenty years old at time of importation are duty free. Photographs less than twenty years old, if suitable for use in production of coffee-table books or art books or other catalog, are imported duty free.[2]

5. *Collages and Assemblages*

§ 6:28 Generally

Collages consisting of "bits and pieces of various animal, vegetable or other materials, assembled as to form a picture or decorative design or motif and glued or otherwise mounted on a backing, e.g., of wood, paper or textile material" are classified under "other"[1] and enter duty free,

---

[Section 6:26]

[1]Harmonized Tariff Schedule of the United States, § XXI, ch. 97, Explanatory Notes on "Works of Art, Collectors' Pieces and Antiques," § 9701.10, at 1616 (1992). These drawings can be classified under Appendix 12. § 49.06.

[Section 6:27]

[1]Chapter 37 covers negatives. Chapter 49 covers printed photographs. *See* Appendix 12.

[2]If the photograph "is suitable for use in the production of articles of 4901," then it is imported duty free.

[Section 6:28]

[1]Harmonized Tariff Schedule of the United States, § XXI, ch. 97, Explanatory Notes on "Works of Art, Collectors' Pieces and Antiques," § 9701.10, at 97.01B (1992). *See* Appendix 12.

including their surrounding frame,[2] if any. Collages enter duty free whether mass produced cheaply "for sale as souvenirs" or rendered with "a high degree of craftsmanship . . . [as] genuine works of art."[3]

Assemblages, constructions, and mobiles, which are not expressly mentioned in HS or annotations, could be classified as collages or sculptures; both sections should be investigated in the tariff schedules.

6. Engravings, Prints, and Lithographs

§ 6:29 Originality requirement

"Engravings, prints and lithographs,[1] . . . whether ancient or modern,[2] . . . irrespective of . . . process or . . . materials . . ." or medium are duty free providing that they "exclude[ ] any mechanical or photomechanical process" and are "originals."[3]

Original has been "judicially defined as original in design, conception and execution." An original for prints is an impression "produced directly, in black and white or in color, from one or several plates wholly executed by hand by the artist,"[4] or for lithographs by transfer technique whereby the artist makes the drawing and then transfers

---

[2]Harmonized Tariff Schedule of the United States, § XXI, ch. 97, Explanatory Notes on "Works of Art, Collectors' Pieces and Antiques," § 9701.10 (1992).

[3]Harmonized Tariff Schedule of the United States, § XXI, ch. 97, Explanatory Notes on "Works of Art, Collectors' Pieces and Antiques," § 9701.10 (1992).

[Section 6:29]

[1]Harmonized Tariff Schedule of the United States (1992), § XXI, ch. 97, Explanatory Notes on "Works of Art, Collectors' Pieces and Antiques," § 9702.00.00.00; *see* Appendix 12.

[2]Harmonized Tariff Schedule of the United States (1992), § XXI, ch. 97, Explanatory Notes on "Works of Art, Collectors' Pieces and Antiques," § 9702.00.00.00 at 1617.

[3]Harmonized Tariff Schedule of the United States (1992), § XXI, ch. 97, Explanatory Notes on "Works of Art, Collectors' Pieces and Antiques," § 9702.00.00.00.

[4]Harmonized Tariff Schedule of the United States (1992), § XXI, ch. 97, Explanatory Notes on "Work of Art, Collectors' Pieces and Antiques," § 97.02; *see* Appendix 12.

it to stone or works directly on the stone.[5] Even if the work has been retouched, it is still classified as an original.[6]

§ 6:30 Processes

Engravings can be done in any process:[1] "line-engraving, dry-point, acquatint (acid process) or stipple-engraving," and the medium can be applied to any support.

Woodcuts and woodblocks, which were expressly mentioned under TSUS,[2] are not recited in HS Section 97.02; they would appear to meet the definition of HS prints, providing that the other requirements are satisfied, as would serigraphs, monoprints, and monotypes.

§ 6:31 Exclusions

Stones and plates, whether they are copper, zinc, wood, or any other material from which the prints are pulled are excluded.[1]

§ 6:32 Frames

Frames, if any, are treated as "part of those articles and classified with them . . . *only* if they are of a kind and of a

---

[5]Harmonized Tariff Schedule of the United States (1992), § XXI, ch. 97, Explanatory Notes on "Work of Art, Collectors' Pieces and Antiques," § 97.02.

[6]Harmonized Tariff Schedule of the United States (1992), § XXI, ch. 97, Explanatory Notes on "Work of Art, Collectors' Pieces and Antiques," § 97.02.

[Section 6:30]

[1]Harmonized Tariff Schedule of the United States (1992), § XXI, ch. 97, Explanatory Notes on "Work of Art, Collectors' Pieces and Antiques," § 97.02, at § 9701.10.00.00.1.

[2]Tariff Schedules of the United States, sched. 7, pt. 11, § 765.10, chart 2 (1982).

[Section 6:31]

[1]Stones and plates are treated under Tariff Schedules of the United States, sched. 7, pt. 11 at § 84.42.

value normal thereto."[1]

7. *Sculptures and Statuary*

§ 6:33 Rule of original plus twelve

Sculpture or statuary, whether ancient or modern must be classified as an original work in the free fine arts for duty-free entry,[1] prepared by a professional artist.[2] The traditional basis for separating commercial sculpture from that of the "free fine arts" is whether or not the object bears the "rare and special genius Congress sought to protect in provided for free entry."[3]

HS allows duty-free entry of the "original sculpture made by the sculptor . . . [and] the first 12 castings, replicas or reproductions made from a sculptor's original work or model are duty free. The 12 may be made by the sculptor himself or by another artist, with or without a change in scale, and whether or not the sculptor is alive at the time the castings, replicas or reproductions are completed."[4]

§ 6:34 Originality requirement

Originality has been defined as original "in conception, execution and design," in contradistinction to artisans or

---

[Section 6:32]

[1]*See* Harmonized Tariff Schedule of the United States, § XXI, ch. 97, Explanatory Notes on "Works of Art, Collectors' Pieces and Antiques," § 97.01B, at 1616 (1992) (emphasis in original); *see* Appendix 12.

[Section 6:33]

[1]H.H. Elder & Co. v. U.S., 53 Cust. Ct. 116, 118, 1964 WL 9758 (Cust. Ct. 3 Div. 1964); Tutton v. Viti, 108 U.S. 312, 2 S. Ct. 687, 27 L. Ed. 737 (1883) ("The instructions of the Treasury Department (pursuant to which these duties were imposed) . . . [are based on] the statutes were made by men not really professional sculptors, though calling themselves such, and were not real works of art, but mere manufactures of marble by good artisans." [offered to jury]).

[2]*See* § 6:39.

[3]Seibert v. U.S., 65 Cust. Ct. 380, 1970 WL 15458 (Cust. Ct. 3 Div. 1970).

[4]Harmonized Tariff Schedule of the United States, Annot., § XXI, 97-1, at ¶ 1 (Addit. notes) (1992); *see* Appendix 12.

skilled craftspersons working in the decorative or industrial arts. Originality has been held to exist where patrons who commission sculpture offer suggestions to artists about form and composition;[1] and where the artist copies the sculpture from photographs rather than artistic designs, providing that artistic interpretation is added and the hand of the artist is palpable.[2]

§ 6:35 Materials

Sculpture can be carved or shaped directly into the materials like "stone, reconstituted stone, terra-cotta, wood, ivory[1], metal, wax."[2] Sculpture can be cast in bronze or plaster or "fired [as in ceramics] or otherwise hardened or maquettes may be reproduced in marble or other materials. Sculpture includes three-dimensional works "in the round," as well as "relief or statues, busts, figurines, groups, representations of animals, reliefs for architectural purposes."[3]

§ 6:36 Rule of fifty

Editions that contain more than 50 copies are classified

[Section 6:34]

[1]53 Cust. Ct. at 118; *but cf.* 65 Cust. Ct. at 380 (fifteen stone lanterns imported from Japan classified as dutiable over protest that they were original works of art where customs inspector was told that importer gave carver pictures and specifications to make earthenware lamps).

[2]53 Cust. Ct. at 120 ("Suggestions as to subject matter do not detract from originality of an artist's work."); *see also* Baldwin Shipping Co. v. U.S., T.D. 40051 (Ct. Cust. App. 1924); *but cf.,* 65 Cust. Ct. at 380 (fifteen carved stone lanterns imported from Japan classified as dutiable over protest that they were original works of art where importer provided carver with pictures and specifications).

[Section 6:35]

[1]Providing import does not violate federal restrictions on ivory importation.

[2]Harmonized Tariff Schedule of the United States (1992), § XXI, ch. 97, Explanatory Notes on "Works of Art, Collectors' Pieces and Antiques," § 97.03, at 1617; *see* Appendix 12.

[3]Harmonized Tariff Schedule of the United States (1992), § XXI, ch. 97, Explanatory Notes on "Works of Art, Collectors' Pieces and Antiques," § 97.03, at 1617.

as commercial works; none, not even the original plus 12, enter duty free.

Editions that contain less than or equal to fifty are classified according to component materials; only the original and the *first* 12 enter duty free. That means if 12 sculptures are imported, but the 12 are 13/50 through 25/50, the 12 would not enter duty free.

§ 6:37 Other exclusions

Duty is imposed on ornamental sculptures, works of conventional craft (ornaments, religious effigies, et cetera) and mass produced reproductions in plaster, cement, paper-mache.[1]

§ 6:38 Pedestals and bases

If sculptures are duty free, so are the pedestals and bases attached to or shipped with them.

§ 6:39 Rule of two es

The sculptor must qualify under U.S. Customs for the sculpture to enter duty free; the artist must have an "e" from either education or exhibition. The U.S. Customs will accept: (1) fine arts education; or (2) exhibition history.

Since sculptures must be established as professional productions to qualify for entry as works of the free fine arts:

> [T]he standard commonly accepted for determining whether the creator of a work is a professional sculptor is that he is a graduate of a course in sculpture at a recognized school of fine art [not industrial or decorative arts] or that he is recognized in art circles as a professional sculptor.[1]

[Section 6:37]

[1]Harmonized Tariff Schedule of the United States (1992), § XXI, ch. 97, Explanatory Notes on "Works of Art, Collectors' Pieces and Antiques," § 97.03, at 1617, at (a)–(c); *see* Appendix 12.

[Section 6:39]

[1]*The Harmonized Commodity Description and Coding System and United States Tariff* (1989), Introduction, W. Von Raab, Commissioner of Customs, at 3; *see also,* 19 U.S.C.A. § 1202, Pt. 11, subpt. A, *citing* Cust. Serv. CSD 81-54 (1980) ("Term 'professional' . . . refers to person

Artist materials relied upon are biography, exhibition catalogs, brochures, and critical reviews.

§ 6:40 Binding ruling classifications

Sculptors who regularly import into the United States may apply to U.S. Customs for a Binding Ruling Classification (BRC) to expedite importation. If the U.S. Customs issues a BRC, the artist does not have to requalify for each entry under the Rule of 2 Es. The BRC is issued by U.S. Customs; once obtained, it binds all U.S. Customs employees at all offices nationwide when presented for customs entry of sculptures. If the applicant changes media, i.e., from marble to bronze, the sculptor must provide U.S. Customs with written notification of the change.

To request a BRC, write to the U.S. Customs Service,[1] and include: (1) artist biography; (2) artist statement about sculptures; (3) identity of medium/media; and (4) excerpts from catalogs, brochures, or critical reviews. Customs has thirty days to respond to the request. It may (1) request more information; (2) issue a BRC; or (3) deny request.

8. Antiques

§ 6:41 100-year minimum

Antiques must be more than 100 years old to be imported duty free,[1] providing the object is not otherwise classified under other art headings discussed above.

§ 6:42 Object list

TSUS Section 9706.00 permits under the heading

---

who either (1) is graduate of course in sculpture at recognized school of free fine art or (2) is recognized in art circles as professional sculptor by acceptance of his works in public exhibitions limited to free fine arts").

[Section 6:40]

[1]BRC requests are processed by U.S. Customs Nat'l Import Specialists for Art and Antiques.

[Section 6:41]

[1]19 CFR § 10.53.

antiques, furniture,[1] frames, paneling, incunabula, books, music, maps, engravings otherwise not covered under art, vases, ceramics, carpets, tapestries, embroideries, laces, other fabrics, jewelry excluding pearls or semiprecious stones, smithworks in gold- or silver-like ewers, cups, candelabra, plates, leaded or stained glass windows, chandeliers and lamps, wares of iron mongers and locksmiths, boxes, sweetmeat boxes, snuff boxes, tobacco graters, caskets, fans, musical instruments, clocks and watches, and glyptographic wares like cameos, carved stones, and sigillographic wares (seals).[2]

In Elkins v. United States,[3] the court had to decide whether three coral and jade carvings of birds in arboreal settings and vases created in the People's Republic of China, imported from Singapore in 1974, should be classified as antiques under TSUS Section 766.25, original works of art under TSUS Section 765.25, original sculptures under TSUS Section 765.15 or—as U.S. Customs classified them—semiprecious stones under TSUS Section 520.61.

To prove the works were more than 100-year old, Elkins retained a curator of far eastern art from the Metropolitan Museum of Art, who compared the works to those in the museum's collection and catalogs and dated the pieces from the eighteenth and nineteenth century. The government's witness, a dealer and appraiser, found marks of modern tools on the birds. Persuaded that the marks were attributable to restoration of the birds' broken tails, not to creation of the birds, the court ordered the works classified as antiques.

§ 6:43 Restoration—Minor restoration

Antiques that have been restored or repaired within 100

[Section 6:42]

[1]Furniture is defined as "movable articles of convenience or decoration for use in furnishing a house, apartment, place of business or accommodation." 19 CFR § 10.53(c).

[2]Harmonized Tariff Schedule of the United States (1992), § XXI, ch. 97, Explanatory Notes on "Works of Art, Collectors' Pieces and Antiques," § 97.06, at 1619–20.

[3]Elkins v. U.S., 83 Cust. Ct. 132, 1979 WL 37208 (Cust. Ct. 1979).

years[1] from the importation date must "retain [their] original character to qualify as duty free antiques."[2] Under regulations interpreting TSUS, antique classifications, if the antique has been repaired with "a substantial amount of additional material, without changing the original form or shape, the original and added portions shall be appraised and reported as separate entities."[3] The basis for reporting shall be plainly indicated on the invoice by the appraiser. Duty is assessable on the restored portion added.[4]

§ 6:44 Restoration—Major restoration: The "identity rule"

If the identity of the antique is changed by repair or restoration, neither the underlying object nor the restored or repaired portion will enter duty free, here termed the "identity rule." If the restoration or repair adds "a feature which changes it substantially from the article originally produced, or if the antique portion has otherwise been so changed as to lose it identity as the article which was in existence" prior to the 100 years, the entire article shall be excluded from duty-free entry.[1]

§ 6:45 Restoration—50 percent rule

Art or antiques that are more than 50 percent restored are subject to reclassification; if presented as authentic from original period, the object would be reclassified as a

---

[Section 6:43]

[1]An example given by U.S. Customs is antique furniture, which incorporate modern manufacture for reinforcement or repair.

[2]Harmonized Tariff Schedule of the United States (1992), § XXI, ch. 97, Explanatory Notes on "Works of Art, Collectors' Pieces and Antiques," § 97.06, at 1620. But restoration and/or repair can affect authenticity; *see* Ch 3.

[3]19 CFR § 10.53(b).

[4]19 CFR § 10.53(b).

[Section 6:44]

[1]19 CFR § 10.53(b).

fake.[1]

§ 6:46 Restoration—Antiques for personal use

Antiques claimed duty free under HS Section 9706.00 may enter duty free if hand-carried by the passenger who executes a passenger declaration that the passenger or person filing the informal entry is the owner of the antiques and that they are for personal use, and not for sale or other commercial use.

9. Tapestries

§ 6:47 Generally

Gobelins tapestries produced at authorized Gobelins factories under the direction and control of the French government are duty free pursuant to TSUS Section 5805.00.10, providing that they are fit only for use as wall-hanging and valued at more than $215 per square meter.[1]

10. Stained Glass

§ 6:48 Generally

Stained glass, painted or colored windows or parts thereof must be made by artists or under their direction to be entered duty free, and their use must be for an institution established solely for religious purposes. U.S. Customs may request proof.[1]

11. Counterfeit Art

§ 6:49 Generally

Fake art or counterfeit art would be ineligible for duty

[Section 6:45]

[1] *See also* 19 CFR § 10.53(f) (object inauthentic by virtue of date).

[Section 6:47]

[1] 19 CFR § 10.54.

[Section 6:48]

[1] 19 CFR § 10.52.

free import under HS.[1] The artist must be identified on all art pursuant to the regulations and headnotes; intentional misidentification for purposes of importation also constitutes criminal fraud.[2]

D. DUTY RATES FOR ART OR ANTIQUE EXCLUSIONS

§ 6:50 "Essential character" doctrine

If the import is not classified as art or antique under HS, then classification is based upon "essential character." Essential character is "not easily defined . . . it has been construed to mean the attribute which strongly marks or serves to distinguish what an article is; that which is indispensable to the structure, core or conditions of the article"; or "determined by the nature of the material or component, its bulk, quantity, weight or value or by the role of a constituent material in relation to the use of goods." "Essential character bears no relationship to component material in chief value, and cannot be resolved on any single factor."[1]

§ 6:51 Raw materials

Raw materials are dutiable depending upon the degree of roughness and extent of processing. Quarry stone [marble] might be classified as a crude mineral substance, but if it were cleaned or slabbed, it might be classified as a processed mineral substance. Duty rates will differ; for the former, the rate is determined by weight; for the latter, rate is a percentage of purchase price. Customs has discretion to make the classification.

[Section 6:49]

[1]Balog v. Center Art Gallery-Hawaii, Inc., 745 F. Supp. 1556, 12 U.C.C. Rep. Serv. 2d 962 (D. Haw. 1990) (U.S. Treasury becomes a victim of art forgery through improper duty-free importation as original artwork under 19 U.S.C.A. § 1201, sched. 7 [now ch. 97]).

[2]*See* §§ 6:52 to 6:53.

[Section 6:50]

[1]*The Harmonized Commodity Description and Coding System and United States Tariff* (1989), Introduction, W. Von Raab, Commissioner of Customs, at 3.

E. FALSE OR IMPROPER CUSTOMS DECLARATIONS

§ 6:52 Federal laws

Several statutory provisions exist for U.S. Customs to monitor imports. Chart 6-1 signals key statutes. Enforcement mechanisms include detention, seizure, forfeiture, and penalties, including fines and imprisonment. Penalties are summarized in Chart 6-2. These are complicated areas, involving mostly policy interpretation, customs directives and few cases. Like virtually every other area in the rapidly developing field of art law, more and more cases, including those on seizure and forfeiture, are being decided.

Chart 6-1: Statutory Provisions Used by U.S. Customs in Monitoring Imports*	
Statute	Subject Matter
18 U.S.C.A. § 541[1]	Entry of goods falsely classified

[Section 6:52]

*Congress has amended major portions of title 18, which affects each of the statutes cited in Chart 6-1. (Pub. L. No. 103-322, tit. XXXIII, § 330016(1)(K)–(L), 108 Stat. 2147 (1994).) Each time a dollar amount appears for a fine in each statute, Congress replaced the words "not more than" and the specified dollar amount with the words, "under this title." Sentencing guidelines appear at the end of title 18.

[1] 18 U.S.C.A. § 541 states: "Whoever knowingly effects any entry of goods . . . upon a false classification as to quality or value, or by the payment of less than the amount of duty legally due, shall be fined not more than $5000 or imprisoned not more than two years, or both."

Chart 6-1: Statutory Provisions Used by U.S. Customs in Monitoring Imports	
Statute	Subject Matter
18 U.S.C.A. § 542[2]	Importation of merchandise by false statement
18 U.S.C.A. § 545[3]	Smuggling
18 U.S.C.A. § 1001[4]	False statements to U.S. Customs

[2] 18 U.S.C.A. § 542 states:

Whoever enters or introduces, or attempts [either], in to the commerce of the United States any imported merchandise by means of any fraudulent or false invoice, declaration, affidavit, letter, paper, or by means of any false statement, written or verbal, or by means of any false or fraudulent practice . . . or makes any false statement in any declaration without reasonable cause to believe the truth of such statement . . . whether or not the United States shall or may be deprived of any lawful duties; or Whoever is guilty of any willful act or omission whereby the United States shall or may be deprived of any lawful duties . . . shall be fined for each offense not more than $5000 or imprisoned not more than two years, or both.

[3] 18 U.S.C.A. § 545 states:

Whoever knowingly and willfully, with intent to defraud the United States, smuggles, or clandestinely introduces into the United States any merchandise which should have been invoiced, or makes out or passes, or attempts to pass, through the customhouse any false, forged, or fraudulent invoice, or other document or paper; or, [w]hoever fraudulently or knowingly imports or brings into the United States, any merchandise contrary to law . . . [s]hall be fined not more than $10,000 or imprisoned not more than five years, or both. Merchandise introduced into the United States in violation of this section . . . shall be forfeited to the United States.

[4] 18 U.S.C.A. § 1001 states:

Whoever, in any matter within the jurisdiction of any department or agency of the United States knowingly and willfully falsifies, conceals or covers up by any trick, scheme, or device a material fact, or makes any false, fictitious or fraudulent statements or representations, or makes or uses any false writing or document knowing the same to contain any false, fictitious or fraudulent statement or entry, . . . shall be fined not more than $10,000 or imprisoned not more than five years, or both.

Chart 6-2: Criminal Import Penalties*			
Statute	Fines	Penalties	Forfeiture
18 U.S.C.A. § 371	Up to $10,000 and/or	imprisonment up to five** years	
18 U.S.C.A. § 541	Up to $5,000 and/or	imprisonment up to two years	
18 U.S.C.A. § 542	Up to $5,000 and/or	imprisonment up to two years	forfeiture
18 U.S.C.A. § 545	Up to $10,000 and/or	imprisonment up to five years	forfeiture
18 U.S.C.A. § 2314	Up to $10,000 and/or	imprisonment up to ten years	forfeiture
18 U.S.C.A. § 2315	Up to $10,000 and/or	imprisonment up to ten years	forfeiture

§ 6:53 Statute of limitations

Section 1621 of title 19 of the U.S. Code provides as follows:

> No suit or action to recover any pecuniary penalty or forfeiture of property accruing under the customs laws shall be instituted unless such suit or action is commenced within five years after the time when the alleged offense was discovered . . .: Provided . . . that any concealment or absence of the property shall not be reckoned within this period of limitation.[1]

The discovery rule aspect of Section 1621, and its concealment exclusionary period, is important for art related cases.

---

* Congress has amended major portions of title 18, which affects each of the statutes cited in Chart 6-2. (Pub. L. No. 103-322, tit. XXXIII, § 330016(1)(K)–(L), 108 Stat. 2147 (1994).) Each time a dollar amount appears for a fine in each statute, Congress replaced the words “not more than” and the specified dollar amount with the words, “under this title.” Sentencing guidelines appear at the end of title 18.

** If offense is misdemeanor, punishment shall not exceed the maximum for that misdemeanor.

[Section 6:53]

[1] 19 U.S.C.A. § 1621.

F. ENFORCEMENT

1. Seizure

§ 6:54 Appraisal

U.S. Customs appraises property seized under customs laws.[1] The procedures for seizure differ depending upon the value of the property.

§ 6:55 Administrative claims: U.S. customs procedures

Persons claiming merchandise seized may file a claim with U.S. Customs within twenty days of notice of seizure and post a bond.[1] Seized property may be released to persons having "substantial interest" in the property who pay "the value of . . . merchandise."[2] U.S. Customs declares the merchandise seized if no claim or bond is filed and is authorized to auction it or dispose of it according to law.[3]

A U.S. Customs declaration of forfeiture has the force and effect of a final decree and order of judicial forfeiture.[4] Title vests in the United States from the date of the act for which the forfeiture was incurred.[5] The burden of proof is on the claimant in forfeiture proceedings.[6] Claimants are not required to exhaust administrative remedies for forfeiture with U.S. Customs before seeking judicial relief in district court.[7]

[Section 6:54]

[1] 19 U.S.C.A. § 1606.

[Section 6:55]

[1] 19 U.S.C.A. § 1608.

[2] 19 U.S.C.A. § 1614.

[3] 19 U.S.C.A. § 1609(a).

[4] 19 U.S.C.A. § 1609(b).

[5] 19 U.S.C.A. § 1609(b).

[6] 19 U.S.C.A. § 1615 (except for actions under 19 U.S.C.A. § 1592).

[7] U.S. v. One Tintoretto Painting Entitled The Holy Family With Saint Catherine and Honored Donor, 691 F.2d 603 (2d Cir. 1982).

§ 6:56 Property valued at less than $10,000

Seized property must be appraised to determine value[1] because procedures differ depending upon the value of the property. If the value of the property does not exceed $10,000, summary seizure without hearing is permitted.[2] Seized property remains in the "custody of the appropriate customs officer for the district in which the seizure was made to await disposition according to law."[3] A person seeking claim to the seized property can post a bond with the district director of customs in order to stop summary forfeiture proceedings.[4] If a bond is posted, the claimant is entitled to assert his interests in court. If no bond is posted, claimant still has administrative remedy. If no petition for relief from forfeiture is made to the Secretary of Treasury, the government can dispose of the property.[5]

§ 6:57 Property valued at $10,000 or more

If the property is valued at $10,000 or more, the district director must file a report with the U.S. Attorney in the district where the property was seized.[1] The U.S. Attorney, not the U.S. Customs, then institutes a forfeiture proceeding in district court.[2] The seized property is within the jurisdiction of the applicable district court.

[Section 6:56]

[1] 19 U.S.C.A. § 1606; 19 CFR § 162.43(a).

[2] 19 U.S.C.A. § 1607 (Supp.); 19 CFR § 162.45. *See* U.S. v. One Tintoretto Painting Entitled The Holy Family With Saint Catherine and Honored Donor, 691 F.2d 603 (2d Cir. 1982).

[3] 19 U.S.C.A. § 1605.

[4] 19 U.S.C.A. § 1608; 19 CFR § 162.47.

[5] 19 U.S.C.A. § 1609; 19 CFR § 162.46(a); *see* U.S. v. One Tintoretto Painting Entitled The Holy Family With Saint Catherine and Honored Donor, 691 F.2d 603 (2d Cir. 1982).

[Section 6:57]

[1] 19 U.S.C.A. § 1610.

[2] 19 U.S.C.A. § 1604; U.S. v. An Antique Platter of Gold, 184 F.3d 131 (2d Cir. 1999), cert. denied, 528 U.S. 1136, 120 S. Ct. 978, 145 L. Ed. 2d 929 (2000) (summary judgment for government in civil forfeiture of an antique gold Sicilian bowl valued at more than $1 million affirmed on appeal).

2. *Forfeiture*

§ 6:58 Civil action in rem

An action for forfeiture is derived from common law. Forfeiture can be sought under a variety of statutes;[1] its purposes are variously stated and depend upon related proceedings and underlying claims.[2] The government procedure is to bring a civil action in rem that "may be . . . quasi-criminal . . . [but] is a separate and distinct proceeding from the criminal proceeding against the offending person [with] forfeiture [being] 'no part of the punishment for the criminal offense.' "[3] The government has the initial burden of establishing probable cause that the property is subject to forfeiture. Section 1615 of title 19 of the U.S. Code imposes on the government the requirement of probable cause to seize the art prior to implementing the forfeiture. Section 1615 provides:

> In all . . . actions . . . brought for the forfeiture of any . . . merchandise. . . seized under the provisions of any law relating to. . . the collection of duties on imports. . . where the property is claimed by any person, the burden of proof shall be upon the claimant. . . *provided,* that probable cause

---

[Section 6:58]

[1]*See, e.g.,* 18 U.S.C.A. §§ 545, 2314-15; 18 U.S.C.A. § 981(a)(1)(C); 19 U.S.C.A. § 1595a(c), 19 U.S.C.A. §§ 2607, 2609 (CPIA); 22 U.S.C.A. § 401 *see also* §§ 6:77 to 6:115 and Ch 11 §§ 11:35 to 11:59.

[2]U.S. v. Portrait of Wally, 105 F. Supp. 2d 288 (S.D. N.Y. 2000) (forfeiture under 19 U.S.C.A. § 1595a(c) and 22 U.S.C.A. § 401(a) sought by government based upon claim that painting by Egon Schiele loaned by Austrian museum to Museum of Modern Art for exhibition was stolen during World War II)(complaint dismissed); U.S. v. An Original Manuscript Dated November 19, 1778, 1999 WL 97894 (S.D. N.Y. 1999) (forfeiture based upon Cultural Property Implementation Act); *see also* §§ 6:93 to 6:99; U.S. v. An Antique Platter of Gold, 991 F. Supp. 222 (S.D. N.Y. 1997), aff'd, 184 F.3d 131 (2d Cir. 1999), cert. denied, 528 U.S. 1136, 120 S. Ct. 978, 145 L. Ed. 2d 929 (2000) (forefeiture proper under 18 U.S.C.A. § 545 based upon material false statements on customs forms); Angel v. Seattle-First Nat. Bank, 653 F.2d 1293 (9th Cir. 1981) ("forfeiture is not to impose punishment without fault on those who are acting 'in good faith and without negligence' ").

[3]U.S. v. One Tintoretto Painting Entitled The Holy Family With Saint Catherine and Honored Donor, 691 F.2d 603 (2d Cir. 1982).

shall be first shown.[4]

Once the government meets its burden, the burden shifts to the claimant to show that the property is not subject to forfeiture.[5] The claimant must demonstrate (1) substantial interest in the seized property, and (2) innocence of the unlawful importation.

In what appears to be the first reported forfeiture under the Cultural Property Implementation Act, a district court, relying upon legislative history, decided that the United States must establish the material is within the scope of the statute[6] and that it was stolen from the institution within the designated time frames.[7]

§ 6:59 Proof of ownership for standing

To establish standing, a claimant must demonstrate some ownership or possessory interest in the property. Such interests may be proven "by actual possession,

---

[4]19 U.S.C.A. § 1615; United States v. Wally, 2002 WL 553552 (S.D.N.Y. 2002) (reviewing constitutionality of probable cause standard and upholding propriety of civil forfeiture against due process challenges); *see also* U.S. v. An Antique Platter of Gold, 991 F. Supp. 222 (S.D. N.Y. 1997), aff'd, 184 F.3d 131 (2d Cir. 1999), cert. denied, 528 U.S. 1136, 120 S. Ct. 978, 145 L. Ed. 2d 929 (2000) (stay granted) (to meet the burden, government must show "reasonable grounds, rising above the level of mere suspicion . . ."); U.S. v. One 18th Century Colombian Monstrance, 797 F.2d 1370, 1 U.C.C. Rep. Serv. 2d 1492 (5th Cir. 1986) (claimant must establish standing before probable cause can be raised).

[5]U.S. v. An Antique Platter of Gold, 991 F. Supp. 222 (S.D. N.Y. 1997), aff'd, 184 F.3d 131 (2d Cir. 1999), cert. denied, 528 U.S. 1136, 120 S. Ct. 978, 145 L. Ed. 2d 929 (2000) (civil forfeiture of antique gold Sicilian bowl affirmed where claimant could not show misstatements on customs forms were immaterial); U.S. v. An Original Manuscript Dated November 19, 1778, 1999 WL 97894 (S.D. N.Y. 1999) (claimant must establish by a preponderance of the evidence that the property is not subject to forfeiture but holding under 19 U.S.C.A. § 2610 CPIA forfeiture, the burden of proof lies with the government); *see also* §§ 6:93 to 6:99.

[6]19 U.S.C.A. §§ 2607, 2609.

[7]U.S. v. An Original Manuscript Dated November 19, 1778, 1999 WL 97894 (S.D. N.Y. 1999) (forfeiture based upon Cultural Property Implementation Act); *see also* §§ 6:93 to 6:99.

dominion, control, title or financial stake."[1] What rises to the level of ownership varies by jurisdiction, particularly interpretation of financial interest.

In United States v. One 18th Century Colombian Monstrance,[2] the country of Colombia and a dealer attempted to claim a jewel encrusted gold holy relic made for a Colombian convent (the monstrance) by challenging judicial forfeiture under Section 545 of title 18 of the U.S. Code based on his authorized interest to sell it. (The importer was indicted for violation of Section 542 of title 18 of the U.S. Code for falsely stating on import documents that the monstrance was imported from Bogota, Spain, when in fact it was imported from Bogota, Colombia; Colombia required export licenses, which would not have been issued.)

Colombia dropped its forfeiture claim when the United States agreed to return the monstrance after an exhibition in the United States. The district court dismissed the dealer's claim, finding the dealer lacked standing because he had neither equitable nor legal ownership in the monstrance. The dealer "was but a broker or consignee, and his financial stake in the Monstrance was not that of ownership but, at most, that a (sic) secured claim or a contingent future interest."

By comparison, in United States v. Two Gandharan Stone Sculptures,[3] which was not a Section 545 seizure, Pakistan sought return of stone sculptures dating from 200 to 300 A.D., which had been imported into the United States by a third party in alleged violation of NSPA. U.S. Customs detained the shipment. Pakistan's ownership claims were rooted in national treasure legislation that

---

[Section 6:59]

[1]U.S. v. An Antique Platter of Gold, 991 F. Supp. 222 (S.D. N.Y. 1997), aff'd, 184 F.3d 131 (2d Cir. 1999), cert. denied, 528 U.S. 1136, 120 S. Ct. 978, 145 L. Ed. 2d 929 (2000) (citations omitted) (actual possession, dominion and control over platter by claimant at his private residence for three-year period established standing to contest government seizure).

[2]U.S. v. One 18th Century Colombian Monstrance, 797 F.2d 1370, 1 U.C.C. Rep. Serv. 2d 1492 (5th Cir. 1986).

[3]U.S. v. Two Gandharan Stone Sculptures, 1986 WL 8344 (N.D. Ill. 1986).

purported to give Pakistan acquisition rights when antiquities were improperly removed from Pakistan. Ruling that Pakistan did not have to make a showing of "how it acquired ownership," the district court stated: "Pakistan has sufficiently alleged its ownership of the sculptures. It need not allege how it acquired title."

§ 6:60 Exhausting administrative remedies

In United States v. One Tinteretto Painting Entitled "The Holy Family with St. Catherine & Honored Donor,"[1] an Israeli national appealed from summary judgment on forfeiture of a Tintoretto painting seized by U.S. Customs under Section 545 of title 18 of the U.S. Code. He claimed ownership at a hearing to enforce the forfeiture on facts that he purchased the painting from a second hand shop in Moscow in 1948, paying the equivalent of $20,000. After owning the picture for thirty years, during which time he openly displayed it, he entrusted it to an art dealer on a commission basis to sell in the United States, contracting to pay any duties owed as well as shipping and other expenses.

The dealer flew to the United States, sending the painting on a different flight, and arranging for a cohort to pick it up at the airport for importation as "personal effects" valued at less than $500. An FBI agent posing as a dealer expressed interest in buying the painting; when the deal was struck at $250,000, the dealer was arrested; he plead guilty to "making false statements in a Customs Bureau document" under Section 542.

The district court held that the claimant was not entitled to a trial because he failed to avail himself of administrative remedy for remission or mitigation of forfeiture provided under Section 1618, title 19 of the U.S. Code. The Second Circuit reversed summary judgment and remanded to the trial court emphasizing that the absence of mandatory terms in Section 1618 like "must"

[Section 6:60]

[1]U.S. v. One Tintoretto Painting Entitled The Holy Family With Saint Catherine and Honored Donor, 691 F.2d 603 (2d Cir. 1982), *questioned by,* U.S. v. An Antique Platter of Gold, 184 F.3d 131, 139 (2d Cir. 1999), cert. denied, 528 U.S. 1136, 120 S. Ct. 978, 145 L. Ed. 2d 929 (2000).

or "shall" gave the claimant right to judicial relief. Claimant had the option to defer judicial relief if he initially proceeded administratively: "[W]here . . . he chooses not to seek administrative relief, his rights in the property are to be determined in the district court proceeding."[2] The Second Circuit found the owner had to present evidence that he did "all that 'reasonably could be expected' of him[3] to avoid the proscribed use of his property" by contracting to pay shipping and duties to import the art into the United States.

§ 6:61 Administrative remedies if no standing

Lesser property interests than ownership are nonetheless recognized in post-forfeiture proceedings. Claimants who cannot prove ownership, and lack standing to challenge forfeiture, still have available the remedy of applying to the Secretary of the Treasury for remission under Section 1617 of title 19 of the U.S. Code after the government acquires title through forfeiture.

§ 6:62 False statements on customs forms

Section 545 of Title 18[1] provides for forfeiture to the United States of merchandise fraudulently imported or imported contrary to law.[2] A district court granted summary judgment for the government in a civil forfeiture proceeding[3] involving a Sicilian gold platter dated from

---

[2]U.S. v. One Tintoretto Painting Entitled The Holy Family With Saint Catherine and Honored Donor, 691 F.2d 603 at 609, (2d Cir. 1982), *questioned by,* U.S. v. An Antique Platter of Gold, 184 F.3d 131, 139 (2d Cir. 1999), cert. denied, 528 U.S. 1136, 120 S. Ct. 978, 145 L. Ed. 2d 929 (2000).

[3]U.S. v. One Tintoretto Painting Entitled The Holy Family With Saint Catherine and Honored Donor, 691 F.2d 603 at 607, (2d Cir. 1982), *questioned by,* U.S. v. An Antique Platter of Gold, 184 F.3d 131, 139 (2d Cir. 1999), cert. denied, 528 U.S. 1136, 120 S. Ct. 978, 145 L. Ed. 2d 929 (2000) (citations omitted).

[Section 6:62]

[1]*See* Chart 6-1 in §§ 6:52 to 6:53 for full text of statute.

[2]*See* § 6:52 for full text of statute.

[3]U.S. v. An Antique Platter of Gold, 991 F. Supp. 222 (S.D. N.Y. 1997), aff'd, 184 F.3d 131 (2d Cir. 1999), cert. denied, 528 U.S. 1136,

the Fifth Century, B.C., affirmed on appeal.[4] The collector who displayed the object in his home for a period of years appealed, challenging the materiality of the misstatements on the customs form under Section 542.[5] The country of origin was misstated, identifying Switzerland instead of Italy, and the value was stated at $250,000 instead of the actual sales price of more than $1 million.

Section 542 includes a materiality requirement in the Second Circuit. In An Antique Platter of Gold, the test for materiality under Section 542 adopted by that Circuit is the natural tendency test.[6] A false statement is material "'if it has the potential significantly to affect the integrity or operation of the importation process as a whole, and that neither actual causation nor harm to the government need be demonstrated.'"[7] The query is whether a "reasonable customs official would consider the statements to be significant to the exercise of . . . official duties."[8]

Relying upon Customs Directive No. 5230-15 advising customs officials to determine whether property is subject to a claim of foreign ownership for purposes of detention and seizure of cultural property, the court held country of origin is material.[9]

---

120 S. Ct. 978, 145 L. Ed. 2d 929 (2000) (antique gold platter of Sicilian origin falsely declared on U.S. Customs documents ordered forefeited to the United States pursuant to 18 U.S.C.A. § 545, 18 U.S.C.A. § 981(a)(1)(C) and 19 U.S.C.A. § 1595a(c)).

[4] U.S. v. An Antique Platter of Gold, 184 F.3d 131 (2d Cir. 1999), cert. denied, 528 U.S. 1136, 120 S. Ct. 978, 145 L. Ed. 2d 929 (2000) (forefeiture proper under 18 U.S.C.A. § 545 based upon material false statements on customs forms).

[5] U.S. v. An Antique Platter of Gold, 184 F.3d 131 (2d Cir. 1999), cert. denied, 528 U.S. 1136, 120 S. Ct. 978, 145 L. Ed. 2d 929 (2000).

[6] U.S. v. An Antique Platter of Gold, 184 F.3d 131 (2d Cir. 1999), cert. denied, 528 U.S. 1136, 120 S. Ct. 978, 145 L. Ed. 2d 929 (2000).

[7] U.S. v. An Antique Platter of Gold, 184 F.3d 131 (2d Cir. 1999), cert. denied, 528 U.S. 1136, 120 S. Ct. 978, 145 L. Ed. 2d 929 (2000) (citations omitted).

[8] U.S. v. An Antique Platter of Gold, 184 F.3d 131 (2d Cir. 1999), cert. denied, 528 U.S. 1136, 120 S. Ct. 978, 145 L. Ed. 2d 929 (2000).

[9] U.S. v. An Antique Platter of Gold, 184 F.3d 131 (2d Cir. 1999), cert. denied, 528 U.S. 1136, 120 S. Ct. 978, 145 L. Ed. 2d 929 (2000).

§ 6:63 Other forfeitures

In United States v. Swetnam,[1] rare Peruvian artifacts were seized under Section 545 when American dealers imported them into the United States by transshipping them from Peru to London, repackaging them in smaller shipments, and labeling them as "personal effects" valued at under $10,000, the amount permitted for permanent residents to import things for personal use, and not commercial resale. The dealers were charged with violating Sections 545 and 1001, one of whom plead guilty to smuggling under Section 545 and served approximately six months imprisonment.

In Angel v. Seattle-First National Bank,[2] paintings were smuggled into the United States by various defendants convicted in separate criminal proceedings. They were targets of an American sting operation undertaken in part in Canada, where undercover agents posing as buyers purchased the paintings from a private citizen. After defendants were convicted, the paintings were forfeited to the government under Sections 1462 and 1581(e) of title 19 of the U.S. Code.

G. ADDITIONAL IMPORT RESTRICTIONS

§ 6:64 Section 305(a) of the Tariff Act of 1930 (19 U.S.C.A. Section 1305)—Seizure authorization

In addition to import restrictions discussed above, Section 305(a) of the Tariff Act of 1930 provides additional restrictions: these include prohibition on importing immoral articles,[1] obscene materials,[2] treasonous materials, and documents of insurrection.[3]

Any material in violation of Section 305(a) "shall be

[Section 6:63]

[1]United States v. Swetnam, 720 F. Supp 810.

[2]Angel v. Seattle-First Nat. Bank, 653 F.2d 1293 (9th Cir. 1981).

[Section 6:64]

[1]19 U.S.C.A. § 1305(a) states: ("All persons are prohibited from importing into the United States from any foreign country . . . any . . . print, picture, drawing, or other representation, figure, or image . . . which is immoral.").

seized [by U.S. Customs] . . . to await the judgment of the district court."[4] The timing of seizure and the institution of judicial proceedings for forfeiture under Section 305 is strictly applied.[5] For obscene material, forfeiture proceedings must begin "no more than 30 days after the time the material is seized."[6] If after seizure the material seized is adjudicated to be in violation of Section 305(a), then "it shall be ordered destroyed and it shall be destroyed."[7] "[W]henever a customs officer discovers any obscene material after such material has been imported or brought into the United States, . . . he may refer to the matter to the U.S. Attorney for . . . forfeiture proceedings."[8] Criminal prosecution can be brought separately under Section 305.[9]

---

[2] 19 U.S.C.A. § 1305(a) states: ("All persons are prohibited from importing into the United States from any foreign country . . . any obscene . . . new print, picture, drawing, or other representation, figure, or image on or of paper or other material, or any cast, instrument or other article which is obscene."); *see also* Parmelee v. U.S., 113 F.2d 729 (App. D.C. 1940) (appellate court reverses libel against importer to destroy six books titled *Nudism in Modern Life* imported via mails and seized by U.S. Customs under 19 U.S.C.A. § 1305(a), stating, "nudity in art has long been recognized as the reverse of obscene. Art galleries and art catalogues contain many nudes, ancient and modern.").

[3] 19 U.S.C.A. § 1305(a) ("All persons are prohibited from importing into the United States from any foreign country any . . . print, picture, or drawing containing any matter advocating or urging treason or insurrection against the United States, or forcible resistance to any law of the United States."); *see also* Cuban Asset Control Regulations, 31 CFR § 515.570, revised after Trading With the Enemy Act (50 U.S.C.A. app. 5(b)(4)) invoked to prohibit Florida museum from exhibiting paintings by Cuban artists who did not denounce Fidel Castro.

[4] 19 U.S.C.A. § 1305(b).

[5] United States v. 37 Photographs, 402 U.S. 363, 91 S. Ct 400 (1971), reh'g denied, 403 U.S. 924,91 S.Ct 2221.

[6] 19 U.S.C.A. § 1305(c).

[7] 19 U.S.C.A. § 1305(b).

[8] 19 U.S.C.A. § 1305(c).

[9] 19 U.S.C.A. §§ 1305(d) et seq.

§ 6:65 Section 305(a) of the Tariff Act of 1930 (19 U.S.C.A. Section 1305)—Obscene materials

In Parmellee v. United States,[1] U.S. Customs seized six books under Section 1305(a) of title 19 of the U.S. Code that were imported via the mails. The title was *Nudism in Modern Life*. Reversing libel against the importer, the appellate court stated: "[N]udity in art has long been recognized as the reverse of obscene. Art galleries and art catalogues contain many nudes, ancient and modern." Although contemporary artwork was seized at the Canadian-American border in the 1990s because of its allegedly obscene content, no charges were filed, and no recent case could be found.

§ 6:66 Unlawful imports of merchandise (19 U.S.C.A. Section 1595)

Even after the import is moved as merchandise into a business, warehouse, facility, or household, U.S. Customs has general authority under warrant to seize merchandise imported unlawfully.[1]

§ 6:67 National Stolen Property Act (18 U.S.C.A. Sections 2314–15)

Customs has the right to detain, seize, and seek forfeiture of property imported in violation of the National Stolen Property Act (NSPA).[1] NSPA art cases are discussed

---

[Section 6:65]

[1]Parmelee v. U.S., 113 F.2d 729 (App. D.C. 1940).

[Section 6:66]

[1]19 U.S.C.A. § 1595 (seizure of unlawfully imported merchandise); *see also* 19 U.S.C.A. § 1615.

[Section 6:67]

[1]18 U.S.C.A. §§ 2314–2315 (NSPA); *see* Ch 11 §§ 11:35 to 11:59 for full text of NSPA. *See, e.g.,* U.S. v. Portrait of Wally, 105 F. Supp. 2d 288 (S.D. N.Y. 2000) (forfeiture under 19 U.S.C.A. 1595a(c) and 22 U.S.C.A. 401(a) sought by government based upon claim that painting by Egon Schiele loaned by Austrian museum to Museum of Modern Art for exhibition was stolen during World War II)(complaint dismissed; U.S. v. Portrait of Wally, A Painting By Egon Schiele, 2002 WL 553532 (S.D. N.Y. 2002) (motions to dismiss third amended complaint denied));

later.[2]

§ 6:68 Unlawful imports of cultural property (19 U.S.C.A. Sections 2601–2613)

Customs has the right to detain, seize, and forfeit cultural property imported in violation of Cultural Property Implementation Act (CPIA),[1] or other special art import control laws. CPIA does not supersede the NSPA.[2] Cultural property is discussed later in this chapter.[3]

Importers should be aware that all art from abroad, regardless of whether it is cultural property, should be brought to the United States with extensive documentation, including deeds of gift or inter vivos transfer, bills of lading, bills of sale, copies of catalogue descriptions, et cetera. The art can be detained by U.S. Customs as cultural property in the absence of documentation; even if admitted into the United States from customs custody, false or improper importation can precipitate seizure at a

---

U.S. v. An Antique Platter of Gold, 991 F. Supp. 222 (S.D. N.Y. 1997), aff'd, 184 F.3d 131 (2d Cir. 1999), cert. denied, 528 U.S. 1136, 120 S. Ct. 978, 145 L. Ed. 2d 929 (2000) (U.S. Attorney instituted forfeiture proceedings under 19 U.S.C.A. § 1595a(c) for a gold Sicilian platter dating from the fourth century B.C. in private possession of an American collector on grounds, *inter alia,* that it constituted stolen property under Italian law for purposes of the NSPA, an issue not reached on appeal); State v. Wilson, 1986 WL 834 (Tenn. Crim. App. 1986) (U.S. Customs detained Pakistani Gandharan sculptures, circa 200–300 A.D., upon importation into the United States in violation of NSPA §§ 2314–2315); U.S. v. Pre-Columbian Artifacts, 845 F. Supp. 544 (N.D. Ill. 1993) (U.S. Customs seized pre- Columbian artifacts from Guatemala upon importation into the United States allegedly in violation of NSPA §§ 2314–2315).

[2]*See* Ch 11 §§ 11:35 to 11:59, for detailed discussion of NSPA as applied to artworks imported from various countries.

[Section 6:68]

[1]CPIA, 19 U.S.C.A. §§ 2601 et seq. *see* §§ 6:77 to 6:115 and Appendix 14.

[2]U.S. v. Schultz, 178 F. Supp. 2d 445 (S.D. N.Y. 2002), aff'd, 333 F.3d 393 (2d Cir. 2003), cert. denied, 124 S. Ct. 1051, 157 L. Ed. 2d 891 (U.S. 2004) (motion to dismiss NSPA charges on ground that civil remedies supersede criminal penalties denied); see also S.Rep.No. 97-564 at 25, 2d. Sess. (1982) (CPIA "neither pre-empts state law in any way, nor modifies any Federal or State remedies. . .").

[3]*See* §§ 6:77 to 6:115.

later date;[4] or the art can be unmarketable because of clouds on title.[5]

§ 6:69 Copyright import prohibitions (17 U.S.C.A. Sections 601–603)

Importation of and unauthorized copies pirated materials are both unlawful.[1] Special bonds are issued to indemnify the United States for detention of copyrighted material alleged to be piratical,[2] and they are ordinarily paid by the copyright owner challenging the importation.[3]

§ 6:70 Imports of false designation, origin, or description (15 U.S.C.A. Section 1125)

Articles having false designations, descriptions, and representations, including symbols, "tending falsely to describe or represent the articles" are prohibited

---

[4]19 U.S.C.A. § 1595 (merchandise unlawfully imported can be seized subsequently).

[5]Jeanneret v. Vichey, 693 F.2d 259, 35 U.C.C. Rep. Serv. 75 (2d Cir. 1982); Autocephalous Greek-Orthodox Church of Cyprus v. Goldberg & Feldman Fine Arts Inc., 717 F. Supp. 1374 (S.D. Ind. 1989), judgment aff'd, 917 F.2d 278 (7th Cir. 1990).

[Section 6:69]

[1]17 U.S.C.A. §§ 601–03; 19 CFR pt. 133; 19 CFR § 11.13. Section 602(a) of the Copyright Act of 1976 provides: "Importation into the [U.S.] without the authority of the owner of copyright . . . of copies . . . of a work that have been acquired outside the [U.S.] is an infringement of the exclusive right to distribute copies . . . under Section 106." 17 U.S.C.A. § 602(a); *see also* H.R. Rep. No. 1476, 94th Cong., 2d Sess. 169, 170 (1976) ("the mere act of importation . . . constitutes an act of infringement."); Parfums Givenchy, Inc. v. C & C Beauty Sales, Inc., 832 F. Supp. 1378 (C.D. Cal. 1993) (unauthorized importation of French perfume through gray market constitutes violation of copyright).

[2]19 CFR § 113.70.

[3]Wildlife Exp. Corp. v. Carol Wright Sales, Inc., 18 F.3d 502 (7th Cir. 1994) (U.S. Customs Service issued notice to defendant-infringer that its importation of duffle bags infringed copyright registered and owned by plaintiff, but U.S. Customs Service cancelled notice when plaintiff did not post bond required to contest the shipment as violative of copyright).

importation.[1] Art has been successfully described as an article with false designation and description under the Lanham Act,[2] but no importation case based on this section could be found.

If objects are detained by U.S. Customs in accordance with federal regulation, and the United States attorney does not prosecute, the objects "shall be seized and forfeited in the usual manner."[3] The district director can release the articles upon a petition from the importer prior to the final disposition of the objects, if the prohibited marking is "removed or obliterated."[4]

II. ART EXPORTS

§ 6:71 National protection laws

America does not have specific laws dedicated to restricting exportation of art, with minor exceptions.[1] NSPA prohibits placement of stolen art in foreign commerce.[2] The Archaeological Resources Protection Act (ARPA)[3] prohibits sale of certain materials and artifacts of indigenous cultures in foreign commerce.[4]

Whether there is an "American" culture of unique national significance is a philosophical as well as a political question. The colonial period is a source of American treasures, particularly the decorative arts, and much "Americana" has ensued since that era. But America has an indigenous culture that predates colonialism, and Native Americans have historically claimed their culture, or

---

[Section 6:70]

[1] 15 U.S.C.A. § 1125; 19 CFR § 11.13; 15 U.S.C.A. §§ 294–96; *see generally,* 19 CFR pt. 133; *see also* 15 U.S.C.A. § 1124.

[2] *See, e.g.,* Romm Art Creations Ltd. v. Simcha Intern., Inc., 786 F. Supp. 1126 (E.D. N.Y. 1992).

[3] 19 CFR § 11.13(c)–(d).

[4] 19 CFR § 11.13(c)–(d).

[Section 6:71]

[1] Bilateral treaties of cooperation have as a goal repatriation of art, discussed in §§ 6:77 to 6:115. *See* Chart 6-9.

[2] *See* Ch 11 for text of NSPA text and discussion; *see also* Chart 6-2.

[3] 16 U.S.C.A. §§ 470aa et seq.

[4] *See* Ch 14.

attempted to do so, well before the advent of contemporary multiculturalism. That culture is increasingly recognized by federal laws.[5]

America's lack of cultural export laws stands in contradistinction to many other countries. Foreign countries often have art protectionist laws, variously referred to as umbrella laws, blanket laws, antiquities laws or patrimony laws. These laws are the means whereby a sovereign asserts, or at least attempts to assert, ownership interest in properties over which it more likely than not lacks possession, custody, or control. Export beyond the territory of the sovereign is prohibited, or at least strictly controlled through export restrictions. The justification is protection of national heritage and the controls are deemed necessary to prevent cultural products from disappearing. Although the justification has some historical and empirical support, the laws are controversial, and American courts have been reluctant to enforce them.[6]

§ 6:72 Export of funds to purchase art abroad

The Currency and Foreign Transactions Reporting Act[1] and implementing regulations require reporting of removal from the United States of currency or monetary instruments to pay for art (or anything) "in an aggregate amount exceeding $10,000 on any one occasion," for anyone who "transports, mails, ships or receives, or attempts, causes or attempts to cause the transportation, mailing, shipping or receiving of currency or monetary instruments in excess of $10,000 for or to a place outside the United States."[2] Incidents of large monetary transfers are common for art purchases abroad.

Withdrawal of the amount in the United States imposes upon the person, not the financial institution from whom the amount is withdrawn, an obligation to complete and file a Currency Monetary Instrument Report (CMIR) re-

---

[5]*See* Ch 13 §§ 13:19 to 13:22, for laws regarding Native American materials.

[6]*See* §§ 6:77 to 6:115.

[Section 6:72]

[1]31 U.S.C.A. §§ 5311–5326.

[2]31 CFR §§ 103 et seq., Customs Form 4790.

cording the transaction.[3] However, where the institution suspects the withdrawal will not be reported properly, procedures exist for it to notify Customs.

Customs Form 4790 must be completed and provided to U.S. Customs upon entering into or departing from the United States.[4] Penalties for violation include fines up to $500,000 and imprisonment up to five years, in addition to seizure and forfeiture of the currency or monetary instrument.[5]

Under the Bank Secrecy Act[6] and implementing regulations, American financial institutions must report deposits or withdrawals in excess of $10,000. The institution is obligated to complete and file a Currency Transaction Report (CTR), IRS Form 4789 for transactions in excess of $10,000.

Dividing large amounts of money into deposits of less than $10,000 among many financial institutions to avoid the reporting requirement is known in law enforcement as "smurfing." One civil suit involving international importation of art describes smurfing without identifying the term.[7] Administrative rulings on financial recordkeeping for these reporting requirements involving foreign transactions state that an institution suspecting smurfing "should immediately contact the IRS Criminal Investigation Division." Other administrative rulings in this area have been made in the arts context.[8]

§ 6:73 Exports of intangible personal property

Export of intangible interests are governed by intellectual property laws and conventions. The United States

---

[3]31 CFR § 103.23.

[4]Report of Int'l Transportation of Currency or Monetary Instruments, U.S. Customs Form 4790, pursuant to 31 CFR §§ 103.23, 103.25; 31 U.S.C.A. § 5316.

[5]31 CFR 103.47–49.

[6]31 U.S.C.A. 5311–5326.

[7]Autocephalous Greek-Orthodox Church of Cyprus v. Goldberg & Feldman Fine Arts Inc., 717 F. Supp. 1374 (S.D. Ind. 1989), judgment aff'd, 917 F.2d 278 (7th Cir. 1990).

[8]31 CFR 103 (artist single deposits at bank in excess of $10,000 during her exhibition should be treated under "know your customer rule").

has not yet sought to protect art specifically. For example, the Smithsonian Institution licensed China to manufacture colonial quilts and classic American objects in its collection.

§ 6:74 Repatriation of art to foreign owners when taken abroad

Art legally sent abroad for mercantile purposes can be done without special export licenses.[1] But if at some point the artworks were unlawfully exported from another country, or subject under foreign law to foreign ownership claims, the exporter incurs a risk that the art will be repatriated to a foreign owner under foreign laws.[2]

§ 6:75 Appropriation of art abroad to determine authenticity

Committees exist in foreign countries to determine authenticity of works of deceased artists. The Comite Picasso, composed of artists and members of the Picasso family, is based in France.[1] The owners of the droit moral for Georges Braque declare authenticity for Braque works. Under foreign laws, if a committee or designate of droit moral considers the art spurious, the art can be seized and destroyed. Persons taking art with them or sending it abroad for authenticity review should request in writing from the committee or designate a statement of policy regarding actions involving works it considers inauthentic and obtain the applicable laws of the respective country.

[Section 6:74]

[1]Art objects that contain or incorporate unlawful components can run afoul of other laws, e.g., restrictions on endangered species, toxic materials, et cetera. *See also* Chs 7 and 9 (organizations exist abroad to protect intellectual property rights of artists worldwide, like Societe des Auteurs des Arts Visuels).

[2]*See, e.g.,* Jeanneret v. Vichey, 693 F.2d 259, 35 U.C.C. Rep. Serv. 75 (2d Cir. 1982).

[Section 6:75]

[1]*See, e.g.,* McCloud v. Lawrence Gallery, Ltd., 1991 WL 136027 (S.D. N.Y. 1991).

§ 6:76 Nonmercantile cultural art import-export agreements

Art imported and exported for exhibitions and educational purposes is covered under HS chapter 98. Permanent Exhibition Bonds are available for art brought in duty free exclusively for no purpose other than exhibition. (Museums do not pay MPF.) Art imported under chapter 98 can be transferred from one organization to another and can remain in the United States for five years. After five years, the art can be exported or sold without penalty. The Art and Artifacts Indemnities Act should be consulted for cultural import-exports.[1]

[Section 6:76]

[1]*See* 20 U.S.C.A. § 974; 45 CFR pt. 1160; *see also* 20 U.S.C.A. § 2459 (immunity from seizure for cultural objects imported for temporary exhibition or display); *see also* Ch 2; Pub. L. No. 94-158, 89 Stat. 844 (Dec. 20, 1975), as amended; Pub. L. No. 96-496, 99-194 § 301, 99 Stat. 1345, Pub. L. No. 100-202, Pub. L. No. 101-512; 20 U.S.C.A. §§ 971–977; 45 CFR § 1160, revised, 60 Fed. Reg. 42464–466 (Aug. 16, 1995); *see also* S. 856, 104th Cong., 1st Sess. (June 1, 1995), a bill to amend NFAH and other arts legislation).

HARMONIZED TARIFF SCHEDULE of the United States (1994)

Annotated for Statistical Reporting Purposes

CHAPTER 98

SPECIAL CLASSIFICATION PROVISIONS

XXII
98-1

U.S. Notes

1. The provisions of this chapter are not subject to the rule of relative specificity in general rule of interpretation 3(a). Any article which is described in any provision in this chapter is classifiable in said provision if the conditions and requirements thereof and of any applicable regulations are met.

2. In the absence of a specific provision to the contrary, the tariff status of an article is not affected by the fact that it was previously imported into the customs territory of the United States and cleared through customs whether or not duty was paid upon such previous importation.

3. Any article exempted under subchapters IV through VII, inclusive, or subchapter IX from the payment of duty shall be exempt also from the payment of any internal-revenue tax imposed upon or by reason of importation.

Heading/ Subheading	Stat. Suffix	Article Description	Units of Quantity	Rates of Duty 1 General	Rates of Duty 1 Special	Rates of Duty 2
9813.00.70	1/	Works of the free fine arts, engravings, photographic pictures and philosophical and scientific apparatus brought into the United States by professional artists, lecturers or scientists arriving from abroad for use by them for exhibition and in illustration, promotion and encouragement of art, science or industry in the United States	......	Free, under bond, as prescribed in U.S. note 1 to this subchapter	Free (CA)	Free, under bond, as prescribed in U.S. note 1 to this subchapter

III. CULTURAL PROPERTY

A. IN GENERAL

§ 6:77 Introduction

Since World War II members of the international community disseminated the idea that some objects are so important that the costs and responsibilities of protection and preservation should be borne by all nations, regardless of the source or site of the objects. Typically these objects embody by reference significant religious, historical, or cultural events, or architectural style or technique, or have innate notable archaeological or ethnographic attributes. The objects are known as cultural property, and the objectives of cultural property laws are to repatriate the objects to the "owner" nation claiming them.

Cultural property is both a larger and smaller category of art and artifact: it is larger in that it includes many more objects than visual art—musical instruments, film, flora, furniture, postage stamps, literary manuscripts; it is smaller in that of the objects encompassed, only listed, designated, or inventoried objects will be eligible for repatriation. The United States, as a recipient nation of artworks from around the world because of its active and developed art markets, is not under any legal obligation to return every cultural object that finds its shores.

Since the postwar era, many international treaties, conventions, and national laws are in place to protect cultural property. In the United States, acts of Congress, executive agreements and bilateral treaties during the last twenty years have produced a body of cultural property regulation, the efficacy of which is in dispute and the revision of which is contemplated.

Cultural property regulation, like the tango, takes two: a claimant nation from whom the cultural property is stolen or exported—albeit unlawfully—and a recipient nation. An export-import type transaction must occur before the United States is bound to act, since the United States's duties under international treaty are triggered only when the cultural property is in the United States, regardless of whether it formally enters or circumvents U.S. Customs.[1] The United States also has a history of voluntary repatriation of cultural property and other national treasures, even if the property is not subject to the regulatory scheme. Museums have also demonstrated increasing willingness to repatriate objects even in the absence of legal obligation, and some institutions have formulated codes of ethics or policy guidelines on acquisition.[2]

This chapter annotates the seminal international agree-

[Section 6:77]

[1]*See* §§ 6:1 to 6:70.

[2]*See* Appendix 15.

ment, the UNESCO Cultural Property Convention,[3] explains key provisions from the Cultural Property Implementation Act in title 19 of the U.S. Code,[4] and identifies the regulations. Criteria to determine which objects are eligible as cultural property are cited and persons and entities who can claim ownership for purposes of repatriation are identified. Mechanisms for import controls in the United States are differentiated, including import restrictions on (1) stolen cultural property, (2) emergency situations, and (3) multilateral treaties. Ways to effectuate repatriation and procedures available to remunerate bona fide purchasers in possession are explained.

§ 6:78 National and international cultural property laws

Cultural property laws are numerous, and their authority reposes in many different legal vehicles: (1) international conventions and treaties;[1] (2) national laws of member states or signators to conventions or treaties based upon requirements of the treaties or linked to their provisions;[2] (3) national laws of foreign countries unrelated to treaties or conventions;[3] (4) customs union agreements, e.g., the Single European Union Treaty establish-

---

[3]*See* Appendix 13.

[4]*See* Appendix 14.

[Section 6:78]

[1]*See* Chart 6-3 and Appendix 13 and 16. A UNIDROIT Multilateral Treaty on the International Return of Stolen or Illegally Exported Cultural Objects, undertaken at the request of UNESCO, was proposed in 1995 for public comment. 60 Fed. Reg. 13202 (Mar. 10, 1995).

[2]UNESCO Handbook of National Legislation (O'Keefe & Prott eds.); an earlier and dated compilation of national legislation is ICOM: The Protection of Cultural Property: Handbook of National Legislations (Burnham ed.). For the most current national laws, contact embassy or consulate.

[3]UNESCO Handbook of National Legislation (O'Keefe & Prott eds.); an earlier and dated compilation of national legislation is ICOM: The Protection of Cultural Property: Handbook of National Legislations (Burnham ed.). For the most current national laws, contact embassy or consulate.

ing the European Economic Community[4] and regional agreements, e.g., the Organization of American States; and (5) bilateral and multilateral agreements.[5]

Each regulatory scheme is different, but in general provisions intended to protect the world's culture are couched in generalities, rely heavily upon voluntarism, lack adequate enforcement measures, and are silent on penalties. UNESCO is the seminal international cultural property convention, and the one to which the United States adheres. The law of the United States is the focus of this chapter, and the mechanics and procedures are discussed below.

For the reader's further information, Chart 6-3 is a sampling of other international actions regarding cultural property.

Chart 6-3: Selected International Cultural Property Agreements, Directives, Recommendations and Regulations

Date	Document
1985	Council of Europe, European Convention on Offenses Relating to Cultural Property
1980	UNESCO Resolution on Protection of Cultural Heritage against Disasters
1981	Council of Europe Parliamentary Assembly Recommendation 921 on Archaeology
1978	Council of Europe Parliamentary Assembly Recommendation 848 on Subaquatic Cultural Heritage

[4]Single European Act, 25 ILM 506 (1986), authorizing the European Union Treaty ("Treaty"), commonly called the Maastracht Treaty after the city where it was signed. *See also* 1993 O.J. (L.74) (Mar. 15, 1993) (The Council of the European Communities adopted a Directive pursuant to Article 36 of the Treaty regarding return of cultural property to Member States, which each Member was allowed to define and to protect after 1992 within the perimeter of the Community.); *see also* Bull. EC 11-1992, 1.3.20–1.3.21 (Regulation EEC No. 3911/92 (conditions for return of cultural property in absence of formal controls at intra-Community frontiers and export licenses for export beyond the Community customs territory).

[5]*See* Chart 6-8.

Date	Document
1976	OAS San Salvador Convention on Protection of Archaeological, Historical and Artistic Heritage of the American Nations
1976	UNESCO Recommendation on safeguarding Historic Areas
1975	European Charter on Architectural Heritage
1974	UNESCO Resolution on Return of Cultural Property to Countries Victims of de facto Expropriation
1972	UNESCO Convention on Protection of World Cultural and Natural Heritage
1970	UNESCO Cultural Property Convention
1969	European Convention on Protection of European Archaeological Heritage
1968	UNESCO Recommendation concerning Preservation of Cultural Property endangered by Public or Private works
1964	UNESCO Recommendation on means of Prohibiting and Preventing Illicit Cultural Property
1956	UNESCO Recommendation on International Principles regarding archaeological excavations
1954	Hague Convention for the Protection of Cultural Property in Event of Armed Conflict
1954	Council of Europe European Cultural Convention

B. FEDERAL LAW

§ 6:79 Cultural property law and regulations

Federal cultural property law derives from the United Nations Education, Scientific and Cultural Organization (UNESCO) 1970 Convention on Means of Prohibiting and Preventing the Illicit Import, Export, and Transfer of Ownership of Cultural Property.[1] Congress ratified a ver-

[Section 6:79]

[1] 823 U.N.T.S. 231 (1972). *See* Appendix 13. The UNESCO Convention is hereinafter referred to as the Convention.

sion of the Convention, titled in the U.S. Code as the Convention on Cultural Property Implementation Act (CPIA).[2] Extensive regulations have been promulgated to implement CPIA[3] and executive orders[4] have adjusted responsibilities among those authorized to supervise its implementation, the Department of Treasury, the Department of State, the U.S. Information Agency, and most recently the Department of Homeland Security. An International Cultural Property Protection web site has been established for information regarding import restrictions.[5]

Cultural property in common parlance is interchangeably used with the terms cultural heritage, national heritage, national treasure, or cultural patrimony.[6] These terms are not precise synonyms; cultural property is used here because it is the designated title of the Convention, the term of art for stolen property under CPIA, and the usage adopted by the CFR.

§ 6:80 Cultural property advisory committee (CPAC)

The CPIA established the Cultural Property Advisory Committee (CPAC) to advise the President regarding specific requests from countries for import restrictions. The director of the U.S. Information Agency is charged with various functions under the CPIA, including providing administrative and technical support for the CPAC. The CPAC is composed of eleven presidential appointees, experts from the areas of archaeology, anthropology, ethnology, international art sales, the museum community, and the public. Members hold staggered terms.

Foreign requests are referred to the CPAC for review

---

[2]Pub.L. 97-446, 19 U.S.C.A. §§ 2601–2613. *See* Appendix 14A (full text).

[3]19 C.F.R. §§ 104 et seq; see *App. 14B* (full text).

[4]Exec. Order 12555 (Mar. 10, 1986).

[5]http://exchanges.state.gov/education/culprop.htm

[6]The term "national treasure" is a term of art in certain countries, like Japan, where living national treasures are persons. National heritage in other countries involves inventories, lists, or designated property. Cultural heritage is used in the Convention in terms of a cultural legacy.

and findings; the CPAC issues a report recommending a course of action. The President is under a mandate to consider the CPAC Report if it is timely submitted within specified periods. The CPAC has reviewed several requests over the years; the status of review and procedures for the CPAC to report findings and recommendations to the various departments are set forth in Chart 6-4 which is current as of 1993. After import restrictions are imposed, the CPAC is responsible for "continual review" by recommending extension or suspension.

Chart 6-4: Timetable for Processing Selected Requests for U.S. Import Bans

*Source: U.S. Information Agency.

	Canada	El Salvador	El Salvador Extension[1]	Bolivia	Bolivia Extension[2]	Peru[3]	Guatemala[4]	Mali
Receipt of Request	10/2/85	3/13/87	12/11/91	5/4/88	11/92	6/15/89	10/3/89	8/10/92[5]
Referred to Committee	4/8/86	4/21/87	12/24/91	5/19/88	11/18/92	6/23/89	11/14/89	9/14/92
Committee Report	10/14/88	7/16/87	1/30/92	8/4/88	2/12/93	9/20/89	2/9/90	12/11/92
USIA Letter Seeking Concurrence	1/15/93	7/31/87	2/92	8/12/88	11/3/89	4/2/90		
State's Concurrence		8/19/87	2/92	1/17/89	12/19/89	11/27/90		

[Section 6:80]

[1]Salvadoran restrictions imposed have been converted into bilateral treaty; *see* § 6:100 *infra*.

[2]Bolivian restrictions have been extended. T.D. No. 93-34.

[3]Peruvian restrictions have been extended. T.D. No. 94-54.

[4]Guatemalan restrictions have been extended. T.D. No. 94-84.

[5]Receipt of request cited as September 4, 1992. 57 Fed. Reg. 43493 (Sept. 21, 1992).

	Canada	El Salvador	El Salvador Extension[1]	Bolivia	Bolivia Extension[2]	Peru[3]	Guatemala[4]	Mali
Treasury's Concurrence		8/21/87	2/92	9/30/88	12/15/89	5/7/90		
Customs Amends Regulations		9/4/87	3/18/92	3/7/89	4/9/90	4/10/91	9/8/93	
Announcement in Federal Register (Effective Date)	4/22/97	9/11/87	3/12/92	3/14/89	5/7/90	4/15/91	9/8/93	

C. ART AS UNIVERSAL HERITAGE

§ 6:81 Policy of cultural property

The policy predicate for all cultural property law is that art is part of a universal heritage and that regardless of whether one country has more or less of it, it is incumbent upon every other country to assure that it is returned to the claimant and does not enter private hands or the black market. That policy in Convention terms requires both the claimant country from whom the property was exported and the recipient country to whom the property was imported be signators to the Convention and have it entered into force.

By the late 1960s, the international view was that market demand for cultural treasures precipitated "rampant pillaging of archaeological and ethnological materials, particularly in countries with few resources to protect their cultural heritage."[1] Market activity may be more the effect of pillaging than its cause. In source countries where local populations live at subsistence levels, the economic incentive to dig and sell booty from archaeological sites, alone or in conjunction with organized domestic or foreign persons, is overwhelming. This activity is not new, and neither are the distribution channels; booty moves to the monied. In contemporary times, this means that the United States, Japan, and some western European countries readily absorb such imports and " . . . cultural treasures . . . [are] not only of importance to the nations where they originate . . . " but to all.[2]

The CPIA does not foreclose criminal prosecution under

[Section 6:81]

[1]U.S. Information Agency, Curbing Illicit Trade in Cultural Property: U.S. Assistance Under the Convention on Cultural Property Implementation Act 2. Economists question whether demand precipitates pillaging. When treasures surface they do transfer into existing chains of distribution.

[2]S. Rep. No. 97-564 at 21 (1982), cited in U.S. v. Schultz, 333 F.3d 393, 408 (2d Cir. 2003), cert. denied, 124 S. Ct. 1051, 157 L. Ed. 2d 891 (U.S. 2004); see App. 14C.

the NSPA or other laws.[3]

Regulatory mechanisms based upon international cooperation were thus created to control pillaging because cultural property has "importance . . . to the greater knowledge and understanding of mankind's common heritage."[4]

§ 6:82 Provenience

Provenience is the archaeological record of the object, its juxtaposition to other objects in situ, its relationship to those objects, and the strata above and below the level at which the object is found in the excavation. Provenience is revealed to scholars and archaeologists by analysis of the archaeological material at its source, providing the syntax and context of the discovery, and preserving the historical record as it is presented at discovery. Analyzing the material at its source, known as the findspot or the situs, is important because it provides a contextual evaluation for historians, sociologists, anthropologists, and others who assess the juxtaposition of objects and structures in relationship to each other and the site, and to the layers of excavation. Objects are ordinarily photographed in situ, excavated, inventoried, and rephotographed, accompanied by field notes, record documents, and other technological documentations. Anyone who participated in a supervised dig or viewed an archaeological site can appreciate the tedious, painstaking and careful custodianship exercised. A moonlit plunder lacks these formalities and destroys the provenience for those objects and that site. That destruction is considered a global cultural and historical loss to everyone, not just to the country in which the findspot is located.

§ 6:83 Dual controls required: Export and import

Cultural property regulation takes two to tango. Duties

---

[3]See Ch 11; U.S. v. Schultz, 333 F.3d 393, 409 (2d Cir. 2003), cert. denied, 124 S. Ct. 1051, 157 L. Ed. 2d 891 (U.S. 2004) (" . . . CPIA does not limit the NSPA's application to antiquities stolen in foreign nations [notwithstanding] . . . potential overlap" of CPIA and NSPA); S. Rep. No. 97-564 at 22 (1982); see App. 14C).

[4]U.S. Information Agency, Curbing Illicit Trade in Cultural Property: U.S. Assistance Under the Convention on Cultural Property Implementation Act 2.

and obligations are imposed upon both the source country and the recipient country, and require a two-part process, one being vigilant internal and export controls, the other being import regulation and repatriation methods. The regulatory process may be premised more upon aspiration than actuality.

Both the source country and the recipient country are supposed to take measures to facilitate the goals of cultural property protection. The source country is required to designate its cultural property by procedures like inventory and registration, to implement prophylactic measures securing unexcavated and newly excavated areas in situ, and to discourage exports by requiring export permits, licenses, or bans. The recipient country is required to restrict import, i.e., declaring the property an unlawful import and seizing it at the border, and establishing mechanisms whereby repatriation can be achieved. The purported objectives contemplate regulatory symbiosis, but since export controls are largely ineffective, the burden to monitor and interdict is shifted to the recipient country. The success of cultural property regulation turns upon the recipient country's ability and willingness to identify and control illicit imports at the border and beyond and to repatriate them. Cultural property law is largely silent about what happens when the object circumvents the import barrier or passes undetected through it, but U.S. Customs laws permit seizure of unlawfully imported merchandise wherever it is found.[1]

Given the substantial amount of illicit cultural property in the markets, one might conclude that neither export nor import controls are particularly successful. That is undoubtedly one aspect, but another is that the universality of protection has not been universally embraced. By 1992, Convention members numbered sixty-nine, including recent signatories Australia,[2] People's Republic of

---

[Section 6:83]

[1]*See* §§ 6:1 to 6:70 and 6:71 to 6:76. The U.S. Customs has policies regarding nonborder intervention.

[2]Australia accepted the Convention on October 30, 1989, and it went into force there on January 30, 1990. 19 CFR § 12.104(b).

China (PRC),[3] and Belize.[4] The United States is virtually alone among the western nations to ratify the Convention.[5] Europe, whatever its view of rampant pillaging, has not agreed to subsidize inadequate security measures of "countries with few resources to protect their cultural heritage." No Convention cultural property intrafrontier border controls are in effect in the European Community.[6]

The Convention by no means reflects all U.N. efforts and activities regarding cultural property controls.[7] The United Nations has issued scores of resolutions regarding cultural property.[8]

---

[3]The PRC accepted the Convention on November 28, 1989, and it went into force there on February 28, 1990. 19 CFR § 12.104(b).

[4]Belize ratified the Convention on January 26, 1990, and it went into force there on April 26, 1990. 19 CFR § 12.104(b).

[5]Neither Australia nor Canada, both signators, compare to the United States as importers or traders of art in volume or dollar amount.

[6]The European Community Cultural Property Regulations and Directives apply to European borders. *See also* 1993 O.J. (L.74) (Mar. 15, 1993) (The Council of the European Communities adopted a Directive pursuant to Article 36 of the Treaty regarding return of cultural property to Member States, which each Member was allowed to define and to protect after 1992 within the perimeter of the Community.); *see also* Bull. EC 11-1992, 1.3.20–1.3.21 (Regulation EEC No. 3911/92 (conditions for return of cultural property in absence of formal controls at intra-Community frontiers and export licenses for export beyond the Community customs territory).

[7]*See* Chart 6-3.

[8]Selected United Nations Resolutions:

Resolution Number	Date
3026A	Dec. 18, 1972
3148	Dec. 14, 1973
3187	Dec. 18, 1973
3391	Nov. 19, 1975
31/40	Nov. 30, 1976
32/18	Nov. 11, 1977
33/50 *	Dec. 14, 1978 **
34/64 *	Nov. 29 1979 **
35/128	Dec. 11, 1980
36/64	Nov. 27, 1981

§ 6:84 Ownership

Behind the policy is the murkier issue of assigning cultural property to a national owner. How does a country come to "own" art? Is Picasso's legacy a cultural treasure for Spain or France? Are the Elgin Marbles British or Greek? Article 4 of the Convention begs the question. The cultural heritage of a state party arise from any of the following territorial nexus: (1) property created by nationals of the state or foreign nationals or stateless persons resident within the territory of the state; (2) property found within the state, which could mean either discovered or situated; (3) property acquired by authorized missions; (4) property received by exchange; and (5) property received as a gift or purchased legally with consent of authorities of country of origin of such property.

The CPIA has built in a territorial relationship because claimants must either have inventoried stolen art through state museums or monuments, or they must have made formal application to the United States for import restrictions. In either case, the claim is sourced to the country's evidentiary trail of ownership.

But even those controls do not completely accommodate the political division of the world at the end of the twentieth century, artificially linking diverse religious, ethnic, and cultural groups. The cultural legacy of an object may have no significance to those in power or the majority of the populous. Events during the early 1990s in former Yugoslavia, the former Soviet Republics, and elsewhere make clear that those in power and possession may have no cultural, religious, or historical interest in the object.

§ 6:85 Burden sharing

If cultural property is voluntarily returned, will preser-

Resolution Number	Date

---

* Resolution subject matter: objets d'art, monuments, museum pieces, manuscripts, documents, and cultural/artistic treasures.

** Date adopted by Assembly.

vation be furthered? The argument often presented is that certain countries are in a better position because of money, human resources, and infrastructure to better restore, maintain, and preserve objects for posterity. Nations who have lost their properties challenge this view as eurocentric, since the countries with relatively more resources for art are typically western and industrialized.[1] The debate continues to this day as to whom should be the preserver of the Elgin Marbles situated in the British Museum—England or Greece.[2] Thomas Bruce, the Scottish Lord Elgin who was British Ambassador to the Ottoman Empire, sold them to the British Museum in 1816, after removing them from the Parthenon in 1801 under a controversial agreement with the occupying Turks. A New Acropolis Museum in Athens designed to house the Elgin Marbles and sculptures from the Parthenon scheduled to open in conjunction with the Athens 2004 Summer Olympic Games has revivified restitution efforts. The plan has revitalized debate on ownership of the Parthenon Marbles, as they are known in Greece. The British Museum has rejected requests to return them or transfer them to Greece on longterm loan. In March 2002, Greek interests and the Parthenon Marbles Trust, joined by a distant relative of Lord Elgin, filed suit against the British government claiming conversion.

Cultural property import-export regulation involves burden sharing, but does not necessarily invoke shared responsibilities for preserving objects. The law is silent as to responsibility for border controls and the extent of prophylactic measures that must be in place before claimants can utilize expedited repatriation.[3] It is not uncommon for the country seeking return of property to have

[Section 6:85]

[1]A Japanese corporation financed restoration of the Sistine Chapel in the Vatican.

[2]Hitchens, C., *Imperial Spoils*: The Curious Case of the Elgin Marbles (Hill&Wang 1987); *UK Team Battles to Return Elgin Marbles to Greece*, The Lawyer (April 1, 2002); *Marbles are back in Play*, Sydney Morning Herald, at 18 (March 19, 2003).

[3]Cultural Property Advisory Committee reviews applications of countries, which specify pillaged sites and properties but do not necessarily recite security measures or border controls.

done little or nothing to secure its own resources until the property has left the country. And although CPIA imposes upon the claimant the costs incident to return of cultural property, it is not clear that such costs have been, or will be, paid.

§ 6:86 Extrajudicial resolution, voluntary repatriation

Even before CPIA, political compromise and diplomatic negotiations resulted in return of cultural objects to claimant countries. Those channels of repatriation are still open after CPIA, and are contemplated in terms of implementation policy by U.S. Customs. Because of the difficulty of conforming cultural property cases to substantive, procedural, and evidentiary requirements of litigation, negotiation is a viable alternative. Some highly publicized examples of cultural property repatriation in the past are a result of negotiations.[1]

D. UNESCO CONVENTION

§ 6:87 Generally

The Convention's legitimacy derives from the UNESCO Constitution, charging UNESCO with a mission to "[M]aintain, increase and diffuse knowledge, . . . by assuring the conservation and protection of the world's inheritance of . . . works of art and monuments of history, . . . and recommending to the nations concerned the necessary international conventions."[1] The Convention is binding upon a member three months after it enters force, subsequent to ratification, acceptance, or accession.

The U.S. Senate ratified the Convention in 1972 subject

[Section 6:86]

[1]Stiftskirche-Domgemeinde v. Meador, No. CA 3-90-1440-D (U.S. Dist. Ct. Dallas Div. June 18, 1990) (out-of-court settlement).

[Section 6:87]

[1]UNESCO Const., art. 1, § 2, cl. c, reprinted in 1946–47 U.N. Year Book 703–04.

to one reservation and six understandings,[2] one of the understandings being that the Convention is not self executing. In international law parlance, Congress has to enact legislation to convert Convention provisions into federal law.[3] (A self-executing international agreement does not require implementation by federal legislation.) The controversiality of bringing the Convention "home" required ten years of political negotiation.[4] The CPIA, passed in December 1982; it was signed into law by President Ronald Reagan on January 12, 1983, and deposited with UNESCO on December 2, 1983.[5] The date of entry into force was set at December 2, 1983;[6] the effective date was set at April 12, 1983. American withdrawal from UNESCO in 1985 did not alter official commitment to the Convention;[7] by its own terms, the Convention permits accession even for nonmembers.

Annotation of UNESCO Convention

Article 1 identifies cultural property categories. This detailed list appears in the regulations to CPIA.

Article 2 contains a statement of purpose regarding protection of cultural heritage.

Article 3 contains a declaration that cultural property exports, imports, and transfers contrary to law are illicit. (United States understanding is that this article does not

---

[2]The U.S. Senate advised and consented to the ratification of the Convention on August 11, 1972.

[3]S. Rep. No 564, 97th Cong., 2d Sess. 24 (1982).

[4]*See* S. 2677, 93d Cong., 1st Sess. (1973); Written Comments on H.R. Rep. No. 14171, Subcomm. on Trade of the House Comm. on Ways and Means, 94th Cong., 2d Sess. 19 (1976); H.R. Rep. No. 615, 9th Cong., 1st Sess. 2–3 (1977); S. Rep. No. 564, 97th Cong., 2d Sess. 22–24 (1982); Misc. Tariff Bills: Hearings on S. 1723 Before Subcomm. on Int'l. Trade, Senate Comm. on Finance, 97th Cong., 2d Sess. 555–556 (1982); see App. 14C (Senate Report 97-564 [full text]).

[5]Pub. L. No. 97-446, 96 Stat. 2329 (1983), *amended by* Pub. L. No. 100-204, 101 Stat. 1331 (1987).

[6]April 12, 1983, is the date provided by the government but the formal deposit was not made until September 1983.

[7]U.S. Information Agency, Curbing Illicit Trade in Cultural Property: U.S. Assistance Under the Convention on Cultural Property Implementation Act 2.

modify property interests in cultural property under the laws of the state party.)

Article 4 describes how cultural property is the heritage of member states.

Article 5 establishes national services with "qualified staff sufficient in number for the effective carrying out" of, among other functions, an updated "national inventory of protected property, a list of important public and private cultural property whose export would constitute an appropriate impoverishment of the national cultural heritage." (The United States reserved this section and to date has no stated cultural property export policy; the requesting country seeking U.S. assistance is not exempt from article 5 and must have inventoried cultural property and designated archaeological and ethnological material in order to obtain assistance from the US.)

Article 6 establishes an export certification system (per Article 5 reservation, this section ipso facto is also reserved).

Article 7

Article 7(a) requires members to take "necessary measures, consistent with national legislation, to prevent museums . . . from acquiring cultural property originating in another State . . . which has been illegally exported." (The United States understands article 7(a) to apply to institutions whose acquisition policy is subject to national control under existing legislation and not to require new legislation to establish national control over other institutions.)

Article 7(b), a key provision of CPIA, prohibits import of stolen cultural property from a museum, religious, secular institution or public monument, or similar institution providing that property is documented as "appertaining to the inventory" of the entity (The United States understands article 7(b) as being without prejudice to other remedies, civil or penal, under laws of state parties, for recovery of stolen cultural property to the rightful owner without payment or compensation,[8] and

Article 7(c) authorizes recovery and repatriation of

[8]The understanding further states, "The [United States] is . . . prepared to take additional steps contemplated by article 7(b)(H) for the return of covered stolen cultural property."

improperly imported cultural property, establishes just compensation for "innocent purchasers" and "persons [with] valid title," and requires the requesting party to "furnish, at its expense, the documentation and other evidence necessary to establish its claim for recovery and return." Requesting party pays all incidental expenses for return and delivery.

Article 8 requires members to "impose penalties or administrative sanctions on any person responsible for infringing the prohibitions . . . of Articles 6(b) and 7(b)."

Article 9. This emergency provision is to control "pillage" of uninventoried archaeological and ethnological materials (not all cultural property) by bilateral or multilateral agreements. Article 9 has been adapted as a key section of CPIA providing for emergency import restrictions for "designated" material.

Article 10 imposes obligation upon source countries to restrict movement of cultural property illegally removed from any state party through education, information, and vigilance, and to increase public awareness on the value of cultural property; as appropriate for each country, it obliges antique dealers, subject to penal or administrative sanctions, to maintain registries recording cultural property sales and data on the transaction. (The United States understands "as appropriate for each country" as permitting each state party to determine the extent of regulation, if any, of antique dealers and to declare that in the United States such determination would by be made by the appropriate authorities of state and municipal governments.)

Article 11 declares illicit occupation activity that results in cultural property transfers.

Article 12 bolsters articles 5 and 10 by mandating that signatories "shall take all appropriate measures to prohibit and prevent the illicit import, export and transfer of ownership of cultural property in [the territories for the international relations of which they are responsible]."

Article 13 authorizes court jurisdiction for cultural property actions: "The Parties . . . , consistent with the laws of each State" must:

(1) prevent transfers of ownership likely to promote illicit import or export;

(2) ensure facilitation of restitution of illegal exports to rightful owners;

(3) "admit actions" for seeking recovery of stolen or lost cultural property not resolved through voluntary repatriation; (subparagraph 3 creates a legal cause of action in the courts; note the understanding in subparagraph 4); and

(4) recognizes "indefeasible right" of each party to declare and classify cultural property as "inalienable" which "ipso facto" should not be exported, and to facilitate recovery of such property where export occurs. (The United States understands article 13(d) applies to objects removed from country of origin after entry into force of Convention, and that means of recovery for cultural property in article 13(d) are judicial actions referred to in article 13(c), such actions are controlled by the law of the recipient state, and the claimant state has to submit necessary proofs.)

Article 14 authorizes and encourages creation of special funds "as far as [members are] able, [to] provide the national services . . . an adequate budget."

Article 15 permits preexisting bilateral and multilateral agreements involving restitution of cultural property entered into before the Convention to continue and new ones to be implemented.

Article 16 establishes a state member's reporting requirement to UNESCO on legislative and administrative implementation of Convention.

Article 17 offers UNESCO's good offices to settle disputes and extend technical assistance.

Article 18 provides for multilingual text.

Article 19 contains ratification and deposit requirements.

Article 20 contains accession provisions for states that are not UNESCO members.

Article 21 establishes timing of effects at inception.

Article 22 contains verbiage extending application to member territories as well as member states.

Article 23 allows members to denounce provisions.

Article 24 contains the notification requirements for the Director General of UNESCO.

Article 25 is a revision binder.

Article 26 establishes registration of members with United Nations.

In basic terms, the Convention can be summarized as follows: If cultural property is imported, exported, or transferred contrary to Convention provisions, the transaction "shall be illicit." Articles 7 and 9 are key in American law. The following explains how the broad mandate of the Convention has been interpreted and implemented.

E. Cultural Property Implementation Act

§ 6:88 Law of sovereigns

Cultural property is the law of nations, and only those nations where the Convention has entered into force.[1] Sovereigns and through them a limited number of approved institutions and entities with documented public collections are the only recognized claimants. The CPIA term for a sovereign is "member" (if it belongs to the Convention) or "state party."[2]

Cultural property regulation requires two parties, a claimant-nation and a recipient-nation based upon an export-import type transaction, even if the unlawful export is not made directly into the United States. The property must ultimately arrive in the United States because America's duties under an international treaty are triggered only when the cultural property is here, regardless of whether it formally enters or circumvents U.S. Customs

§ 6:89 Cultural property definitions and descriptions—Convention

Cultural property is nowhere specifically defined. What

[Section 6:88]

[1]Private property claims are not authorized by CPIA or envisioned by the Convention. Proposals to create treaties to redress private property losses have been circulated but to date none has been signed by the United States. *See, e.g.,* the International Institute for the Unification of Private Law, (UNIDROIT), a draft for private rights of action to recover cultural property.

[2]Recall that even nonmembers can accede to the Convention; *see* article 20 at § 6:87.

the Convention text[1] contains are specifically designated categories, reciting at Article 1: "[t]he term 'cultural property' means property, which on religious or secular grounds, is specifically designated *and* which belongs to the following categories." The Convention categories are broad.[2] A cursory glance at article 1 reveals these objects: art, antiques, flora, fauna, coins, furniture, musical instruments, books and manuscripts, postage, archives, historical properties, ethnological objects, et cetera.[3]

§ 6:90 Cultural property definitions and descriptions—CPIA and CFR

Article 1 (a1-k) categories are expressly referred to in CPIA[1] at Section 302(6), and listed in Section 12.104 of title 19 of the CFR.[2] CPIA drops the Convention requirement that the state party must specifically designate the property. The article 1 list includes, inter alia, antiquities more than 100-years old, original works of sculpture, original engravings, prints, lithographs, artistic assemblages and montages, products of archaeological excavations, and dismembered elements of artistic or archaeological monuments.

Section 12.104(a) establishes categories of and criteria for archaeological material[3] at subpart (1) and ethnological material[4] at subpart (2). Archaeological material must be at least 250 years old.[5] (No parallel age requirements exist for ethnological material or cultural property under CPIA.) The "age" of cultural property under the national laws of state parties varies.

[Section 6:89]

[1] *See* Appendix 13 and 14A.

[2] Convention, art. 1 (Emphasis added.)

[3] Convention, art. 1 (a1-k).

[Section 6:90]

[1] *See* Appendix 14A.

[2] *See* Appendix 14B.

[3] 12 CFR § 12.104(a)(1).

[4] 12 CFR § 12.104(a)(2).

[5] 19 U.S.C.A. § 2601.

F. DIFFERENTIAL IMPORT RESTRICTIONS: Section 12.104a of title 19 of the Code of Federal Regulations Categories

§ 6:91 Stolen property

CPIA does not treat importation of all cultural property equally in terms of imposing import restrictions. If the property is stolen from a museum, a religious, secular, or public monument, or similar institution in any state party, "[n]o [such] article documented as appertaining to the inventory [of such institution] may be imported into the U.S.," pursuant to Section 12.104a(a) of title 19 of the Code of Federal Regulations. A museum is defined as a private or public nonprofit institution organized on a permanent basis for educational or aesthetic purposes that, in conjunction with a professional staff, owns, utilizes, cares for, and exhibits to the public on a regular basis tangible objects.[1]

§ 6:92 Archaeological and ethnological materials

Archaeological and ethnological materials, defined at Section 12.104a(b) of the CFR, are subject to different import controls. Unless an export certificate or other document certifies lawful exportation, no archaeological or ethnographic material that is designated "may be imported in the U.S. . . . (whether or not such exportation is to the U.S.)," pursuant to Section 12.104a(b). Designated material means it is covered by an import agreement under Section 303[1] (no such agreements exist to date)[2] or subject to emergency import restrictions under Section 304.[3] Chart 6-5 identifies the countries for which emergency import

---

[Section 6:91]

[1] 19 CFR § 12.104(e).

[Section 6:92]

[1] 19 U.S.C.A. § 2602.

[2] In 1995 the first import agreement pursuant to Section 303 was entered into between the United States and El Salvador, for which emergency import restrictions already were in place. *See* Chart 6-5 for types of materials covered, and *see* § 6:100 for discussion of this import agreement.

[3] 19 U.S.C.A. § 2603.

restrictions are in effect.

Chart 6-5: CPIA Import Restrictions***

Country	Cultural Property	T.D. No.**
Canada	Archaeological Artifacts and Ethnological Material Culture of Canadian Origin	T.D. 97-31
El Salvador	Archaeological material representing Prehispanic cultures of El Salvador	T.D. 95-20 extended by T.D. 00-16
Guatemala	Archaeological material from sites in the Peten Lowlands of Guatemala, and related Pre-Columbian material from the Highlands and the Southern Coast of Guatemala	T.D.97-81
Italy	Archaeological Material of pre-Classical, Classical, and Imperial Roman periods ranging approximately from the 9th century B.C. to the 4th century A.D.	T.D. 01-06
Mali	Archaeological material from the Niger River Valley Region, Mali, and the Bandiagara Escarpment (Cliff) forming part of the remains of the sub-Sahara culture.	T.D. 97-80
Nicaragua	Archaeological Material of pre-Columbian cultures ranging approximately from 8000 B.C. to 1500 A.D	T.D. 00-75
Peru	Archaeological artifacts and ethnological material from Peru	T.D. 97-50
Bolivia(e)*	Antique ceremonial textiles from Coroma.	T.D. 89-37 extended by 93-34
Cambodia(e)*	Khmer stone archaeological material from Cambodia	T.D. 99-88
Cyprus(e)*	Byzantine ecclesiastical and ritual ethnological materials from Cyprus	T.D. 99-35

Country	Cultural Property	T.D. No. **

*** See App. 14B (current status of import restrictions).

** T.D. refers to Treasury Decisions which contain complete descriptions of the cultural property. The Office of Homeland Security assumed oversight effective 2004. CPB Decision Numbers now replace T.D.s.

* "e" signifies emergency import restrictions.

G. STOLEN CULTURAL PROPERTY IMPORT CONTROLS

§ 6:93 Evidentiary requirements

Section 308 of CPIA prohibits entry into the United States of cultural property stolen from museums, religious or secular monuments, or similar institutions, providing that the property is "documented as appertaining to the inventory" of such institutions.[1] Whenever stolen cultural property is imported into the United States, U.S. Customs is under mandate to seize and forfeit it.[2]

§ 6:94 Applicable dates and timing of thefts

Section 308 applies to thefts occurring after the "effective date [of CPIA] or . . . the date of entry into force of the Convention" for the state party, "whichever is later."[1] The USIA establishes April 12, 1983, as the effective date for CPIA, and that thefts must occur on or after that date, or the later date applicable to the state party see king return of the property.[2]

[Section 6:93]

[1] 19 U.S.C.A. § 2607.

[2] 19 CFR § 12.104e(b).

[Section 6:94]

[1] 19 U.S.C.A. § 2607.

[2] U.S. Information Agency, Curbing Illicit Trade in Cultural Property: U.S. Assistance Under the Convention on Cultural Property Implementation Act 7. The date of U.S. acceptance was not until September 2, 1983, and date of entry into force was December 2, 1983,

§ 6:95 Seizure and forfeiture—Authority

CPIA authorizes seizure and forfeiture of stolen cultural property imported into the United States in violation of Section 2607 of title 19 of the U.S. Code. "All provisions of law relating to seizure, forfeiture, and condemnation for violation of the customs laws shall apply to seizures and forfeitures incurred, or alleged to have been incurred, under [CPIA]"[1] and are authorized seized by Section 2609(c).

§ 6:96 Seizure and forfeiture—Proof

Section 311 of CPIA requires the United States to establish as a matter of evidence in a forfeiture action that the property was "documented as appertaining to the inventory" and was stolen after the applicable date.[1] To date, no appellate cases have been reported, but a district court recently interpreted these provisions.[2] In a forfeiture case involving a manuscript by Junipero Serra consigned for sale to an auction house by claimant, the government met its burden of probable cause by offering an affidavit from a scholar that it was part of the Mexican National Archives and the fact of its recordation in the museum's microfilm inventory. In Autocephalous Church,[3] where Byzantine mosaics were stolen in the 1970s prior to CPIA's effective date of 1983, the church's registration of an ownership certificate with the Cypriot government and the photographing and publication of books on the mosaics would appear to satisfy the spirit and letter of the documenta-

---

according to the UNESCO Lists of States having deposited an instrument . . . as of May 1990. Pursuant to article 21, entry of force is three months after deposit. The issue is the delay in deposit in September 1983.

[Section 6:95]

[1] 19 U.S.C.A. § 2609(a).

[Section 6:96]

[1] 19 U.S.C.A. § 2610.

[2] U.S. v. An Original Manuscript Dated November 19, 1778, 1999 WL 97894 (S.D. N.Y. 1999).

[3] Autocephalous Greek-Orthodox Church of Cyprus v. Goldberg & Feldman Fine Arts Inc., 717 F. Supp. 1374 (S.D. Ind. 1989), judgment aff'd, 917 F.2d 278 (7th Cir. 1990).

tion function.

§ 6:97 Seizure and forfeiture—Just compensation with proof of title

In a forfeiture action to recover stolen property imported in violation of Section 308, a claimant can establish valid title to the property, "under applicable law, as against the institution from which the article was stolen."[1] If the claimant establishes title, "forfeiture shall not be decreed unless the State Party to which the article is to be returned pays the claimant just compensation." Just compensation presumably refers to fair market value or something comparable, without limitation to purchase price, which is deemed permissible remuneration where title cannot be proven.

§ 6:98 Seizure and forfeiture—Purchase price for innocent purchasers

If the claimant cannot establish valid title but he or she purchased for value without "knowledge or reason to believe it was stolen," there will not be forfeiture unless: (1) the state party pays the claimant an amount equal to the claimant's purchase price; or (2) the United States establishes that the state party, "as a matter of law or reciprocity, would in similar circumstances recover and return an article stolen from an institution in the United States without requiring the payment of compensation."[1] Evidence of reciprocity should be supplied by the state party in the form of governmental decrees, proclamations, or other writings.[2] However, the affirmative defense of innocent purchaser was rejected where the buyer failed to inquire into provenance or request written documentation of provenance, and the buy was a cash deal consummated

---

[Section 6:97]

[1] 19 U.S.C.A. § 2609(c)(1).

[Section 6:98]

[1] 19 U.S.C.A. § 2609(c)(1)(B).

[2] U.S. Customs Directive, Policies and Procedures Manual, Apr. 18, 1991 No. 5230-15, at p 6.

in a hotel room.[3] Compensation was refused under section 2609(c)(1)A because the buyer was not deemed an innocent purchaser.[4]

§ 6:99 Seizure and forfeiture—Return and delivery expenses, disposal

If the property is forfeited to the United States, it shall "first be offered for return to the State Party in whose territory is situated the [Section 308] institution" and returned if that party "bears the expenses incident to such return and delivery."[1] If it is not returned to the state party, the property shall be "disposed of in the manner prescribed by law for articles forfeited in violation of the customs laws."[2]

Not one case has been decided pursuant to Section 308, nor at the time of this writing has there been a report of any cultural property requested or returned thereunder.[3]

H. ARCHAEOLOGICAL AND ETHNOLOGICAL MATERIALS IMPORT RESTRICTIONS

§ 6:100 Section 303: Bilateral and multilateral import restrictions

Article 9 of the Convention discusses import-export restrictions on uninventoried archaeological and ethnographic materials in jeopardy of pillage. CPIA Section 303 elaborates upon and implements procedures for dealing with these materials by authorizing import restrictions on certain identifiable materials or categories of materials.

---

[3]U.S. v. An Original Manuscript Dated November 19, 1778, 1999 WL 97894 (S.D. N.Y. 1999).

[4]U.S. v. An Original Manuscript Dated November 19, 1778, 1999 WL 97894 (S.D. N.Y. 1999). (discussion of compensation denial based upon reciprocity grounds).

[Section 6:99]

[1]19 CFR § 12.104e(b)(1)(i).

[2]19 CFR § 12.104e(b)(1)(ii).

[3]None has been disclosed by U.S. Information Agency. *Cf.* Autocephalous Greek-Orthodox Church of Cyprus v. Goldberg & Feldman Fine Arts Inc., 717 F. Supp. 1374 (S.D. Ind. 1989), judgment aff'd, 917 F.2d 278 (7th Cir. 1990) (mentions Convention in dicta but CPIA inapplicable because theft occurred prior to 1983).

To obtain import restrictions under Section 303, a state party must submit a formal written request to the director of the U.S. Information Agency. The request must contain five detailed findings as follows:

(1) the cultural patrimony of the requesting nation must be in "jeopardy" due to the "pillage" of its archaeological or ethnological material;[1]

(2) the requesting nation must have taken actions of its own to protect its cultural property;[2]

(3) restrictions must have a "substantially beneficial effect" in preventing a "serious situation of pillage" if within a reasonable time other nations with a significant import trade apply similar restrictions for the same archaeological or ethnological material;[3]

(4) remedies less drastic than the application of import restrictions are not available;[4] and

(5) application of import restrictions must be consistent with the general interest of the international community.[5]

If these five preconditions are satisfied, the director of the U.S. Information Agency, acting in consultation with the Secretary of State and the Secretary of the Treasury,[6] is authorized to enter into a bilateral or multilateral agreement prohibiting importation of the endangered archaeological or ethnological material. The United States has entered into bilateral agreements with the countries, or "state parties" listed in Chart 6-5 covering a broad range of materials.

§ 6:101 Section 304: Emergency import restrictions—Designated materials

If property is designated under emergency restrictions,

[Section 6:100]

[1] 19 U.S.C.A. § 2602(a).

[2] 19 U.S.C.A. § 2602(a).

[3] 19 U.S.C.A. § 2602(a).

[4] 19 U.S.C.A. § 2602(a).

[5] 19 U.S.C.A. § 2602(a).

[6] Exec. Order 12555 (Mar. 10, 1986).

then its importation is severely limited, but is not proscribed outright.[1] Basically, emergency restrictions follow agreement requests, but must specifically ask for, and identify, emergency conditions and state that U.S. restrictions on a temporary basis would, in whole or in part, reduce the incentive for pillage, dismantling, dispersal, or fragmentation. Section 304 defines "emergency condition" as follows:

> (a) Emergency Condition Defined . . . means, with respect to any archaeological or ethnological material of any State Party, that such material is (1) a newly discovered type of material which is of importance for understanding of the history of mankind . . . (2) identifiable as coming from any site recognized to be of high cultural significance if such site is in jeopardy from pillage, dismantling, dispersal, or fragmentation which is, or threatens to be, of crisis proportion; or (3) a part of the remains of a particular culture or civilization, the record of which is in jeopardy from pillage, dismantling, dispersal, or fragmentation which is, or threatens to be, of crisis proportions; . . . and . . . [section 307] restrictions would "reduce the incentive" for such pillage. The regulations require that the particular property be designated under 19 CFR 12.104g(b). The seizure and forfeiture provisions described in section 5.20C apply equally to emergency import restrictions.

Chart 6-6 illustrates the weaknesses of this by tracing Peru's application for import restrictions, made two years after plunder of archaeological findspots. At the time the federal government was gearing up to impose restrictions, the criminal justice system was returning to defendants the very objects illegally exported and unlawfully imported. Since emergency restrictions did not yet exist, the defendant was charged under Sections 371, 545, and 1001 of Title 18 of the U.S. Code.

[Section 6:101]

[1] *See* 19 CFR § 12.104c.

Chart 6-6: Intertwining Criminal Justice System and CPIA Section 304 Application by Peru Involving Sipan Artifacts

Event	Date
Peru accedes to Convention	10/24/79
Convention enters into force in Peru	1/24/80
Tombs discovered	1986
Tombs plundered	1986–87
Unlawful importations	May–Oct. 1987
Criminal indictment of defendant	Nov. 1988
Order Granting Motion for Return of Property	12/20/88
Guilty Plea	5/12/89
Peru applies to the United States to impose emergency restrictions on Moche culture materials from the Sipan Region[2]	6/15/89
Notice of request published re CPIA § 303(f)(1)	6/23/89
Request referred to CPAC	6/23/89
Judgment and Probation Commitment Order	6/26/89
Request submitted through diplomatic channels under CPIA § 303(a)(3) to the President through the Director of USIA	
CPAC reviews eligibility of request for emergency import controls under CPIA § 306(f) and its findings referred to the Deputy Director of USIA, the presidential designate, and Congress[3]	

[2]54 Fed. Reg. 26,462–63 (1989).

[3]The functions conferred upon the President regarding emergency import restrictions under CPIA § 304 are delegated to the director of the U.S. Information Agency (the deputy director actually handles this designated function). Exec. Order 12555, 51 Fed. Reg. 8475 (1986).

Event	Date
Order granting Motion for Return of Property[4]	7/26/89
Defendant surrenders to U.S. Marshal	9/6/89
Order to continue surrender date	9/8/89
CPAC submits report on Peru[5]	9/20/89
Defendant surrenders	9/25/89
Peru files civil suit against importers/ collectors[6]	1989
Deputy Director seeks concurrence	11/3/89
(1) in consultation with the Secretary of State, and	12/19/89
(2) the Secretary of the Treasury	12/15/89
Defendant released from federal facility	3/25/90
Consultation with Commissioner of Customs to prepare list of categories of cultural property for public notice and use by U.S. Customs[7]	4/9/90
Import restrictions become effective on date of announcement in Federal Register	5/7/90
Twenty-three objects returned to Peru	1990
Order Granting Motion for Return of Property	

§ 6:102 Section 304: Emergency import restrictions—Authorized import of designated materials—Certification

Designated material "will be permitted entry" if it is accompanied by a certificate or other documentation issued

[4]All Sipan material returned to defendant except the objects specified in indictment.

[5]*See* Chart 6-4. If CPAC's report is timely submitted within ninety days from the date CPAC receives the request, then the President or designate "must consider" the report. CPAC timely submitted every report based upon requests received from Bolivia, Canada, El Salvador, and Guatemala.

[6]Government of Peru v. Johnson, 720 F. Supp. 810 (C.D. Cal. 1989), aff'd sub nom. Peru v. Wendt, 933 F.2d 1013 (9th Cir. 1991).

[7]19 CFR § 12.104(g).

by the country of origin that the exportation was not in violation of the laws of the country; otherwise the property will be seized and subject to forfeiture. The form of certification is not specified but examples include affidavits, export licenses, and export permits authorized by a state official under seal and expressly reciting the certification of lawful export.

§ 6:103 Section 304: Emergency import restrictions—Authorized import of designated materials—Satisfactory evidence

Even if certification is lacking, if the importer can provide "satisfactory evidence" (one or more declarations under oath) that the material was exported from the party nation more than ten years before the date of importation and that the importer had not owned it for more than one year (accompanied by a statement from the seller), then the material can be still be imported. A similar exception is provided if the material were exported on or before the date the import restrictions became effective.[1]

§ 6:104 Forfeiture of designated materials

Designated materials without certification that attempt to obtain certification or other evidence "shall be seized and summarily forfeited. If forfeited, the material is first offered for return to the state party, or if not returned to the state party, to a claimant if the claimant establishes valid title and that he or she is bona fide purchaser, providing that expenses of return and delivery are paid."[1] Otherwise, the forfeited articles are disposed of in the manner prescribed by customs laws.

I. IMPORT EXEMPTIONS: Section 312

§ 6:105 Immunity from seizure

Regulations exclude certain materials and properties

[Section 6:103]

[1] 19 U.S.C.A. § 2604; 19 CFR § 12.104c(b).

[Section 6:104]

[1] 19 CFR § 12.104e(a).

from import restrictions. Any archaeological or ethnological material or any cultural property imported into the United States for temporary exhibition or display is exempt from regulations, if it is immune from seizure under judicial process pursuant to Section 2459 of title 22 of the U.S. Code.[1]

§ 6:106 Museum exemptions—Acquisition policies: Convention article 7(a)

Article 7(a) of the Convention recited the understanding upon Senate ratification that its application is only to institutions "whose acquisitions policy is subject to national control." The United States is, with minor exception, a nation of nongovernmental museums, and acquisition policies are not federal. Federal entities like the Smithsonian Institution and the Library of Congress do exist, and much debate has occurred on whether even these federal entities are subject to national controls regarding acquisition policies. The practical point to extrapolate from the understanding is simply that no additional federal legislation was implemented or contemplated to regulate cultural property acquisition policies of the nation's thousandfold museums. The absence of federal law can be mooted somewhat because museums themselves, through their directors, curators, registrars, have established independent scrutiny by enacting codes of ethics and passing resolutions pertaining to acquisition of cultural properties.

§ 6:107 Museum exemptions—Museum acquisition guidelines

The International Council of Museums has enacted an ethical acquisition code. The American Association of Museums and the Association of Art Museum Directors, among others, adopted a resolution in 1973 which was ratified by their respective memberships. Individual

---

[Section 6:105]

[1] 19 CFR § 12.104h(a); *see* § 6:132.

museums can have their own policies and codes.[1]

Museums have various ways to exempt objects already accessioned from the effect of CPIA Section 312 and the implementing regulations.[2] Section 312 provides multiple exemptions on various bases, exempting some cultural property in museum collections from sovereign claimants. A summary of these rules is provided in Chart 6-7.

Chart 6-7: Regulations for Exemptions Under Section 312 for Museum Collections

Rule	Regulations
Three-Year Rule	(1) U.S. site—three-year minimum (2) BFP status (3) Publication or public exhibit (one year) or catalogue (two years)
Five- and Ten-Year Rule	(1) Public exhibit—five-year minimum (2) U.S. site—ten-year minimum
Ten-Year Rule Plus Fair Notice	(1) U.S. site—ten-year minimum (2) Fair notice via publication or other means
Twenty-Year Rule	(1) U.S. site—twenty-year minimum (2) BFP status

§ 6:108 Museum exemptions—CPIA three-year rule

Designated material and cultural property are exempt if they have been held in the United States for a period of not less than three consecutive years by a recognized museum, religious or secular monument, or similar institution and was purchased by that institution for value, in good faith, and without notice that the material or article was imported in violation of the Act or regula-

[Section 6:107]

[1] *See* Appendix 15.

[2] 19 U.S.C.A. § 2611; 19 CFR § 12.104h.

tions, "but only if" the museum or entity complies with one of the following requirements:[1]

(1) The acquisition of the material was reported in a publication of the museum, any regularly published newspaper or periodical with a circulation of at least 50,000, or a periodical or exhibition catalogue "concerned" with type of property sought to be exempt;
(2) The material is exhibited to the public for at least one year during the three-year period; or
(3) The material is cataloged, and the catalog is available to the public upon request for at least two years of the three years.[2]

§ 6:109 Museum exemptions—CPIA five- and ten-year rule

If the museum cannot meet one of the aforementioned three requirements, the property is still exempt if it has been in the United States for a period not less than ten consecutive years and exhibited in a recognized museum or comparable institution for at least five of those ten years.

§ 6:110 Museum exemptions—CPIA ten-year plus fair notice rule

Property can still be exempt if it has been in the United States for a period not less than ten consecutive years and the requesting nation has received or should have received fair notice of its location.

§ 6:111 Museum exemptions—CPIA twenty-year rule

The property is exempt if it has been in the United States for a period not less than twenty consecutive years and the claimant establishes that it purchased for value without knowledge or reason to believe that it was

---

[Section 6:108]

[1] 19 CFR § 12.104h(b).

[2] 19 CFR § 12.104h(b)(1)(i).

imported in violation of law.

J. MISCELLANEOUS ISSUES

§ 6:112 Pre-columbian sculpture and murals

The Pre-Columbian Monumental, Architectural Sculpture or Murals Act of 1972[1] was enacted by Congress to discourage illicit plunder, looting and trade in pre-Columbian artifacts after publicized incidents involving thefts of major works from Central and South America. Regulations were promulgated to implement the Pre-Columbian Monuments Act.[2]

No object described under the regulations exported from its country of origin after June 1, 1973, regardless of whether the export is to the United States, can be imported into the United States.[3] The "country of origin" is defined as the country where the object was first discovered.[4] The following countries are specifically identified as sources of pre-Columbian materials: Belize, Bolivia, Colombia, Costa Rica, Dominican Republic, Ecuador, El Salvador, Guatemala, Honduras, Mexico, Panama, Peru, and Venezuela.

The types of property included are broad, inter alia, stone carvings, murals, wall art, columns, obelisks, aqueducts, buildings, doorways, plazas, architectural masks, glyphs, graffiti, moldings, and fragments.

Importation is permitted only by certification or satisfactory evidence.[5] The objects will be detained if the importer cannot produce the certificate or evidence at the time of importation; the importer has ninety days to produce the information after the object is taken into customs

---

[Section 6:112]

[1] 19 U.S.C.A. §§ 2091–95 (the Pre-Columbian Monumental, Architectural Sculpture or Murals Act of 1972 is hereinafter cited and referred to throughout this treatise as the Pre-Columbian Monuments Act).

[2] 19 CFR §§ 12.105 et seq.

[3] 19 CFR § 12.106.

[4] 19 CFR § 12.105(c).

[5] 19 CFR § 12.107. *See also* §§ 6:102 to 6:103.

custody, unless a longer period is allowed for good cause.[6]

Seizure and forfeiture provisions are authorized in accordance with Section 2093 of title 19 of the U.S. Code. In many respects, the procedures parallel those for cultural property in that objects are offered to the country of origin and returned if the country bears all expenses incident to return.[7]

No cases could be found reported under the Pre-Columbian Monuments Act. The Pre-Columbian Monuments Act apparently provided successful notification to the trade of intended federal action on specific works of definitive dates from particular sources. The effect was deterrence. CPIA does not have that kind of specificity, either temporally or categorically, and its efficacy is undermined by its broad, amorphous provisions.

§ 6:113 Postborder interdiction

Many objects, if not most, escape border interdiction because they are not declared. If U.S. Customs is notified by informants or citizens or through undercover operations that cultural property has surreptitiously entered U.S. commerce, it has authority to act by making a request for voluntary return, seizing it as evidence of a crime, or undertaking an undercover purchase. Arrest and search warrants can be issued under various laws.[1]

§ 6:114 Other cultural property treaties and agreements

The United States has signed agreements and treaties with Ecuador, Guatemala, Mexico, and Peru regarding cultural property regulation, identified in Chart 6-8.

---

[6] 19 CFR § 12.108.

[7] *See* 19 CFR § 12.109.

[Section 6:113]

[1] *See* §§ 6:1 to 6:70.

Chart 6-8: U.S. Agreements and Treaties on Cultural Property Regulation*

Agreement/Treaty	Date
Agreement Between the United States and the Republic of Guatemala for Recovery and Return of Stolen Archaelogical, Historical and Cultural Properties	May 21, 1984, entered into force Aug. 12, 1984
Agreement Between the United States and Ecuador for Recovery and Return of Stolen Archaelogical, Historical and Cultural Properties	Nov. 12, 1983, entered into force Jan. 14, 1987
Agreement Between the United States and Republic of Peru for Recovery and Return of Stolen Archaelogical, Historical and Cultural Properties, T.I.A.S. No. 10136, 33 U.S.T. 1608	Sept. 15, 1981, entered into force Sept. 15, 1981
Treaty of Cooperation Between United States and United Mexican States providing for Recovery and Return of Stolen Archaeological, Historical and Cultural Properties, T.I.A.S. No. 7088, 22 U.S.T. 494	July 17, 1970, entered into force Mar. 24, 1971

* Excluding CPIA.

If any property has been returned by the United States under these agreements, it has not been publicly reported.

§ 6:115 Diplomatic cooperation

Virtually all the importation violations under title 18 of the U.S. Code[1] can be used to interdict cultural property and return it through diplomatic channels to claimant countries: aiding and abetting (Section 2); conspiracy (Section 371), false classifications of value or quality or

[Section 6:115]

[1] *See also* 19 U.S.C.A. §§ 1595, 2606.

underpayment of duty (Section 541); false statements (Section 542); smuggling (Section 545); and false statements to customs (Section 1001).[2] The National Stolen Property Act[3] is also a criminal predicate for stolen goods valued at more than $5,000 in interstate or foreign commerce. Title 19 of the U.S. Code, Sections 1497 and 1595,[4] can also be used in conjunction with diplomatic arrangement. U.S. Customs, as a matter of policy, notifies the cultural attache of the respective embassy after the country of origin is determined. If the embassy requests that the property be returned, the request is treated as a petition for relief under remission or mitigation of penalties provisions set forth in Section 1618 of title 19 of the U.S. Code.[5] Return of the object must await criminal action, forfeiture proceedings, or interpleader action, if any such related actions are planned or pending.

IV. INTERNATIONAL TRANSACTIONS

A. IN GENERAL

§ 6:116 Introduction

All cultural property of a foreign country is not subject to American cultural property law under the Cultural Property Implementation Act (CPIA):[1] the property may have been stolen before CPIA's effective time period; the property may not conform to cultural property classifications; no emergency import restrictions on designated materials may exist, or the import restrictions may have been imposed after the unlawful activity occurred.

In other words, practitioners need to be familiar with alternative legal routes for recovery of personal property located in the United States. In the past, foreigners seeking redress on American soil did not ordinarily fare well. Recent revelations, or at least public acknowledgements,

---

[2] *See* Charts 6-1 and 6-2.

[3] 18 U.S.C.A. §§ 2314–15.

[4] *See* §§ 6:1 to 6:70.

[5] *See, e.g.,* U.S. v. Two Gandharan Stone Sculptures, 1986 WL 8344 (N.D. Ill. 1986).

[Section 6:116]

[1] *See* §§ 6:77 to 6:115.

about Nazi dealings during World War II have forced a public accounting on American and international entities. As a result of intense media coverage, restitution is being sought and granted in the twenty-first century for some of the War's victims or their heirs.

The spillover effect has been felt strongly in the arts. It is an open secret that many artworks in the collections of major museums were acquired after World War II without adequate investigation into provenance or perhaps without any. For the first time, in a very public way, major American institutions are attempting to correct possible improper acquisitions relating to this era and to quell once and for all old claims, by posting on web sites lists of objects that have gaps in provenance. As these sites proliferate, some museums are entering negotiated settlements with litigants or potential litigants in response to ownership claims that otherwise might be defeated by traditional defenses like the statute of limitations. Tribunals and conferences have been established to "repatriate" owners with artworks dispossessed by the Nazis or as a result of forced sales during the War. Chart 6-9 shows that litigants have not had successful recovery rates through the early 1990s. But the tide of public opinion appears to be changing. This may explain why some potential defendants are making extrajudicial settlements. In addition there appears to be some moral reflection at the institutional level.

Regardless, buyers of art with an international provenance should make detailed inquiries prior to purchase. World War II is but one small period, albeit sensationalized, where ownership problems occur for international objects. Property is regularly stolen or wrongfully exported from the nations of the world, ranging from artifacts unlawfully excavated at archaeological digs to spiritual or sacred works of indigenous peoples.[2] Litigating these cases is expensive, often requiring testimony of foreign experts on the laws of their respective countries, as well as resolution of ill-defined international legal principles involving choice of laws, conflicts of law, international law, laws of transshipment countries, as well as U.S. law and equity. Although some facts give rise to criminal prosecutions

[2] *See* Ch 13.

against importers or recipients, more often than not the action is a civil one.

The seminal cases are analyzed here. Checklists for collectors prior to purchase offer possible channels of inquiry about art with an international provenance.

§ 6:117 Illicit international trade

The "exotic . . . international art trade" has global significance;[1] every nation is a source of private and public bounty. Illicit art is big business and makes good press; what the real numbers are in dollar terms is not known, and purported estimates are simply speculations. What is known is the sources of these international properties, and the reasons they are considered illicit: unauthorized removals from authorized archaeological sites;[2] unauthorized excavations;[3] "appropriation" arising from war and occupation;[4] looting of religious sanctuaries and shrines;[5] "discovery" of objects "missing" since World War II,[6] smuggling and in certain circumstances, illegal exports,[7] and thefts from museums, private and public institutions, and

---

[Section 6:117]

[1]Mucha v. King, 792 F.2d 602 (7th Cir. 1986).

[2]*See, e.g.,* Government of Peru v. Johnson, 720 F. Supp. 810 (C.D. Cal. 1989), aff'd, 933 F.2d 1013 (9th Cir. 1991).

[3]*See, e.g.,* U.S. v. Hollinshead, 495 F.2d 1154, 1156 (9th Cir. 1974).

[4]*See, e.g.,* Stroganoff-Scherbatoff v. Weldon, 420 F. Supp. 18 (S.D. N.Y. 1976).

[5]Autocephalous Greek-Orthodox Church of Cyprus v. Goldberg & Feldman Fine Arts Inc., 717 F. Supp. 1374 (S.D. Ind. 1989), judgment aff'd, 917 F.2d 278 (7th Cir. 1990).

[6]See DeWeerth v. Baldinger, 658 F. Supp. 688 (S.D. N.Y. 1987), judgment rev'd on other grounds, 836 F.2d 103 (2d Cir. 1987); Kunstsammlungen Zu Weimar v. Elicofon, 536 F. Supp. 829 (E.D. N.Y. 1981), aff'd, 678 F.2d 1150 (2d Cir. 1982); Menzel v. List, 22 A.D.2d 647, 253 N.Y.S.2d 43 (1st Dep't 1964). The reunification of Germany and increasing access to records of former East Germany may reveal more art that disappeared during World War II. The exhibition "Hidden Treasures Revealed," consisting of Impressionist and Post-Impressionist paintings "removed" from Germany by the Russians in World War II, held at the Hermitage Museum in St. Petersburg from 1994–1996, refocused public attention on the issues of wartime appropriation.

[7]See 6:119.

private citizens. The reunification of Germany, the balkanization of Europe, the dissolution of the former soviet republics, the war in Iraq, and instability elsewhere has brought into the market unprecedented quantity, variety, and quality of national treasures and cultural properties. Charts 6.9 and 6.10 provides a sample of litigation in U.S. courts involving diverse artworks, claimants, and countries.

Chart 6-9: Civil Litigation in U.S. Courts

Case	Court	Action	Claimant	Result
Church of Cyprus v. Goldberg[8]	7th Cir.	replevin	church and Cyprus	property returned
Quedlinburg v. Maedon[9]	Texas (fed)	return of property	church (in former East Germany)	out of court settlement, property returned
DeWeerth v. Baldinger[10]	2d Cir.	return of property	private party (German)	property kept by Δ 1987, appeal by π 1992; F.R.Civ.P. 60 motion granted
Government of Peru v. Johnson[11]	9th Cir.	return of property	Peru	limited voluntary property repatriation
Kunts-ammlungen Zu Weimar v. Elicofon[12]	2d Cir.	return of property	museum (former East Germany)	property returned

[8]Autocephalous Greek-Orthodox Church of Cyprus v. Goldberg & Feldman Fine Arts Inc., 717 F. Supp. 1374 (S.D. Ind. 1989), judgment aff'd, 917 F.2d 278 (7th Cir. 1990), reh'g denied, (Nov. 21, 1990).

[9]Stiftskirche-Domgemeinde v. Meador; No. CA 3-90-144-D (U.S. Dist. Ct. Dallas Div. June 18, 1990) (out-of-court settlement).

[10]DeWeerth v. Baldinger, 658 F. Supp. 688 (S.D.N.Y.), rev'd, 836 F.2d 103 (2d. Cir.), cert. denied, 486 U.S. 1056 (1988), order amplified, 804 F. Supp. 539 (S.D.N.Y. 1992), rev'd, 38 F.3d 1266 (2d Cir.), cert denied, 513 U.S. 1001 (1994).

[11]Government of Peru v. Johnson, 720 F. Supp. 810 (C.D. Cal. 1989), aff'd, 933 F.2d 1013 (9th Cir. 1991).

[12]Kuntsammlungen Zu Weimar v. Elicofon, 536 F. Supp. 829 (E.D.N.Y. 1981), aff'd, 678 F.2d 1150 (2d. Cir. 1982).

Case	Court	Action	Claimant	Result
Netherlands v. Woodner[13]	S.D.N.Y. (fed)	return of property	Netherlands	———
Turkey v. Metropolitan Museum of Art[14]	S.D.N.Y. (fed)	conversion recoveryof chattel	Turkey	case settled; property returned
Jeanneret v. Vichey[15]	2d Cir.	private party (Swiss)	property returned	
Republic of Turkey v. OKS Partners[16]	D. Mass. (fed)	replevin	Turkey	———
Stroganoff-Scherbatoff v. Weldon[17]	S.D.N.Y. (fed)	conversion	private party (Russian)	property kept by ≜s
Lebanon v. Sotheby's[18]	N.Y. App. Div.	rights of possession	Lebanon	———
Menzel v. List[19]	N.Y. App. Div.	replevin	Belgium	property returned
Patriarchate v. Christie's[20]	S.D.N.Y. (fed)	return of property	Religious entity	property kept by ≜s
Rosenberg v. Seattle[21]	W.D. Wash. (fed)	return of property	private party (US)	property returned

[13]Netherlands v. Woodner, No. 89 Civ. 7425 (S.D.N.Y.Dec. 1989).

[14]Republic of Turkey v. Metropolitan Museum of Art, 762 F. Supp. 44 (S.D.N.Y. 1990).

[15]Jeanneret v. Vichey, 693 F.2d 259 (2d Cir. 1982).

[16]Republic of Turkey v. OKS Partners, 146 F.R.D. 24 (D. Mass. 1993).

[17]Stroganoff-Scherbatoff v. Weldon, 420 F. Supp 18 (S.D.N.Y. 1976).

[18]Republic of Lebanon v. Sotheby's, 167 A.D.2d 142, 561 N.Y.S.2d 566 (1990).

[19]Menzel v. List, 22 A.D.2d 647 (1964), on remand, 267 N.Y.S.2d 608 (1966), modified on other grounds, 28 A.D.2d 516 (1967), modification rev'd, 246 N.E.2d 742 (1969).

[20]Greek Orthodox Patriarchate of Jerusalem v. Christie's, Inc., 1999 WL 673347 (S.D.N.Y. 1999).

[21]Rosenberg v. Seattle Art Museum, 42 F. Supp. 2d 1029, motion to dismiss granted, 70 F. Supp. 2d 1163 (W.D. Wash. 1999) (third party defendant's motion for summary judgment against third party plaintiff museum on fraud claim granted and other claims dismissed for lack of personal jurisdiction).

Case	Court	Action	Claimant	Result
Altmann v. Austria[22]	9th Cir.	return of property	private party	cert. granted

Chart 6-10: Criminal Prosecutions in U.S. Courts

Case	Court	Action	Country	Result
United States v. Hollins-head[23]	9th Cir.	NSPA 18 U.S.C.A. §§ 2314–15	Guatemela	Convicted
United States v. Mc-Clain[24]	5th Cir.	NSPA 18 U.S.C.A. §§ 2314–15	Mexico	Convicted only on con-spiracy
United States v. Swetnam[25]	C.D. Cal. (fed)	NSPA 18 U.S.C.A. §§ 2, 371, 545, 1001	Peru	Guilty Plea on 18 U.S.C.A. §§ 2, 345
United States v. An-tique Plat-ter[26]	2d Cir.	18 U.S.C.A. §§ 545, 542	Italy	civil forfei-ture
United States v. Portrait of Wally[27]	S.D.N.Y. (fed)	forfeiture	USA	in litigation under pri-vate settle-ment

[22]Altmann v. Republic of Austria, 317 F.3d 954 (9th Cir. 2002), opinion amended on denial of reh'g, 327 F.3d 1246 (9th Cir. 2003), cert. granted in part, 124 S. Ct. 46, 156 L. Ed. 2d 703 (U.S. 2003) and aff'd, 2004 WL 1238028 (U.S. 2004) and cert. granted in part, 124 S. Ct. 46, 156 L. Ed. 2d 703 (U.S. 2003)

[23]United States v. Hollinshead, 495 F.2d 1154 (9th Cir. 1974).

[24]United States v. McClain, 545 F.2d 988 (5th Cir.), reh'g denied, 551 F.2d 52 (5th Cir. 1977), rev'd in part, aff'd in part, 593 F.2d 658, 664 (5th Cir. 1979), cert denied, 444 U.S. 918 (1979).

[25]United States v. Swetnam, Indictment CR 88-914 RG (C.D. Cal. Nov. 1988).

[26]United States v. Antique Platter of Gold, 184 F.3d 131 (2d Cir. 1999), cert. denied, 68 U.S.L.W. 3479 (U.S. 2000).

[27]United States v. Portrait of Wally, 105 F.Supp.2d 288 (S.D.N.Y. 2000) (complaint dismissed); U.S. v. Portrait of Wally, 2000 WL 1890403 (S.D. N.Y. 2000) (motion to file third amended complaint granted); (motions to dismiss third amended complaint denied).

Case	Court	Action	Country	Result
United States v. Schultz[28]	2d Cir.	18 U.S.C.A. § § 371, 2315	USA	Convicted

If the underlying removal is illicit, i.e., looting, plunder, pillage, and unlawful export, claims by the dispossessed for return or property located in the United States are not necessarily actionable in U.S. courts. The reason is situated in property law, due process, the rules of evidence and procedure, and a strictly construed and broadly applied concept of private ownership.

In civil actions, conversion, replevin or return of personal property under applicable state law is ordinarily the type of relief sought.[29] Art has not been routinely traded or transferred under an organized system of recordation or even documentation. This can make the task of proving sufficient ownership interest difficult for private claimants. When a sovereign seeks recovery, additional issues arise, particularly when the property was never reduced to possession.[30]

U.S. courts require proof of ownership as a predicate to recovery. Proving art ownership is difficult; as discussed earlier,[31] art is not transferred under a system of recordation, making title an elusive concept. Even when art is traded, the documentation record is sparse, often nothing more than a handwritten note devoid of particulars[32] or

---

[28]U.S. v. Schultz, 333 F.3d 393 (2d Cir. 2003), cert. denied, 124 S. Ct. 1051, 157 L. Ed. 2d 891 (U.S. 2004)

[29]See Chart 6-9.

[30]See § 6:119.

[31]*See* § 6:1; *see also* Chs 1, 2, and 4.

[32]Jafari v. Wally Findlay Galleries, 1989 WL 116437 (S.D. N.Y. 1989) (handwritten invoice for Salvador Dali painting: "Item: S. Dali 'Grand Opera' 1957, $210,000, Terms, Wire transfer, . . . Note: Painting is sold with photo certificate from Alex Maguy, Paris."); *cf.* Greenberg Gallery, Inc. v. Bauman, 817 F. Supp. 167 (D.D.C. 1993), order aff'd, 36 F.3d 127 (D.C. Cir. 1994) (invoice for Alexander Calder mobile recites, "black sheet metal and steel wire hanging mobile, 31″ × 65″, titled *Rio Nero,* signed 'AC' ").

just a handshake.[33]

The problems are logarithmic when the claimants are foreign, particularly sovereign. Private claimants have discovered that U.S. courts suspect their ownership credentials;[34] sovereign claimants may never have had actual possession;[35] the law whereby the sovereign claims ownership may not identify the property at issue;[36] the claimant may not be recognized by the United States as a sovereign, de facto or de jure, under international legal principles;[37] and the claimant may not have exercised sufficient "rights incident to ownership."[38]

§ 6:118 Choice of law and conflict of law

Trade transactions involving cultural properties traverse multiple jurisdictions, giving rise to the issue of whose law should apply and when and where the pivotal transactions occurred: negotiations; sale; delivery; export; location of defendant and property when action filed; and transship-

---

[33]Community for Creative Non-Violence v. Reid, 652 F. Supp. 1453 (D.D.C. 1987), judgment rev'd, 846 F.2d 1485 (D.C. Cir. 1988) and judgment aff'd, 490 U.S. 730, 109 S. Ct. 2166, 104 L. Ed. 2d 811 (1989) (sculpture commission without written agreement between parties).

[34]DeWeerth v. Baldinger, 658 F. Supp. 688 (S.D. N.Y. 1987), judgment rev'd on other grounds, 836 F.2d 103 (2d Cir. 1987) ("Key documents, including DeWeerth's father's will . . . are missing. [Her] claim of superior title is supported largely by hearsay testimony of questionable value.").

[35]Government of Peru v. Johnson, 720 F. Supp. 810 (C.D. Cal. 1989), aff'd, 933 F.2d 1013 (9th Cir. 1991); U.S. v. McClain, 545 F.2d 988 (5th Cir. 1977).

[36]Government of Peru v. Johnson, 720 F. Supp. 810 (C.D. Cal. 1989), aff'd, 933 F.2d 1013 (9th Cir. 1991).

[37]See, e.g., Autocephalous Greek-Orthodox Church of Cyprus v. Goldberg & Feldman Fine Arts Inc., 717 F. Supp. 1374 (S.D. Ind. 1989), judgment aff'd, 917 F.2d 278 (7th Cir. 1990) (Turkish occupying forces in Cyprus not recognized by court); *cf.* Stroganoff-Scherbatoff v. Weldon, 420 F. Supp. 18 (S.D. N.Y. 1976) (Soviet state recognized after Russian Revolution); *see also* Kunstsammlungen Zu Weimar v. Elicofon, 536 F. Supp. 829 (E.D. N.Y. 1981), aff'd, 678 F.2d 1150 (2d Cir. 1982) (discussion of American-East German relations and recognition during Cold War).

[38]Government of Peru v. Johnson, 720 F. Supp. 810 (C.D. Cal. 1989), aff'd, 933 F.2d 1013 (9th Cir. 1991).

ment countries.[1] The law of the situs of the art at the time of removal or export is invariably evaluated to assist in the determination of the claimant's ownership rights.[2]

A federal court sitting in diversity jurisdiction must follow the choice-of-law rules of the state in which it sits to determine which substantive law to apply.[3] The court decides the appropriate jurisdiction as a matter of law. Some federal district courts backstop the opinion by analyzing the law under alternating jurisdictions.[4]

[Section 6:118]

[1]Autocephalous Greek-Orthodox Church of Cyprus v. Goldberg & Feldman Fine Arts Inc., 717 F. Supp. 1374 (S.D. Ind. 1989), judgment aff'd, 917 F.2d 278 (7th Cir. 1990) (law of Switzerland analyzed where mosaics pass through duty-free part of Geneva airport to be viewed by defendant, money is wired to Switzerland and paid to sellers in Switzerland); Jeanneret v. Vichey, 693 F.2d 259, 35 U.C.C. Rep. Serv. 75 (2d Cir. 1982) (art delivered, sold and paid for in Switzerland but where parties assume New York law applies because negotiations occurred there, court "shall follow them in assumption").

[2]Jeanneret v. Vichey, 693 F.2d 259, 35 U.C.C. Rep. Serv. 75 (2d Cir. 1982) (laws of Italy analyzed where sale took place in Switzerland and New York law applied); Autocephalous Greek-Orthodox Church of Cyprus v. Goldberg & Feldman Fine Arts Inc., 717 F. Supp. 1374 (S.D. Ind. 1989), judgment aff'd, 917 F.2d 278 (7th Cir. 1990) (laws of Cyprus and Turkey occupying forces and military powers analyzed where sale occurred in Switzerland and Indiana law applied); Stroganoff-Scherbatoff v. Weldon, 420 F. Supp. 18 (S.D. N.Y. 1976) (laws of Soviet analyzed where art auctioned by Soviets in Berlin and artwork sold to defendants in Europe and New York law applied); DeWeerth v. Baldinger, 658 F. Supp. 688 (S.D. N.Y. 1987), judgment rev'd on other grounds, 836 F.2d 103 (2d Cir. 1987) (laws of National Socialist Party, occupying forces, and military laws analyzed where theft occurred in East Germany, sale occurred in United States and New York law applied).

[3]Autocephalous Greek-Orthodox Church of Cyprus v. Goldberg & Feldman Fine Arts Inc., 717 F. Supp. 1374 (S.D. Ind. 1989), judgment aff'd, 917 F.2d 278 (7th Cir. 1990) (federal court applies law of Indiana to determine where wrong was committed); *see also* Hoelzer v. City of Stamford, Conn., 933 F.2d 1131 (2d Cir. 1991) (in an action not involving cultural property of a sovereign, but arguably American cultural property—WPA murals—"analysis of this choice of law issue under New York's 'interest analysis' or 'significant relationship' test seems appropriate.").

[4]*See, e.g.,* Autocephalous Greek-Orthodox Church of Cyprus v. Goldberg & Feldman Fine Arts Inc., 717 F. Supp. 1374 (S.D. Ind. 1989), judgment aff'd, 917 F.2d 278 (7th Cir. 1990).

B. PATRIMONY LAWS

§ 6:119 Definition

Some countries have implemented restrictions on ownership and/or export variously referred to as patrimony, umbrella, retention or blanket laws.[1] The objective of such laws ordinarily is to vest in the sovereign state title of objects like antiquities, historic, religious and artistic objects—the so-called cultural patrimony of the country. The properties may be movables or immovables, privately owned or undiscovered, described generally or with specificity. In this manner, governments assert ownership although they may lack possession.

The form of these patrimony controls varies. In some instances the law is a legislative enactment, supplemented by export restrictions, enforced by regulations, sanctions and penalties. In others, the "law" may be a mere decree, proclamation, or newspaper notice.

Putative state ownership under such patrimony laws is scrutinized in American courts when the property becomes involved in civil litigation or criminal prosecution.[2] Courts have emphasized various issues to determine whether the patrimony law vests a cognizable ownership interest in the state or merely operates as an export restriction. Considerations include whether or not the law includes recitations of a clear and unequivocal declaration of ownership that survives translation; provisions for sanctions, seizures, and other legitimate penalties; procedures for domestic enforcement; and, other acts, activities and conduct consistent with the incidents of ownership.

Broad declarations of national ownership recited in foreign laws suffice in some jurisdictions and under certain circumstances.[3] Egypt's patrimony law declaring all antiquities public property, whether in private possession

---

[Section 6:119]

[1]The author reviewed approximately 100 national cultural property laws in English translation in Prott & O'Keefe, *Handbook of National Regulations Concerning the Export of Cultural Property*.

[2]See Ch 11 (criminal prosecutions).

[3]U.S. v. Schultz, 333 F.3d 393 (2d Cir. 2003), cert. denied, 124 S. Ct. 1051, 157 L. Ed. 2d 891 (U.S. 2004) (conviction upheld on a count of conspiracy for receiving stolen property transported in interstate and

or not, was deemed to "vest absolute and true ownership of all antiquities" in the Egyptian government.[4]

The property "blanketed" by the law may be broadly described.[5] Classification may include age.[6]

Although sovereign ownership rights "by legislative fiat" may be recognized in American courts even when property remains in private hands, the governmental intention must be clear and unequivocal.[7] Private ownership did not undermine an Egyptian law that expressed a "clear declaration of national ownership" define[d] antiquity' [and] set[] forth serious criminal penalties . . . licens[ed] . . . foreign archaeological missions . . . [was] directed at [domestic] activities . . . as well as export . . . and [was] active[ly] enforce[d] [including seizing discovered objects].[8]

However, regulation alone will not bootstrap otherwise deficient declarations of ownership into something more than export laws. Notwithstanding a century of governmental regulation of pre-Columbian artifacts that included systems of registration, export licensing and other controls, Mexico's laws until 1972 failed to establish the requisite incantation of national ownership. "The State

---

foreign commerce under 18 U.S.C.A. §§ 371, 2315 [Egyptian sculptures and antiquities]); U.S. v. McClain, 545 F.2d 988 (5th Cir. 1977) [McClain 1]; U.S. v. McClain, 593 F.2d 658 (5th Cir. 1979) [McClain 2] (convictions upheld on conspiracy counts for receiving, concealing and selling stolen property in interstate and foreign commerce under 18 U.S.C.A. §§ 2314, 2315 but reversed on substantive NSPA violations [pre-Columbian artifacts]); U.S. v. Hollinshead, 495 F.2d 1154 (9th Cir. 1974) (conviction upheld on conspiracy count for transporting stolen property in interstate and foreign commerce under 18 U.S.C.A. § 2314 [Mayan stela]).

[4]U.S. v. Schultz, 333 F.3d 393, 405 (2d Cir. 2003), cert. denied, 124 S. Ct. 1051, 157 L. Ed. 2d 891 (U.S. 2004), Law 117 ["Law 117"] on Protection of Antiquities, Art. 6 ("All antiquities are considered to be public property . . . ").

[5]Law 117, Art. 1 (antiquity is "any . . . product of the various civilizations or any of the arts, sciences, humanities and religions . . . from prehistoric times . . .).

[6]Law 117, Art. 1 (objects at least one hundred years old).

[7]McClain 1, 545 F.2d at 992 ("possession. . .is not the *sine qua non* of ownership . . .," discussing Mexican laws that "specifically recognized" private ownership.).

[8]U.S. v. Schultz, 333 F.3d 393, 402 (2d Cir. 2003), cert. denied, 124 S. Ct. 1051, 157 L. Ed. 2d 891 (U.S. 2004).

comes to own property only when it acquires such property in the general manner by which private persons come to own property, or when it declares itself the owner . . . ."[9]

The legal viability of patrimony laws has been generally acknowledged[10] but substantive criminal counts have yet to be imposed. Where an ambiguity exists about which patrimony law was being applied, a substantive NSPA conviction against a dealer was reversed. "Mexico [may] have considered itself the owner of all pre-Columbian artifacts for almost 100 years [but] . . . it has not expressed that view with sufficient clarity to survive translation into terms understandable by and binding upon American citizens. [O]ur basic standards of due process and notice preclude us from characterizing the artifacts as 'stolen.'"[11]

Peru's patrimony laws were deemed insufficient to establish ownership in pre-Columbian artifacts seized from the collection of an American dealer.[12] Peru's conversion claim was based upon a decree providing that pre-Hispanic artistic objects "belonging to the nation's cultural wealth are untouchable" and prohibiting their removal from Peru. The court concluded Peru had merely implemented an export restriction. "[A]rtistic objects [that are] 'part of the national cultural wealth, . . . untouchable, inalienable and inprescriptable,' and . . . [where] removal from [Peru] is 'categorically forbidden' . . . [gives] no indication in the record that Peru ever has sought to exercise its ownership

[9]McClain 1, 545 F.2d at 998-1000, 1002 (" . . . the state's power to regulate [exports] is not ownership . . . a declaration of national ownership [combined with a restriction on export] is necessary before illegal exportation of an article can be considered theft . . . .").

[10]McClain 2, 593 F.2d at 659 (" . . . artifacts were 'stolen' only in the sense that Mexico generally declared itself owner of all pre-Columbian artifacts within its borders . . . anyone who digs up or finds such an item and deals in it without governmental permission has unlawfully converted the item from its proper owner.").

[11]McClain 2, 593 F.2d at 670-71 ("The law unequivocally establishes for the first time [in 1972] what Dr. Gertz testified had been the case since 1897 . . . [but][o]nly after . . . 1972 . . . would . . . Mexico . . . have ownership of the . . . artifacts . . . in this case . . . .' ").

[12]Government of Peru v. Johnson, 720 F. Supp. 810 (C.D. Cal. 1989), aff'd, 933 F.2d 1013 (9th Cir. 1991).

rights in such property, so long as there is no removal].”[13]

Guatemala's patrimony law was deemed sufficient to declare ownership of an in situ pre-Columbian stela taken from a documented Mayan monument in the jungle and ultimately imported by a dealer into the United States.[14] Experts testified that under Guatemalan law such artifacts were “property of the Republic” and could not be exported without government permission.[15]

Sourcing the property obviously affects ownership claims.[16]

§ 6:120 Private ownership under patrimony laws

Patrimony laws may have de minimis effect on private ownership within the state's borders.[1] Although possession is not the “*sine qua non*” of ownership, when the property remains in private hands without more, the “domestic effect of such a pronouncement may be extremely limited.”[2]

The fact that privately possessed objects may be

---

[13]Government of Peru v. Johnson, 720 F. Supp. 810, 814 (C.D. Cal. 1989), aff'd, 933 F.2d 1013 (9th Cir. 1991) (“[Supreme Decree (Feb. 27, 1985)] [contains] declarations . . . concerned with protection [that] do not imply ownership. [The law of 1929] does proclaim . . . artifacts in historical monuments as ‘the property of the State’ and that unregistered artifacts ‘shall be considered to be the property of the State . . . .The laws of Peru concerning its artifacts could reasonably be considered to have no more effect than export restrictions.”).

[14]U.S. v. Hollinshead, 495 F.2d 1154 (9th Cir. 1974) (Mayan stela reduced and divided into smaller parts shipped as personal effects from a fish packing plant in Belize).

[15]U.S. v. Hollinshead, 495 F.2d 1154, 1155 (9th Cir. 1974).

[16]Government of Peru v. Johnson, 720 F. Supp. 810, 812 (C.D. Cal. 1989), aff'd, 933 F.2d 1013 (9th Cir. 1991) (“[Peru's expert] . . . admitted that an item may have come from Ecuador or Columbia or Mexico or even Polynesia . . . [T]his court can not base a finding of ownership upon such subjective conclusions.”).

[Section 6:120]

[1]720 F. Supp. at 810, aff'd, 933 F.2d at 1013 (“[N]o indication in the record that Peru ever . . . sought to exercise its ownership rights in such property.”).

[2]Government of Peru v. Johnson, 720 F. Supp. 810, 814 (C.D. Cal. 1989), aff'd, 933 F.2d 1013 (9th Cir. 1991) (“This Decree does not clearly establish state ownership of any such art objects . . . .if any artifacts here were concerned were privately excavated between January 5 and

transferred by gift, bequest or intestate succession would seemingly undermine national ownership claims."[3] But when an art dealer convicted on conspiracy for receiving smuggled antiquities contended Egypt's patrimony law was merely an export restriction because privately owned objects prior to 1983 could remain in private possession and be transferred or disposed of, the potential for residual private control was not considered enough to undermine national ownership.[4]

Considerations include whether the property subject to the law can be exchanged commercially for private profit within the state, transferred by gift, devise or intestacy; provisions to escheat properties to the state upon death or other event; existence of state registry; procedures tosafeguard, insure, or otherwise secure properties; and to penalize and fine for violation. Some laws do not even contain penalty provisions. Some penalty provisions simply are not enforced, or are insignificant or insubstantial. If the law has no domestic effect, it is much more likely to be considered as only an export restriction.

§ 6:121 Sanctions and penalties

The existence of sanctions and penalties in a patrimony law is an important factor, in addition to the actual degree of hardship imposed by such penalties and the level of

---

June 22, 1985, they would constitute private property, rather than being owned by Peru.")

[3]Government of Peru v. Johnson, 720 F. Supp. 810, 814 (C.D. Cal. 1989), aff'd, 933 F.2d 1013 (9th Cir. 1991) (" . . . no indication . . . that Peru . . . sought to exercise its ownership rights in such property, so long as there [was] no removal . . . [having] no more effect than export restrictions . . . .").

[4]U.S. v. Schultz, 333 F.3d 393, 403-406 (2d Cir. 2003), cert. denied, 124 S. Ct. 1051, 157 L. Ed. 2d 891 (U.S. 2004) ("[effective 1983 Law 117, Art. 7] . . . prohibit[s] trade in antiquities" [and Art. 8] [prohibits] " . . . possession of antiquities [except those in ownership or possession prior to 1983] . . . ." means " . . . it would be possible for Egyptian authorities to leave antiquities in the possession of private individuals, [but] no evidence that the authorities ever *actually* had *permitted* an individual to retain an antiquity found after 1983 . . . ."[emphasis in original]).

enforcement for domestic and export violations.[1]

Although cases of this kind are often presented in an idiosyncratic procedural context, the following basic questions should ordinarily be considered by claimants bringing an action in American courts for return of property and/or investigated by buyers and sellers of art with international provenance:[2]

(1) Does the state have a "law" purporting to declare ownership in tangible personal property?
(2) Has the law been translated into English?
(3) Does an unequivocal right to ownership of property survive translation?
(4) Does the law relate to the property at issue?
(5) What are the effective dates of the law?
(6) What acts did the state exercise incident to ownership?
(7) Did export regulations applicable to the property exist, and if so, what effective dates?
(8) Was the property transshipped through other countries? If so, those laws and export regulations may need to be investigated.

In *Schultz*[3] the Second Circuit decided a patrimony law satisfied ownership requirements under a substantially lower threshold. Egypt's patrimony law declared all antiquities discovered after 1983 property of the government.[4] The law provided that antiquities privately owner prior to 1983 were to be registered. The law prohibited removal of registered items. Neither registra-

---

[Section 6:121]

[1]U.S. v. Schultz, 333 F.3d 393, 400 (2d Cir. 2003), cert. denied, 124 S. Ct. 1051, 157 L. Ed. 2d 891 (U.S. 2004) (sanctions including imprisonment for a minimum five year term and fines of 3000 pounds Egyptian for thefts within Egypt and prison terms with hard labor and fines ranging from 5000 to 50,000 pounds Egyptian for smuggling deemed hardships).

[2]*See* Ch 11.

[3]U.S. v. Schultz, 333 F.3d 393 (2d Cir. 2003), cert. denied, 124 S. Ct. 1051, 157 L. Ed. 2d 891 (U.S. 2004).

[4]Law on Protection of Antiquities, Art. 6 ("All antiquities are considered to be public property . . . "); Art. 7 ("[effective 1983]. . .it is prohibited to trade in antiquities . . . "); Art. 8 (" . . . possession of

tion of pre-1983 privately owned properties, or enforcement of those provisions, was discussed. Persons in possession could transfer, dispose of or relocate antiquities with notification. Notification procedures were not mentioned. Sanctions included imprisonment and fines.[5] Testimony by experts from the Egyptian government stated that investigations and prosecutions of persons trafficking in antiquities within Egypt had occurred, although no number was specified.

Deciding that "Egypt ha[d] made a clear declaration of national ownership," the court wrote:

> "Law 117 defines 'antiquity'. . .it sets forth serious criminal penalties. . .it provides licensure of . . . foreign archaeological missions . . . [It] is directed at activities within Egypt as well as export . . . [w]e conclude that Law 117 is clear and unambiguous . . . the antiquities . . . were owned by the Egyptian government."[6]

Sanctions included imprisonment and fines.[7] Testimony by experts from the Egyptian government stated that when the Egyptian government learned of a discovery, it seized and registered the antiquity, and that investigations and prosecutions of persons trafficking in antiquities within Egypt had occurred, although no number was specified (defendant's expert's opinion that Law 117 was "ambiguous [could] not overcome the combination . . . plain text . . . and [official] testimony.").

In *McClain*,

> The law defined antiquities as Testimony by experts from the Mexican government stated that when Mexico

See §§ 6:123 to 6:125 (Act of State Doctrine).

Legal barriers have been somewhat circumvented or ameliorated as a result of, among other factors, diplomacy,

---

antiquities [except those in ownership or possession prior to 1983] shall be prohibited . . . ").

[5]U.S. v. Schultz, 333 F.3d 393, 400 (2d Cir. 2003), cert. denied, 124 S. Ct. 1051, 157 L. Ed. 2d 891 (U.S. 2004) (fines ranged from 100 to 50,000 pounds Egyptian).

[6]U.S. v. Schultz, 333 F.3d 393, 402 (2d Cir. 2003), cert. denied, 124 S. Ct. 1051, 157 L. Ed. 2d 891 (U.S. 2004).

[7]U.S. v. Schultz, 333 F.3d 393, 400 (2d Cir. 2003), cert. denied, 124 S. Ct. 1051, 157 L. Ed. 2d 891 (U.S. 2004) (fines ranged from 100 to 50,000 pounds Egyptian).

private negotiation, judicial and private settlements, public awareness, media coverage, political pressures, and industry guidelines and institutional codes of ethics regarding return and repatriation of cultural works.[8] Furthermore, sovereigns may be able to allege ownership at the pleading stage under lesser standards under the federal rules of notice pleading.[9]

C. EXPORT REGULATION

§ 6:122 Generally

Export regulation is a national mechanism to prohibit or restrict extraterritorial transfers. Nations have a basic right to control persons and properties that pass their borders; one of the first acts of Congress was to secure import-export regulation, establishing customs houses and raising revenues.

Sovereigns have implemented export restrictions to control extraterritorial transfer of cultural properties,[1] but export regulation alone is considered insufficient to inhere ownership in a sovereign state.[2] Export restrictions vary from country to country: outright bans, licenses, permits, product passports.[3]

---

[8]See App. 15 and 16.

[9]U.S. v. Two Gandharan Stone Sculptures, 1986 WL 8344 (N.D. Ill. 1986).

Republic of Turkey v. OKS Partners, 146 F.R.D. 24 (D. Mass. 1993); 720 F. Supp. at 810, aff'd, 933 F.2d at 1013; U.S. v. McClain, 545 F.2d 988 (5th Cir. 1977); U.S. v. An Antique Platter of Gold, 991 F. Supp. 222 (S.D. N.Y. 1997), aff'd, 184 F.3d 131 (2d Cir. 1999), cert. denied, 528 U.S. 1136, 120 S. Ct. 978, 145 L. Ed. 2d 929 (2000) (Italian ownership of antique gold platter of Sicilian origin falsely declared on U.S. Customs documents demonstrated by, inter alia, expert opinion of Italian lawyer pursuant to Article 44, No. 1089 (June 1, 1939)).

[Section 6:122]

[1]*See* Prott & O'Keefe, *Handbook of National Regulations Concerning the Export of Cultural Property*.

[2]The U.S. government has not classified any property as "cultural property," for export, except for short-term exports involving exhibition, education, and scientific purposes; see also § 6:71 (ARPA).

[3]Some countries, predominantly in western Europe, have licensing or registration systems in lieu of laws, which vest in government or

D. ACT OF STATE DOCTRINE

§ 6:123 Premise

Sovereign claimants in theory have special status with respect to ownership claims under an established principle of international law known as the Act of State Doctrine. A basic premise of state sovereignty is that territorial jurisdiction is exercised by the state over all persons and all property therein to the exclusion of external control of and by all other states.[1] That premise gives rise to the doctrine that acts of state by the sovereign should be honored in extraterritorial litigation; in the context of property ownership this means that when a state declares ownership of cultural property in its territory, that act should suffice to confer ownership without relitigating the legality of the act when an ownership dispute is adjudicated in the United States. The district court in New York has phrased the doctrine this way:

> The act of state doctrine requires [U.S.] courts to refrain from independent examination of the validity of a taking of property by a sovereign state where 1) the foreign government is recognized by the United States at the time of the lawsuit, and 2) the taking of the property by the foreign sovereign occurred within its own territorial boundaries.[2]

Since the premise is that every state must respect the validity of public acts promulgated by another state, the means to accomplish this is by not testing the legality or constitutionality of foreign state acts according to the legal measure of the domestic judicial arena.[3] Thus, " '[T]he courts of one country will not sit in judgment on the acts of the government of another, done within its own

---

designated agencies something equivalent to rights of first refusal to purchase properties intended for export.

[Section 6:123]

[1]*See generally* Williams, The International and National Protection of Movable Cultural Property 54.

[2]Stroganoff-Scherbatoff v. Weldon, 420 F. Supp. 18 (S.D. N.Y. 1976).

[3]Williams, The International and National Protection of Movable Cultural Property 10.

territory.' "[4]

§ 6:124 Confiscatory decrees

The Act of State Doctrine has been applied to ownership claims.[1] Where a private party claiming lineage to Russian royalty sought recovery in the 1970s of a portrait by Sir Anthony Van Dyck and a bust by Jean Houdon from an American museum and private American owners, defendants moved successfully for summary judgment by reason of the Act of State Doctrine. The district court reasoned as follows:

> It appears that the Triest Portrait and the Diderot bust were transported to Berlin for public sale in May 1931 at the direction of the Soviet Government . . . recognized by the U[ ]S[ ] as the de jure government of Russia in 1933. The sale of the Stroganoff Collection was held by order of the . . . Soviet Government. While the actual sale . . . occurred in Berlin, the property had been seized in Russia by the Soviet Government.[2]

The Act of State Doctrine was held inapplicable where plaintiffs' painting by Marc Chagall was appropriated by the Nazis in Belgium during the occupation after they had fled. A New York state court decided that the appropriation was by an organ of a political party, not a recognized government, that the Belgian king in exile was the recognized government, and that it occurred outside territorial limits.[3]

§ 6:125 Lex situs

Lex situs is the law of the place where tangible, mov-

---

[4]Stroganoff-Scherbatoff v. Weldon, 420 F. Supp. 18 (S.D. N.Y. 1976), *citing* Underhill v. Hernandez, 168 U.S. 250, 18 S. Ct. 83, 42 L. Ed. 456 (1897).

[Section 6:124]

[1]Stroganoff-Scherbatoff v. Weldon, 420 F. Supp. 18 (S.D. N.Y. 1976) (Act of State Doctrine applied, plaintiff denied recovery of art); Menzel v. List, 22 A.D.2d 647, 253 N.Y.S.2d 43 (1st Dep't 1964) (Act of State Doctrine not applied, plaintiff recovered art).

[2]420 F. Supp at 21 (Soviet government was recognized as the de jure government of Russia by the United States in 1933).

[3]Menzel v. List, 22 A.D.2d 647, 253 N.Y.S.2d 43 (1st Dep't 1964).

able property is situated at the time of transfer.[1] In conjunction with the Act of State Doctrine, patrimony laws have been viewed as valid lex situs transfers. The interface of act of state, lex situs and umbrella laws "may . . . give effect to . . . a foreign state'[s] . . . transfer of ownership of property . . . [otherwise] controversial . . . where . . . the foreign law violates fundamental principles of national law."[2]

E. DISCOVERY MOTIONS ON RETENTION LAWS

§ 6:126 Foreign law as matter of law

Federal Rule of Civil Procedure Rule 44.1, as adopted in 1966, and amended in 1987, is considered a watershed for proving foreign law in U.S. courts. The reason is that Rule 44.1 treats foreign law as a matter of law instead of a question of fact. Rule 44.1 provides:

> A party who intends to raise an issue concerning the law of a foreign country shall give notice by pleadings or other reasonable written notice. The court, in determining foreign law, may consider any relevant material or source, including testimony, whether or not submitted by a party or admissible under the Federal Rules of Evidence. The court's determination shall be treated as a ruling on a question of law.

By so doing, the court can consider any and all relevant material without regard to admissibility for factual materials under the Federal Rules of Evidence.[1]

Comparable provisions appear in the Federal Rules of

[Section 6:125]

[1]Williams, The International and National Protection of Movable Cultural Property 55.

[2]Ott, *Public International Law in the Modern World.*

[Section 6:126]

[1]Republic of Turkey v. OKS Partners, 146 F.R.D. 24 (D. Mass. 1993); U.S. v. Pre-Columbian Artifacts, 845 F. Supp. 544 (N.D. Ill. 1993) (construction of Guatemalan law is a "legal question," and under Rule 44.1 court can also consider "any relevant material or source . . . in establishing foreign law.").

Criminal Procedure.[2]

§ 6:127 Expert testimony and legal materials

Foreign law is often proved in the federal courts by "written or oral expert testimony according to extracts from foreign legal materials,"[1] and foreign case law decisions, treatises, and learned articles.

§ 6:128 Unpublished legislation

Rule 44.1 was interpreted in an action brought by Turkey for replevin of 2,000 rare ancient Greek and Lycian silver coins and other objects known as the Elmali Hoard in the possession of an American partnership, which Turkey claimed under patrimony laws.[1] The coins were unlawfully excavated in 1984, illegally removed from Turkey, and ultimately ended up in defendants' possession. Defendants claimed that Turkey never acquired title.

Before the evidentiary hearing to resolve Turkish law, defendants sought the unpublished legislative history of one of the laws at issue, the Protection of Cultural and Natural Properties (July 23, 1983). Rule 44.1, although broad, removes from consideration by the court anything that is not "relevant." In determining the relevance of the unpublished materials, the court decided it would examine what a Turkish court would do in interpreting Turkey's

---

[2]Fed. R. Crim. P. 26.1 ("issues of foreign law are questions of law"); U.S. v. Schultz, 333 F.3d 393 (2d Cir. 2003), cert. denied, 124 S. Ct. 1051, 157 L. Ed. 2d 891 (U.S. 2004) (de novo review of Egyptian law on appeal).

[Section 6:127]

[1]146 F.R.D. at 27; U.S. v. Pre-Columbian Artifacts, 845 F. Supp. 544 (N.D. Ill. 1993) (Guatemalan law); U.S. v. Schultz, 333 F.3d 393 (2d Cir. 2003), cert. denied, 124 S. Ct. 1051, 157 L. Ed. 2d 891 (U.S. 2004) (Egyptian law [Secretary General of Supreme Council of Antiquities and Director of Criminal Investigations for Egyptian Antiquities Police]); Government of Peru v. Johnson, 720 F. Supp. 810 (C.D. Cal. 1989), aff'd, 933 F.2d 1013 (9th Cir. 1991) (Peruvian law [former chief justice of Peru Supreme Court]); U.S. v. McClain, 593 F.2d 658 (5th Cir. 1979) (Mexican law [Mexican Bar Association Formal Opinion]); U.S. v. Hollinshead, 495 F.2d 1154 (9th Cir. 1974) (Guatemalan law)..

[Section 6:128]

[1]Republic of Turkey v. OKS Partners, 146 F.R.D. 24 (D. Mass. 1993).

laws, and decided that Turkey would not, at that point in the discovery process, order release of unpublished materials, especially where the defendants already had obtained published legislative histories. "Discovery [under Rule 44.1] should not be enlarged merely because the sovereign is a party to the litigation in a court in the United States."[2]

§ 6:129 Discovery upon preliminary showing

A party seeking discovery of foreign law under Rule 44.1 must make a preliminary showing demonstrating necessity.[1]

F. MISCELLANEOUS ISSUES

§ 6:130 Due diligence[1]

Due diligence, or lack thereof, is a common issue in replevin actions for return of internationally traded cultural materials, ordinarily raised in conjunction with statute of limitations defense and now viable—and defeatable—in some jurisdictions in connection with the equitable defense of laches. The reason due diligence figures prominently in many international cases is that when the former owner or dispossessed party seeks recovery of the object in American courts, the statute of limitations has expired, particularly for acts of World War II vintage and others relating to political upheavals, wars and civil disruptions. Tracing and tracking personal property, and particularly art, can be difficult under ordinary conditions, and impractical when the dispossessed have more pressing concerns and needs. Thus time goes by while the statutory clock continues to tick.

New developments that mark a sea change for recovery of artworks from World War II have opened new avenues to claimants that may reduce or eliminate diligence defenses. Historically, the few international art claims arising from the War were disposed of by some type of dil-

---

[2]Republic of Turkey v. OKS Partners, 146 F.R.D. 24 (D. Mass. 1993).

[Section 6:129]

[1]Republic of Turkey v. OKS Partners, 146 F.R.D. 24 (D. Mass. 1993).

[Section 6:130]

[1]*See* Ch 2 §§ 2:67 to 2:71.

igence analysis. For example, in Elicofon where a German museum claimed that Durer paintings were stolen during World War II, federal courts found its efforts to locate the art diligent, and allowed an otherwise untimely replevin action to stand by accruing the action from the date of reasonable discovery of the owner.[2] In DeWeerth,[3] the Second Circuit, reversing the district court, held that plaintiff's lack of due diligence in pursuing claims to a Claude Monet painting *Champs de Ble a Vetheuil,* which disappeared in 1945 when American soldiers were quartered in the family castle in southern Germany, terminated her rights to recover it under New York law. But, in Solomon R. Guggenheim Foundation v. Lubell,[4] a case involving domestic recovery of artwork unrelated to war, a unanimous New York Court of Appeals ruled that no duty of due diligence existed under New York law for legal claims: "We have examined the relevant New York case law and we conclude that the Second Circuit should not have imposed a duty of reasonable diligence on the owners of stolen art work for purposes of the statute of limitations."[5]

In 1991 DeWeerth moved the Second Circuit to vacate its judgment in view of the Guggenheim decision, which was denied without opinion. In 1992 the district court vacated the judgment subsequently reversed by the Second Circuit.[6] Due diligence was imposed on out-of-possession owners in other cases and jurisdictions prior to the

---

[2]Kunstsammlungen Zu Weimar v. Elicofon, 536 F. Supp. 829 (E.D. N.Y. 1981), aff'd, 678 F.2d 1150 (2d Cir. 1982).

[3]DeWeerth v. Baldinger, 658 F. Supp. 688 (S.D. N.Y. 1987), judgment rev'd, 836 F.2d 103 (2d Cir. 1987) (action for recovery of stolen property brought within state three-year limitations period from demand under demand and refusal rule, but demand unreasonably delayed by lack of plaintiff's due diligence).

[4]Solomon R. Guggenheim Foundation v. Lubell, 153 A.D.2d 143, 550 N.Y.S.2d 618 (1st Dep't 1990), order aff'd, 77 N.Y.2d 311, 567 N.Y.S.2d 623, 569 N.E.2d 426 (1991) (museum entitled to recovery of Marc Chagall gouache rediscovered after a twenty-year loss).

[5]Diligence may still have relevance for the equitable affirmative defense of laches, which involves prejudicial undue delay. In Lubell, due diligence was disposed of in the context of statutes of limitations.

[6]Although the Second Circuit refused to vacate its judgment upon DeWeerth's post-Guggenheim motion, the district court did so on the grounds that federal courts should conform to state court legal interpretations of state law, and that the district court was the more

Guggenheim case.[7]

§ 6:131 Criminal cases[1]

Cultural property has been the subject of criminal actions brought under national laws involving stolen property or unlawfully imported property; in these cases the United States, not the out-of-possession sovereign, is the claimant.[2] Recovery of the property is obtained by seizure and forfeiture to the United States, and transferred through diplomatic channels to the sovereign.

§ 6:132 Immunity from Seizure Act

In 1965, Congress enacted the Immunity from Seizure

---

appropriate forum for the procedure. The judgment was subsequently reversed. DeWeerth v. Baldinger, 24 F.3d 416, 28 Fed. R. Serv. 3d 1231 (2d Cir. 1994), for superseding opinion, see 38 F.3d 1266 and withdrawn from bound volume.

[7]Seventh Circuit: Autocephalous Greek-Orthodox Church of Cyprus v. Goldberg & Feldman Fine Arts Inc., 717 F. Supp. 1374 (S.D. Ind. 1989), judgment aff'd, 917 F.2d 278 (7th Cir. 1990); Second Circuit: Golden Budha Corp. v. Canadian Land Co. of America, N.V., 931 F.2d 196, 20 Fed. R. Serv. 3d 388 (2d Cir. 1991); Hoelzer v. City of Stamford, Conn., 933 F.2d 1131 (2d Cir. 1991).

[Section 6:131]

[1]*See* Ch 11.

[2]U.S. v. Hollinshead, 495 F.2d 1154 (9th Cir. 1974) (return of stelae to Guatemala); United States v. Swetnam, Indictment CR 88-914 RG (C.D. Cal. Nov. 1988); Government of Peru v. Johnson, 720 F. Supp. 810 (C.D. Cal. 1989), aff'd, 933 F.2d 1013 (9th Cir. 1991) (civil defendants voluntarily repatriated undisclosed number of objects and criminal defendant returned approximately 22 items to Peru); U.S. v. McClain, 545 F.2d 988 (5th Cir. 1977); U.S. v. Pre-Columbian Artifacts, 845 F. Supp. 544 (N.D. Ill. 1993) (United States filed interpleader action to determine who is entitled to pre-Columbian artifacts seized from defendants by U.S. Customs because they were allegedly stolen from Guatemala in violation of Guatemala law, constituting violation of National Stolen Property Act, 18 U.S.C.A. §§ 2314–2315); U.S. v. An Antique Platter of Gold, 991 F. Supp. 222 (S.D. N.Y. 1997), aff'd, 184 F.3d 131 (2d Cir. 1999), cert. denied, 528 U.S. 1136, 120 S. Ct. 978, 145 L. Ed. 2d 929 (2000) (summary judgment granted for government; United States sought forefeiture on behalf of Italy of 5th Century B.C. phiale removed from Italy and deemed owned by Italy under its cultural property laws).

Act (IFSA).[1] Section 2459 of IFSA provides:

> Whenever any work of art or other object of cultural significance is imported into the United States from any foreign country, pursuant to an agreement entered into between the foreign owner . . . and the United States or one or more cultural or educational institutions within the United States providing for the temporary exhibition or display thereof within the United States at any cultural exhibition . . . administered, operated or sponsored, without profit, by any such cultural or educational institution, no court of the United States, any State, the District of Columbia, or any territory or possession of the United States, may issue or enforce any judicial process, or enter any judgment, decree or order, for the purpose or having the effect of depriving such institution, or any carrier engaged in transporting such work or object within the United States, of custody or control of such object if before the importation of such object the President or his designee has determined that such object is of cultural significance and that the temporary exhibition or display thereof within the United States is in the national interest, and notice to that effect has been published in the Federal Register.[2]

The IFSA protects artworks on loan from any foreign country for exhibition in American not-for-profit cultural institutions against civil and criminal process, if certain requirements are satisfied prior to importation. The work must be on temporary loan, the exhibition must be not-for-profit, the USIA must determine that the artwork is of "cultural significance," and that the temporary exhibition is in the "national interest." In addition, public notice of the USIA decision must be published in the Federal Register.[3] If protection is granted, artworks are not subject to any judicial process, state or federal. The IFSA has been held not to preempt a state law that also regulated artworks on loan from a foreign museum for an art

[Section 6:132]

[1]H.R. Rep. No. 89-1070, 89th Cong., 1st Sess. (Sept. 22, 1965); 22 U.S.C.A. § 2459.

[2]22 U.S.C.A. § 2459.

[3]Exec. Order No. 12047, sec. 1, 43 Fed. Reg. 13, 359 (1978), *amended by* Exec. Order No. 12388, 47 Fed. Reg. 46, 245 (1982).

exhibition.[4]

§ 6:133 Museums

New York State has a law pertaining to loans of artworks to cultural institutions in the state.[1] Section 12.03 provides:

> No process of attachment, execution, sequestration, replevin, distress or any kind of seizure shall be served or levied upon any work of fine art while the same is en route to or from, or while on exhibition or deposited by a nonresident exhibitor at any exhibition held under the auspices or supervision of any museum, college, university or other nonprofit art gallery, institution or organization within any city or county of this state for any cultural, educational, charitable or other purpose not conducted for profit to the exhibitor, nor shall such work of fine art be subject to attachment, seizure, levy or sale, for any cause whatever in the hands of the authorities of such exhibition or otherwise.

The law has been applied to protect from the subpeona power of a Grand Jury paintings by Egon Schiele loaned by the Leopold Museum in Austria to the Museum of Modern Art for exhibition.[2]

---

[4]In Matter of Application to Quash Grand Jury Subpoena Duces Tecum Served on Museum of Modern Art, 177 Misc. 2d 985, 677 N.Y.S.2d 872 (Sup 1998), rev'd, 253 A.D.2d 211, 688 N.Y.S.2d 3 (1st Dep't 1999), rev'd, 93 N.Y.2d 729, 697 N.Y.S.2d 538, 719 N.E.2d 897 (1999) (IFSA provides "floor of protection that does not preclude states from providing greater protections from judicial process for paintings on loan from foreign museums").

[Section 6:133]

[1]NY Arts & Cult. Aff. § 12.03.

[2]In Matter of Application to Quash Grand Jury Subpoena Duces Tecum Served on Museum of Modern Art, 177 Misc. 2d 985, 677 N.Y.S.2d 872 (Sup 1998), rev'd, 253 A.D.2d 211, 688 N.Y.S.2d 3 (1st Dep't 1999), rev'd, 93 N.Y.2d 729, 697 N.Y.S.2d 538, 719 N.E.2d 897 (1999) (subpoena quashed where American citizens claimed ownership of paintings allegedly stolen or misappropriated by the Nazis from their respective families during the annexation of Austria).

§ 6:134 Jurisdiction

The Foreign Sovereign Immunities Act[1] has been held to confer jurisdiction over foreign parties for purposes of an action to recover paintings allegedly "Aryanized" by the Nazis during World War II.[2] Jurisdiction in this context was held to satisfy due process requirements under the Fifth Amendment.[3]

[Section 6:134]

[1]28 U.S.C.A. §§ 1602 to 1611.

[2]Altmann v. Republic of Austria, 317 F.3d 954 (9th Cir. 2002), opinion amended on denial of reh'g, 327 F.3d 1246 (9th Cir. 2003) (FSIA expropriation exception applied to alleged wrongful appropriation of Gustav Klimt paintings by Austria and state-owned gallery); cert. granted, 125 S.Ct. 46 (2003).

[3]Altmann v. Republic of Austria, 317 F.3d 954 (9th Cir. 2002), opinion amended on denial of reh'g, 327 F.3d 1246 (9th Cir. 2003) (publishing and marketing books and tourist brochures about the Klimt paintings and other consular and trade activities established sufficient minimum contacts for personal jurisdiction).

Chapter 7

Copyright

I. GENERALLY

II. HISTORY OF VISUAL ART AND COPYRIGHT LAW

A. CONSTITUTIONAL BASIS

B. JUDICIAL EXPANSION

C. STATUTORY EVOLUTION OF ART COPYRIGHT

III. ART ISSUES IN COPYRIGHT

A. IDEA/EXPRESSION DICHOTOMY

B. IMAGERY

IV. STATUTORY BASICS

A. NOTICE

B. REGISTRATION

1. In General

2. Deposit

a. Identifying Material (I.D. Material)

b. Copies

3. Certificate of Registration

C. PUBLICATION

1. 1909 Act

2. 1976 Act

V. COPYRIGHT ELIGIBILITY

A. GENERAL

1. Reproducing Art in Different Media or Size

2. Functional Art

B. OWNERSHIP OF COPYRIGHT

C. WORK MADE FOR HIRE

D. TRANSFERRING OWNERSHIP, ASSIGNMENTS

1. Writing Requirement

2. First Sale Doctrine

VI. COPYRIGHT INFRINGEMENT

A. IN GENERAL

B. COPIES

C. DISTRIBUTION

D. DERIVATIVE WORKS

E. DISPLAY

VII. FAIR USE

A. Section 107

B. PURPOSE AND CHARACTER OF USE

C. NATURE OF COPYRIGHTED WORK

D. VOLUME OF TAKING: AMOUNT AND SUBSTANTIALITY

E. MARKET EFFECT AND OTHER FACTORS

VIII. SPECIFIC ART FORMS

A. CARTOONS AND COMIC STRIP CHARACTERS

B. PHOTOGRAPHY

C. CATALOGUE RAISONNE

IX. ARCHITECTURE

A. IN GENERAL

B. PLANS, DRAWINGS

C. BUILDINGS

I. GENERALLY

§ 7:1 Introduction

Copyright is codified in Title 17 of the U.S. Code. Copyright arises from the fixation of images in specified forms. The legal requirements are relatively straightforward: Copyright provides a limited monopoly for limited duration[1] to the creator, its assigns, or survivors for works of original authorship fixed in a tangible medium of expression. The copyright owner has the power to exploit individually or collectively an exclusive bundle of divisible rights during the limited time period. Subject matter of copyright includes pictorial, graphic, and sculptural works (PGS).

Section 102 of the U.S. Code[2] provides that "copyright protection subsists . . . in original works of authorship fixed in any tangible medium of expression, now known or later developed," which includes "pictorial, graphic and sculptural works,"[3] and "architectural works."[4] Note that the Section 102 subject matter of copyright does not now include, and never included, the term "visual art."

To succeed in a copyright action, the plaintiff must prove ownership of a valid copyright and infringement of the copyright by unauthorized use. Injunctive relief, actual damages, and, in some instances, statutory damages, attorneys' fees, and costs are available.

The copyright concept of limited monopoly to regulate use of visual imagery is alien to artmaking, which has evolved over thousands of years based upon the principle and practice of copying—quotation, imitation and appropriation. Unauthorized copying, for which no fees are paid or licenses obtained, is the basis of art apprenticeship, art technique, and art education. "Copied" art is stock-in-trade in the art markets. After thousands of years of artmaking, only the last decade has produced case law that has the profound potential of imposing new costs upon

---

[Section 7:1]

[1] 1989 H.R. Rep. No. 2589, 105th Cong., 2d Sess. (1988) (The Sonny Bono Copyright Term Extension Act (CTEA), approved by Congress in 1998, extends copyright from life plus fifty to seventy years for general works and joint works created since 1978, and extends time periods for works made-for-hire and other works, in addition to making substantive changes in duration of copyright for subsisting copyrights). The constitutionality of CTEA has been upheld. Eldred v. Ashcroft, 537 U.S. 186, 123 S. Ct. 769, 154 L. Ed. 2d 683, 65 U.S.P.Q.2d (BNA) 1225 (2003) (Bryer, J. and Stevens, J., dissenting).

[2] 17 U.S.C.A. § 102; *see also* 17 U.S.C.A. § 101, definition revised by Act of Oct. 31, 1988, Pub L. No. 100-568.

[3] 17 U.S.C.A. § 102(5).

[4] 17 U.S.C.A. § 102(8).

artists for that revered pedagogical, tutorial, and historical methodology integral to the evolution of art: copying.

The societal goal underlying copyright is to stimulate and encourage progress in the arts.[5] Copyright supposedly sparks creative impulse through economic impetus. Conversely, unauthorized copying inhibits creativity. No empirical study supports this assertion for visual art, and history suggests the contrary; the compulsion to create without remuneration survives even when impecunious circumstances dictate otherwise. The greatest gifts of artistic genius have come down to us through the millennia without copyright motivation. Master artworks from ages past might not have been created if copyright costs had been imposed for visual arts. Aside from the artists themselves, copyright imposes a cost upon their patrons, private and institutional collectors.

Copyright is a structure for economically rewarding activity (not creativity) in commerce. Claims that copyright is impetus and reward for creative exploitation are simply not borne out upon review of art cases. Culture does not easily track economic models nor is it clear that copyright policy should apply to cultural commerce. Nonetheless, Congress and the courts have chosen to bring art under the copyright umbrella, or at least some of it. The cases compel the lawyer to differentiate fine art—which in this chapter only refers to object oriented, one-of-a-kind works, and editions of extremely limited number, from commercial art—works whose primary value is not intrinsic to the object, but is dependent upon reproductive values through usage, whether it is derivation, reproduction, and/or display, including expanded meanings of these terms to encompass internet use. That scrutiny must be paid to differentiate art for purposes of copyright is ironic

[5]Eldred v. Ashcroft, 123 S. Ct. 769, 154 L. Ed. 2d 683, 65 U.S.P.Q. 2d (BNA) 1225 (U.S. 2003) (Bryer, J. and Stevens, J., dissenting)("'[t]he economic philosophy behind the [Copyright] Clause . . . is the conviction that encouragement of individual effort by personal gain is the best way to advance public welfare through the talents of authors . . . ' [the] law 'celebrates the profit motive, recognizing that the incentive to profit from the exploitation of copyrights will redound to the public benefit by resulting in the proliferation of knowledge. . . . ' [R]ewarding authors for their creative labor and 'promoting . . . Progress' are thus complementary.' ")

for several reasons: distinctions between fine and commercial art are, and have been, blurring; technology conflates product and process, undermining formal categorizations as it creates new categories; the jurisprudence that brought art within the copyright umbrella purported to eschew just such line drawing.

Copyright has historically been incongruous with art history, where copying is a mainstay, but novelty is a hallmark. Technology, advances in digitalization and the internet, innovative multisite installations, and encoded Net art are changing basic concepts and beliefs in the visual arts, and challenging the attendant policies of copyright. Whether artists making one-of-a-kind artworks will use copyright to stop cultural progeny from copying their art is unclear, but not one such case could be found.

The cases overwhelmingly demonstrate that copyright can provide legal relief for commercial artists, graphic artists, and photographers, who typically receive little or no remuneration for the tangible work produced, and rely for livelihood upon licensing fees for copying, reproduction, and display of artworks. Even when relief is granted, damages awards may not compensate a plaintiff unless damages are fairly interpreted to adjust financial inequities between commercial artists and high end arts infringers. The internet impacts not only basic tenets of copyright but the relief awarded to those infringed.[6]

This chapter does not recite the law of copyright nor is it intended to do so; comprehensive treatises and hornbooks devoted exclusively to copyright are readily available. Familiarity with the law of copyright is assumed. What follows in §§ 7:2 to 7:11, a subset of art copyright; §§ 7:12 to 7:19, a summary evolution of art within copyright law; §§ 7:20 to 7:43, a practice and procedure guide for registering art and providing notice on artworks; §§ 7:44 to 7:70, an analysis of how copyright issues have been applied to the arts; §§ 7:71 to 7:86, a case analysis presented by copyright issues; §§ 7:87 to 7:102, the fair use defense as applied to art and its relationship to the first amendment; §§ 7:102 to 7:112, specific types of art, like cartoons and comic strips, photography; §§ 7:114

[6]See, e.g., In re Napster, Inc. Copyright Litigation, 191 F. Supp. 2d 1087 (N.D. Cal. 2002).

to 7:127, laws and cases involving architectural copyright, including buildings and plans from before and after enactment of AWCPA; §§ 7:128 to 7:136, remedies available, civil and criminal offenses including actual damages, statutory damages, and injunctive relief, and attorney's fees and costs; and § 7:137, insurance.

Many of the applicable statutory sections and regulations for the Revised Copyright Act of 1976 and subsequent amendments are quoted for the reader's convenience. Where relevant, prior versions of copyright law, e.g., the Act of 1909, and legislative history are quoted or identified.

Title 17 of the U.S. Code is the repository of copyright law, and Congress chose to include there two Berne Convention rights some European countries provide to visual artists: (1) the right of attribution and (2) the right of integrity. Those rights do not bestow copyright to visual art; they do not expand copyright protection to visual art; they are not "subject matter" of copyright; they are not subject to most copyright procedures and requirements; and they are unrelated to the prevailing policies underlying copyright. These rights are mentioned in §§ 7:2 to 7:11 in the context of art copyright evolution, and are fully addressed as artist's rights.[7]

II. HISTORY OF VISUAL ART AND COPYRIGHT LAW

A. CONSTITUTIONAL BASIS

§ 7:2 Generally

Article I, section 8, clause 8 of the U.S. Constitution is the constitutional predicate for federal copyright and patent law.[1] Congress has the power "[t]o promote the . . . useful Arts by securing for limited Times to Authors and Inventors the exclusive Right to their respective Writings

---

[7]*See* Ch 9.

[Section 7:2]

[1]Patent law is not discussed in this chapter. For patents, *see* 35 U.S.C.A. §§ 101 et seq. Patent does not preclude copyright of art work attached to, part of, or on the patented work; *see, e.g.,* Application of Yardley, 493 F.2d 1389 (C.C.P.A. 1974) (artwork on the face of Spiro Agnew watch was copyrightable even though watch was patentable); *accord,* Mazer v. Stein, 347 U.S. 201, 74 S. Ct. 460, 98 L. Ed. 630

and Discoveries."[2] Visual art was certainly not within the scope of the drafters' imaginations or intentions; *The Federalist Papers* are silent on this issue.[3] The pre-Revolutionary English Statute of Anne,[4] the cornerstone from which American copyright originates, did not encompass visual art: "An Act for the encouraging of learning, by vesting of the copies of printed books in the authors or purchasers of such copies, during the times . . . mentioned."[5] Nor did visual art appear in letter or spirit in the first copyright law of 1790; 200 years elapsed before the Visual Artists Rights Act of 1990 codified the term "visual art" in federal copyright.[6] The following sections summarize what occurred during these two centuries to bring the law to its current, and continuously evolving, state.

B. JUDICIAL EXPANSION

§ 7:3 Originality, authorship, novelty

Copyright protection exists in original works of authorship fixed in any tangible medium of expression codified in title 17 of the U.S. Code.[1] "Copyright protection subsists . . . in original works of authorship fixed in any tangible medium of expression, now known or later developed," which includes "pictorial, graphic and sculptural works"

(1954) (sculptural base of table lamps that were patentable did not prevent copyright protection as works of art).

[2]U.S. Constitution, Art. I, § 8, cl. 8 ("The Congress shall have Power . . . To Promote the . . . useful Arts . . . (for purposes of copyright protection)").

[3]The Federalist Papers No. 43 (Madison).

[4]Act of Anne 8, Ch. 19, (1710) (authors and their heirs had sole right to print or copy work for fourteen years).

[5]Act of Anne 8, ch. 19, (1710); *see* Eldred v. Ashcroft, 123 S. Ct. 769, 154 L. Ed. 2d 683 (U.S. 2003) (history of Statute of Anne); *but cf.* Burrow-Giles Lithographic Co. v. Sarony, 111 U.S. 53, 4 S. Ct. 279, 28 L. Ed. 349 (1884) (mention of early king's bench and queen's bench cases cited for proposition that courts applied copyright to intellectual products)

[6]Pub. L. No. 101-650, 104 Stat. 3048 (1990).

[Section 7:3]

[1]All sections refer to title 17 of the U.S. Code, the revised 1976 Copyright Act, and subsequent amendments, unless otherwise specified.

(PGS)[2] and "architectural works."[3] Those two categories, PGS and architectural works, contain most of the subject matter of this work.[4] Artworks were presumably not within the contemplation of the drafters of the Constitution or the members of the First Congress.[5]

The expansive view of copyright to umbrella the arts evolved over many, many years, and continues to this day. Initially, the courts grappled with what constituted originality[6] and authorship to satisfy the Constitution.

Originality is a legal term of art under copyright that is not coterminous with artistic originality recognized in the arts. The requirement of originality is judicially imposed based upon interpretation of copyright protection for "authors;" authors, for purposes of clause 8, are originators. Originality is considered a constitutional imprimatur "read into the Copyright Act" so that the requirement of originality is both constitutional and statutory.

Determining originality is a matter of law.[7] Ch 1 emphasized the difficulty of generally defining "originality" in an arts context. *Baker v. Selden*[8] in the 19th century made clear the Court's position that originality does not require something novel or new. More than 100 years later, the Court is still grappling with definitions: Originality is satisfied if there is "independent creation and a modicum of creativity."[9]

The threshold for originality is generally considered so

---

[2]17 U.S.C.A. § 102(a)(5).

[3]17 U.S.C.A. § 102(a)(8).

[4]*See* §§ 7:103 to 7:113.

[5]*See* § 7:2. Benjamin Franklin, who dabbled in watercolors, was an art aficionado, and other authors had common knowledge of painting and sculpture; *see also,* Burrow-Giles Lithographic Co. v. Sarony, 111 U.S. 53, 4 S. Ct. 279, 28 L. Ed. 349 (1884) (framers did not include photography in 1780s because it did not exist at the time).

[6]*See* §§ 7:44 to 7:53 (discussion of requirements of "original works of authorship").

[7]Hearn v. Meyer, 664 F. Supp. 832, 839 (S.D. N.Y. 1987).

[8]Baker v. Selden, 101 U.S. 99, 102–03, 25 L. Ed. 841 (1879).

[9]Feist Publications, Inc. v. Rural Telephone Service Co., Inc., 499 U.S. 340, 111 S. Ct. 1282, 1287–88, 113 L. Ed. 2d 358 (1991); *see also* Acuff-Rose Music, Inc. v. Jostens, Inc., 155 F.3d 140, 41 Fed. R. Serv.

low it has been held to be "little more than a prohibition of actual copying."[10] Although novelty, inventiveness, and aesthetic merit[11] are not required in the sense of striking uniqueness or ingeniousness, "the 'author' [must] contribute [ ] something more than a 'merely trivial' variation, something recognizably 'his own.' "[12] "The requisite level of creativity is extremely low; even a slight amount will suffice. The vast majority of works make the grade quite easily, as they possess some creative spark, 'no matter how crude, humble or obvious' it might be."[13]

In *Bleistein*,[14] where circus posters were protected, the Court found originality could be supported in imagery, whether taken from life, natural realism, or by pure invention. Life drawing, model portraiture, and pure fantasy were equally protectible. There, lithography company employees created advertising posters based upon descriptions of circus acts made by the shop's customer—the circus owner—the Court asserted that life drawing and live performance were also protected: "a portrait by Velasquez or Whistler [is not] common prop-

---

3d 1368 (2d Cir. 1998) (although independent creation can create copyright even if work is identical to preexisting work, song lyrics "You've Got to Stand For Something/Or You'll Fall For Anything" lacked requisite originality where defendant's evidence showed widespread public usage).

[10]Alfred Bell & Co. v. Catalda Fine Arts, 191 F.2d 99, 103 (2d Cir. 1951).

[11]Bleistein v. Donaldson Lithographing Co., 188 U.S. 239, 23 S. Ct. 298, 47 L. Ed. 460 (1903) (circus posters copyrightable as works "connected with the fine arts" under statute no longer in force).

[12]L. Batlin & Son, Inc. v. Snyder, 536 F.2d 486, 490 (2d Cir. 1976), *quoting* Alfred Bell & Co. v. Catalda Fine Arts, 74 F. Supp. 973 (S.D. N.Y. 1947), decision supplemented, 75 U.S.P.Q. (BNA) 283, 1947 WL 3391 (S.D. N.Y. 1947), decision supplemented, 86 F. Supp. 399 (S.D. N.Y. 1949), judgment modified, 191 F.2d 99 (2d Cir. 1951); Bridgeman Art Library, Ltd. v. Corel Corp., 36 F. Supp. 2d 191 (S.D. N.Y. 1999) ("slavish" copying insufficient to support originality); E. Mishan & Sons, Inc. v. Marycana, Inc., 662 F. Supp. 1339, 1342 (S.D. N.Y. 1987) (although Americana-style calico and lace kitchen magnets did not have high degree of novelty and plaintiff failed to show magnets lacked "independent authorship").

[13]Feist Publications, Inc. v. Rural Telephone Service Co., Inc., 499 U.S. 340, 345, 111 S. Ct. 1282, 113 L. Ed. 2d 358 (1991).

[14]Bleistein v. Donaldson Lithographing Co., 188 U.S. 239, 23 S. Ct. 298, 47 L. Ed. 460 (1903).

erty because others . . . try their hand on the same face. Others are free to copy the original. They are not free to copy the copy [created by the author]. There is no reason to doubt that these prints in their *ensemble* and in all their details . . . are . . . original."[15]

The Supreme Court has recently reaffirmed originality's minimal threshold.[16] Thus the use of a petroglyph as the middle two zeros in a "2000" calendar had the "requisite originality."[17]

"Authorship," a key copyright term, has been expanded incrementally by judicial interpretation. In Burrow-Giles,[18] where a particular portrait photograph of Oscar Wilde copied by a lithography company was proffered by the artist as protectible material, the Supreme Court emphasized that authorship simply means the copyrighted work originates with that person: "An author . . . is an . . . originator . . . maker . . . By writings . . . is meant the literary productions of those authors . . . and Congress . . . properly . . . declared these to include all forms of writing, printing, engraving, etching etc., by the ideas in the mind of the author are given visible expression."

Chart 7-1: Origination of Artwork Copyrights Under Federal Law Prior to 20th Century

Year	Law	Protectible Works
1789	U.S. Constitution, Art. 1, § 8, cl. 8	useful arts, writings

[15] Bleistein v. Donaldson Lithographing Co., 188 U.S. 239, 23 S. Ct. 298, 47 L. Ed. 460 (1903) (emphasis in original).

[16] Eldred v. Ashcroft, 123 S. Ct. 769, 154 L. Ed. 2d 683 (U.S. 2003), citing Feist Publ., Inc. v. Rural Telephone Service Co., 499 U.S. 340, 345, 359 (1991) ("[T]he *sine qua non* of copyright is originality . . . [but] [o]nly "a narrow category of works in which the creative spark is utterly lacking or so trivial as to be virtually nonexistent" will not be original.).

[17] Willard v. Estern, 206 F. Supp. 2d 723 (D.V.I. 2002) (summary judgment denied because combined petroglyph and calendar date reflected artist's decision and creation).

[18] Burrow-Giles Lithographic Co. v. Sarony, 111 U.S. 53, 57–58, 4 S. Ct. 279, 28 L. Ed. 349 (1884) (holding constitutional R.S. Stat 1874 making "photographs and the negatives thereof" copyrightable).

Year	Law	Protectible Works
1790	1 Stat. 124 (First Congress)	authors of maps, charts, books; fourteen-year protection from publication, renewable for 14 years
1802	2 Stat. 171	fourteen-year protection extended to inventors and designers who engrave, etch or work historical or other prints
1831	4 Stat. 436*	twenty-eight-year protection added for prints and engravings (and all above) from publication, renewable for 14 years
1865	13 Stat. 540	"photographs and the negatives thereof"
1874	R.S. Stat. 4952	prints, paintings, drawings, cuts, chromo engravings, photographs, statues, statuary, and models or designs (intended to be perfected as works of the fine arts)
1874	18 Stat. 78–79	"fine arts" restriction for prints, cuts, and engravings
1884	*Burrow-Giles***	Sup. Ct. applies R.S. Stat. 4952 to photographs
1909	35 Stat. 1080–1081	28 years from publication, renewable 28 years

Year	Law	Protectible Works
1976	Pub. L 94–553	Pictorial, Graphic, Sculptural {PGS} works: life plus fifty years from creation for persons; anonymous, pseudonymous and work for hire, 75 years from publication or 100 years from creation, whichever expires first
1990	AWCPA AWCPA Pub. L 101-650	plans, designs, drawings, buildings
1998	CTEA*** Pub.L. 105-298 § 102(b) and (d)	life plus seventy from creation for persons; anonymous, pseudonymous and work for hire, 95 years from publication or 120 years from creation, whichever expires first

* First use of term "copyright" in federal legislation (repeals Acts of 1790 and 1802).

** Burrow-Giles Lithographic Co. v. Sarony, 111 U.S. 53, 58 (1884) ("The Constitution is broad enough to cover an act authorizing copyright of photographs, so far as they are representatives of original intellectual conceptions of the author.").

*** Eldred v. Ashcroft, 123 S. Ct. 769, 154 L. Ed. 2d 683 (U.S. 2003) (CTEA constitutionality upheld).

After *Burrow-Giles*, authors were no longer limited to creators of "writings;" visual artists, designers, engravers, photographers, lithographers, and others who did not make "writings" could now qualify as "authors."

The foregoing seemingly simple oft-quoted propositions establish the scope and tone of copyright that persists to the present day. These rules have become veritable adages. In each case the artwork at issue should be evaluated within the particular facts and circumstances, enabling practitioners to draw successfully from general copyright principles to the specifics of the case or matter.

§ 7:4 "Useful" art, fine art

The Constitution expressly modifies "arts" by the adjective "useful." The fine arts are not useful; indeed, a common definition of fine art is work created to fulfill no utilitarian purpose. That has not presented a constitutional hurdle because the requirement of usefulness was disposed of early on in *Bleistein v. Donaldson Lithographing Co.*[1] There, the Court had to determine whether advertising posters were useful arts or were related to the fine arts. The posture of that case, which required the Supreme Court to accomplish two different (and incompatible) goals, should be thoroughly understood because it dramatically affects art copyright to the present day.

Bleistein did not involve aesthetics, or one-of-a-kinds. *Bleistein* involved two commercial printers, and is about business. One lithographing company charged another with infringing copyright for reproducing, in reduced form, lithographs prepared for a customer to advertise his circus. The circus owner himself appeared in the corner of each of the posters, which depicted a ballet, a family of cyclists, and a group of statuesque persons. The defendant's directed verdict, which was upheld by the Sixth Circuit, went up on appeal to the Supreme Court which had to respond to the defendant's seemingly foolproof claim that the posters were neither "useful," and therefore were not among "useful arts" identified in the Constitution, nor "fine art." If either argument were upheld, defendant would win.

The Court's predicament was twofold: (1) The constitutional adjective "useful" describing "Arts" had to be explained away for advertising, where in fact it has usefulness; (2) Advertising had to be classified as pictorial illustration related to the fine arts to comply with the copyright statute. If the posters were deemed useful as advertising, then how could the advertising be "fine art?"

The Court broadened the constitutional meaning of "useful arts," but it did so summarily and conclusively: "We shall do no more than mention the suggestion that a paint-

[Section 7:4]

[1]Bleistein v. Donaldson Lithographing Co., 188 U.S. 239, 23 S. Ct. 298, 47 L. Ed. 460 (1903).

ing and engraving, unless for a mechanical end, are not among the useful arts . . . . The Constitution does not limit the useful to that which satisfies immediate bodily needs."[2] The ambiguity has various interpretations: Pictures feed the soul, and therefore have a spiritual utility cognizable in copyright, or advertising stimulates economic demand and generates business revenues, and therefore has an economic utility.

Next the Court considered the fine art aspects of advertising posters. The statute before the Court provided: "in the construction of this act, the words 'engraving,' 'cut,' 'print' shall be applied only to pictorial illustrations or works *connected with the fine arts.*"[3] The Court initially limited the prepositional phrase to "works." But assuming, arguendo, it applied to "pictorial illustrations," the Court broadened the term fine arts, or eviscerated it, depending on one's point of view:

> [T]he act . . . does not mean that ordinary posters are not good enough [as fine art]. The antitheses to "illustrations or works connected with the fine arts" is not works of little merit or of humble degree, or illustrations addressed to the less educated classes; it is prints or labels designed to be used for . . . articles of manufacture. Certainly works are not the less connected with the fine arts because their pictorial quality attracts the crowd, and therefore gives them a real use—if use means to increase trade and to help make money. A picture is nonetheless . . . a subject of copyright, that it is used for an advertisement.[4]

In this passage, the Court coalesced two distinct requirements of copyright—useful art and pictorial illustration related to the fine arts—by equating usefulness and advertising with fine art. By so doing, the Court obtained protection in copyright for something shrewdly understood as having profound economic import on trade practices in a young mercantile country on the brink of the new century: Commercial advertising.

The Court seemed to recognize its own coup. At the end

---

[2]Bleistein v. Donaldson Lithographing Co., 188 U.S. 239 at 248, 23 S. Ct. 298, 47 L. Ed. 460 (1903).

[3]Bleistein v. Donaldson Lithographing Co., 188 U.S. 239 at 248, 23 S. Ct. 298, 47 L. Ed. 460 (1903) (emphasis added).

[4]Bleistein v. Donaldson Lithographing Co., 188 U.S. 239 at 248, 23 S. Ct. 298, 47 L. Ed. 460 (1903).

of the opinion, in language almost ruminating, the Court writes: "Yet if [the posters] command the interest of any public, they have a commercial value [usefulness]—it would be bold to say that they have not an aesthetic and educational value—and the taste of any public is not to be treated with contempt."[5] *Bleistein* is about advertising, not art, and yet it is a sine qua non in art law cases as the source of a subsequently named antidiscrimination rule. The rule democratizes visual art for purposes of copyright.

§ 7:5 Connoisseurship and the antidiscrimination rule

Copyrightability of visual art, in theory, is not supposed to be contingent upon quality, critical acclaim, medium, aesthetics, or public acceptance. At the turn of the Twentieth Century in *Bleistein*, the Supreme Court, speaking through Justice Holmes, admonished the courts from making value judgments on art:

> It would be a dangerous undertaking for persons trained only in the law to constitute themselves final judges of the worth of pictorial illustrations. . . . At one extreme some works of genius would be sure to miss appreciation. Their very novelty would make them repulsive until the public had learned the new language in which their author spoke . . . At the other . . . copyright would be denied to pictures which appealed to a public less educated than the judge.[1]

The retroactive rule espoused by subsequent courts is that visual art is entitled to federal copyright protection without regard to quality, subject matter, or aesthetic appeal. "[W]hat is good art . . . varies with individuals as it does from one generation to another."[2] "One man's mu-

---

[5]Bleistein v. Donaldson Lithographing Co., 188 U.S. 239 at 248, 23 S. Ct. 298, 47 L. Ed. 460 (1903).

[Section 7:5]

[1]Bleistein v. Donaldson Lithographing Co., 188 U.S. 239, 23 S. Ct. 298, 47 L. Ed. 460 (1903). Antidiscrimination is, at best, a misnomer and, at worst, misleading because copyright law inherently values and prioritizes artworks.

[2]Hannegan v. Esquire, Inc., 327 U.S. 146, 157, 66 S. Ct. 456, 90 L. Ed. 586 (1946).

ral is another's graffiti."[3] *Bleistein* is a nonconnoisseurship rule, an admonition to the courts not to interpose their value judgments upon the artworks before them. *Bleistein* and its progeny do not create antidiscriminatory rules, nor could they; the court must, as a matter of law, make determinations on originality and authorship that require discriminatory judgments.

What is significant about *Bleistein* from a visual arts perspective is its vanguard position of the need to accept new artists. Yet during ninety years of prolix citings, *Bleistein* has not been used for the proposition Justice Holmes posited: Would the "etchings of Goya or the paintings of Manet . . . have been sure of protection when seen for the first time?"[4]

Bleistein is also noteworthy from a visual arts perspective for its unequivocal position to incorporate into pictorial usage new technological applications. But, for all its democratizing principles, *Bleistein* is not so much about differential treatment of good art and bad art (for which it is cited), as its affect on protecting the commerce of art, historically centered in, but not limited to, graphic arts, posters, advertisements, and mass produced prints, and the evolving computer technology of the twenty first century.

Whether Bleistein is read as a nonconnoisseurship rule or an antidiscrimination rule, copyright law today is not supposed to preconceive any particular type of artwork or "enshrine" any particular definition of art. Describing art by Section 101 was not intended to imply "criterion of artistic taste, aesthetic value, or intrinsic quality."[5] Nonetheless, copyright applied to the arts creates de facto discriminatory distinctions. The effect of this de facto discrimination has been well recognized in the cases—although never phrased in discriminatory terms—in the form of the idea-expression dichotomy.[6]

---

[3]Hannegan v. Esquire, Inc., 327 U.S. 146, 157, 66 S. Ct. 456, 90 L. Ed. 586 (1946).

[4]Bleistein v. Donaldson Lithographing Co., 188 U.S. 239, 23 S. Ct. 298, 47 L. Ed. 460 (1903).

[5]H.R. Rep. No. 94-1476, at 54, 1976 U.S.C.C.A.N. 5659, 5667.

[6]*See* §§ 7:12 to 7:19.

C. STATUTORY EVOLUTION OF ART COPYRIGHT

§ 7:6 Laws prior to 1909

The first Copyright Act, enacted May 31, 1790,[1] was limited to: "maps, charts, and books." The first indicia of visual art as protectible subject matter under copyright occurred in 1802 when Congress added "engravings, etchings and prints."[2] As the Nineteenth Century progressed, federal law afforded copyright protection to an "author, designer, or proprietor . . . of any engraving, cut, print [or] chromo[lithograph]"[3] Federal copyright was amended by the Act of 1874,[4] which clarified that "in the construction of this act, the words 'engraving,' 'cut,' and 'print' shall be applied only to pictorial illustrations or works connected with the fine arts.' " The law was further amended several times throughout the nineteenth century.[5]

§ 7:7 Copyright Act of 1909

Congress, by the Copyright Act of 1909 and regulations promulgated thereunder, made art eligible for copyright registration pursuant to Section 5[1] as follows: eligibility was clarified in Section 5(a); models or designs for works of art were covered under Section 5(g); reproductions of a work of art were defined under Section 5(h); drawings or plastic works of a scientific or technical character were described in Section 5(i); photographs were covered in Section 5(j); prints and pictorial illustrations, including prints or labels used for articles of merchandise were included in Section 5(k).

In 1910, copyright regulations defined "works of art" as

[Section 7:6]

[1] 1 Stat. 124. *See* Chart 7-1 in § 7:3.

[2] 2 Stat. 171.

[3] US Rev. Stat. § 4952, US Comp. Stat. 1901, at 3406.

[4] 18 Stat. at L. 78, 79, ch. 301, § 3, US Comp. Stat. 1901, at 3412.

[5] Act of March 3, 1891, 26 Stat. at L. 1109, ch. 565; Act of March 2, 1895, 26 Stat. at L. 965, ch. 194. *See* Chart 7-1.

[Section 7:7]

[1] 17 U.S.C.A. § 5 (under the 1909 Act).

"all works belonging fairly to the so-called fine arts [paintings, drawings, and sculpture]. Productions of the industrial arts utilitarian in purpose and character are not subject to copyright registration, even if artistically made or ornamented."[2] The definition was further clarified: "Works of art [Class G] General. This class includes works of artistic craftsmanship, in so far as their form but not their mechanical or utilitarian aspects are concerned . . . as well as . . . paintings, drawings, and sculpture."[3]

§ 7:8 Revised Copyright Act of 1976 and amendments

The Revised Copyright Act of 1976, which became effective on January 1, 1978, federalized all copyright law.[1] Prior to 1978, there were separate schemes covering statutory copyright and common-law copyright.[2] Copyright after 1978 inheres in all works fixed in a tangible medium of expression from the moment the work is fixed, without an interlude between reduction to the medium and publication. Section 102[3] now provides that "copyright protection subsists . . . in original works of authorship fixed in any tangible medium of expression, now known or later developed," which includes "pictorial, graphic and sculptural works,"[4] and "architectural works."[5] Note that Section 102 subject matter of copyright does not now include, and never did include the express term, "visual art."

Section 101 defines, or more accurately describes, "pictorial, graphic and sculptural works" (PGS) as "includ[ing] "

---

[2]Registration of Claims to Copyright, Bulletin No. 15 (1910), at 8.

[3]Copyright Act of 1909, 37 C.F.R. § 202.10 (revoked 1978).

[Section 7:8]

[1]17 U.S.C.A. §§ 101 et seq.

[2]For a discussion of prior law, *see* Playboy Enterprises, Inc. v. Dumas, 831 F. Supp. 295 (S.D. N.Y. 1993), opinion modified on reargument, 840 F. Supp. 256 (S.D. N.Y. 1993) and judgment aff'd in part, rev'd in part, 53 F.3d 549, 132 A.L.R. Fed. 703 (2d Cir. 1995).

[3]17 U.S.C.A. § 102.

[4]17 U.S.C.A. § 102(5); *see also* 17 U.S.C.A. § 101, definition revised by Act of Oct. 31, 1988, Pub. L. No. 100-568, 102 Stat. 2853, 2854.

[5]17 U.S.C.A. § 102(8); Appendix 18B.

the following:

> [T]wo-dimensional and three-dimensional works of fine, graphic, and applied art, photographs, prints and art reproductions, maps, globes, charts, diagrams, models, and technical drawings, including architectural plans. Such works shall include works of artistic craftsmanship insofar as their form but not their mechanical or utilitarian aspects are concerned.

§ 7:9 Berne Convention Implementation Act of 1988 (BCIA)

The Berne Convention Implementation Act of 1988 (BCIA)[1] implemented the Convention for the Protection of Literary and Artistic Works, signed at Berne, Switzerland, on September 9, 1886, and its subsequent amendments.[2] "Any rights in a work eligible for protection under title 17" that arise under title 17, federal, state, or common law, "shall not be expanded or reduced by virtue of . . . the Berne Convention. . . ."[3]

When Congress implemented the Berne Convention, it specifically excluded article 6bis.[4] Article 6bis provides rights of artists "to claim authorship of the work; or to object to any distortion, mutilation, or other modification of, or other derogatory action in relation to, the work, that would prejudice the author's honor of reputation."[5] Congress added those rights in 1990 by enactment of the Visual Artists Rights Act of 1990 (VARA), which added rights analogous to those of article 6bis of Berne.[6]

§ 7:10 Architectural Works Copyright Protection Act of 1990

The Architectural Works Copyright Protection Act

[Section 7:9]

[1]Pub. L. No. 100-568 (Oct. 31, 1988).

[2]Pub. L. No. 100-568 § 2(1) (Oct. 31, 1988).

[3]17 U.S.C.A. § 104(c).

[4]§ 9:78.

[5]Pub. L. No. 100-568, § 3.

[6]17 U.S.C.A. § 106A; see Ch 9 § 9:78; § 7:11.

(AWCPA),[1] added as a subject matter of copyright "architectural works."[2] Section 101 was amended to describe "architectural works" as "includ[ing]" the following:

> [A]n architectural work is the design of a building as embodied in any tangible medium of expression, including a building [providing that it is erected in a country adhering to the Berne Convention], architectural plans, or drawings. The work includes the overall form as well as the arrangement and composition of spaces and elements in the design, but does not include individual standard features.[3]

Architectural works unconstructed before the effective date of AWCPA, December 1, 1990, but embodied in drawings or plans as of the effective date, are protected against unauthorized copying on or after that date, as are unconstructed architectural works created after the effective date.[4] The copyright protection for unconstructed works embodied in unpublished plans or drawings terminates on December 31, 2002, unless the work is constructed by that date.[5]

§ 7:11 Visual Artists Rights Act of 1990 (VARA)

VARA codified a right of attribution and a limited right of integrity for visual artists,[1] which apply only to "visual art," as that term is defined in title 17 of the U.S. Code.[2] Although commonly referred to as moral rights, nowhere in the federal statute or in the Regulations does that designation appear, and it is disfavored and not used by certain commentators. The neutral term "inherent" rights is used here to describe these personal rights which inhere

---

[Section 7:10]

[1]Pub. L. No. 101-650, §§ 701, 702, 704, 104 Stat. 5133, §§ 7:114 to 7:127; *also* Appendix 18B.

[2]17 U.S.C.A. § 102(8).

[3]17 U.S.C.A. § 101.

[4]Pub. L. No. 101-650, § 706(2), 104 Stat. 5133, 5134 (1990); H.R. Rep. No. 101-735.

[5]Pub. L. No. 101-650, § 706(2), 104 Stat. 5133, 5134 (1990); H.R. Rep. No. 101-735. See § 7.09.

[Section 7:11]

[1]Discussed in §§ 9:66 and 9:67.

[2]17 U.S.C.A. § 101.

in the artist in relationship to the work. Inherent rights are dealt with later, where they are treated for what they are: artists' rights.[3]

VARA does not expand copyright protection for visual art; the term visual art is not among the enumerated subject matter of copyright under Section 102. VARA recognizes distinct and limited rights of visual artists in certain copyrightable visual art works.

Against the foregoing piecemeal statutory background, the courts have cobbled together art and copyright. Copyright, in one very real sense, is antithetical to the creation and transfer of art. Technique, process, skill, and knowledge are passed from one art generation to another by copying. The professional contribution of artists to society consists of the creative dialogue of stating and restating ideas and images in visual media, linking historical tradition with technology, and tying the past to contemporaneous events. At its core, this interactive exchange salutes art history through copying.

III. ART ISSUES IN COPYRIGHT

A. IDEA/EXPRESSION DICHOTOMY

§ 7:12 Ideas

The expression/idea dichotomy originated in case law and was codified in the 1976 Act under Section 102(b). Section 102(b) states: "In no case does copyright protection for an original work of authorship extend to any idea, procedure, process, system, method of operation, concept . . . regardless of the form in which it is described, explained, illustrated, or embodied."[1] This is the statutory source of the idea/expression dichotomy. Only expression is protected. The "'idea/expression dichotomy strikes a definitional balance between the First Amendment and the Copyright Act by permitting free communication of facts while still protecting an author's expression.'. . . [E]very idea, theory, and fact in a copyrighted work becomes instantly available for public exploitation at the

---

[3]Ch 9.

[Section 7:12]

[1]17 U.S.C.A. § 102(b).

of moment of publication."[2]

Art is a visual expression of concept and process, which transmits ideas and/or emotions that may or may not be intended by the creator or understood by the viewer. The precise mix of factors in the creativity formula is incalculable: Pablo Picasso "found his creative powers 'un mystere totale.' "[3] Of this spectrum of expression, copyright is restricted to the expression of ideas, and only where the ideation expressed in the work is "original" within that term's meaning under copyright.[4]

The court's task is to determine in an infringement action if there has been copying of expression or merely an idea. No set formula exists to determine Section 102(b) line-drawing, considered to be one of degree resolved on an ad hoc, case-by-case basis under the particular facts and circumstances. Courts have rejected the following as mere ideas under Section 102(b): a heart-shaped picture of the earth (no copyright);[5] a naked floating baby against a blank background (no copyright);[6] five interlocking rings (no copyright);[7] Holstein cow black splotches on white background (no copyright);[8] restaurants' combining sales of food and art (no copyright).[9] Similarly, a photograph of a cemetery sculpture on a book cover was considered an

---

[2]Eldred v. Ashcroft, 123 S. Ct. 769, 154 L. Ed. 2d 683 (U.S. 2003) (citations omitted).

[3]Boorstin, The Creators 728.

[4]*See, e.g.,* Austin Productions, Inc. v. F.D.F. Design Studio, Inc., 1991 Copr. L. Dec. ¶ 26662, 1990 WL 198741 (E.D. N.Y. 1990).

[5]Meade v. U.S., 27 Fed. Cl. 367 (1992), aff'd, 5 F.3d 1503 (Fed. Cir. 1993).

[6]Gentieu v. John Muller & Co., 712 F. Supp. 740 (W.D. Mo. 1989).

[7]Arthur v. American Broadcasting Companies, Inc., 633 F. Supp. 146 (S.D. N.Y. 1985).

[8]Beaudin v. Ben and Jerry's Homemade, Inc., 95 F.3d 1 (2d Cir. 1996) (the idea of placing black splotches on a white background is not the subject of copyright, which does not protect ideas; therefore artist who sold, along with copyrighted artwork, "cow" hats that had Holstein spots on white background could not enforce infringement action against ice cream makers when they sent hats he sold them to manufacturers for mass production).

[9]Sweet v. City of Chicago, 953 F. Supp. 225 (N.D. Ill. 1996) (plaintiffs' complaint dismissed with prejudice where allegation was that outdoor art fair combining restaurants and art exhibitions in

unprotected idea by the district court in suit against a movie studio that used a similar depiction of the sculpture to promote a film based upon the book.[10] The Eleventh Circuit reversed:[11]

> . . . mood is not so much an independent aspect of his photograph protected by copyright, as the effect created by the lighting, shading, timing, angle and film. The same holds true for the overall combination of elements in the photograph. As long as the analysis is not overly detached and technical, it can adequately address both the effect of the protected, original elements of Leigh's photograph on the viewer and the contribution of those elements to the work as a whole . . . The . . . moss provides a border. . .the location of the statue and the lighting . . . lends a spiritual air . . . the [hidden] bowls contribute to the mystery and symbolic meaning of the images.

Other instances where courts have found copyright include: glass rectangles constructed in spiral (copyright);[12] a rose blossom over an abstract background design (copyright for the blossom only).[13]

Section 102(b) has been more effectively used as a shield to defeat copyright claims for artworks than any other rule, and it is among the most nettlesome for art. The dichotomy is accute in the arts, where concept and expression are often inextricably linked, if they are not one and the same. Art can (1) convey ideas without images; (2) copy images using different processes to convey new ideas; and (3) depict no imagery and ostensibly contain no ideas.

---

single event infringed plaintiffs' guidebook, which listed city bars and restaurants displaying artworks, because copyright does not protect idea of connecting art and food).

[10]Leigh v. Warner Bros., a Div. of Time Warner Entertainment Co., L.P., 10 F. Supp. 2d 1371, 48 U.S.P.Q. 2d (BNA) 1172 (S.D. Ga. 1998) ("idea of a forlorn cemetery statue as representing 'final judgment' cannot be protected by copyright")

[11]Leigh v. Warner Bros., a Div. of Time Warner Entertainment Co., L.P, 212 F.3d 1210 (11th Cir. 2000) (reversing summary judgment on copyright claim for single-frame image where expressive elements of artistic craft were copyrightable).

[12]Runstadler Studios, Inc. v. MCM Ltd. Partnership, 768 F. Supp. 1292 (N.D. Ill. 1991).

[13]Folio Impressions, Inc. v. Byer California, 752 F. Supp. 583, 31 Fed. R. Evid. Serv. 1320 (S.D. N.Y. 1990), judgment aff'd, 937 F.2d 759, 33 Fed. R. Evid. Serv. 569 (2d Cir. 1991).

These explorations are typical among fine artists and those involved in one-of-a-kind object-making, but such works might be hard-pressed to receive copyright.

The limitation of copyright protection to expression of an idea is based upon the societal interest in competition.[14] The policy is to balance the interests of artistic exploitation against the free flow of creativity, and to encourage original works without restricting subsequent creators who build upon work of others. The distinctions offer little guidance when applied to the arts because the policy speaks largely to commercial products, not artistic ones. Copyright does not necessarily offer the visual artist, as the individual exploiter, or society, the national inheritor of cultural heritage, the best protection.

§ 7:13 Process

Art has always involved process, and, as technology is increasingly incorporated in artmaking, and process itself is presented as art, product and process conflate. Process, without more, however, is expressly not copyrightable under Section 102(b).[1] Courts have distinguished certain exceptions, but have applied the exceptions inconsistently.

In Alfred Bell,[2] the plaintiff's verbatim copying of masterwork paintings into etchings was considered original because of the painstaking technical process applied to produce the works in a new medium. In Hearn,[3] the plaintiff-artist's use of technology to reproduce illustrations by W.W. Denslow from the out-of-print "Wonderful World of Oz," published in 1900, for Hearn's own book on Oz was not considered original.

---

[14]Austin Productions, Inc. v. F.D.F. Design Studio, Inc., 1991 Copr. L. Dec. ¶ 26662, 1990 WL 198741 (E.D. N.Y. 1990) (citations omitted).

[Section 7:13]

[1]§ 7:12 and §§ 7:104 to 7:112.

[2]Alfred Bell & Co. v. Catalda Fine Arts, 74 F. Supp. 973 (S.D. N.Y. 1947), decision supplemented, 75 U.S.P.Q. (BNA) 283, 1947 WL 3391 (S.D. N.Y. 1947), decision supplemented, 86 F. Supp. 399 (S.D. N.Y. 1949), judgment modified, 191 F.2d 99 (2d Cir. 1951) (copyrights infringed).

[3]Hearn v. Meyer, 664 F. Supp. 832, 835 (S.D. N.Y. 1987) (since Hearn did not transfer Denslow's illustrations "in another medium or form" the reproductions were not original as a matter of law).

Computers have so changed the nature of creation, communication and production by the end of the twentieth century that the impact of applying and adapting existing technology and developing new technology in the twenty-first cannot be overstated. Artists push the envelope; laws lag behind. Where artists venture has not necessarily been anticipated by copyright law or even encompassed within existing principles. Today's technology changes the balance of equities and goals historically fundamental to copyright. Congress is responsible for evaluating whether the constitutional basis and the judicial interpretations are diverging. Meanwhile, courts fashion rules responsive to new technology based on longstanding principles.

B. IMAGERY

§ 7:14 Forms of expression

Art imagery historically was divided, somewhat loosely, into two basic forms, representational and abstract. These terms apply to the image regardless of what "school" the work is classified under or what "movement" the art is affiliated with, i.e., conceptual art can be representational or abstract, or combine elements of both; a realist landscape is a representational work.

Abstraction per se is not a new development in art, but its adaptation and incorporation by Western European and nonindigenous North American artists is relatively recent in art historical terms. The evolution of abstraction has been comprehensively analyzed by art scholars[1] and is well beyond the scope of this chapter. Without wishing to misstate by simplification the complex evolution of modernism, suffice it to say that popular lineology of Western art invariably credits Cezanne as a precipitator of cubism and the modern abstractionism that followed.[2] His recomposition and flattening of the picture plane into geometric shapes and multiple perspectives in the Nineteenth

---

[Section 7:14]

[1]Biblio-II.

[2]*See also* Boorstin, The Creators 729 ("[C]ubism was a product of many influences—trends in science and mathematics, African sculpture, the personal experiments of Cezanne, Henri Rousseau, Seurat . . . 'Cubism,' like names for other schools of modern painting, began in

Century stimulated a chain of events that unleashed art from 500 years of service to classical ideals. His imagination is still impressed upon the art world in the twenty-first century.

Today some critics and scholars use the terms objective and nonobjective to refine, replace, and recategorize representational and abstract. Again, art criticism and art historical scholarship are beyond the focus of this chapter and writings in those areas should be consulted.

Such a condensation of the art timeline is not offered as an artistic analysis, but simply to make a key historical point: Modern abstract art did not exist during the origination of common-law copyright law and its domestic development in the United States in the 1800s and 1900s.[3] To this day, copyright law treats art containing certain abstract imagery differently from art containing representational imagery. The distinctions stem from the purpose and protection that copyright was intended to afford.

§ 7:15 Abstract art—Geometric shapes

Certain forms and ideas are deemed commercially necessary so that even limited monopolistic control by copyright is precluded or restricted. Generic geometric shapes, i.e., squares, triangles, circles, rectangles, and certain abstract symbols are ordinarily not copyrightable and are considered to be in the public domain; but some courts have accepted as original works of authorship geometric patterns,[1] and combinations of shapes otherwise in the

---

derision. In 1908, when Braque's paintings were being hung for exhibition, a critic exclaimed . . . 'Encore des cubes? Assez de cubisme!' ").

[3] Chart 7-1.

[Section 7:15]

[1] Mulberry Thai Silks, Inc. v. K & K Neckwear, Inc., 897 F. Supp. 789 (S.D. N.Y. 1995), adhered to on reconsideration, (Oct. 10, 1995) (court will not look beyond "certificate of registration [as] prima facie evidence of validity, and "therefore, . . . originality"); *but cf.* Runstadler Studios, Inc. v. MCM Ltd. Partnership, 768 F. Supp. 1292 (N.D. Ill. 1991) (inconsistencies of copyright registration for geometrics and abstract shapes).

public domain.[2] In *Arthur v. American Broadcasting Cos.*,[3] the court considered a copyrighted sculpture of five welded interlocking bronze rings. The artist sued for infringement, alleging that American Broadcasting's logo of the Olympic interlocking rings symbol imposed over lowercase "a, b, c" was copied from sketches and photos he had sent them years before they developed the logo.[4] The court dismissed the action, concluding interlocking circles were mere ideas:

> [S]ince "[i]n no case does copyright protection . . . extend to any idea, concept, principle, . . . " 17 U.S.C.A. 102(b), the copyright office correctly rejected Arthur's first sketches as lacking originality. These bare outlines of five interlocking rings, the upper three of which have been modified to a lower case a, b and c, contain no more than the bare idea or concept of superimposing the two logos.[5]

§ 7:16 Abstract art—Combining shapes

Unique combinations of standard shapes may possess the requisite creativity necessary for protection. A sculpture composed of standard shapes—39 clear glass rectangles—overlaying each other to form a spiral was held to possess the requisite creativity to qualify an origi-

[2]Mulberry Thai Silks, Inc. v. K & K Neckwear, Inc., 897 F. Supp. 789 (S.D. N.Y. 1995), adhered to on reconsideration, (Oct. 10, 1995); *see* § 7:16; Tompkins Graphics, Inc. v. Zipatone, Inc., 1984 Copyright Law Decisions, ¶ 25,698 (E.D. Pa. 1984) (basic geometric shapes in public domain); *but cf.* Reader's Digest Ass'n, Inc. v. Conservative Digest, Inc., 821 F.2d 800 (D.C. Cir. 1987) (magazine cover incorporating shapes and common forms in public domain was copyrightable original work of art based upon arrangement and presentation).

[3]Arthur v. American Broadcasting Companies, Inc., 633 F. Supp. 146 (S.D. N.Y. 1985).

[4]Arthur v. American Broadcasting Companies, Inc., 633 F. Supp. 146 at 148 n.2 (S.D. N.Y. 1985) ("Query whether plaintiff has even this right [to sculptural execution of five interlocking rings] in his sculpture . . . in view of the exclusive rights to the interlocking rings accorded the [U.S.] Olympic Committee.").

[5]Arthur v. American Broadcasting Companies, Inc., 633 F. Supp. 146 at 148 (S.D. N.Y. 1985).

nal work,[1] even though the defendant's alleged copy was refused registration by the copyright office. The following have been considered sufficient factors to support originality in abstract sculpture using uncopyrightable geometric shapes: choice of dimensions, location, and orientation of rectangles, and degree of arc.[2] If copyright is found, it extends only to that which is original in the combination of shapes, not to the standard shapes alone.

§ 7:17 Representational art—Photorealism, naturalism

Photographic realism, naturalism, and other precise renderings are considered a convergence of idea and expression with limited copyrightability. Where the particularized expression and the idea are close, or coalesce, the copyright, in trademark terminology, is considered "thin"[1] or "weak."[2] In *Franklin Mint*, the Third Circuit concluded no protectible expression existed in life-like renderings of birds by wildlife artists, explaining the difficulty of dividing idea from expression for realistic artworks:

> Precision in marking the boundary between the unprotected idea and the protected expression . . . are rarely possible . . . . Isolating the idea from the expression and determining the extent of copying required for unlawful appropriation necessarily depends to some degree on whether the subject matter is words or symbols . . . or paint brushed onto canvas.
>
> [I]n the world of fine art, the ease with which a copyright may be delineated may depend on the artist's style. A painter like Monet . . . is apt to create a work which can

---

[Section 7:16]

[1]Runstadler Studios, Inc. v. MCM Ltd. Partnership, 768 F. Supp. 1292 (N.D. Ill. 1991).

[2]Runstadler Studios, Inc. v. MCM Ltd. Partnership, 768 F. Supp. 1292 (N.D. Ill. 1991).

[Section 7:17]

[1]Feist Publications, Inc. v. Rural Telephone Service Co., Inc., 499 U.S. 340, 111 S. Ct. 1282, 113 L. Ed. 2d 358 (1991).

[2]Franklin Mint Corp. v. National Wildlife Art Exchange, Inc., 195 U.S.P.Q. (BNA) 31, 1977 WL 22706 (E.D. Pa. 1977), judgment aff'd, 575 F.2d 62, 65 (3d Cir. 1978).

> make infringement attempts difficult [in the impressionist's work the lay observer will be able to differentiate more readily between the because] reality of subject matter and subjective effect of the artist's work. [A]n artist who produces a rendition with photograph-like clarity and accuracy may be hard pressed to prove unlawful copying by another who uses the same subject matter and the same technique.[3]

In *Concrete Machinery*,[4] where fabricators of deer, swan, and monkey animal sculptures were held not to infringe on the competitor's copyright in similar stone animals, the court found real animals can be expressed in only so many ways: "Some ideas admit of only limited number of expressions. When there is essentially only one way to express an idea, the idea and its expression are inseparable and copyright is no bar to copying that expression."[5]

§ 7:18 Representational art—Archetypal imagery

Copyright typically does not allow artists to monopolize archetypal icons, images, and imagery. Art is replete with veritable archetypes, virtually universal and timeless: the recumbent nude, groups of and single bathers, the Crucifixion, sunsets, pastoral landscapes, children strolling through fields of flowers, boats moored at a pier, or fishing off a bridge. "[S]hared culture and common media exposure have invested certain objects and events in our society with a universal meaning."[1] The familiar idea may not be protected, but the artist's particular means of

---

[3]575 F.2d at 65.

[4]Concrete Machinery Co., Inc. v. Classic Lawn Ornaments, Inc., 843 F.2d 600 (1st Cir. 1988) (swans, monkeys, and deer held to be common images subject to limited expression, such that plaintiff could not enjoin defendant from creating animals, even if they were similar to plaintiff's copyrighted animals, absent physical evidence of copying).

[5]Concrete Machinery Co., Inc. v. Classic Lawn Ornaments, Inc., 843 F.2d 600 at 606–07 (1st Cir. 1988); *accord,* Flag Fables, Inc. v. Jean Ann's Country Flags and Crafts, Inc., 730 F. Supp. 1165, 1179 (D. Mass. 1989); Austin Productions, Inc. v. F.D.F. Design Studio, Inc., 1991 Copr. L. Dec. ¶ 26662, 1990 WL 198741 (E.D. N.Y. 1990) ("expression of reindeer" on sculptures is limited).

[Section 7:18]

[1]Leibovitz v. Paramount Pictures Corp., 137 F.3d 109 (2d Cir. 1998) (". . . the basic pose of a nude, pregnant body and the position of the hands [one covering the breast and the other holding distended stom-

expressing it is.[2] Digital reproductions of city skyline photographs copied protected expression.[3]

Recurring themes are ordinarily not copyrightable, although decisions may be based more upon the merging of idea and expression than on the acknowledged recognition of archetypes.[4]

Although not necessarily presented in archetypal terms, a loosely analogous concept known as "scenes a faire" exists in copyright. Scenes a faire, which originated in a literary context, has been described variously as "often-recurring themes" and "common stock," typically not protected by copyright to avoid economic monopolies on ideas, presented in different jurisdictions under various rationales.[5]

The First Circuit wrote in *Woolworth*: "Copyright on a work of art does not protect a subject, but only the treatment of a subject."[6] But treatment of certain subject matter may have limited protection under an archetypal

---

ach], if ever protectible, [was] placed into the public domain by painters and sculptors long before Botticelli's 'Birth of Venus' . . . "); *see, e.g.*, Washegesic v. Bloomingdale Public Schools, 813 F. Supp. 559, 81 Ed. Law Rep. 96 (W.D. Mich. 1993), order aff'd, 33 F.3d 679, 94 Ed. Law Rep. 32, 1994 FED App. 310P (6th Cir. 1994).

[2]Silberman v. Innovation Luggage, Inc., 67 U.S.P.Q.2d (BNA) 1489, 2003 WL 1787123 (S.D. N.Y. 2003) (Manhattan skyline photographed at dusk as common cityscape.").

[3]Silberman v. Innovation Luggage, Inc., 67 U.S.P.Q.2d (BNA) 1489, 2003 WL 1787123 (S.D. N.Y. 2003) (defendants "appropriated . . . the particular [expression] . . . precisely as [the artist] composed and created it.").

[4]Walker v. Time Life Films, Inc., 784 F.2d 44, 48 (2d Cir. 1986) (recurring themes are not protectible "except to the extent they are given unique—and therefore protectible—expression in an original creation.").

[5]*See, e.g.,* Ets-Hokin v. Skyy Spirits, Inc., 225 F.3d 1068, 2000 (9th Cir. 2000) (scenes a faire held to be defenses to infringement rather than issues of copyrightability); Williams v. Crichton, 84 F.3d 581 (2d Cir. 1996) (author of children's books on dinosaurs seeking infringement action against author of Jurassic Park); Beal v. Paramount Pictures Corp., 20 F.3d 454, 459–60 (11th Cir. 1994) (mosque palace with minarets considered scenes a faire in story about arabic royalty).

[6]F. W. Woolworth Co. v. Contemporary Arts, 193 F.2d 162, 164 (1st Cir. 1951), cert. granted, 343 U.S. 963, 72 S. Ct. 1061, 96 L. Ed. 1360 (1952) and judgment aff'd, 344 U.S. 228, 73 S. Ct. 222, 97 L. Ed. 276 (1952).

analysis. The Third Circuit wrote in *Franklin Mint*: "The fact that the same subject matter may be present in two paintings does not prove copying or infringement."[7] But in *Leigh*,[8] the Eleventh Circuit reversed a district court determination that an eerie, spiritual mood of a photograph taken in a cemetery for the cover of a best selling novel was scenes a faire commonly associated with graveyards and not protected by copyright.

§ 7:19 Return to theme, variations on a theme

Courts have held that artists need freedom to return to subjects and techniques they have previously explored. "[S]ome painters return to certain basic themes time and time again. Winslow Homer's Schoolboys, Monet's Facade of Rouen Cathedral [these] are examples of 'variations on a theme' . . . examples of the freedom which must be extended to artists to utilize basic subject matter more than once."[1]

No copying was found in the following cases because the courts found the artist was returning to a theme or exploring a variation: (1) "techniques" used by alleged infringer that had been used by him in his earlier works prior to creation of the plaintiff's work,[2] and (2) reusing some of the same source material for wildlife paintings already

---

[7]Franklin Mint Corp. v. National Wildlife Art Exchange, Inc., 575 F.2d 62, 64 (3d Cir. 1978); Leigh v. Warner Bros., Inc., 212 F.3d 1210, 2000 (11th Cir. 2000).

[8]Leigh v. Warner Bros., a Div. of Time Warner Entertainment Co., L.P., 10 F. Supp. 2d 1371, 1999 (S.D. Ga. 1998), aff'd in part, rev'd in part, 212 F.3d 1210 (11th Cir. 2000) (". . . there is no need to determine whether scenes a faire applies in this case. . . ," analyzing the moody spiritual aspect of the photograph as the artistic expression of the "photographer's craft.").

[Section 7:19]

[1]Franklin Mint Corp. v. National Wildlife Art Exchange, Inc., 195 U.S.P.Q. (BNA) 31, 1977 WL 22706 (E.D. Pa. 1977), judgment aff'd, 575 F.2d 62 (3d Cir. 1978).

[2]Gentieu v. John Muller & Co., Inc., 712 F. Supp. 740 (W.D. Mo. 1989).

licensed.[3] Copying was found where a photographer reshot the same model with some similar accessories two years after shooting the original photo.[4]

Franklin Mint,[5] relied upon "variations on a theme" as examples of artistic freedom which enable artists to utilize basic subject matter more than once. The plaintiff, who held a valid assignment of "all rights-reproduction" contract with the artist, was not entitled to damages for copyright infringement when the artist used the same sources to produce works for others. A recognized wildlife artist painted "Cardinals on Apple Blossom," which he licensed to plaintiff for $1,500; the licensee produced and sold a limited edition of 300 prints of the painting, and registered the copyright. Some years later, the artist painted a series of four paintings, including one titled "The Cardinal," for Franklin Mint, using some of the same source material. Franklin made engravings of the paintings and sold four engravings as a set. The licensee sued Franklin Mint for copyright infringement, but the district court found, inter alia, that the artist was entitled to reuse his source materials and return to themes.

But, in *Gross v. Seligman*,[6] an artist was found to have infringed a copyright involving his own work after he licensed his art to the plaintiff. The defendant-photographer sold all rights in a photograph of a young girl to the plaintiff. Some years later he photographed the same girl, in a similar position, with the same or similar accessories. "Whether the model in the second [photo] was posed . . . with a copy of the first photograph physically present . . . or whether [the artist's] mental reproduction of the exact combination he had already once effected was so clear and vivid that he did not need the physical reproduction [is] immaterial."

---

[3]Franklin Mint Corp. v. National Wildlife Art Exchange, Inc., 195 U.S.P.Q. (BNA) 31, 1977 WL 22706 (E.D. Pa. 1977), judgment aff'd, 575 F.2d 62, 64 (3d Cir. 1978).

[4]Gross v. Seligman, 212 F. 930 (C.C.A. 2d Cir. 1914).

[5]Franklin Mint Corp. v. National Wildlife Art Exchange, Inc., 575 F.2d 62, 64 (3d Cir. 1978).

[6]Gross v. Seligman, 212 F. 930 (C.C.A. 2d Cir. 1914).

IV. STATUTORY BASICS[7]

A. NOTICE

§ 7:20 Formality

Notice of copyright is no longer required after the United States adhered to the Berne Convention, but it is still recommended.[1] Where notice is required, e.g., pre-Berne works, or voluntarily, formalities must be observed. Failure to comply with notice formalities in circumstances where notice is required may result in loss of copyright protection. The 1976 Act specifies ways in which improper, defective or omitted notice can be cured.[2] Even where notice is voluntary, it should still comply with the established formalities.

The form of notice for copyright is specified by Section 401, supplemented by the Code of Federal Regulations.[3] The three requisite elements are (1) a symbol for the letter C in a circle "©" or symbol substitute, i.e., "copyright", or "copr.", (2) the year of first publication,[4] and (3) the name of the copyright owner, an abbreviation by which the name can be recognized or a generally known alternative designation.[5]

Notice can be placed on publicly distributed copies from

---

[7]*See* Appendix 19.

[Section 7:20]

[1]*See* § 7:21.

[2]*See* § 7:21.

[3]17 U.S.C.A. § 401(b); 37 C.F.R. Part 201. Examples of acceptable formal notice are: Joe Artist. ©1993; J. Artist. copr. 1993; Joe. copyright. 1993 (if artist is recognized or known as "Joe"). Publication without notice resulted in forfeiture of copyright under the Act of 1909; *see* Simon v. Birraporetti's Restaurants, Inc., 720 F. Supp. 85 (S.D. Tex. 1989) (creator of original photograph in 1977 that was published without notice had no copyright interest because photo entered the public domain).

[4]*See* §§ 7:38 to 7:43, (many issues exist as to when, and under what circumstances, PGS works are "published" within the meaning of copyright); *see also* Appendix 19-1, § 3 (Form VA requires a date of completion for all visual works of art, and requests publication only if the work has been published).

[5]Ronald Litoff, Ltd. v. American Exp. Co., 621 F. Supp. 981 (S.D. N.Y. 1985) (defendants challenge that jewelry designer was recognized or generally known by initials "RL").

which it is "visually perceptible, either directly or with the aid of a machine or device."[6] The law requires giving only reasonable notice of copyright, but notice must be permanently legible for ordinary use of the work and affixed in such a way and position that it is not concealed from view upon reasonable examination.[7]

Chart 7-2: Guide for Affixing Copyright Notice to PGS Works[8]		
Type of Work	How to Notice	Location of Notice
2D works	Notice front or back durably attached	On copies, backing, mounting, mats, frames, etc.
3D works	Notice on any visible portion of work durably attached	On base, mounting, framing, or other material
Works of special size or physical requirements	Tag notice, durable material attached with sufficient durability to remain w/copy in normal channels of commerce	Tags

Whether reasonable notice has been given is a question of fact for the finder of fact.[9] Where notice is provided, the year of first publication is ordinarily required. For unpublished PGS works, what date should be used? The date the work leaves the control of the author or copyright owner has been suggested by the Copyright Office, and the notice can so recite.[10] The date the work is completed, commonly used by some artists, is another option, although this poses artistic as well as legal concerns.[11] Cases

[6] 17 U.S.C.A. § 401(a).

[7] 17 U.S.C.A. § 401(c); 37 C.F.R. § 201.20, ¶ 12,040.

[8] Chart created from information contained in 37 C.F.R. § 201.20(i).

[9] Chart created from information contained in 37 C.F.R. § 201.20(i).

[10] Example: Copyright. Unpublished [work]. 1995. Art Artist.

[11] *See* Chs 1 to 2.

regarding perceptibility of notice on PGS works are few: notice on a sculpture placed 20 feet above eye level was inadequate;[12] notice on the back of a sculpture plaque was inadequate;[13] notice on jewelry although "somewhat difficult to read" was adequate.[14]

Where the artist's name is omitted from notice but the publisher's name appears, the artist's rights may still be protected.[15] The year of first publication may be omitted where a PGS category work is reproduced under certain circumstances on greeting cards, postcards, or any useful article.[16] Section 405 provides specifically for omissions of

---

[12]Scherr v. Universal Match Corp., 417 F.2d 497, 11 A.L.R. Fed. 447 (2d Cir. 1969) (copyright notice placed on the backpack of a 25 foot-high monumental sculpture was invalid notice).

[13]Coventry Ware, Inc. v. Reliance Picture Frame Co., 288 F.2d 193 (2d Cir. 1961).

[14]Ronald Litoff, Ltd. v. American Exp. Co., 621 F. Supp. 981 (S.D. N.Y. 1985) (defendants contest notice of jewelry designers); *accord,* Encore Shoe Corp. v. Bennett Industries, Inc., 18 U.S.P.Q.2d (BNA) 1874, 1991 WL 27412 (D. Mass. 1991) (notice on shoe ornaments adequate even though less than 8/100th of an inch in diameter).

[15]Dauman v. Andy Warhol Foundation for Visual Arts, Inc., 43 U.S.P.Q.2d (BNA) 1221, 1997 WL 337488 (S.D. N.Y. 1997) (general copyright notice in name of Time Inc. sufficient to allege copyright ownership by photographer of President John F. Kennedy's funeral published in Life magazine, in a complaint brought by Time and photographer against foundation and estate of Andy Warhol, who allegedly used Life photographic images for composite portrayals of Jacqueline Kennedy); *see also* Goodis v. United Artists Television, Inc., 425 F.2d 397 (2d Cir. 1970) (where a magazine purchased rights of first publication, copyright notice in the name of the magazine was sufficient to obtain valid copyright on behalf of the author); Varon v. Santa Fe Reporter, 1983 Copyright Law Decisions ¶ 25,499 (D. N. Mex. 1982) (in action decided under Section 19 of Copyright Act of 1909, which required notice of name of copyright proprietor, omission of artist's name still satisfied Section 19 because art publisher name appeared, and publication of artist's photograph was a one-time rental).

[16]17 U.S.C.A. § 401(b)(2) (Identification of the year of publication is not required for notices affixed to "pictorial, graphic, or sculptural work . . . reproduced in or on . . . any useful articles."); *see also* E. Mishan & Sons, Inc. v. Marycana, Inc., 662 F. Supp. 1339 (S.D. N.Y. 1987) (affixing defendant's artwork to magnets constituted a design feature separately identifiable from useful article, and excused omission from notice of dates of first publication under § 401(b)(2); *but cf.,* Langman Fabrics v. Samsung America, Inc., 967 F. Supp. 131 (S.D. N.Y. 1997), clarified in part, 997 F. Supp. 479 (S.D. N.Y. 1998) and rev'd, 160 F.3d

notice.[17]

§ 7:21 Notice voluntary after berne

Works first published after March 1, 1989—the date BCIA became effective—are not required to bear notice of copyright as a condition for maintaining copyright protection.[1] In conjunction with this, Sections 401 and 405 of title 17 of the U.S. Code were amended by removing the requirement of notice for post-Berne works.[2] (Works first published between January 1, 1978 and February 28, 1989, are subject to notice provisions of the 1976 Act.) If notice were sufficient for pre-Berne publications, the omission of notice in post-Berne publications does not require cure, but if pre-Berne publications bear defective notice, reasonable efforts must be made to add notice to all copies after defective notice is discovered, even if discovery occurs after March 1, 1989.[3] The Uruguay Round Agreements Act (URAA) restores copyright in certain foreign works originally published without notice before March 1, 1989 that otherwise would have entered the public domain in the United States.

---

106 (2d Cir. 1998), opinion amended, 169 F.3d 782 (2d Cir. 1998) (no loss of copyright for fabric designs because they were "useful articles").

[17] 17 U.S.C.A. § 405 (". . . [t]he omission of a copyright notice . . . from copies . . . publicly distributed by authority of the copyright owner does not invalidate the copyright in a work if (1) the notice has been omitted from no more than a relatively small number of copies . . . distributed to the public; or (2) registration for the work has been made before or is made within five years after the publication without notice, and a reasonable effort is made to add notice to all copies or phonorecords that are distributed to the public in the United States after the omission has been discovered . . ."); *see, e.g.,* E. Mishan & Sons, Inc. v. Marycana, Inc., 662 F. Supp. 1339 (S.D. N.Y. 1987) (no loss of copyright for works distributed without notice for two years due to small number of copies distributed and erroneous date of first publication not prejudicial).

[Section 7:21]

[1] Pub. L. No. 100-568 (Oct. 31, 1988).

[2] Pub. L. No. 100-568 (Oct. 31, 1988); 17 U.S.C.A. §§ 401, 405.

[3] *See, e.g.,* Encore Shoe Corp. v. Bennett Industries, Inc., 18 U.S.P.Q.2d (BNA) 1874, 1991 WL 27412 (D. Mass. 1991).

§ 7:22 Evidentiary weight of notice for innocent infringer defense

Although notice is not required for post-Berne works, notice is recommended because of its evidentiary weight for the innocent infringer defense in mitigation of actual or statutory damages, in addition to the general benefits of giving public information that the work is protected, identifying the author or copyright owner, and, as applicable, evidencing the year of first publication. If notice appears on the copy to which defendant had access, "no weight" shall be given to defendant's defense "based on innocent infringement in mitigation of actual or statutory damages."[1]

§ 7:23 Willful interference with notice

Intentionally removing a notice or otherwise obliterating a notice for purposes of copying, or instructing others to copy, supports a finding of defendant's willful and intentional copying,[1] relevant to bad faith and unfair use.[2] In the *Koons* cases,[3] artist Jeff Koons tore off copyright notices from published copyrighted photographs by other artists before sending them to fabricators with instructions to copy the photos in detail.

[Section 7:22]

[1]17 U.S.C.A. § 401(d).

[Section 7:23]

[1]Rogers v. Koons, 751 F. Supp. 474 (S.D. N.Y. 1990), amended on reargument, 777 F. Supp. 1 (S.D. N.Y. 1991) and judgment aff'd, 960 F.2d 301 (2d Cir. 1992) (defendant artist tore off plaintiff-artist's notice from a museum postcard before sending it to overseas fabricators to copy as a sculpture).

[2]*See* §§ 7:87 to 7:102.

[3]Rogers v. Koons, 751 F. Supp. 474 (S.D. N.Y. 1990), amended on reargument, 777 F. Supp. 1 (S.D. N.Y. 1991) and judgment aff'd, 960 F.2d 301 (2d Cir. 1992); United Feature Syndicate, Inc. v. Koons, 817 F. Supp. 370 (S.D. N.Y. 1993); Campbell v. Koons, 1993 WL 97381 (S.D. N.Y. 1993).

B. REGISTRATION

1. *In General*

§ 7:24 Statutory prerequisite for suit, damages, costs, and fees

Congress created a statutory system to register a copyright claim, which may be made at any time during the life of the copyright. Although under Section 102(a) "copyright protection subsists . . . in original works of authorship fixed in any tangible medium of expression" and a creator is not required to register,[1] registration entitles the copyright owner to benefits and is required prior to bringing suit.

Registration, including payment of fees and deposit of copies, is the statutory prerequisite to filing a cause of action for infringement.[2] Registration enables registrants to seek statutory damages under Section 504(c), and costs and attorney's fees under Section 505.[3] In 1992, the number of registrations for "works of visual art," including pictorial, graphic, and sculptural works, totalled 77,900, and almost 75 percent of those were published works.[4] The Office of Copyright registers claims to copyright and issues certificates of registration.

§ 7:25 Form VA

Registration for visual art is made by filing with the

[Section 7:24]

[1]17 U.S.C.A. § 102(a); *cf.,* Copyright Act of 1909 (publication without notice resulted in forfeiture of copyright).

[2]17 U.S.C.A. § 411(a) ("no action for infringement of the copyright in any work shall be instituted until registration of the copyright claim has been made.").

[3]17 U.S.C.A. § 412 ("no award of statutory damages or of attorney's fees, as provided by sections 504 and 505 shall be made for * * * (2) any infringement of copyright commenced after first publication of the work and before the effective date of registration, unless such registration is made within three months after the first publication of the work."); Mackie v. Rieser, 296 F.3d 909 (9th Cir. 2002), cert. denied, 123 S. Ct. 1259, 154 L. Ed. 2d 1022 (U.S. 2003) (artist could not use statutory damages because of failure to register prior to infringement).

[4]Report of the Register of Copyrights 1992, at 34 (53,253 works published and 24,647 unpublished; data includes registrations of labels and applied art).

Copyright Office a properly completed Form VA, including payment of a filing fee, in conjunction with making deposit of "identifying material" or copies of the visual art.[1] The procedures for registering and depositing are specified by the Copyright Office in detailed circulars and brochures, prepared so that artists could comply with the registration process without assistance of counsel. However, artists who work collaboratively, artists who are hired by others or who hire others to fabricate or process their works, artists who make multiples or use the services of others to do so, and artists who make abstract art, minimalist art, functional art, conceptual art, computer art, or photography might wish to understand the legal implications of registration as indicated in case law.

An artist's failure to use Form VA did not invalidate his copyright in sculpture in the absence of fraud where he attached to Form TX (textual materials) pictures of his sculpture, and the certificate issued.[2] The effective date of registration is the day on which an application, deposit, and fee, which are later determined to be acceptable for registration, have all been received by the Copyright Office.[3]

2. *Deposit*

a. *Identifying Material (I.D. Material)*

§ 7:26 Description

Deposit is part of the registration process; the appropriate deposit is usually one complete copy of the work, for unpublished works, and two complete copies of the best edition, if the work was first published in the United States. Since the Copyright Office is not a depository for artwork, nor is it possible for one-of-a-kind artworks to be physically deposited, the Copyright Office mandates the deposit of "identifying material" or "I.D. material" for certain works of art, and permits it for others.

[Section 7:25]

[1] *See* Appendix 19 for Form VA.

[2] Runstadler Studios, Inc. v. MCM Ltd. Partnership, 768 F. Supp. 1292 (N.D. Ill. 1991).

[3] 17 U.S.C.A. § 410(d).

The I.D. material used is ordinarily two dimensional reproductions or renderings of artwork in the form of photographic prints, photographic transparencies, photocopies, or drawings that show the complete copyrightable content of the registered work. If I.D. material is submitted, only one set is required, but it must be complete, i.e., if multiple views are required to show the entire copyrightable content of the work, they must be submitted. The image should "show clearly" the entire copyrightable content of the work.

§ 7:27 Size

The I.D. material must be visually perceptible without the aid of machine or device. Photographic transparencies must be at least 35 mm; if 3" × 3" or less, transparencies must be fixed in cardboard, plastic or similar mounts; transparencies larger than 3" × 3" should be mounted. All I.D. material, other than photographic transparencies, must be at least 3" × 3" and not more than 9" × 12". The Copyright Office recommends 8" × 10" I.D. material for everything other than transparencies.

§ 7:28 Color

If the work is pictorial or graphic, the I.D. material should present the actual colors used. In all other instances, the I.D. material may be either black and white or color.

§ 7:29 Title and dimension

At least one piece of ID material must provide the title of the work on the front, back, or mount, and the exact measurement of one or more dimensions.

§ 7:30 Required

The Copyright Office requires the deposit of I.D. material for published or unpublished three-dimensional works of visual art, and for any PGS work that exceeds ninety-six inches in any dimension.

§ 7:31 Permitted

Pursuant to regulations, the Copyright Office permits

I.D. material instead of an actual copy for certain unpublished two-dimensional "pictorial or graphic" works, including drawings, paintings, illustrations.[1] I.D. material is also permitted for published "pictorial or graphic work," including limited edition prints, in lieu of two actual copies, "where an individual author is the owner of copyright and either: less than five copies of the work have been published; or the work has been published and sold or offered for sale in a limited edition consisting of no more than 300 numbered copies."[2]

b. Copies

§ 7:32 Generally

A "copy" is an actual copy of the work, not a scale rendering or a photograph. The preceding sections indicate when I.D. material is required or permitted, but a copy can be used on deposit as Chart 7-3 makes clear, and indicates how many copies are required and what the copy should consist of (the number in parentheses indicates the number of copies required for deposit).[1]

Chart 7-3: Use of Copies as Deposit of I.D. Material

Artwork	Number of Copies	Explanatory Note
Architectural works (unconstructed building)	One copy of architectural drawing or blueprint showing overall form of building and any interior arrangement of spaces and/or design element in which copyright claimed	Work must have been created on or after December 1, 1990 or have been unconstructed and embodied only in unpublished drawings as of December 1, 1990

[Section 7:31]

[1]37 C.F.R. § 202.20.

[2]37 C.F.R. § 202.20.

[Section 7:32]

[1]*See* 37 C.F.R. § 202.20.

Artwork	Number of Copies	Explanatory Note
Architectural works (constructed building)	One complete copy per unconstructed building above plus I.D. material in form of photographs clearly identifying the architectural work	Work must have been created on or after December 1, 1990 or have been unconstructed and embodied only in unpublished drawings as of December 1, 1990
(1) Published limited edition posters, prints, etchings	(1) one	Etching is a form of printmaking; limited means published in quantities of less than five or if artist is copyright owner, copies of 300 or less
(2) Published photographs, posters, prints, exhibition catalogues	(2) two	
(3) Unpublished photographs	(3) one (copy of proofs, photocopy, or contact sheets)	
Published drawings, paintings, illustrations or other pictorial or graphic works	two	
Unpublished drawings, paintings, illustrations or other pictorial or graphic works	one	
Contributions to collective works, photographs or drawings	one complete copy of the best edition of the entire collective work or one photocopy of contribution as it was published)	

For work deposited in a three-dimensional hologram, the copy shall be accompanied by precise instructions for displaying the image fixed in the hologram, and photographs or other I.D. material "complying with section 202.21 and clearly showing the displayed image."

3. *Certificate of Registration*

§ 7:33 Registrations and refusals

The Copyright Office does not grant or issue copyright; it registers claims to copyright, or refuses to register. The precise extent of its role in determining the originality requirement of artwork, and its practical ability to do so, is debatable.[1] The Register of Copyright is guided by the Office Compendium of Policies and Practices and the Code of Federal Regulations. Rule 202.10(a) offers limited guidance: "[T]o be acceptable as a pictorial, graphic or sculptural work, the work must embody some creative authorship in its delineation or form."[2] Rule 202.1 offers as examples of noncopyrightability for which "applications for registration of such works cannot be entertained . . . (b) ideas, plans, methods, systems, or devices, as distinguished from the particular manner in which they are expressed or described."[3] The Register of Copyrights can refuse registration of Form VA applications if it finds the works are not copyrightable under these guidelines.[4] The Supreme Court has recognized the limited role of the Copyright Office in registering copyright: Virtually no prior governmental review occurs before a copyright claim is registered for applicants who are required to meet only

---

[Section 7:33]

[1]Mazer v. Stein, 347 U.S. 201, 74 S. Ct. 460, 98 L. Ed. 630 (1954) (Register does not determine originality); *cf.,* Arthur v. American Broadcasting Companies, Inc., 633 F. Supp. 146 (S.D. N.Y. 1985) (Register correctly rejected artist's works in registration application as "lacking originality.").

[2]37 C.F.R. § 202.10.

[3]37 C.F.R. § 202.1(b).

[4]17 U.S.C.A. § 411(a) ("where . . . registration has been refused, the applicant is entitled to institute an anction for infringement."); Runstadler Studios, Inc. v. MCM Ltd. Partnership, 768 F. Supp. 1292 (N.D. Ill. 1991) (registration refused for abstract geometric shapes because geometric shapes are in the public domain); Esquire, Inc. v. Ringer, 414 F. Supp. 939 (D.D.C. 1976), judgment rev'd, 591 F.2d 796 (D.C. Cir. 1978) (registration refused for modern abstract sculptural form based on utilitarian function; register did not abuse its discretion in denying copyright registration to the artistic design of a lighting fixture under 37 C.F.R. § 202.10(c) (1976) (utilitarian articles)).

minimal standards.[5] Rejected applicants can seek a writ of mandamus[6] and can file infringement actions.[7] If a valid and complete application were refused, judicial review extends to denial of registration as well as infringement.[8]

The opinions are inconsistent on the issue of whether the certificate reflects prima facie evidence of copyright validity in general or a particular verification of originality.

§ 7:34 Automatic admissibility and prima facie evidence

Section 410(c) of title 17 provides:

> In any judicial proceedings the certificate of a registration, made before or within five years after first publication of the work shall constitute prima facie evidence of the validity of the copyright and of the facts stated in the certificate. The evidentiary weight to be accorded the certificate of a registration made thereafter shall be within the discretion of the court.

Where registration is filed before or within the time period specified, the certificate of registration is automatically admissible in the action and "constitute[s] prima facie evidence of the validity of the copyright and of the facts stated in the certificate."[1] This has been interpreted as showing that the owner is the proprietor of the copyright and holds title to the copyright.[2] The presumption of validity "order[s] the burdens of proof."[3] Where "other evidence in the record casts doubt on the question, validity will not be

[5]Feist Publications, Inc. v. Rural Telephone Service Co., Inc., 499 U.S. 340, 111 S. Ct. 1282, 1287–88, 113 L. Ed. 2d 358 (1991).

[6]Esquire, Inc. v. Ringer, 414 F. Supp. 939 (D.D.C. 1976), judgment rev'd on other grounds, 591 F.2d 796 (D.C. Cir. 1978).

[7]17 U.S.C.A. § 411.

[8]Esquire, Inc. v. Ringer, 414 F. Supp. 939 (D.D.C. 1976), judgment rev'd on other grounds, 591 F.2d 796 (D.C. Cir. 1978).

[Section 7:34]

[1]17 U.S.C.A. § 410(c).

[2]Academy of Motion Picture Arts and Sciences v. Creative House Promotions, Inc., 944 F.2d 1446 (9th Cir. 1991) (statutory presumption is rebuttable).

[3]Sapon v. DC Comics, 62 U.S.P.Q.2d (BNA) 1691, 2002 WL 485730 (S.D. N.Y. 2002); Estate of Hogarth v. Edgar Rice Burroughs, Inc., 62

assumed."[4] The burden shifts to the defendant to rebut the presumption of ownership and validity.[5] If the defense evidence rebuts the presumption, the plaintiff must present independent evidence to support his copyright.[6]

§ 7:35 Originality

The United States Supreme Court has recognized that originality is a substantive issue of copyright subject to independent judicial determination.[1] Revisions to the Copyright Act do not indicate that judicial review has been superseded or displaced by the administrative registration process that underlies the Section 410(c) certificate. The lower court opinions are inconsistent, or silent, on the

---

U.S.P.Q.2d (BNA) 1301, 2002 WL 398696 (S.D. N.Y. 2002) (citations omitted).

[4]Estate of Hogarth v. Edgar Rice Burroughs, Inc., 62 U.S.P.Q.2d (BNA) 1301, 2002 WL 398696 (S.D. N.Y. 2002), judgment aff'd, 342 F.3d 149, 68 U.S.P.Q.2d (BNA) 1065 (2d Cir. 2003), cert. denied, 124 S. Ct. 1660, 158 L. Ed. 2d 357 (U.S. 2004); Sapon v. DC Comics, 62 U.S.P.Q.2d (BNA) 1691, 2002 WL 485730 (S.D. N.Y. 2002) (presumption is light and rebuttable by some evidence "as opposed to a mere assertion of noncopyrightability. . . ." (citations omitted)).

[5]Rogers v. Koons, 751 F. Supp. 474 (S.D. N.Y. 1990), amended on reargument, 777 F. Supp. 1 (S.D. N.Y. 1991) and judgment aff'd, 960 F.2d 301 (2d Cir. 1992); Academy of Motion Picture Arts and Sciences v. Creative House Promotions, Inc., 944 F.2d 1446 (9th Cir. 1991) (burden shifts to defendant to show that Oscar statuette entered the public domain); Ets-Hokin v. Skyy Spirits Inc., 1998 WL 690856 (N.D. Cal. 1998), rev'd on other grounds, 225 F.3d 1068 (9th Cir. 2000) ("an infringement defendant must simply offer some evidence or proof to dispute or deny the plaintiff's . . . case . . .").

[6]Sapon v. DC Comics, 62 U.S.P.Q.2d (BNA) 1691, 2002 WL 485730 (S.D. N.Y. 2002) (prima facie status of registration rejected because of errors in application); *cf.* Tiffany Design, Inc. v. Reno-Tahoe Specialty, Inc., 55 F. Supp. 2d 1113, 51 U.S.P.Q.2d (BNA) 1651 (D. Nev. 1999) (certificate inaccuracies were not significant).

[Section 7:35]

[1]Mazer v. Stein, 347 U.S. 201, 74 S. Ct. 460, 98 L. Ed. 630 (1954) (decided under the Copyright Act of 1909); Bridgeman Art Library, Ltd. v. Corel Corp., 36 F. Supp. 2d 191, 199 (S.D. N.Y. 1999) (a certificate of registration "is prima facie evidence of the validity of the copyright, including the originality of the work . . . a rebuttable presumption").

issue.[2]

What does the defendant have to proffer or show to trigger adjudicatory review? To survive summary judgment, defendants must present a triable issue of fact to support a bona fide defense.[3]

§ 7:36 Copies attached to certificate—Deposited copies

What neither title 17 nor the legislative history make clear is the admissibility and evidentiary weight of the copies deposited in conjunction with the registration. In *Seiler*,[1] a graphic artist sued LucasFilm for copyright infringement of his drawings of science fiction creatures used in a film, "The Empire Strikes Back." The artist did not have the original drawings; he attempted to introduce in court reconstructions he had used to obtain his copyright registration after the film was released. The district court found that the artist had lost or destroyed the originals in bad faith, and that no reconstruction was admissible under the best evidence rule, and granted summary judgment to LucasFilm.

---

[2]Mulberry Thai Silks, Inc. v. K & K Neckwear, Inc., 897 F. Supp. 789 (S.D. N.Y. 1995), adhered to on reconsideration, (Oct. 10, 1995) (certificate is prima facie evidence of originality); *cf.,* Home Art v. Glensder Textile Corp., 81 F. Supp. 551 (S.D. N.Y. 1948) (certificate demonstrates prima facie evidence of title, proprietary interest and validity).

[3]*See, e.g.,* Ets-Hokin v. Skyy Spirits Inc., 1998 WL 690856 (N.D. Cal. 1998), (defendants' submission of photographs of underlying work and plaintiff's work was sufficient evidence that plaintiff's work was derivative to rebut the statutory presumption of validity), rev'd, 225 F.3d 1068 (9th Cir. 2000) ("an infringement defendant must simply offer some evidence or proof to dispute or deny the plaintiff's . . . case . . ."); Home Art v. Glensder Textile Corp., 81 F. Supp. 551 (S.D. N.Y. 1948) (defendants were required to present facts that their artwork was copied from an original painting, rather than from plaintiff's copyrighted designs, to survive summary judgment).

[Section 7:36]

[1]Seiler v. Lucasfilm, Ltd., 808 F.2d 1316, 22 Fed. R. Evid. Serv. 601 (9th Cir. 1986).

§ 7:37 Copies attached to certificate—Best evidence rule

Rules 1001 to 1008 of the Federal Rules of Evidence (FRE) contain provisions codifying common law, these are referred to collectively as the original document rule or best evidence rule. Rule 1002 requires production of the original, with certain exceptions, "to prove the content of a writing." Rule 1001 describes "writing": " 'writings' consist of letters, words, sounds, or numbers, or their equivalent, set down." When the Seiler case[1] went on appeal, drawings were held to be writings for purposes of Rule 1001 under the phrase "writings . . . or their equivalent." The Ninth Circuit explained:

> A creative literary work, which is artwork, and a photograph whose contents are sought be proved, as in copyright . . . are both covered by the best evidence rule . . . . We would be inconsistent to apply the rule to artwork which is literary or photographic but not to artwork of other forms. Furthermore, blueprints, . . . architectural designs may all lack words or numbers yet still be capable of copyright.[2]

Although the plaintiff contended Section 410(c) mandates automatic admission of the certificate,[3] "when the deposited copies are subject to evidentiary challenge under the best evidence rule, the copies are not deemed to be incorporated into the certificate and are not therefore automatically admissible under [Section] 410(c)."[4] In a best evidence situation, deposited copies attached to the certificate have been held not automatically admissible and carry no presumption of validity or ownership.[5]

[Section 7:37]

[1]Seiler v. Lucasfilm, Ltd., 808 F.2d 1316, 22 Fed. R. Evid. Serv. 601 (9th Cir. 1986).

[2]Seiler v. Lucasfilm, Ltd., 808 F.2d 1316, at 1320 22 Fed. R. Evid. Serv. 601 (9th Cir. 1986).

[3]Seiler v. Lucasfilm, Ltd., 808 F.2d 1316, at 1321 22 Fed. R. Evid. Serv. 601 (9th Cir. 1986).

[4]Seiler v. Lucasfilm, Ltd., 808 F.2d 1316, 22 Fed. R. Evid. Serv. 601 (9th Cir. 1986).

[5]Seiler v. Lucasfilm, Ltd., 808 F.2d 1316, 22 Fed. R. Evid. Serv. 601 (9th Cir. 1986).

C. PUBLICATION

1. *1909 Act*

§ 7:38 General and limited publication

Publication affects the number of copies and type of material that must be deposited when registering work, affects duration of copyright for certain works and transfers, and triggers dates for certain damages and fees. Publication in the United States of some works also invokes mandatory deposit requirements in the Library of Congress, violation of which results in fines and penalties.

The 1909 Act did not define the term "publication." Under the 1909 Act, publication without notice ordinarily injected work into the public domain; anyone thereafter could publish it for his or her own benefit. In other words, a general publication divested the work of copyright unless the author converted the common law copyright into a federal copyright by complying with federal statute.[1] To protect against forfeiture of common law copyrights, judicial rules developed distinctions between general and limited publications. A general publication transferred the work to the public domain but a limited one did not.

The distinction between general and limited is therefore of great legal import notwithstanding that definitions of general publication are various: "General publication has been stated to be 'such a dissemination of the work of art itself among the public, as to justify the belief that it took place with the intention of rendering such work common property;' "[2] "[P]ublication occurs when by the consent of the copyright owner, the original or tangible copies of a work are sold, leased, loaned, given away, or otherwise made available to the general public, or when an authorized offer is made to dispose of the work in any such manner, even if a sale or other disposition does not in fact oc-

---

[Section 7:38]

[1]Estate of Martin Luther King, Jr., Inc. v. CBS, Inc., 194 F.3d 1211, 1999 (11th Cir. 1999) (citations omitted)(reversing and remanding summary judgment for defendant).

[2]American Tobacco Co. v. Werckmeister, 207 U.S. 284, 299–300, 28 S. Ct. 72, 52 L. Ed. 208 (1907) (display of painting in gallery did not constitute general publication placing work into public domain because of gallery's enforced policy of disallowing copying).

cur;"[3] general publication occurs at an exhibition coupled with concomitant-wide and unlimited reproduction and dissemination or "when a work is made available to members of the public at large without regard to their identity or what they intend to do with the work . . ."[4] A distinction between general and limited publication under the 1909 Act has been recently revisited.[5]

A limited publication has been defined as one that "communicates the contents of a [work] to a definitely selected group and for a limited purpose, and without the right of diffusion, reproduction, distribution, or sale . . . and which does not result in the loss of the author's common law copyright to his work."[6] To establish a limited publication, the creator in some jurisdictions had to make an express limitation or reservation regarding terms. Actions and omissions by copyright holders can divest a work of common law copyright protection. Under the 1909 law, copyright was presumed to transfer with the object unless creators reserved or limited their rights at the time of

---

[3]Kramer v. Newman, 749 F. Supp. 542, 549 (S.D. N.Y. 1990).

[4]LaCienega Music Co. v. ZZ Top, 53 F.3d 950 (9th Cir. 1995) (rejected so-called minority rule that sale of phonograph records does not constitute publication under Copyright Act of 1909); Estate of King v. CBS, Inc., 13 F. Supp. 2d 1347 (N.D. Ga. 1998), rev'd, 194 F.3d 1211 (11th Cir. 1999), *disapproving* King v. Mister Maestro, Inc., 224 F. Supp. 101 (S.D.N.Y. 1963) (oral delivery of Martin Luther King's "I Have a Dream" speech to vast audience found to be limited publication, even though press was given copies of speech for reprinting) (citations omitted) (copyright infringement action against television corporation for use of "I Have a Dream" 1963 speech in historical documentary aired in 1994), rev'd and remanded, Estate of Martin Luther King, Jr., Inc. v. CBS, Inc., 194 F.3d 1211, 1999 Copr.L.Dec. ¶ 27,983, 52 U.S.P.Q.2d 1656, 27 Media L. Rep. 2473, 13 Fla. L. Weekly Fed. C 121 (11th Cir. 1999).

[5]Estate of King v. CBS, Inc., 13 F. Supp. 2d 1347 (N.D. Ga. 1998), (public delivery of a famous civil rights speech, distributed in advance in written form to the press and in a newsletterm "constituted a general publication of the speech so as to place it in the public domain."), rev'd, 194 F.3d 1211 (11th Cir. 1999) (release to news media for contemporary coverage of newsworthy event is a limited publication).

[6]Estate of King v. CBS, Inc., 13 F. Supp. 2d 1347 (N.D. Ga. 1998), rev'd on other grounds, 194 F.3d 1211 (11th Cir. 1999) (citations omitted); Academy of Motion Picture Arts and Sciences v. Creative House Promotions, Inc., 944 F.2d 1446 (9th Cir. 1991).

transfer.[7] Although in some circumstances limited publication might be inferred, an exhibition to the general public without reservation of rights has been held a general publication.[8]

In *Pushman*,[9] the court considered reservation of rights when an artist sold his painting through an agent to a university; the artist sued when the university had it reproduced. The court held that "an artist must, if he wishes to retain or protect the reproduction right, make some reservation of that right when he sells the painting . . . an ordinary . . . bill of sale shows an intention to convey the artist's whole property in his picture. Here there is no substantial proof of contrary intent."

§ 7:39 Display of art as publication

Reservation of interest or limitation of display could effectively restrict publication of art as well as reproduction of it. In *American Tobacco Co. v. Werckmeister*,[1] an English artist transferred copyright in his painting to a

---

[7]Pushman v. New York Graphic Soc., Inc., 287 N.Y. 302, 39 N.E.2d 249 (1942); *accord,* Crimi v. Rutgers Presbyterian Church in City of New York, 194 Misc. 570, 89 N.Y.S.2d 813 (Sup 1949) ("when the artistic work [by Alfred Crimi] has been completed and delivered to the patron and accepted . . . there is no right whatever in and to the subject matter of the painting reserved to the artist in the absence of a specific agreement providing therefor."); Grandma Moses Properties v. This Week Magazine, 117 F. Supp. 348 (S.D. N.Y. 1953); *see also* Hughes v. Design Look Inc., 693 F. Supp. 1500 (S.D. N.Y. 1988) (under the 1909 Act, distribution of multiples to the public, museums, and galleries, without recitation of artist restrictions or limitations, constituted sale of the artist's rights in the images depicted). *See* Bib. II for information on artists.

[8]Estate of King v. CBS, Inc., 13 F. Supp. 2d 1347 (N.D. Ga. 1998), rev'd on other grounds, 194 F.3d 1211 (11th Cir. 1999) (no express, tacit or implied limitations given to press or others regarding speech, and no objections made to mass coverage).

[9]Pushman v. New York Graphic Soc., Inc., 287 N.Y. 302, 39 N.E.2d 249 (1942).

[Section 7:39]

[1]American Tobacco Co. v. Werckmeister, 207 U.S. 284, 28 S. Ct. 72, 52 L. Ed. 208 (1907); *see also* Crimi v. Rutgers Presbyterian Church in City of New York, 194 Misc. 570, 89 N.Y.S.2d 813 (Sup 1949); *accord,* Estate of King v. CBS, Inc., 13 F. Supp. 2d 1347 (N.D. Ga. 1998), (exhibition coupled with concomitant-wide and unlimited reproduction and

company, which made copies bearing copyright notice. The artist, who retained ownership, exhibited the painting without notice at the Royal Academy in London, where guards enforced the Academy policy of refusing permission to copy. The American Tobacco Company argued that the exhibition constituted publication, placing the image in the public domain, and making the plaintiff's copyright invalid. But the court concluded only a limited publication occurred since no copying was permitted. In dicta, the court stated that public exhibition of a painting or sculpture might constitute publication if it were situated where all could see it and freely copy it.

Publication was held to have occurred in *Letter Edged in Black Press*,[2] where Chicago's building commission installed in front of the civic center a monumental sculpture fabricated from a maquette given to the city by Pablo Picasso. The maquette had been publicly displayed without copyright notice or restrictions on copying. In 1968, some years after the maquette and monumental sculpture were displayed and exhibited, the Commission filed and received a certificate of copyright registration.

The plaintiff, a publisher who wanted to make copies of the sculpture, sought a declaratory judgment invalidating the defendant's copyright; he contended the display constituted general publication, injecting the art into the public domain. The court concluded that there had been an unrestricted display of the maquette, which on the facts had also been reproduced and distributed without notice in magazines, postcards, drawings, and photographs. Specifically, without reproduction restrictions the city had publicized the sculpture, exhibited the maquette at a

---

dissemination constitutes general publication) rev'd, 194 F.3d 1211 (11th Cir. 1999) (release to news media for contemporary coverage of newsworthy event is a limited publication).

[2]Letter Edged in Black Press, Inc. v. Public Bldg. Commission of Chicago, 320 F. Supp. 1303 (N.D. Ill. 1970) (". . . every citizen was free to copy the maquette for his own pleasure and camera permits were available to members of the public."); *accord,* Estate of King v. CBS, Inc., 13 F. Supp. 2d 1347 (N.D. Ga. 1998) ("lack of restriction on copying and Commission's free allowance of reproduction by the press" coupled with public exhibition constituted general publication and loss of common law copyright protection), rev'd, 194 F.3d 1211 (11th Cir. 1999) (release to news media for contemporary coverage of newsworthy event is a limited publication).

museum, provided the public with photographs, organized photo opportunities for the media, sold postcards featuring the sculpture, and distributed promotional materials reproducing the sculpture. No efforts were made to curtail copying or photographing by the public. Therefore, publication had occurred. Since the monumental work was considered a mere copy of the maquette, publication placed both artworks in the public domain.[3]

2. *1976 Act*

§ 7:40 Statute

Publication under the 1976 Act is defined as "the distribution of copies . . . of a work to the public by sale or other transfer of ownership, or by rental, lease, or lending. The offering to distribute copies to a group of persons for further distribution or for public display constitutes publication. A public . . . display of a work does not *of itself* constitute publication."[1]

§ 7:41 Exceptions for artworks

Section 102(a) of the Copyright Act states "copyright protection subsists . . . in original works of authorship . . . ." Artwork under the 1976 Act is purportedly subject to separate rules that would otherwise satisfy the requirements of publication under legislative history and copyright office circulars. A one-of-a-kind art object is not considered published when the single copy is sold or offered for sale through a dealer, a gallery, or an auction. A statue installed in a public place is not necessarily published. Multiples are published when the reproductions are publicly distributed or offered to a group for further distribution or public display.

---

[3]Letter Edged in Black Press, Inc. v. Public Bldg. Commission of Chicago, 320 F. Supp. 1303 (N.D. Ill. 1970). *But cf.* Alva Studios, Inc. v. Winninger, 177 F. Supp. 265 (S.D. N.Y. 1959) (scaled down sculpture constituted original work, not a mere copy).

[Section 7:40]

[1]17 U.S.C.A. § 101 (emphasis added).

§ 7:42 Delivery of art

In a case decided under the 1976 Act,[1] delivery of slides without notice to defendant who intended to, and did publish the works, did not constitute publication.[2] In Vane, a photographer delivered slides to the defendants for the limited purposes of reproduction in mailers. No copyright notice was affixed to the slides at the time of delivery, nor did the defendant use a copyright notice when the mailers were distributed. When the photographer discovered the slides were being used for television commercials without his authorization he sued for infringement.

The defendant contended that the photographer forfeited his copyright by failing to affix notice prior to publication, and dated the publication to the date of slide delivery to the defendant. The court found, as a matter of law, that delivery was not a publication. Alternatively, the court concluded that if plaintiff were deemed to have made publication when defendant reproduced them, the artist's copyright was valid because he registered within five years after publication under Section 405(a)(2) of title 17 of the U.S. Code.

§ 7:43 Exhibition catalogues

Where the artist exhibited his works at an exhibition for three months, the defendant allegedly infringed in the month following closing. The plaintiff had registered the exhibited works in the month thereafter. The court found, for purposes of the fair use defense, that the plaintiff's works were "published in the catalogue," without reference to any publication date.[1]

[Section 7:42]

[1]Vane v. The Fair, Inc., 676 F. Supp. 133 (E.D. Tex. 1987), judgment aff'd, 849 F.2d 186 (5th Cir. 1988).

[2]Vane v. The Fair, Inc., 676 F. Supp. 133 (E.D. Tex. 1987), judgment aff'd, 849 F.2d 186 (5th Cir. 1988) (publication of artist's slides occurs for the first time when defendant publishes them in mailers, not when artist delivers them without copyright notices to defendant).

[Section 7:43]

[1]Wojnarowicz v. American Family Ass'n, 745 F. Supp. 130 (S.D. N.Y. 1990) (an ambiguity exists as to whether the court's reference to

V. COPYRIGHT ELIGIBILITY

A. GENERAL

§ 7:44 Originality

Originality arises in different contexts in copyright litigation: qualifying for copyright protection;[1] a Section 102(b) defense to rebut the presumption of validity;[2] derivative work from copyrighted work;[3] or derivative work in the public domain.[4] Although the rote copier or reproducer of reproductions ordinarily is not an author of original work,[5] courts have made exceptions on various grounds.

1. *Reproducing Art in Different Media or Size*

§ 7:45 Process as basis for originality

Art, like law, involves substance and process. The pro-

---

published work included, or was meant to include, publication as a term of art. No evaluation of publication dates was made in the case because the court found that defendants' use was fair. But the query remains: If public display, which does not constitute publication, is seen as an interval, would catalogs documenting the display be viewed as transcending the interval, creating a publication interlude between opening and closing dates of exhibitions? Will it matter what type of catalog, i.e., museum catalog or dealer's catalog? Or will catalog publication be insufficient even when offerings are intended for sale under the art exceptions?).

[Section 7:44]

[1]Reader's Digest Ass'n, Inc. v. Conservative Digest, Inc., 821 F.2d 800 (D.C. Cir. 1987).

[2]Gentieu v. John Muller & Co., Inc., 712 F. Supp. 740 (W.D. Mo. 1989).

[3]Gracen v. Bradford Exchange, 698 F.2d 300 (7th Cir. 1983).

[4]Alfred Bell & Co. v. Catalda Fine Arts, 74 F. Supp. 973 (S.D. N.Y. 1947), decision supplemented, 75 U.S.P.Q. (BNA) 283, 1947 WL 3391 (S.D. N.Y. 1947), decision supplemented, 86 F. Supp. 399 (S.D. N.Y. 1949), judgment modified, 191 F.2d 99 (2d Cir. 1951).

[5]L. Batlin & Son, Inc. v. Snyder, 536 F.2d 486, 489–90 (2d Cir. 1976); Hearn v. Meyer, 664 F. Supp. 832, 835 (S.D. N.Y. 1987) (reproductions of illustrations in plaintiff's *The Annotated Wizard of Oz,* from reproductions of illustrations in *The Wonderful World of Oz* in the public domain not original as a matter of law); Bridgeman Art Library, Ltd. v. Corel Corp., 36 F. Supp. 2d 191 (S.D. N.Y. 1999) (transparencies from photographs of a painting in the public domain, *The Laughing Cavalier,* lacked originality as a matter of law).

cess of creating and fabricating art is not ordinarily considered separately in art law disputes, but a bifurcated analysis may be essential in copyright for originality.[1] Courts have considered whether the process of transformation converting a work from one medium to another will suffice for originality.[2] Reproduction of art in one medium to a different medium, conversion of a two-dimensional design to a three-dimensional one, reproducing illustrations using technological capabilities, or scaling reproductions to sizes different from the original have been considered under originality standards, as the following discussion indicates.[3] Were a pure antidiscrimination rule or nonconnoisseurship rule applied for artworks, the Section 102(b) defense would be greatly eroded.

§ 7:46 Intramedium transfer—Skill of artisan

In *Alfred Bell*,[1] the court found originality in mezzotint engravings copied from old master paintings that were in the public domain; the mezzotints were reproduced by engravers for a British print publisher. In the 1940s, this print producer and dealer copyrighted the eight mezzotint engravings and sued a color lithographer and dealer of lithographs who produced and sold color lithographs of the mezzotints. The British publisher won, based upon the skill of the artisan. Since the mezzotints were identical

---

[Section 7:45]

[1]And to analyze joint authorship. *See* §§ 7:54 to 7:57.

[2]Courts have consistently rejected as a defense the substituted medium, where the defendant contends his copying did not infringe upon plaintiff's copyright because the copied work is produced in a different medium; *see* Rogers v. Koons, 751 F. Supp. 474 (S.D. N.Y. 1990), amended on reargument, 777 F. Supp. 1 (S.D. N.Y. 1991) and judgment aff'd, 960 F.2d 301 (2d Cir. 1992); King Features Syndicate v. Fleischer, 299 F. 533 (C.C.A. 2d Cir. 1924).

[3]L. Batlin & Son, Inc. v. Snyder, 536 F.2d 486, 491 (2d Cir. 1976); Durham Industries, Inc. v. Tomy Corp., 630 F.2d 905, 911 (2d Cir. 1980); Hearn v. Meyer, 664 F. Supp. 832, 835 (S.D. N.Y. 1987).

[Section 7:46]

[1]Alfred Bell & Co. v. Catalda Fine Arts, 74 F. Supp. 973 (S.D. N.Y. 1947), decision supplemented, 75 U.S.P.Q. (BNA) 283, 1947 WL 3391 (S.D. N.Y. 1947), decision supplemented, 86 F. Supp. 399 (S.D. N.Y. 1949), judgment modified, 191 F.2d 99 (2d Cir. 1951).

copies of the old master paintings, the district court predicated its protection on the originality of the engravers' treatment and handling of process in the new medium, engraving, by transposing the old medium, oil on canvas, and described in comprehensive detail the engraving process used.[2]

> [T]he ideas for the subject are entirely those of the first artist, the painter. What is original with the engraver is the handling of the paintings in another medium . . . . The engraver is not trying to alter or improve on the old master. He is trying to express in another medium what the original artist expressed in oils . . . . It is only this treatment in another medium which is original [description of the engraving process].[3]

The Second Circuit affirmed infringement and in a footnote made a reference to the skill of the artisan:

> [A]n engraver is almost invariably a copyist, but although his work may infringe copyright in the original . . . his work may still be original in the sense that he has employed skill and judgment in its production [he] produces his effects by the management of light and shade . . . produced by different lines and dots.[4]

In *Batlin*,[5] the court denied copyright to the plaintiff, concluding that originality was not satisfied in a plastic Uncle Sam bank copied from a metal bank in the public domain. The plaintiff had reproduced the bank for distribution and sale in a smaller scale and with exterior changes. The Second Circuit held that some "substantial variation" from the underlying work was required: "The

---

[2]Alfred Bell & Co. v. Catalda Fine Arts, 74 F. Supp. 973 (S.D. N.Y. 1947), decision supplemented, 75 U.S.P.Q. (BNA) 283, 1947 WL 3391 (S.D. N.Y. 1947), decision supplemented, 86 F. Supp. 399 (S.D. N.Y. 1949), judgment modified, 191 F.2d 99 (2d Cir. 1951).

[3]Alfred Bell & Co. v. Catalda Fine Arts, 74 F. Supp. 973 at 975–76 (S.D. N.Y. 1947), decision supplemented, 75 U.S.P.Q. (BNA) 283, 1947 WL 3391 (S.D. N.Y. 1947), decision supplemented, 86 F. Supp. 399 (S.D. N.Y. 1949), judgment modified, 191 F.2d 99 (2d Cir. 1951).

[4]Alfred Bell & Co. v. Catalda Fine Arts, 74 F. Supp. 973 (S.D. N.Y. 1947), decision supplemented, 75 U.S.P.Q. (BNA) 283, 1947 WL 3391 (S.D. N.Y. 1947), decision supplemented, 86 F. Supp. 399 (S.D. N.Y. 1949), judgment modified, 191 F.2d 99 (2d Cir. 1951).

[5]L. Batlin & Son, Inc. v. Snyder, 536 F.2d 486, 489–90 (2d Cir. 1976).

requirement of originality [cannot] be satisfied simply by the demonstration of 'physical skill' or 'special training.' A considerably higher degree of skill is required, true artistic skill, to make the reproduction copyrightable."[6]

§ 7:47 Intramedium transfer—Litigation deterrent

In *Gracen*,[1] an artist claimed copyright in her painting of Dorothy from the "Wizard of Oz" that she had created using a photograph made during the film. The artist's Dorothy held Toto the dog in her left hand, instead of the waving arm in the photograph, and depicted a background of the yellow-brick road and rainbow, nowhere reproduced in the photograph. Common to both works was Dorothy's location in a cornfield and a basket on her right arm. The Seventh Circuit refused protection on the ground that the artist's contribution was too trivial, and that the uncopied background containing the yellow brick road was not original since it was part of the movie set. Judge Posner added a twist to the originality requirement of portent to the arts: Originality "is not to guide aesthetic judgments but to ensure a sufficiently gross difference between the underlying and the derivative work to avoid entangling subsequent artists depicting the underlying work in copyright problems."[2]

§ 7:48 Intermedium transfer—Process of design and illustration

In *Hearn v. Meyer*,[1] the plaintiff-artist applied the reasoning of Alfred Bell to his reproductions of illustrations by W.W. Denslow from the "Wonderful World of Oz" published in 1900 that Hearn published in his book. The defendants reproduced Hearn's illustrations in their own book, "A Treasury of the Great Children's Illustrators,"

---

[6]L. Batlin & Son, Inc. v. Snyder, 536 F.2d 486, 489–90 (2d Cir. 1976).

[Section 7:47]

[1]Gracen v. Bradford Exchange, 698 F.2d 300 (7th Cir. 1983).

[2]Gracen v. Bradford Exchange, 698 F.2d 300 at 303 (7th Cir. 1983).

[Section 7:48]

[1]Hearn v. Meyer, 664 F. Supp. 832, 835 (S.D. N.Y. 1987).

and Hearn sued. The defendants moved for summary judgment on the ground that, inter alia, Hearn's work was not original.

Hearn explained the technical and artistic processes and renderings that took more than one year: He (1) used pen and ink on acetate and hand drew every mark two or three times to reproduce a single color; (2) traced or redrew every color; (3) printed primary colors on top of each other to make secondary colors; (4) pulled proofs at each stage to check the register and density of color; and (5) constantly redrew and reapplied mylar. In terms comparable to the engraving process description in Alfred Bell, Hearn related the processes and steps used to recreate the Denslow illustrations. The court found that Alfred Bell did not apply since, there, originality was based upon a process of converting oil painting to engraving. Since Hearn did not use a process to transfer Denslow's illustrations "in another medium or form," Hearn's reproductions, as a matter of law, were not original.

In *Millworth Converting*,[2] the Second Circuit held that a three-dimensional embroidery effect on flat fabric, copied from a two-dimensional fabric design in the public domain, "required effort and skill" to meet the modest requirement of "not merely trivial" originality. In *Millworth*, the work was not converted from one medium to another or even one process to another. The *Hearn* court appears to have distinguished *Millworth* on the ground that the "effect" of dimensionality was achieved through copying, even though no change of medium or dimension occurred.

§ 7:49 Intermedium transfer—Process of scaling reproductions

In *Alva Studios*,[1] a copy of a museum sculpture that was one-third of the original size and in the public domain was entitled to copyright protection because of the artistic and technical skill the court found in the size reduction which preserved the "character" of the original. The

---

[2]Millworth Converting Corp. v. Slifka, 276 F.2d 443, 445 (2d Cir. 1960).

[Section 7:49]

[1]Alva Studios, Inc. v. Winninger, 177 F. Supp. 265 (S.D. N.Y. 1959).

plaintiff was a fabricator who, in conjunction with a museum, made replicas of museum owned sculptures for retail sale. The plaintiff copyrighted its reproduction of "Hand of God" by Auguste Rodin which is in the public domain, and then sued the defendant for infringement based upon its copying of plaintiff's replica. Originality was satisfied because the plaintiff's "accurate scale" required "great skill and originality . . . to produce a scale reduction of a great work with exactitude [and] also lies in the treatment of the rear side of the base [by] clos[ing] it [when] the original base is open." The court relied on expert testimony of museum officials, that had ordered the models and approved the replicas, which the court equated with a stamp of approval of originality on the replicas.

But, in *Batlin*, the Second Circuit did not find the special training, the "true artistic skill" for originality. There, the plaintiff scaled and reduced in size from eleven to nine inches plastic replicas of a metal Uncle Sam bank that was in the public domain.[2]

§ 7:50 Technological processes

Today, artists regularly utilize technology in both the process and substance of their works. Would a court today find skill of the artisan if specifications for the scaled replicas in *Alva Studios* were computer-generated? *Alva Studios* was discussed approvingly in *Hearn*; the sculpture fabricator was distinguished from Hearn in that "creativity [was required] to interpret, project and transpose the original Rodin work . . . and 'substantial differences' existed in appearance . . . and the accrediting of the reproduction by a [museum] expert." Hearn took advantage of contemporary technology available in the graphic arts to bring the artwork to market; perhaps the role of counsel for artists using new technologies is to educate the court. The creativity and skill of the artisan should be expanded to include the creativity and technique of the technology.

---

[2]L. Batlin & Son, Inc. v. Snyder, 536 F.2d 486, 491 (2d Cir. 1976); *but cf.*, M. Kramer Mfg. Co. v. Andrews, 783 F.2d 421 (4th Cir. 1986) (plaintiff not required to add true artistic skill to computer program).

§ 7:51 Creator's time and efforts

Time and effort invested by the creator is not enough to confer originality. Where an author of books on children's illustration sued another author and publisher about use of his "Wizard of Oz" illustrations, the plaintiff argued he had made a great investment of time (more than one year) and extensive artistic efforts to create the illustrations. The district court was not impressed with the time spent, and did not consider time a factor supporting originality, stating that "plaintiff's contribution is merely the reproduction of the original reproductions."[1]

2. *Functional Art*

§ 7:52 Generally

Chart 7-4: Sample of Functional Objects Protected Under Copyright

Object	Copyright	Case	Act
Abstract sculptural elliptical housings for outdoor lights	No	Esquire, Inc. v. Ringer, 591 F.2d 796 (9th Cir. 1978), cert. denied, 440 U.S. 908 (1979)	1909
figurative sculptural bases for table lamps	Yes	Mazer v. Stein, 347 U.S. 201 (1954)	1909
shoe sole	No	SOCA Industries, Inc. v. Famolare, Inc., 192 U.S.P.Q. 216 (S.D.N.Y. 1976)	1909
reproduction antique telephone housing pencil sharpener	Yes	Ted Arnold, Ltd. v. Silvercraft Col., 259 F. Supp. 733 (S.D.N.Y. 1966)	1909

[Section 7:51]

[1] Hearn v. Meyer, 664 F. Supp. 832, 839 (S.D. N.Y. 1987).

Object	Copyright	Case	Act
refrigerators, clocks, stoves, oil dispensers	No	Mazer v. Stein, 347 U.S.* 201 (1954).	1909
silver belt buckles	Yes	Kieselstein-Cord v. Accessories by Pearl, Inc., 632 F.2d 989 (2d Cir 1980)	1976
candlesticks	Yes	Esquire, Inc. v. Ringer, 591 F.2d 796 (9th Cir. 1978). [1]	1976
bicycle rack	No	Brandir International, Inc. v. Cascade Pacific Lumber Co., 834 F.2d 1142 (1987)	1976
mannequins	No	Carole Barnhart, Inc. v. Economy Cover Corp., 773 F.2d 411 (2d Cir. 1985), petition for certiorari filed (April 29, 1996)	1976

* Refers to such objects and their judicial disposition.

The Supreme Court ruled in *Mazer v. Stein*[1] that the patentability of utilitarian designs does not abrogate copyrightability of their artistic aspects that are otherwise eligible for registration as works of art, even if the object is commercially viable as a mass-produced utilitarian item. The Court considered statuettes of Balinese dancing figures created for reproduction as bases for table lamps; nothing in copyright law, concluded the Court, prohibited registration of artworks intended for commercial and

[Section 7:52]

[1]Mazer v. Stein, 347 U.S. 201, 74 S. Ct. 460, 98 L. Ed. 630 (1954).

industrial use.[2]

At the time *Mazer* was decided by the Court, Section 5(g) permitted registration of "models or designs for works of art." Section 202.10 of the Code of Federal Regulations, enacted after *Mazer* to affirm that commercial use will not disqualify an otherwise registrable work of art, interprets the Copyright Act of 1909:

> In order to be acceptable as a work of art, the work must embody some creative authorship in its delineation or form. The registrability of a work of art is not affected by the intention of the author as to the use of the work, the number of copies reproduced, or the fact that it appears on a textile . . . . The potential availability of protection under the design patent law will not affect registrability of a work of art.
>
> If the *sole* intrinsic function of an article is its utility, the fact that the article is unique and attractively shaped will not qualify it as a work of art. However, if the shape of a utilitarian article incorporates . . . artistic sculpture, carving or pictorial representation, which can be identified separately and are capable of existing independently as a work of art, such features will be eligible for registration.[3]

Copyright was amended by the 1976 Act to reclassify "works of art" from the 1909 Act as "pictorial, graphic, and sculptural works" (PGS) under Section 102.[4] Section 101 defines PGS by incorporating language from the Regulations under the 1909 Act:

> Such [PGS] works shall include works of artistic *craftsmanship insofar as their form but not their mechanical or utilitarian aspects are concerned;* the design of a useful article . . . shall be considered [PGS] only if, and only to the extent that, such design incorporates [PGS] features that *can be identified separately from, and are capable of existing inde-*

[2] Mazer v. Stein, 347 U.S. 201 at 218, 74 S. Ct. 460, 98 L. Ed. 630 (1954).

[3] 37 C.F.R. § 202.10(b) and 202.10(c). The italicized word "sole" was removed from the definition by 1976 Act § 101.

[4] 17 U.S.C.A. § 102(a)(5). H.R. Rep. No. 94-1476, at 53–59, 1976 U.S.C.C.A.N. 5659, 5666–73 (the definition of pictorial, graphic, and sculptural works has been clarified in an attempt to distinguish between protectible works of applied art and industrial designs not subject to protection.).

pendently of, the utilitarian aspects of the article.[5]

Section 101 defines "useful article" as follows: One "having an intrinsic utilitarian function that is not merely to portray the appearance of the article or to convey information. An article that is normally a part of a useful article is considered a 'useful article.'"

Congress acknowledged the problem of delineating between the aesthetic and the functional for purposes of copyright protection when revisions were made in 1976.[6] As explained in the legislative history of the 1976 revisions: "Unless the shape of [the functional item] contains some element that, physically or conceptually, can be identified as separable from the utilitarian aspects of [the item], the design would not be copyrighted under the bill."[7]

Copyright rules are stretched to rational limits when utilitarian rules and tests are applied to works of art. Artists merge form and function; their ability to link form and function in a single work of art is a matter of artistic resolution. If copyright is, as the commentators and judges have repeatedly stated, an economic impetus and reward for artistic exploitation, then functional art is the crucial area where copyright should be available to artists. Copyright demands separability of art and function. The utilitarian exclusion in copyright means most functional art is

---

[5]17 U.S.C.A. § 101 (italicized portions refer to text incorporated into this Section from former 37 C.F.R. § 202.10(a) and 202.10(c)).

[6]H.R. Rep. No. 94-1476, at 55, reprinted at 1976 U.S.C.C.A.N. 5659, 5668 ("although the shape of an industrial product may be aesthetically satisfying and valuable, the Committee's intention is not to offer it copyright protection . . . The test of separability and independence from 'the utilitarian aspects' does not depend upon the nature of the design . . . Even if the appearance of an article is determined by esthetic . . . considerations, only elements . . . which can be identified separately from the useful article . . . are copyrightable . . . And even if the three dimensional design contains some such element . . . copyright protection would extend only to that element, and would not cover the over-all configuration of the utilitarian article as such.").

[7]H.R. Rep. No. 94-1476, at 55, reprinted at 1976 U.S.C.C.A.N. 5659, 5668.

beyond copyright protection. *Bleistein*[8] instructs that the purpose for which the visual art is used should not affect its copyright protection.

Mazer v. Stein[9] is the signal case where the Supreme Court held that the sculptural base of an electric lamp was a work of art independent and separate from the utilitarian function of the lamp, and therefore copyrightable. This rule, already adopted by the Copyright Office in regulations, was codified in the Revised Copyright Act of 1976.[10] The rule authorizes copyright protection for the art portion of the utilitarian work if the art embellished or adorned the article "without losing its ability to exist independently as a work of art." That the artist's internal resolution of form and function could be served in one product was explicitly removed from copyright protection in the collective legislative view expressed in the House Report, which stated: "The test of separability and independent from the utilitarian aspect of the article does not depend upon nature of the design— . . . even if the appearance of an article is determined by aesthetic . . . considerations, only elements, if any, which can be identified separately . . . are copyrightable."[11]

In *Esquire*,[12] the Register of Copyright was compelled by the district court, under writ of mandamus, to issue a certificate of copyright for Esquire's abstract modern art form lighting fixture designs. The court held, "the forms of the articles here in dispute are clearly art," and concluded they were "entitled to same recognition afforded more traditional sculpture."

The Ninth Circuit, in *Barnhart, Inc. v. Economy Cover Corp.*,[13] affirmed a summary judgment of noncopyrightability of four life-sized mannequins of partial human torsos. The plaintiff contended they were artistic sculp-

---

[8]Bleistein v. Donaldson Lithographing Co., 188 U.S. 239, 23 S. Ct. 298, 47 L. Ed. 460 (1903).

[9]Mazer v. Stein, 347 U.S. 201, 74 S. Ct. 460, 98 L. Ed. 630 (1954).

[10]17 U.S.C.A. §§ 101 et seq.

[11]H.R. Rep. No. 1476 at 54, reprinted in 1976 U.S.C.C.A.N. 5667.

[12]Esquire, Inc. v. Ringer, 414 F. Supp. 939 (D.D.C. 1976), judgment rev'd, 591 F.2d 796 (D.C. Cir. 1978).

[13]Carol Barnhart Inc. v. Economy Cover Corp., 594 F. Supp. 364 (E.D. N.Y. 1984), judgment aff'd, 773 F.2d 411 (2d Cir. 1985).

tures that were infringed by the defendant based on the sculpted details and anatomical features that differentiated them from other mannequins. She provided, as evidence of artistic merit, art gallery invitations to exhibit them. The court applied the conceptual separability test, stating: "The question, then, is not whether the forms are original, the product of creativity or have aesthetic value, it is whether there are physically or conceptually separable works of art that can exist independently of the function . . . . What stands before the court are four aesthetically designed utilitarian display forms."[14]

In *Brandir*,[15] the Second Circuit reexamined functionality issues presented in the form of a bent tubing bicycle rack known as a ribbon rack, which was based on wire sculptures that the designer had created. Some years after displaying the sculpture in his home, he and a friend explored fabricating it as a bicycle rack, and the Brandir Ribbon Rack was promoted for national sale. When the plaintiffs discovered three years later that the defendant was selling a similar product, they attempted five registrations, all of which were denied, and brought suit for declaration of copyright ownership and infringement. Brandir claimed its rack was minimalist sculpture. Experts testified about minimalist art, known for simplification of forms devoid of ornamentation, and compared it to Richard Serra's sculpture, Tilted Arc. Notwithstanding its footnote reference to antidiscrimination cases,[16] the court found "form and function are inextricably intwined in the rack, its ultimate design being as much the result of utilitarian pressures as aesthetic choices." Declaring the rack not copyrightable, the court wrote: "The form of the rack is influenced in significant measure by utilitarian concerns and thus any aesthetic elements cannot be said to be conceptually separable from the utilitarian . . . . This is true even though the sculptures . . . may well have been—the issue of originality aside—copyrightable. [T]he designer has clearly adapted . . . aesthetic elements to ac-

[14]Carol Barnhart Inc. v. Economy Cover Corp., 594 F. Supp. 364 at 370–71 (E.D. N.Y. 1984), judgment aff'd, 773 F.2d 411 (2d Cir. 1985).

[15]Brandir Intern., Inc. v. Cascade Pacific Lumber Co., 834 F.2d 1142 (2d Cir. 1987).

[16]*See* § 7:5.

commodate . . . a utilitarian purpose."[17]

B. OWNERSHIP OF COPYRIGHT

§ 7:53 Joint authors: Interdependent and inseparable whole

Artwork can, and often does, have co-creators, producers of a collaborative effort conceived and created by two or more artists. Copyright recognizes multiple contributors to a single work, providing the work qualifies as a joint work, a term of art. "A 'joint work' is a work prepared by two or more authors with the intention that their contributions be merged into inseparable or interdependent parts of a unitary whole."[1] Authors of a joint work are co-owners of copyright,[2] but each author "must make an independently copyrightable contribution."[3] The contribution must be fixed, independent, and interdependent. An author, for purposes of joint works, is one who "actually create[s] the work . . . , a person who translates an idea into a fixed, tangible expression entitled to copyright protection."[4]

The proverbial "idea man" does not rise to the level of authorship for purposes of a joint work. If the contribution is classified as a mere idea, process, or concept under Section 102(b), the joint authorship claim can be disposed of as a matter of law by summary judgment.[5] Each joint author has an unrestricted right to use the copyright; a joint author may license the work.[6] A joint author, without joinder by co-authors, may sue for infringement of a joint

---

[17]834 F.2d at 1147.

[Section 7:53]

[1]17 U.S.C.A. § 101.

[2]17 U.S.C.A. § 201(a).

[3]Ashton-Tate Corp. v. Ross, 916 F.2d 516, 521 (9th Cir. 1990).

[4]Community for Creative Non-Violence v. Reid, 652 F. Supp. 1453 (D.D.C. 1987), judgment rev'd, 846 F.2d 1485 (D.C. Cir. 1988) and judgment aff'd, 490 U.S. 730, 109 S. Ct. 2166, 104 L. Ed. 2d 811 (1989).

[5]Community for Creative Non-Violence v. Reid, 490 U.S. 730, 109 S. Ct. 2166, 104 L. Ed. 2d 811 (1989); Johannsen v. Brown, 797 F. Supp. 835, 841 (D. Or. 1992).

[6]Leicester v. Warner Bros., 232 F.3d 1212 (C.D. Cal. May 29, 1998) (co-author may grant only nonexclusive license).

work, but the issue of liability of licensees remains unsettled.[7]

§ 7:54 Commissioning art, supervising preparation, and specifying suggestions as joint work

In *Community for Creative Non-Violence v. Reid*,[1] the defendant, artist James Reid, created a sculpture titled "Third World America" commissioned by the Creative Center for Non-Violence (CCNV), a nonprofit entity in Washington, D.C., dedicated to causes for the poor. The director of CCNV conceived of a modern day nativity scene depicting a homeless family and paid Reid costs to fabricate the sculpture. No written agreement existed. Both Reid and CCNV registered competing copyright claims. When Reid refused to return the sculpture after he regained possession to make minor repairs, CCNV sued Reid for declaration of copyright ownership, claiming co-authorship based upon the director's following contributions: he conceived the idea of a black homeless family in lieu of the Holy Family; he suggested using life-size figures and installing them huddled over a steam grate; he rejected the artist's sketches of a family carrying luggage and instructed substitution of a shopping cart; he controlled fabrication of the pedestal and installation for the sculpture; he titled the piece; and he wrote the legend for the statue, "and still there is no room at the inn." The Supreme Court[2] concluded some of those facts created an issue as to whether the sculpture constituted a joint work co-authored by the artist and CCNV, remanding the case to the district court for determination under the Section 101 "inseparable and interdependent definition" for joint

---

[7]Leicester v. Warner Bros., 232 F.3d 1212 (C.D. Cal. May 29, 1998) (failure of co-author to join suit did not prevent suit, but no infringement was found).

[Section 7:54]

[1]Community for Creative Non-Violence v. Reid, 652 F. Supp. 1453 (D.D.C. 1987), judgment rev'd, 846 F.2d 1485 (D.C. Cir. 1988) and judgment aff'd, 490 U.S. 730, 109 S. Ct. 2166, 104 L. Ed. 2d 811 (1989).

[2]Community for Creative Non-Violence v. Reid, 652 F. Supp. 1453 (D.D.C. 1987), judgment rev'd, 846 F.2d 1485 (D.C. Cir. 1988) and judgment aff'd, 490 U.S. 730 at 742, 109 S. Ct. 2166, 104 L. Ed. 2d 811 (1989).

work.

In *Johannsen v. Brown*,[3] an officer of a magazine named as a defendant in a copyright infringement action claimed he was a coauthor of "American Relix," a send-up of "American Gothic" by artist Grant Wood. The plaintiff-artist created a pencil and graphite illustration used on the cover of "Relix"—the defendants' magazine—substituting two skeletons for Grant's husband and wife farmers and a guitar for the farmer's pitchfork. "American Relix" was distributed on posters without the artist's authorization and without crediting him.

The defendant contended that he had suggested the concept of "American Relix" to the artist and did the following in terms of its preparation and execution: instructed the couple be represented as skeletons, specified the pitchfork substitution, titled the piece, and selected colors, hair styles, and jewelry. But the court found these contributions were not enough to constitute a joint work because the defendant had merely described how the work should look, but did not reduce his description into tangible expression. The court concluded that the defendant merely offered ideas or concepts to which copyright protection would not be extended under Section 102(b): "[Defendant's] conception . . . is insufficient as a matter of law, to make him a joint author . . . 'regardless of the form in which [they are] described, explained, illustrated, or embodied.' "[4]

In *Morita*,[5] the defendant-photographer claimed he could not have infringed the plaintiff's poster containing the defendant's photograph because he was a joint author, entitled to publish his photographs without the designer's permission. The photographer, who donated his services and received credit on the poster, took six photographs, each arranged and composed by Morita, who claimed the photographer was a mere technician. The court found material issues of fact to preclude summary judgment.

---

[3]Johannsen v. Brown, 797 F. Supp. 835 (D. Or. 1992).

[4]Johannsen v. Brown, 797 F. Supp. 835 at 842 (D. Or. 1992).

[5]Morita v. Omni Publications Intern., Ltd., 741 F. Supp. 1107 (S.D. N.Y. 1990), consent judgment approved, 760 F. Supp. 45 (S.D. N.Y. 1991).

§ 7:55 Creating concept and title

In *Johannsen v. Brown*,[1] the district court found that conceiving a work and titling it would not be enough for joint authorship. Citing *Ashton-Tate*[2] and *Whelan Associates*,[3] the court emphasized that the contribution must be "independently copyrightable." Similarly, in *Community for Creative Non-Violence v. Reid*,[4] where the commissioning plaintiff created the concept of a modern nativity scene, titled the sculpture, and wrote the legend for the base, the Court concluded those acts alone would not be enough to satisfy co-authorship, but it remanded for a finding of joint authorship based upon other contributions made by the plaintiff.

§ 7:56 Fabrication and installation

Where the commissioning party fabricates a sculpture pedestal and a mount in conjunction with installing and engineering the installation of the sculpture, such contributions may support a joint work.[1]

C. WORK MADE FOR HIRE

§ 7:57 Statutory basis

Ownership of copyright ordinarily vests in the author of the work. Copyright provides a notable exception for works

---

[Section 7:55]

[1]Johannsen v. Brown, 797 F. Supp. 835 (D. Or. 1992).

[2]Ashton-Tate Corp. v. Ross, 916 F.2d 516, 521 (9th Cir. 1990).

[3]Whelan Associates, Inc. v. Jaslow Dental Laboratory, Inc., 609 F. Supp. 1307 (E.D. Pa. 1985), judgment amended, 609 F. Supp. 1325, 91 A.L.R. Fed. 827 (E.D. Pa. 1985) and judgment aff'd, 797 F.2d 1222, 21 Fed. R. Evid. Serv. 571 (3d Cir. 1986).

[4]Community for Creative Non-Violence v. Reid, 490 U.S. 730, 109 S. Ct. 2166, 104 L. Ed. 2d 811 (1989).

[Section 7:56]

[1]Community for Creative Non-Violence v. Reid, 490 U.S. 730, 109 S. Ct. 2166, 104 L. Ed. 2d 811 (1989) (remanded to district court on issue of co-authorship).

made for hire, commonly called work for hire.[1] If the work is prepared for an employer or other person, that person may be the author by operation of law, and holds ownership of the copyright, unless there exists a signed written agreement to the contrary.[2]

17 U.S.C.A. § 201(b) recites: "In the case of a work made for hire, the employer or other person for whom the work was prepared is considered the author . . . , and, *unless the parties have expressly agreed otherwise in a written instrument signed by them,* owns all of the rights comprised in the copyright."[3] A "work made for hire" is defined at Section 101 as:

(1) a work prepared by an employee within the scope of his or her employment; or

(2) a work specially ordered or commissioned for use as a contribution to a collective work, as a part of a motion picture or other audiovisual work, as a translation, as a supplementary work, as a compilation, as an instructional text, . . . if the parties expressly agree in a written instrument signed by them that the work shall be considered a work made for hire.

The economic drive of copyright underwrites work for hire: "In the work for hire context, the law directs its incentives towards the person who initiates, funds and guides the creative activity, namely, the employer, ..."[4]

Section 201(b) work for hire issues can be avoided if the parties execute an express written agreement, as the emphasized language quoted above recites. Typically, no agreement exists with the visual artist, and work for hire claims do not arise until the deal sours, the artist sues, and the defendant asserts copyright ownership under work

---

[Section 7:57]

[1]This discussion addresses the 1976 Act unless otherwise specified.

[2]17 U.S.C.A. § 201(b).

[3]17 U.S.C.A. § 201(b) (Emphasis added).

[4]Estate of Hogarth v. Edgar Rice Burroughs, Inc., 62 U.S.P.Q.2d (BNA) 1301, 2002 WL 398696 (S.D. N.Y. 2002), judgment aff'd, 342 F.3d 149, 68 U.S.P.Q.2d (BNA) 1065 (2d Cir. 2003), cert. denied, 124 S. Ct. 1660, 158 L. Ed. 2d 357 (U.S. 2004) (artist's heirs copyright claims to artwork in Tarzan books declared works for hire under Act of 1909).

for hire.

Work for hire is a question of fact; however, appellate courts have considered the issue a mixed one of law and fact, reviewing de novo whether the facts, as a matter of law, support the work for hire findings.[5] Summary judgment may be appropriate where, as a matter of law, the creator is deemed an independent contractor.[6] No work for hire existed for the following: photographs and slides prepared at the defendant's request for advertising in its brochures;[7] sculpture commissioned by a nonprofit organization;[8] drawings prepared by artist in his studio that were voluntarily forwarded to defendant for possible use in its magazine;[9] and fabric designs using illustrations and designs created by a freelance artist under the directive of the textile company owner.[10]

---

[5]Playboy Enterprises, Inc. v. Dumas, 831 F. Supp. 295 (S.D. N.Y. 1993), opinion modified on reargument, 840 F. Supp. 256 (S.D. N.Y. 1993) and judgment aff'd in part, rev'd in part on other grounds, 53 F.3d 549, 132 A.L.R. Fed. 703 (2d Cir. 1995).

[6]Johannsen v. Brown, 797 F. Supp. 835 (D. Or. 1992) (a rational trier of fact could not find that artist was anything but an independent contractor); Langman Fabrics v. Samsung America, Inc., 967 F. Supp. 131 (S.D. N.Y. 1997), clarified in part, 997 F. Supp. 479 (S.D. N.Y. 1998) and rev'd, 160 F.3d 106 (2d Cir. 1998), opinion amended, 169 F.3d 782 (2d Cir. 1998) (summary judgment granted where fabric design involving "high degree of creative skill" was created by freelance artist as independent contractor).

[7]Vane v. The Fair, Inc., 676 F. Supp. 133 (E.D. Tex. 1987), judgment aff'd, 849 F.2d 186 (5th Cir. 1988) (not a work for hire because the defendant did not have right to supervise and direct, the artist selected and posed models, provided his own materials, and had full discretion for artistic result).

[8]Community for Creative Non-Violence v. Reid, 490 U.S. 730, 109 S. Ct. 2166, 104 L. Ed. 2d 811 (1989) (remanded on other grounds).

[9]Johannsen v. Brown, 797 F. Supp. 835 (D. Or. 1992).

[10]Langman Fabrics v. Samsung America, Inc., 967 F. Supp. 131 (S.D. N.Y. 1997), clarified in part, 997 F. Supp. 479 (S.D. N.Y. 1998) and rev'd, 160 F.3d 106 (2d Cir. 1998), opinion amended, 169 F.3d 782 (2d Cir. 1998) (while evidence existed that owner "exercised some control" over design details, the "extent of control" is not dispositive).

§ 7:58 Section 101(1)—Commissioning artworks

In *Community for Creative Non-Violence v. Reid,*[1] where no written agreement was executed, and copyright was not mentioned, the Community Center commissioned the sculptor Reid to create a modern nativity scene titled "Third World America" (TWA). CCNV agreed to pay $15,000 for costs and Reid agreed to donate his services. The issue was whether the artist's sculpture had been a work for hire, which became a major issue when a dispute arose as to ownership and control of the sculpture. Reid, unhappy with an exhibition itinerary CCNV planned for the work, took possession of the sculpture for minor repairs and kept it, refusing to return it, and registered the copyright. CCNV then registered a competing copyright, and sued Reid for return of the sculpture and determination of copyright ownership.[2]

The district court declared CCNV the copyright owner under work for hire; the appellate court reversed and remanded, holding that Reid owned the copyright because TWA was not a work for hire. The Supreme Court, granting certiorari to resolve conflicts among the Courts of Appeal, held that to determine if artwork constitutes work for hire under Section 101(1), a court should evaluate nonexhaustive guidelines under the common law of agency recited in the *Restatement Second of Agency,* with no one factor being determinative:

(1) hiring party's right to control manner and means by which product is made;
(2) skill required;
(3) source of tools;
(4) location of work;
(5) duration of relationship between the parties;
(6) whether the hiring party has the right to assign

[Section 7:58]

[1]Community for Creative Non-Violence v. Reid, 490 U.S. 730, 732, 109 S. Ct. 2166, 104 L. Ed. 2d 811 (1989), is not a Section 101(2) commission case because it does not fall within any of the section's enumerated categories: "sculpture is not one of the nine categories of works enumerated in § 101(2)."

[2]*See* §§ 7:73 to 7:80, for a discussion regarding the right of display.

additional projects to the hired party;
(7) the hired party's discretion over work hours;
(8) method of payment;
(9) the hired party's role in hiring and paying assistants;
(10) whether the work is part of the regular business of hiring party;
(11) whether the hiring party is in business;
(12) payment of employee benefits;
(13) tax treatment of hired party.[3]

Based on the facts of the case, the Supreme Court affirmed the Court of Appeals decision that Reid was an independent contractor, "a sculptor, a skilled occupation." He supplied his own tools, worked in his own studio in a different city from CCNV making daily supervision impractical, worked for only two months, maintained freedom to decide when and how long to work, hired and fired his own assistants, and was paid a sum dependent on completion of a specific job. CCNV was not in the regular business of making art, did not pay taxes, or provide employee benefits or contribute to other worker funds.

Artists appear to have an additional judicial dispensation as independent contractors because of their creativity and skills, and the proficiency required to create artwork.[4] Supervising creation or preparation of artwork does not

---

[3]Some courts use only some factors, and weight others. *See, e.g.,* Langman Fabrics v. Samsung America, Inc., 967 F. Supp. 131 (S.D. N.Y. 1997), clarified in part, 997 F. Supp. 479 (S.D. N.Y. 1998) and rev'd, 160 F.3d 106 (2d Cir. 1998), opinion amended, 169 F.3d 782 (2d Cir. 1998) (Second Circuit has adopted five factors and a "weighted approach").

[4]Johannsen v. Brown, 797 F. Supp. 835, 840 (D. Or. 1992) (artists deemed independent contractors where they worked from their own studios with their own tools and hired their own assistants, had no duty to produce artwork, and no payroll or social security taxes, unemployment insurance, worker's compensation, or other employee benefits were paid or accrued on their behalf); Community for Creative Non-Violence v. Reid, 490 U.S. 730, 735, 109 S. Ct. 2166, 104 L. Ed. 2d 811 (1989) (Supreme Court rejected contention that use of word "employ" or "employment" in contract created employee relationship as a matter of law); Carter v. Helmsley-Spear, Inc., 71 F.3d 77, 138 A.L.R. Fed. 711 (2d Cir. 1995) (artists commissioned to design, create, and install sculpture and other installations in a commercial lobby had

bring it under the work for hire doctrine.[5] The issue has been examined for commercial photographers who prepare slides for corporate advertising. In *Vane*,[6] a photographer delivered slides to the defendants for the limited purpose of reproduction in mailers. When they made unauthorized use for television ads, the plaintiff sued. The defendant argued that the slide photography was work for hire, and therefore it was entitled to the copyright. The defendant had been present during the photo sessions and made suggestions, but it did not supervise and it did not have a contractual right of supervision. Finding no work for hire, the court highlighted the artist's work: the photographer (1) selected and posed the models, (2) provided his own materials, and (3) had full discretion to implement the defendant's desired effect.

Work for hire in the visual arts context was reexamined in *Carter v. Helmsley-Spear, Inc.*,[7] where three artists were commissioned to design, create, and install sculpture and other installations in the lobby of a commercial building in Queens, New York. The artists were paid weekly, based upon a 40-hour week, and by contract agreed that they would only undertake other work beyond the forty-hour basis if it would not interfere with their services to the defendants. The defendants paid payroll and social security taxes, provided employee benefits such as life, health, and liability insurance and paid vacations and contributed to unemployment insurance and workers' compensation funds, and two artists claimed unemployment benefits naming the defendants as former employers. The defen-

---

artistic control and freedom, a "central factor" in court's inquiry into "manner and means by which the product is accomplished"); Langman Fabrics v. Samsung America, Inc., 967 F. Supp. 131 (S.D. N.Y. 1997), clarified in part, 997 F. Supp. 479 (S.D. N.Y. 1998) and rev'd, 160 F.3d 106 (2d Cir. 1998), opinion amended, 169 F.3d 782 (2d Cir. 1998) (artist who selected brushes, pencils, other art supplies, and the art supplier might not be "skilled [like] Picasso" but was "skilled in the sense that Reid, the sculptor in the CCNV case, was skilled.") (citations omitted).

[5]Community for Creative Non-Violence v. Reid, 490 U.S. 730, 109 S. Ct. 2166, 104 L. Ed. 2d 811 (1989).

[6]Vane v. The Fair, Inc., 676 F. Supp. 133 (E.D. Tex. 1987), judgment aff'd, 849 F.2d 186 (5th Cir. 1988).

[7]Carter v. Helmsley-Spear, Inc., 71 F.3d 77, 138 A.L.R. Fed. 711 (2d Cir. 1995).

dants also supplied the artists with supplies, and controlled their ability to hire paid assistants. Reversing the district court's decision, the Second Circuit held, on balancing the Reid factors, that the artists were employees, and the sculptures were "work for hire as a matter of law."[8]

§ 7:59 Section 101(2)—Specially ordered or commissioned

In *Playboy Enterprises v. Dumas*,[1] the Second Circuit evaluated whether a series of artworks used by a magazine, which the parties agreed was a "collective work" for purposes of Section 101(2), were: (1) "specially ordered or commissioned" and (2) whether the parties expressly agreed in a signed writing as to each work that that work was to be considered a work for hire.

The Supreme Court has interpreted "specially ordered or commissioned" as denoting a commercial relationship in which a hiring party pays an independent contractor for work.[2] The Second Circuit has expanded the variables to resurrect a test used in some jurisdictions under the 1909 Act, the "instance and expense test."[3] Artistic control may not be determinative of whether or not a special order or commission has occurred.[4]

---

[8]Carter v. Helmsley-Spear, Inc., 71 F.3d 77, 138 A.L.R. Fed. 711 (2d Cir. 1995) (lower court rejected contention that use of word "employ" or "employment" in the contracts created employee relationship or was of legal significance).

[Section 7:59]

[1]Playboy Enterprises, Inc. v. Dumas, 53 F.3d 549, 132 A.L.R. Fed. 703 (2d Cir. 1995).

[2]Community for Creative Non-Violence v. Reid, 490 U.S. 730, 742–43, 109 S. Ct. 2166, 104 L. Ed. 2d 811 (1989).

[3]Playboy Enterprises, Inc. v. Dumas, 53 F.3d 549, 132 A.L.R. Fed. 703 (2d Cir. 1995) (remanded for further finding on facts as to whether artist who regularly submitted works to magazine depicting nude women was working at "instance" of publisher after a period of years when, without direction, he continued to submit artwork of female nudes).

[4]Playboy Enterprises, Inc. v. Dumas, 53 F.3d 549, 132 A.L.R. Fed. 703 (2d Cir. 1995).

§ 7:60 Section 101(2)—Writing requirement—Timeliness

Section 101(2) requires a writing executed by each party, or its agent, but does not specify when that writing should occur. Some authority exists for the proposition that the writing must precede creation of the work.[1] The arguments in favor of precreation are congressional goals of predictability for use and identifying authorship, thus avoiding one "author" before the writing and one after. The Second Circuit has concluded that the parties must agree before creation that a work will be considered a work for hire, but that the writing can be executed after the work is created, "if the writing confirms a prior agreement, either explicit or implicit, made before the creation of the work."[2]

This issue seems far from resolved generally, and an open field for art specifically. Lawyers are advised to examine the law of the applicable jurisdiction.

§ 7:61 Section 101(2)—Writing requirement—Content

What language must a Section 101(2) writing recite to satisfy the statutory requirement that the work shall be a work for hire? The verbiage of legends and endorsement stamps on the back of checks paid to the artist or its agent were examined in some detail by the Second Circuit in *Playboy Enterprises v. Dumas*.[1] One legend recited the phrase ". . . payee acknowledges payment in full for services rendered on a work-made-for-hire basis in connection with the work named on the face of this check, and confirms ownership by [name] of all right, title and inter-

---

[Section 7:60]

[1] H.R. Rep. No. 51-374, 89th Cong., 1st Sess., Pt. 5, 1964 Revision Bill w/Discussion and Comments, at 145 (1965); Schiller & Schmidt, Inc. v. Nordisco Corp., 969 F.2d 410 (7th Cir. 1992).

[2] Playboy Enterprises, Inc. v. Dumas, 53 F.3d 549, 132 A.L.R. Fed. 703 (2d Cir. 1995).

[Section 7:61]

[1] Playboy Enterprises, Inc. v. Dumas, 831 F. Supp. 295 (S.D. N.Y. 1993), opinion modified on reargument, 840 F. Supp. 256 (S.D. N.Y. 1993) and judgment aff'd in part, rev'd in part, 53 F.3d 549, 132 A.L.R. Fed. 703 (2d Cir. 1995).

est . . . , including all rights of copyright, in and to the work."[2] This was held to pass technical muster as a writing, but still insufficient, without more, to satisfy Section 101(2). A determination still had to be made regarding whether the parties intended *before the creation of the work* that a work for hire was contemplated.[3]

In addition, the intent of the party seeking a finding of work for hire is not dispositive, even where it comports with regular business practices of that party. Nor has custom and usage in an industry been persuasive. Thus, even where checks with endorsements reciting work-for-hire terms were negotiated and deposited by an artist after a period of years during which he submitted artwork under work for hire to a magazine publisher, the first check bearing the endorsement was not sufficient evidence of the parties' intent because the court could not infer "pre-creation consent."[4] Further, where the artist's authorized agents deposited checks with such legends after the artist had similarly done so, negotiation and use of funds was not found necessarily to infer precreation consent of the artist, although the artist had made such deposits.[5]

A legend that assigned "all right, title, and interest" to a magazine in a specified artwork, but omitted work-for-hire language, was inadequate to create a work for hire.[6]

Crucial is the intent of the parties themselves; when one considers that the artist's intent is often not easily

---

[2]Playboy Enterprises, Inc. v. Dumas, 831 F. Supp. 295 (S.D. N.Y. 1993), opinion modified on reargument, 840 F. Supp. 256 (S.D. N.Y. 1993) and judgment aff'd in part, rev'd in part, 53 F.3d 549, 132 A.L.R. Fed. 703 (2d Cir. 1995).

[3]Playboy Enterprises, Inc. v. Dumas, 831 F. Supp. 295 (S.D. N.Y. 1993), opinion modified on reargument, 840 F. Supp. 256 (S.D. N.Y. 1993) and judgment aff'd in part, rev'd in part, 53 F.3d 549, 132 A.L.R. Fed. 703 (2d Cir. 1995) (remanded to district court for further findings).

[4]Playboy Enterprises, Inc. v. Dumas, 831 F. Supp. 295 (S.D. N.Y. 1993), opinion modified on reargument, 840 F. Supp. 256 (S.D. N.Y. 1993) and judgment aff'd in part, rev'd in part, 53 F.3d 549, 132 A.L.R. Fed. 703 (2d Cir. 1995).

[5]Playboy Enterprises, Inc. v. Dumas, 831 F. Supp. 295 (S.D. N.Y. 1993), opinion modified on reargument, 840 F. Supp. 256 (S.D. N.Y. 1993) and judgment aff'd in part, rev'd in part, 53 F.3d 549, 132 A.L.R. Fed. 703 (2d Cir. 1995).

[6]Playboy Enterprises, Inc. v. Dumas, 831 F. Supp. 295 (S.D. N.Y. 1993), opinion modified on reargument, 840 F. Supp. 256 (S.D. N.Y.

resurrected at the time of the dispute because when the artist is dead, and the trail of evidence is paltry,[7] then defining intent and describing it sufficiently so that it will satisfy evidentiary concerns becomes increasingly important. When assignees and surviving spouses are added, nonspecific intent can easily become a malleable concept.

§ 7:62 Advertising

The critical issue after the Revised Copyright Act of 1976 is not whether the work is an advertisement, but whether or not it is a work for hire. In the absence of an agreement, the fact that work is an advertisement or used for an advertisement does not mean it is work for hire.

D. TRANSFERRING OWNERSHIP, ASSIGNMENTS

1. *Writing Requirement*

§ 7:63 Generally

Section 204(a) provides "A transfer of copyright ownership, other than by operation of law, is not valid unless an instrument of conveyance, or a note or memorandum of the transfer, is in writing and signed by the owner of the rights conveyed or such owner's duly authorized agent."[1]

A document transferring ownership of copyright may be recorded in the Copyright Office if the document bears the actual signature of the person who executed it, or if it is joined with a sworn or official certification that it is a true copy of the original signed document.[2] Courts decide as a matter of law whether the documentation of transfer satisfies the statute.

The Section 204 requirement is based on the policy that reducing words to writing "forces parties to clarify their thinking and consider problems that potentially could

---

1993) and judgment aff'd in part, rev'd in part, 53 F.3d 549, 132 A.L.R. Fed. 703 (2d Cir. 1995).

[7] *See* Ch 9 §§ 9:58 to 9:71.

[Section 7:63]

[1] 17 U.S.C.A. § 204(a).

[2] 17 U.S.C.A. § 205(a).

arise."[3] The writing requirement has been satisfied in various ways: by a valid written contract;[4] through an oral contract or license followed by a written memorialization;[5] or by a check legend, notation or endorsement, or other legend or endorsement agreement.[6]

The transfer is not valid where the precise understanding of the owner and the transferee regarding the copyright transfer cannot be adduced by the writing. Writings purporting to transfer must explicitly recite transfer of the particular copyright interest(s) conveyed and the scope and extent of use, or will be vulnerable to interpretation that the interests transferred relate to the object, not to the copyright or to one-time use.[7] Parol evidence may be admissible "to help guide the court" where the writing is not clear.[8]

Writings that were held sufficient to satisfy Section

---

[3]Effects Associates, Inc. v. Cohen, 908 F.2d 555 (9th Cir. 1990).

[4]*See* Dean v. Burrows, 732 F. Supp. 816 (E.D. Tenn. 1989).

[5]*See* Effects Associates, Inc. v. Cohen, 908 F.2d 555 (9th Cir. 1990); Playboy Enterprises, Inc. v. Dumas, 831 F. Supp. 295 (S.D. N.Y. 1993), opinion modified on reargument, 840 F. Supp. 256 (S.D. N.Y. 1993) and judgment aff'd in part, rev'd in part, 53 F.3d 549, 132 A.L.R. Fed. 703 (2d Cir. 1995); Kenbrooke Fabrics, Inc. v. Soho Fashions, Inc., 690 F. Supp. 298 (S.D. N.Y. 1988).

[6]Franklin Mint Corp. v. National Wildlife Art Exchange, Inc., 195 U.S.P.Q. (BNA) 31, 1977 WL 22706 (E.D. Pa. 1977), judgment aff'd, 575 F.2d 62 (3d Cir. 1978) (artist's claim that he had reserved copyright for himself rejected where the legend recited: "For . . . painting . . . including all rights-reproduction, etc."); *but cf.* Playboy Enterprises, Inc. v. Dumas, 831 F. Supp. 295 (S.D. N.Y. 1993), opinion modified on reargument, 840 F. Supp. 256 (S.D. N.Y. 1993) and judgment aff'd in part, rev'd in part, 53 F.3d 549, 132 A.L.R. Fed. 703 (2d Cir. 1995).

[7]Kenbrooke Fabrics, Inc. v. Soho Fashions, Inc., 690 F. Supp. 298 (S.D. N.Y. 1988) (letter transferring all ownership interest in screens for fabric reproduction held not to transfer the copyright interest, even though the screens had only marginal value without the rights of reproduction of the patterns on the screens); Playboy Enterprises, Inc. v. Dumas, 831 F. Supp. 295 (S.D. N.Y. 1993), opinion modified on reargument, 840 F. Supp. 256 (S.D. N.Y. 1993) and judgment aff'd in part, rev'd in part, 53 F.3d 549, 132 A.L.R. Fed. 703 (2d Cir. 1995).

[8]Playboy Enterprises, Inc. v. Dumas, 831 F. Supp. 295 (S.D. N.Y. 1993), opinion modified on reargument, 840 F. Supp. 256 (S.D. N.Y. 1993) and judgment aff'd in part, rev'd in part on other grounds, 53 F.3d 549, 132 A.L.R. Fed. 703 (2d Cir. 1995).

204(a) were: a pro forma, one-line writing;[9] and a check notation for pig sculpture "mold designs and molds," where a written transfer of the copyright agreement was prepared in the same month as the check and was recorded in the Copyright Office.[10] Writings that were held insufficient to satisfy Section 204(a) were: a transfer by legend check endorsement reciting "payee acknowledges payment in full for the assignment . . . of all right, title and interest" in a work;[11] and a transfer by bill of sale of "bargained, sold, granted and conveyed . . . all my right title and interest in and to a certain negative of motion picture film dealing with animal study in Africa . . . , and also one positive of the same negative film."[12]

§ 7:64 Undocumented transfers

Courts have been confronted with ownership disputes in the copyright context involving undocumented transfers of valuable art in the possession of the putative owner for more than incidental periods of time. One case involved original Disney artwork and animation celluloids (cels) given to a former employee. When the employee kept them for thirty years, the art was deemed a gift.[1] Another case concerned original sculpture by John Chamberlain created

---

[9]Effects Associates, Inc. v. Cohen, 908 F.2d 555 (9th Cir. 1990) (in case where no writing was offered, the court stated the transfer "doesn't have to be the Magna Carta; a one-line pro forma statement will do.").

[10]Dean v. Burrows, 732 F. Supp. 816 (E.D. Tenn. 1989).

[11]Playboy Enterprises, Inc. v. Dumas, 831 F. Supp. 295 (S.D. N.Y. 1993), opinion modified on reargument, 840 F. Supp. 256 (S.D. N.Y. 1993) and judgment aff'd in part, rev'd in part on other grounds, 53 F.3d 549, 132 A.L.R. Fed. 703 (2d Cir. 1995) (since transfer of the object does not transfer the copyright, the legend did not reveal what the parties intended as to the transfer of copyright).

[12]Davenport Quigley Expedition v. Century Productions, 18 F. Supp. 974 (S.D. N.Y. 1937).

[Section 7:64]

[1]Walt Disney Productions v. Basmajian, 600 F. Supp. 439 (S.D. N.Y. 1984) (the defendant "has established that the [art] collection now in his possession was a gift from Disney. His claim that he was given this material by persons at Disney . . . has not been rebutted. . . . As lawful possessor . . . [he] has right to consign it to Christie's," and under 17 U.S.C.A. § 109(a), the first sale doctrine, plaintiff had the right to sell the collection without infringing Disney's copyright).

for and installed in a new restaurant in which the artist's son was a partner. The sculpture was displayed for two or three years and thereafter removed, the artist contending it was merely on loan.[2]

§ 7:65 Writings under state law

Artists have attempted to argue in cases that did not involve a copyright ownership dispute that state statutes mimicking many copyright provisions create a higher writing standard for transfer than that established by Section 204. The argument was that those state law requirements created statutes of fraud for artworks, and, in the absence of a writing satisfying the stricter state statute, the artwork itself had not been transferred.[1]

2. *First Sale Doctrine*

§ 7:66 Transfers constituting "sale"

The exclusive right "to distribute copies . . . by sale or other transfer of ownership" set forth in § 106(3) is limited by the judicial "first sale" doctrine, codified by statute. The first sale doctrine states that where the copyright owner sells, transfers, or gives a particular copy of a work, the owner is divested of the exclusive right in that copy;[1] the right to resell or retransfer passes to the transferee.[2] Section 109(a) provides that "the owner of a particular copy . . . or any person authorized by such owner, is entitled,

---

[2]Chamberlain v. Cocola Associates, 958 F.2d 282 (9th Cir. 1992) (the right to display did not confer property rights in the sculpture, and on the record it could not be determined whether a loan or sale had occurred).

[Section 7:65]

[1]Chamberlain v. Cocola Associates, 958 F.2d 282 (9th Cir. 1992).

[Section 7:66]

[1]17 U.S.C.A. § 109.

[2]17 U.S.C.A. § 109(a). The first sale doctrine does not give the transferee the right to prepare derivative works; *see also* Quality King Distributors, Inc. v. L'anza Research Intern., Inc., 523 U.S. 135, 118 S. Ct. 1125, 140, 140 L. Ed. 2d 254 (1998) (first sale doctrine applies to imported copies in action brought by California manufacturer of hair products against distributor who reimported them into the United States and sold them to unauthorized retailers).

without the authority of the copyright owner, to sell or otherwise dispose of the possession of that copy."

What else constitutes an eligible transfer for purposes of the first sale doctrine is a matter of law for the courts. Transfer of title clearly triggers the first sale doctrine. Proof of ownership through title is particularly slippery for art, where documented transactions are not the norm, particularly for putative "sales" that occur outside established trade, i.e., dealers, auctioneers, and many gifts and loans.[3] Courts have examined what other types of art transfers will qualify to trigger the first sale doctrine.

§ 7:67 Undocumented gifts

In *Walt Disney v. Basmajian*,[1] where Disney sought to enjoin a former employee in the animation department from auctioning Disney celluloids (cels) he had been given when Disney managers were ready to discard them, the court, considering the "arrangement at issue,"[2] found a first sale had occurred. "Basmajian has established that the collection now in his possession was a gift from Disney . . . . As lawful possessor [he] has right to consign it to Christie's for auction."

§ 7:68 Undocumented loans, undocumented partnership transfers

The artist who does not document a loan or a business interest transfer operates at his peril. In *Chamberlain v. Cocola Associates*,[1] where the first sale doctrine was implicitly at issue, the court was confronted with an undocumented transfer of a large sculpture from the artist to the defendant-restaurant, and a documented partnership

---

[3]*See* Mac'Avoy v. The Smithsonian Inst., 757 F. Supp. 60 (D.D.C. 1991) (determining whether artwork was a gift or loan to the National Gallery of Art).

[Section 7:67]

[1]Walt Disney Productions v. Basmajian, 600 F. Supp. 439 (S.D. N.Y. 1984).

[2]Walt Disney Productions v. Basmajian, 600 F. Supp. 439 at 442 (S.D. N.Y. 1984).

[Section 7:68]

[1]Chamberlain v. Cocola Associates, 958 F.2d 282 (9th Cir. 1992).

agreement that allocated shares to the artist's son. The partners in the restaurant (which was named after the painting) contended the son's contribution to the partnership was the artwork and his services. The Ninth Circuit held that triable issues of fact existed on whether transfer of ownership or a loan had occurred.

§ 7:69 Preemption—Copyright

Section 301 provides in part:

> (a) On or after January 1, 1978, all legal or equitable rights that are equivalent to any of the exclusive rights within the general scope of copyright as specified by section 106 in works of authorship that are fixed in a tangible medium of expression and come within the subject matter of copyright as specified by sections 102 and 103, whether created before or after that date and whether published or unpublished, are governed exclusively by this title. Thereafter, no person is entitled to any such right or equivalent right in any such work under the common law or statutes of any State.
>
> (b) Nothing in this title annuls or limits any rights or remedies under the common law or statutes of any State with respect to—
>
> (1) subject matter that does not come within the subject matter of copyright as specified by sections 102 and 103, including works of authorship not fixed in any tangible medium of expression; or
>
> (2) any cause of action arising from undertakings commenced before January 1, 1978;
>
> (3) activities violating legal or equitable rights that are not equivalent to any of the exclusive rights within the general scope of copyright as specified by section 106;
>
> (4) State and local landmarks, historic preservation, zoning, or building codes, relating to architectural works protected under section 102(a)(8).

The Copyright Act is intended to govern the exclusive rights specified in Section 106. Any state law rights that are "equivalent" to the exclusive rights are preempted by federal copyright. The state rights must be qualitatively different than those under Section 106. Equivalency is evaluated on a case-by-case basis through examination of the underlying acts and conduct that form the basis of the claim.

VI. COPYRIGHT INFRINGEMENT

A. IN GENERAL

§ 7:70 Exclusive rights under Section 106

Section 106 provides the owner of copyright "the exclusive rights to do and to authorize any of the following:

> 1. to reproduce the copyrighted work in copies . . .
>
> 2. to prepare derivative works based upon the copyrighted work;
>
> 3. to distribute copies . . . of the copyrighted work to the public by sale or other transfer of ownership . . . .
>
> . . . .
>
> 5. in the case of . . . [PGS works,] . . . to display the copyrighted work publicly."[1]

An infringement of copyright is based upon violation of one or more of these enumerated exclusive rights, providing that the work in question is within the subject matter of copyright, and other factors discussed throughout this chapter, are satisfied.

§ 7:71 The infringement claim

To prevail on a copyright infringement claim, plaintiff must establish ownership of a valid registered copyright in the protected work and violation(s) of any one or more of the exclusive rights under Section 106. Section 501 states: "Anyone who violates any of the exclusive rights of the copyright owner as provided by Sections 106 through 118 or of the author as provided in section 106A . . . is an infringer of the copyright or rights of the author."[1] Plaintiffs must show not unlawful "copying" but unlawful use within the meaning of the exclusive right allegedly

---

[Section 7:70]

[1] 17 U.S.C.A. § 106.

[Section 7:71]

[1] 17 U.S.C.A. § 501(a).

infringed.[2]

Galleries and dealers that promote and market the infringing artworks may themselves be liable as direct infringers even if they had no knowledge of infringement. Where a gallery invoiced sales of infringing artworks and received sales commissions, the gallery was held a direct infringer.[3] Museums, artist foundations and other entities may be liable.[4]

B. COPIES

§ 7:72 Generally

What is a copy? Section 101 describes "copies" as "material objects . . . in which a work is fixed by any method now known or later developed, and from which the work can be perceived, reproduced, or otherwise communicated, either directly or with the aid of a machine or device. The term 'copies' includes the material object, . . . in which the work is first fixed."[1] Case law on use of copyrighted visual work in other visual work has been limited. Before the digital age, analysis focused on whether an artwork on television or videography constituted a "copy."[2] The

---

[2]17 U.S.C.A. § 106(3), (5). The Greenwich Workshop, Inc. v. Timber Creations, Inc., 932 F. Supp. 1210 (C.D. Cal. 1996) ("Copying refers to the infringement of any of the copyright owner's five exclusive rights . . ."); Country Kids 'N City Slicks, Inc. v. Sheen, 77 F.3d 1280 (10th Cir. 1996) ("'Copying' is regularly used as a shorthand to refer to the infringement of a copyright holder's exclusive rights under a copyright." (citations omitted)).

[3]Rogers v. Koons, 777 F. Supp. 1 (S.D. N.Y. 1991), modifying 751 F. Supp. 474, 19 Media L. Rep. (BNA) 1586, 20 U.S.P.Q.2d (BNA) 1054 (S.D. N.Y. 1990) (advertising and display of infringing sculpture contributed to infringing conduct).

[4]Dauman v. Andy Warhol Foundation for Visual Arts, Inc., 43 U.S.P.Q.2d (BNA) 1221, 1997 WL 337488 (S.D. N.Y. 1997) (photograph of Jacqueline Kennedy published in Life magazine allegedly appropriated in 45 Warhol works and reproduced by museum in calendars and catalogues.).

[Section 7:72]

[1]17 U.S.C.A. § 101.

[2]Kelly v. Arriba Soft Corp., 280 F.3d 934, 61 U.S.P.Q.2d (BNA) 1564 (9th Cir. 2002), opinion withdrawn and superseded on denial of reh'g, 336 F.3d 811, 67 U.S.P.Q.2d (BNA) 1297 (9th Cir. 2003)(reversed on

Internet presents the conceptual issue of the cyber-copy.[3] Scanning copyrighted material into a computer, however briefly it resides in RAM, has been held to constitute infringing copying.[4]

§ 7:73 Direct evidence

Copying may be proven by either: (1) direct evidence of copying, or (2) by showing defendant (a) had access to the copyrighted work, and (b) the copyrighted work and the infringing work are substantially similar. Substantial similarity is an issue of fact for the trier of fact; motions for summary judgment involving the issue nonetheless have been granted.[1]

---

other grounds and remanded) (inline linked and framed copyrighted image of others obtained from trolling websites [copy]); *see also* Jackson v. Warner Bros. Inc., 993 F. Supp. 585 (E.D. Mich. 1997) (summary judgment for defendant based upon fair use of plaintiff-artist's copyrighted lithographs used "as props" in movie "Made in America"); Amsinck v. Columbia Pictures Industries, Inc., 862 F. Supp. 1044 (S.D. N.Y. 1994) (televising artist's copyrighted teddy bear mobile [no copy]); *distinguished in* Ringgold v. Black Entertainment Televison, Inc., 126 F.3d 70, 150 A.L.R. Fed. 813 (2d Cir. 1997) (poster of artist's silkscreened quilt used as set decoration on television series [copy]).

[3]Tiffany Design, Inc. v. Reno-Tahoe Specialty, Inc., 55 F.Supp. 2d 1113 (D.Nev. 1999) (computer scan of computer-enhanced photographic images as precursor to graphical manipulation [copy]).

[4]Tiffany Design, Inc. v. Reno-Tahoe Specialty, Inc., 55 F.Supp. 2d 1113 (D.Nev. 1999) (loading protected visual imagery into computer's RAM in preparation for manipulation constituted infringement).

[Section 7:73]

[1]Kaplan v. Stock Market Photo Agency, Inc., 133 F. Supp. 2d 317 (S.D. N.Y. 2001) (defendants' motion for summary judgment granted in copyright infringement action where works were not substantially similar because either no reasonable trier could find photographs substantially similar or similarity affected noncopyrightable elements of underlying work); Hearn v. Meyer, 664 F. Supp. 832, 835 (S.D. N.Y. 1987) (a reasonable fact-finder could not find similarity); *see also* Durham Industries, Inc. v. Tomy Corp., 630 F.2d 905, 911 (2d Cir. 1980) (trier of fact would not be permitted to find substantial similarity as a matter of law); Walker v. Time Life Films, Inc., 784 F.2d 44, 48 (2d Cir. 1986) (lack of substantial similarity must fall outside the range of disputed facts); Arthur v. American Broadcasting Companies, Inc., 633 F. Supp. 146 (S.D. N.Y. 1985) (rough finished brass interlocking rings "so strikingly different" from ABC's polished and modern interlocking rings that there was no similarity as a matter of law).

Ordinarily evidence of copying is a significant factor for the plaintiff to prove, but in art, where copying is a mainstay, defendants often admit to copying.[2] Where no direct evidence exists, failure to find substantial similarity defeats the claim, even if defendant had access to the original.[3]

§ 7:74 Access

Although the rules are refined in various jurisdictions, access is generally shown when plaintiff can demonstrate with particularity that the defendant had a reasonable opportunity to see the work. Access was found in the following: where defendant admitted digitizing the copyrighted work into its computer's random access memory;[1]where defendant admitted that it viewed the plaintiff's rose design before creating its own;[2] where defendant provided fabricators with plaintiff's copyrighted

---

[2]Silberman v. Innovation Luggage, Inc., 67 U.S.P.Q.2d (BNA) 1489, 2003 WL 1787123 (S.D. N.Y. 2003) (defendant admitted copying a catalogue reproduction of photographer's "Manhattan Skyline"); Flack v. Friends of Queen Catherine Inc., 139 F. Supp. 2d 526 (S.D. N.Y. 2001) (defendants admitted copying the artist's work); Rogers v. Koons, 751 F. Supp. 474 (S.D. N.Y. 1990), amended on reargument, 777 F. Supp. 1 (S.D. N.Y. 1991) and judgment aff'd, 960 F.2d 301 (2d Cir. 1992) (defendant admitted he instructed the fabricator to copy closely the plaintiff's work); United Feature Syndicate, Inc. v. Koons, 817 F. Supp. 370 (S.D. N.Y. 1993) (uncontroverted direct evidence of copying existed where the defendant admitted the sculpture design came from a color picture of "Odie," which he directed the fabricator to copy without seeking authorization).

[3]Folio Impressions, Inc. v. Byer California, 752 F. Supp. 583, 31 Fed. R. Evid. Serv. 1320 (S.D. N.Y. 1990), judgment aff'd, 937 F.2d 759, 33 Fed. R. Evid. Serv. 569 (2d Cir. 1991) (plaintiff failed to sustain its burden of proof, resulting in dismissal of the infringement claim, and dissolution of the preliminary injunction).

[Section 7:74]

[1]Kelly v. Arriba Soft Corp., 280 F.3d 934, 61 U.S.P.Q.2d (BNA) 1564 (9th Cir. 2002), opinion withdrawn and superseded on denial of reh'g, 336 F.3d 811, 67 U.S.P.Q.2d (BNA) 1297 (9th Cir. 2003) (reversed on other grounds and remanded) (search engine program crawled the web, downloading full-sized images onto its server and generating lower resolution thumbnails).

[2]Folio Impressions, Inc. v. Byer California, 752 F. Supp. 583, 31 Fed. R. Evid. Serv. 1320 (S.D. N.Y. 1990), judgment aff'd, 937 F.2d 759, 33 Fed. R. Evid. Serv. 569 (2d Cir. 1991); *see also* United Feature

notecards as prototypes for defendant's sculptures;[3] where retailer suggested to defendant that it produce visual designs patterned after plaintiff's.[4]

§ 7:75 Substantial similarity—Plaintiff's burden

The plaintiff has the burden of establishing that the infringing work is "substantially similar" to the copyrighted work to prove infringement.[1] Substantial similarity is decided by the trier of fact,[2] and the factfinder's task is to predict the probable reaction of the "ordinary observer" or "ordinary lay observer." Summary adjudication may be appropriate where as a matter of law a trier of fact would not be permitted to find substantial similarity. "Lack of substantial similarity between the protectible aspects of the works [must be] 'so clear as to fall outside the range of disputed fact questions' requiring resolution at trial."[3]

Syndicate, Inc. v. Koons, 817 F. Supp. 370 (S.D. N.Y. 1993) (artist admitted he had access to copyrighted work).

[3]Rogers v. Koons, 751 F. Supp. 474 (S.D. N.Y. 1990), amended on reargument, 777 F. Supp. 1 (S.D. N.Y. 1991) and judgment aff'd, 960 F.2d 301 (2d Cir. 1992).

[4]Mulberry Thai Silks, Inc. v. K & K Neckwear, Inc., 897 F. Supp. 789 (S.D. N.Y. 1995), adhered to on reconsideration, (Oct. 10, 1995).

[Section 7:75]

[1]Ringgold v. Black Entertainment Television, Inc., 126 F.3d 70, 74, 150 A.L.R. Fed. 813 (2d Cir. 1997) (distinguishing similarity required for indirect evidence of copying once access has been shown from similarity required for actionable copying after fact of copying has been established).

[2]Kisch v. Ammirati & Puris Inc., 657 F. Supp. 380 (S.D. N.Y. 1987) (rational trier of fact could find substantial similarity).

[3]Kaplan v. Stock Market Photo Agency, Inc., 133 F. Supp. 2d 317 (S.D. N.Y. 2001) (defendants' motion for summary judgment granted in copyright infringement action where similarity involved noncopyrightable elements of underlying work); Kisch v. Ammirati & Puris Inc., 657 F. Supp. 380 (S.D. N.Y. 1987). In Sid & Marty Krofft Television Productions, Inc. v. McDonald's Corp., 562 F.2d 1157 (9th Cir. 1977), the Ninth Circuit offered the extrinsic test, backed up by the intrinsic test. Essentially, the extrinsic test rested upon supposedly objective criteria analyzed by expert witnesses. The decision as to whether or not the ideas of the two works satisfied the extrinsic test was often decided as a matter of law. If the works were similar in idea, then the similarity

§ 7:76 Substantial similarity—De minimis

The concept of *de minimis non curat lex* in the copyright context, as explicated by the Second Circuit at the end of the twentieth century, has a plurality of meanings: trivial technical violations without legal consequence; copying that is not quantitatively or qualitatively sufficient to support the requisite "substantial similarity" for actionable infringement; copying that relates to the volume and substantiality of the fair use defense.[1]

To determine whether the amount of copying is de minimis for actionable copying, quantitative and qualitative components are examined.[2] The qualitative component involves "the copying of expression"; the quantitative component involves the amount of the copyrighted work used and its observability in the allegedly infringing work. The amount may not be de minimis even if only a relatively small portion of the total work is copied. If the material is central and significant to the composition, it may be enough.[3] The de minimis measure for substantial similarity has been generally distinguished from the measuring

---

of their expression was tested by the ordinary observer test, a question of fact for the trier of fact.

[Section 7:76]

[1]Ringgold v. Black Entertainment Televison, Inc., 126 F.3d 70 at 75–76, 150 A.L.R. Fed. 813 (2d Cir. 1997) ("the [de minimis] concept is an inappropriate one to be enlisted in fair use analysis" because "[i]f the infringing work makes such a quantitatively insubstantial use of the copyrighted work to fall below the threshold required for actionable copying, it makes more sense to reject the claim . . . and find no infringement . . . than undertake a . . . fair use analysis. . . ."); Sandoval v. New Line Cinema Corp., 147 F.3d 215 (2d Cir. 1998) ("Where unauthorized use . . . is de minimis, [a] determination of . . . fair use . . . is unnecessary"); *but cf.* Jackson v. Warner Bros. Inc., 993 F. Supp. 585 (E.D. Mich. 1997) (analyzing under de minimis measures use of plaintiff's work in defendants' film under the amount and substantiality prong of fair use).

[2]Ringgold v. Black Entertainment Televison, Inc., 126 F.3d 70, 76, 150 A.L.R. Fed. 813 (2d Cir. 1997) ("In cases involving visual works . . . the quantitative component of substantial similarity also concerns the observability of the copied work . . .").

[3]Silberman v. Innovation Luggage, Inc., 67 U.S.P.Q.2d (BNA) 1489, 2003 WL 1787123 (S.D. N.Y. 2003) (defendants copied seven buildings from center portion of artist's photograph of Manhattan skyline and Brooklyn Bridge but that was "central to the composition.").

concepts used for a third factor analysis of fair use, and specifically disapproved.

§ 7:77 Substantial similarity—Observability

Observability becomes an important factor when the actual visual artwork is reproduced in toto, or in part, in media like film and videotape. Observability has been described as the length of time the copied work is viewable in the other media, influenced by other factors like visibility, discernible detail, focus, lighting, camera angles, prominence, and repetition.[1] The cumulative effect of repeating short or partially obscured works has been deemed a factor that might provide prominence to otherwise incidental views.[2] Grainy textures and reduced tonality did not "diminish observable similarities" where the copying was "clearly visible."[3]

In assessing length of observable time, some courts use the timing categories provided in the royalty schedule for public broadcasting companies for use of published visual and pictorial works issued by the Librarian of Congress.[4] Although observability may be couched in quantitative

---

[Section 7:77]

[1]*See* Ringgold v. Black Entertainment Televison, Inc., 126 F.3d 70, 150 A.L.R. Fed. 813 (2d Cir. 1997); Sandoval v. New Line Cinema Corp., 147 F.3d 215 (2d Cir. 1998).

[2]Ringgold v. Black Entertainment Televison, Inc., 126 F.3d 70, 150 A.L.R. Fed. 813 (2d Cir. 1997) (brief repeated shots reinforced prominence).

[3]Silberman v. Innovation Luggage, Inc., 67 U.S.P.Q.2d (BNA) 1489, 2003 WL 1787123 (S.D. N.Y. 2003) (a lay observer would be able to recognize the source).

[4]37 C.F.R. § 253.8; 17 U.S.C.A. § 118(b) ("featured" displays are "full-screen or substantially full-screen for more than three seconds"); ("background" displays are "any display less than full-screen or substantially full-screen, or full-screen for three seconds or less"); Ringgold v. Black Entertainment Televison, Inc., 126 F.3d 70, 150 A.L.R. Fed. 813 (2d Cir. 1997) (four to five-second segment of off-focus full visibility of plaintiff's poster in television feature, reinforced by brief segments of partial visibility totalling twenty-six seconds, was not de minimis); Sandoval v. New Line Cinema Corp., 147 F.3d 215 (2d Cir. 1998) (use of plaintiff's transparencies on a light box for thirty-five seconds in a feature film, of which longest uninterrupted view was for six seconds, and other views which were barely discernible, briefly visible, and partly or fully obscured, was considered de minimis); *see also* Jackson

terms by the courts, the analysis includes qualitative aspects. Similarly, qualitative sufficiency challenges have been based upon so-called quantitative observability factors. A qualitative sufficiency challenge that viewers could only see a vague stylistic painting, but no protectible expression, was rejected by the Second Circuit:

> . . . [A] visual work, though selected by production staff for thematic relevance, or . . . decorative value, might ultimately be filmed at such a distance and so out of focus that a typical . . . viewer . . . would not discern any decorative effect that the work contributes to the set. But that is not the case. The painting . . . is recognizable as a painting, and with sufficient observable detail for the "average lay observer."[5]

§ 7:78 Substantial similarity—Copyright viewer

Who the ordinary observer or lay observer is has been variously stated as: One who, unless charged with detecting "disparities," would overlook them in favor of viewing the "aesthetic appeal" of the copyrighted work and the infringing work as the same;[1] one who, by an ocular comparison, would have a "spontaneous response" that

---

v. Warner Bros. Inc., 993 F. Supp. 585 (E.D. Mich. 1997) (favoring fair use on amount and substantiality factor where lithographs were visible in background in movie for less than sixty seconds).

[5]Ringgold v. Black Entertainment Televison, Inc., 126 F.3d 70, 150 A.L.R. Fed. 813 (2d Cir. 1997); *cf.* Sandoval v. New Line Cinema Corp., 147 F.3d 215 (2d Cir. 1998) ("Sandoval's photographs . . . are not displayed with sufficient detail for the average lay observer to identify even the subject matter . . . , much less style.. . . [They] are displayed in poor lighting and at great distance . . . out of focus and . . . only briefly in eleven different shots . . . and have no cumulative effect because the images contained [therein] are not distinguishable").

[Section 7:78]

[1]Kaplan v. Stock Market Photo Agency, Inc., 133 F. Supp. 2d 317 (S.D. N.Y. 2001) ("substantial similarity does not require literally identical copying of every detail."); Austin Productions, Inc. v. F.D.F. Design Studio, Inc., 1991 Copr. L. Dec. ¶ 26662, 1990 WL 198741 (E.D. N.Y. 1990); United Feature Syndicate, Inc. v. Koons, 817 F. Supp. 370 (S.D. N.Y. 1993) ("The Second Circuit has [used] 'whether an average lay observer would recognize the alleged copy as having been appropriated from the copyrighted work'; . . . whether the 'ordinary observer, unless he set out to detect the disparities, would be disposed to overlook them, and regard their aesthetic appeal as the same.' " (citations omitted)).

the two works were substantially similar; one who would recognize the copy as having been appropriated from the copyrighted work;[2] one who, upon "closer inspection, more attentive to detail" than a "generalized impression," sees copying;[3] or one who would "conclude that the accused work is so similar to the plaintiff's work . . . that the defendant unlawfully appropriated the plaintiff's protectible expression by taking material of substance and value."[4] The rule "must be applied with caution in the context of graphic or three-dimensional works."[5]

Neither a connoisseur nor an artist has ever been held a proper ordinary viewer in an arts case, but a "sophisticated observer"[6] has been.[7] Some courts have focused upon aspects of aesthetic appeal[8] or appropriation of copyrighted

[2]Kaplan v. Stock Market Photo Agency, Inc., 133 F. Supp. 2d 317 (S.D. N.Y. 2001); Past Pluto Productions Corp. v. Dana, 627 F. Supp. 1435, 1443, 83 A.L.R. Fed. 827 (S.D. N.Y. 1986), citing Ideal Toy Corp. v. Fab-Lu Limited (Inc.), 360 F.2d 1021, 1022 (2d Cir. 1966).

[3]First Am. Artificial Flowers, Inc. v. Joseph Markovits Inc., 342 F. Supp. 178, 186 (S.D. N.Y. 1972).

[4]Wildlife Exp. Corp. v. Carol Wright Sales, Inc., 18 F.3d 502 (7th Cir. 1994) (citations omitted) (side by side comparison of parties' soft sculpture panda bear, brown bear, duck and elephant duffel bags support finding of same "aesthetic appeal").

[5]United Feature Syndicate, Inc. v. Koons, 817 F. Supp. 370, 377 (S.D. N.Y. 1993), *citing* Warner Bros. Inc. v. American Broadcasting Companies, Inc., 720 F.2d 231, 242 (2d Cir. 1983) ("elusive distinction" rule between characters).

[6]Beaudin v. Ben and Jerry's Homemade, Inc., 95 F.3d 1 (2d Cir. 1996) (applying the ordinary observer in a "more discerning" manner appropriate to visual art); Kaplan v. Stock Market Photo Agency, Inc., 133 F. Supp. 2d 317 (S.D. N.Y. 2001) (citations omitted) (the "discerning" ordinary observer test excludes from comparison unprotectible elements.).

[7]Runstadler Studios, Inc. v. MCM Ltd. Partnership, 768 F. Supp. 1292 (N.D. Ill. 1991).

[8]Peter Pan Fabrics, Inc. v. Martin Weiner Corp., 274 F.2d 487, 489 (2d Cir. 1960) ("the ordinary observer unless . . . set out to detect the disparities, would be disposed to overlook them, and regard their aesthetic appeal as the same."); Folio Impressions, Inc. v. Byer California, 752 F. Supp. 583, 31 Fed. R. Evid. Serv. 1320 (S.D. N.Y. 1990), judgment aff'd, 937 F.2d 759, 33 Fed. R. Evid. Serv. 569 (2d Cir. 1991); Kenbrooke Fabrics, Inc. v. Holland Fabrics, Inc., 602 F. Supp. 151, 153 (S.D. N.Y. 1984) (fabric designs); Mulberry Thai Silks, Inc. v. K & K

work by infringing copy;[9] however, a general impression of similarity is not enough.[10] Some jurisdictions consider what kind of scrutiny the observer will give the works, given the works' intended uses.[11] The ordinary observer does not have to "confuse" the copy with the protected work, or find that the copied work is a "virtual copy" in order to find substantial similarity.[12]

Identifying the test is incidental to its application. The comparison between the works should evaluate whether substantial similarity exists between protectible aspects of the copyrighted work and the allegedly infringing work. To the extent that the similarities between works constitute elements unprotectible under copyright, they must be disregarded by the eye of the ordinary observer. The "protectible" restricter has often been ignored, and sometimes with good reason. Nonprotectible elements, for example, may be combined in certain circumstances into a protectible arrangement.

Although these rules sound like semantic perturbation, they arguably have some merit in application.[13] Were this limitation uniformly applied in practice, the narrower scope of the observer's examination would often affect substantial similarity.

The ordinary observer initially views similarities, as the tests utilized by the courts in the arts context demonstrate.[14] Substantial similarity is not intended to focus upon dissimilarities or disparities between the works. As a practical matter, the differences cannot be

---

Neckwear, Inc., 897 F. Supp. 789 (S.D. N.Y. 1995), adhered to on reconsideration, (Oct. 10, 1995) (court "finds that the aesthetic appeal [of geometric fabric patterns] is substantially the same.")

[9]Ideal Toy Corp. v. Fab-Lu Limited (Inc.), 360 F.2d 1021, 1022 (2d Cir. 1966).

[10]Durham Industries, Inc. v. Tomy Corp., 630 F.2d 905 (2d Cir. 1980).

[11]Folio Impressions, Inc. v. Byer California, 752 F. Supp. 583, 31 Fed. R. Evid. Serv. 1320 (S.D. N.Y. 1990), judgment aff'd, 937 F.2d 759, 33 Fed. R. Evid. Serv. 569 (2d Cir. 1991).

[12]Country Kids 'N City Slicks, Inc. v. Sheen, 77 F.3d 1280 (10th Cir. 1996) (vacated and remanded to district court where ruling recited an ordinary observer would not "confuse" the works" or find a "virtual copy.")

[13]*See* § 7:78.

[14]*See* §§ 7:75 to 7:76.

cleanly dissected. The courts often do note differences,[15] sometimes as minor variations[16] or new material in conjunction with copied material.[17]

At what point do differences legally undermine a finding of substantial similarity? Where dissimilarity exceeds similarity, and the similarities are "of small import quantitatively or qualitatively [in comparison to the original work], no infringement is appropriate.[18]

No substantial similarity was found between two photographs, each depicting a businessman contemplating a leap from a tall building onto a busy city street below, because the similarities arose from uncopyrightable ideas—explained how dissimilarities may help courts delineate between protected expression and unprotected idea:

> The determination of which elements of a work are protectible is also an inexact science, and is case-specific . . . . [F]undamental . . . [to copyright law] is . . . that an idea or concept [is not protected] but only the expression of that idea or concept . . . . The distinction between an idea and its expression is 'elusive' and is often an 'impenetrable inquiry.' [Without] . . . firm gauge to enable the Court to determine when an 'imitator has gone beyond [an idea] . . . and has borrowed . . . expression, . . . the level of abstraction or generalization [may be important].'

Where substantial or significant differences exist, such that no substantial similarity could be found, the matter

---

[15]Leigh v. Warner Bros., Inc., 212 F.3d 1210, 2000 (11th Cir. 2000) (defendant's photos differed from plaintiff's in that statue was "smaller and more distant," lighting contrast was "more extreme" and involved additional light beams and obscure shadowing, and new elements had been added, including colors, flora, a cross, movie cast).

[16]United Feature Syndicate, Inc. v. Koons, 817 F. Supp. 370 (S.D. N.Y. 1993) (ordinary observer would not notice different length of copied cartoon character's tongue where defendant's sculpture otherwise was an "exact reproduction").

[17]United Feature Syndicate, Inc. v. Koons, 817 F. Supp. 370 at 376 (S.D. N.Y. 1993) ("no plagiarist can excuse the wrong by showing how much of his work he did not pirate").

[18]Kaplan v. Stock Market Photo Agency, Inc., 133 F. Supp. 2d 317 (S.D. N.Y. 2001) ("[D]issimilarity can be important in determining whether there is . . . substantial similarity.").

has been disposed of by summary judgment.[19] If substantial similarity is satisfied, the burden shifts to the defendant to prove the infringing work is an independent creation.[20] To determine independence, the trier of fact may consider the "defendant's training [and] his past conduct in independently creating works."[21]

§ 7:79 Limited modes of expression

Substantial similarity may not constitute infringement where the similarities arise from expression of themes, ideas, concepts or archetypes.[1]

---

[19]Creations Unlimited, Inc. v. McCain, 112 F.3d 814 (5th Cir. 1997) (to determine whether . . . copying is legally actionable, a side-by-side comparison must be made between the original and the copy to determine whether a layman would view the two works as "substantially similar"); Leigh v. Warner Bros., 10 F. Supp.2d 1371 (S.D. Ga. 1998) (plaintiff cannot copyright subject matter of photograph depicting cemetery statue), rev'd in part, aff'd in part, Leigh v. Warner Bros., Inc., 212 F.3d 1210, 2000 Copr.L.Dec. ¶ 28,087, 54 U.S.P.Q.2d 1865, 28 Media L. Rep. 1961, 13 Fla. L. Weekly Fed. C 689 (11th Cir. 2000) (". . . a jury ultimately may conclude that the similarities . . . are not 'substantial'. . . [b]ut they are significant enough . . . to preclude summary judgment . . . [which is] a question of fact . . ."); Gund, Inc. v. Smile Intern., Inc., 691 F. Supp. 642, 645 (E.D. N.Y. 1988), judgment aff'd, 872 F.2d 1021 (2d Cir. 1989) (inquiry on similarity must be on specific features copied from floppy stuffed toy dog that do not pertain to general idea of dogs "flopping" on their stomachs); *see also* E. Mishan & Sons, Inc. v. Marycana, Inc., 662 F. Supp. 1339, 1344 (S.D. N.Y. 1987) (tests for determining substantial similarity in face of differences).

[20]John L. Perry Studio, Inc. v. Wernick, 597 F.2d 1308 (9th Cir. 1979) (no copyright infringement of registered seagull sculptures where the defendant showed his progenitor of seagulls preexisted the plaintiff's seagulls and showed, along with testimony, independent creation); Davidov v. Tapemeasure Enterprises, Inc., 27 U.S.P.Q.2d (BNA) 1382, 1993 WL 88234 (S.D. N.Y. 1993) (evidence of independent creation may rebut prima facie case of infringement).

[21]Austin Productions, Inc. v. F.D.F. Design Studio, Inc., 1991 Copr. L. Dec. ¶ 26662, 1990 WL 198741 (E.D. N.Y. 1990) (citation omitted).

[Section 7:79]

[1]*See* Franklin Mint Corp. v. National Wildlife Art Exchange, Inc., 195 U.S.P.Q. (BNA) 31, 1977 WL 22706 (E.D. Pa. 1977), judgment aff'd, 575 F.2d 62 (3d Cir. 1978) (substantially similar paintings of birds by realist painters resulted from the limited ways in which to depict subject matter in realistic styles); Cory Van Rijn, Inc. v. California Raisin Advisory Bd., 697 F. Supp. 1136 (E.D. Cal. 1987) (parties' respec-

In *Folio*,[2] the court, "using its layman's eye," found two rose textile patterns were not substantially similar based on aesthetic appeal. The court found sharper edges and more geometric styling in one, and a "softer looking . . . more painterly . . . and well rounded" style in the other. That court's vision may be much more acute than any lay observer; under any of the foregoing tests the two fabric patterns (in black and white photoreproduction) are similar. Once the disparities are extrapolated, the differences become more apparent, although not readily so. If one has spent time looking at patterned fabrics, even those differences might be minimal:

In *Leigh*,[3] the court painstakingly compared differences and similarities between a photographer's shot for the cover of a best selling novel and a film's promotional materials:

> Although it may be easy to identify [significant] differences . . . the Warner Brothers images also have much in common with the elements protected by Leigh's copyright. All . . . are taken from a low position, angled up slightly at the Bird Girl so that the contents of the bowls in her hands remain hidden. Hanging Spanish moss borders the tops . . . The statue is close to centered . . . Light shines down and envelopes the statue in all of the images . . . all . . . are

---

tive "raisin people" not substantially similar due to the limited number of ways of creating the image of "humanized" raisins); John L. Perry Studio, Inc. v. Wernick, 597 F.2d 1308 (9th Cir. 1979) (sculptures of seagulls in flight fabricated from white plastic held not to infringe copyrighted seagulls because there are only so many ways to realistically portray such birds in flight); Gund, Inc. v. Smile Intern., Inc., 691 F. Supp. 642 (E.D. N.Y. 1988), judgment aff'd, 872 F.2d 1021 (2d Cir. 1989) (no infringement based upon similar floppy stuffed toy dogs because similarities based upon common ideas); *see also* Hennon v. Kirklands, Inc., 870 F. Supp. 118 (W.D. Va. 1994), aff'd, 64 F.3d 657 (4th Cir. 1995) (motion for preliminary injunction denied to prevent inexpensive "knock-offs" of plaintiff's copyrighted Christmas carol figurines, where mouths open in song, clothing and facial expressions constituted unprotectible expression of Victorian carolers).

[2]Folio Impressions, Inc. v. Byer California, 752 F. Supp. 583, 31 Fed. R. Evid. Serv. 1320 (S.D. N.Y. 1990), judgment aff'd, 937 F.2d 759, 33 Fed. R. Evid. Serv. 569 (2d Cir. 1991).

[3]Leigh v. Warner Bros., Inc., 212 F.3d 1210, 2000 (11th Cir. 2000) (reversing summary judgment on copyright claim for single-frame image) (" . . . a jury ultimately may conclude that the similarities . . . are not 'substantial' . . . [b]ut they are significant enough . . . to preclude summary judgment . . . [which is] a question of fact . . . ").

monochromatic. These expressive elements all make the pictures more effective.

C. DISTRIBUTION

§ 7:80 Generally

The copyright owner has the right "to distribute copies . . . of the copyrighted work to the public by sale or other transfer of ownership . . ." or by rental, lease or lending.[1] Distribution for PGS works has occurred on the Internet, through the uploading of pictorial images on a subscription electronic bulletin board service accessible to subscribers by modem.[2]

D. DERIVATIVE WORKS

§ 7:81 More than minimal contribution—Taking work out of public domain

The copyright owner has the exclusive "right to prepare derivative works based upon the copyrighted work."[1] Section 101 defines a derivative work as one "based upon one or more preexisting works, such as a translation, musical arrangement, dramatization, fictionalization, motion picture version, sound recording, art reproduction, abridgement, condensation, or any other form in which a work may be recast, transformed, or adapted."[2] A work consisting of editorial revisions, annotations, elaborations, or other modifications which, as a whole, represent an original work of authorship, is a "derivative work." According to the legislative history Congress intended a

---

[Section 7:80]

[1]17 U.S.C.A. § 106(3).

[2]Playboy Enterprises, Inc. v. Chuckleberry Pub., Inc., 939 F. Supp. 1032 (S.D. N.Y. 1996) (by soliciting American subscribers to foreign internet site, defendant had distributed copyrighted images in United States within meaning of copyright injunction); Playboy Enterprises, Inc. v. Frena, 839 F. Supp. 1552, 1554 (M.D. Fla. 1993) (unauthorized uploading of copyrighted images with knowledge that images would be downloaded by subscribers constituted distribution).

[Section 7:81]

[1]17 U.S.C.A. § 106(2).

[2]17 U.S.C.A. § 101.

violation to occur where "the infringing work incorporate[s] a portion of the copyrighted work in some form."[3]

Section 103, titled "compilations and derivative works," recites:

> The copyright in a derivative work "extends only to the material contributed by the author of such work, as distinguished from the preexisting material employed in the work, and does not imply any exclusive right in the preexisting material. The copyright in such work is independent of, and does not affect or enlarge the scope, duration, ownership, or subsistence, of any copyright protection in the preexisting material."[4]

To qualify a derivative work for separate copyright protection, the new work must meet the requirement that the "material contributed" be original. The issue is whether "a genuine difference [exists] between the underlying work of art and the copy . . . for which protection is sought."[5] Some jurisdictions require substantial variation of the derivative work from the original,[6] and a higher threshold of artistic skill. In the Second Circuit the key is "whether the new work is an independent creation [containing] a modicum of creativity."[7]

The following were deemed derivative works: cropped and enlarged photographic image transferred to silkscreen upon which large red blocks were superimposed with text;[8] defendants' transfer of plaintiff's small scale reproductions from books onto canvases or mats for sale to public as

---

[3]H.R. Rep. No. 1476, 94th Cong., 2d Sess. (1976), reprinted at 1976 U.S.C.C.A.N. 5659, 5675.

[4]17 U.S.C.A. § 103(b).

[5]Hearn v. Meyer, 664 F. Supp. 832, 840 (S.D. N.Y. 1987).

[6]Lee v. A.R.T. Co., 125 F.3d 580 (7th Cir. 1997) ("'originality' is essential to a derivative work."); L. Batlin & Son, Inc. v. Snyder, 536 F.2d 486 (2d Cir. 1976); Gracen v. Bradford Exchange, 698 F.2d 300 (7th Cir. 1983).

[7]Sapon v. DC Comics, 62 U.S.P.Q.2d (BNA) 1691, 2002 WL 485730 (S.D. N.Y. 2002) (citations omitted).

[8]Hoepker v. Kruger, 200 F. Supp. 2d 340, 30 Media L. Rep. (BNA) 1737, 63 U.S.P.Q.2d (BNA) 1168 (S.D. N.Y. 2002) (rejecting claim that Barbara Kruger's use of plaintiff's photograph was a reproduction that lacked sufficient additional creativity to qualify as a derivative).

framed artworks;[9] defendant's transfer of plaintiff's artworks reproduced in a commemorative book into tiles for sale;[10] and a rose configuration on textiles superimposed upon a documentary design that was in the public domain.[11] The following were not deemed derivative works: a photograph by an artist copied from a poster by the same artist;[12] the transfer of Disney characters into plastic wind-up toys;[13] copying of architectural drawings from brochure in public domain;[14] the remounting of copyrighted

[9]Greenwich Workshop, Inc. v. Timber Creations, Inc., 932 F. Supp. 1210 (C.D. Cal. 1996) (recasting and transforming copyrighted works by physically removing pages and mounting them under glass to hang on wall constituted derivative work infringing plaintiff's copyrights in the bookplates as well as original artwork).

[10]Mirage Editions, Inc. v. Albuquerque A.R.T. Co., 856 F.2d 1341, 1343 (9th Cir. 1988) (by removing plaintiff's images and gluing them onto sheets of plastic for sale, defendant created derivative works infringing plaintiff's copyrights); *contra* Lee v. A.R.T. Co., 125 F.3d 580 (7th Cir. 1997) (defendants' remounting of plaintiff's registered notecards and prints on ceramic tiles covered with transparent epoxy resin did not constitute derivative works).

[11]Folio Impressions, Inc. v. Byer California, 752 F. Supp. 583, 31 Fed. R. Evid. Serv. 1320 (S.D. N.Y. 1990), judgment aff'd, 937 F.2d 759, 33 Fed. R. Evid. Serv. 569 (2d Cir. 1991) (unrebutted testimony that the rose was originally designed); *see also* Harvey Cartoons v. Columbia Pictures Industries, Inc., 645 F. Supp. 1564 (S.D. N.Y. 1986).

[12]Simon v. Birraporetti's Restaurants, Inc., 720 F. Supp. 85 (S.D. Tex. 1989) (copyright held invalid for lack of originality, where the plaintiff created a poster identical to a photograph he made some years earlier, where no evidence was introduced to support originality and the poster and photograph were identical).

[13]Durham Industries, Inc. v. Tomy Corp., 630 F.2d 905 (2d Cir. 1980).

[14]Harris Custom Builders, Inc. v. Hoffmeyer, 92 F.3d 517 (7th Cir. 1996) (no protection for derivative work where plaintiff-copyright owner of unpublished drawings published a brochure containing adapted drawings without pre-Berne Convention mandatory copyright notice, the defective notice injecting the work into the public domain, and thus no infringement of plaintiff's architectural plans); Sweet v. City of Chicago, 953 F. Supp. 225 (N.D. Ill. 1996) (outdoor city art fair was not a derivative work of a guidebook, which listed city bars and restaurants that exhibited artworks: "[E]ven if [art fair] . . . indicates which restaurants . . . display art for sale, . . . that would be merely the expression of an idea.").

notecards and lithographs on ceramic tiles;[15]and mirrored eyeglasses and computer controlled wings on Black Bat character adapted from Batman.[16]

§ 7:82 More than minimal contribution—Unauthorized use of copyrighted artwork

In *Mirage*,[1] the defendant removed pages from art books depicting artist Patrick Nagel's artwork and glued each page onto ceramic tiles, which it offered for sale in retail markets. Nagel's licensee sued. The district court concluded that the resulting ceramic products comprised derivative works, infringing Nagel's copyright. On appeal the defendant claimed the tiles could not be derivative works because it had not "reproduced" Nagel's art, but the Ninth Circuit found that by making another version of Nagel's art by permanently bonding the artwork to the tile, the work had been transformed, adapted, and recast within the terms of the law.

But in *Lee*, where an artist sued the same *Mirage* defendants for mounting her copyrighted notecards and lithographs on ceramic tiles using transparent epoxy, the Seventh Circuit disagreed, expressly disapproving the *Mirage* opinion.[2] The artist argued the transpositioning of her art constituted a "preparation" in violation of her exclusive right to prepare derivative works under Section 106(2). The district court concluded that the tile-mounted artwork was not an "original work of authorship" under the second sentence of the Section 101 definition of derivative works, and that mounting the work on tile was legally indistinguishable from framing a copyrighted painting, which has not been considered an infringement under the "recasting, transforming, and adapting" requirements of

---

[15]Lee v. A.R.T. Co., 125 F.3d 580 (7th Cir. 1997) (holding that tiles were not art "reproductions" and that bonding artworks to a slab by epoxy did not "recast, transform[] or adapt[]" them under Section 101).

[16]Sapon v. DC Comics, 62 U.S.P.Q.2d (BNA) 1691, 2002 WL 485730 (S.D. N.Y. 2002) (additions made to Bat character were "trivial differences insufficient to support a copyright claim.").

[Section 7:82]

[1]Mirage Editions, Inc. v. Albuquerque A.R.T. Co., 856 F.2d 1341 (9th Cir. 1988).

[2]Lee v. A.R.T. Co., 125 F.3d 580 (7th Cir. 1997).

the first sentence.

The Seventh Circuit affirmed, stating, "If the framing process does not create a derivative work, then mounting art on a tile, which serves as a flush frame, does not create a derivative work. . . . [T] he Ninth Circuit erred in assuming that normal means of mounting and displaying are easily reversible."[3]

E. DISPLAY

§ 7:83 Generally

The copyright owner has the exclusive right under Section 106(g) to display and authorize display of the copyrighted work publicly, a right which did not exist before the Act of 1976.[1] Display is defined as showing a copy of the copyrighted work, directly or indirectly by films, slides, television, or other device or process.[2] Section 106 makes actionable public display defined in Section 101:

> To . . . display a work "publicly" means—
>
> (1) to . . . display it at a place open to the public or at any place where a substantial number of persons outside of a normal circle of a family and its social acquaintances is gathered; or
>
> (2) to transmit or otherwise communicate a . . . display of the work to a place specified by clause (1) or to the public, by means of any device or process, whether the members of the public capable of receiving the . . . display receive it in the same place or in separate places and at the same time or at different times.[3]

The exclusive right of display applies to original works

---

[3]Lee v. A.R.T. Co., 125 F.3d 580 at 581 (7th Cir. 1997).

[Section 7:83]

[1]H.R. Rep. No. 1476, 94th Cong., 2d Sess. at 63 (1976), reprinted at 1976 U.S.C.C.A.N. 5659, 5676.

[2]17 U.S.C.A. § 101.

[3]*See also* Thomas v. Pansy Ellen Products, Inc., 672 F. Supp. 237, 239–41 (W.D. N.C. 1987) (giving literal construction to Congress' definition of audience beyond familial circle and social acquaintances, notwithstanding other restrictions on entrance).

of art and art reproductions.[4] By operation of law, owners of the object itself—the tangible personal property—have the right to display it without the authorization of the copyright owner.[5]

Ownership of the copyright is distinct from ownership of the material object.[6] The right to display the work publicly is vested in ownership of the material object, or the "copy" of a copyrightable work.[7]

Display is indispensable to art; therefore the meaning and interpretation of the display right is crucial to artists and institutional and private collectors. However, the legislative history and the Register's reports indicate that the display right was not enacted or intended to benefit primarily PGS category works, and its meaning has been more fully explored in terms of the entertainment industry than the visual arts:

> In our earlier drafting efforts we had assumed that, since the bill considers the showing of a motion picture as a "performance" rather than an "exhibition," the only classes of works that needed the exhibition right were those created to be looked at (pictorial, graphic, and sculptural works) . . . We have now come to realize . . . that . . . textual or notated works . . . may well be given wide public dissemination by exhibition on mass communications devices.[8]

---

[4]H.R. Rep. No. 1476, 94th Cong., 2d Sess. at 64 (1976); S. Rep. No. 473, 94th Cong., 2d Sess.; 17 U.S.C.A. § 101; Burwood Products Co. v. Marsel Mirror and Glass Products, Inc., 468 F. Supp. 1215 (N.D. Ill. 1979) (right infringed by display of prototypes of copyrighted work); Kelly v. Arriba Soft Corp., 280 F.3d 934 (9th Cir. 2002) (importation of images from plaintiff's web site infringed upon exclusive right of public display).

[5]17 U.S.C.A. § 109(c).

[6]17 U.S.C.A. § 202.

[7]Community for Creative Non-Violence v. Reid, 846 F.2d 1485, 1489 (D.C. Cir. 1988) and judgment aff'd, 490 U.S. 730, 109 S. Ct. 2166, 104 L. Ed. 2d 811 (1989) (artist-copyright holder who retook possession of a sculpture owned by the plaintiff because of a copyright dispute has no legal right to the artwork under section 202 and 109(c), noting the display right exists for the "copy" including the original "copy," the ". . . distinction between ownership of a particular copy and ownership of a copyright . . ."); *see also* §§ 7:73 to 7:80.

[8]Supp. Report of Register of Copyrights on General Revision of U.S. Copyright Law: 1965 Revision Bill, 89th Cong., 1st Sess. (1965).

§ 7:84 Internet display

The internet has the potential of having substantial impact on display rights. Courts have held that showing images on a computer screen constitute display, and that the display is public even absent proof that potential recipients were receiving the image or even using receiving apparatus at the time of transmission.[1]

A professional photographer displayed copyrighted images of the American West on his web site and sites of others with whom he had licensing agreements. He sued the operator of a search engine for copyright infringement when he discovered the defendant crawled the web and downloaded full-sized copies of his images onto its server. Defendant generated smaller lower resolution images from the copies, displaying them on its web site in the form of small pictures termed "thumbnails."[2]

Defendant used inline linking, the direct importation of an image from one web site to another without actually copying the image onto its web site. As a result of inline linking, defendant's users could access a full-sized image of plaintiff's images, flanked by defendant's banner and advertising, supplemental text, and a link to the originating site. Defendant used the technique of framing whereby users accessing the thumbnail could view two new windows on defendant's web page, one containing the full-sized imported image, and another window displaying the originating web page.

The Ninth Circuit, reversing the district court, held that defendant created a public display of the larger images of plaintiff's works and infringed his display right by making the images available to any viewer. It was immaterial whether anyone actually saw the images. Capability was

---

[Section 7:84]

[1]Kelly v. Arriba Soft Corp., 280 F.3d 934 (9th Cir. 2002) (by making plaintiff's full-sized images available on its web site, defendant enabled unrestricted public access to anyone with internet access and computer capability).)

[2]Kelly v. Arriba Soft Corp., 280 F.3d 934 (9th Cir. 2002) (fair use defense for thumbnails affirmed on appeal).

enough to establish infringment.[3]

Few cases relevant to art are reported. Courts have deemed that a public display under Section 101(1) occurred in the following: a brochure mailed to association members and newspapers, containing reproductions of plaintiff's copyrighted artworks;[4] exhibit of copyrighted "cute" bear designs on nursery jars at a trade show where entrance was restricted to buyers and association members;[5] display and offering for sale of plaintiff's copyrighted wicker mirror prototypes at a trade show;[6] and the performance of copyrighted songs at a private club.[7]

Courts have deemed no public display occurred in the following: where a copyrighted turkey decoy was used on a hunting party.[8]

In a twist on the display issue, courts have examined as a defense to an infringement of derivative works the assertion that tearing copyrighted images from copyrighted books and mounting them in glass frames for sale creates an alternative form of public display.[9] Although not clearly enunciated, defendant's position was that display would be permissible under the first sale doctrine codified at section 109(a) of the Copyright Act.[10] Without addressing the issue of whether or not the plaintiff's display rights were infringed, the court responded: "Defendants' practice of

---

[3]Kelly v. Arriba Soft Corp., 280 F.3d 934 (9th Cir. 2002) (number of viewers affected amount of damages); accord, Playboy Enterprises, Inc. v. Russ Hardenburgh, Inc., 982 F. Supp. 503 (N.D. Ohio 1997) (electronic bulletin board operated by defendants that accepted uploaded copyrighted images from subscribers and moved selected ones into files for downloading constituted a display regardless of whether the images were seen).

[4]Wojnarowicz v. American Family Ass'n, 745 F. Supp. 130 (S.D. N.Y. 1990).

[5]Thomas v. Pansy Ellen Products, Inc., 672 F. Supp. 237, 239–241 (W.D. N.C. 1987).

[6]Burwood Products Co. v. Marsel Mirror and Glass Products, Inc., 468 F. Supp. 1215 (N.D. Ill. 1979).

[7]Ackee Music, Inc. v. Williams, 650 F. Supp. 653 (D. Kan. 1986).

[8]Streeter v. Rolfe, 491 F. Supp. 416, 421 (W.D. La. 1980).

[9]Greenwich Workshop, Inc. v. Timber Creations, Inc., 932 F. Supp. 1210 (C.D. Cal. 1996).

[10]"The owner of a particular copy . . . lawfully made . . . , or any person authorized by such owner, is entitled, without the authority of

removing from plaintiff's copyrighted book reduced-scale versions of . . . artwork, which were intended solely for inclusion in the books, is not equivalent to simply framing a work of art for display purposes."[11]

§ 7:85 Display of material object by owner—Statute

A major exception to the display right is the owner's legal capacity to display by virtue of his effective title. Section 109(c) provides, in part, "notwithstanding the provisions of section 106(5) [display rights], the owner of a particular copy . . . or any person authorized by such owner, is entitled, without the authority of the copyright owner, to display that copy publicly, either directly or by the projection of no more than one image at a time, to viewers present at the place where the copy is located."[1] Similarly, Section 202 states, "ownership of a copyright, or of any of the exclusive rights under a copyright, is distinct from ownership of any material object in which the work is embodied." The right to display inheres in ownership of the object and is automatically transferred to the owner of the material object by operation of law.

A museum has the right to display artwork it owns, without the permission of the artist or copyright holder. An artist who objects to exhibition venues for his artwork cannot prevent owners from displaying it at such sites.[2] Terms of payment or financial arrangements agreed upon do not affect ownership rights for purposes of the display right.[3]

---

the copyright owner, to sell or to otherwise dispose of the possession of that copy . . . ."

[11]Greenwich Workshop, Inc. v. Timber Creations, Inc., 932 F. Supp. 1210 (C.D. Cal. 1996).

[Section 7:85]

[1]17 U.S.C.A. § 109(c).

[2]Hoepker v. Kruger, 200 F. Supp. 2d 340, 30 Media L. Rep. (BNA) 1737, 63 U.S.P.Q.2d (BNA) 1168 (S.D. N.Y. 2002) (MOCA had right to display artist's work without permission).

[3]Hoepker v. Kruger, 200 F. Supp. 2d 340, 30 Media L. Rep. (BNA) 1737, 63 U.S.P.Q.2d (BNA) 1168 (S.D. N.Y. 2002) (sculpture commission based on payment of fabrication costs).

§ 7:86 Display of material object by owner—Commissioned art: No written agreement, services volunteered, and costs paid

In Community for Creative Non-Violence v. Reid,[1] the artist retook possession of a sculpture from the plaintiff, for whom it was commissioned in return for payment of fabrication costs, and refused to return it because he objected to plaintiff's planned exhibition schedule for the work. The artist did not dispute that CCNV had paid him in full the amount agreed upon, but sought to terminate its ability to display. The Supreme Court made clear that the artist, even if he is sole copyright owner, has no post-sale display rights to the material object, absent violations of VARA or contractual restrictions. Once ownership transfers, the artist by operation of law does not have any exclusive rights under copyright to restrict the owner's display.

VII. FAIR USE

A. Section 107

§ 7:87 Generally

The equitable doctrine of fair use, codified in Section 107, allows others to use copyrighted works in a reasonable manner without authorization of the copyright owner under limited circumstances and for certain purposes. The doctrine is intended to "preserve values enshrined in the first amendment."[1] The defendant must establish by a preponderance of the evidence that it made fair use of the copyrighted material under Section 107, which provides:

> [T]he fair use of a copyrighted work, including such use by reproduction in copies . . . or by any other means . . . for

---

[Section 7:86]

[1]Community for Creative Non-Violence v. Reid, 652 F. Supp. 1453 (D.D.C. 1987), judgment rev'd, 846 F.2d 1485 (D.C. Cir. 1988) and judgment aff'd, 490 U.S. 730, 109 S. Ct. 2166, 104 L. Ed. 2d 811 (1989) (artist had no post-sale display rights in material object).

[Section 7:87]

[1]Elvis Presley Enterprises, Inc. v. Passport Video, 357 F.3d 896, 898 (9th Cir. 2004) (citing Eldred v. Ashcroft, 537 U.S. 186, 219-220, 123 S. Ct. 769, 154 L. Ed. 2d 683, 65 U.S.P.Q.2d (BNA) 1225 (2003).

> purposes such as criticism, comment, news reporting, teaching . . . scholarship, or research, is not an infringement of copyright. In determining whether the use made . . . in any particular case is a fair use the factors to be considered shall include—
>
> 1. the purpose and character of the use, including whether such use is of a commercial nature or is for nonprofit educational purposes;
> 2. the nature of the copyrighted work;
> 3. the amount and substantiality of the portion used in relation to the copyrighted work as a whole; and
> 4. the effect of the use upon the potential market for or value of the copyrighted work.

Fair use presents a mixed question of fact and law, which must be considered on the facts of each case as evaluated by the nonexhaustive four factors, with no single factor negating fair use or creating fair use per se.[2]

B. PURPOSE AND CHARACTER OF USE

§ 7:88 Commerciality

The purpose and character of unauthorized use examines whether the copyrighted work was copied "in good faith to benefit the public or primarily for the commercial interests of the infringer."[1] The Supreme Court has made clear that whether use is fair requires an evaluation through the prism of the "determinative factors," explored and weighed together, on a "case-by-case analysis," under

---

[2]Campbell v. Acuff-Rose Music, Inc., 510 U.S. 569, 114 S. Ct. 1164, 127 L. Ed. 2d 500 (1994) ("The task [for evaluating fair use] is not to be simplified with bright-line rules, for the statute, like the doctrine it recognizes, calls for case-by-case analysis . . . . Nor may the four statutory factors be treated in isolation, one from another. All are to be explored, and the results weighed together, in light of the purposes of copyright.").

[Section 7:88]

[1]Rogers v. Koons, 751 F. Supp. 474 (S.D. N.Y. 1990), amended on reargument, 777 F. Supp. 1 (S.D. N.Y. 1991) and judgment aff'd, 960 F.2d 301 (2d Cir. 1992).

the purposes of copyright law.[2] The Section 107 preamble of uses is deemed suggestive and "illustrative" rather than exclusive. Appellate opinions have faulted district courts for failure to consider whether use fell within, or "was similar to" the "illustrative" categories set out in the preamble.[3] The fair use doctrine, generally, and the preamble's recited categories of Section 107, including comment and criticism, implicate the critical free flow of ideas and information in a pluralistic society, thus providing public benefit and underwriting the principle of copyright law as fostering and fomenting creativity.[4]

The first factor, purpose and character of use, invites a weighing of the "commercial nature" or "nonprofit educational purposes" of the use. Even within the confines of subsection 1, courts have made clear that the choice is not bipolar. Commercial use is "a matter of degree, not an absolute."[5]

Commerciality inquiries traditionally focused, albeit not exclusively, on economic incentives and remuneration, bottom-line motivations and monetary returns, such as

---

[2] Harper & Row Publishers, Inc. v. Nation Enterprises, 471 U.S. 539, 560, 105 S. Ct. 2218, 85 L. Ed. 2d 588 (1985) (citations omitted) ("Since the [fair use] doctrine is an equitable rule of reason, no generally applicable definition is possible, and each case raising the question must be decided on its own facts"); Campbell v. Acuff-Rose Music, Inc., 510 U.S. 569, 114 S. Ct. 1164, 127 L. Ed. 2d 500 (1994).

[3] Ringgold v. Black Entertainment Televison, Inc., 126 F.3d 70, 78, 150 A.L.R. Fed. 813 (2d Cir. 1997) ("though . . . criticism, comment, news reporting, teaching, scholarship, and research . . . have an 'illustrative and not limitative' function . . . the [preamble] categories should not be ignored.").

[4] *See, e.g.,* Wojnarowicz v. American Family Ass'n, 745 F. Supp. 130, 143 (S.D. N.Y. 1990) (fair use of artist's paintings in brochure proselytizing against federal funds for art).

[5] Kelly v. Arriba Soft Corp., 280 F.3d 934, 61 U.S.P.Q.2d (BNA) 1564 (9th Cir. 2002), opinion withdrawn and superseded on denial of reh'g, 336 F.3d 811, 67 U.S.P.Q.2d (BNA)(reversed on other grounds and remanded) 1297 (9th Cir. 2003) (commercial use of plaintiff's images in defendant's search engine database was "more incidental and less exploitative"; because images were not highly exploitative, commercial nature weighed "only slightly against a finding of fair use"); Higgins v. Detroit Educational Television Foundation, 4 F. Supp. 2d 701 (E.D. Mich. 1998) (citations omitted)(public television station claimed fair use in copyright infringement brought by performer for unauthorized use of his music as background in a teen-targeted feature broadcast).

the copier's profits, price disparities between the underlying work and the copied work, and other quantifiable factors.[6] Neither profit motive nor monetary gain, however, established commerciality, and a per se concept is at odds with a malleable weighing of factors urged by the Court.[7] Conversely, nonprofit educational use is not converted into commercial use because the user makes a profit or charges for the work.[8] Even where use is deemed commercial, the notion that "every commercial use of copyrighted material is presumptively unfair"[9] was dispelled by the United States Supreme Court in favor of evaluating commercial use as a "separate factor that tends to weigh against fair use, a 'tendency' that varies with the context of the use."[10]

The internet is providing challenges to the concept of balancing and weighing this factor. An internet search engine that displayed its results in the form of small pictures, known as thumbnails, was sued by a photographer for copying photographs displayed on his and other web sites licensed by him.[11] The operator of the search engine created its data base by copying, downloading and indexing images from the other sites for its web users. Defendant's commercial purpose was deemed "incidental" because it did not promote its own web site nor profit by

---

[6]Rogers v. Koons, 960 F.2d 301 (2d Cir. 1992).

[7]Campbell v. Acuff-Rose Music, Inc., 510 U.S. 569, 577, 114 S. Ct. 1164, 127 L. Ed. 2d 500 (1994) ("the mere fact that a use is educational and not for profit does not insulate it from a finding of infringement, any more than the commercial character of a use bars a finding of fairness"); Haberman v. Hustler Magazine, Inc., 626 F. Supp. 201 (D. Mass. 1986) (publisher's reproduction of artist's sculptures in adult entertainment magazine was not "commercial"); *see also* Harper & Row Publishers, Inc. v. Nation Enterprises, 471 U.S. 539, 562, 105 S. Ct. 2218, 85 L. Ed. 2d 588 (1985) (the sole motive is not monetary gain but "whether the user stands to profit from exploitation . . . without paying the customary price").

[8]Higgins v. Detroit Educational Television Foundation, 4 F. Supp. 2d 701 (E.D. Mich. 1998) (use of plaintiff's music by public television stations that grossed $2,000 did not convert use to commercial).

[9]Sony Corp. of America v. Universal City Studios, Inc., 464 U.S. 417, 451, 104 S. Ct. 774, 78 L. Ed. 2d 574 (1984).

[10]Campbell v. Acuff-Rose Music, Inc., 510 U.S. 569, 114 S. Ct. 1164, 127 L. Ed. 2d 500 (1994).

[11]Kelly v. Arriba Soft Corp., 336 F.3d 811, 67 U.S.P.Q.2d (BNA) 1297 (9th Cir. 2003).

selling the images.[12]

§ 7:89 Transformation

First factor analysis—purpose and character of use—appears to be shifting in response to *Campbell v. Acuff-Rose Music, Inc.* The Supreme Court invoked commercial considerations under Section 107(1), but focused on "transformative use."[1] The query articulated by the Court to determine if the copier has transformed the original into some other legally cognizable thing is as follows:

> Is the work one that "merely 'supersedes the objects' of the original . . . , or adds something new, with a further purpose or different character, altering the first with a new expression, meaning or message?" . . . Although such transformative use is not absolutely necessary for a finding of fair use . . . the goal of copyright, to promote science and the arts, is generally furthered by the creation of transformative works . . . .[2]

Campbell creates a sliding scale for commerciality, measured in inverse proportion by the degree or extent of transformation: "the more transformative the new work, *the less will be the significance of other factors, like commercialism,* that may weigh against a finding of fair use."[3] Emphasis on the transformative thus affects all "other factors," as expressly noted by the Court, and lays the

---

[12]Kelly v. Arriba Soft Corp., 336 F.3d 811, 818, 67 U.S.P.Q.2d (BNA) 1297 (9th Cir. 2003).

[Section 7:89]

[1]Campbell v. Acuff-Rose Music, Inc., 510 U.S. 569, 577, 114 S. Ct. 1164, 127 L. Ed. 2d 500 (1994); *see* §§ 7:88 to 7:96.

[2]Campbell v. Acuff-Rose Music, Inc., 510 U.S. 569, 577, 579 114 S. Ct. 1164, 127 L. Ed. 2d 500 (1994) (citations omitted).

[3]Campbell v. Acuff-Rose Music, Inc., 510 U.S. 569, 577, 579 114 S. Ct. 1164, 127 L. Ed. 2d 500 (1994) (emphasis added); Sandoval v. New Line Cinema Corp., 973 F. Supp. 409 (S.D. N.Y. 1997), aff'd, 147 F.3d 215 (2d Cir. 1998) (transformation neutralized commercialism of production company's use of plaintiff's photographs when used in furtherance of a "distinct visual aesthetic and overall mood" of movie); *but cf.* Leibovitz v. Paramount Pictures Corp., 137 F.3d 109, 115 (2d Cir. 1998) (parodic advertisement created for commercial film product lessened the weight of first factor analysis in favor of defendants, but "less indulgence does not mean no indulgence at all," tipping first factor toward fair use).

groundwork for a marked new fair use calculus of all factors.

Although the Campbell opinion is a benchmark in parody, a subsection of commentary and criticism, Campbell is not limited in substantive scope to parody cases and has had substantive application to the arts, image conversions to television media and the internet.[4]

Ordinarily reproducing work in a different medium is not transformative.[5] But if the function is changed by the new medium, then transformation may be sustained.[6] Even exact replicas may be transformative under certain conditions. Thumbnails of an artist's photographs displayed on search engine web sites have been considered sufficiently transformative:

> "Kelly's images are artistic works intended to inform and to engage the viewer in an aesthetic experience. His images are used to portray scenes from the American West in an aesthetic manner. [Defendant's] use of the [artist's] images in the thumbnails is unrelated to any aesthetic purpose.

---

[4]Kelly v. Arriba Soft Corp., 280 F.3d 934, 61 U.S.P.Q.2d (BNA) 1564 (9th Cir. 2002), opinion withdrawn and superseded on denial of reh'g, 336 F.3d 811, 818, 67 U.S.P.Q.2d (BNA) 1297 (9th Cir. 2003)(reversed on other grounds and remanded) (applying Campbell transformative test for fair use in infringement action involving unauthorized display of plaintiff's copyrighted photographs on the internet); Ringgold v. Black Entertainment Televison, Inc., 126 F.3d 70, 150 A.L.R. Fed. 813 (2d Cir. 1997) (applying Campbell transformative test for fair use in nonparodic infringement action involving unauthorized display of plaintiff's licensed poster in commercial television sitcom); Higgins v. Detroit Educational Television Foundation, 4 F. Supp. 2d 701 (E.D. Mich. 1998) (applying Campbell transformative test for fair use in nonparodic infringement action involving unauthorized use of music in audio-visual public television feature); Mattel, Inc. v. Pitt, 229 F. Supp. 2d 315 (S.D. N.Y. 2002) (applying Campbell transformative test for fair use in infringement action involving customized Barbie doll figures in sadomasochistic costumes and in sexual slavery storylines on website); Mattel, Inc. v. Walking Mountain Productions, 353 F.3d 792, 69 U.S.P.Q.2d (BNA) 1257 (9th Cir. 2003) (applying *Campbell* transformative test for fair use in infringement action involving photographs of Barbie doll in absurd and often sexualized situations printed on postcards and posted on website).

[5]See 7:45 to 7:46.

[6]Elvis Presley Enterprises, Inc. v. Passport Video, 357 F.3d 896 (9th Cir. 2004) (voice-overs accompanying photographs in a biographical documentary video sufficiently transformed copyrighted photos into something new).

> * * *
>
> This . . . [is] more than mere[] retransmission of [the artist's] images in a different medium. Arriba's use . . . serves a different function than [the artist's]-improving access to information on the internet versus artistic expression. [Such] use is not superseding . . . but . . . has created a different [transformative] purpose."[7]

In the absence of fungible end-use, the work is considered more transformative than superseding. Thus, where subsequent downloads by search engine subscribers enlarging thumbnails from web site would be grainy, the court concluded they would not be substitutes for illustration or aesthetic viewing.[8]

The internet has been considered a "tool" to "improve access to images" on the internet, fulfilling underlying goals of copyright that benefit both public and artist. Display of copyrighted photographs as thumbnails on a web site was transformative:

> The thumbnails do not stifle artistic creativity because they are not used for illustrative or artistic purposes and . . . do not supplant the need for the originals . . . [T]hey benefit the public by enhancing information gathering techniques on the internet.[9]

However, the court concluded that the full-sized images on the web site were "end product[s]" because framing the images and adding datum text did not add new expression or transform meaning.

§ 7:90 Parody—Generally

In *Campbell v. Acuff-Rose*, the United States Supreme Court unequivocally endorsed parody as a potential fair use consistent with comment and criticism, referencing

---

[7]Kelly v. Arriba Soft Corp., 336 F.3d 811, 818-819, 67 U.S.P.Q.2d (BNA) 1297 (9th Cir. 2003).

[8]Kelly v. Arriba Soft Corp., 336 F.3d 811, 819, 67 U.S.P.Q.2d (BNA) 1297 (9th Cir. 2003) (enlarging copies "sacrifices" clarity); Elvis Presley Enterprises, Inc. v. Passport Video, 357 F.3d 896 (9th Cir. 2004) (Elvis fans wanting photos would not find television documentary displaying them a "viable substitute.").

[9]Kelly v. Arriba Soft Corp., 336 F.3d 811, 820, 67 U.S.P.Q.2d (BNA) 1297 (9th Cir. 2003).

the public benefit that underlies the equitable doctrine.[1] In *Rogers v. Koons*,[2] the Second Circuit described parody for purposes of the fair use defense:

> Parody or satire . . . is when one artist, for comic effect or social commentary, closely imitates the style of another artist, and in so doing creates a new art work that makes ridiculous the style and expression of the original. . . . [P]arody and satire are valued forms of criticism, encouraged because this sort of criticism itself fosters the creativity protected by the copyright law.[3]

Although the Supreme Court denied certiorari in *Rogers v. Koons*, shortly thereafter in *Campbell v. Acuff-Rose Music, Inc.*,[4] the Court endorsed the defense:

> [P]arody has an obvious claim to transformative value. . . . Like less ostensibly humorous forms of criticism, [parody] can provide social benefit by shedding light on an earlier work, and in the process creating a new one. We thus line up with the courts that have held that parody, like other comment or criticism, may claim fair use under section 107 [of title 17].[5]

[Section 7:90]

[1]Campbell v. Acuff-Rose Music, Inc., 510 U.S. 569, 577, 114 S. Ct. 1164, 127 L. Ed. 2d 500 (1994); *see also* § 8:8, (parody evaluated in trademark infringement cases in the context of whether or not the parodist's goods confuse customers under the "likelihood of confusion" element).

[2]Rogers v. Koons, 751 F. Supp. 474 (S.D. N.Y. 1990), amended on reargument, 777 F. Supp. 1 (S.D. N.Y. 1991) and judgment aff'd, 960 F.2d 301 (2d Cir. 1992).

[3]Rogers v. Koons, 751 F. Supp. 474 (S.D. N.Y. 1990), amended on reargument, 777 F. Supp. 1 (S.D. N.Y. 1991) and judgment aff'd, 960 F.2d 301 at 309 (2d Cir. 1992).

[4]Campbell v. Acuff-Rose Music, Inc., 510 U.S. 569, 114 S. Ct. 1164, 127 L. Ed. 2d 500 (1994) (parody defense asserted in action for copyright infringement brought by owner of copyright to Roy Orbison song, "Oh, Pretty Woman," against musical group 2 Live Crew for its unauthorized "rap" version).

[5]Campbell v. Acuff-Rose Music, Inc., 510 U.S. 569, 114 S. Ct. 1164, 127 L. Ed. 2d 500 at 516 (1994). *See also* Hustler Magazine v. Falwell, 485 U.S. 46, 108 S. Ct. 876, 99 L. Ed. 2d 41 (1988) (parody recognized for its sociocultural and historical value in a democratic society but Supreme Court did not expressly rule on the defense); Benny v. Loew's Inc., 239 F.2d 532 (9th Cir. 1956), cert. granted, 353 U.S. 946, 77 S. Ct. 824, 1 L. Ed. 2d 856 (1957) and judgment aff'd, 356 U.S. 43, 78 S. Ct.

The "threshold question . . . is whether a parodic character may reasonably be perceived."[6] The resolution of whether a work is parody is a matter of law.[7] Parody, by definition, requires an appropriation to some degree of a preexisting work, but the appropriation must both conjure up the underlying work and transform it to produce the requisite parodic ridicule. Transformation is key.[8]

The Supreme Court reaffirmed the importance of the transformative factor, writing:

> For the purposes of copyright law, the nub of the definitions, and the heart of any parodist's claim to quote from existing material, is the use of some elements of a prior author's composition to create a new one that, at least in part, comments on that author's works. . . . Parody needs to mimic an original to make its point, and so has some claim to use the creation of its victim's . . . imagination.[9]

Parody as a "'form of social . . . criticism [has] significant value as free speech under the First Amendment.' "[10] Since the core of copyright is promotion of the arts by protecting artistic works and encouraging new development, parody is one instance where fair use limits "the rights of [] copyright owner[s] [in] works that build upon, reinterpret, and reconceive existing works."[11] However, parody does not create a presumption of fair use; although parodists are accorded "significant leeway" with respect to the extent and nature of copying because of the perceived

---

667, 2 L. Ed. 2d 583 (1958) (parody considered but no opinion rendered on fair use).

[6]Campbell v. Acuff-Rose Music, Inc., 510 U.S. 569, 114 S. Ct. 1164, 127 L. Ed. 2d 500 (1994).

[7]Mattel, Inc. v. Walking Mountain Productions, 353 F.3d 792, 69 U.S.P.Q.2d (BNA) 1257 (9th Cir. 2003) ("parody is a question of law, not a matter of public . . . opinion.").

[8]Rogers v. Koons, 960 F.2d 301 (2d Cir. 1992) ("whimsical image . . . of eight . . . puppies cuddled side-by-side in the arms of their owners" in Koons' sculptures, reinforced and recaptured both the image and the message)..

[9]Campbell v. Acuff-Rose Music, Inc., 510 U.S. 569, 114 S. Ct. 1164, 127 L. Ed. 2d 500 (1994).

[10]Mattel, Inc. v. Walking Mountain Productions, 353 F.3d 792, 801, 69 U.S.P.Q.2d (BNA) 1257 (9th Cir. 2003) (citation omitted).

[11]Mattel, Inc. v. Walking Mountain Productions, 353 F.3d 792, 799, 69 U.S.P.Q.2d (BNA) 1257 (9th Cir. 2003).

social value of such criticism. The parody still must be examined in the context of fair use factors,[12] "work[ing] its way through the relevant facts, and be judged case by case in light of the ends of the copyright law."[13]

§ 7:91 Parody—Object of the parody

The parody must "conjure up" the original work[1] and transform and ridicule it in a perceptible way, the so-called object of the parody rule. "It is [the] joinder of reference and ridicule that marks off the author's choice of parody from the other types of comment and criticism that . . . have had a claim to fair use protection as transformative works."[2]

That combination of parodic perception and commentary on the underlying author's work has been examined in the arts.[3] If the object of the parody is not the underlying work, courts do not consider the rule satisfied. The parody may "loosely target" the original as long as it "can reasonably be perceived" as comment or criticism of the original.[4] In contrast, a general critique or commentary using another's work will not be enough for purposes of parody since fair use is intended to credit originator and parodist.

Context has been used to evaluate whether the original

---

[12]Campbell v. Acuff-Rose Music, Inc., 510 U.S. 569 at 79, 114 S. Ct. 1164, 127 L. Ed. 2d 500 (1994); *see also* Fisher v. Dees, 794 F.2d 432, 435 (9th Cir. 1986).

[13]Fisher v. Dees, 794 F.2d 432, 435 (9th Cir. 1986), *see also* Berlin v. E. C. Publications, Inc., 329 F.2d 541, 9 A.L.R.3d 612 (2d Cir. 1964).

[Section 7:91]

[1]Rogers v. Koons, 751 F. Supp. 474 (S.D. N.Y. 1990), amended on reargument, 777 F. Supp. 1 (S.D. N.Y. 1991) and judgment aff'd, 960 F.2d 301, 310 (2d Cir. 1992); United Feature Syndicate, Inc. v. Koons, 817 F. Supp. 370 (S.D. N.Y. 1993).

[2]Campbell v. Acuff-Rose Music, Inc., 510 U.S. 569, 582, 114 S. Ct. 1164, 127 L. Ed. 2d 500 (1994); Mattel, Inc. v. Walking Mountain Productions, 353 F.3d 792, 802, 69 U.S.P.Q.2d (BNA) 1257 (9th Cir. 2003).

[3]*See* § 7:92.

[4]Mattel, Inc. v. Walking Mountain Productions, 353 F.3d 792, 801, 69 U.S.P.Q.2d (BNA) 1257 (9th Cir. 2003) (the "original need not be the sole object" of the parody).

is being parodied. Photographs of a Barbie doll nude or dressed in bizarre outfits and staged in curious or sexualized domestic scenarios was deemed a parody of Mattel's "ideal American" girl doll. By re-contextualizing Barbie, successfully marketed in couture ensembles associated with a lifestyle of glamour, wealth and beauty, the artist was commenting on Barbie's adverse influence on gender, class, sexuality and the social role of women.[5]

In contrast, if the new work is parodying societal ills or general issues, then even direct quotation of the original may be insufficient for purposes of the object of the parody rule. Thus, copying a whimsical photograph of puppies into sculpture did not parody the underlying image where the artist's commentary was about mass production and the declining quality of modern life.

In *Campbell v. Acuff-Rose*,[6] a rap group's use of the hit song "Oh, Pretty Woman," by Roy Orbison was deemed a parody in that it conjured up the original both lyrically and, to some degree, musically, even though the lyrics departed from the original after the first few lines. The 2-Live Crew rendition commented on the naivet? of the nostalgic, sentimental love of the original " . . . that ignore[d] the ugliness of street life . . . ." Parody does not require the new work to be "the irreplaceable object for its form of social commentary" as long as the underlying work is "' . . . at least in part the target of the . . . satire.' "[7]

Quotation and contrast have been sufficient to conjure up the original for parody. A composite photograph portraying the face of smirking comedian Leslie Nielsen attached to the body of a very pregnant model was deemed a parody of the Demi Moore photograph on the Vanity Fair cover by renowned artist Annie Liebovitz. By adding new elements and replicating the stylized Renaissance

[5]Mattel, Inc. v. Walking Mountain Productions, 353 F.3d 792, 802, 69 U.S.P.Q.2d (BNA) 1257 (9th Cir. 2003)(" . . . lighting, background, props, and camera angles all serve to create a context for Mattel's copyrighted work that transform Barbie's meaning.").

[6]Campbell v. Acuff-Rose Music, Inc., 510 U.S. 569, 114 S. Ct. 1164, 127 L. Ed. 2d 500 (1994).

[7]Mattel, Inc. v. Walking Mountain Productions, 353 F.3d 792, 802, 69 U.S.P.Q.2d (BNA) 1257 (9th Cir. 2003) (quoting Dr. Seuss Enterprises, L.P. v. Penguin Books USA, Inc., 109 F.3d 1394, 1400, 25 Media L. Rep. (BNA) 1641, 42 U.S.P.Q.2d (BNA) 1184 (9th Cir. 1997)).

pose of the original, the studio's advertisement for a new film

The Second Circuit clarified why the policies and purposes underlying the parody defense require conjuring up the original work:

> If an infringement of copyrightable expression could be justified as fair use solely on the basis of the infringer's claim to a higher or different artistic issue—without insuring public awareness of the original work—there would be no practicable boundary to the fair use defense. . . . The [object of the parody] rule's function is to insure that credit is given where credit is due. By requiring that the copied work be an object of the parody, we merely insist that the audience be aware that underlying the parody there is an original and separate expression, attributable to a different artist.[8]

In *United Features Syndicate, Inc. v. Koons*,[9] Koons admitted that the infringing sculpture "Wild Boy and Puppy" was not intended to be a parody of the "Garfield" comic strip character "Odie:"

> Given that Koons admits that other images or figures could have been used in the sculpture besides "Odie," it becomes even more obvious that the sculpture cannot be a comment, criticism, or parody directed, in any way, at "Odie" and there is no justification for the parody defense. . . . "Odie" is not an object of the parody but merely is claimed to be "an animal figure" that is part of a more general parody on the banality of life.[10]

§ 7:92 Parody—Amount and substantiality of parodic copying

Classifying the work as parody does not immunize the work from an analysis of the degree of taking in both amount and substantiality, the former a quantitative test and the latter a qualitative one. The rules and applications for this factor differ, however, for parody than for

---

[8]Rogers v. Koons, 960 F.2d 301, 310 (2d Cir. 1992).

[9]United Feature Syndicate, Inc. v. Koons, 817 F. Supp. 370 (S.D. N.Y. 1993).

[10]United Feature Syndicate, Inc. v. Koons, 817 F. Supp. 370 at 384 (S.D. N.Y. 1993).

fair use in general.[1] Before *Campbell*, jurisdictions applied varying tests to determine whether too much had been taken. *Campbell* recognized a flexibility for evaluating parodic copying and acknowledged that the facts and circumstances of each case would impact upon the "' . . . extent of permissible copying [that would] var[y] with the purpose and character of use,' "[2]

No formula exists for determining the propriety of the extent and degree of the taking.[3] Where the underlying work is not naturally severable, copying all of it may be justified.[4] Nor is the parodist required to copy the absolute minimum.[5] Verbatim copying may be permissible in certain situations, like where the purpose of the work dif-

---

[Section 7:92]

[1]*See* §§ 7:99 to 7:100.

[2]Mattel, Inc. v. Walking Mountain Productions, 353 F.3d 792, 803, 69 U.S.P.Q.2d (BNA) 1257 (9th Cir. 2003)(quoting Campbell v. Acuff-Rose Music, Inc., 510 U.S. 569, 586-587, 114 S. Ct. 1164, 127 L. Ed. 2d 500, 22 Media L. Rep. (BNA) 1353, 29 U.S.P.Q.2d (BNA) 1961 (1994)) (examination of the "'persuasiveness of a parodist's justification for the particular copying done.' ").

[3]Rogers v. Koons, 751 F. Supp. 474 (S.D. N.Y. 1990), amended on reargument, 777 F. Supp. 1 (S.D. N.Y. 1991) and judgment aff'd, 960 F.2d 301 (2d Cir. 1992) (rejecting the artist's claim of parody defense, where the wholesale copying of the underlying work would not constitute comment and criticism, because of unfamiliarity with that work); Walt Disney Productions v. Air Pirates, 581 F.2d 751 (9th Cir. 1978) (if the copying is "excessive" in conjuring up the original, fair use may be precluded in the Ninth Circuit; *but cf.* Leibovitz v. Paramount Pictures Corp., 137 F.3d 109 (2d Cir. 1998) (interpreting Campbell as rejecting Walt Disney Productions v. Air Pirates rule that "no more than an amount sufficient to conjure up" is permitted in favor of the Second Circuit's rule that the parody can conjure up "at least enough" of the original).

[4]Mattel, Inc. v. Walking Mountain Productions, 353 F.3d 792, 803, 69 U.S.P.Q.2d (BNA) 1257 (9th Cir. 2003) (where copyrighted material is plastic doll and infringing photographs depict doll, artist does not need to sever parts of doll).

[5]Mattel, Inc. v. Walking Mountain Productions, 353 F.3d 792, 804, 69 U.S.P.Q.2d (BNA) 1257 (9th Cir. 2003) (once the underlying work is conjured up, "how much more is reasonable will depend . . . on purpose and character or . . . likelihood that parody may serve as a market substitute . . . ," quoting Campbell, 510 US at 587).

fers from the original.[6] But some courts have fine-tuned *Campbell* by evaluating the quantity of material copied as well as its "quality and importance" in the underlying work; as well as he reasonableness of additional copying of the underlying work.[7] The evaluation is subjective in scale and scope, and highly contextual.

"Taking the heart" of the copyrighted work may be fair copying in some circumstances, particularly in parody where the "heart is also what most readily conjures up the [original] for parody, and it is the heart at which parody takes aim. . . . Copying does not become excessive in relation to parodic purpose merely because the portion taken was the original's heart."[8]

The inquiry in heart-taking parodic cases is "what else the parodist did besides go to the heart of the original."[9] Taking more than is necessary to conjure up the original, however, does not necessarily tip the third factor against fair use. The reasonableness of additional taking depends on the "overriding purpose and character of the copy to the original and the likelihood that the parody may serve as a market substitute for the original."[10] Even where defendants exceeded copying "to an extreme degree" using digital computer enhancement and copied the heart of a photograph of a nude pregnant actress, the third factor was given little weight.[11] No fair use defense for parody was found where a comic strip character was copied in

[6]Mattel, Inc. v. Walking Mountain Productions, 353 F.3d 792, 803, 69 U.S.P.Q.2d (BNA) 1257 (9th Cir. 2003) (quoting Kelly v. Arriba Soft Corp., 336 F.3d 811, 821, 67 U.S.P.Q.2d (BNA) 1297 (9th Cir. 2003)) (artist did not make a verbatim copy of Barbie doll).

[7]Leibovitz v. Paramount Pictures Corp., 137 F.3d 109 (2d Cir. 1998) (summary judgment in favor of studio on grounds of its fair use of nude photograph of pregnant actress upheld on appeal).

[8]Campbell v. Acuff-Rose Music, Inc., 510 U.S. 569, 588, 114 S. Ct. 1164, 127 L. Ed. 2d 500 (1994) (defendant musical group copied opening bass riff and first lyrical line of Roy Orbison song, but thereafter departed from original lyrics and tune).

[9]Campbell v. Acuff-Rose Music, Inc., 510 U.S. 569, 588, 589, 114 S. Ct. 1164, 127 L. Ed. 2d 500 (1994).

[10]Leibovitz v. Paramount Pictures Corp., 137 F.3d 109, 116 (2d Cir. 1998).

[11]Leibovitz v. Paramount Pictures Corp., 137 F.3d 109 (2d Cir. 1998) (". . . the third factor [has] little, if any, weight against fair use so long

toto in sculpture,[12] or where a photograph of puppies was copied in sculpture.[13]

§ 7:93 Parody—Market effect

In evaluating the effect of use on the potential market for, or value of the work, courts consider the extent of actual market harm caused by the infringer and whether such conduct would have a substantial adverse impact on potential markets.[1] Thus, analysis of effect on the market for the original, and the derivative markets, is required.

For parody, analysis of the fourth factor, like the third, has its own particularities. The law recognizes no derivative market for critical works, under the theory that imaginative authors would rarely create or license a derivative market critical of their work. "The market for potential derivative uses includes only those that creators of original works would in general develop or license others to develop."[2] The issue is not whether parody, by ridicule or criticism, impairs the original market or the market for derivative uses; "[t]he only harm to [be considered in this context] . . . is the harm of market

---

as the first and fourth factors favor the parodist"); *cf.* Ringgold v. Black Entertainment Televison, Inc., 126 F.3d 70, 150 A.L.R. Fed. 813 (2d Cir. 1997) (finding of fair use reversed and remanded on all factors in nonparodic case, but district court weighted the third factor toward defendants based upon brevity of intervals in which plaintiff's poster was visible on television, and potentially imprecise focus of near-full views of her poster in other segments).

[12]United Feature Syndicate, Inc. v. Koons, 817 F. Supp. 370 (S.D. N.Y. 1993).

[13]Rogers v. Koons, 751 F. Supp. 474 (S.D. N.Y. 1990), amended on reargument, 777 F. Supp. 1 (S.D. N.Y. 1991) and judgment aff'd, 960 F.2d 301 (2d Cir. 1992).

[Section 7:93]

[1]*See generally* § 7:101, Campbell v. Acuff-Rose Music, Inc., 510 U.S. 569, 590, 114 S. Ct. 1164, 127 L. Ed. 2d 500 (1994).

[2]Campbell v. Acuff-Rose Music, Inc., 510 U.S. 569, 590, 114 S. Ct. 1164, 127 L. Ed. 2d 500 (1994) ("no protectible derivative market for criticism"); *see also* Leibovitz v. Paramount Pictures Corp., 137 F.3d 109, 116 (2d Cir. 1998) ("[A]ny lost revenue Leibovitz might experience due to celebrities' reluctance to be photographed for fear of enduring parodies is not cognizable harm under the fourth fair use factor.").

substitution."[3] Thus, it is important that the proper derivative markets be identified.[4]

Misinterpretations of evidentiary presumptions of unfair use on market effect where use is commercial have been clarified by the Court, and all but disposed of except for market substitution, a verbatim copying when "use amounts to a mere duplication of the entirety of an original."[5] For transformative works generally, and parodic ones particularly, no presumption of unfair use is applicable.

Similarly, where there is a "silent record" on unexplored identified markets or misidentified markets, summary judgment has been held inappropriate for defendants who carry the burden of affirmative defense.[6] But where use admittedly does not interfere with potential markets for the copied work or derivative works based on it, defendant has no obligation to present evidence showing lack of harm in derivative markets.[7]

§ 7:94 Parody—Author's comments

Appropriating visual imagery is commonplace. Artists

---

[3]Campbell v. Acuff-Rose Music, Inc., 510 U.S. 569, 592, 114 S. Ct. 1164, 127 L. Ed. 2d 500 (1994).

[4]Campbell v. Acuff-Rose Music, Inc., 510 U.S. 569, 592, 114 S. Ct. 1164, 127 L. Ed. 2d 500 (1994) ("no evidence that potential rap market was harmed in any way by [defendants'] parody, rap version"); Mattel, Inc. v. Pitt, 229 F. Supp. 2d 315 (S.D. N.Y. 2002) (sadomasochistic Barbie dolls "do not . . . pose any danger of usurping demand for Barbie dolls in the children's toys market [nor does] sale or display of 'adult' dolls . . . appear to be a use Mattel would likely develop or license others to develop.") ; Mattel, Inc. v. Walking Mountain Productions, 353 F.3d 792, 803, 69 U.S.P.Q.2d (BNA) 1257 (9th Cir. 2003) (unlikely that Mattel would market or license works like those of the artist that lampooned Barbie); see also Kelly v. Arriba Soft Corp., 336 F.3d 811, 821, 67 U.S.P.Q.2d (BNA) 1297 (9th Cir. 2003) (transformative non-parodic thumbnails of artist's photographs on defendant's web site did not harm artist's market or licensees).

[5]Campbell v. Acuff-Rose Music, Inc., 510 U.S. 569, 591, 592, 114 S. Ct. 1164, 127 L. Ed. 2d 500 (1994).

[6]Campbell v. Acuff-Rose Music, Inc., 510 U.S. 569, 591, 592, 114 S. Ct. 1164, 127 L. Ed. 2d 500 (1994).

[7]Leibovitz v. Paramount Pictures Corp., 137 F.3d 109, 116 (2d Cir. 1998) (plaintiff sought licensing fee for use of her work in an advertisement).

have, for a long time, copied works of contemporaries and predecessors, and both apprenticeship and academicism utilize copying for pedagogical purposes.[1] Many contemporary art historians, critics, curators, and traders, to some degree and in various ways, acknowledge "appropriation" as an identifiable movement or category.

Appropriation juxtaposes antecedent imagery, structure, and composition, embedded in the historical, social, and cultural context of its creator, to the contemporary context of the copier. Appropriation in contemporary times refers loosely to the borrowing of preexisting imagery, advertising, artwork, or other sources created in one context to reconfigure a new artwork in a new context, with the intention of revealing different meanings and associations. Some critics emphasize that this reevaluation of meanings and associations must apply to *both* the underlying work and the copied work.

Jurisprudence and criticism generally track each other on a key point that the new work must transform the copied work to create a new work with a different message. But the law has never required that the parodist must also trigger a retroactive evaluation of the underlying work. From the legal perspective, the social benefits of parody are present and future-oriented; parody, like "originality," functions as a creative precipitator, consistent with the constitutional fostering of the arts codified in copyright law,[2] and thus eligible for fair use.

While the single act of relocating an image out of one era and into another might be sufficient from an artistic perspective to significantly change the message and meaning of both the copier's work and the copied work, no court has yet allowed for such a pure platonic appropriation. Something more is required of copiers to situate themselves within the legal paradigm for parody. The Supreme Court appears to have broadened the view of what consti-

---

[Section 7:94]

[1]*See* § 7:1.

[2]*See* §§ 7:2 to 7:11.

tutes recontextualizing a creative work,[3] signaling perhaps a judicial willingness to lower the threshold that the copier must cross to transform meaning for fair use purposes.

§ 7:95 Defendant's conduct

Some courts consider good faith as part of the first fair use factor—purpose and character—and others separate it as an additional factor. Wherever situated, it has been held an appropriate aspect of review. For courts in the former category, the view is that relevant to characterizing use as commercial or for public benefit is the defendant's conduct in effectuating use. In *Rogers v. Koons*,[1] the court found artist Jeff Koons had acted in bad faith by tearing off plaintiff Rogers' copyright notice before he sent plaintiff's photograph to Italian fabricators with instructions to copy the photo in detail. In *Haberman v. Hustler Magazine, Inc.*,[2] the court found Hustler Magazine had not acted in bad faith because it credited Haberman's copyright and informed readers how they could purchase postcards and photographs directly from the artist.

§ 7:96 Artistic purpose

That the infringing material is "art" is not "a shield to salvage an otherwise defective fair use defense."[1] Artists have positioned their unauthorized use of other creators' artworks in the context of art history. In *United Features v. Koons*, the court explained:

> The fact that the infringing copy can be classified as "art" or as being part of an "artistic tradition" cannot be used as a

---

[3]Campbell v. Acuff-Rose Music, Inc., 510 U.S. 569, 114 S. Ct. 1164, 127 L. Ed. 2d 500 (1994).

[Section 7:95]

[1]Campbell v. Acuff-Rose Music, Inc., 510 U.S. 569, 114 S. Ct. 1164, 127 L. Ed. 2d 500 (1994).

[2]Haberman v. Hustler Magazine, Inc., 626 F. Supp. 201 (D. Mass. 1986).

[Section 7:96]

[1]United Feature Syndicate, Inc. v. Koons, 817 F. Supp. 370 (S.D. N.Y. 1993); *see also* Rogers v. Koons, 751 F. Supp. 474 (S.D. N.Y. 1990), amended on reargument, 777 F. Supp. 1 (S.D. N.Y. 1991) and judgment aff'd, 960 F.2d 301 (2d Cir. 1992).

shield. . . . The creation of music[ ] . . . films, plays, and literature can all be characterized as "art". . . . If . . . "art" automatically immunized such work under the fair use doctrine . . . it would virtually eviscerate the protection afforded by the Copyright Act. Instead, the fair use analysis properly focuses . . . on whether the work is "of a commercial nature" which looks primarily at whether the defendant stands to profit from the use . . . without paying for such usage.[2]

C. NATURE OF COPYRIGHTED WORK

§ 7:97 Factual or creative

The nature of a work refers to its content, whether it is factual, or a product of imagination. Fair use is more likely to be found where the copied work is informational or factual, like directories, textbooks, guidebooks, how-to books, or telephone books; fair use is less likely to be found where the work is creative or imaginative, like artworks or cartoon characters. The law recognizes a greater need to disseminate fact, giving broader berth for fair use where the copyrighted work is factual material.[1]

In this limited context of fair use, courts usually recognize that art is "creative, imaginative, and original . . . represent[ing] a substantial investment of time and labor in anticipation of financial return, among other things,"[2] which militate against finding fair use. Courts have specifically considered the following factors to determine if

---

[2]United Feature Syndicate, Inc. v. Koons, 817 F. Supp. 370, 379 (S.D. N.Y. 1993).

[Section 7:97]

[1]Campbell v. Acuff-Rose Music, Inc., 510 U.S. 569, 114 S. Ct. 1164, 127 L. Ed. 2d 500 (1994) (comparing factual and fictional works for fair use defense); Stewart v. Abend, 495 U.S. 207, 237–38, 110 S. Ct. 1750, 109 L. Ed. 2d 184 (1990) (fictional story and factual work); Harper & Row Publishers, Inc. v. Nation Enterprises, 471 U.S. 539, 563–64, 105 S. Ct. 2218, 85 L. Ed. 2d 588 (1985) (about-to-be published memoir and published speech); Sony Corp. of America v. Universal City Studios, Inc., 464 U.S. 417, 455 n.40, 104 S. Ct. 774, 78 L. Ed. 2d 574 (1984) (motion picture and news broadcast); Feist Publications, Inc. v. Rural Telephone Service Co., Inc., 499 U.S. 340, 348-41, 111 S. Ct. 1282, 113 L. Ed. 2d 358 (1991) (creative work with factual compilation).

[2]Haberman v. Hustler Magazine, Inc., 626 F. Supp. 201 (D. Mass. 1986).

a work is creative in nature and "closer to the core of intended copyright protection: art is creative and imaginative (militates against fair use);[3] art represents an investment of time in anticipation of financial return (militates against fair use);[4] art contains a political message (militates against fair use because art is "no less creative" because of its message);[5] art provides aesthetics and information (search engine providing public benefit favors fair use);[6] and whether or not the work has been published or unpublished (published work favors fair use).[7]

§ 7:98 Publication

Whether or not the copied work has been published is critical to its nature. Courts have concluded that the scope of fair use should be broader, even for imaginative artwork, if the art has been publicly released by the artist.[1]

---

[3]United Feature Syndicate, Inc. v. Koons, 817 F. Supp. 370, 380 (S.D. N.Y. 1993).

[4]Rogers v. Koons, 751 F. Supp. 474 (S.D. N.Y. 1990), amended on reargument, 777 F. Supp. 1 (S.D. N.Y. 1991) and judgment aff'd, 960 F.2d 301 (2d Cir. 1992).

[5]Wojnarowicz v. American Family Ass'n, 745 F. Supp. 130, 144 (S.D. N.Y. 1990).

[6]Kelly v. Arriba Soft Corp., 336 F.3d 811, 820, 67 U.S.P.Q.2d (BNA) 1297 (9th Cir. 2003).

[7]Kelly v. Arriba Soft Corp., 280 F.3d 934, 61 U.S.P.Q.2d (BNA) 1564 (9th Cir. 2002), opinion withdrawn and superseded on denial of reh'g, 336 F.3d 811, 67 U.S.P.Q.2d (BNA) 1297 (9th Cir. 2003) (reversed on other grounds and remanded) ("Published works are more likely to qualify as fair use because the first appearance of the artist's expression has already occurred.").

[Section 7:98]

[1]Kelly v. Arriba Soft Corp., 336 F.3d 811, 820, 67 U.S.P.Q.2d (BNA) 1297 (9th Cir. 2003) (creativity balanced by publication weighed factor "only slightly in favor of [artist]"); Haberman v. Hustler Magazine, Inc., 626 F. Supp. 201 (D. Mass. 1986); Wojnarowicz v. American Family Ass'n, 745 F. Supp. 130, 143–44 (S.D. N.Y. 1990); Higgins v. Detroit Educational Television Foundation, 4 F. Supp. 2d 701 (E.D. Mich. 1998) (second fair use factor tipped for plaintiff because his musical compositions were creative, but factor was not weighed heavily because music was previously published); Ringgold v. Black Entertainment Televison, Inc., 126 F.3d 70, 150 A.L.R. Fed. 813 (2d Cir. 1997) (second factor weighed in favor of plaintiff because her work was creative, without

D. VOLUME OF TAKING: AMOUNT AND SUBSTANTIALITY

§ 7:99 Amount

The third factor asks whether "the amount of substantiality of the portion used in relation to the copyrighted work as a whole" is reasonable in relation to the purpose of copying.[1] In determining how much has been used, the focus is not on how much was taken, but how much was taken of the protected elements in the original.[2]

The amount and substantiality of use involves a qualitative and quantitative analysis.[3] No set formula exists for determining the percentage amount of copying that will fall within or without a fair use finding. The "extent of permissible copying varies with the purpose and character of use."[4]; however, courts make certain repeated observations: (1) the greater the amount of copying, the less likelihood it constitutes fair use; and (2) copying the "heart" of the copyrighted work diminishes fair use.[5] The rules for assessing the volume of the taking are modified for parody.[6]

The opinions are not consistent on the degree of use: Extensive and verbatim copying precludes fair use;[7] copy-

---

referencing that copyrighted painting had already been published as a licensed poster).

[Section 7:99]

[1]Campbell v. Acuff-Rose Music, Inc., 510 U.S. 569, 586, 114 S. Ct. 1164, 127 L. Ed. 2d 500 (1994).

[2]Leibovitz v. Paramount Pictures Corp., 137 F.3d 109 (2d Cir. 1998) (plaintiff was not entitled to protection for the appearance of a nude, pregnant body); *see also* §§ 7:104 to 7:112 (discussing what photographic elements are copyrightable).

[3]*See also* § § 7:89, 7:90 to 7:94.

[4]Kelly v. Arriba Soft Corp., 280 F.3d 934 (9th Cir. 2002) (copying the entire image was fair use because it enabled internet users to decide whether to access the originating web site or obtain more information).

[5]Leibovitz v. Paramount Pictures Corp., 137 F.3d 109 (2d Cir. 1998).

[6]*See* §§ 7:90 to 7:94.

[7]Weissmann v. Freeman, 868 F.2d 1313, 1325, 101 A.L.R. Fed. 91 (2d Cir. 1989).

ing an entire work does not preclude fair use;[8] copying an entire work in reduced size does not preclude fair use;[9] copying small percentages, e.g., 3.3% of artwork, favors fair use;[10] and copying an entire image with cropping or reductions is fair use;[11] quantitative copying totaling 16 percent of copyright music without copying the lyrics tipped fair use factor in favor of defendants;[12] intermittent two to three-second partial on-screen views of plaintiff's poster used as set decoration in television program tipped fair use factor in favor of defendants.[13] Even if artwork is reproduced in its entirety, that fact may not weigh against fair use if the usage is criticism and commentary or parody. The amount used is a function of the portion used in relation to the copyrighted work, not in relationship to the infringing work. This means that if an artist appropriates a substantial portion of the copyrighted work, the fact that the copied portion may only constitute a tiny percentage of the new work is irrelevant; what has been taken from the copyrighted work in relationship to the totality of that work is the crucial factor.

§ 7:100 Copying the heart

Copying that goes to the heart of the copyrighted work, even if the copying is quantitatively small, militates

---

[8]Hustler Magazine Inc. v. Moral Majority Inc., 796 F.2d 1148, 1155 (9th Cir. 1986).

[9]Haberman v. Hustler Magazine, Inc., 626 F. Supp. 201 (D. Mass. 1986) (fine art postcard).

[10]Wojnarowicz v. American Family Ass'n, 745 F. Supp. 130, 144 (S.D. N.Y. 1990).

[11]Haberman v. Hustler Magazine, Inc., 626 F. Supp. 201 (D. Mass. 1986).

[12]Higgins v. Detroit Educational Television Foundation, 4 F. Supp. 2d 701 (E.D. Mich. 1998) (qualitative analysis also tipped in favor of defendants).

[13]Ringgold v. Black Entertainment Televison, Inc., 126 F.3d 70, 150 A.L.R. Fed. 813 (2d Cir. 1997) (twenty-six seconds total of nine intermittent on-screen partial views, the longest of which was five seconds showing 80 percent of poster, tipped fair use factor in favor of defendants, but decision reversed and remanded).

against finding fair use.[1] Summary judgment was upheld on the amount factor in cases where the amount copied in a sculpture was "nearly in toto" the copyrighted photograph;[2] the amount copied in a sculpture was the entirety of a comic strip character;[3] the portion copied in a sculpture was at "the heart of" the copied work depicting two boys in a farmyard pushing a large beribboned pig into a gift box, even though the box and one boy were not copied.[4]

E. MARKET EFFECT AND OTHER FACTORS

§ 7:101 Market effect

The fourth factor is "the effect of the use upon the potential market for or value of the copyrighted work."[1] Considerations include actual market harm caused by the use and whether such use would materially and adversely affect potential markets for the original.

Considered of singular importance, but not sole or primary importance after *Campbell*, "effect of the use" on the market value of the original must be considered by striking a balance between the benefit gained by the copyright owner when the copying is unfair use and the benefit gained by the public when the use is fair. Plaintiff need only show by a preponderance of the evidence that some "meaningful likelihood of future harm exists."[2]

The inquiry "must take account not only of harm to the original but also of harm to the market for derivative

---

[Section 7:100]

[1]Campbell v. Koons, 1993 WL 97381 (S.D. N.Y. 1993) (photograph).

[2]Rogers v. Koons, 751 F. Supp. 474 (S.D. N.Y. 1990), amended on reargument, 777 F. Supp. 1 (S.D. N.Y. 1991) and judgment aff'd, 960 F.2d 301 (2d Cir. 1992).

[3]United Feature Syndicate, Inc. v. Koons, 817 F. Supp. 370 (S.D. N.Y. 1993).

[4]Campbell v. Koons, 1993 WL 97381 (S.D. N.Y. 1993).

[Section 7:101]

[1]17 U.S.C.A. § 107(4); *see also* § 7:87.

[2]Wojnarowicz v. American Family Ass'n, 745 F. Supp. 130, 145 (S.D. N.Y. 1990) (citation omitted).

works."[3] Transformation affects market analysis. The more transformative the work, the more likely the market is arguably different from that of the original work. Conversely, non-transformative works that have the same purpose as the original negatively impact markets for the original work.[4]

When evaluating a potential market, consideration by some courts is given "only [to] traditional, reasonable, or likely to be developed markets."[5] Failure to show that the use had a likelihood of adversely affecting sales of the copied work is not dispositive in instances where the plaintiff is alleging appropriation without paying a licensing fee.[6] The less the impact on the owner's market or potential market, the less public benefit need be shown for noncommercial fair use.[7]

In *Rogers v. Koons*,[8] the Second Circuit found the use by Koons and Sonnabend Gallery commercial, and plaintiff's market prejudiced, notwithstanding the transfer of medium which fed two different markets, the high-end sculpture market and the low-end postcard and fine art photography market. The court found the plaintiff's derivative market would be adversely curtailed by the defendant's activity, since by derivation the plaintiff and/or his licensees could exploit any medium.

In *Kelly v. Arribasoft Corp.*,[9] the Ninth Circuit considered the artist's potential multiple markets impacted by

---

[3]Harper & Row Publishers, Inc. v. Nation Enterprises, 471 U.S. 539, 568, 105 S. Ct. 2218, 85 L. Ed. 2d 588 (1985). Campbell v. Acuff-Rose Music, Inc., 510 U.S. 569, 590, 114 S. Ct. 1164, 127 L. Ed. 2d 500 (1994) (the law recognizes no derivative market for critical works, but such works, including parody, may have effects in protectible markets for derivative works).

[4]Kelly v. Arriba Soft Corp., 280 F.3d 934 (9th Cir. 2002).

[5]Ringgold v. Black Entertainment Televison, Inc., 126 F.3d 70, 80, 150 A.L.R. Fed. 813 (2d Cir. 1997).

[6]Ringgold v. Black Entertainment Televison, Inc., 126 F.3d 70, 80, 150 A.L.R. Fed. 813 (2d Cir. 1997).

[7]Rogers v. Koons, 751 F. Supp. 474 (S.D. N.Y. 1990), amended on reargument, 777 F. Supp. 1 (S.D. N.Y. 1991) and judgment aff'd, 960 F.2d 301 (2d Cir. 1992).

[8]Ringgold v. Black Entertainment Televison, Inc., 126 F.3d 70, 80, 150 A.L.R. Fed. 813 (2d Cir. 1997).

[9]Kelly v. Arriba Soft Corp., 280 F.3d 934 (9th Cir. 2002).

defendant's use of his photographs on the internet. Plaintiff was a professional photographer who maintained a web site and licensed other sites to show his works. The defendant operated a search engine that displayed results from "crawling" the internet and offering users image-based results. Smaller versions of plaintiff's copyrighted images appeared on defendant's web site. Users could download the "thumbnails" to disks or print them but enlargement resulted in loss of clarity. Affirming the district court's finding of fair use of the thumbnails, the Ninth Circuit explained:

> Kelly's images are related to several potential markets. One purpose . . . is to attract internet users to his web site, where he sells advertising space as well as books and travel packages . . . . [K]elly could sell or license his photographs to other web sites or to a stock photo database, which [in turn] could offer the images to its customers. [Defendant's] use of Kelly's images does not harm [his] market . . . or the value of his images . . . . [t]he search engine . . . guide[s] users to Kelly's web site rather than away from it. Even if users were more interested in the image itself rather than the information on the web page, they would still have to go to Kelly's site to see the full-sized image. The thumbnails [are] not a substitute for the full-sized images because when . . . enlarged, they lose . . . clarity.

But the Ninth Circuit reversed a finding of fair use for the full-sized images, holding the artist's display right was infringed:

> By giving users access to Kelly's full-sized images on its own web site, [defendant] harms all of Kelly's markets. Users will no longer have to go to Kelly's web site to see the full-sized images, therby deterring people from visiting his . . . site. In addition, users would be able to download the full-sized images from [defendant's] site and then sell or license those images themselves, reducing Kelly's opportunity to sell or license his own images. If the display . . . became widespread [on] other web sites, it would reduce the number of visitors to Kelly's web site even further and increase the chance of others exploiting his images. These actions would result in substantial adverse effects to the potential markets for Kelly's original works.

§ 7:102 Additional factors

Fair use analysis includes the four factors, but is in no

way limited to them. The four factors can be considered the "above the line" legal prerequisites, supplemented, as appropriate, by additional points and issues, or the "below the line" supplementary factors. The defendant asserting the affirmative defense ordinarily should be prepared to bootstrap its position with additional points. The following factors considered in addition to the four fair use factors in art copyright suits are estoppel; unclean hands; and the First Amendment.[1]

But the majority of courts have refused to entertain assertions of First Amendment rights separate and distinct from the fair use defense. First Amendment issues are considered incorporated within the fair use analysis. Thus the courts have rejected artistic speech and political speech as separate factors under fair use.

VIII. SPECIFIC ART FORMS

A. CARTOONS AND COMIC STRIP CHARACTERS

§ 7:103 Generally

Cartoon characters and comic strip characters are eligible for protection as original works of authorship: "protection exists . . . because cartoon characters . . . have 'physical as well as conceptual qualities' that are 'more likely to contain some unique elements of expression.'"[1] Distinctive cartoon characters are protectible, but those "that embody little more than an unprotected

---

[Section 7:102]

[1]Wojnarowicz v. American Family Ass'n, 745 F. Supp. 130, 146 (S.D. N.Y. 1990).

[Section 7:103]

[1]Chase-Riboud v. Dreamworks, Inc., 987 F. Supp. 1222 (C.D. Cal. 1997) (citations omitted); *see, e.g.,* I.R.V. Merchandising Corp. v. Jay Ward Productions, Inc., 856 F. Supp. 168 (S.D. N.Y. 1994) (Rocky the Flying Squirrel, Bullwinkle, Boris and Natasha, and Dudley Do-Right); ARP Films, Inc. v. Marvel Entertainment Group, Inc., 952 F.2d 643, 21 Fed. R. Serv. 3d 887 (2d Cir. 1991) (Spiderman); Detective Comics v. Bruns Publications, 111 F.2d 432 (C.C.A. 2d Cir. 1940) (Superman); King Features Syndicate v. Fleischer, 299 F. 533 (C.C.A. 2d Cir. 1924) (Spark Plug); Walt Disney Productions v. Air Pirates, 581 F.2d 751 (9th Cir. 1978) (Mickey Mouse); United Feature Syndicate, Inc. v.

idea are not."[2] To determine "whether a character in a second work infringes a cartoon character, courts have generally considered not only the visual resemblance but also the totality of the characters' attributes and traits."[3]

Can fictional characters become so incorporated into the American cultural landscape that their use is as iconographic as famous natural landmarks and[4] does not require authorization? The question does not appear to have been posited precisely this way, but courts have examined whether commercial success of fictional characters transforms them into factual entities for purposes of analyzing the nature of the work under fair use defense. The district court in United Features, rejecting the artist's contention that the comic strip character Odie had a "factual existence" as a successful Garfield character, responded:

> [U]nlike a trade name that loses its protection under the Lanham Act when it becomes generic, these imaginative characters do not lose copyright protection as a result of their incorporation into American culture. [citation omitted] No matter how popular a character may become, the copyright owner is entitled to guard against the unauthorized commercial exploitation of that character.[5]

B. PHOTOGRAPHY

§ 7:104 Elements

Section 101 expressly identifies "photographs" as PGS

Koons, 817 F. Supp. 370 (S.D. N.Y. 1993) (Odie); *see also* Sapon v. DC Comics, 62 U.S.P.Q.2d (BNA) 1691, 2002 WL 485730 (S.D. N.Y. 2002) (Batman).

[2]Kouf v. Walt Disney Pictures & Television, 16 F.3d 1042 (9th Cir. 1994).

[3]Ollie v. Domino's Pizza, Inc., 44 U.S.P.Q.2d (BNA) 1042, 1997 WL 529049 (S.D. N.Y. 1997), citing Warner Bros. Inc. v. American Broadcasting Companies, Inc., 720 F.2d 231, 240 (2d Cir. 1983) (cartoon characters under copyright and the Lanham Act).

[4]*But see* Pebble Beach Co. v. Laub America Corp., 1985 WL 5584 (N.D. Cal. 1985) (abstract rendering of famous cypress trees used by corporation enjoined under Lanham Act where plaintiff had been using its own version as a corporate logo long before defendant).

[5]United Feature Syndicate, Inc. v. Koons, 817 F. Supp. 370, 380 (S.D. N.Y. 1993).

works,[1] eligible for protection under Section 102(a)(5). The popularity and prevalence of the new medium for documenting the Civil War resulted in statutory copyright protection for photographs.[2] The United States Supreme Court addressed the medium directly in the seminal case of *Burrow-Giles*[3] holding that a photographic portrait of Oscar Wilde was protected. Regulations provide guidelines for photography.[4] Cases discussing photography include originals, slides, book and magazine reproductions, posters, advertising.[5] Certain photographs made for exhibition purposes are also eligible for protection under VARA.[6]

Photography and its technological progeny have anchored the contemporary art scene for many years yet only recently has the medium been widely recognized as a discrete museum department for specific curatorial focus. Major photography exhibitions are regularly mounted drawing large crowds. Art photography is a vital evolving field that brings rich talent to the arts, and many contemporary artists have explored and creatively exploited the medium; i.e., digitalized transmissions, xerographic collages, large format installations, and assemblages. Although it appeals to the small community of artists for the

---

[Section 7:104]

[1]17 U.S.C.A. § 101.

[2]Act of March 3, 1865, 13 Stat. 540.

[3]Burrow-Giles Lithographic Co. v. Sarony, 111 U.S. 53, 4 S. Ct. 279, 28 L. Ed. 349 (1884).

[4]*See* 37 C.F.R. § 202.

[5]Vane v. The Fair, Inc., 676 F. Supp. 133 (E.D. Tex. 1987), judgment aff'd, 849 F.2d 186 (5th Cir. 1988); Heyman v. Salle, 743 F. Supp. 190 (S.D. N.Y. 1989); Simon v. Birraporetti's Restaurants, Inc., 720 F. Supp. 85 (S.D. Tex. 1989); Stuff v. E.C. Publ., Inc., 342 F.2d 143 (S.D.N.Y. 1962) (print showing Alfred E. Neuman titled "Me Worry?" entitled to protection); Morita v. Omni Publications Intern., Ltd., 741 F. Supp. 1107 (S.D. N.Y. 1990), consent judgment approved, 760 F. Supp. 45 (S.D. N.Y. 1991) (poster designer could not claim copyright interest in the photographer's outtakes, prepared in conjunction with shooting the poster photograph); Joshua Ets-Hokin v. Skyy Spirits, Inc., 225 F.3d 1068 (9th Cir. 2000) (photographs of vodka bottle used in various ad campaigns); Leigh v. Warner Bros., Inc., 212 F.3d 1210 (11th Cir. 2000) (book cover)

[6]VARA extends protection to still photographs produced for exhibition purposes only, signed by the author, and existing in a single copy. 17 U.S.C.A. § 101.

diversity and innovation it affords, photography is a democraticizing medium, as accessible to the Sunday shutter-bug as to the connoisseur.

Well-settled since the late 1800s is the concept that a photographer's "intellectual conceptions" makes photography a proper subject of copyright.[7] The twentieth century is in accord, considering photography an "exercise of artistic talent."[8] Notwithstanding judicial approbations of photographic artistry, the overwhelming . . . maxim . . . is that a copyright resides in technique. Skepticism about the medium for purposes of originality seems to feed such an assumption. At its inception, photography was primarily used to reproduce or recapture an underlying reality, be it a person, object or scene. To find the requisite originality, courts focused on what the photographer did that was evinced in the work and subsumed it under technique.

What is meant by technique? Courts and commentators regularly recite some or all of these factors: Selection of posing and arrangement, including background, accessories, light and shade;[9] lighting, shading, positioning, and timing;[10] angle of photograph, lighting, and timing; pose, background, light, and shade;[11] type of camera, film and lens, situs, and camera position;[12] tone, mood, camera position, angle, and lighting;[13] lighting, angle selection of film and camera, evoking a desired expression[14] lighting,

[7]Burrow-Giles Lithographic Co. v. Sarony, 111 U.S. 53, 4 S. Ct. 279, 28 L. Ed. 349 (1884).

[8]Gross v. Seligman, 212 F. 930 (C.C.A. 2d Cir. 1914).

[9]Burrow-Giles Lithographic Co. v. Sarony, 111 U.S. 53, 4 S. Ct. 279, 28 L. Ed. 349 (1884); Kisch v. Ammirati & Puris Inc., 657 F. Supp. 380 (S.D. N.Y. 1987).

[10]Pagano v. Chas. Beseler Co., 234 F. 963, 964 (S.D. N.Y. 1916).

[11]Gross v. Seligman, 212 F. 930, 931 (C.C.A. 2d Cir. 1914).

[12]Time Inc. v. Bernard Geis Associates, 293 F. Supp. 130, 141 (S.D. N.Y. 1968).

[13]Kisch v. Ammirati & Puris Inc., 657 F. Supp. 380 (S.D. N.Y. 1987).

[14]Rogers v. Koons, 751 F. Supp. 474 (S.D. N.Y. 1990), amended on reargument, 777 F. Supp. 1 (S.D. N.Y. 1991) and judgment aff'd, 960 F.2d 301 (2d Cir. 1992).

shading angle, background[15] All factors need not co-exist to support originality, and less than a handful may be enough. Courts have not focused upon whether a single aspect from the foregoing will support a finding of originality, but given the overall minimal degree of creativity generally required,[16] some courts have concluded that "the slightest artistic touch will meet the originality test for a photograph."[17] The catch-all term is technique, distilled as a common denominator, long considered the tried and true protectible element.[18]

The foregoing approach bears scrutiny. Techniques described above by the courts[19] are extremely similar to and almost indistinquishable from unprotected processes under Section 102(b), which states, "in no case does copyright protection . . . extend . . . to any idea,procedure, process, system, method of operation, concept, principle . . . regardless of the form in which it is . . . embodied in such work." Process and product have been conflated in the twenty-first century. Even by "traditional" standards, protected technique and unprotected process are sometimes inextricably intertwined.[20] Computers, sophisticated software and digital technologies provide users with practices and techniques that enable modulation and manipulation in ways beyond the court's reckoning to date, no

[15]Joshua Ets-Hokin v. Skyy Spirits, Inc., 225 F.3d 1068 (9th Cir. 2000).

[16]*See* Ch 7 §§ 7:44 to 7:45.

[17]Joshua Ets-Hokin v. Skyy Spirits, Inc., 225 F.3d 1068 (9th Cir. 2000).

[18]Burrow-Giles Lithographic Co. v. Sarony, 111 U.S. 53, 4 S. Ct. 279, 28 L. Ed. 349 (1884); Kisch v. Ammirati & Puris Inc., 657 F. Supp. 380 (S.D. N.Y. 1987).

[19]This cumulative list of factors has been considered in these, among other, cases: Vane v. The Fair, Inc., 676 F. Supp. 133 (E.D. Tex. 1987), judgment aff'd, 849 F.2d 186 (5th Cir. 1988); Gross v. Seligman, 212 F. 930, 931 (C.C.A. 2d Cir. 1914); Rogers v. Koons, 751 F. Supp. 474 (S.D. N.Y. 1990), amended on reargument, 777 F. Supp. 1 (S.D. N.Y. 1991) and judgment aff'd, 960 F.2d 301 (2d Cir. 1992); Pagano v. Chas. Beseler Co., 234 F. 963, 964 (S.D. N.Y. 1916); *accord* Time Inc. v. Bernard Geis Associates, 293 F. Supp. 130, 141 (S.D. N.Y. 1968).

[20]Kelly v. Arriba Soft Corp., 336 F.3d 811, 820, 67 U.S.P.Q.2d (BNA) 1297 (9th Cir. 2003); Hearn v. Meyer, 664 F. Supp. 832, 835 (S.D. N.Y. 1987) (hand coloring and hand drawing are unprotected processes for reproduction of illustrations).

doubt affecting legal line-drawing in this area.

Some contemporary courts are encompassing more forward thinking on the copyrightable elements of photography, although they recite the maxims quoted above. Current analysis appears to incorporate the view that appropriation of the photographer's ideas and concepts should be recognized.[21] Recent opinions reflect greater awareness of how photography is created, made, used, and commercially exploited. Although the more recent opinions couch the analysis in traditional verbiage, the result is nonetheless much broader protection for concept as that concept is reflected in the imagery, consistent with the view that art copying involves more than "tracing the original line by line . . . it includes the appropriation of the artist's thought in creating his own form of expression."[22]

The Eleventh Circuit, for example, stated it this way:

> Although some cases . . . evaluate[ ] 'mood' . . . independently . . . it is safest to focus on the more concrete elements of the photographer's craft . . . [t]he mood is not so much an independent aspect of his photograph protected by copyright, as the effect created by the lighting, shading, timing, angle, and film. The same holds true for the overall combination of elements in the photograph. *As long as the analysis is not overly detached and technical, it can adequately address both the effect of the protected, original elements of [the] photograph on the viewer and the contribution of those elements to the work as a whole.*[23]

A case for this proposition is *Rogers v. Koons*,[24] where the holding is more significant than the verbiage. The Second Circuit, after citing the protectible litany—film, camera, angle, lighting—continued: "To the extent that these factors are involved, 'Puppies' is the product of

[21]Rogers v. Koons, 960 F. 2d 301 (2d Cir. 1992), cert. denied, 113 S. Ct. 365 (1992) (elements of originality include "almost any . . . variant involved.").

[22]Franklin Mint Corp. v. National Wildlife Art Exchange, Inc., 195 U.S.P.Q. (BNA) 31, 1977 WL 22706 (E.D. Pa. 1977), judgment aff'd, 575 F.2d 62, 65 (3d Cir. 1978) (paintings).

[23]Leigh v. Warner Bros., Inc., 212 F.3d 1210 (11th Cir. 2000) (emphasis added).

[24]Rogers v. Koons, 751 F. Supp. 474 (S.D. N.Y. 1990), amended on reargument, 777 F. Supp. 1 (S.D. N.Y. 1991) and judgment aff'd, 960 F.2d 301 (2d Cir. 1992).

plaintiff's artistic creation. Rogers' inventive efforts in posing the group, taking the picture, and printing . . . suffices to meet the original work of art criteria."[25] However, evaluating substantial similarity between the photo and the infringing sculpture the court wrote: "[I]t is not the idea of the couple with eight small puppies seated on a bench that is protected, but . . . Rogers' expression of this idea . . . had [Koons] simply used the idea presented by the photo, there would not have been an infringing copy."[26] The court's assertion belies a belief that a couple and eight puppies on a single bench is outside expression. Future art cases may decide otherwise.

Leigh, for example, describes the integration among expression, imagery and technical selection in its evaluation of the protected elements of the photographer's work common to defendant's work:

> All of the photographs are taken from a low position, angled up . . . so that the contents of the bowls . . . remain hidden. Hanging Spanish moss borders the tops of . . . the photographs . . . Light shines down and envelopes the statue . . . leaving the surrounding cemetery in darkness . . . . These expressive elements all make the pictures more effective. The Spanish moss provides a . . . border . . . The location of the statue and the lighting . . . draw the viewer's attention . . . and lends a spiritual air . . . the angle contributes to the mystery and symbolic meaning . . . .[27]

A review of the cases indicates that those who convert the maxims to artistic standards by which the photograph can be evaluated as a PGS work produce comprehensive, integrated arguments.

§ 7:105 Publication—Delivery of slides to publisher

Delivery of slides to a publisher without copyright notice, even though the recipient intends to publish them,

---

[25] Rogers v. Koons, 751 F. Supp. 474 (S.D. N.Y. 1990), amended on reargument, 777 F. Supp. 1 (S.D. N.Y. 1991) and judgment aff'd, 960 F.2d 301 (2d Cir. 1992).

[26] Rogers v. Koons, 751 F. Supp. 474 (S.D. N.Y. 1990), amended on reargument, 777 F. Supp. 1 (S.D. N.Y. 1991) and judgment aff'd, 960 F.2d 301 (2d Cir. 1992).

[27] Leigh v. Warner Bros., Inc., 212 F.3d 1210 (11th Cir. 2000) (reversing summary judgment for defendant on single frame images for purposes of copyright infringement).

does not constitute publication. In *Vane v. The Fair, Inc.*,[1] a photographer delivered slides to the defendants for the limited purposes of reproduction in mailers. No copyright notice was affixed to the slides at the time of delivery, nor did the defendant use a copyright notice in the mailers. When the photographer discovered the slides were being used without his authorization for television commercials, he sued for infringement. Defendants contended that the photographer had forfeited his copyright by failing to affix notice prior to publication, dating the publication at the date of slide delivery to the defendant. The court concluded that delivery was not publication, but even if it were, the artist's copyright was still valid because he registered within five years after publication under Section 405(a)(2).[2]

§ 7:106 Publication—Reproduction in magazines, books, catalogs, newspapers

Publication in magazines, books, or catalogs ordinarily constitutes publication of a previously unpublished photograph.[1]

§ 7:107 Publication—Studio sales

An artist selling a limited number of photos or even one to an individual at the studio may constitute publication.

[Section 7:105]

[1]Vane v. The Fair, Inc., 676 F. Supp. 133 (E.D. Tex. 1987), judgment aff'd, 849 F.2d 186 (5th Cir. 1988) (in a case decided under the 1976 Act, publication of artist slides occurred for the first time when the defendant published them in mailers, not when the artist delivered them, without copyright notices, to the defendant).

[2]For copies distributed before the effective date of BCIA, omission of notice does not invalidate the copyright if "registration for the work has been made before or is made within five years after the publication without notice." 17 U.S.C.A. § 405(a)(2).

[Section 7:106]

[1]Schatt v. Curtis Management Group, Inc., 764 F. Supp. 902 (S.D. N.Y. 1991) (defendant's motion for summary judgment denied where the issue of date of publication arose because the photographer failed to renew his copyright under the Act of 1909, leading to forfeiture).

In *Schatt*,[1] the plaintiff, known for his seminal images of James Dean, sold only one photo between 1955 and 1962 to a Dean fan who visited the studio. The artist claimed a "congenial strangers" exception to general publication, because studio visitors were a limited class of individuals to whom communication was restricted, and that the single sale was not enough to constitute publication. The court responded to the former claim by stating, "plaintiff's arbitrary test of those fans 'worthy' of the opportunity to purchase his work could not have sufficiently limited the scope of publication."[2] The single sale was enough because the photo bore notice: "[P]laintiff elected to proceed by sale with a copyright notice, his claim to copyright must be measured from the year stated in the notice."[3]

§ 7:108 Obtaining valid copyright without registration—Compilations and collections

Form VA is used to register photography. If the photographer has omitted registration, he or she may still have a valid copyright under different theories. Section 103(a) extends copyright to compilations. A compilation is defined as "a work formed by the collection and assembling of preexisting materials . . . that are selected, coordinated, or arranged in such a way that the resulting work as a whole constitutes an original work of authorship."[1] Compilations include collective works. Collective works are defined as a "work . . . in which a number of contributions, constituting separate and independent works in themselves, are assembled into a collective whole."[2] Photographs reproduced in books, magazines, and other publications and periodicals may be eligible for protection

[Section 7:107]

[1]Schatt v. Curtis Management Group, Inc., 764 F. Supp. 902 (S.D. N.Y. 1991).

[2]Schatt v. Curtis Management Group, Inc., 764 F. Supp. 902 at 911 n.12 (S.D. N.Y. 1991).

[3]Schatt v. Curtis Management Group, Inc., 764 F. Supp. 902 at 911 n.12 (S.D. N.Y. 1991).

[Section 7:108]

[1]17 U.S.C.A. § 101.

[2]17 U.S.C.A. § 101

under these sections. Furthermore, separate contributions in a collective work do not require independent notice. Section 404(a) provides, "A separate contribution to a collective work may bear its own notice. . . . However, a single notice applicable to the collective work as a whole is sufficient . . . with respect to the separate contributions it contains."

§ 7:109 Obtaining valid copyright without registration—Reproduction in magazines, brochures, books, catalogs, newspapers

Photography is frequently published in compilations and collective works. Many works were published before art law became an official part of media reporting, i.e., before awareness seeped into the consciousness of artists that prophylactic measures need to be employed to protect their works under copyright. Nonetheless, photographers may have protection by virtue of the foregoing sections.

Photographs in copyrighted art catalogs are protected where the catalog contains notice. In *Heyman v. Salle*,[1] Heyman, a professional photographer, sued appropriationist artist David Salle for his use of Heyman's photograph of the Scull family, famous Pop art collectors, sitting at a table with portions of a James Rosenquist painting visible on the wall. The photo was reproduced in a Pop Art catalog copyrighted in 1965. No copyright was obtained for the photo. Salle used the photo to copy the image onto a theatrical backdrop, which in turn was published by another photographer, who was paid for a reproduction in a monograph on Salle. In 1986 a museum used that photo again in an exhibition catalog prepared for a Salle show. Salle admitted copying, but contended that Heyman never copyrighted the Scull photo, and that the compilation extension could not be made to the photo under Section 103(b), which states that copyright in a compilation "extends only to the material contributed by the author of such work," not to preexisting material used in the work. Since the Scull photo preexisted, it should not be protected.

The court found the Pop Art book was a compilation of

[Section 7:109]

[1]Heyman v. Salle, 743 F. Supp. 190 (S.D. N.Y. 1989).

photographs. Further, it found the Scull photo was an original work by Heyman which he contributed to the catalog, implicitly in line with the plaintiff's contention that since he was the photo author, the copyright of Pop Art extended to the photo as a component part of the author's contribution. The court further found that Section 404 notice protected the book and its contents, refusing to grant summary judgment for defendants.

§ 7:110 Copying

Copying occurs in various ways: Photo-to-photo; photo-to-sculpture;[1] photo-to-poster;[2] and photo-to-catalog-to-theatrical backdrop.[3] How the copying is executed by the alleged infringer should not affect the underlying copyright, but medium transfers do pertain to similarity issues,[4] and have been used to undercut the artist's own ability to create derivative works.[5]

§ 7:111 Substantial similarity

Substantial similarity presents a particular hurdle in photography, although even in courts where the only copyrightable aspect of a photograph is deemed technique, the intentional copying of a set-up shot may support a

---

[Section 7:110]

[1]Campbell v. Koons, 1993 WL 97381 (S.D. N.Y. 1993) (farmboys and pig); Rogers v. Koons, 751 F. Supp. 474 (S.D. N.Y. 1990), amended on reargument, 777 F. Supp. 1 (S.D. N.Y. 1991) and judgment aff'd, 960 F.2d 301 (2d Cir. 1992) (couple and puppies).

[2]Morita v. Omni Publications Intern., Ltd., 741 F. Supp. 1107 (S.D. N.Y. 1990), consent judgment approved, 760 F. Supp. 45 (S.D. N.Y. 1991) (photo to poster to magazine cover); Simon v. Birraporetti's Restaurants, Inc., 720 F. Supp. 85 (S.D. Tex. 1989) (photo to poster).

[3]Heyman v. Salle, 743 F. Supp. 190 (S.D. N.Y. 1989).

[4]*See, e.g.,* Heyman v. Salle, 743 F. Supp. 190 (S.D. N.Y. 1989) (Intra-medium transfers changing the look, so that lay observers would not find the art similar); *cf.,* Campbell v. Koons, 1993 WL 97381 (S.D. N.Y. 1993) (intra-medium transfer from 2-D to 3-D that "goes to heart" of the photo shows similarity).

[5]Simon v. Birraporetti's Restaurants, Inc., 720 F. Supp. 85 (S.D. Tex. 1989) (addition of text to a poster created by the artist when he reproduced his own work contained nothing original).

finding of substantial similarity.[1] In *Heyman v. Salle*,[2] the court found enough similarities between a photo and a theatrical backdrop, depicting a family of famous collectors sitting before a work by a famous contemporary artist, to deny defendants summary judgment notwithstanding the differences: Substantial capture of image but no direct copying; size (backdrop was 50 feet, photo 5½ inches); length of time exposed to audience (5 minutes); composite presentation (backdrop was for an opera, and only a component of a larger ensemble production set); different medium, giving different appearance; and colors (backdrop orange, photo black and white).

In *Rogers v. Koons*,[3] the Second Circuit upheld the district court's summary judgment for plaintiff on undisputed direct evidence of copying of the plaintiff's black and white photograph, "Puppies," of a couple seated on a bench with eight german shepherd puppies. Koons copied the photo by converting it with a base to an almost lifesize polychromed wood sculpture. Buttressing its ruling on additional grounds of substantial similarity, the court found identical expression, composition, and poses. In *Campbell v. Koons*,[4] where once again Koons copied a plaintiff's black and white photograph, "Boys with Pig," into a polychromed sculpture that was exhibited and sold at the same show as "Puppies," the court found "exact duplication of the central subject matter of Campbell's photograph—the boy pushing the pig—was not only a substantial portion . . . but the 'heart' of it."

§ 7:112 Derivative works

Derivative works, like works taken from the public

[Section 7:111]

[1]Kisch v. Ammirati & Puris Inc., 657 F. Supp. 380 (S.D. N.Y. 1987) (motion to dismiss denied where the trier of fact could find that the defendant's photograph was similar to the plaintiff's, where the lighting, camera angles, and positioning appear to be the same, but also finding that the mood and tone evoked were similar).

[2]Heyman v. Salle, 743 F. Supp. 190 (S.D. N.Y. 1989).

[3]Rogers v. Koons, 751 F. Supp. 474 (S.D. N.Y. 1990), amended on reargument, 777 F. Supp. 1 (S.D. N.Y. 1991) and judgment aff'd, 960 F.2d 301 (2d Cir. 1992).

[4]Campbell v. Koons, 1993 WL 97381 (S.D. N.Y. 1993).

domain, are vulnerable to originality claims. The additional matter added to such works must be more than "a minimal contribution." Too minimal for copyright were a painting of Dorothy in the Wizard of Oz based upon a photograph taken from the film, creating a new background and adding Toto the dog;[1] and an art poster created by an artist by reproducing his own original photograph with added text.[2]

In Simon,[3] where the defendant restaurant admitted using the artist's photographic poster for an advertising campaign, the court held no copyright protection existed because the work was in the public domain. Some years before, the artist had created an original photograph depicting an elderly gentleman in a Santa Claus suit rummaging through Christmas ornaments in an attic, which he authorized for publication in a magazine. Publication occurred without notice. Two years later, the artist created a photographic poster from the photograph. After the artist refused defendant's offer to purchase the rights to the poster, the restaurant hired a designer, providing the poster as the model. The court applied no presumption of validity to the registration, and instead of placing the burden on the defendant to rebut the presumption,[4] it found the plaintiff had failed to introduce evidence to support originality. The court concluded that if originality would not attach to mechanical photocopying by xeroxing or reprinting a negative, nor by photographing a print, then it could not apply to an artist who rephotographed

---

[Section 7:112]

[1]Gracen v. Bradford Exchange, 698 F.2d 300 (7th Cir. 1983); *see also* L. Batlin & Son, Inc. v. Snyder, 536 F.2d 486 (2d Cir. 1976) (change in medium from metal to plastic); Durham Industries, Inc. v. Tomy Corp., 630 F.2d 905 (2d Cir. 1980) (creating Walt Disney characters in the form of plastic wind-up toys); Shapiro, Bernstein & Co. v. Jerry Vogel Music Co., 73 F. Supp. 165 (S.D. N.Y. 1947) (new title and change in rhythm for musical number).

[2]Simon v. Birraporetti's Restaurants, Inc., 720 F. Supp. 85 (S.D. Tex. 1989).

[3]Simon v. Birraporetti's Restaurants, Inc., 720 F. Supp. 85 (S.D. Tex. 1989).

[4]The opinion does not report, but it may have relied on the public domain arguments as the rebuttal.

his work for a poster.[5] Although the rule seems proper as applied in the case, where "neither party disputes the identical nature of the photograph and the poster," it is important to distinguish what contribution, however "trivial," is made by the photographer in the development and production stages so that derivative works may be exploited. Photographing a print could add something new to the existing print if it were developed and produced to result in a derived image or manipulated photograph common in the arts.

C. CATALOGUE RAISONNE

§ 7:113 Generally

A catalogue raisonne has been considered a compilation of historical facts. Compilations are eligible for protection under Section 103. Subject matter extends "only to the material contributed by the author of such work, as distinguished from the preexisting material."[1]

In *Mount v. Ormond*,[2] the New York district court rejected an attempt by an author of books and catalogs about the artist John Singer Sargent to enjoin a museum director from publishing a catalogue raisonne on Sargent:

> [Plaintiff] has no rights in or to [the artist's] work or any existing historical material . . . The works of [the artist] and the facts regarding his life and work are matters of history. . . . A second author may make significant use of a prior work devoted to a historical subject, provided "he does not bodily appropriate the expression of another." Further, a catalogue raisonne, a listing of the "authentic" works of Sargent, while it may enjoy some copyright protection as a compilation, such protection "extends only to the material contributed by the author for such work as distinguished from the preexisting material employed in the work and does not imply any exclusive right in the preexisting material."[3]

---

[5]The court did not independently examine these propositions.

[Section 7:113]

[1]17 U.S.C.A. § 103(b).

[2]Mount v. Ormand, 1991 WL 191228 (S.D. N.Y. 1991).

[3]Mount v. Ormand, 1991 WL 191228 (S.D. N.Y. 1991).

IX. ARCHITECTURE

A. IN GENERAL

§ 7:114 Generally

It is not surprising given the debate about the borders of art and process and art and non-art that sooner or later a court would be confronted with the issue of whether the work is art or architecture, a distinction that has a critical impact on copyright outcomes. Classifying the work has been a held a question of fact.[1] Similarly, a factual question is presented by the issue of whether copyrightable expression by two authors has merged into a unitary whole.[2]

§ 7:115 PGS works under 1976 Act

Congress intended the Copyright Act of 1976 to protect architects from unauthorized copying of their plans and drawings.[1] Prior to BCIA,[2] the Act contained no reference to plans, although case law provided protection within the

---

[Section 7:114]

[1]Leicester v. Warner Brothers, 47 U.S.P.Q.2d (BNA) 1501, 1998 WL 468754 (C.D. Cal. 1998), aff'd, 232 F.3d 1212 (9th Cir. 2000) (lantern towers and landscape features prepared under percent for art program by artist determined by district court as streetwall see that comprised building design of architect).

[2]Leicester v. Warner Brothers, 47 U.S.P.Q.2d (BNA) 1501, 1998 WL 468754 (C.D. Cal. 1998), aff'd, 232 F.3d 1212 (9th Cir. 2000) (standard of review is clear error).

[Section 7:115]

[1]17 U.S.C.A. §§ 101, 102(a)(5); H.R. No. 1476, 94th Cong., 2d Sess. (1976) ("[a]n architect's plans and drawings would, of course, be protected by copyright."); 37 C.F.R. § 202.3(b)(iii); 37 C.F.R. 202.12(a)(blueprints as drawings) *cf.* Robert H. Jacobs, Inc. v. Westoaks Realtors, Inc., 159 Cal. App. 3d 637, 205 Cal. Rptr. 620 (2d Dist. 1984) (no common law copyright for unauthorized use of architectural plans after the Copyright Act of 1976 became effective, because of federal preemption under 17 U.S.C.A. § 301.); 17 U.S.C.A. § 5(i) (superseded) ("drawings . . . of a . . . technical character" were copyrightable).

[2]*See* § 7:9.

scope of PGS.[3] After BCIA, the PGS category was expressly amended to include "diagrams, models, and technical drawings, including architectural plans."[4] Conversely, the definition for visual art under Section 101 specifically excludes technical drawings; to date, no judicial opinion has so extended VARA.[5]

In 1990, Congress enacted the Architectural Works Copyright Protection Act.[6] Section 101 describes architectural works as follows:

> [A]n architectural work is the design of a building as embodied in any tangible medium of expression, including a building [providing that it is erected in a country adhering to the Berne Convention], architectural plans, or drawings. The work includes the overall form as well as the arrangement and composition of spaces and elements in the design, but does not include individual standard features.[7]

Architectural copyright law tracks two different types of cases—those before AWCPA[8] and those after. By identifying the interests—buildings, unconstructed buildings, or plans and designs—and ascertaining the timing of claims (AWCPA has an effective date and, for unconstructed works, a future reach), the practitioner can expedite his research. For convenience, the architectural materials are combined in this section.Recent cases discussed below provide judicial interpretation of the statutory provisions.

---

[3]Imperial Homes Corp. v. Lamont, 458 F.2d 895, 896 (5th Cir. 1972); Arthur Rutenberg Corp. v. Parrino, 664 F. Supp. 479, 480 (M.D. Fla. 1987); Kent v. Revere, 229 U.S.P.Q. (BNA) 828, 1985 WL 6453 (M.D. Fla. 1985); *see also* Robert H. Jacobs, Inc. v. Westoaks Realtors, Inc., 159 Cal. App. 3d 637, 205 Cal. Rptr. 620 (2d Dist. 1984).

[4]Pub. L. No. 100-568, 102 Stat. 2853, *amending* 17 U.S.C.A. § 101.

[5]Eales v. Environmental Lifestyles, Inc., 958 F.2d 876 (9th Cir. 1992), cert. denied, 113 S. Ct. 605 (1992) (The "useful article" exception, interposed as a defense barrier to plans and drawings, has been disposed of by the court because the intrinsic function of such plans is to "enable the reader to construct a building."), disapproved on other grounds, Hunt v. Pasternak, 179 F.3d 683 (9th Cir. 1999).

[6]*See* § 7:10.

[7]17 U.S.C.A. § 101; Architectural Works Copyright Protection Act, Pub. L. No. 101-650, §§ 701, 702, 704, 104 Stat. 5089, 5133 (1990). *See* Appendix 18B.

[8]*See* § 7:10.

§ 7:116 Authorship and originality

Copyright protection is available to architects; its scope has extended from drawings and blueprints to plans and buildings. The architect "who originates a set of blueprints for a dwelling is as much an author for copyright purposes as the writer who creates an original novel."[1]

In *Eales*,[2] the Ninth Circuit affirmed an infringement action against a real estate developer in favor of an architect. The developer had hired a California architectural firm to prepare construction plans and drawings for homes to be built in Arizona. After construction began, an Arizona architect was needed to conform the plans to the Scottsdale building code, and Eales was hired. She did not seek the permission of the California architectural firm to use its plans in constructing the homes. She viewed the plans, returned them to the developer, visited the site, examined the footprints of partially constructed homes, and prepared her own construction plans to comport with the existing footprint and local codes. The developer went out of business, and its former employees built a house on the same site for buyers using Eales' plans without her permission, and she sued. Defendants contended that Eales' work was not original because of her reliance upon the California plans. Citing the Bleistein standard that work need only manifest something "irreducible, which is one man's alone, not that the work be novel," the Ninth Circuit found originality "is met when the work is the result of independent creation." Since the plaintiff did not copy the plans and created the layout without consulting them, originality was satisfied.

B. PLANS, DRAWINGS

§ 7:117 Access, copying—Floor plan registered

Before AWCPA, copyright allowed architects to prevent copying of their floor plans, architectural drawings, and

---

[Section 7:116]

[1]Imperial Homes Corp. v. Lamont, 458 F.2d 895, 897 (5th Cir. 1972).

[2]Eales v. Environmental Lifestyles, Inc., 958 F.2d 876 (9th Cir. 1992), as amended, (May 11, 1992), cert den. 113 S. Ct 605, 506 U.S. 1001.

blueprints; post-AWCPA, protection has been further extended.[1] Access, which is not required on direct evidence of copying, has been found where defendants visited a model home,[2] and obtained brochures depicting floor plans without seeing architectural drawings.[3] The floor plan does not have to be registered so long as the architectural drawings from which the plan is generated are, and vice versa. In *Rutenberg Corp. v. Parrino*,[4] a bench trial resulted in judgment against defendants, who built their home by copying a reproduction of a simplified floor plan from plaintiff's advertising brochure. Although the floor plan was registered and the brochure recited copyright notice, the architectural drawings were not registered. Defendants argued that they could not have had access to the actual drawings to copy them, and that copyright protection did not extend to depiction of the floor plan. The court found that the opportunity to view the copyrighted work through the brochure constituted "access," and found wilful infringement by the homeowner. In Rutenberg Corp. v. Dawney,[5] judgment was entered against defendants, where they built their home by copying a reproduction of plaintiff's floor plan, which recited the proper copyright

---

[Section 7:117]

[1]*See* § 7:10; *see also* Hunt v. Pasternack, 179 F.3d 683 (9th Cir. 1999), opinion amended and superseded on denial of reh'g, 192 F.3d 877 (9th Cir. 1999) (AWCPA applies to works embodied in buildings, plans or drawings, a clarification of dicta in Eales v. Environmental Lifestyles, Inc., 958 F.2d 876 (9th Cir. 1992), as amended, (May 11, 1992)).

[2]Imperial Homes Corp. v. Lamont, 458 F.2d 895 (5th Cir. 1972); Arthur Rutenberg Corp. v. Parrino, 664 F. Supp. 479 (M.D. Fla. 1987); Eales v. Environmental Lifestyles, Inc., 958 F.2d 876 (9th Cir. 1992), as amended, (May 11, 1992) cert den. 113 S. Ct 605, 506 U.S. 1001.

[3]Imperial Homes Corp. v. Lamont, 458 F.2d 895 (5th Cir. 1972); Kent v. Revere, 229 U.S.P.Q. (BNA) 828, 1985 WL 6453 (M.D. Fla. 1985) (floor plans contained sufficient information for a designer to produce technical drawings from which a house could be constructed).

[4]Arthur Rutenberg Corp. v. Parrino, 664 F. Supp. 479 (M.D. Fla. 1987).

[5]Arthur Rutenberg Corp. v. Dawney, 647 F. Supp. 1214 (M.D. Fla. 1986).

notice.[6]

§ 7:118 Access, copying—Architectural drawing registered

In *Evans v. Continental Homes*,[1] an architect sued a builder for, inter alia, copyright infringement of residential homes by copying registered plans in brochures that failed to recite notice. The district court found access based upon the defendants' admitted copying of the brochure drawings, but defendants claimed that since they lacked access to the copyrighted technical working drawings attached to the registration, no infringing copying could have occurred. The Eleventh Circuit affirmed on that issue.[2]

§ 7:119 Access, copying—No registration

In *Jacobs v. Westoaks Realtors*,[1] an architect whose plans were used without his authorization by an assignee of the developer, sued the developer for, inter alia, breach of contract, civil conspiracy, and common law copyright infringement. The trial court entered judgment for the developer, affirmed on appeal, finding that defendant had a license to use and transfer the plans permissible by the absence of contractual prohibitions.[2]

Use of the plans in the absence of copying them outright by constructing a building based upon them has been more

---

[6]Arthur Rutenberg Corp. v. Dawney, 647 F. Supp. 1214 (M.D. Fla. 1986).

[Section 7:118]

[1]Donald Frederick Evans and Associates, Inc. v. Continental Homes, Inc., 785 F.2d 897 (11th Cir. 1986).

[2]Donald Frederick Evans and Associates, Inc. v. Continental Homes, Inc., 785 F.2d 897 (11th Cir. 1986).

[Section 7:119]

[1]Robert H. Jacobs, Inc. v. Westoaks Realtors, Inc., 159 Cal. App. 3d 637, 205 Cal. Rptr. 620 (2d Dist. 1984) (no breach of contract found where the contract was silent regarding prohibitions on alteration of the plans or proscriptions on assignment of license to use the plans, and the architect had objected to such assignments on prior transactions with the same developer).

[2]Robert H. Jacobs, Inc. v. Westoaks Realtors, Inc., 159 Cal. App. 3d 637, 205 Cal. Rptr. 620 (2d Dist. 1984).

problematic, as the following section indicates.[3]

§ 7:120 Use

Copyrighted architectural plans do not give architects exclusive rights to reproduce the buildings depicted. Others may construct buildings using the plans, at least to some degree. Plans or drawings that are copied or "imitated or transcribed in whole or in part" have been considered as infringing the copyright owner's rights.[1] A plaintiff builder developed architectural plans for residential dwellings, and registered copyright in the drawings. The copyrighted floor plan was reproduced in a brochure distributed to the public.[2] Defendants visited one of the model homes, obtained the brochure, and developed their own drawings with a builder to duplicate the model, which they had measured on their visit. After the duplicate home was built, Imperial sought injunctive relief and damages. The defense was that they copied only the floor plan in the brochure, not the copyrighted drawings to which they had had no access. The district court entered judgment for the defendants, but the Fifth Circuit reversed and remanded, acknowledging that constructing a substantially identical residential dwelling is not prohibited by copyrighted architectural plans, but holding that if the builders had copied, imitated, or transcribed in whole or in part the floor plan in the brochure, that would constitute infringement.

§ 7:121 Substantial similarity

The fact-finder examines different material to evaluate substantial similarity of plans or drawings than it does for

---

[3]Demetriades v. Kaufmann, 680 F. Supp. 658 (S.D. N.Y. 1988); East/West Ventures v. Wurmfeld Assoc., P.C., 722 F. Supp 1064 (S.D.N.Y. 1989); Imperial Homes Corp. v. Lamont, 458 F.2d 895 (5th Cir. 1972).

[Section 7:120]

[1]Imperial Homes Corp. v. Lamont, 458 F.2d 895 (5th Cir. 1972).

[2]Imperial Homes Corp. v. Lamont, 458 F.2d 895 (5th Cir. 1972); *but cf.* Scholz Homes, Inc. v. Maddox, 379 F.2d 84, 3 A.L.R. Fed. 787 (6th Cir. 1967) (infringer was not liable even if brochure floor plans copied because copyright protected brochure, an advertising medium, not rights in the plans depicted therein).

art, although viewing the criteria as a lay observer is theoretically the same. Checklist 7-1 extrapolates some types of architectural factors and features examined.

Checklist 7-1: Architectural Factors and Features Evaluated in Plans and Drawings for Issue of Substantial Similarity

(1) layout;
(2) proportions;
(3) number of floors;
(4) location of master bedroom;
(5) tubs/showers in particular bathrooms;
(6) fireplace location;
(7) combined areas, e.g., dining room and living room;
(8) window placements and window types, i.e., bay windows;
(9) stair locations;
(10) roof lines;
(11) appliance locations;
(12) door placements, door types, i.e., French doors, door orientation, i.e., right hanging or left hanging;
(13) location and orientation of deck, pool, spa, balconies;
(14) use of glass, e.g., mitred, bevelled;
(15) garage (three car);
(16) television niche; and
(17) skylights.

In *Howard v. Sterchi,*[1] the Eleventh Circuit reexamined the district court's examination of similarities and dissimilarities between two plans of log cabins, finding that although the floor plans and layout were visually similar, the "dissimilarities were significant." Noting that log houses and country style frame houses dictate square angles only, innocent similarities can occur, and "modest

[Section 7:121]

[1]Howard v. Sterchi, 974 F.2d 1272 (11th Cir. 1992).

dissimilarities are more significant than . . . in other types of art works."[2] In Rutenberg, the court's review of the final plans for the infringing home and the copyrighted architectural drawings "reveal[ed] a remarkable number of similarities."[3]

§ 7:122 Abandonment

In *Imperial Homes*, decided under the 1909 Act, the district court concluded that publication of a floor plan in an advertising brochure constituted waiver and abandonment of copyright. The Fifth Circuit reversed and remanded, writing, "Rather than the publication of the instant booklet evincing abandonment, the opposite intention is disclosed because in the brochure Imperial expressly claimed that the floor plan design was the subject of copyright."[1]

C. BUILDINGS

§ 7:123 Generally

As a result of the Architectural Works Copyright Protection Act, Section 120 was added to Title 17, which provides the scope of exclusive rights in architectural works as follows:

> (a)—The copyright in an architectural work that has been constructed does not include the right to prevent the making, distributing, or public display of pictures, paintings, photographs, or other pictorial representations of the work, if the building in which the work is embodied is located or ordinarily visible from a public place.[1]
>
> (b)—Notwithstanding [the right to prepare derivative works], the owners of a building embodying an architectural work may, without the consent of the author or copyright owner of the architectural work, make or authorize the making of alterations to such building, and destroy or authorize

---

[2]Howard v. Sterchi, 974 F.2d 1272 at 1276 (11th Cir. 1992).

[3]Arthur Rutenberg Corp. v. Parrino, 664 F. Supp. 479, 481 (M.D. Fla. 1987).

[Section 7:122]

[1]Imperial Homes Corp. v. Lamont, 458 F.2d 895, 898 (5th Cir. 1972).

[Section 7:123]

[1]17 U.S.C.A. § 120(a) ("Public place" is not defined in Section 101).

the destruction of such building."[2]

For buildings constructed after October 1990, the law protects "overall form," the "arrangement and composition of spaces and elements in the design," but not "individual standard features."

The issue of when a building is "constructed" within the meaning of the regulations[3] implementing AWCPA has been reviewed on appeal. An architect filed an infringement action for a house he designed and began building in 1990.[4] He obtained copyrights in the architectural drawings for that house and copyright in the architectural work. After he filed a complaint alleging others infringed his copyrights by building similar houses, a district court held that the term "constructed" in the regulations means "substantially completed" as opposed to "finished."[5] The plaintiff's house was substantially completed as of December 1, 1990, and therefore ineligible for copyright protection under AWCPA.[6] The Second Circuit affirmed, conceding that although neither the term "constructed" in the regulation nor "unconstructed" in AWCPA is defined, a more practical definition of the regulatory term should be "substantially constructed."[7] Section 120(a) has been held a limitation on the copyright afforded, thus allowing publicly visible buildings to be freely photographed

[2] 17 U.S.C.A. § 120(b); Leicester v. Warner Brothers, 47 U.S.P.Q.2d (BNA) 1501, 1998 WL 468754 (C.D. Cal. 1998), aff'd, 232 F.3d 1212 (9th Cir. 2000).

[3] 37 C.F.R. § 202.11; *see* Appendix 18B.

[4] Richard J. Zitz, Inc. v. Dos Santos Pereira, 232 F.3d 290, 2000 (2d Cir. 2000).

[5] *See* Appendix 18B, 37 C.F.R. § 202.11(d)(3).

[6] Richard J. Zitz, Inc. v. Dos Santos Pereira, 232 F.3d 290, 2000 (2d Cir. 2000); *see also*, Bryce & Palazzola Architects and Associates, Inc. v. A.M.E. Group, Inc., 865 F. Supp. 401, 406, (E.D. Mich. 1994).

[7] Richard J. Zitz, Inc. v. Dos Santos Pereira, 232 F.3d 290, 2000 (2d Cir. 2000) ("If we are to understand "constructed" as having the same significance as "publication" [in copyright], then . . . the equivalent of publication occurs when others can readily see—and copy—the work in question. On that basis, habitability and final completion seem much less significant . . .").

without ad hoc determinations of fair use.[8]

§ 7:124 Integrated art and architectural projects

The protection of architectural works under Section 102(a)(8) has been held an exclusive remedy for PGS works embodied in architectural works, a position supported by legislative history.[1]

§ 7:125 Plans

Valid copyright can subsist in plans for an unconstructed architectural work for purposes of AWCPA.[1] An architect prepared and registered plans for defendants' restaurant. Subsequent architects built the restaurant from the design embodied in the plans. The Ninth Circuit held that a valid copyright existed in the plans although the building had not yet been constructed.[2]

---

[8]Leicester v. Warner Brothers, 47 U.S.P.Q.2d (BNA) 1501, 1998 WL 468754 (C.D. Cal. 1998), aff'd, 232 F.3d 1212 (9th Cir. 2000) (Section 120(a) permits the public the right to photograph unitary architectural work, including building and streetwall embodying architectural work).

[Section 7:124]

[1]H.R. Rep, No. 101-735, at 6950–52 (1990); Leicester v. Warner Brothers, 47 U.S.P.Q.2d (BNA) 1501, 1998 WL 468754 (C.D. Cal. 1998), aff'd, 232 F.3d 1212 (9th Cir. 2000); *but see* C.J. Tashima, *concurrence* ("where a joint architectural/artistic work functions as part of a building . . . I agree with that conclusion in the narrow circumstances . . .) and *cf.*, C.J. Fisher, *dissent* (where copyrightable architectural works contain conceptually separable PGS elements, the latter are entitled to protection under section 102(a)(5) without the exclusive remedy bar of section 102(a)(8)).

[Section 7:125]

[1]Hunt v. Pasternack, 179 F.3d 683 (9th Cir. 1999), opinion amended and superseded on denial of reh'g, 192 F.3d 877 (9th Cir. 1999), *disapproving* Eales v. Environment Lifestyles, Inc., 958 F.2d (9th Cir. 1992) (reversing and remanding summary judgment for defendants, and holding that AWCPA applies to plans).

[2]H.R. Rep. No. 101-735 at 19 (1990) (congressional redraft of "architectural work" such that "a work of architecture may be embodied in the built design . . . or in plans, drawings, or in 'any tangible medium of expression,' such as a blueprint or computer disk").

D. STATE LAWS

§ 7:126 Resale royalties

Architectural drawings are not included within the meaning of California state statutory definitions of "fine art" and therefore have been held ineligible for state resale royalties.[1]

§ 7:127 Artists' rights

Many state art protection laws exclude from the definition of fine art works that are prepared in a commercial context. In *Robert H. Jacobs, Inc. v. Westoaks Realtors, Inc.*,[1] an architect contended that the California Art Preservation Act[2] applied to architectural plans, and that the defendant's alterations of his plans at the building site entitled him to renounce authorship. The California Court of Appeal held that the plaintiff's architectural plans were prepared in a commercial context, an express exclusion under California statute. Conceding that architectural drawings might be as creative as types of fine art protected under the statute, the court wrote: "Even if the inspiration that produces an architect's plans may be ignited by the same creative spark that inspires poetry . . . , we must follow [Cal. Civ. Code] section 987. Jacobs' contentions are best addressed to the legislature."[3]

§ 7:128 Preemption—Architectural Works

Section 301, the preemption provision of the Copyright

[Section 7:126]

[1]Robert H. Jacobs, Inc. v. Westoaks Realtors, Inc., 159 Cal. App. 3d 637, 205 Cal. Rptr. 620 (2d Dist. 1984); *see* Ch 9 (resale royalties).

[Section 7:127]

[1]Robert H. Jacobs, Inc. v. Westoaks Realtors, Inc., 159 Cal. App. 3d 637, 205 Cal. Rptr. 620 (2d Dist. 1984).

[2]Cal. Civ. Code § 987.

[3]159 Cal. App. 3d at 643.

Act.[1]

X. REMEDIES

A. INJUNCTION

§ 7:129 Generally

Injunction is an appropriate relief for copyright infringement.[1] Injunction has been ordered in cases to terminate manufacture, sale, and distribution by a publisher of a posthumous collection of an artist's silkscreens made for magazine publication but never authorized for separate sale as an art collection;[2] to terminate the manufacture, sale, distribution, and display of sculpture by an artist copied from a photograph copyrighted by the creator-artist;[3] to terminate unauthorized use by reproduction, publication, and distribution of an artist's religious images on greeting cards and prayer cards, which use was exclusively granted to plaintiff in conjunction with its purchase of the original paintings.[4]

B. DAMAGES

§ 7:130 Section 504

Section 504(a) provides, in pertinent part, as follows:

> an infringer of copyright is liable for either—
>
> (1) the copyright owner's actual damages and any additional profits of the infringer . . . [under 504(b)]; or

---

[Section 7:128]

[1]See § 7:69. expressly excludes at § 301(b)(4) state and local regulation of "architectural works."

[Section 7:129]

[1]17 U.S.C.A. § 502.

[2]Playboy Enterprises, Inc. v. Dumas, 831 F. Supp. 295 (S.D. N.Y. 1993), opinion modified on reargument, 840 F. Supp. 256 (S.D. N.Y. 1993) and judgment aff'd in part, rev'd in part on other grounds, 53 F.3d 549, 132 A.L.R. Fed. 703 (2d Cir. 1995).

[3]Rogers v. Koons, 751 F. Supp. 474 (S.D. N.Y. 1990), amended on reargument, 777 F. Supp. 1 (S.D. N.Y. 1991) and judgment aff'd, 960 F.2d 301 (2d Cir. 1992); Campbell v. Koons, 1993 WL 97381 (S.D. N.Y. 1993).

[4]Reproducta Co., Inc. v. Kellmark Corp., 1994 WL 719705 (S.D. N.Y. 1994).

(2) statutory damages . . . [under 504(c)].[1]

The complexity that can occur in calculating copyright damages ordinarily requires a fact-specific, case-by-case analysis. The following sections illustrate some examples from art copyright. The purpose of awards is "to prevent the infringer from unfairly benefiting from a wrongful act."[2]

§ 7:131 Actual damages

Section 504(b) provides:

> The copyright owner is entitled to recover the actual damages suffered by him or her as a result of the infringement, and any profits of the infringer that are attributable to the infringement and are not taken into account in computing the actual damages. In establishing the infringer's profits, the copyright owner is required to present proof only of the infringer's gross revenue, and the infringer is required to prove his or her deductible expenses and the elements of profit attributable to factors other than the copyrighted work.

In short, the plaintiff is entitled to actual damages and apportionment of the infringer's profits.[1] Calculation of actual damages is based upon the "extent to which the market value of the copyrighted work at the time of infringement has been injured or destroyed by the infringement."[2]

Market value is based on objective analysis.[3] To deter-

[Section 7:130]

[1]17 U.S.C.A. § 504(a).

[2]H.R. Rep. No. 94-1476, 94th Cong., 2d Sess (1976), reprinted at 1976 U.S.C.C.A.N. 5659, 5777.

[Section 7:131]

[1]Arthur Rutenberg Corp. v. Dawney, 647 F. Supp. 1214 (M.D. Fla. 1986) (plaintiffs recovered defendant's profits of $134,750).

[2]Rogers v. Koons, 960 F.2d 301 (2d Cir. 1992); see also Rogers v. Koons, 777 F. Supp. 1, 19 Media L. Rep. (BNA) 1586, 20 U.S.P.Q.2d (BNA) 1054 (S.D. N.Y. 1991) (gallery that invoiced sculptures and retained profit percentage as direct infringing seller).

[3]Mackie v. Rieser, 296 F.3d 909 (9th Cir. 2002), cert. denied, 123 S. Ct. 1259, 154 L. Ed. 2d 1022 (U.S. 2003) (artist's subjective views

mine market value at the time of infringement, courts have used "what a willing buyer would have been reasonably required to pay to a willing seller for [the] work."[4] Where the infringement does not affect the work's market value, calculating a licensing fee has been upheld as a permissible basis for estimating actual damages. In *Rogers v. Koons*,[5] the Second Circuit, remanding for damages, offered as an approximation of the plaintiff's market injury a "reasonable license fee" for his photograph. Actual damages award based on licensing fees were upheld notwithstanding the artist's personal objections to the manner of unauthorized use.[6] Other courts have simply stated the value of the use without explaining it.[7]

The fair market value of plans has been upheld as a permissible basis for actual damages in an architectural infringement action. In *Eales*,[8] the Ninth Circuit affirmed damages based on the market value of architectural plans calculated by multiplying the number of square feet in the home by the architect's price per square foot.

Actual damages cannot be based upon an assumption that a customer who buys an infringing artwork would have purchased a similar but more expensive work of art.[9]

---

objecting to how his art was appropriated are irrelevant to the calculation).

[4]Mackie v. Rieser, 296 F.3d 909 (9th Cir. 2002), cert. denied, 123 S. Ct. 1259, 154 L. Ed. 2d 1022 (U.S. 2003) (citations omitted).

[5]Rogers v. Koons, 960 F.2d 301 (2d Cir. 1992); Silberman v. Innovation Luggage, Inc., 67 U.S.P.Q.2d (BNA) 1489, 2003 WL 1787123 (S.D. N.Y. 2003) (licensing fee for photograph of " a relatively standard image of New York" would probably be insubstantial).

[6]Mackie v. Rieser, 296 F.3d 909 (9th Cir. 2002), cert. denied, 123 S. Ct. 1259, 154 L. Ed. 2d 1022 (U.S. 2003) ($1000 was proper licensing fee for reproducing public artwork in promotional brochure).

[7]Vane v. The Fair, Inc., 676 F. Supp. 133, 136 (E.D. Tex. 1987), judgment aff'd, 849 F.2d 186 (5th Cir. 1988) (value of slides used in television ads set at $60,000).

[8]Eales v. Environmental Lifestyles, Inc., 958 F.2d 876 (9th Cir. 1992), as amended, (May 11, 1992), cert. denied, 506 U.S. 1001 (1992).

[9]Dumas v. Dagl, 1990 WL 258343 (S.D. N.Y. 1990) (customers who bought for $32 infringing titles depicting the artist's work would not necessarily have purchased silkscreens for $200–$400).

§ 7:132 Profits

When the injured party elects Section 504(b), he or she is entitled to the infringer's profits that derive from the infringement, as well as actual damages. The rule, summarily stated, is "plaintiff's loss plus defendant's gain."[1] Profits recoverable are those attributable to infringing use of the protected work.

Section 504(b) does not distinguish direct profits and indirect profits. In certain circuits, a threshold finding of a causal link between the infringement and subsequent indirect profits is required.[2] The Ninth Circuit affirmed summary judgment disposing of an artist's claims for indirect profits where revenues for a municipal orchestra could not be causally linked to the infringing use of his artwork in a direct mail brochure.[3]

To sustain an award of damages based on profits, the plaintiff is required to prove the infringer's gross revenues; the burden is on the infringer to establish deductions for expenses, or to demonstrate that the profits claimed by the plaintiff and the elements of profit are not attributable to infringing use.[4]

Profits have been held applicable for infringement of architecture plans.[5] Courts have calculated direct profits for architects by measuring the amount an architect would have made had he or she sold the building based upon the

---

[Section 7:132]

[1]Walker v. Forbes, Inc., 28 F.3d 409 (4th Cir. 1994).

[2]Mackie v. Rieser, 296 F.3d 909 (9th Cir. 2002), cert. denied, 123 S. Ct. 1259, 154 L. Ed. 2d 1022 (U.S. 2003) ("sufficient non-speculative evidence" must support causal relationship between infringement and indirect profits).

[3]Mackie v. Rieser, 296 F.3d 909 (9th Cir. 2002), cert. denied, 123 S. Ct. 1259, 154 L. Ed. 2d 1022 (U.S. 2003) (individual's ticket purchasing decisions based on factors like musicians, conductor, concert dates, programs, new symphony hall unrelated to artist's work).

[4]Vane v. The Fair, Inc., 676 F. Supp. 133 (E.D. Tex. 1987), judgment aff'd, 849 F.2d 186 (5th Cir. 1988) (plaintiff failed to present sufficient proof of the defendant's gross revenue attributable to the infringement, so no recovery was allowed for profits).

[5]Russell v. Price, 612 F.2d 1123 (9th Cir. 1979); Robert R. Jones Associates, Inc. v. Nino Homes, 858 F.2d 274, 281, 26 Fed. R. Evid. Serv. 1245, 100 A.L.R. Fed. 241 (6th Cir. 1988).

copied plans;[6] and by taking the sales price of the infringing home and deducting building costs.[7] If the infringer's records are inadequate, doubt is supposed to be resolved in favor the copyright owner.[8] If the infringer cannot satisfy the burden, the gross figure is left to stand as the profit factor. A homeowner's testimony of costs to build a home that infringed on an architect's copyrighted plans was considered adequate, and resulted in a $200,000 reduction of profits.[9]

From the entertainment field has emerged the rule that those excludable elements of profit not attributable to infringing use may include the infringer's own notoriety and his ability to command high-end prices. The Supreme Court decided that in apportioning profits, star power of motion picture actors and their popular draw were proper elements to consider.[10] In *Rogers v. Koons*, the Second Circuit suggested that the defendant might avoid Roger's claim for $367,000 of infringing profits "[t]o the extent that Koons is able to prove that the profits at issue derive solely from his own position in the art world, [in which case] he should be allowed to retain them."[11]

In Walker v. Forbes, Inc.,[12] plaintiff's photograph of a local textile magnate appeared in a local paper, bearing his copyright. Forbes, a magazine publisher, ran a cropped version of the photograph when it featured the subject of the photo as one of seven extended profiles in Forbes 400,

---

[6]Eales v. Environmental Lifestyles, Inc., 958 F.2d 876 (9th Cir. 1992), as amended, (May 11, 1992), cert. denied, 506 U.S. 1001 (1992)(Section 504(b) prohibition on recovering twice for the same damages, by compensatory damages and profits, is not implicated because "Eales is not in the business of selling her services as a homebuilder . . . [so it does not] constitute forbidden double damages.").

[7]Arthur Rutenberg Corp. v. Dawney, 647 F. Supp. 1214, 1215 (M.D. Fla. 1986).

[8]Roulo v. Russ Berrie & Co., Inc., 886 F.2d 931 (7th Cir. 1989).

[9]Arthur Rutenberg Corp. v. Dawney, 647 F. Supp. 1214, 1215, (M.D. Fla. 1986).

[10]Sheldon v. Metro-Goldwyn Pictures Corporation, 309 U.S. 390, 407, 60 S. Ct. 681, 84 L. Ed. 825 (1940) (apportioning profits in movie "Letty Lynton" that infringed play "Dishonored Lady").

[11]Rogers v. Koons, 960 F. 2d 301 at 313, 20 Media L. Rep. (BNA) 1201, 22 U.S.P.Q. 2d 1492 (2d Cir. 1992).

[12]Walker v. Forbes, Inc., 28 F.3d 409 (4th Cir. 1994).

"The Richest People in America" (the 400), a special annual issue. Forbes neither sought authorization nor credited the photographer.

Forbes' fair use defense failed at trial, and plaintiff was awarded approximately $5,800 in damages. The photographer appealed on the issue of damages only, raising improper introduction of evidence and erroneous jury instruction on the issue of apportionment.[13]

The extrapolation of nonattributable profits from the apportionment rule to the visual arts can produce anomalous results. The reasons for this are numerous, but stem, in part, from a hierarchy that stacks "fine" art above commercial art. The result becomes apparent when the copier and the copied are both artists, the copied primarily doing business in the commercial aspects of artmaking, e.g., reproduction-based revenue through licensing, and the copier receiving sales-based revenues of high-end priced one-of-a-kinds, or expensive and extremely limited editions. If the copier can effectively retain profits reaped by virtue of the notoriety of his appropriation and his ability to exploit it, the damages provisions are undermined. If damages are limited to licensing fees as a result of the nonattributable profits portion of the apportionment rule, then the fee becomes a mere cost of doing business that the copier can pass on by incorporating it into the sales price.

For example, were damages in the *Koons* case to be restricted to a licensing fee, that licensing fee is minimal in relationship to the price at which sculptures copied from those photographs were sold, i.e., $100,000 to $300,000 each, in editions of three or four. Had Koons contacted Rogers before the copying occurred, Rogers could have attempted to strike a deal, negotiating a price that was reasonable for him at that time, when the risk and reward of copying had economic uncertainty. The economic analysis dramatically changes when the deal is struck after the copying by adjudicatory forces rather than those of the marketplace. A precopying negotiated fee in the former instance might be some thousand dollars, whereas a postcopying fee in a judicial context for the same work might only be a few hundred dollars. Even if no deal is

---

[13]Walker v. Forbes, Inc., 28 F.3d 409, 415 (4th Cir. 1994).

struck because the would-be copier finds the market price too costly and is willing to use other work or to take his or her chances of being sued, the transaction still has informational value for the copyright holder; the holder can then seek its own licensee, or undertake its own work. This raises, among other issues, which set of circumstances better serves the market, furthers the constitutional and congressional objectives, and obtains or facilitates cultural values. Should copyright law in the visual arts context encourage the appropriating artist or the good-faith mime?

To apportion profits based on nonattributable factors in the visual arts is to reward the "successful" appropriating artist, because damages that are effectively limited to licensing fees could be de minimis.

The reputation factor further establishes an insurmountable hurdle for the low profile artist who consistently makes a livelihood from art but is not part of the "glitz" of the "art world." Finally, the unknown or less established or less successful appropriating artist ironically would be subject to greater payment of profits than the successful one. Arguably, it is the latter's exploitation that poses far greater detriment to the plaintiff's market. Nowhere do such unexpected and surely unintended results appear in the statute, nor are they contemplated in the legislative history.

However, where the copier is not another artist, the apportionment rule can have a favorable economic result for the plaintiff-artist. In *Walker v. Forbes*,[14] the plaintiff photographer's award was almost $6,000, even after apportionment, significantly higher than average photographic licensing fees or royalties. Where apportionment is based on quantifiable data, like advertising revenues and sales, the reproduction revenue-based artist is not effectively penalized under the nonattributable profits portion of the apportionment rule as he or she can be when the defendant is an artist. Note that the plaintiff's perception may not be susceptible to numerical data; the photographer in *Walker v. Forbes* appealed for a higher damages award.

---

[14]Walker v. Forbes, Inc., 28 F.3d 409 (4th Cir. 1994).

§ 7:133 Statutory damages

In place of actual damages and profits, a copyright owner may elect at any time before final judgment is rendered an award of statutory damages under Section 504(c), which originally provided:

> (1) . . . an award of statutory damages for all infringements involved . . . with respect to any one work, for which any one infringer is liable individually, or for which any two or more infringers are liable jointly and severally, in a sum of not less than $500 or more than $20,000 as the court considers just.
>
> (2) . . . [if] infringement was committed willfully, the court in its discretion may increase the award of statutory damages to a sum of not more than $100,000.

Section 504(c), as amended, increased the statutory damages range from $750 to $30,000, and raised the maximum for willful infringement to $150,000.[1] The trial court has broad discretion to determine whether allowable recovery should be based upon actual damages and profits, based upon the evidence, or by statutory damages, ascertained by the court.[2] "[T]he court's conception of what is just in the particular case, considering the nature of the copyright, the circumstances of the infringement . . . is made the measure of the damages to be paid, but with the express qualification that in every case the assessment must be within the prescribed limitations, . . . neither more than the maximum nor less than the minimum."[3] Plaintiffs who elect statutory damages are not guaranteed

---

[Section 7:133]

[1]Pub.L. 105-80, 111 Stat. 1535; Pub.L. 105-298, 112 Stat.2833; Pub.L. 106-160, 113 Stat. 1774.

[2]F. W. Woolworth Co. v. Contemporary Arts, 344 U.S. 228, 231, 73 S. Ct. 222, 97 L. Ed. 276 (1952); Mackie v. Rieser, 296 F.3d 909 (9th Cir. 2002), cert. denied, 123 S. Ct. 1259, 154 L. Ed. 2d 1022 (U.S. 2003) (statutory damages not available where plaintiff's copyright not registered at time of infringement); Silberman v. Innovation Luggage, Inc., 67 U.S.P.Q.2d (BNA) 1489, 2003 WL 1787123 (S.D. N.Y. 2003) (statutory damages and attorneys' fees denied where infringement began before artist registered copyright).

[3]F. W. Woolworth Co. v. Contemporary Arts, 344 U.S. 228, 231, 73 S. Ct. 222, 97 L. Ed. 276 (1952) (trial court should receive into evidence proof of sales and other records supporting actual damages for probative value, even if statutory damages are elected).

that the statutory award will exceed actual damages and profits. An architect who presented testimony alleging $20,000 in lost profits elected statutory damages and received only $5000.[4] Nor does the defendant's gross profit establish the maximum available for statutory damages.[5]

Willfulness may be considered in determining the amount of statutory damages under Section 504(c)(2). Willfulness, which is not defined in Title 17, is determined by the trier of fact in some jurisdictions, and reviewed under the "clearly erroneous" standard.[6] The trier of fact may consider whether the defendant ignored the plaintiff's notification;[7] failed to seek advice of an attorney after the plaintiff's notification;[8] or considered the plaintiff's notice a mere nuisance.[9] In *Rogers v. Koons*,[10] the Second Circuit noted that defendant's wilful and "egregious" behavior in tearing off copyright notices before instructing copying should be considered by the district court for enhanced statutory damages under Section 504(c)(2).

C. ATTORNEY'S FEES AND COSTS

§ 7:134 Attorney's fees

Reasonable attorney fees may be awarded to the prevail-

---

[4]Arthur Rutenberg Corp. v. Parrino, 664 F. Supp. 479, 482 (M.D. Fla. 1987).

[5]F. W. Woolworth Co. v. Contemporary Arts, 344 U.S. 228, 231, 73 S. Ct. 222, 97 L. Ed. 276 (1952) ($5000 statutory damages were awarded for infringement of small dog sculptures and figurines, where the defendants' gross profit was only $899).

[6]*See, e.g.,* Wildlife Exp. Corp. v. Carol Wright Sales, Inc., 18 F.3d 502 (7th Cir. 1994).

[7]Dumas v. Dagl, 1990 WL 258343 (S.D. N.Y. 1990) (maintaining and continuing the infringing activity after receipt of notice from plaintiff's counsel is also pertinent).

[8]Wildlife Exp. Corp. v. Carol Wright Sales, Inc., 18 F.3d 502 (7th Cir. 1994).

[9]Wildlife Exp. Corp. v. Carol Wright Sales, Inc., 18 F.3d 502 at 512 (7th Cir. 1994).

[10]Rogers v. Koons, 751 F. Supp. 474 (S.D. N.Y. 1990), amended on reargument, 777 F. Supp. 1 (S.D. N.Y. 1991) and judgment aff'd, 960 F.2d 301 (2d Cir. 1992); cf. Silberman v. Innovation Luggage, Inc., 67 U.S.P.Q.2d (BNA) 1489, 2003 WL 1787123 (S.D. N.Y. 2003) (statutory damages generally achieve purpose of "punitive" damages in preventing malicious conduct and punishing).

ing party in the discretion of the court as part of the costs of action.[1] The court has broad discretion in making the award.[2] The award has been considered by some courts as compensating the plaintiff and deterring future violations by the defendant.[3] Awards of fees are considered "particularly appropriate" where the infringement is wilful.[4] The Supreme Court rejected a dual standard for plaintiffs and defendants in evaluating awards of attorney's fees under Section 505 of Title 17, and held that the parties should be treated alike.[5] The "equitable discretion" of the courts under Section 505 is to be exercised in accordance with nonexclusive factors.[6]

The underlying premise is whether defense of the action "furthered the purposes of the [Copyright] Act."[7] If the district court fails to provide reasons for the basis of denying attorney's fees, the appellate court may remand "if the record does not support the district court's decision."[8] A defendant may prevail if the plaintiff's claims objectively lack reasonable merit, are baseless, frivolous, or brought

---

[Section 7:134]

[1]17 U.S.C.A. § 505.

[2]Martin v. City of Indianapolis, 28 F. Supp. 2d 1098 (S.D. Ind. 1998) (award of fees evaluated by applying lodestar, multiplying number of hours billed by reasonable hourly rates.)

[3]Kenbrooke Fabrics, Inc. v. Holland Fabrics, Inc., 602 F. Supp. 151 (S.D. N.Y. 1984).

[4]Dumas v. Dagl, 1990 WL 258343 (S.D. N.Y. 1990).

[5]Fogerty v. Fantasy, Inc., 510 U.S. 517, 114 S. Ct. 1023, 127 L. Ed. 2d 455 (1994).

[6]Fogerty v. Fantasy, Inc., 510 U.S. 517 at 534, n. 19, 114 S. Ct. 1023, 127 L. Ed. 2d 455 (1994) ("frivolousness, motivation, objective unreasonableness, and . . . need . . . to advance . . . compensation and deterrence. . . .").

[7]Mattel, Inc. v. Walking Mountain Productions, 353 F.3d 792, 816, 69 U.S.P.Q.2d (BNA) 1257 (9th Cir. 2003) (distinguishing between defense of the action and amount of the fee award).

[8]Mattel, Inc. v. Walking Mountain Productions, 353 F.3d 792, 815, 69 U.S.P.Q.2d (BNA) 1257 (9th Cir. 2003) (remanded for reconsideration of denial of attorney's fees where reasoning for conclusions not provided and record did not support conclusions).

in bad faith.[9] In other situations, the defendant need not make a bad faith showing.[10]

Attorney's fees were considered proper in the following cases: fees attributable to determination of copyright ownership in an infringement counterclaim, even where elements of proof of ownership comprised part of a declaratory judgment claim for which no attorney fees were proper.[11] Attorney's fees were not awarded in the following cases: determination of copyright ownership in a declaratory relief claim, where there were questions of first impression and custom and usage of industry;[12] and determination of infringement, where colorable claims were raised that "section 505 is intended to encourage."[13]

§ 7:135 Costs

Section 505 provides, "the court in its discretion may allow the recovery of full costs by or against any party." Costs were awarded where the infringement was wilful in actions for infringement of an architect's plans;[1] and infringement of an artist's prints.[2]

---

[9]Folio Impressions, Inc. v. Byer California, 752 F. Supp. 583, 592, 31 Fed. R. Evid. Serv. 1320 (S.D. N.Y. 1990), judgment aff'd, 937 F.2d 759, 33 Fed. R. Evid. Serv. 569 (2d Cir. 1991).

[10]Donald Frederick Evans and Associates, Inc. v. Continental Homes, Inc., 785 F.2d 897, 916 (11th Cir. 1986) (no fees were awarded to the defendant because "colorable" claims existed).

[11]Playboy Enterprises, Inc. v. Dumas, 831 F. Supp. 295 (S.D. N.Y. 1993), opinion modified on reargument, 840 F. Supp. 256 (S.D. N.Y. 1993) and judgment aff'd in part, rev'd in part on other grounds, 53 F.3d 549, 132 A.L.R. Fed. 703 (2d Cir. 1995).

[12]Playboy Enterprises, Inc. v. Dumas, 831 F. Supp. 295 (S.D. N.Y. 1993), opinion modified on reargument, 840 F. Supp. 256 (S.D. N.Y. 1993) and judgment aff'd in part, rev'd in part on other grounds, 53 F.3d 549, 132 A.L.R. Fed. 703 (2d Cir. 1995).

[13]Donald Frederick Evans and Associates, Inc. v. Continental Homes, Inc., 785 F.2d 897, 916 (11th Cir. 1986).

[Section 7:135]

[1]Arthur Rutenberg Corp. v. Parrino, 664 F. Supp. 479, 482 (M.D. Fla. 1987).

[2]Dumas v. Dagl, 1990 WL 258343 (S.D. N.Y. 1990).

§ 7:136 Criminal infringement

Criminal infringement is provided under Section 506(a) for any person "who infringes a copyright willfully and for purposes of commercial advantage or private financial gain shall be punished as provided in section 2319 of Title 18,"[1] and the court in its judgment of conviction shall order forfeiture and destruction of infringing copies when any person is convicted of violation of Section 506(a).[2] Title 17 penalties are specified for fraudulent copyright notice, fraudulent removal of notice, and false representation.[3] Section 506(f) expressly excludes criminal offenses for infringement of rights under VARA.[4]

XI. INSURANCE

§ 7:137 Generally

Insurance exists for copyright infringement.[1] When the insurer's obligation to defend is triggered depends on the terms and conditions of the underlying policy.[2]

[Section 7:136]

[1]17 U.S.C.A. § 506(a) (punishment under 18 U.S.C.A. § 2319 provides, "Whoever violates section 506(a) . . . shall be in addition to any other provisions of title 17 or any other law.").

[2]17 U.S.C.A. § 506(b).

[3]17 U.S.C.A. § 506(c)–(e); *see also* U.S. v. Powell, 701 F.2d 70 (8th Cir. 1983) (higher penalties and fines under title 18 for sound recordings and motion pictures).

[4]17 U.S.C.A. § 506(f).

[Section 7:137]

[1]*See, e.g.,* Andy Warhol Foundation for Visual Arts, Inc. v. Federal Ins. Co., 189 F.3d 208 (2d Cir. 1999) (reversal of summary judgment for insurance company denying coverage to Warhol estate where underlying claim involved a copyright infringement action brought by photographer and magazine against Warhol's estate based upon the artist's unauthorized use of plaintiff-photographer's copyrighted photograph of Jacqueline Kennedy).

[2]Ziman v. Fireman's Fund Ins. Co., 73 Cal. App. 4th 1382, 87 Cal. Rptr. 2d 397 (2d Dist. 1999) (no duty to defend insured in copyright infringement action under advertising injury coverage provision in general comprehensive liability policy where complaint alleged insured copied a painting loaned by artist for building lobby; the display was deemed a property improvement, not an advertisement); Cort v. St.

Paul Fire and Marine Ins. Companies, Inc., 311 F.3d 979 (9th Cir. 2002) (no duty to defend building owners for personal injury claims where underlying action brought by artists charged that owners violated VARA and state libel and privacy laws when wall mural was coated in white sealant); *see* Ch 9.

Chapter 8

Trademark and Unfair Competition

I. GENERALLY

II. Lanham Act

A. SECTION 43(A)

B. TRADE MARK AND TRADE DRESS

C. APPLICABILITY OF SECTION 43(A) TO ART

D. RELATIONSHIP TO COPYRIGHT AND VARA

E. NAME AND USE: ARTISTS AND MUSEUMS

F. ALTERATIONS, GARBLED VERSIONS

G. COPYING OR SIMILARITY

H. FALSE ADVERTISING

I. OTHER ISSUES

J. REMEDIES

K. Federal Trademark Dilution Act of 1995

III. STATE UNFAIR COMPETITION LAWS

I. GENERALLY

§ 8:1 Overview

Artists and art publishers, distributors and sellers are pleading federal, state and common law unfair competition laws with increasing frequency. Claims are based on diverse conduct and activities, including attribution or misattribution; authenticity or lack thereof; unauthorized use of artist signature; copying or similarity; fabrication; advertising; and alteration. Federal claims are often plead in conjunction with infringement actions under copyright and VARA, although some judicial authority now suggests that certain trade claims formerly wed with copyright may be preempted by VARA. Recent cases demonstrate the intention of corporations and celebrities to enforce proprietary trade interests even when visual artists are using the mark, dress or likeness in artworks ordinarily considered noncommercial speech.

Sections 8:2 to 8:38 introduces art as protectible mark under federal trademark law, commonly called the Lanham Act, by briefly summarizing principles of trademark and trade dress as applied to art and architecture. Although the number of reported cases is limited, the holdings are notable, and recent opinions by the Supreme Court involving visual imagery as protectible mark portend potential expansion. These sections also evaluate federal false advertising and false description claims under Section 43(a) of the Lanham Act. The relationship of VARA to the Lanham Act is discussed, including recent judicial views of VARA's preemptive scope. The new federal antidilution provisions added by the Federal Trademark Dilution Act of 1995 have been tested by celebrities and others claiming artistic use infringes their marks, dress, images or likenesses, triggering a new and growing genre of false endorsement claims under Lanham and related state right of publicity claims and other cases against visual artists for use in their artworks. Such claims trigger First Amendment issues, in the context of commercial and non-commercial speech, addressed in Sections §§ 8:11 to 8:12.

Sections §§ 8:39 to 8:45 identifies unfair competition claims under state and common law affiliated with art production, promotion, distribution and sale. Depending upon the jurisdiction, claims may sound in dilution, misappropriation, or false advertising.

II. Lanham Act

A. SECTION 43(A)

§ 8:2 Generally

Section 43(a) of the Lanham Act[1] provides a federal statutory remedy for either "false designation of origin" or "false description or representation" in connection with goods or services in interstate commerce.[2] In short, false origin, association, or endorsement and false advertising are each cognizable legal claims.[3] Section 43(a), which applies whether or not a trademark is registered, provided, prior to amendment, that:

> Any person who shall affix, apply or annex, or use in connection with any goods or services, . . . a false designation

---

[Section 8:2]

[1] 15 U.S.C.A. § 1125(a).

[2] 15 U.S.C.A. § 1114(1)(b).

[3] *See, e.g.,* Lord Simon Cairns v. Franklin Mint Co., 24 F. Supp. 2d 1013 (C.D. Cal. 1998) (recognizing celebrity false endorsement claims under section 43(a) in a trademark action brought by the estate regarding name use of Princess Diana); ETW Corp. v. Jireh Pub., Inc., 332 F.3d 915, 925, 67 U.S.P.Q.2d (BNA) 1065, 2003 FED App. 0207P (6th Cir. 2003) (false designation of origin claim by celebrity based on artist's depiction of Tiger Woods in print edition treated as false endorsement claim under Section 43(a)).

of origin, or any false description or representation, including words or other symbols tending falsely to describe or represent the same, and shall cause such goods or services to enter into commerce, and any person who shall with knowledge of the falsity of such designation of origin or description or representation cause or procure the same to be transported or used, shall be liable in a civil action.

Until 1988 Section 43(a) covered only misrepresentations about the producer's own products, and did not apply to disparagement of a competitor's products. Section 43(a) was amended in 1988[4] to include misrepresentation about plaintiff's goods by defendant:

(1) Any person who, on or in connection with any goods or services, uses in commerce any word, term, name, symbol, or device, or any combination thereof, or . . . any false designation of origin, false or misleading description of fact, or false or misleading representation of fact, which

(A) is likely to cause confusion, or to cause mistake, or to deceive as to the . . . origin, sponsorship, or approval of his or her goods, services, or commercial activities by another person, or

(B) in commercial advertising or promotion, misrepresents the nature, characteristics, qualities or geographic origin of his or her or another person's goods, services, or commercial activities, shall be liable in a civil action by any person who believes that he or she is likely to be damaged by such act.

The Lanham Act, deemed a remedial statute that should be broadly construed, was intended to make "actionable the deceptive and misleading use of marks" in a wide variety of commercial practices, "to protect persons engaged in . . . commerce against unfair competition,"[5] and to act as

[4]Pub. L. No. 100-667, tit. I, § 132, 102 Stat. 3946 (effective Nov. 16, 1989).

[5]15 U.S.C.A. § 1127.

a curative remedy for false and misleading advertising.[6]

The purpose of the Act is to "secure to the owner of the mark the goodwill of his business and to protect the ability of consumers to distinguish among competing producers,"[7] as well as to source accurately goods, services and commercial activities.[8] Thus, it is intended to protect "merchants against unfair competition and . . . the public against deceptive advertising and marketing."[9]

The nexus between the mark and the product, business or service is considered crucial: Trademark rights are not considered platonic or abstract rights that may be acquired as distinct assets independent of existing commercial activity. The right asserted is a transferable property right that derives from the use of a mark that symbolizes a product, service or business in the public's mind.

The general interpretation of Lanham's purpose is that it is designed to "'exclusively protect the interests of a purely commercial class against unscrupulous commercial conduct.' "[10] In the arts context, application of Lanham has taken interesting judicial spins, not surprising given the

---

[6]Hofmann v. Kleinhandler, 1994 WL 240335 (S.D. N.Y. 1994) (dealer's alteration of another dealer's promotional brochures depicting artworks as false advertising).

[7]S. Rep. No. 1333, 79th Cong., 2d Sess. 3–5 (1946).

[8]S. 100-515, U.S.C.C.A.N. 5577, 5603 (1988).

[9]McMahon v. City of Chicago, 1999 WL 342712 (N.D. Ill. 1999) (artist's Lanham Act claims based on rejected public art proposal dismissed by court as attempt to create hybrid "federal tort of misrepresentation . . ."). Claims are loosely bracketed as false association or false endorsement under subparagraph A, referring to deceptive or misleading use of plaintiff's marks in relationship to defendant's products, and false advertising under subparagraph B.

[10]Boule v. Hutton, 70 F. Supp. 2d 378 (S.D. N.Y. 1999) (citations omitted); aff'd in part, vacated and remanded in part, 328 F.2d 84 (2d Cir. 2003) (art magazine articles about authenticity dispute involving works of deceased Russian artist between major collectors and artist's heirs was not commercial speech for purposes of Lanham Act claim but remanded to determine if certain false statements violated state unfair competition statutes); Gmurzynska v. Hutton, 355 F.3d 206, 69 U.S.P.Q.2d (BNA) 1477 (2d Cir. 2004) (museum catalogue and magazine article on authenticity was not commercial speech, advertising or promotion under Lanham Act);.

vagaries of art trading.[11] Collectors with sufficient market position have qualified as having sufficient "commercial" interests to satisfy the Lanham Act.[12] Art is generally not considered a typical Lanham Act commercial product. Even when an artist is situated within Lanham's commercial predicates, the issue remains whether or not, or to what degree, the artwork or visual is disparate from the product or service.

The Supreme Court has endorsed visual imagery as viable trade dress, but the visual images that constituted the dress were separate and distinct.

The concern is that trade law will be misused by artists seeking unavailable copyright protection. Simultaneous developments in the arts like increasing commercialization of artwork, artwork fabricated and promoted as product endorsement, and artists as merchandisers, suggest that Lanham could be appropriate in certain circumstances.

The fear that the Lanham Act is being improperly expanded as a statutory salvage dump for copyright claims is unwarranted. Misplead Lanham Act claims can and do occur within and without the arts; procedures are available, and regularly used, to summarily dispose of masqueraded copyright claims.

Not-for-profit organizations utilize marks, which can create revenue-generating opportunities that transcend financially circumscribed art fundraising committees and extend the reach of the organization beyond the patron and traditional donor communities. They are also seeking protection for their marks.[13]

The Lanham Act remains a somewhat anomalous rem-

---

[11]*See* Ch 2 §§ 2:1 to 2:11.

[12]Boule v. Hutton, 70 F. Supp. 2d 378 (S.D. N.Y. 1999) (collectors who own a "significant percentage of extant works attributed to one artist . . . who promoted their collection . . . and contracted to sell substantial numbers of such works . . . have a sufficient commercial interest"), 138 F. Supp. 2d 491 (S.D. N.Y. 2001) (plaintiffs failed to sustain their burden of proof by a preponderance of evidence that defendants' statements about the artworks were false); aff'd in part, vacated and remanded in part, 328 F.2d 84 (2d Cir. 2003) (*ARTnews* article on fraud in the art market was not commercial speech).

[13]Lord Simon Cairns v. Franklin Mint Co., 24 F. Supp. 2d 1013 (C.D. Cal. 1998) (the use of profits for charitable purposes is "immaterial" if a

edy for visual arts, in the context of claiming art as mark or dress, but an unbiased evaluation and examination is indicated based upon the facts and circumstances, rather than a blanket exclusion of visual art claims. The issues have not yet been squarely addressed in a visual arts context by precedential authorities, although some authority exists for the viability of Lanham Act claims in this new and developing area.

A separate genre of cases involves the evolving boundary between Lanham Act protection and protected artistic expression under the First Amendment umbrella. Corporate cultural icons like the Barbie doll and sports celebrities like Tiger Woods have sought Lanham remedies for infringement of their mark, dress, likeness or image depicted in works of visual art.[14]

B. TRADE MARK AND TRADE DRESS

§ 8:3 Elements

A trademark is defined at 15 U.S.C.A. § 1127[1] as "any word, name, symbol or device or any combination thereof" adopted and used by any person "to identify and distinguish his goods, including a unique product, from those manufactured or sold by others and to indicate the source of the goods, even if that source is unknown." Some marks are classified as inherently distinctive and protectible but not all inherently distinctive symbols or words on products function as trademarks. A designation must create "'a separate and distinct commercial impression which performs the trademark function of identifying the source of the merchandise to the customers.' "[2] Thus, color by itself has been held by a unanimous Supreme Court to constitute the basis of a registrable trademark, where the color has

---

commercial interest is satisfied under section 43(a)); see also Cairns v. Franklin Mint Co., 292 F.3d 1139, 63 U.S.P.Q.2d (BNA) 1279 (9th Cir. 2002) (no liability for false endorsement under Lanham Act based on memorabilia bearing the late Princess Diana's name and likeness).

[14]See § 8:11.

[Section 8:3]

[1]15 U.S.C.A. § 1127.

[2]Rock and Roll Hall of Fame and Museum, Inc. v. Gentile Productions, 134 F.3d 749 (6th Cir. 1998) (citations omitted).

attained secondary meaning.[3]

Section 43(a) extends beyond registered marks to trade dress. Trade dress initially referred to the way an item was "dressed" for market, like labelling, packaging, display. Trade dress has been broadened to include overall product presentation, including the "total image" in design, appearance and particulars that presents to the customer. Trade dress is generally accepted as the "total image" of the good and "overall appearance," including, inter alia, words, symbols, size and shape,[4] colors,[5] collections of colors, color combinations,[6] textures, graphics and designs, advertising materials or techniques,[7] brochures[8] and catalogs, associated by the public with a single source.[9]

---

[3]Qualitex Co. v. Jacobson Products Co., Inc., 13 F.3d 1297 (9th Cir. 1994), cert. granted in part, 512 U.S. 1287, 115 S. Ct. 40, 129 L. Ed. 2d 935 (1994) and rev'd, 514 U.S. 159, 115 S. Ct. 1300, 131 L. Ed. 2d 248 (1995) (in an action between two competing manufacturers of dry cleaning press pads, the Supreme Court held that the Lanham Act "permits the registration of a trademark that consists, purely and simply, of a color").

[4]Fotomat Corp. v. Photo Drive-Thru, Inc., 425 F. Supp. 693 (D.N.J. 1977) (size, shape and coloration of quick-film development kiosks).

[5]Fotomat Corp. v. Photo Drive-Thru, Inc., 425 F. Supp. 693 (D.N.J. 1977); Qualitex Co. v. Jacobson Products Co., Inc., 514 U.S. 159, 115 S. Ct. 1300, 131 L. Ed. 2d 248 (1995)(color).

[6]Carillon Importers Ltd. v. Frank Pesce Group, Inc., 913 F. Supp. 1559 (S.D. Fla. 1996), aff'd, 112 F.3d 1125 (11th Cir. 1997) (combinations of colors on bottle label and in script on labels).

[7]Original Appalachian Artworks, Inc. v. Toy Loft, Inc., 684 F.2d 821 (11th Cir. 1982) (dolls using an "adopt me" promotion); Romm Art Creations Ltd. v. Simcha Intern., Inc., 786 F. Supp. 1126 (E.D. N.Y. 1992) (lithographs using tear sheets).

[8]Hofmann v. Kleinhandler, 1994 WL 240335 (S.D. N.Y. 1994) (brochures promoting artist and dealer).

[9]Reader's Digest Ass'n, Inc. v. Conservative Digest, Inc., 821 F.2d 800, 803 (D.C. Cir. 1987) (trade dress is total image of a product including size, shape, color combinations, texture and graphics); John H. Harland Co. v. Clarke Checks, Inc., 711 F.2d 966, 980 (11th Cir. 1983) (trade dress refers to total image of a product, including individual features); Hofmann v. Kleinhandler, 1994 WL 240335 (S.D. N.Y. 1994) (dealer's promotional brochure for artist with whom it had exclusive sales agreement constitutes trade dress); Mattel, Inc. v. Walking Mountain Productions, 353 F.3d 792, 808, 69 U.S.P.Q.2d (BNA) 1257 (9th Cir. 2003) (discussion without decision on Barbie doll's overall appearance and Superstar Barbie head as trade dress).

Whether registered mark or trade dress, the "[same] general principles . . . are for the most part applicable in determining whether an unregistered mark [trade dress] is entitled to protection under § 43(a)."[10] The purpose of trademark and trade dress protection is to afford business an efficient identification system to enable the public to source a given product to the business through the use, inter alia, of its design and visual insignia. Plaintiff must show that it has used the designation as a mark and that defendant has done the same with a similar designation, and that the likelihood exists such that consumers will be confused as to sponsorship or production of the goods or services.[11]

The traditional elements needed to prevail on a trade dress claim were: (1) the trade dress was nonfunctional; (2) the trade dress had acquired secondary meaning; and (3) the defendant's use of trade dress was likely to confuse or mislead the public. "Functionality" is a term of art that refers to whether the trade dress is essential to the use or purpose of the product or affects its cost or quality. "Secondary meaning" is a term of art that means the public has come to recognize the common features of the trade dress as distinctive of or associated with the plaintiff's goods in commerce.[12] The Supreme Court has emphasized that crucial to secondary meaning is the public's association with the product source.[13]

In 1992 the U.S. Supreme Court disposed of the plaintiff's burden of proving secondary meaning for inherently

---

[10]Two Pesos, Inc. v. Taco Cabana, Inc., 505 U.S. 763, 112 S. Ct. 2753, 120 L. Ed. 2d 615 (1992); Mattel, Inc. v. Walking Mountain Productions, 353 F.3d 792, 808, 69 U.S.P.Q.2d (BNA) 1257 (9th Cir. 2003) ("'trade dress is protectable (sic) if 'nonfunctional and has acquired secondary meaning and if its imitation creates a likelihood of consumer confusion.'").

[11]Rock and Roll Hall of Fame and Museum, Inc. v. Gentile Productions, 134 F.3d 749 (6th Cir. 1998); *see* 15 U.S.C.A. §§ 1114(1), 1125(a)(1).

[12]15 U.S.C.A. § 1052 (e–f); Reader's Digest Ass'n, Inc. v. Conservative Digest, Inc., 821 F.2d 800, 803 (D.C. Cir. 1987).

[13]Qualitex Co. v. Jacobson Products Co., Inc., 514 U.S. 159, 115 S. Ct. 1300, 131 L. Ed. 2d 248 (1995) (color that has acquired secondary meaning is appropriate for trademark registration).

distinctive trade dress in *Two Pesos*,[14] a decision involving two competitive nationwide restaurant chains' decorative ambiance. The Court, confronted with conflicting decisions in the circuit courts of appeal, held that Section 43(a) protects inherently distinctive trade dress without proof of secondary meaning,[15] noting that the terms "trademark," "trade dress," and "secondary meaning" do not appear in Section 43(a): "We see no basis for requiring secondary meaning for inherently distinctive trade dress protection under section 43(a) but not for other distinctive words, symbols, or devices capable of identifying a producer's product."[16]

§ 8:4 Burden of proof

The burden is on the party seeking relief under the Lanham Act to prove its case by a preponderance of the evidence.[1]

§ 8:5 Inherently distinctive

Generic trade marks, like generic trade dress, are

---

[14]Two Pesos, Inc. v. Taco Cabana, Inc., 505 U.S. 763, 112 S. Ct. 2753, 120, 120 L. Ed. 2d 615 (1992).

[15]*See also* Romm Art Creations Ltd. v. Simcha Intern., Inc., 786 F. Supp. 1126 (E.D. N.Y. 1992) (inherently distinctive is "proof of secondary meaning"); *cf.* Vibrant Sales, Inc. v. New Body Boutique, Inc., 652 F.2d 299 (2d Cir. 1981) (unregistered marks require proof of secondary meaning).

[16]Two Pesos, Inc. v. Taco Cabana, Inc., 505 U.S. 763, 112 S. Ct. 2753, 120 L. Ed. 2d 615, 627, (1992). To demonstrate protectibility of unregistered marks against challenge, users must show that they are the first user and that they intend to continue commercial use of the mark. *See, e.g.,* Swanson v. Georgetown Collection, Inc., 1995 WL 72717 (N.D. N.Y. 1995) (small but continuous use of soft sculpture dolls acceptable).

[Section 8:4]

[1]Lish v. Harper's Magazine Foundation, 807 F. Supp. 1090, 1107 (S.D. N.Y. 1992), order amended on other grounds, 20 Media L. Rep. (BNA) 2228, 25 U.S.P.Q.2d (BNA) 1556, 1993 WL 7576 (S.D. N.Y. 1993); Playboy Enterprises, Inc. v. Dumas, 831 F. Supp. 295 (S.D. N.Y. 1993), opinion modified on reargument, 840 F. Supp. 256 (S.D. N.Y. 1993) and judgment aff'd in part, rev'd in part on other grounds, 53 F.3d 549, 132 A.L.R. Fed. 703 (2d Cir. 1995); *see also* King v. Allied Vision, Ltd., 807 F. Supp. 300 (S.D. N.Y. 1992), order aff'd in part, rev'd in part on other grounds, 976 F.2d 824 (2d Cir. 1992).

ordinarily not protected. A generic mark "refers to the genus or class of which a particular product is a member" and trade dress is considered generic if "well-known . . . common . . . refinement of a commonly adopted and well-known form of ornamentation . . . or a common basic shape or design . . . [not] refined in precisely the same way."[1] Trademark protection is available to marks without proof of secondary meaning if they are inherently distinctive, which means the mark is "fanciful," "arbitrary," "otherwise distinctive," or "suggestive."[2] Plaintiff must prove its trade dress is inherently distinctive. The key to distinctiveness is that the customer is "automatically" informed that a brand or a product source is the intended reference.[3] Distinctiveness turns upon the combination of elements rather than the distinctiveness of each element of the trade dress.[4] The following visuals have been considered inherently distinctive trade dress: A restaurant's festive ambiance created by bright colors, paintings

[Section 8:5]

[1]Ale House Management, Inc. v. Raleigh Ale House, 205 F.3d 137 (4th Cir. 2000) (citations omitted) (affirming summary judgment for defendants on trade dress of restaurant interiors where plaintiff did not uniformly configure its various establishments and did not use "unique or unusual" design features).

[2]Knitwaves, Inc. v. Lollytogs Ltd. (Inc.), 71 F.3d 996 (2d Cir. 1995) (adopting a new test in a sweater design case for determining whether product features are inherently distinctive for purposes of obtaining trade dress protection; test focuses solely on whether the images were likely to serve primarily as an indicator of source rather than the recited list previously used in the Second Circuit and other jurisdictions, as well as by the United States Supreme Court); *accord,* New York Racing Ass'n, Inc. v. Perlmutter Pub., Inc., 959 F. Supp. 578 (N.D. N.Y. 1997) (noting both Knitwaves test and Two Pesos test to determine if images were inherently distinctive, but applying sole criterion of the former).

[3]Qualitex Co. v. Jacobson Products Co., Inc., 514 U.S. 159, 115 S. Ct. 1300, 131 L. Ed. 2d 248 (1995).

[4]Jeffrey Milstein, Inc. v. Greger, Lawlor, Roth, Inc., 58 F.3d 27 (2d Cir. 1995) (photographs on die-cut cards did not qualify for trade dress because die-cut photographic greeting cards constituted unprotectible concept or idea).

and murals, awnings, umbrellas and artifacts;[5] greeting cards depicting a few cursive lines of text, common shapes like stripes and dots, flanked by colored stripes printed on cream-colored textured paper;[6] and visual imagery of cafe scenes reproduced in commercial prints, in combination with graphic art, margins and tear sheets.[7]

No precedential ruling to date expressly holds that a visual image per se is trade dress. In the limited number of cases considering the issue, no clear cut markers emerge. One district court, applying Section 43(a) in an action for infringement of commercial reproductions of artworks, found visual imagery, reproduced in combination with graphic art, distinctive borders, margins, and tear sheets, inherently distinctive trade dress.[8]

§ 8:6 Artistic style, visual imagery

Is a visual image or artistic style protectible under the Lanham Act? The district courts have been divided. Until recently, no precedent-setting opinion directly addresses the issue in terms of the visual arts. The background of such cases discussed below focused on style, overall imagery or pastiche of visuals rather than any particular or specific image. But at least one jurisdiction has more

---

[5]Two Pesos, Inc. v. Taco Cabana, Inc., 505 U.S. 763, 112 S. Ct. 2753, 120 L. Ed. 2d 615 (1992).

[6]Roulo v. Russ Berrie & Co., Inc., 886 F.2d 931 (7th Cir. 1989) (greeting card designer sued a greeting card manufacturer for whom she had previously created cards for trademark infringement, alleging its cards incorporated the trade dress of her cards, which she marketed herself and through others).

[7]Romm Art Creations Ltd. v. Simcha Intern., Inc., 786 F. Supp. 1126 (E.D. N.Y. 1992).

[8]Romm Art Creations Ltd. v. Simcha Intern., Inc., 786 F. Supp. 1126 at 1137 (E.D. N.Y. 1992) (analyzing the strength of the senior user's mark, the court adopted findings that ". . . as imaginative, artistic portraits, the [plaintiff's] images are strong marks"); see also Mattel, Inc. v. Walking Mountain Productions, 353 F.3d 792, 808, 69 U.S.P.Q.2d (BNA) 1257 (9th Cir. 2003) (discussion without decision on Barbie doll's overall appearance and Superstar Barbie head as trade dress).

directly confronted the issue.[1] The photographer of a Bird Girl statue taken in a Savannah cemetery that served as the cover of a best seller, claimed trademark in the photograph. The defendant made a film based upon the novel and used images of the statue in the film and promotional materials. Entering summary judgment for defendant, the district court found that the artist was impermissibly attempting to use the Lanham Act to protect visual style.

On appeal, the artist claimed he used the Bird Girl photograph as a "source identifier" to promote workshops and sales. But none of the advertising, flyers, materials, exhibits, or web sites was dated before release of the movie. As a matter of law, the evidence thus failed to establish the artist's trademark rights before defendant's use. The court further observed that the photographic use was descriptive, failing to function as a separate mark. The purported mark in the photograph was the "good" itself, since the photograph was also offered for sale in connection with the sales materials.[2] In the absence of connection of disparate product or service, no "mark" was established.

The result comports with a limited chain of cases involving integrated blends of mark and imagery or blends of imagery and other visual components that marketed a disparate good. Opinions finding trade dress examine the combination of visual and graphic elements rather than any one item. For example, where a series of greeting cards incorporated common shapes and features, i.e., stripes, dots, and handwriting, the court concluded, "[t]he fact that her cards incorporated common, indistinct elements such as lines and handwriting does not refute the

---

[Section 8:6]

[1]Leigh v. Warner Bros., a Div. of Time Warner Entertainment Co., L.P., 10 F. Supp. 2d 1371 (S.D. Ga. 1998), aff'd in part, rev'd in part, 212 F.3d 1210 (11th Cir. 2000) (photograph of the Bird Girl statue on the cover of the best-seller, *Midnight in the Garden of Good and Evil*).

[2]Leigh v. Warner Bros., a Div. of Time Warner Entertainment Co., L.P., 10 F. Supp. 2d 1371 (S.D. Ga. 1998), aff'd in part, rev'd in part, 212 F.3d 1210 (11th Cir. 2000) (print ads showed photograph as an "example" of works available; art center displays showed photograph along with others to promote workshops; thumbnail reproduction on gallery web site rotated five photos).

fact that Roulo's combination of these elements was sufficiently unique to warrant trade-dress protection."[3] The appellate court qualified protection of the imagery to the context of the overall look and feel of the card, the combined dress. "[Plaintiff] has not been granted exclusive rights in an artistic style or some concept, idea, or theme of expression. Rather it is [the] specific artistic expression in combination with other features to produce an overall . . . look that is being protected."[4]

Similarly, an abstract rendition of a lone cypress tree (based upon a landmark tree) and v-shaped waves, used by the owners of the famous Pebble Beach golf course in connection with the sale of related products and services, was found to be a "highly fanciful" and "distinctive" mark entitled to far reaching protection. The trial court permanently enjoined another defendant corporation located near the tree from making any commercial use of a similar abstract mark that was developed ten years after the Pebble Beach mark was in use.[5]

Other courts have not been willing to consider visual impression, imagery or artistic style as protectible trade dress.[6] Where plaintiff alleged that works by surrealist artist Salvador Dali were inherently distinctive trade dress—"particular lines, unique figural constellation, colors, stylistic features and design of a certain subject in an image created by Dali . . . Each one . . . unique image constitutes a valid trademark . . . [as] the image or the configuration of the drawing applied to paper"—the court granted defendant's motion to dismiss the trademark claim on the grounds that it was a copyright claim

[3]Roulo v. Russ Berrie & Co., Inc., 1988 WL 64094 (N.D. Ill. 1988), decision aff'd, 886 F.2d 931 (7th Cir. 1989).

[4]Hartford House, Ltd. v. Hallmark Cards, Inc., 846 F.2d 1268, 1274 (10th Cir. 1988).

[5]Pebble Beach Co. v. Laub America Corp., 1985 WL 5584 (N.D. Cal. 1985).

[6]*See, e.g.*, Heyman v. Salle, 743 F. Supp. 190 (S.D. N.Y. 1989); Galerie Furstenberg v. Coffaro, 697 F. Supp. 1282 (S.D. N.Y. 1988); and Hughes v. Design Look Inc., 693 F. Supp. 1500 (S.D. N.Y. 1988); *see also* § 8:15.

masquerading as trademark.[7] When the estate of Andy Warhol claimed trade dress existed in specific images as well as the "unique style" of Warhol imagery, seeking damages and injunction against a calendar publisher based on its use of twelve uncopyrighted images depicting Marilyn Monroe and Campbell's Soup cans, the court refused to enjoin the publisher;[8] the art did not constitute "marks" used by the artist or estate to promote products or business. Without analyzing the availability of trade dress protection for visual images, the court explained:

> Despite the fact that these particular works have not been used as marks, the Plaintiffs still claim protection because of the unique style of Andy Warhol and because these images—particularly Marilyn and Campbell's Soup—have come to represent Warhol. However, there is no question [about that] . . . To prevail, Plaintiffs must show not that these images have come to signify Andy Warhol as the artist, but plaintiffs as the source of the product, the calendars.[9]

Where a professional photographer sued a painter under Section 43(a) for copying his photo from a Pop Art book to prepare a theatrical backdrop in a stage production (the photo was republished in monographs and catalogues), the court granted the painter's motion for summary judgment, stating "it is difficult to comprehend how . . . a photograph published in this manner can be subject to trademark."[10]

Supreme Court holdings have focused upon the interface and combination of colors, patterns, and objects rather than any particular work of art, but such holdings have significant application to visual art, where cases have been summarily adjudicated because secondary meaning could not be shown.[11] If the Court has upheld interior decor of a restaurant as inherently distinctive trade dress, then presumably many types of artwork of unique visual combina-

---

[7]Galerie Furstenberg v. Coffaro, 697 F. Supp. 1282 (S.D. N.Y. 1988) (query such a district court result after the Court's decision in Qualitex Co. v. Jacobson Products Co., Inc., 514 U.S. 159, 115 S. Ct. 1300, 131 L. Ed. 2d 248 (1995)).

[8]Hughes v. Design Look Inc., 693 F. Supp. 1500 (S.D. N.Y. 1988).

[9]Hughes v. Design Look Inc., 693 F. Supp. 1500 (S.D. N.Y. 1988).

[10]Heyman v. Salle, 743 F. Supp. 190 (S.D. N.Y. 1989).

[11]Hughes v. Design Look Inc., 693 F. Supp. 1500, 1507 (S.D. N.Y. 1988) (the court held no marks existed in the works of Andy Warhol, negating any possibility of secondary meaning:

tion and composition of colors, symbols, shapes and the like could qualify as trade dress, assuming that the circumstances survive the commercial nexus imposed by most courts on Section 43(a) claims.

New tests for inherently distinctive are apparently being created as this is written.[12] Redefining the term "inherently distinctive" will also affect what visual imagery qualifies as dress.[13]

§ 8:7 Functionality

In simplest terms, the trademark functionality doctrine seeks to prevent a competitor from "inhibiting legitimate competition . . . by allowing [it] to control . . ." a particular functional, or useful, feature of a product.[1] In *Qualitex*, the Supreme Court held that the functionality doctrine would not automatically prevent registering as a trademark pure color, which had acquired secondary meaning, in instances where the color is not "essential to a product's

---

Plaintiffs have not made any showing of secondary meaning . . . these images were never used by Warhol or the plaintiffs in association with the promotion of any goods or services . . . . in light of the fact that the Plaintiffs have to date produced no similar products, indeed no products at all, bearing similar images, secondary meaning cannot be claimed. In the absence of secondary meaning, there is no question but that a claim of consumer confusion cannot be made out.).

[12]*See, e.g.,* Knitwaves, Inc. v. Lollytogs Ltd. (Inc.), 71 F.3d 996 (2d Cir. 1995) (adopting a new test in a sweater design case for determining whether product features are inherently distinctive for purposes of obtaining trade dress protection; test focuses solely on whether the images were likely to serve primarily as an indicator of source rather than the categorizations ["generic, descriptive, suggestive, arbitrary or fanciful"] previously used in the Second Circuit and other jurisdictions, as well as by the United States Supreme Court); *accord,* New York Racing Ass'n, Inc. v. Perlmutter Pub., Inc., 959 F. Supp. 578 (N.D. N.Y. 1997).

[13]*See, e.g.,* Knitwaves, Inc. v. Lollytogs Ltd. (Inc.), 71 F.3d 996 (2d Cir. 1995) (adopting a new test in a sweater design case for determining whether product features are inherently distinctive for purposes of obtaining trade dress).

[Section 8:7]

[1]Qualitex Co. v. Jacobson Products Co., Inc., 514 U.S. 159, 115 S. Ct. 1300, 131 L. Ed. 2d 248 (1995).

use or purpose and does not affect cost or quality."[2] Plaintiff had used the green-gold color on its dry-cleaning press pads since the 1950s and sought to prevent a competitive manufacturer from using the same color.

In *Two Pesos*,[3] a Section 43(a) action involving two commercial restaurant chains using similar decor and themes, the Court held that visual images in combination create a nonfunctional visual impression. The nonfunctional trade dress there consisted of a restaurant's festive ambiance, created by bright colors, paintings and murals, awnings, umbrellas and artifacts.[4]

Similarly, the sleek gold Oscar statuette presented by the Academy of Motion Picture Arts and Sciences was deemed a nonfunctional distinctive design because "an achievement award need not have those particular characteristics."[5]

§ 8:8 Color and imagery

To what extent imagery alone in a visual arts context will constitute protectible dress is unresolved.[1] Color has been held to constitute trade dress or trademark. Noting that registration has issued for sound, fragrance, and shapes, the Supreme Court found color satisfactory "to identify and distinguish [one's] goods, . . . including a unique product, from those manufactured or sold by others, and to indicate the source of the goods, even if that

---

[2]Qualitex Co. v. Jacobson Products Co., Inc., 514 U.S. 159, 115 S. Ct. 1300, 131 L. Ed. 2d 248 (1995) ("doctrine of 'functionality' does not create an absolute bar to the use of color alone as a mark . . .").

[3]Two Pesos, Inc. v. Taco Cabana, Inc., 505 U.S. 763, 112 S. Ct. 2753, 120 L. Ed. 2d 615 (1992).

[4]*See also* Fuddruckers, Inc. v. Doc's B.R. Others, Inc., 826 F.2d 837 (9th Cir. 1987).

[5]Academy of Motion Picture Arts and Sciences v. Creative House Promotions, Inc., 944 F.2d 1446 (9th Cir. 1991) (the "Oscar" entitled to protection under the Lanham Act in action brought against distributor of shiny metallic figurines marketed as trophies for business achievement).

[Section 8:8]

[1]*See* § 8:5.

source is unknown."[2] Color in combination with objects[3] or in connection with artworks[4] previously has been held to constitute protectible trade dress.

Color and imagery can constitute protectible trade dress. In *Two Pesos*,[5] the overall image of a restaurant, including its artworks, artifacts, and ambiance, was held to be trade dress.[6] In *Romm Art Creations*,[7] posters and prints of stylized portraits of women sitting in cafes, in combination with the promotional presentation of tear sheets and borders, were considered trade dress.[8] In a case involving premium imported vodkas, conventionally shaped clear glass wine bottles, packaged with black labels reciting the product name in white and gold lettering, black neck wrappers, and black neck labels comprised of overlapping gold medallions, were considered trade dress.[9]

§ 8:9 Likelihood of confusion—Viewer standard

Federal law prohibits imitations that confuse, deceive, or mislead consumers.[1] Plaintiffs must show not only valid mark or trade dress, but also the likelihood of public confusion.

Likelihood of confusion has been expressed in various

[2]Qualitex Co. v. Jacobson Products Co., Inc., 514 U.S. 159, 115 S. Ct. 1300, 131 L. Ed. 2d 248 (1995) (citing 15 U.S.C.A. § 1127).

[3]Two Pesos, Inc. v. Taco Cabana, Inc., 505 U.S. 763, 112 S. Ct. 2753, 120 L. Ed. 2d 615 (1992).

[4]Romm Art Creations Ltd. v. Simcha Intern., Inc., 786 F. Supp. 1126 (E.D. N.Y. 1992).

[5]Two Pesos, Inc. v. Taco Cabana, Inc., 505 U.S. 763, 112 S. Ct. 2753, 120 L. Ed. 2d 615 (1992).

[6]Two Pesos, Inc. v. Taco Cabana, Inc., 505 U.S. 763, 112 S. Ct. 2753, 120 L. Ed. 2d 615 (1992).

[7]Romm Art Creations Ltd. v. Simcha Intern., Inc., 786 F. Supp. 1126 (E.D. N.Y. 1992).

[8]Romm Art Creations Ltd. v. Simcha Intern., Inc., 786 F. Supp. 1126 (E.D. N.Y. 1992).

[9]Carillon Importers Ltd. v. Frank Pesce Group, Inc., 913 F. Supp. 1559 (S.D. Fla. 1996), aff'd, 112 F.3d 1125 (11th Cir. 1997) (Stolichnaya Cristall vodka obtained injunction to prevent Cristal Moscow vodka from using similar packaging).

[Section 8:9]

[1]15 U.S.C.A. §§ 1114(1)(a), 1125(a).

ways among the courts. Regardless of the particular set of factors applied, the basic issues are whether the public has a mistaken belief as to the source of the product—for example, where the consumer believes the defendant's product is the plaintiff's product, or the product sources to the same supplier; or the public believes the plaintiff "is in some way related to or connected or affiliated with, or sponsor[s] . . ." defendant's product.[2]

Plaintiff must establish the likelihood of consumer confusion, although competing goods generally require less proof of confusion than noncompeting goods.[3] Likelihood of confusion has been decided as a mixed question of fact and law, an issue of fact subject to the clearly erroneous standard, or a conclusion of law, subject to review de novo.[4]

Where sufficiently sharp differences exist between the nature of the goods and services, courts have decided they are unrelated as a matter of law.[5] Likelihood of confusion has been tested in some jurisdictions under the "ordinarily

---

[2]Nike, Inc. v. Just Did It Enterprises, 6 F.3d 1225 (7th Cir. 1993).

[3]Durham Industries, Inc. v. Tomy Corp., 630 F.2d 905, 911 (2d Cir. 1980) (no Lanham Act violation where there is no likelihood of consumer confusion).

[4]Durham Industries, Inc. v. Tomy Corp., 630 F.2d 905, 911 (2d Cir. 1980); Champions Golf Club, Inc. v. The Champions Golf Club, Inc., 78 F.3d 1111, 1996 FED App. 94P (6th Cir. 1996) (vacating and remanding for review of facts and law district court decision that no likelihood of confusion existed between two championship golf clubs); Lord Simon Cairns v. Franklin Mint Co., 24 F. Supp. 2d 1013 (C.D. Cal. 1998) (likelihood of confusion is primarily factual in nature, but resolution, as matter of law, on summary judgment may be appropriate where the products or marks are so dissimilar that no question of fact is presented).

[5]*See, e.g.,* Toho Co., Ltd. v. Sears, Roebuck & Co., 645 F.2d 788, 791 (9th Cir. 1981) (dismissal of complaint by distributor of reptilian fictional monster "Godzilla," "King of the Monsters," against American retailer producing and selling "monstrously strong," "Bagzilla" garbage bags upheld on appeal because consumers [were] not likely to be confused as to source or sponsorship."); Hooker v. Columbia Pictures Industries, Inc., 551 F. Supp. 1060 (N.D. Ill. 1982) (dismissal of complaint by woodcarver named T.J. Hooker doing business eponymously against entertainment entity using same name for series starring fictional California policeman on grounds that products were unrelated and were marketed in entirely different channels, the latter by network television and the plaintiff's through specialty catalogues); Sweet v.

prudent purchaser" standard: Are "an appreciable number of ordinarily prudent purchasers . . . likely to be misled, or indeed simply confused, as to the source of the goods in question."[6]

§ 8:10 Likelihood of confusion—Factors considered

Courts use a variety of factors to determine whether or not there is a likelihood of confusion. Some circuits use commonly-cited lists within their own jurisdiction, others borrow from elsewhere. The factors, like the fair use defense in copyright, are expressly nonexhaustive, with no one factor controlling.[1] A summary of the circuits in which visual art has been tested are recited below.

The Second Circuit uses factors recited in Polaroid Corp. v. Polarad Electronics Corp.,[2] sometimes referred to as the "Polaroid Factors": (1) strength of senior user's mark; (2) degree of similarity between the two marks; (3) competitive proximity of the two products; (4) likelihood plaintiff will 'bridge the gap';[3] (5) evidence of actual confusion; (6) junior user's good faith; (7) quality of junior user's prod-

---

City of Chicago, 953 F. Supp. 225 (N.D. Ill. 1996) (art fair that was ancillary to outdoor food festival as a matter of law was unrelated to guidebook providing information about restaurants that displayed art, and no likelihood of confusion existed as to origin or sponsorship).

[6]Academy of Motion Picture Arts and Sciences v. Creative House Promotions, Inc., 944 F.2d 1446 (9th Cir. 1991) (in action involving Oscar statuette and similar-looking metal figurine, actual confusion not required so long as "consumers are likely to assume that the mark is associated with another source or sponsor because of similarities between the two marks"); *cf.*, Leigh v. Warner Bros., Inc., 212 F.3d 1210, 2000 (11th Cir. 2000) (actual confusion required, and proof must be more than de minimus); Romm Art Creations Ltd. v. Simcha Intern., Inc., 786 F. Supp. 1126, 1136 (E.D. N.Y. 1992); Swanson v. Georgetown Collection, Inc., 1995 WL 72717 (N.D. N.Y. 1995).

[Section 8:10]

[1]*See, e.g.,* Nike, Inc. v. Just Did It Enterprises, 6 F.3d 1225 (7th Cir. 1993).

[2]*See* Polaroid Corp. v. Polarad Elecs. Corp., 287 F.2d 492, 4 Fed. R. Serv. 2d 81 (2d Cir. 1961) (Polaroid Factors applied in Romm Art Creations Ltd. v. Simcha Intern., Inc., 786 F. Supp. 1126, 1136 (E.D. N.Y. 1992).

[3]"Bridging the gap" refers to the likelihood that the senior user will enter the junior user's market.

uct; and (8) sophistication of purchasers.[4]

The Seventh Circuit relied on these factors to determine likelihood of confusion in a case where greeting cards were at issue because of the similarity of their artwork and scripted messages: (1) similarity of trade dress; (2) type of products to which trade dress attaches; (3) area and manner of concurrent use; (4) degree of care likely to be exercised by consumers; (5) strength of plaintiff's trade dress; (6) actual confusion; and (7) intent on part of infringer to pass off its goods as those of plaintiff's.[5]

The Seventh Circuit found similarity of trade dress based upon a side-by-side comparison of the two greeting cards, the fact that the cards were sold as impulse items through the same retailers, evidence from which a jury could discern an intent to imitate plaintiff's cards, as well as the strength of plaintiff's mark. "The strength of a particular trade dress relates in part to its uniqueness . . . [testimonial] evidence [showed] that [plaintiff's] card [ ] was the 'finest sensitive verse greeting card line ever released.' "[6]

The First Circuit factors that follow were applied in a case where a museum's use of its own name, "Mystic Seaport," on beverages was challenged by a beverage distributor using the registered mark "Mistic": (1) similarity of the marks; (2) similarity of the goods; (3) relationship between the parties' channels of trade; (4) relationship between the parties' advertising; (5) classes of prospective purchasers; (6) actual confusion; (7) strength of the plaintiff's mark; and (8) defendant's intent in adopting the mark.[7]

The district court decided as issues of fact that a likelihood of confusion existed because the beverages were low-priced items, traded in the same channels, and purchased

---

[4]Romm Art Creations Ltd. v. Simcha Intern., Inc., 786 F. Supp. 1126, 1139 (E.D. N.Y. 1992) (Polaroid Factors applied to posters and limited edition prints with an average price of $30).

[5]Roulo v. Russ Berrie & Co., Inc., 886 F.2d 931 (7th Cir. 1989); Nike, Inc. v. Just Did It Enterprises, 6 F.3d 1225 (7th Cir. 1993).

[6]886 F.2d at 937.

[7]Best Flavors, Inc. v. Mystic River Brewing Co., 886 F. Supp. 908 (D. Me. 1995).

by a similar clientele.[8]

The Ninth Circuit recognizes several different tests to determine likelihood of confusion, no list exhaustive or intended for mechanistic application: (1) strength of the mark; (2) similarity in appearance, sound and meaning between the two marks; (3) class of goods; (4) marketing channels; (5) evidence of actual confusion; (6) defendant's intent in selecting the mark; (7) likely degree of purchaser care; and (8) likelihood of product expansion lines.[9] The Eleventh Circuit uses the following factors to test confusion: (1) type of trademark; (2) similarity of design; (3) similarity of the product; (4) identity of retail outlets and purchasers; (5) similarity of advertising media used; (6) defendant's intent; and (7) actual confusion.[10]

§ 8:11 First Amendment exceptions—Generally

The First Amendment is as applicable to works of art as other forms of expression.[1] Thus, an artist's use of a mark or dress in a work of creative expression resonates with First Amendment considerations. Commercial use or sale of expressive works does not negate the protection to which such works are otherwise entitled.[2] When a Lanham claim is based upon an artwork that is considered speech

---

[8]Best Flavors, Inc. v. Mystic River Brewing Co., 886 F. Supp. 908 (D. Me. 1995).

[9]*See, e.g.,* Academy of Motion Picture Arts and Sciences v. Creative House Promotions, Inc., 944 F.2d 1446 (9th Cir. 1991) (evaluating whether a shiny metal muscular male figurine holding a star in its hand on a circular gold mount created a likelihood of confusion with the Oscar statuette awarded in the entertainment industry); Lord Simon Cairns v. Franklin Mint Co., 24 F. Supp. 2d 1013 (C.D. Cal. 1998) (reciting all factors to test likelihood of confusion).

[10]Leigh v. Warner Bros., Inc., 212 F.3d 1210, 2000 (11th Cir. 2000) (summary judgment in favor of defendant film company in trade dress infringement action brought by photographer because no likelihood of confusion between a photograph that depicted a noted sculpture, which was commissioned for the cover of a bestselling novel, and defendant's photographs of a sculptural replica used for merchandising and promotion of a movie based upon the same book).

[Section 8:11]

[1]See Ch 10.

[2]Comedy III Productions, Inc. v. Gary Saderup, Inc., 25 Cal. 4th 387, 408, 106 Cal. Rptr. 2d 126, 21 P.3d 797, 29 Media L. Rep. (BNA)

protected by the first amendment, the analysis of unauthorized use of the marks or dress changes. However, "'[t]rademark protection "is not lost simply because the allegedly infringing use is in connection with a work of artistic expression.""[3]

The First Amendment "confers a measure of protection for the unauthorized use of trademarks when that use is part of the expression of a communicative message . . . ."[4] Nor has Section 43(a) been broadened to "stifle criticism of goods or services" by noncompetitors. It is not intended "to limit political speech, consumer or editorial comment, parodies, satires, or other constitutionally protected material . . . [it] is narrowly drafted to encompass only clearly

---

1897, 58 U.S.P.Q.2d (BNA) 1823 (2001), cert. denied, 534 U.S. 1078, 122 S. Ct. 806, 151 L. Ed. 2d 692 (2002) (commercial enterprise profiting from sale of multiple reproductions that contain "significant creative elements" as "entitled to first amendment protection as an original work of art.").

[3]Parks v. LaFace Records, 329 F.3d 437, 31 Media L. Rep. (BNA) 1897, 66 U.S.P.Q.2d (BNA) 1735, 2003 FED App. 0137P (6th Cir. 2003), cert. denied, 124 S. Ct. 925, 157 L. Ed. 2d 744 (U.S. 2003) (citations omitted)(". . .the First Amendment cannot permit anyone who cries 'artist' to have carte blanche when it comes to naming and advertising . . . works, art though it may be.").

[4]ETW Corp. v. Jireh Pub., Inc., 332 F.3d 915, 925, 67 U.S.P.Q.2d (BNA) 1065, 2003 FED App. 0207P (6th Cir. 2003) (where "colorable claim that . . .use of. . .celebrity's identity is protected by. . .First Amendment. . .likelihood of confusion test is not appropriate); Mattel, Inc. v. Walking Mountain Productions, 353 F.3d 792, 69 U.S.P.Q.2d (BNA) 1257 (9th Cir. 2003) ("public interest in free and artistic expression greatly outweighs. . .interest in potential consumer confusion about Mattel's sponsorship of [artist's] works"); Gmurzynska v. Hutton, 355 F.3d 206, 69 U.S.P.Q.2d (BNA) 1477 (2d Cir. 2004) (journalist's article on authenticity dispute between competing galleries was not commercial speech, advertising or promotion but opinion protected under first amendment); Boule v. Hutton, 328 F.3d 84, 91, 31 Media L. Rep. (BNA) 1793, 66 U.S.P.Q.2d (BNA) 1659 (2d Cir. 2003) (statements in arts magazine article on authenticity disputes were not commercial speech); Yankee Pub. Inc. v. News America Pub. Inc., 809 F. Supp. 267, 275 (S.D. N.Y. 1992) (*New York Magazine's* use of Old Farmers Almanac registered cover design on its Christmas issue cover was a "joke," not a parody, but still entitled to some measure of First Amendment protection); *accord,* New York Racing Ass'n, Inc. v. Perlmutter Pub., Inc., 959 F. Supp. 578 (N.D. N.Y. 1997) (First Amendment bar to plaintiff's trademark infringement claims based upon paintings of Saratoga Race Course used on his souvenirs).

false or misleading commercial speech."[5]

The mark itself may have transmogrified for purposes of legal analysis. When marks assume cultural or other significance, they "'enter the public discourse and become an integral part of [the] vocabulary [performing] . . . a role outside the bounds of trademark law.'"[6] In the words of the Ninth Circuit, "[t]he trademark owner does not have the right to control public discourse whenever the public imbues [the] mark with a meaning beyond its source."[7]

Courts have considered a variety of contexts for First Amendment claims in artistic works. Focusing on visual art imagery, trademark protection has been evaluated in the following: likeness portrayal of celebrities[8]

---

[5]S. 1883, 101st Cong., 1st Sess., 135 Cong. Rec. 1207, 1217 (Apr. 13, 1989); Wojnarowicz v. American Family Ass'n, 745 F. Supp. 130 (S.D. N.Y. 1990) (dismissal of artist's Lanham Act claim against non-profit organization that distributed brochures containing his paintings and critical of public funding for such artworks).

[6]Mattel, Inc. v. Walking Mountain Productions, 353 F.3d 792, 69 U.S.P.Q.2d (BNA) 1257 (9th Cir. 2003)(citations omitted).

[7]Mattel, Inc. v. Walking Mountain Productions, 353 F.3d 792, 69 U.S.P.Q.2d (BNA) 1257 (9th Cir. 2003) (citations omitted).

[8]15 U.S.C.A. § 1125(a)] (no protection for {unregistered}mark) ETW Corp. v. Jireh Pub., Inc., 332 F.3d 915, 922, 67 U.S.P.Q.2d (BNA) 1065, 2003 FED App. 0207P (6th Cir. 2003) (trademark is not "right in gross" that allows Woods "to constitute himself as a walking, talking trademark" because images and likenesses do not perform designation function or identify source of goods), Clay, J. dissenting, 332 F.3d at 940 (". . .if plaintiff alleging infringement in the unregistered mark of his image or likeness . . .[presents] evidence of consumer confusion, then the image or likeness. . .may very well be functioning 'as a trademark' for purposes of § 1125(a)."); [15 U.S.C.A. § 1125(a)](no false endorsement) ETW Corp. v. Jireh Publ. Inc., 332 F.3d at 926, 937 (6th Cir. 2003) (Tiger Woods' image in painting "The Masters of Augusta" had artistic relevance and did not explicitly mislead public as to source of work, applying balancing test of Rogers v. Grimaldi, 875 F.2d 994, 999, 16 Media L. Rep. (BNA) 1648, 10 U.S.P.Q.2d (BNA) 1825 (2d Cir. 1989) (prohibiting application of Lanham Act to titles of artistic works unless title 'has no artistic relevance. . .[or if some relevance]. . . unless. . . title explicitly misleads as to. . .source or content. . ..."), Clay, J. dissenting, 332 F.3d at 943 (arguing Rogers limited to title cases and urging application of [Ohio's] eight-factor likelihood of confusion test to evidence of consumer confusion regarding Woods' sponsorship of artist's prints); [state/common law](no right of publicity)] ETW Corp. v. Jireh Publ. Inc., 332 F.3d at 937-38 (6th Cir.

and portrayals of cultural icons.[9] Certain circuits have held that a person's image or likeness "cannot function as a trademark."[10] Courts have also considered use of the mark in, on or packaged with artworks.[11]

There are several tests utilized by courts in considering

2003)[Ohio](celebrities embody societal ideas, ideals and values through "pervasive media presence" and serve as "'important element[s] of shared communicative . . .[cultural] resources. . .'")(citations omitted), Clay, J. dissenting, 332 F.3d at 960(". . .the [Rush] prints gain their commercial value by exploiting the fame and celebrity status that Woods has worked to achieve; [therefore] the right of publicity is not outweighed by the right of free expression."); see also Comedy III Productions, Inc. v. Gary Saderup, Inc., 25 Cal. 4th 387, 396, 106 Cal. Rptr. 2d 126, 21 P.3d 797, 29 Media L. Rep. (BNA) 1897, 58 U.S.P.Q.2d (BNA) 1823 (2001), cert. denied, 534 U.S. 1078, 122 S. Ct. 806, 151 L. Ed. 2d 692 (2002) [California] (applying transformative effects test to decide whether artist's charcoal drawings of Three Stooges reproduced in prints and on T-shirts by commercial enterprise for profit were entitled to first amendment protection as "expressive works. . .not advertisement[s] or [product] endorsement[s]. . . ").

[9]Mattel, Inc. v. Walking Mountain Productions, 353 F.3d 792, 808, 69 U.S.P.Q.2d (BNA) 1257 (9th Cir. 2003) [parodic portrayals of "Barbie" doll in photographs and on website](trade dress) ("Arguably, the Barbie trade dress also plays a role in our culture similar to [that of] Barbie trademark-[] symbolization of an unattainable ideal of femininity for some women, [and thus the artist's] use of the Barbie trade dress. . .would present First Amendment concerns similar to those that made us reluctant to apply the Lanham Act as a bar to the artistic uses of Mattel's Barbie trademark," finding nominative fair use without applying first amendment balancing test); see also 8: 13.

[10]ETW Corp. v. Jireh Pub., Inc., 332 F.3d 915, 67 U.S.P.Q.2d (BNA) 1065, 2003 FED App. 0207P (6th Cir. 2003), citing Pirone v. MacMillan, Inc., 894 F.2d 579, 583, 17 Media L. Rep. (BNA) 1472, 13 U.S.P.Q.2d (BNA) 1799 (2d Cir. 1990) (no trademark rights in calendar photograph of Babe Ruth-a "larger than life hero to millions and an historical figure[.]"-because photograph was not an identifier); but cf. Presley's Estate v. Russen, 513 F. Supp. 1339, 1363-64, 211 U.S.P.Q. (BNA) 415 (D.N.J. 1981) (particular image of Elvis Presley consistently used in advertising and sales could function as identifier but rejecting general claim that all Presley's images and likenesses without more were marks).

[11]Mattel, Inc. v. Walking Mountain Productions, 353 F.3d 792, 807, 69 U.S.P.Q.2d (BNA) 1257 (9th Cir. 2003) (where use of mark in titles of works and on website described subject of photographs depicting and parodying Barbie, the "public interest in free and artistic expression greatly outweighs. . .interest in potential consumer confusion about Mattel's sponsorship of [artist's] works."); ETW Corp. v. Jireh Pub., Inc., 332 F.3d 915, 937, 67 U.S.P.Q.2d (BNA) 1065, 2003 FED App.

Lanham Act claims involving artistic use: the standard likelihood of confusion factors,[12] the balancing test (sometimes referred to as the *Rogers* test),[13] the "alternative avenues" test,[14] and the transformative effects test.[15]

The balancing test derived from *Rogers* appears currently to predominate in cases involving visual arts. Free expression trumps proprietary interests under the balancing test if the use "has artistic relevance, unless i[t's] use. . ..explicitly misleads as to the source of the work.[16] The [Lanham] Act should be construed to apply to artistic works only where the public interest in avoiding consumer confusion outweighs the public interest in free expression."[17] The use of the balancing test would seem to

---

0207P (6th Cir. 2003) (use of sports celebrity name registered mark "Tiger Woods" in artist's statement and packaging of prints)(fair use); see also 8:13.

[12]See 8:9 to 8:10.

[13]Rogers v. Grimaldi, 875 F.2d 994, 16 Media L. Rep. (BNA) 1648, 10 U.S.P.Q.2d (BNA) 1825 (2d Cir. 1989)(balancing test formulated in case involving titles); Parks v. LaFace Records, 329 F.3d 437, 31 Media L. Rep. (BNA) 1897, 66 U.S.P.Q.2d (BNA) 1735, 2003 FED App. 0137P (6th Cir. 2003), cert. denied, 124 S. Ct. 925, 157 L. Ed. 2d 744 (U.S. 2003) (applying balancing); ETW Corp. v. Jireh Pub., Inc., 332 F.3d 915, 67 U.S.P.Q.2d (BNA) 1065, 2003 FED App. 0207P (6th Cir. 2003) (majority applying balancing); Mattel, Inc. v. Walking Mountain Productions, 353 F.3d 792, 69 U.S.P.Q.2d (BNA) 1257 (9th Cir. 2003) (applying balancing).

[14]Parks v. LaFace Records, 329 F.3d 437, 31 Media L. Rep. (BNA) 1897, 66 U.S.P.Q.2d (BNA) 1735, 2003 FED App. 0137P (6th Cir. 2003), cert. denied, 124 S. Ct. 925, 157 L. Ed. 2d 744 (U.S. 2003) (expressive works not protected from false advertising if sufficient alternative means exist for artist to convey idea).

[15]ETW Corp. v. Jireh Publ. Inc., Clay, J. dissent (applying transformative test of Comedy III Productions, Inc. v. Gary Saderup, Inc., 25 Cal. 4th 387, 106 Cal. Rptr. 2d 126, 21 P.3d 797, 29 Media L. Rep. (BNA) 1897, 58 U.S.P.Q.2d (BNA) 1823 (2001), cert. denied, 534 U.S. 1078, 122 S. Ct. 806, 151 L. Ed. 2d 692 (2002) (right of publicity)(rendering was not transformative when "unadorned, nearly photographic reproduction" that "capitalized on a literal depiction" without artist's own "significant creative component," making it more likely to interfere with economic interests protected by right of publicity.).

[16]ETW Corp. v. Jireh Pub., Inc., 332 F.3d 915, 928, 67 U.S.P.Q.2d (BNA) 1065, 2003 FED App. 0207P (6th Cir. 2003).

[17]ETW Corp. v. Jireh Pub., Inc., 332 F.3d 915, 928, 67 U.S.P.Q.2d (BNA) 1065, 2003 FED App. 0207P (6th Cir. 2003) (likelihood of confu-

effectively preclude application of the likelihood of confusion factors. But some courts use both or multiple combinations or permutations of the tests, the result of which, notwithstanding putative choice, is often a blend of various considerations.

§ 8:12 First Amendment exceptions—Parody

Parodic artistic use for non-commercial speech has been directly addressed.[1] In other cases, parody has been incorporated into the likelihood of confusion factors.[2] here Parody alone in this context has not disposed of or trumped any other factor, the courts limning the boundary between parody and economic appropriation:

> The keystone of parody is imitation. . . . A parody must convey two simultaneous—and contradictory—messages: "that it is the original, but also that it is not the original and is instead a parody". . . . The parody has to be a take-

---

sion factors not applied); Mattel, Inc. v. Walking Mountain Productions, 353 F.3d 792, 69 U.S.P.Q.2d (BNA) 1257 (9th Cir. 2003); Yankee Pub. Inc. v. News America Pub. Inc., 809 F. Supp. 267 (S.D. N.Y. 1992) (*New York Magazine*'s comic commentary on Christmas issue cover that used part of registered cover design for *Old Farmer's Almanac* outweighed "minor injury" to trademark), *citing,* Rogers v. Grimaldi, 875 F.2d 994 (2d Cir. 1989); *see also* New York Racing Ass'n, Inc. v. Perlmutter Pub., Inc., 959 F. Supp. 578 (N.D. N.Y. 1997) (first amendment protection for T-shirt reproductions of paintings incorporating trademarks).

[Section 8:12]

[1]See § 8:11.

[2]People for Ethical Treatment of Animals v. Doughney, 263 F.3d 359, 60 U.S.P.Q.2d (BNA) 1109 (4th Cir. 2001) (peta.org domain name used to create website purportedly spoofing animal rights was not parody of registered mark PETA); Nike, Inc. v. Just Did It Enterprises, 6 F.3d 1225 (7th Cir. 1993) (First Amendment allows ridicule by parody of manufacturers' and merchants' corporate symbols, logos and marks in the national spotlight); *see also* Jordache Enterprises, Inc. v. Hogg Wyld, Ltd., 828 F.2d 1482, 92 A.L.R. Fed. 1 (10th Cir. 1987) ("Lardashe" on large sized jeans as parody of Jordache jeans trademark); Tetley, Inc. v. Topps Chewing Gum, Inc., 556 F. Supp. 785 (E.D. N.Y. 1983) (Petly Flea Bags as parody of Tetley tea bags); *cf.* Yankee Pub. Inc. v. News America Pub. Inc., 809 F. Supp. 267 (S.D. N.Y. 1992) (*New York* magazine's use of Old Farmers Almanac registered cover design on its Christmas issue cover was a "joke," not a parody, but still entitled to some measure of First Amendment protection); Eveready Battery Co., Inc. v. Adolph Coors Co., 765 F. Supp. 440 (N.D. Ill. 1991).

off, not a ripoff.[3]

§ 8:13 Fair use

Fair use of a mark may exist where the use ". . .is descriptive of and used fairly and in good faith only to describe the goods or services of such party. . .."[1] The defense is applied where use "'does not imply sponsorship or endorsement of the product because the mark is used only to describe the thing, rather than to identify its source.'"[2] Fair use has been applied to artworks containing marks and dress.[3]

C. APPLICABILITY OF SECTION 43(A) TO ART

§ 8:14 Overview

There is division among jurisdictions as to whether or not the Lanham Act is applicable to art, and if so, under what facts and circumstances.[1] Courts have accepted various grounds for dismissing Lanham Act claims: artwork is

---

[3]Nike, Inc. v. Just Did It Enterprises, 6 F.3d 1225, 1228 (7th Cir. 1993) (citations omitted) (reversed summary judgment for plaintiff because of disputed or undetermined facts regarding confusion).

[Section 8:13]

[1]15 U.S.C.A. § 1115(b)(4).

[2]ETW Corp. v. Jireh Pub., Inc., 332 F.3d 915, 925, 67 U.S.P.Q.2d (BNA) 1065, 2003 FED App. 0207P (6th Cir. 2003) (fair use of registered mark "Tiger Woods" in artist's statement about his work depicting The Masters Tournament and printed under an envelope flap containing his prints where artwork signed by artist and other materials identified him as source).

[3]Mattel, Inc. v. Walking Mountain Productions, 353 F.3d 792, 69 U.S.P.Q.2d (BNA) 1257 (9th Cir. 2003) (nominative fair use by artist of trade dress in Barbie doll for his parodic photographs depicting her); Rock and Roll Hall of Fame and Museum, Inc. v. Gentile Productions, 134 F.3d 749, 45 U.S.P.Q.2d (BNA) 1412, 1998 FED App. 0020P (6th Cir. 1998) (fair use by artist of museum's name on borders of artworks depicting museum); see also Rogers v. Grimaldi, 875 F.2d 994, 16 Media L. Rep. (BNA) 1648, 10 U.S.P.Q.2d (BNA) 1825 (2d Cir. 1989) (Ginger Rogers' name used in title of artistic work).

[Section 8:14]

[1]Schatt v. Curtis Management Group, Inc., 764 F. Supp. 902 (S.D. N.Y. 1991) (Section 43(a) claims preserved for trial based upon distribution of falsely attributed copyrighted photographs, even if the artist

not protectible mark or dress; artwork is not disparate from the mark or dress; artists are not competitors of the corporate or commercial defendants they sue; artists are not engaged in producing commercial products for market; nor in business.[2]

Caution is required in this area as the law is rapidly changing and developing, even as this is being written, and it is highly recommended that the most current law of the applicable jurisdiction be ascertained in conjunction with Supreme Court authority. Preemption provisions under copyright law generally and VARA specifically may bar certain types of claims. Judicial disposition of various types of activities historically underlying Lanham Act claims is set out below.

Lanham Act Section 43(a) was considered proper in the following types of claims:

Attribution, misattribution, or attribution omission: Fail-

---

no longer owned the copyright); Galerie Furstenberg v. Coffaro, 697 F. Supp. 1282 (S.D. N.Y. 1988) (Section 43(a) claim dismissed in action brought by producers and distributors of Salvador Dali works against others producing, distributing and selling allegedly fake Dali works); Wojnarowicz v. American Family Ass'n, 745 F. Supp. 130 (S.D. N.Y. 1990) (Section 43(a) claim dismissed in an action brought by an artist against defendants based upon the unauthorized reproduction and distribution of excised portions of his artwork attributed to him, in a brochure mailed to defendants' association members as part of a campaign to terminate public funding for the arts); Playboy Enterprises, Inc. v. Dumas, 831 F. Supp. 295 (S.D. N.Y. 1993), opinion modified on reargument, 840 F. Supp. 256 (S.D. N.Y. 1993) and judgment aff'd in part, rev'd in part, 53 F.3d 549, 132 A.L.R. Fed. 703 (2d Cir. 1995) (Section 43(a) claim dismissed in action brought by an artist's licensee against a publisher for posthumous reproduction of artworks in an altered form); Campbell v. Koons, 1993 WL 97381 (S.D. N.Y. 1993) (Lanham Act claims reserved for trial in an action based upon the defendant's unauthorized copying of plaintiff's photograph).

[2]Tracy v. Skate Key, Inc., 697 F. Supp. 748 (S.D. N.Y. 1988) (artist was not a competitor of the skating rink company that allegedly appropriated designs for its own promotional materials from a mural he made under commission); Hughes v. Design Look Inc., 693 F. Supp. 1500 (S.D. N.Y. 1988); *see also* Leigh v. Warner Bros., a Div. of Time Warner Entertainment Co., L.P., 10 F. Supp. 2d 1371 (S.D. Ga. 1998), aff'd in part, rev'd in part, 212 F.3d 1210 (11th Cir. 2000) (photograph was neither a mark nor trade dress for artist).

ure to credit the artist's copyright on photographs[3] or the intentional use of a name other than the artist's as copyright owner on goods.[4]

Alteration or modification of artwork by reproduction, advertising or fabrication: Alteration of an artist's photographs through unauthorized distribution;[5] and inferior unauthorized publication of an artist's work advertised in a brochure.[6]

Quality differential: Advertising an artist's works and selling them as high quality when production was of inferior quality.[7]

Copying or similarity: Distribution of prints by competitor print publishers and distributors of posters and prints similar to plaintiff's, although the prints were created by different artists;[8] artist's limited edition sculptures created by copying the plaintiff's photograph;[9] an artist's limited edition sculptures created by copying the plaintiff's comic strip character;[10] abstract renderings of a famous landmark cypress tree independently created and used as a logo on T-shirts and merchandise by two different corporations located in the vicinity of the tree;[11] combination of features on nonoccasion fine art greeting cards by

---

[3]Schatt v. Curtis Management Group, Inc., 764 F. Supp. 902, 913 (S.D. N.Y. 1991) (factual issues preclude summary judgment on plaintiff's Lanham Act claims).

[4]Schatt v. Curtis Management Group, Inc., 764 F. Supp. 902, 913 (S.D. N.Y. 1991).

[5]Schatt v. Curtis Management Group, Inc., 764 F. Supp. 902, 913 (S.D. N.Y. 1991).

[6]Wildlife Internationale, Inc. v. Clements, 591 F. Supp. 1542 (S.D. Ohio 1984).

[7]Wildlife Internationale, Inc. v. Clements, 591 F. Supp. 1542 (S.D. Ohio 1984).

[8]Romm Art Creations Ltd. v. Simcha Intern., Inc., 786 F. Supp. 1126 (E.D. N.Y. 1992).

[9]Campbell v. Koons, 1993 WL 97381 (S.D. N.Y. 1993) (summary judgment for plaintiff on copyright claims; Lanham Act claims reserved for trial).

[10]United Feature Syndicate, Inc. v. Koons, 817 F. Supp. 370 (S.D. N.Y. 1993) (summary judgment on copyright; Section 43(a) claims reserved).

[11]Pebble Beach Co. v. Laub America Corp., 1985 WL 5584 (N.D. Cal. 1985).

one manufacturer that were similar in look and feel to another manufacturer's greeting cards.[12]

Lanham Act Section 43(a) claims were, however, dismissed or summarily adjudicated in the following types of claims:

Attribution, misattribution, or attribution omission: Attribution to an artist of excised artworks depicting pornographic details from large multimedia works containing political and cultural statements in a brochure, which urged recipients to terminate public funding;[13] no attribution to a photographer by an artist who copied his work in a theatrical backdrop for a stage production, which was reproduced in artist monograph;[14] no attribution to a graphic artist for a photograph used on a magazine cover;[15] and catalogue raisonne listing painting owned by plaintiff as spurious.[16]

Quality differential: Publication on a magazine cover of an outtake photograph, which was among the photographs shot for an award-winning poster associated with the plaintiff, where the outtake photo was inferior to the one selected for the original poster;[17] and the unauthorized reproduction of an artist's works using different litho-

---

[12]Hartford House, Ltd. v. Hallmark Cards, Inc., 846 F.2d 1268 (10th Cir. 1988); *see also* Hughes v. Design Look Inc., 693 F. Supp. 1500 (S.D. N.Y. 1988) (analysis of Lanham Act application to a poster calendar depicting Andy Warhol artworks).

[13]Wojnarowicz v. American Family Ass'n, 745 F. Supp. 130 (S.D. N.Y. 1990).

[14]Heyman v. Salle, 743 F. Supp. 190 (S.D. N.Y. 1989).

[15]Morita v. Omni Publications Intern., Ltd., 741 F. Supp. 1107 (S.D. N.Y. 1990), order vacated, 760 F. Supp. 45 (S.D. N.Y. 1991) (consent decree entered).

[16]Vitale v. Marlborough Gallery, 32 U.S.P.Q.2d (BNA) 1283, 1994 WL 654494 (S.D. N.Y. 1994) (Section 43(a) claim dismissed because to the extent based upon catalogue publication in 1978, it was barred by state six-year statue of limitations for fraud, and to the extent based upon future catalogue revisions or editions alledgedly in preparation, the issues were premature for adjudication).

[17]Morita v. Omni Publications Intern., Ltd., 741 F. Supp. 1107 (S.D. N.Y. 1990), order vacated, 760 F. Supp. 45 (S.D. N.Y. 1991) (consent decree entered).

graphic plates.[18]

Alteration or modification of artwork: The publication of altered artist's prints by a limited licensee;[19] excised artwork taken from large multimedia artworks with attribution to artist and no disclosure of excising.[20]

Copying or similarity: Publication and distribution by unauthorized distributors and publishers of Salvador Dali prints;[21] unauthorized reproduction and distribution of excised portions of an artist's paintings in a pamphlet because the pamphlet lacked the requisite "advertising or promotion" of goods or services;[22] the unauthorized copying of a photograph for a pro-nuclear purpose, when plaintiff-artist had prepared the photo to advocate an anti-nuclear sentiment and to commemorate the bombing of Hiroshima;[23] humanoid raisin characters used by different advertisers.[24]

§ 8:15 Commercial predicates

The text of Section 43(a) refers to use "in commerce." The commercial predicate of Section 43(a) requires at a minimum commercial context of product use and commercial conduct of the parties. Particular sourcing and product qualifications have also been recognized, at least in the arts context. The Supreme Court has interpreted trademark law as generally requiring a nexus to trade or business: "There is no such thing as property in a

[18]Galerie Furstenberg v. Coffaro, 697 F. Supp. 1282 (S.D. N.Y. 1988).

[19]Playboy Enterprises, Inc. v. Dumas, 831 F. Supp. 295 (S.D. N.Y. 1993), opinion modified on reargument, 840 F. Supp. 256 (S.D. N.Y. 1993) and judgment aff'd in part, rev'd in part on other grounds, 53 F.3d 549, 132 A.L.R. Fed. 703 (2d Cir. 1995) (no false advertising as to origin or misuse of the artist's name).

[20]Wojnarowicz v. American Family Ass'n, 745 F. Supp. 130 (S.D. N.Y. 1990).

[21]Galerie Furstenberg v. Coffaro, 697 F. Supp. 1282 (S.D. N.Y. 1988).

[22]Wojnarowicz v. American Family Ass'n, 745 F. Supp. 130 (S.D. N.Y. 1990).

[23]Morita v. Omni Publications Intern., Ltd., 741 F. Supp. 1107 (S.D. N.Y. 1990), order vacated, 760 F. Supp. 45 (S.D. N.Y. 1991)(consent decree entered).

[24]Cory Van Rijn, Inc. v. California Raisin Advisory Bd., 697 F. Supp. 1136 (E.D. Cal. 1987) (Lanham Act claim dismissed).

trademark except as a right appurtenant to an established business or trade in connection with which the mark is employed . . . the right to a particular mark grows out of its use, not its mere adoption, . . . it is not the subject of property except in connection with an existing business."[1]

The general rule is that both plaintiff and defendant must be involved in commercial conduct, consistent with keeping a clean marketplace by discouraging dishonest and unfair trade practices.[2]

Collectors with sufficient market position have been held to have sufficient "commercial" interests to satisfy the Lanham Act, even though they were not professional traders.[3] Where defendants are not selling a product or service, or advertising or promoting work, or are otherwise not engaged in a commercial venture, use or misuse of plaintiff's artwork has not been held actionable under Section 43(a).[4] And even artists who earn a livelihood making art are not always considered engaged in a trade or business producing a publicly identifiable product for purposes of seeking protection of their work under the Act.[5] Some opinions underscore competition among the commercial entities, but the merging and blurring of markets in the 1980s and 1990s appears to have recharacterized clear-

---

[Section 8:15]

[1]Rock and Roll Hall of Fame and Museum, Inc. v. Gentile Productions, 134 F.3d 749 (6th Cir. 1998) (citation omitted).

[2]Hofmann v. Kleinhandler, 1994 WL 240335 (S.D. N.Y. 1994) (competing dealers selling artworks by same artist); *cf.* Boule v. Hutton, 70 F. Supp. 2d 378 (S.D. N.Y. 1999) (plaintiffs were collectors selling their own collection of artworks by Lazar Khidekel and defendants were gallery owners who claimed exclusive representation).

[3]Boule v. Hutton, 70 F. Supp. 2d 378 (S.D. N.Y. 1999) (collectors who own a "significant percentage of extant works attributed to one artist . . . who promoted their collection. . . . and contracted to sell substantial numbers of such works . . . have a sufficient commercial interest"); *see also* Ch 2 §§ 2:1 to 2:11.

[4]*See* Wojnarowicz v. American Family Ass'n, 745 F. Supp. 130 (S.D. N.Y. 1990).

[5]*See, e.g.,* Hughes v. Design Look Inc., 693 F. Supp. 1500 (S.D. N.Y. 1988) (discussion of Andy Warhol name and artworks as marks in commerce); *cf.* Leigh v. Warner Bros., a Div. of Time Warner Entertainment Co., L.P., 10 F. Supp. 2d 1371 (S.D. Ga. 1998), aff'd in part, rev'd in part, 212 F.3d 1210 (11th Cir. 2000) (photographer-plaintiff engaged in promotional sales and merchandising of his work).

line concepts of competition.

How does the commercial nexus translate into the visual arts? Where the estate of Pop artist Andy Warhol brought a Section 43(a) action against publishers of a calendar depicting twelve uncopyrighted Warhol images, the federal district court in New York, however, would not consider the Warhol style or artistic images "marks," because they had not been used in commerce:

> Here . . . there was no mark created to transfer. No evidence was presented to show that any of these twelve images had ever been associated with any product or service put out by Warhol. Thus, no goodwill is associated with these particular images. . . . the works themselves in issue *were not used for commercial as opposed to artistic purposes.* In fact, Warhol sold these images outright, in some cases without retaining a copy.[6]

Posthumous merchandising will have to determine where, if at all, the Warhol oeuvre can be situated within the Lanham Act. Warhol's use of others' marks, dress or images or likenesses has been considered.[7]

Is the underlying category of business activity relevant? Generally, the Lanham Act would not appear to distinguish among commerce, but recent developments in the law, in the market, and in the arts, require qualifying any short answer. The corporatization and commercialization of visual icons have lead artists to seek trade protections. But the courts have distinguished between protections granted for the visuals used in mass merchandising by megabusiness and the protections sought by individual

---

[6]Hughes v. Design Look Inc., 693 F. Supp. 1500, at 1506 (S.D. N.Y. 1988) (emphasis added) (transfers occurred prior to the Revised Copyright Act of 1976, when the presumption existed that rights transferred upon sale unless expressly reserved by the artist).

[7]Comedy III Productions, Inc. v. Gary Saderup, Inc., 25 Cal. 4th 387, 408-409, 106 Cal. Rptr. 2d 126, 21 P.3d 797, 29 Media L. Rep. (BNA) 1897, 58 U.S.P.Q.2d (BNA) 1823 (2001), cert. denied, 534 U.S. 1078, 122 S. Ct. 806, 151 L. Ed. 2d 692 (2002) (Warhol's "distortion. . .and manipulation of context" might make literal reproduction of celebrity images "a form of ironic social comment on the dehumanization of celebrity itself. . ."); but see Dauman v. Andy Warhol Foundation for Visual Arts, Inc., 43 U.S.P.Q.2d (BNA) 1221, 1997 WL 337488 (S.D. N.Y. 1997) (copyright infringement action by artist and magazine based on unauthorized use of Jacqueline Kennedy photographs).

artists for intermittent, quixotic and relatively small-scale market entries. Thus, if the underlying activity involves visual art, categorization can be important, particularly in terms of product output.

The term "disparate" has not been used by the courts in the Lanham Act context. But if the term is not identified in the opinions, the necessity for product separate and distinct from the visual and beyond the one-of-a-kind has been articulated in some jurisdictions. Is disparateness also required between the product and the image? Although the issue has not been squarely addressed in the visual arts context at the appellate level, a handful of opinions among district courts provide limited guidance. Under this interpretation, protection is not valid for visuals, visual imagery, graphics or visual style unless a separate and distinct product or service is being sourced and identified in commerce. Thus, the *Hughes* court wrote: "None of the specific works in question have ever been used by Warhol himself to promote any products except that one Marilyn [Monroe] was used in the late 1970s in a Sony advertisement and another used by a Japanese advertising company in a calendar to promote its services."[8]

More recently, a court addressed whether photographic imagery depicting a locally known sculpture *in situ* emphasizing natural and preternatural aspects of a cemetery site commissioned for the cover of a best-selling novel could, without more, be trade dress. The court decided it could not.[9] The photograph was catapulted to fame as a result of the book's success. The photographer sued the film studio when the advertising and promotional campaign for a movie based upon the book used as its cornerstone a photographic replica of the sculpture that it, too, sited in the same cemetery. Ordering summary judgment for defendant on the trademark claims, the court wrote: "Plaintiff *cannot* show that he has a valid trademark, service mark or trade dress because trademark law *should not* be used to protect his visual style. Such a use

---

[8] Hughes v. Design Look Inc., 693 F. Supp. 1500 (S.D. N.Y. 1988).

[9] Leigh v. Warner Bros., a Div. of Time Warner Entertainment Co., L.P., 10 F. Supp. 2d 1371 (S.D. Ga. 1998), aff'd in part, rev'd in part, 212 F.3d 1210 (11th Cir. 2000).

would ignore the identification requirement of trademark . . . extend [its] reach . . . and . . . circumvent copyright law's prohibition on the protection of ideas."

The caveat is that the visual or dress typically is intended to identify the source of the product or service, and not be coextensive. When they are coextensive, the identification sources to the artist, according to courts subscribing to such views. "[I]f a picture or a work of art merely identifies the artist rather than any product or service, it cannot be protected as a mark."[10] The Leigh photographer, apparently, did not produce or license anything using the visual imagery; others, meanwhile, were marketing merchandise like bags, keychains, t-shirts, and postcards using his work.

D. RELATIONSHIP TO COPYRIGHT AND VARA

§ 8:16 Relationship to copyright law

A valid copyright is not a prerequisite for bringing an action under the Lanham Act,[1] although both claims are often conjunctively plead.[2] The Lanham Act requires a modicum of source identification for products and services, and informed—if limited—veracity in advertising and promotion, a different premise than that of federal

---

[10]Leigh v. Warner Bros., a Div. of Time Warner Entertainment Co., L.P., 10 F. Supp. 2d 1371 at 1380 (S.D. Ga. 1998), aff'd in part, rev'd in part, 212 F.3d 1210 (11th Cir. 2000) (emphasis added).

[Section 8:16]

[1]Rosenfeld v. W.B. Saunders, a Div. of Harcourt Brace Jovanovich, Inc., 728 F. Supp. 236, 243 (S.D. N.Y. 1990), decision aff'd, 923 F.2d 845 (2d Cir. 1990) ("Copyright ownership or lack of such ownership is not a disposition of the issue of unfair competition under the Lanham Act."); Boston Professional Hockey Ass'n, Inc. v. Dallas Cap & Emblem Mfg., Inc., 510 F.2d 1004 (5th Cir. 1975) (disapproved of by, University of Pittsburgh v. Champion Products, Inc., 566 F. Supp. 711 (W.D. Pa. 1983)) (the Lanham right asserted is a property right that arises from a mark symbolizing "a product or business in the public mind."); Hughes v. Design Look Inc., 693 F. Supp. 1500 (S.D. N.Y. 1988) (Lanham Act claim based upon uncopyrighted artworks).

[2]Kisch v. Ammirati & Puris Inc., 657 F. Supp. 380 (S.D. N.Y. 1987) (denial of motion to dismiss a Lanham Act claim where copyright claims exist).

copyright.[3] Title 17, Section 301(d), the federal preemption provision in copyright, expressly allows federal claims like Lanham to coexist with copyright: "Nothing in this title annuls or limits any rights or remedies under any other Federal statute."[4] But "the Lanham Act should not be distorted to provide a remedy for a failed claim of copyright infringement,"[5] or "enforce . . . a copyright claim through the mechanism of trademark protection."[6] Thus, a false copyright notice actionable under copyright was held not to constitute a false designation of origin within the meaning of the Lanham Act.[7]

The correct analysis is whether or not the facts pled independently support a Lanham Act claim. The courts have not made differentiation easier, notwithstanding quotable rhetoric. That courts use the copyright tests to analyze claims under the Lanham Act can further contribute to confusion.[8] Factual support for the claims and discrete legal analysis of the elements of the claims will assist lawyers in pleading the separate causes of action. By care-

---

[3]Waldman Pub. Corp. v. Landoll, Inc., 43 F.3d 775 (2d Cir. 1994) ("[T]he Copyright Act and the Lanham Act address different harms. Through a copyright infringement action, a copyright owner may control who publishes, sells or otherwise uses a work. Through a Lanham Act action, an author may ensure that his or her name is associated with a work when the work is used.").

[4]17 U.S.C.A. § 301(d). *See also* Tracy v. Skate Key, Inc., 697 F. Supp. 748 (S.D. N.Y. 1988).

[5]Morita v. Omni Publications Intern., Ltd., 741 F. Supp. 1107, 1114 (S.D. N.Y. 1990), order vacated, 760 F. Supp. 45 (S.D. N.Y. 1991) (consent decree entered) (court awarded plaintiff ownership of the copyright in lithograph, photograph and sculpture, and decreed defendant-photographer as co-author only of the photograph, assigning to plaintiff all right, title, interest, including copyrights, in photograph).

[6]Galerie Furstenberg v. Coffaro, 697 F. Supp. 1282 (S.D. N.Y. 1988).

[7]Lipton v. The Nature Co., 71 F.3d 464 (2d Cir. 1995) (no violation of Section 43(a) where false copyright notice was sole basis of claim for false designation of origin); Kregos v. Associated Press, 937 F.2d 700 (2d Cir. 1991) (plaintiff's copyrighted baseball statistical form copied by defendants was held to infringe copyright, but did not convert into viable Lanham Act claim).

[8]Waldman Pub. Corp. v. Landoll, Inc., 43 F.3d 775 (2d Cir. 1994) (a trade dress action borrowing definition of "original" and "derivative" from copyright, borrowing standard of substantial similarity from copyright, borrowing concept of "author" from copyright); Jeffrey Milstein, Inc. v. Greger, Lawlor, Roth, Inc., 58 F.3d 27 (2d Cir. 1995) (applying

fully distinguishing the underlying acts and effects, one can differentiate the unfair competition claims from those of copyright.

§ 8:17 Relationship to VARA

Congress enacted the Visual Artists Rights Act (VARA), codified at Title 17 of the U.S. Code,[1] to protect artists against misuse or misattribution of their name and alteration or distortion of their work to the damage of their reputation through rights of attribution and integrity.[2] VARA is so new that reported cases could not be found until recently that alleged both Section 43(a) and VARA.[3] By VARA definitions of, and exclusions from, the term "visual art" recited in 17 U.S.C.A. § 101, the circumstances and conditions for compatible claims appears circumscribed.[4] In fact, authority now exists for the proposition that VARA preempts Section 43(a) claims involving attribution and integrity rights.[5]

Before VARA, application of the Lanham Act was extended by some courts to protect creative rights in the context of production and distribution of entertainment properties, such as films, television productions and the like. The authority for Lanham as an artists' rights law is

---

copyright concept of idea/expression dichotomy to determine protectible elements of trade dress); *see* Ch 7 §§ 7:12 to 7:19.

[Section 8:17]

[1]See Appendix 17.

[2]*See* Chs 7 and 9.

[3]Board of Managers of Soho International Arts Condominium v. City of New York, 2003 WL 21403333 (S.D. N.Y. 2003) (VARA preempted Lanham false designation claim); Grauer v. Deutsch, 64 U.S.P.Q.2d (BNA) 1636, 2002 WL 31288937 (S.D. N.Y. 2002) (attribution omission of allegedly co-authored photographs as basis of false designation of origin and as VARA violation); *cf.* Gegenhuber v. Hystopolis Productions, Inc., 1992 WL 168836 (N.D. Ill. 1992) (alleged attribution omission for puppet production brought by puppeteer under VARA and state laws).

[4]*See* Ch 9.

[5]Board of Managers of Soho International Arts Condominium v. City of New York, 2003 WL 21403333 (S.D. N.Y. 2003) ("VARA is the sole remedy for artists seeking to protect the . . .rights of attribution and integrity under state or federal law."), citing 17 U.S.C.A. § 301; see Ch 9, § 9:9, and Appendix 17.

often sourced to *Gilliam v. American Broadcasting Cos.*,[6] where Lanham was viewed by the court as a law that should protect the creative output of television writers involved in Monty Python programs. The plaintiffs claimed that the extent of network editing distorted their work and misrepresented it to the public, the so-called garbled version rule.[7] But to rely upon Gilliam as a springboard for the proposition that Lanham is a visual artists' rights law is inapt. Enactment of VARA would seem to address this. Specifically, *Gilliam* has been analyzed post-VARA and rejected as authority for a "noncommercial" right of integrity in visual art.[8]

Courts before VARA nonetheless have considered artist protection of integrity rights as an appropriate aspect of the Lanham Act. In a case where the court decided Lanham Act claims applied to unauthorized reproductions, alterations and distributions on posters, calendars, magnets and t-shirts of an artist's photographs of James Dean taken from his book, *James Dean: A Portrait,* the opinion urged expansive artistic protection:

> The Lanham Act . . . is designed not only to protect the public and the artist from misrepresentations of the artist's contribution to a finished work, but also to vindicate 'the author's personal right to prevent the presentation of his work to the public in a distorted form.'[9]

In a case involving competitors' manufacture of look-alike greeting cards, the district court—without citing corroborating legislative history—wrote, "one salutary purpose of the Lanham Act . . . is to protect a creative artists' rights in his or her creation and thus provide incentive to be

[6]Gilliam v. American Broadcasting Companies, Inc., 538 F.2d 14, 24 (2d Cir. 1976).

[7]See § 8:24

[8]Board of Managers of Soho International Arts Condominium v. City of New York, 2003 WL 21403333 (S.D. N.Y. 2003) (". . . if *Gilliam* gave artists a noncommercial moral right to protect their works through [section 43(a)]-preemption would be mandatory since VARA's preemption clause expressly preempts a federal right 'equivalent' to . . . VARA . . . .").

[9]Schatt v. Curtis Management Group, Inc., 764 F. Supp. 902 (S.D. N.Y. 1991), *quoting* Gilliam v. American Broadcasting Companies, Inc., 538 F.2d 14, 24 (2d Cir. 1976).

creative."[10]

Note that in these cases, although the language of the courts supported Lanham as a basis for artistic protection or creative incentive, the claims centered upon commercial products.[11] Caution should be used in taking out of context artist protection language and applying it to visual art.

E. NAME AND USE: ARTISTS AND MUSEUMS

§ 8:18 Attribution and misattribution

There is division among jurisdictions regarding application of the Lanham Act to attributions and misattributions of authorship. VARA, which codifies attribution and attribution omission rights for visual artists under federal copyright, may eventually clarify such claims, by preemption or otherwise, but thus far appears to have further clouded an area of existing multiple claims.[1] Attribution[2] is pled under various aspects of Section 43(a): "false designation of origin";[3] or false impression.[4] Some cases hold that Section 43(a) of the Lanham Act does not create an express duty of attribution but protects against misattribution. The cases involving visual art offer mixed

---

[10]Hartford House Ltd. v. Hallmark Cards Inc., 647 F. Supp. 1533, 1540 (D. Colo. 1986), judgment aff'd, 846 F.2d 1268 (10th Cir. 1988) ("By protecting and fostering creativity, a product with features different . . . to the [copied] product may well be developed. Offering consumers a choice . . . stimulates, rather than stifles competition.").

[11]Allen v. National Video, Inc., 610 F. Supp. 612 (S.D. N.Y. 1985) (use of a Woody Allen look-alike on a poster to endorse defendants' video products violative of the Lanham Act).

[Section 8:18]

[1]*See* § 8:17.

[2]*E.g.,* attribution, misattribution, or attribution omission.

[3]Waldman Pub. Corp. v. Landoll, Inc., 43 F.3d 775 (2d Cir. 1994) (remanding claim of false designation of origin as applied to a "misattribution" of authorship of books, that was, in fact, reverse passing off claim; i.e., according to court, defendant's books published under defendant's name were sold with a "false designation of origin" because books could have originated with plaintiff).

[4]Wildlife Internationale, Inc. v. Clements, 591 F. Supp. 1542 (S.D. Ohio 1984) (prints published by defendant bearing artist's signature violated Section 43(a) because signature infer that quality of publication reflect artistic standards).

support.[5]

Artist Patrick Nagel's heir and licensee alleged Lanham Act violations based upon an attribution in an action against a magazine publisher for its distribution and sale of silkscreens and other posters at $30 to $175, created by Nagel for inclusion in Playboy magazine.[6] After Nagel died, the publisher sold copies of the works as "The Playboy Collection by Patrick Nagel." Four of ten posters were altered for publication; female breasts were covered in three and only the top half of the fourth poster was reproduced. The licensee contended that the use of Nagel's name misidentified him as the author or creator of the works, and that alterations to the works created a false impression of origin.[7] The court concluded that no Lanham Act violations existed based upon use of the artist's name, because there was no false advertising misidentifying him as the creator; Nagel had prepared the works for Playboy and the collection so identified him.

§ 8:19 Attribution omission

Attribution omission claims for visual artists under Section 43(a) require the same showing as other Lanham Act

---

[5]Playboy Enterprises, Inc. v. Dumas, 831 F. Supp. 295 (S.D. N.Y. 1993), opinion modified on reargument, 840 F. Supp. 256 (S.D. N.Y. 1993) and judgment aff'd in part, rev'd in part, 53 F.3d 549, 132 A.L.R. Fed. 703 (2d Cir. 1995) (attribution); Morita v. Omni Publications Intern., Ltd., 741 F. Supp. 1107 (S.D. N.Y. 1990), order vacated, 760 F. Supp. 45 (S.D. N.Y. 1991) (attribution omission); Cleary v. News Corp., 30 F.3d 1255 (9th Cir. 1994) (attribution omission); Schatt v. Curtis Management Group, Inc., 764 F. Supp. 902 (S.D. N.Y. 1991) (attribution omission); Grauer v. Deutsch, 64 U.S.P.Q.2d (BNA) 1636, 2002 WL 31288937 (S.D. N.Y. 2002) (attribution omission) .

[6]Playboy Enterprises, Inc. v. Dumas, 831 F. Supp. 295 (S.D. N.Y. 1993), opinion modified on reargument, 840 F. Supp. 256 (S.D. N.Y. 1993) and judgment aff'd in part, rev'd in part, 53 F.3d 549, 132 A.L.R. Fed. 703 (2d Cir. 1995).

[7]Playboy Enterprises, Inc. v. Dumas, 831 F. Supp. 295 (S.D. N.Y. 1993), opinion modified on reargument, 840 F. Supp. 256 (S.D. N.Y. 1993) and judgment aff'd in part, rev'd in part, 53 F.3d 549, 132 A.L.R. Fed. 703 (2d Cir. 1995); *see also* King v. Allied Vision, Ltd., 807 F. Supp. 300 (S.D. N.Y. 1992), order aff'd in part, rev'd in part on other grounds, 976 F.2d 824 (2d Cir. 1992) (where a well-known writer had not been involved with a screenplay or approved it, a possessory credit using his name on the movie was misleading and likely to mislead consumers under the Lanham Act).

claims and have been allowed to co-exist at the pleading stage with VARA claims.[1]

The Lanham Act historically has not been singularly successful for omission cases claiming false designation of origin.[2] The court concluded that the result would be different if there were other photographers involved who were not credited, relying upon a Ninth Circuit holding in a case where a songwriter published a song without naming other writers of the song.[3] For claims involving false designation, omitted contributors may also have to be competitors. The Ninth Circuit required "conduct . . . not only . . . unfair but must in some discernable [*sic*] way be competitive."[4] Where an artist did not allege that he was in competition with the photographer, the court dismissed the false designation claim.[5]

A district court allowed an artist-plaintiff to present evidence on the issue of whether the photographs of James Dean, copied by the defendant, were so associated in the public mind with him as the photographer that the distortion, without attribution to him or with attribution to others, violated the Lanham Act.[6]

[Section 8:19]

[1]Grauer v. Deutsch, 64 U.S.P.Q.2d (BNA) 1636, 2002 WL 31288937 (S.D. N.Y. 2002) (exhibition of photographs under only one of alleged co-authors' names plead as a false designation of origin survived summary judgment but plaintiff would have to prove it was something more than VARA claim).

[2]Morita v. Omni Publications Intern., Ltd., 741 F. Supp. 1107 (S.D. N.Y. 1990), order vacated, 760 F. Supp. 45 (S.D. N.Y. 1991)(consent decree entered) ("In order for Morita to state a claim . . . the Lanham Act must create a duty of express attribution. Morita points to no language in the statute itself from which such a duty could flow . . . the cases he cites in support . . . involve misattributions, not omissions.").

[3]Lamothe v. Atlantic Recording Corp., 847 F.2d 1403 (9th Cir. 1988).

[4]Lamothe v. Atlantic Recording Corp., 847 F.2d 1403 at 1406 (9th Cir. 1988).

[5]Morita v. Omni Publications Intern., Ltd., 741 F. Supp. 1107 (S.D. N.Y. 1990), order vacated, 760 F. Supp. 45 (S.D. N.Y. 1991) (consent judgment entered).

[6]Schatt v. Curtis Management Group, Inc., 764 F. Supp. 902 (S.D. N.Y. 1991).

§ 8:20 Signature

Section 43(a) applies to "innuendo, indirect intimation and ambiguous suggestions" regarding origin. The court found that offering for sale two prints bearing the artist's signature violated Section 43(a) in that it suggested, by "indirect intimation," that the prints reflected the artistic standards of the artist, and that the artist had approved the standards of the print.[1] This false impression, coupled with the likelihood of consumer confusion, would be sufficient to warrant injunctive relief. The court also found that the defendant's distribution of old brochures, which reproduced the artist's prints bearing his signature and depicted his likeness, tacitly indicated his approval, creating a false impression and public confusion in violation of Section 43(a).

§ 8:21 Artist's name as mark

Artists' names are appropriate marks.[1] The name must serve to identify a source and distinguish it from other sources.[2] When the artist's name is a registered trademark, a prima facie case of trademark infringement is shown where defendant's use is likely to confuse consumers as to

---

[Section 8:20]

[1]Wildlife Internationale, Inc. v. Clements, 591 F. Supp. 1542 (S.D. Ohio 1984).

[Section 8:21]

[1]Hughes v. Plumsters Ltd., 17 Media L. Rep. (BNA) 1188, 13 U.S.P.Q.2d (BNA) 1253, 1989 WL 418804 (N.D. Cal. 1989) (use of Andy Warhol name on tee-shirt that also depicted imagery in artist's style); Grandma Moses Properties v. This Week Magazine, 117 F. Supp. 348 (S.D. N.Y. 1953) ("Grandma Moses" as registered trademark); McMahon v. City of Chicago, 1999 WL 342712 (N.D. Ill. 1999) (artist's name as service mark); Hughes v. Design Look Inc., 693 F. Supp. 1500, 1505 (S.D. N.Y. 1988); (defendants "changed the name of its product to 'Pop Art' to avoid use of any mark attached to the Warhol name"); *see also* Allen v. National Video, Inc., 610 F. Supp. 612 (S.D. N.Y. 1985) (Woody Allen look-alike used on a poster to endorse defendants' video products)

[2]ETW Corp. v. Jireh Publ. Inc., 332 F.3d 915, 922 (6th Cir. 2003)(a name does not qualify as a mark unless it "performs job of identification.").

source of the product.[3] However, where consent to use the artist's name is expressly given and arbitrarily terminated after the user has relied, the equitable defense of acquiescence may estop enjoining the defendant's use. Where an artist expressly authorized the defendants to use her name in connection with marketing a line of products, and provided her signature to appear on the product line, the artist was estopped from seeking an injunction against defendants who had manufactured mugs and calendars in reliance on the artist's consent.[4]

§ 8:22 Museum name as mark

Museums and other not-for-profit arts institutions are seeking new revenue sources as federal funding of the arts decreases, and corporate support is spread ever thinner.[1] Commercial ventures to sell products related to the mission of the institution are increasingly important. Use of the name of the museum or institution is often integral to promoting and marketing products. Competing interests arise when use of a museum name is made in artworks for which the institution seeks protection under Lanham.[2]

A museum's use of its name on a line of historic root beers was challenged successfully in a trademark infringement suit brought by a producer of nonalcoholic beverages.[3] Mystic Seaport Museum in Connecticut, which had been using the name MYSTIC SEAPORT since World War II, launched a line of spruce and birch beers as part

---

[3]15 U.S.C.A. § 1114(1).

[4]Ladas v. Potpourri Press, Inc., 846 F. Supp. 221 (E.D. N.Y. 1994) (injunctive relief denied to terminate defendant's use of "Christina" collections that plaintiff-artist created for $100,000 per year, where she had encouraged defendant to use her name on its product line, but subsequently terminated her relationship with defendant and trademarked her name).

[Section 8:22]

[1]*See* Ch 1 §§ 1:37 to 1:41.

[2]See 8:13.

[3]Best Flavors, Inc. v. Mystic River Brewing Co., 886 F. Supp. 908 (D. Me. 1995).

of its retail line based on nineteenth-century products.[4] MYSTIC SEAPORT was registered as a mark in 1968, but the mark had not yet been registered for beverages at the time of the suit. The plaintiff's mark, MISTIC, was registered in the early 1990s and used on its carbonated beverages; it planned to launch a root beer under the mark in 1995. Finding a likelihood of confusion, the district court enjoined the museum from using its current label on the root beers, but refused to enjoin the museum's use of MYSTIC SEAPORT in connection with the future sale of beverages under a different label.

§ 8:23 Museum building design

A landmark museum facility designed by I.M. Pei was the center of a trademark infringement action when a local artist photographed the building at sunset and featured it on posters sold for under $50. The front view of the building was framed by a border that read "Rock N' Roll Hall of Fame, Cleveland."[1] The museum argued that the poster infringed its mark in the building and that the border text infringed its registered service mark in "THE ROCK AND ROLL HALL OF FAME." The museum merchandised its own poster of the museum at sunset with its mark. The district court agreed, enjoining the artist from further infringement and ordering destruction of all posters in the artist's possession.[2]

The Sixth Circuit vacated and remanded, finding no evidence in the record of public recognition of the building design as a Museum mark.

> We are not persuaded that the Museum uses its building design as a trademark . . . A picture or a drawing of the Museum is not fanciful in the same way that a word like Exxon is when . . . coined as a service mark. Such a word is distinctive as a mark because it readily appears to a

---

[4]Best Flavors, Inc. v. Mystic River Brewing Co., 886 F. Supp. 908 (D. Me. 1995).

[Section 8:23]

[1]Rock and Roll Hall of Fame and Museum, Inc. v. Gentile Productions, 134 F.3d 749 (6th Cir. 1998).

[2]Rock and Roll Hall of Fame and Museum Inc. v. Gentile Productions, 934 F. Supp. 868 (N.D. Ohio 1996), judgment vacated, 134 F.3d 749 (6th Cir. 1998).

> consumer to have no other purpose. In contrast, a picture of the Museum on a product might be more readily perceived as ornamentation than as an identifier of source. . . . Although the Museum has used [versions] of the building design on various goods, it has not done so with any consistency. . . . In reviewing the Museum's disparate uses of several different perspectives of its building design, we cannot conclude that they create a consistent and distinct commercial impression as an indicator of a single source of origin or sponsorship . . . *We cannot conclude . . . that the Museum has established a valid trademark in every photograph . . . which prominently displays the front of the [ ] building.*[3]

On remand, the district court found the building design had not been used as a trademark by the Museum or the artist, entering summary judgment for defendants.[4]

F. ALTERATIONS, GARBLED VERSIONS

§ 8:24 Generally

Section 43(a) has been alleged as a predicate for unauthorized alterations to reproductions of works of visual art. *Gilliam v. American Broadcasting Cos.*,[1] a Monty Python case, is most often cited for the proposition that alteration of visual art is actionable under the Lanham Act, but *Gilliam* did not involve visual art.

In *Gilliam*, a scheduled network broadcast of edited Monty Python work was challenged by writers and performers in the Python group, who sought to enjoin the broadcast because the truncated version distorted their work before the public.[2] The Second Circuit held that "an allegation that a defendant has presented to the public a 'garbled' distorted version of plaintiff's work seeks to

---

[3]Rock and Roll Hall of Fame and Museum, Inc. v. Gentile Productions, 134 F.3d 749 (6th Cir. 1998) (emphasis added).

[4]Rock & Roll Hall of Fame and Museum, Inc. v. Gentile Productions, 71 F. Supp. 2d 755 (N.D. Ohio 1999) (reiterating inconsistent use of views of building on merchandise).

[Section 8:24]

[1]Gilliam v. American Broadcasting Companies, Inc., 538 F.2d 14 (2d Cir. 1976); see § 8:17.

[2]Gilliam v. American Broadcasting Companies, Inc., 538 F.2d 14, 24 (2d Cir. 1976).

redress the very rights sought to be protected by the Lanham Act." Discussing the absence of moral rights for literary authors, screenwriters and playwrights, the court said that garbled public presentation of writers' programs "*should be* recognized as stating a cause of action" under Lanham.[3]

The "garbled" standard has not yet been proven in the visual arts context. A graphic artist alleged that the use by a photographer of an outtake photograph, shot for the plaintiff's award-winning poster and rejected by plaintiff in favor of another, garbled his anti-nuclear message. The outtake was published on a magazine cover in conjunction with nuclear advocacy, whereas plaintiff's use of the award-winning poster photograph commemorated the nuclear bombing of Hiroshima. The court responded, "the theory of Gilliam does not apply here because unlike the truncated version of Monty Python show, the photograph at issue was not altered in any way."[4]

Another court concluded that Lanham Act Section 43(a) could apply to alteration of silkscreens and prints if the alteration constituted "a false reference to the origin of a work, or a reference which, while not literally false, is misleading or likely to confuse."[5]

G. COPYING OR SIMILARITY

§ 8:25 Generally

A Section 43(a) claim based on unauthorized proven copying of visual art has not yet succeeded,[1] although cases

[3]Gilliam v. American Broadcasting Companies, Inc., 538 F.2d 14, 24 (2d Cir. 1976) (emphasis added) (issuing preliminary injunction without deciding substantive claims).

[4]Morita v. Omni Publications Intern., Ltd., 741 F. Supp. 1107 (S.D. N.Y. 1990), order vacated, 760 F. Supp. 45 (S.D. N.Y. 1991) (consent decree entered).

[5]Playboy Enterprises, Inc. v. Dumas, 831 F. Supp. 295 (S.D. N.Y. 1993), opinion modified on reargument, 840 F. Supp. 256 (S.D. N.Y. 1993) and judgment aff'd in part, rev'd in part on other grounds, 53 F.3d 549, 132 A.L.R. Fed. 703 (2d Cir. 1995).

[Section 8:25]

[1]*See* §§ 8:2 to 8:45; *see, e.g.,* Kisch v. Ammirati & Puris Inc., 657 F. Supp. 380, 384–85 (S.D. N.Y. 1987) (motion to dismiss a Lanham Act

exist in which the issue is raised.[2]

H. FALSE ADVERTISING

§ 8:26 Generally

The proscription of Lanham Act Section 43(a) on the "false designation of origin, false or misleading description of fact . . . in commercial advertising or promotion [that] misrepresents the nature, characteristics, qualities or geographic origin of . . . another person's goods, services, or commercial activities" has been extended to fraudulent misrepresentation, deceptive advertising, and merchandising,[1] that is "likely to cause confusion[,] . . . mistake[,] . . . or decei[t]."[2] Section 43(a) in some jurisdictions applies not only to "literal falsehoods" but also to "innuendo, indirect intimations and ambiguous suggestions."[3] Plaintiffs must show either that the advertising was false or that it was true but likely to mislead or confuse consumers. In the latter case, "proof that the advertising conveyed an implied message and . . . deceived a significant portion of the recipients is critical."[4] "The essence of a Lanham Act claim for false advertising is deception of the American public."[5]

The following was deemed sufficient at the pleading

---

claim granted, in an action involving a photographic scene allegedly copied by a commercial advertiser).

[2]United Feature Syndicate, Inc. v. Koons, 817 F. Supp. 370 (S.D. N.Y. 1993); Campbell v. Koons, 1993 WL 97381 (S.D. N.Y. 1993).

[Section 8:26]

[1]Hofmann v. Kleinhandler, 1994 WL 240335 (S.D. N.Y. 1994) (defendant's copying of plaintiff's promotional brochure containing eleven full-color reproductions of artist's paintings, biographical, and bibliographical information and excision of plaintiff's name, address, and telephone number and exclusivity statement constitute false misrepresentations for purposes of Section 43(a)).

[2]15 U.S.C.A. § 1125(a).

[3]Hofmann v. Kleinhandler, 1994 WL 240335 (S.D. N.Y. 1994) (citations omitted).

[4]Lord Simon Cairns v. Franklin Mint Co., 24 F. Supp. 2d 1013 (C.D. Cal. 1998) (citations omitted) A presumption that consumers were deceived may be enough where defendant intentionally mislead them.

[5]Vitale v. Marlborough Gallery, 32 U.S.P.Q.2d (BNA) 1283, 1994 WL 654494 (S.D. N.Y. 1994).

stage to survive summary judgment: use of one dealer's promotional brochure prepared on behalf of an artist with whom it had an exclusive sales agreement by another dealer to market the artist's work;[6] removal by defendant-dealer of plaintiff-dealer's name, address, and phone number and recitation of exclusive representation in plaintiff's promotional brochure for an artist;[7] backdating of paintings by an artist to recite a different year than the one in which the paintings were made[8] and, catalogue prepared in conjunction with gallery exhibition for purpose of sale and promotion.[9] Claims that defendants made allegedly false and disparaging comments about artworks owned and sold by plaintiffs to plaintiff's customers and arranged for false articles to be published did not survive dismissal because none was in commercial competition with plaintiff.[10]

§ 8:27 Text with visuals

In *Wildlife International*,[1] plaintiff, an artist of original wildlife paintings, and co-plaintiff, his company, which reproduced the artist's original art as lithographs and other prints, entered into an agreement with defendant,

---

[6]Vitale v. Marlborough Gallery, 32 U.S.P.Q.2d (BNA) 1283, 1994 WL 654494 (S.D. N.Y. 1994) (constitutes deceptive practice in that consumers may have been misled that plaintiff was no longer representing artist).

[7]Vitale v. Marlborough Gallery, 32 U.S.P.Q.2d (BNA) 1283, 1994 WL 654494 (S.D. N.Y. 1994) (constitutes allegations of false representations regarding availability of paintings depicted in brochure and identity of sales distributors for artist's works).

[8]Vitale v. Marlborough Gallery, 32 U.S.P.Q.2d (BNA) 1283, 1994 WL 654494 at ¶ 15 (S.D. N.Y. 1994) (constitutes false impression, false description, and false representation of material fact that paintings were created at a certain point in artist's career when in fact they were painted at a different time, leading to consumer confusion about dates, values, and artistic style).

[9]Boule v. Hutton, 70 F. Supp. 2d 378 (S.D. N.Y. 1999) (catalogue is "commercial advertising").

[10]Gmurzynska v. Hutton, 2003 WL 1193727 (S.D. N.Y. 2003) (defendants were art experts).

[Section 8:27]

[1]Wildlife Internationale, Inc. v. Clements, 591 F. Supp. 1542 (S.D. Ohio 1984).

president of a company that agreed to reproduce certain paintings by plaintiff.[2] After the contract expired, defendant reproduced plaintiff's art in advertising brochures without authorization. The court ruled that a Section 43(a) violation could be found based upon false advertising regarding print quality; the brochure statement that the prints were the "highest quality printing of any fine art prints on the market" was false.

§ 8:28 Text obfuscation or alteration

Where a dealer who had an exclusive representation agreement with an artist published nationwide a promotional brochure depicting the artist's works, the defendant's unauthorized whiting or inking out the plaintiff's exclusivity legend on the brochure to promote the same artist, thus obfuscating the plaintiff's name and address, were sufficient to withstand a motion to dismiss.[1]

I. OTHER ISSUES

§ 8:29 False description, false representation

Backdating certain artworks for sale in interstate commerce has been the basis of a claim for false description and false representation of fact under Section 43(a). A competing dealer allegedly backdated an artist's paintings that had actually been made in 1992 and after, to appear as if they were created in 1991 or before, so that the paintings would appear to be dated before the artist's exclusive representation agreement with plaintiff took effect in 1992. The court decided that if such date-changing had occurred, it would misrepresent the nature of the work, falsely represent the dates on which the works were created, and confuse buyers about the evolution and change in the

---

[2]Wildlife Internationale, Inc. v. Clements, 591 F. Supp. 1542 (S.D. Ohio 1984).

[Section 8:28]

[1]Hofmann v. Kleinhandler, 1994 WL 240335 (S.D. N.Y. 1994).

artist's style and techniques.[1]

Statements about the artist in a catalogue prepared in conjunction with a gallery exhibition regarding his work and dealer representation were statements of fact regarding "goods" to support a false advertising claim under the Lanham Act.[2] Section 42(a) does not extend to unsolicited inquiries from the press seeking comments on issues of public concern.[3]

§ 8:30 Architecture

Section 43(a) of the Lanham Act has been used by architects to protect against false designation of their plans.[1] Acts that have been held sufficient to implicate a Section 43(a) violation include a single filing of architectural plans with a governmental agency;[2] and a single filing, supplemented by amended filings, with a local plan-

---

[Section 8:29]

[1]Hofmann v. Kleinhandler, 1994 WL 240335 (S.D. N.Y. 1994) (in the Second Circuit, Section 43(a) applies to falsehoods and "embraces 'innuendo, indirect intimations, and ambiguous suggestions.' ").

[2]Boule v. Hutton, 70 F. Supp. 2d 378, 52 U.S.P.Q.2d (BNA) 1808 (S.D. N.Y. 1999), aff'd, 328 F.3d 84, 31 Media L. Rep. (BNA) 1793, 66 U.S.P.Q.2d (BNA) 1659 (2d Cir. 2003) (to constitute "commercial advertising" the "statement must be disseminated sufficiently to the relevant purchasing public") (statements in repudiation letter about museum exhibition catalogue were not factual assertions about another's goods because statements of opinion under Lanham are not actionable if they cannot "'reasonably be seen as stating or implying provable facts' about a competitor's good or services.").

[3]Boule v. Hutton, 70 F. Supp. 2d 378 (S.D. N.Y. 1999) (defendants' economic interest in art magazine comments did not alone transform them into "commercial advertising").

[Section 8:30]

[1]East/West Venture v. Wurmfeld Associates, P.C., 722 F. Supp. 1064 (S.D. N.Y. 1989); Demetriades v. Kaufmann, 680 F. Supp. 658, 664 (S.D. N.Y. 1988); Joseph J. Legat Architects, P.C. v. U.S. Development Corp., 625 F. Supp. 293, 300 (N.D. Ill. 1985) (disapproved of by Easter Seal Soc. for Crippled Children and Adults of Louisiana, Inc. v. Playboy Enterprises, 815 F.2d 323 (5th Cir. 1987)).

[2]Joseph J. Legat Architects, P.C. v. U.S. Development Corp., 625 F. Supp. 293, 300 (N.D. Ill. 1985) (disapproved of by Easter Seal Soc. for Crippled Children and Adults of Louisiana, Inc. v. Playboy Enterprises, 815 F.2d 323 (5th Cir. 1987)).

ning board.[3] Even one false designation may create confusion.

§ 8:31 Statute of limitations

The Lanham Act contains no statute of limitations provision, so courts borrow analogous state statutes of limitations.[1] Selecting the appropriate limitations period depends upon the claim. In some cases, courts have applied the state limitations period for fraud.[2] In some jurisdictions the statute of limitations may be raised by the court sua sponte even when not plead as an affirmative defense.[3]

§ 8:32 Attorney's fees

The Lanham Act allows courts to award attorney fees to

---

[3]Joseph J. Legat Architects, P.C. v. U.S. Development Corp., 625 F. Supp. 293, 300 (N.D. Ill. 1985) (disapproved of by Easter Seal Soc. for Crippled Children and Adults of Louisiana, Inc. v. Playboy Enterprises, 815 F.2d 323 (5th Cir. 1987)) (denial of motion to dismiss Lanham Act claims).

[Section 8:31]

[1]Board of Managers of Soho International Arts Condominium v. City of New York, 2003 WL 21403333 (S.D. N.Y. 2003) (applying three-year state anti-dilution law, the "most analogous" New York statute, to artist's federal anti-dilution claim under § 1125(c)).

[2]Vitale v. Marlborough Gallery, 32 U.S.P.Q.2d (BNA) 1283, 1994 WL 654494 (S.D. N.Y. 1994) (analogous cause of action for Section 43(a) claim under New York state law was fraud where claims based upon recitation in Jackson Pollock catalogue raisonne that painting owned by plaintiff was spurious); Johannsen v. Brown, 797 F. Supp. 835, 839 (D. Or. 1992); *cf.* Agency Holding Corp. v. Malley-Duff & Associates, Inc., 483 U.S. 143, 107 S. Ct. 2759, 97 L. Ed. 2d 121 (1987) (federal statutes of limitations should govern Section 43(a) claims); Construction Technology, Inc. v. Lockformer Co., Inc., 704 F. Supp. 1212, 1221 (S.D. N.Y. 1989) (New York statute of limitations for injury to property used for Lanham Act claims).

[3]Board of Managers of Soho International Arts Condominium v. City of New York, 2003 WL 21403333 (S.D. N.Y. 2003) (statute of limitations raised sua sponte to time-bar artist's antidilution claim presented 15 years later and omitted in his pleadings) (magazine publisher affixed its copyright notice to artist's work).

the prevailing party "in exceptional cases."[1] No fees were awarded in cases involving unauthorized posthumous distribution and sale of altered art posters by the defendant-publisher introducing new issues for determination;[2] or the production by a greeting card manufacturer of a card line creating similar and dissimilar trade dress than plaintiff's cards.[3] But if a Lanham claim is "groundless or unreasonable, vexatious, or pursued in bad faith," attorney's fees may be appropriate.[4]

J. REMEDIES

§ 8:33 Damages

The plaintiff has the burden of proving damages under Section 43(a).[1] The Lanham Act expressly provides for awarding profits in the discretion of the judge, subject to principles of equity.[2] To sustain awards of damages based on profits, the parties do not need to be in direct competition or prove that the infringement was willful; such awards have been based in different jurisdictions upon unjust enrichment, deterrence and compensation. The plaintiff is required to prove the infringer's gross revenues, with the burden on the infringer to establish deductions for expenses or to demonstrate that the profits claimed by the plaintiff were not attributable to infringing use under

---

[Section 8:32]

[1]15 U.S.C.A. § 1117.

[2]Playboy Enterprises, Inc. v. Dumas, 831 F. Supp. 295 (S.D. N.Y. 1993), opinion modified on reargument, 840 F. Supp. 256 (S.D. N.Y. 1993) and judgment aff'd in part, rev'd in part, 53 F.3d 549, 132 A.L.R. Fed. 703 (2d Cir. 1995).

[3]Roulo v. Russ Berrie & Co., Inc., 886 F.2d 931 (7th Cir. 1989).

[4]Mattel, Inc. v. Walking Mountain Productions, 353 F.3d 792, 69 U.S.P.Q.2d (BNA) 1257 (9th Cir. 2003) (citations omitted) (vacating and remanding denial of attorney's fees in trademark and trade dress action against artist for expressive speech where court failed to provide reason for denial)

[Section 8:33]

[1]Schatt v. Curtis Management Group, Inc., 764 F. Supp. 902 (S.D. N.Y. 1991) (testimony of the author of the definitive book on James Dean is not sufficient proof of damages to permit summary resolution, since he is not a representative sample of marketplace consumers).

[2]Roulo v. Russ Berrie & Co., Inc., 886 F.2d 931 (7th Cir. 1989).

the Lanham Act.

None of the visual art cases cited involve damage awards. However, *Roulo v. Russ Berrie & Co.*,[3] a greeting card trade dress case, is instructive. The trial court awarded the plaintiff a joint sum for Section 43(a) and copyright infringement in the amount of $4.3 million, based upon defendant's profits. Roulo's expert, a certified public accountant, testified that proceeds from defendant's sale of the cards were $5.9 million, minus direct production costs of $945,000. Defense witnesses testified that profits were only $2.9 million, and that after deductions plaintiff was only entitled to $38,601, but defendant's data was defective in that, among other things, it deducted fixed costs from the profits. The Seventh Circuit upheld the award on the basis of either deterrence or unjust enrichment, even though the plaintiff's actual damages, which she did not demonstrate, "may have been less."

§ 8:34 Injunction

A party is entitled to preliminary injunctive relief under the Lanham Act when it can show irreparable harm and likelihood of success on the merits.[1] A showing of likelihood of confusion as to source establishes the requisite likelihood of success on the merits and risk of irreparable harm under Lanham Act claims.[2] Plaintiff need only establish "likelihood that an appreciable number of ordinary prudent purchasers are likely to be misled, or indeed

---

[3]Roulo v. Russ Berrie & Co., Inc., 886 F.2d 931 (7th Cir. 1989).

[Section 8:34]

[1]King v. Allied Vision, Ltd., 807 F. Supp. 300 (S.D. N.Y. 1992), order aff'd in part, rev'd in part on other grounds, 976 F.2d 824 (2d Cir. 1992) (sufficiently serious questions going to the merits to make the claim fair grounds for litigation, and the balance of hardships tipped decidedly toward the party requesting relief as alternative grounds for preliminary injunction).

[2]Romm Art Creations Ltd. v. Simcha Intern., Inc., 786 F. Supp. 1126 (E.D. N.Y. 1992); King v. Allied Vision, Ltd., 807 F. Supp. 300 (S.D. N.Y. 1992), order aff'd in part, rev'd in part on other grounds, 976 F.2d 824 (2d Cir. 1992) (irreparable harm presumed where plaintiff demonstrated probability of success on Lanham Act claims).

simply confused, as to the source of the goods in question."[3]

The court granted injunctive relief to an artist-publisher who sued a publisher with whom he had an agreement to reproduce his paintings in lithographs, where that publisher was distributing the artist's works and likeness in advertising brochures and representing falsely that the lithographs were of a superb printing quality.[4] Another court granted preliminary injunction against a producer of a record titled *George Benson, Erotic Moods*, where the jacket cover displayed a large recent photograph of jazz musician Benson and prominently displayed his name in bold letters.[5] The recording, based upon one made by Benson many years earlier, was over-dubbed, accented and altered using sexual noises without Benson's knowledge. The recording was advertised as "new" material although it was old and altered, which the court found deceptively portrayed the album as a current release.[6] A court granted injunctive relief to a print publisher to prevent distribution and sale of certain prints by other artists whose works were similar to plaintiff's.[7]

---

[3]Schatt v. Curtis Management Group, Inc., 764 F. Supp. 902 (S.D. N.Y. 1991) (citations omitted) (entitlement to damages requires plaintiff to prove actual consumer confusion resulting from false designation of origin; proof should focus upon representative samples of the marketplace, not experts in the field).

[4]Wildlife Internationale, Inc. v. Clements, 591 F. Supp. 1542 (S.D. Ohio 1984).

[5]Benson v. Paul Winley Record Sales Corp., 452 F. Supp. 516 (S.D. N.Y. 1978).

[6]Benson v. Paul Winley Record Sales Corp., 452 F. Supp. 516 (S.D. N.Y. 1978) (irreparable injury found where consumers disappointed in style and content would be deterred from purchasing future releases); *cf.* CBS, Inc. v. Gusto Records, Inc., 403 F. Supp. 447 (M.D. Tenn. 1974) (no injunction where an album bore the likeness of Charlie Rich, contained Rich songs recorded fifteen years earlier, and where Rich was the principal performer who exercised technical and stylistic control over production of the work; the court ordered a decal affixed to the album to clarify contents, thus alleviating harm).

[7]Romm Art Creations Ltd. v. Simcha Intern., Inc., 786 F. Supp. 1126 (E.D. N.Y. 1992).

K. Federal Trademark Dilution Act of 1995

§ 8:35 Generally

The Federal Trademark Dilution Act of 1995[1] added Section 43(c) to the Lanham Act,[2] providing federal antidilution protection for famous marks, effective January 16, 1996. Although twenty-five states have existing dilution statutes, which are not pre-empted by this federal law, Congress enacted nationwide protection to provide consistent dilution protection for such marks.[3]

Section 1125(c) provides, in pertinent part, as follows:

> The owner of a famous mark shall be entitled, subject to the principles of equity and upon such terms as the court deems reasonable, to an injunction against another person's commercial use in commerce of a mark or trade name, if such use begins after the mark has become famous and causes dilution of the distinctive quality of the mark . . .

To state a cause of action under Section 43(c), a party must show that the mark is famous, that defendant's use began after the mark became famous and that the complainant's use is commercial, and likely to cause dilution. Specific exclusions exist for fair use in comparative advertising, noncommercial use, news reporting, and commentary.[4]

A list of nonexhaustive factors is provided to determine the distinctiveness and fame of the mark:

(A) The degree of inherent or acquired distinctiveness of the mark
(B) The duration and extent of use of the mark in connection with the goods or services with which the mark is used
(C) The duration and extent of advertising and publicity of the mark
(D) The geographical extent of the trading area in which the mark is used

---

[Section 8:35]

[1] Pub. L.104-98, sec. 3(a), 109 Stat. 985 (Jan. 16, 1996).

[2] 15 U.S.C.A. § 1125(c).

[3] H.R. Rep. No. 374, 104th Cong. 1st Sess. (1995).

[4] 15 U.S.C.A. § 1125(c)(4).

(E) The channels of trade for the goods and services with which the mark is used
(F) The degree of recognition of the mark in the trading areas and channels of trade used by the marks' owner and the person against whom the injunction is sought
(G) The nature and extent of use of the same or similar marks by third parties
(H) Whether the mark was registered under the [federal Acts], or on the principal register[5]

Dilution is defined as "the lessening of the capacity of a famous mark to identify and distinguish goods or services, regardless of the presence or absence of (1) competition between the owner of the famous mark and other parties, or (2) likelihood of confusion, mistake, or deception."[6] The definition recognizes that "a cause of action for dilution may exist whether or not the parties market the same or related goods [or services] or whether or not a likelihood of confusion exists."[7]

Courts have described it, more simply, as a "gradual 'whittling away' of a trademark's value . . . ."[8] "blurring . . . uniqueness . . . or tarnishing [by] . . . negative association[]."[9]

Dilution has only been applied to "commercial" speech defined by the Supreme Court and progeny as speech that does 'no more than propos[e] a commercial transaction.'"[10] Creative expression ordinarily is not considered commercial speech. Thus, artistic or parodic artistic use of marks or dress has not been actionable under antidilution

[5]15 U.S.C.A. § 1125(c)(1)(A)–(H).

[6]15 U.S.C.A. § 1127.

[7]H.R. Rep. No. 374, 104th Cong. 1st Sess. (1995).

[8]Playboy Enterprises, Inc. v. Welles, 279 F.3d 796 (9th Cir. 2002) (discussing blurring and tarnishment as forms of dilution).

[9]Mattel, Inc. v. Walking Mountain Productions, 353 F.3d 792, 69 U.S.P.Q.2d (BNA) 1257 (9th Cir. 2003) (citations omitted) (no dilution of Barbie doll mark and dress by artist's photographs); H.R.Rep.No. 104-374 at 3 (1995) (". . . to protect famous trademarks from subsequent uses that blur the distinctiveness of the mark or tarnish or disparage it, even in the absence of a likelihood of confusion.").

[10]ETW Corp. v. Jireh Pub., Inc., 332 F.3d 915, 925, 67 U.S.P.Q.2d (BNA) 1065, 2003 FED App. 0207P (6th Cir. 2003) (citations omitted).

statutes because of the first amendment speech interests.[11] If no mark or dress is established, dilution is inapplicable.[12]

Dilution is aimed at avoiding misappropriation.[13] The harm of dilution is that it creates in the public "an association between a mark and a different good or service."[14]

Section 1125 exempts users who compare their products in "commercial advertising or promotion to identify the competing goods or services of the owner of the famous mark."[15] Courts have applied that principle to exempt nominative uses of trademark.[16]

§ 8:36 Remedies

The remedy for dilution is generally restricted to the court's equitable power of injunction.[1] The owner of a mark qualifying under Section 43(c) is ordinarily only entitled relief for use beginning after the mark has become famous.[2] An artist's attempt to have his work restored to a building

---

[11]Mattel, Inc. v. Walking Mountain Productions, 353 F.3d 792, 812, 69 U.S.P.Q.2d (BNA) 1257 (9th Cir. 2003) ("Parody is a form of noncommercial speech if it does more than propose a commercial transaction.").

[12]ETW Corp. v. Jireh Pub., Inc., 332 F.3d 915, 923, 67 U.S.P.Q.2d (BNA) 1065, 2003 FED App. 0207P (6th Cir. 2003) (dilution claim dismissed by summary judgment because Tiger Woods' likeness portrayed in limited edition prints "does not function as a trademark . . . subject to protection . . . under Lanham . . . ."), Clay, C.J. dissenting, 332 F.3d at 939 (question of fact exists whether Woods' likeness is mark).

[13]Playboy Enterprises, Inc. v. Welles, 279 F.3d 796 (9th Cir. 2002)("' . . . the issue at stake is not . . . the signaling function but [the] . . . free rid[e] on . . . investment. . .'").

[14]Playboy Enterprises, Inc. v. Welles, 279 F.3d 796 (9th Cir. 2002); ETW Corp. v. Jireh Pub., Inc., 332 F.3d 915, 67 U.S.P.Q.2d (BNA) 1065, 2003 FED App. 0207P (6th Cir. 2003) (risk of misidentification of source minimal where artist's name recited in merchandising materials, statement and artist's signature on face of artworks).

[15]15 U.S.C.A. § 1125(c)(4)(A).

[16]Playboy Enterprises, Inc. v. Welles, 279 F.3d 796 (9th Cir. 2002) (nominative use identifying plaintiff as a former Playboy playmate of the year did not dilute defendant's product or create an association between a new product and defendant's mark).

[Section 8:36]

[1]15 U.S.C.A. § 1125(c).

[2]15 U.S.C.A. §§ 1125, 1127.

exterior after it was completely removed under a theory of dilution was denied where the remedy sought was not the statutory injunction to protect against further dilution but re-installment of his work.[3]

Where the complainant can prove that the person "willfully intended to trade on the owner's reputation or to cause dilution, the owner of the famous mark shall also be entitled to the remedies set forth in sections 35(a) and 36, subject to the discretion of the court and the principles of equity."

§ 8:37 Commerce

Noncommercial uses of famous marks are expressly excluded.[1] The type of activities that will constitute "commercial use in commerce" under Section 43(c) has been subject to judicial interpretation.

The following have been determined use "in commerce": unauthorized use of a domain name, which includes a protected trademark; to engage in commercial activity on the Internet;[2] and dissemination of a registered mark on the Internet.[3]

Use of the "com" suffix on a registered domain name in the Internet has not, of itself, been considered commercial use, but the intention to arbitrage, sell, or license domain names has been found commercial use within the meaning of the Lanham Act.[4]

§ 8:38 Internet

Section 43(c) has been applied to cases involving registration of trademarked names as domain names on

[3]Board of Managers of Soho International Arts Condominium v. City of New York, 2003 WL 21403333 (S.D. N.Y. 2003) (". . .the connection between the alleged violation [of § 1125(c)] and the redress sought [is] wholly untenable.").

[Section 8:37]

[1]15 U.S.C.A. § 1125(c)(4)(B).

[2]Cardservice Intern., Inc. v. McGee, 950 F. Supp. 737 (E.D. Va. 1997), aff'd, 129 F.3d 1258 (4th Cir. 1997).

[3]Intermatic Inc. v. Toeppen, 947 F. Supp. 1227 (N.D. Ill. 1996) (Lanham's "in commerce" requirement should be broadly construed).

[4]Intermatic Inc. v. Toeppen, 947 F. Supp. 1227 (N.D. Ill. 1996).

the Internet.[1]

III. STATE UNFAIR COMPETITION LAWS

§ 8:39 Deceptive trade practices: Generally

Where artwork is sold, advertised, fabricated, or promoted contrary to contract or authorization, claims for unfair competition may lie under common law or state statute,[1] e.g., misappropriation, dilution, or "passing off."[2] Some states may have criminal penalties for manufactur-

---

[Section 8:38]

[1]Intermatic Inc. v. Toeppen, 947 F. Supp. 1227 (N.D. Ill. 1996) (injunction issued under Section 43(c) to prohibit defendant's use of "intermatic.com" for sale of computer software, where Intermatic was plaintiff's registered mark); Hasbro, Inc. v. Internet Entertainment Group, Ltd., 1996 WL 84858 (W.D. Wash. 1996) (injunction issued under Section 43(c) to prohibit defendant's use of "http://candyland.com" for a sexually explicit Internet site, where Candyland was plaintiff's registered mark.)

[Section 8:39]

[1]Austin Productions, Inc. v. F.D.F. Design Studio, Inc., 1991 Copr. L. Dec. ¶ 26662, 1990 WL 198741 (E.D. N.Y. 1990) (unfair competition claims under state law dismissed); Galerie Furstenberg v. Coffaro, 697 F. Supp. 1282 (S.D. N.Y. 1988) (injury to business reputation claims under state law dismissed); Reproducta Co., Inc. v. Kellmark Corp., 1993 WL 385779 (S.D. N.Y. 1993) (state unfair competition claims alleged based upon unauthorized manufacture and marketing of an artist's religious scenes on greeting cards); Shaheen v. Stephen Hahn, Inc., 1994 WL 854659 (S.D. N.Y. 1994) (claim for violation of state deceptive business practices law (N.Y. Gen. Bus. L. § 349) based upon sale of a painting purportedly by Mary Cassatt dismissed where authenticity in question because "sale of a unique painting, that does not affect the public interest and is not one of a recurring nature, falls outside [the statute]"), *citing* Gumowitz v. Wildenstein & Co., 10229/92, slip op. at 7 (Sup. Ct., N.Y. Co. July 31, 1992) (sale of painting by George Seurat not type of transaction within purview of N.Y. Gen. Bus. L. § 349); Jeffrey Milstein, Inc. v. Greger, Lawlor, Roth, Inc., 58 F.3d 27 (2d Cir. 1995) (affirming denial of motion for preliminary injunction based, inter alia, upon common law unfair competition claim under New York law, which requires plaintiff to show either actual confusion in action for damages or likelihood of confusion in action for equitable relief).

[2]Claims may also lie under consumer fraud laws, tortious interference with business relations, contract or prospective economic advantage, conversion, unjust enrichment, and state artists' rights laws. *See* Appendix 20.

ing or selling counterfeit marks "registrable" under the Lanham Act.[3]

§ 8:40 Federal relationship—Preemption under copyright and VARA

Section 301(f) of Title 17 provides:

> [A]ll legal or equitable rights that are equivalent to any of the rights conferred by section 106A [VARA] with respect to works of visual art to which the rights conferred by section 106A apply are governed exclusively by section 106A and section 113(d) and the provisions of this title relating to such sections. Thereafter, no person is entitled to any such right or equivalent right in any work of visual art under the common law or statutes of any State.

Section 106A provides artists the right to claim authorship, prevent the use of the artist's name as the author of works the artist has not created, and to prevent the use of the artist's name as the author of visual art in the event of distortion, mutilation, or other modification prejudicial to the artist's honor or reputation.[1] These claims sound similar to those alleged under unfair competition, and they are. VARA has been held to preempt the Lanham Act.[2] Even before VARA, courts regularly held that state claims were preempted by federal copyright, including claims under state artists' rights laws.[3]

Preemption analysis under VARA is similar to that

---

[3] *See, e.g.,* Cal. Penal Code § 350.

[Section 8:40]

[1] 17 U.S.C.A. § 106A. *See* § 8:17 and §§ 9:11 to 9:35.

[2] Board of Managers of Soho International Arts Condominium v. City of New York, 2003 WL 21403333 (S.D. N.Y. 2003) (VARA's preemption clause is intended to preempt state, common law and all other federal remedies for rights of attribution and integrity.).

[3] Villa v. Brady Pub., 63 U.S.P.Q.2d (BNA) 1603, 2002 WL 1400345 (N.D. Ill. 2002) (graffiti artist's claims for violation of state business practices and privacy laws based on unauthorized reproduction of his outdoor mural in guidebook were "qualitatively identical" to copyright infringement).

under copyright.[4] Section 301 provides a two-pronged test to determine when a state claim is preempted: First, is the art within the subject matter of copyright, and second, are the rights granted by the state law equivalent to the rights protected by copyright. The test has been restated variously: If the state law has an "extra element" absent from copyright, then the state law is not preempted; if the state law would be infringed by an act, which of itself infringes a protected right under copyright, then the state law is preempted. Since federal preemption occurs only if the right allegedly infringed is equivalent to that conferred in copyright, analyzed as above, preemption under VARA has unique limitations absent from copyright law that bear upon state unfair competition claims. First, only certain artworks are defined as "visual works of art" in Section 101 of title 17; preemption of state claims would only affect those works that fall within the copyright definition of "visual works of art" for purposes of VARA. Second, VARA does not create a right of survivorship, but many state laws do. Section 301 expressly recognizes that provisions in common law and state statutes are not "annul[ed] or limit[ed] with respect to "activities violating legal or equitable rights which extend beyond the life of the author."[5] Finally, unlike other copyright interests, VARA rights are not assignable or transferable; federal inherent rights are considered personal rights in relationship to the work that vest exclusively with and in the artist. Claims by licensees, transferees, and others impermissible under VARA are actionable under applicable state law.

VARA was held to preempt an artist's Lanham claim for false designation against a condominium board and others for removing his work of art from the exterior of a building.[6]

---

[4]H.R.Rep.No. 101-514 at 21 (1990) (VARA preemption clause [App. 18-5] ". . . follows principles . . . [in] . . . [Copyright Act] preemption [provisions].")

[5]17 U.S.C.A. § 301(f)(2)(C).

[6]Board of Managers of Soho International Arts Condominium v. City of New York, 2003 WL 21403333 (S.D. N.Y. 2003) (no possibility of confusion to the public even if VARA did not preempt Lanham because

§ 8:41 Federal relationship—Supplemental jurisdiction

Title 28 U.S.C.A. § 1367 allows a district court to exercise supplemental jurisdiction over pendent state claims when it has jurisdiction over associated federal claims that "form part of the same case or controversy."[1] In the absence of preemption, state claims for unfair competition may, in the court's discretion, be pled with federal claims under the Lanham Act if they comply with the same case or controversy requirement.[2]

§ 8:42 Misappropriation

Misappropriation claims involving art have been rejected on various theories, including an absence of competitive products or businesses, and preemption under Section 301 of federal copyright law.[1] Misappropriation claims have been dismissed as preempted under federal copyright law where the "misappropriation" claimed by plaintiffs was a substitute for reproduction,[2] or copying of art.[3] Misappropriation claims were not dismissed and not preempted where plaintiffs alleged a breach of fiduciary duty under

---

artist's work was entirely removed and was no longer publicly displayed).

[Section 8:41]

[1]28 U.S.C.A. § 1367.

[2]McMahon v. City of Chicago, 1999 WL 342712 (N.D. Ill. 1999) (supplemental jurisdiction of state claims for defamation and commercial disparagement declined after Lanham Act claims dismissed); Hofmann v. Kleinhandler, 1994 WL 240335 (S.D. N.Y. 1994) (supplemental jurisdiction proper where basis of state unfair competition claims related to Lanham Act); Vitale v. Marlborough Gallery, 32 U.S.P.Q.2d (BNA) 1283, 1994 WL 654494 (S.D. N.Y. 1994) (federal court that has jurisdiction over certain claims may properly assert jurisdiction over state aspects of the case if claims "share a common nucleus of operative facts," dismissing pendent state claims where it dismissed federal claims).

[Section 8:42]

[1]17 U.S.C.A. § 301(f).

[2]Galerie Furstenberg v. Coffaro, 697 F. Supp. 1282 (S.D. N.Y. 1988) (distinguishing between New York law of unfair competition claims and New York misappropriation claims, but concluding that federal preemption under copyright would require dismissal of both); *accord,* Kisch v. Ammirati & Puris Inc., 657 F. Supp. 380 (S.D. N.Y. 1987)

state law, an extra element absent from a copyright infringement action.[4]

Misappropriation claims were dismissed on other grounds where the defendant publisher produced a calendar depicting twelve images by Andy Warhol.[5] Although the estate of Warhol had entered into an agreement to produce a calendar in the future using the images, no competing product existed at the time of the defendant's products. Multiplicity of sources for the unprotected images Warhol sold to the public precluded a finding that consumers would be misled into identifying Warhol as the creator of the calendar.

§ 8:43 Dilution

Dilution is a "whittling down" of the identity or reputation of a mark, "blurring . . . uniqueness . . . or tarnishing [by] . . . negative association[]."[1]. Approximately half the states have antidilution statutes, supplemented by the Federal Trademark Dilution Act of 1995, providing federal antidilution protection for famous marks, effective January 16, 1996.[2] State laws are not pre-empted by the new federal law.[3]

Dismissal of dilution claims under California's antidilu-

(cause of action for misappropriation under New York law preempted by federal copyright law).

[3]Kisch v. Ammirati & Puris Inc., 657 F. Supp. 380, 384 (S.D. N.Y. 1987).

[4]Ronald Litoff, Ltd. v. American Exp. Co., 621 F. Supp. 981 (S.D. N.Y. 1985).

[5]Hughes v. Design Look Inc., 693 F. Supp. 1500, 1508 (S.D. N.Y. 1988) (coalescing as a single cause of action New York law of unfair competition claims and New York misappropriation claims).

[Section 8:43]

[1]Mattel, Inc. v. Walking Mountain Productions, 353 F.3d 792, 69 U.S.P.Q.2d (BNA) 1257 (9th Cir. 2003) (citations omitted); see § 8:35 (federal).

[2]Pub. L. No. 104-98, sec. 3(a), 109 Stat. 985 (Jan. 16, 1996), 15 U.S.C.A. § 1125(c); *see* §§ 8:35 to 8:38.

[3]*See* §§ 8:35 to 8:38; although federal law does not require that the goods or services be competitive to claim dilution, state law provisions vary.

tion statute[4] was reversed and remanded in a case involving the Oscar statuette and a look-alike used by defendants for business trophies.[5] A publisher's use of Andy Warhol images in a calendar did not dilute the works or undervalue the Warhol reputation: "The calendar purports to celebrate . . . the work of this artist. In the absence of proof of a blurring or tarnishing of the Warhol reputation, no claim is stated under [New York dilution law]."[6]

Dilution claims were dismissed under New York law where the defendants distributed and sold, without authorization, allegedly fake Salvador Dali artworks, because the court concluded that Dali's unique style did not constitute a mark.[7] State dilution claims arising from Internet use have been joined with federal ones in many recent cases involving pictorial images, domain names, and other applications.[8]

§ 8:44 False advertising

State law may provide a private right of action for persons injured by advertising that is materially false or misleading;[1] some state statutes protect competitors as well as consumers. False advertising claims, relating to defendants' distribution of allegedly fake artworks represented to be by Salvador Dali were dismissed as preempted under federal copyright.[2] False advertising claims were not dismissed and not preempted where defendants' alleged false advertising of plaintiffs' jewelry was pled in terms "qualitatively different" than copyright

---

[4]Cal. Bus. & Prof. Code § 14330.

[5]Academy of Motion Picture Arts and Sciences v. Creative House Promotions, Inc., 944 F.2d 1446, 1456 (9th Cir. 1991) (plaintiff only needs to show the distinctive value of its mark is likely to be diluted; actual injury or monetary damages not required).

[6]Hughes v. Design Look Inc., 693 F. Supp. 1500 at 1509 (S.D. N.Y. 1988).

[7]Galerie Furstenberg v. Coffaro, 697 F. Supp. 1282 (S.D. N.Y. 1988).

[8]*See* §§ 8:35 to 8:38.

[Section 8:44]

[1]*See, e.g.*, N.Y. Gen. Bus. Law, § 350 (1968).

[2]Galerie Furstenberg v. Coffaro, 697 F. Supp. 1282 (S.D. N.Y. 1988) (false advertising claim dismissed).

claims.[3]

§ 8:45 Passing off

Passing off, also called "palming off," is a state tort claim under common law and statutory unfair trade practices.[1] Passing off involves misrepresentation whereby the defendant places in commerce goods that resemble or appear to be the plaintiff's, which are passed off to buyers without identifying the plaintiff or distinguishing that the products have separate sources. An example is *A* selling its products under the name of *B*.[2] Some jurisdictions recognize "reverse passing off," where *A* sells a product of *B* under *A*'s name,[3] typically changing or modifying the product somewhat, or otherwise "directly misappropriates goods or services of another."[4] The tort may survive a federal preemption claim under copyright[5] even if the underlying acts involve copying, providing the state claim is not considered an "equivalent right" of the exclusive rights under copy-

---

[3]Ronald Litoff, Ltd. v. American Exp. Co., 621 F. Supp. 981 (S.D. N.Y. 1985).

[Section 8:45]

[1]Gegenhuber v. Hystopolis Productions, Inc., 1992 WL 168836 (N.D. Ill. 1992); Ronald Litoff, Ltd. v. American Exp. Co., 621 F. Supp. 981 (S.D. N.Y. 1985); *see, e.g.,* Summit Mach. Tool Mfg. Corp. v. Victor CNC Systems, Inc., 7 F.3d 1434, 1437 (9th Cir. 1993) (federal circuit courts of appeal established their own tests for proving "reverse passing off" for claims brought under Section 43(a) of the Lanham Act).

[2]Waldman Pub. Corp. v. Landoll, Inc., 43 F.3d 775 (2d Cir. 1994) (action under Section 43(a) of the Lanham Act on misattribution of authorship of written work, remanded to trial court); *see also* Ronald Litoff, Ltd. v. American Exp. Co., 621 F. Supp. 981, 985–86 (S.D. N.Y. 1985).

[3]Waldman Pub. Corp. v. Landoll, Inc., 43 F.3d 775 (2d Cir. 1994) (citing Restatement (Third) of Unfair Competition § 5 (Tentative Draft No. 1 (1988)).

[4]Summit Mach. Tool Mfg. Corp. v. Victor CNC Systems, Inc., 7 F.3d 1434, 1437 (9th Cir. 1993) ("Express reverse passing off," where one purchases or obtains another person's goods, removes that person's name "and markets the product . . . as its own" is recognized by some courts).

[5]17 U.S.C.A. § 301; *see* §§ 8:39 to 8:45.

right, or contains qualitatively different elements.[6]

Where a grafitti and graphic artist, commissioned to paint a mural for a skating rink, alleged Lanham Act violations and state passing off claims against the owner of the rink, who allegedly copied his design on T-shirts and promotional materials to advertise the rink,[7] the court held that the passing off claim was not preempted by federal copyright because passing off required the extra element of deception absent from copyright. In *Gegenhuber v. Hystopolis Productions, Inc.*,[8] professional artists and puppeteers brought suit against a puppet theater under Illinois' deceptive practices statute, because the theater omitted attribution in playbills advertising an award-winning puppet show that they and others had collaboratively developed, directed, and produced. Defendants were allegedly "passing off" the puppet show to the public as their own by failing to give proper credit, a claim held not preempted by federal copyright, and proper for state court resolution, and in certain circumstances, the Lanham Act.[9]

---

[6]Waldman Pub. Corp. v. Landoll, Inc., 43 F.3d 775, 781 (2d Cir. 1994) ("claim of 'reverse passing off' is separate and distinct from a claim of copyright infringement"); Kisch v. Ammirati & Puris Inc., 657 F. Supp. 380 (S.D. N.Y. 1987).

[7]Tracy v. Skate Key, Inc., 697 F. Supp. 748 (S.D. N.Y. 1988).

[8]Gegenhuber v. Hystopolis Productions, Inc., 1992 WL 168836 (N.D. Ill. 1992) (plaintiffs' motion to remand to state court granted).

[9]*See* §§ 8:17, 8:23 to 8:29; *see also* Waldman Pub. Corp. v. Landoll, Inc., 43 F.3d 775 (2d Cir. 1994) (action under Section 43(a) of the Lanham Act on misattribution of authorship of written work, remanded to trial court).